The World's Greatest Hoaxes

The World's Greatest Hoaxes

Geoff Tibballs

BARNES & NOBLE
NEW YORK

This edition published by Barnes & Noble Publishing, Inc.

2006 Barnes & Noble Publishing

ISBN-13: 978-0-7607-8222-4
ISBN-10: 0-7607-8222-9

Printed and bound in the European Union

06 07 08 09 10 11 M 9 8 7 6 5 4 3 2 1

Contents

SECTION ONE: HOAXERS

SECTION TWO: CON ARTISTS

SECTION THREE: IMPOSTORS

Introduction

By any standards it was an audacious prank. Theodore Hook, author and compulsive hoaxer, was walking along London's Berners Street one day in 1809 when his companion, playwright Samuel Beazley, remarked on how quiet and nondescript the street was. Never able to resist a challenge, Hook immediately bet his friend a guinea that by the end of the week he could make 54 Berners Street the most talked about house in the city.

Having ascertained that the occupant of number 54 was an elderly widow called Tottingham, whose life had hitherto been singularly uneventful, Hook proceeded to write nigh on a thousand letters in her name, requesting various items to be sent to that address at prearranged times of the day. With Mrs Tottingham blissfully unaware that her home was about to be descended upon by dozens of tradesmen, Hook and Beazley rented a room across the street – a vantage point from where they could readily observe the fun.

The activity commenced at nine o'clock in the morning with the arrival at number 54 of a dozen chimney sweeps who were less than pleased when the occupant revealed that she had not ordered their services. Next two dozen wagons, each carrying a ton of coal, drew up outside the house, only for their drivers to meet with a brusque response from a bewildered Mrs Tottingham. They were followed in quick succession by separate coaches bringing two doctors, a dentist and a midwife, then a hearse bearing a coffin, accompanied by appropriate funeral coaches. No sooner had these unexpected visitors been sent on their way by the irate householder than a wagon arrived stacked with hundreds of crates of beer. Cartloads of furniture appeared, along with deliveries of potatoes, clocks, flooring, and a huge pipe organ, which needed six men just to unload it.

As Berners Street started to become congested, the steady flow of tradesmen showed no sign of abating – butchers, wigmakers, hairdressers, opticians, clockmakers and salesmen. On Mrs Tottingham's behalf, Hook had placed job advertisements in assorted publications with the result that all manner of domestic staff came to apply for posts. He had also written to several civic dignitaries stating that Mrs Tottingham had a large fortune that she was eager to dispose of. Since money has a habit of attracting money, it should have come as no surprise that she soon received visits from the Governor of the Bank of England, the Archbishop of Canterbury, the Lord Mayor of London and the Lord Chief Justice. After this the Duke of York arrived, with an escort of cavalry, having been informed that one of his mistresses lay dying at 54 Berners Street and wished to see him.

By now the street was full to saturation point. As wheels locked together, wagons overturned. Tempers became frayed and fights broke out. While Mrs Tottingham cowered inside her house, no doubt dreading the next knock on the door, sightseers gathered, the whole charade watched from a safe distance by Hook and Beazley.

The chaos and confusion lasted the entire day. Hook won his bet although he was forced to go into hiding for some days after the Lord Mayor, who was familiar with the author's 'boisterous buffooneries', had concluded that Hook was responsible for the mayhem. When the furore had subsided, Hook was appointed Accountant-General of Mauritius on a healthy salary of £2,000 a year. Hoaxing can pay.

The Berners Street affair demonstrates the extraordinary lengths to which hoaxers will go in order to achieve their goal. A good hoax (and by that I do not mean malevolent calls that senselessly waste the time and resources of the emergency services) can be enormously rewarding. Indeed in the hands of such seasoned practitioners as Alan Abel and Joey Skaggs, it has become something of an art. It is essentially a cerebral form of the banana skin – an extension and refinement of the schoolboy practical joke. In its most popular guise, it aims to cause maximum embarrassment to figures or sections of authority – people whose pomposity is, in the eyes of the hoaxer, simply waiting to be pricked.

In 1902 the 'Jolly Eight', a group of Yale University undergraduates dedicated to the promotion of smoking, drinking and non-stop partying, decided to deflate the temperance movement that was rapidly gaining momentum in the United States. Falsely describing themselves as 'a party of Yale men who have banded together to promote the cause of total abstinence', they invited militant temperance crusader Carry Nation to address their number. After she had finished her speech denouncing the evils of alcohol and tobacco, the students asked her to pose for a photograph, toasting to temperance with a glass of water while they stood behind her empty-handed. In its relative infancy, indoor photography required all lights to be put out and, as soon as the room was plunged into darkness, the students grabbed a quantity of beer bottles, cigarettes and pipes, which they had secreted beforehand. Miss Nation was horrified to see the resultant photograph in the *Yale Record* for it appeared to show her blowing three smoke rings and being cheered on by her drinking buddies!

Similarly the Beringer Stones stemmed from the desire to ridicule an eminent archaeologist; the poet Ern Malley was created to expose the pretensions of Australian literary circles; and the Sokal Affair represented one American physicist's wish to draw attention to the perceived shortcomings of a scientific journal. Hoaxing may be fun but it often carries a serious message.

The clever hoax may not only be a perfectly acceptable means of propaganda, it can also be totally justifiable. Never was this better illustrated than at the height of the Second World War when, in the story that became known as The Man Who Never Was, Allied leaders invented a fictitious officer to fool the Germans and save thousands of lives in the process. On the other hand, some hoaxes in sport are simply euphemisms for cheating. By the nature of their hoaxes, athletes Rosie Ruiz and Fred Lorz, jockey Sylvester Carmouche and sailor Donald Crowhurst have gone down in the annals of sport as blatant cheats rather than lovable pranksters.

The dividing line between a hoaxer and a con artist is perilously thin. As a rule – and there are notable exceptions such as Konrad Kujau, forger of the 'Hitler Diaries', and shameless showman P.T. Barnum – hoaxers are not driven by financial gain. The successful performance of an ingenious, well-crafted plan with egg left on the faces of the right people is generally reward enough. This is partly why, even though the hoax itself may have gone undetected, hoaxers are often only too happy to admit to their sins once the fuss has died down and there is no risk of prosecution. Many possess a need to be acknowledged for their skills and, of course, to let their victims know that they have been tricked. Part of the satisfaction is in witnessing the discomfort of those who were meant to suffer. Con artists, however, are in it purely for the money, although their schemes may be sufficiently intricate as to be worthy of the most accomplished hoaxer. Step forward Victor Lustig, Frank Abagnale and Oscar Hartzell.

Abagnale was also a good example of a con man versed in the art of imposture. Almost everyone has adopted another persona at some time in life. It may be the guy on a date who tries to be as cool as Brad Pitt or George Clooney, the politician who blusters with Churchillian rhetoric or the karaoke singer who convinces herself she is Madonna. With the exception of actors, whose careers entail slipping in and out of different characters, these impersonations are invariably fleeting, yet there are those who have maintained impostures for months or even years. In 1975, 19-year-old Roberto Coppola was arrested in Rome after impersonating a priest for the previous two years. In that time he had heard countless confessions and performed numerous wedding ceremonies; the news that he was a fake forced many frantic Italian couples to renew their marriage vows. An Egyptian merchant seaman spent two years in the United States masquerading as Harrods owner Mohamed Al-Fayed, only to be undone when a freelance photographer innocently sent the real Al-Fayed pictures of the impostor on tour with the rock group Duran Duran. The accompanying note read: 'Mo – here are a couple of prints from the Duran tour.' Not only is Al-Fayed never addressed as 'Mo', but he had never been on tour with Duran Duran. He spent half a million dollars tracking down the impostor to a hotel in New Orleans. But these pale alongside the likes of the woman calling herself 'Anna Anderson' who spent over 60 years trying to convince the world that she was the Romanov heiress, the Grand Duchess Anastasia.

Impostors' motives vary. Some take on a different identity simply to carry out a harmless hoax, such as Horace Cole who, with a group of friends, dressed up as an official Abyssinian delegation to make fools out of the British Navy. Then there are career impostors – like Dennis Roark, Gerald Barnbaum and Marvin Hewitt – who, thwarted in their chosen profession for one reason or another, try to fulfil their dreams by pretending to be doctors, lawyers or teachers. When finally arrested after years of posing as assorted college professors across the United States, Hewitt wailed that he meant no harm – he just wanted to be taken seriously as a teacher. In fact, despite having to rely on bogus qualifications, some acquit themselves admirably in their chosen field. Hewitt proved a more than capable professor while Fred Demara – 'The Great Impostor' — was outstanding as surgeon, prison officer and schoolteacher.

The likes of Michael Backman and Brian MacKinnon went back to school to achieve their goals – thirtysomethings posing as young students – while others took more drastic measures. Denied the opportunity to break into the male-dominated world of jazz, Dorothy Tipton dressed as a man and spent the last 60-odd years of her life as pianist and saxophonist Billy Tipton. Over a century earlier Deborah

Sampson chose to circumnavigate the rule that forbade women from serving as soldiers in the US Army by joining up as 'Robert Shurtleff'. She went on to distinguish herself by her gallantry – but not her sex – for the best part of 18 months.

Some impostors were driven by the familiar motive of monetary gain (the Tichborne Claimant) while for others wealth was secondary to the prospect of achieving fame and standing within the community, as with David Hampton, who passed himself off as the son of actor Sidney Poitier, and Wilhelm Voigt, the infamous Captain of Köpenick. Finally there have been pretenders to the throne, including England's Lambert Simnel and Perkin Warbeck and Russia's False Dmitry, whose quests for power were habitually orchestrated by self-serving nobles.

Whatever their aspirations, hoaxers and impostors are more active today than ever, profiting from the opportunities afforded by the new mediums of electronic mail and the Internet. To their victims, they are irritating, even criminal, but to the dispassionate onlooker they can sometimes provide a breath of fresh air in a world of stifling bureaucracy. And just occasionally those who have been duped admit to a grudging admiration.

Research for this book was made all the more pleasurable by the friendly assistance of the staffs at Nottingham Library, Westminster Library and the British Newspaper Library, Colindale. I would also like to thank Robinson commissioning editor Krystyna Green for keeping the wheels of production oiled with her usual sound advice, calm reassurance and a particularly good Chilean Chardonnay.

Geoff Tibballs

SECTION ONE

Hoaxers

Chapter 1

Business

The Final Curtain

'Death got you down?' asked an advertisement which ran in a number of American weekly magazines around March 1999. 'At last an alternative!'

The website in question announced 'an iconoclastic concept for the new millennium – The Final Curtain – a revolutionary, world-wide memorial theme park mall and timeshare plan for the deceased that will replace the cemetery and funeral industry as we know it.'

The Final Curtain aimed to put the fun back into dying. It sought to encourage artists of all kinds – painters, sculptors, graffiti artists, photographers, filmmakers, writers, actors, dancers, musicians or performance artists – to design their own graves before they died, to serve as a homage to their lives and spirits. A chain of Final Curtain cemeteries was envisaged throughout the world, allowing the deceased to be transported from one to another, if they so desired, for the rest of time.

The website explained: 'Death faces all of us. But there's a lack of imagination which accompanies our passage. Until now, the handling of death has been regimented and boring, limited by those who control it, whether the State, Church, morticians or our survivors. At The Final Curtain, we are throwing away all the rules. The Final Curtain is a series of memorial parks dedicated to creative souls, soon to be built in great metropolitan cities around the world. Those who are laid to rest here are memorialized by their own creations, which serve as both tomb and eternal exhibit of their most personally meaningful work. Or, if they prefer to become a perpetually kinetic testament to life as they knew it, they may join the Timeshare Program through which we transport the remains to several of our parks on a rotational basis. For example, a client might spend autumn in New York, summer in California, spring in Paris, and winter in Florida. Member of The Final Curtain's Timeshare Program will experience mobility after death as they travel through the hereafter in perpetual luxury and comfort, enabling them to be a free spirit for eternity.

'The Final Curtain provides a unique bridge between the living and the dead. The jewel-like physical settings of our memorial parks encourage joyful contemplation of the triumph of the creative spirit. Visitors are invited to enjoy and interact with the artists' own celebrations of their lives in an environment where life will be immortalized with irreverence and humor rather than by the morbid display of funereal pomp. An amphitheater for memorial performances and concerts, a museum featuring rotating client exhibitions, and a selection of on-site restaurants and shops complete the memorial experience.'

These on-site restaurants bore names such as the Heaven's Gate Café and Dante's Grill where diners could feast on Cajun and South American cuisine while watching wax figures of art critics roast in a simulated inferno. Gift shops would sell mausoleum replica key chains and coffee mugs while the restrooms were equipped with 'a perpetually flowing drinking fountain of nondenominational holy water.' The website also displayed entries already submitted by artists for inclusion at The Final Curtain. Among the more imaginative were:

- Kim Markegard who would fashion his gravesite as a 10 ft square dance floor and jukebox, 'an outlet for enemies and adversaries to express their feelings for me . . . for my loved ones, to allow them to celebrate my escape from this world.'
- Mary Dresser would mix her ashes with the soil of a large ant-farm.
- Nick Gaetano would display the message 'Nick is Dead' in blue neon lights.
- Joseph Sullivan would show a live video feed of his decomposing body.
- Alex Repasky would mix his ashes with iron filings and display them in the form of a giant Etch-a-sketch.
- Dennis Overman would place his ashes in an electric blender that anyone could turn on in order to whip him into a frenzy.

The plan was to build the first Final Curtain in New York. The website contained an official business plan where it noted that 'death is a growth business' and suggested that the theme park environment would help attract 'visitors beyond just the friends and families of the deceased.' The concept included artist-designed adventure rides such as the 'roller coaster of life and death' and an interactive playground where children could dance on artists' gravesites.

A company called Investors Real Estate Development, based in New Jersey, was initially providing funding for the construction of the cemeteries. The contact for interested parties was given as Marketing Director Stuart MacLelland. What nobody realized at that stage was that Stuart MacLelland was the latest alias of inveterate practical joker and hoaxer Joey Skaggs.

For nearly 40 years Skaggs, who trained in advertising and fine art, has been fooling newspapers, TV stations and wire services with his elaborate pranks. His aim has never been to make money, simply to use humour 'to show the system for what it is.'

Back in 1976 he posed as one Giuseppe Scagolli, purveyor of 'certified and authenticated rock star sperm.' He appealed to women who wanted children with sperm provided by the likes of John Lennon, Bob Dylan and Jimi Hendrix, and the story of a sperm bank robbery was picked up by several wire services and *Ms* magazine.

Five years on, Skaggs emerged as Dr Josef Gregor, a Colombian entomologist who extolled the virtue of consuming cockroach hormones as a cure for colds, acne, anaemia, and menstrual pains. The doctor was interviewed on US television, his cover only being blown when Skaggs played his organization's theme song, 'La Cucaracha'.

In 1986 Skaggs assumed the role of Joe Bones, a former Marine Corps drill sergeant who was head of a group of fictional weight-watchers called 'The Fat Squad'. He told ABC's *Good Morning America* that for '$300 a day plus expenses' his commandos would disarm any dieter who tried to sneak a cookie before bedtime. After Skaggs exposed the hoax, *Good Morning America* publicly apologized for not doing more homework before booking guests. Host David Hartman confessed: 'We were had, in spades.'

Come 1990 and Skaggs was reincarnated as Sy Sperling, head of Hair Today Ltd, a firm specializing in a cure for baldness by taking follicle transplants from the dead. Sperling said the ideal recipients would be salesmen or TV news anchors who needed to 'look their best' and could afford the $3,500 price tag. A number of newspapers and TV stations fell for the story.

Skaggs travelled to England as Baba Wa Simba (Swahili for 'The Lion King'), a healer who taught a new form of therapy which would soothe the 'wounded animal inside us all'. The therapy simply involved behaving like a lion. More than one news presenter got down on all fours and began roaring as the cameras rolled.

Skaggs was also the mastermind behind the Hippie Bus Tour to Queens, which involved a busload of freaks turning the tables on rubbernecking suburban tourists, and a bogus attempt to become the first person to windsurf from Hawaii to California. Both events attracted widespread media attention.

One of Skaggs's most outrageous alter-egos was Kim Yung Soo, President of Kea So Joo Incorporated, a company that sent 1,500 letters to dog shelters across America, soliciting all their unwanted hounds for $10 per pound in order to put the dog meat into soup. The letter, written in fractured English, went: 'We buy all dog, regardless of size or color. We prefer big, young strong dog, but we take all dog from your dog shelter. Lot people eat dog. Dog is healthy for you. You make more money, more people happy. You get cleaner air. No burn up dog. No waste dog. People pet no disappear. Everybody happy.' Kea So Joo's telephone rang incessantly. The outgoing message, in both Korean and English, was punctuated by the sound of barking dogs in the background. Dog lovers sent angry messages and faxes. The media picked up on the story and although Skaggs never returned any of the calls or faxes, several TV and newspaper reporters claimed that they had indeed spoken with representatives of the company and were shocked at what they had discovered.

Skaggs was now so notorious that when the US television show *Entertainment Tonight* planned a special programme on famous media hoaxes and how the mainstream media had been duped by such pranks, it invited him on for an exclusive interview. However, the elusive Skaggs used the situation as the basis for another piece of deception, sending along a friend to take his place. It was only after the interview had been broadcast that the producers were informed that the real Joey Skaggs had been 3,000 miles away in New York at the time.

Skaggs puts a great deal of time, trouble and money into his hoaxes. 'The ideas result from my reflections, observations and criticisms of society,' he says. 'They're quirky, odd, and sometimes funny, but usually a literal or abstract interpretation of a social issue. I'm plugged into mass media and I know how it works. I look at the news as if it's a commercial and commercials as if they're news. I know exactly how they're both constructed and towards what end.

'What makes a prank difficult and challenging is the execution. Hoaxes have to be executable in a way that fool wise men and fools alike. And they have to have universal appeal on a budget and in a time frame. If a hoax doesn't take off immediately, you have to nurse it along making improvisational changes as you go. It's like doing a film or theatrical production, where all the elements have to work together.'

Skaggs viewed the death care industry 'as a giant corporate scam, exquisitely successful at commercializing death', a world where funeral directors persuade the bereaved to part with their dollars on lavish coffins and headstones because it is considered to be the right thing to do. So in the summer of 1998 he assembled an international team of around 50 volunteer artists, writers and designers to create The Final Curtain website, the ultimate satire on all things funereal. To perpetuate the hoax, Skaggs set up a bogus office with a telephone and an answering machine so that he could respond to requests for interviews with Investors Real Estate Development. He proceeded to play all of the company's executives – managing director Michael Varley, marketing director Stuart MacLelland, and associate marketing director Paul Corey. Nobody made the connection.

No sooner had the first advertisements appeared in various publications than the story of this unusual venture was picked up by newspapers, magazines, TV and radio stations across the United States. Beneath the headline GO OUT WITH A BANG: CUTTING-EDGE TOMBSTONES IN A THEME-PARK SETTING, the *Los Angeles Times* dedicated three columns to the press release for this 'Coney Island for corpses'. The article noted that 'Currently, only artists are being accepted as clients, in order to achieve "a higher-quality product that will set new standards for the death-care industry."'

Landscape Architecture magazine also devoted many column inches to the concept, describing how each Final Curtain park would be designed in the shape of an artist's palette 'with plantings carefully chosen to display different colors at different times of year.' It went on: 'Clearly, the five-hundred-acre parks will not be designed for the easily offended. The nearly thirty monument proposals on-line so far range from mildly humorous to somewhat sinister to considerably ribald. For example, mixed-media artist Jolly Bodine (somewhat ironically named) has designed a figure crushed by guilt – for "things done and not done" – whereas graphic artist Peter Markus's design features a dog urinating on a fire hydrant, an admission that "we are all alone and we are doomed" . . . Paul Corey, The Final Curtain's associate marketing director, says that more ideas are on the horizon. The company envisions including interactive kiosks where family members might be able to express their longing or grief and get pre-recorded messages from the deceased in return. He adds that Final Curtain artists can be commissioned to create fittingly irreverent resting places for non-creative types as well.'

Although Skaggs had poured a lot of dollars into the prank, the aim was not to make money so when venture capitalists expressed interest in investing in The Final Curtain, their offers were politely declined. The website received tens of thousands of hits, artists submitted burial concepts in the hope of being selected by the company for a free grave site, and funeral directors purred at the prospect of their industry moving into the megabucks world of entertainment. Some members of the public were less enthusiastic about the morbid theme parks, branding them tasteless, but everybody was united in one respect – they all thought the idea was genuine. This was despite the fact that, as always, Skaggs had left a clue in the hoax. In this case, it was Skaggs's own picture on the website as Joseph Sullivan, the man who morphed from flesh to bone with a worm crawling in one eye and out of his mouth. Ironically Sullivan's was one of the most written-about monuments.

In October 1999 the management of The Final Curtain issued a press release announcing that they had been contacted by the maker of Uncle Milton's Ant Farms with regard to the use of the trademarked term 'Ant Farm' on the website. The manufacturer of the Ant Farms had pointed out that 'Ant Farm' is not a descriptive phrase but an incontestable trademark that identifies Uncle Milton Industries. The threat of litigation between The Final Curtain and Uncle Milton's Ant Farms induced a new wave of media coverage.

By May 2000 some 40 newspapers, 19 radio stations, ten magazines and six television stations had reported on The Final Curtain. Two European TV crews had requested permission to shoot a documentary about the exciting new venture, and an unsuspecting student at the University of Chicago had asked to use The Final Curtain as the basis for her master's thesis on social art. The student's involvement was partly responsible for Skaggs calling a halt to the hoax. After all, it was one thing to dupe the media; but another to play games with a graduate student. Besides the joke had been running for two years, which was long enough to satisfy Skaggs's sense of mischief.

So on 14 May 2000 (Mother's Day), The Final Curtain issued another press release revealing that the whole thing had been a hoax. Skaggs explained that while he intended his hoax to be viewed as a form of performance art, he had also wanted to draw attention to the excesses of the death-care industry. Most of the media chose to ignore the retraction, smarting as they were from being the victims of another Joey Skaggs prank.

A Slice of Manhattan

The Center Market was one of the great gathering points in the New York City of the early 1800s. Located at the junction of Baxter, Center and Grand Streets, it was an area where people went not only to buy goods and pass a few hours in idle conversation but also to hold forth on issues of the day. It even had its own soapbox upon which the small businessmen who frequented the market would put the world to right.

Among their number was a retired ships' carpenter known only as Lozier, a highly educated man with a flair for oration. Every day he could be found at the market debating a particular topic, be it political, topical or financial. He always had a ready answer, and his word was treated as gospel, not least because he had convinced the market regulars that he mixed in high places. According to Lozier, it was he who had advised President Monroe on issuing his famous doctrine. His fellow debaters held him in considerable awe.

Lozier's habitual associate was a retired butcher, John DeVoe, but in July 1824 the pair became conspicuous by their absence from the market. When they returned several days later, Lozier was not his usual extrovert self, instead sitting silently in the corner with the troubles of the world seemingly on his shoulders. And for once he did not appear to have a solution. If anyone approached him, he would demand to be left alone. His friends deliberated for weeks on end as to what might be causing his depression until eventually they summoned up the courage to send a delegation. A captive audience was precisely what Lozier had been waiting for. He began to explain that it was not only his problem but one that would affect everyone present. His words created such an immediate air of anticipation that the crowd surrounding him quickly multiplied. What they heard next sent a shiver of trepidation down their spines. For Lozier revealed that he had been holding urgent talks with Mayor Stephen Allen who had warned him that Manhattan was in grave peril.

In a carefully rehearsed speech he informed the multitude that, as a result of all the large buildings erected on the Battery end of Manhattan over recent years, the island was starting to tilt dangerously and that it would be only a matter of time before the lower end broke off into the sea with a horrendous loss of life. A few of the audience appeared disbelieving, so Lozier offered them conclusive proof. He told the crowd to look down the road. Sure enough, from City Hall to the opposite end was downhill. It was true, they gasped. The island was sinking!

With blind panic threatening to overwhelm the throng, Lozier produced words of reassurance. He had almost worked out a solution, he said, but needed a little more time before he could reveal his master plan.

A few days later word got around that Lozier was preparing to make a speech that afternoon. Hundreds turned out to hear him explain how Manhattan Island could be saved from disaster. He announced that the plan was to saw the island off at its northern end, at the Kingsbridge, and tow it past both Governor's Island and Ellis Island, and out into the bay. There the severed section would be turned around and reattached to the mainland, in the opposite direction to before. So now the heavy end would be the one adjoining the mainland, making the island much more stable. The idea was the work of a genius.

According to Lozier, Mayor Allen had been concerned that it would first be necessary to detach Long Island from its moorings and tow it out of the way, but Lozier was happy to assure the crowd that there was plenty of room in New York Bay to perform this complicated manoeuvre without having to disturb Long Island.

A few harboured doubts as to the feasibility of such an undertaking, but Lozier reminded them that the Erie Canal was nearing completion even though that, too, had been labelled an engineering impossibility. His silver tongue also convinced onlookers that he and DeVoe had been given the job of sawing off Manhattan as private contractors in order to speed up the process. After all, time was of the essence.

Naturally the dismantling was at the top of the marketeers' agenda for debate over the ensuing days. All were anticipating Lozier's next move; they did not have long to wait. The next time he arrived at Center Market, he started to sign up labourers to work on the project. He recruited 300 on the first day alone – mostly immigrants just arrived in the city from Ireland and desperate for work. Carpenters were hired to build a large barracks and mess hall to accommodate and feed the workforce while butchers were invited to submit their prices for 500 head of cattle, 500 hogs, and 3,000 chickens. The mass order sent meat prices rocketing in the city. Blacksmiths were contracted to make fifteen, 100 ft long crosscut saws, each saw tooth being 3 ft high. Lozier estimated that it would need 50 men to operate each saw. He also employed skilled craftsmen to build 1,500 boats to tow the island, several miles of heavy chain to link the boats to trees on the island, and massive anchors to prevent Manhattan from being swept right out to sea in the event of a storm occurring before reattachment.

The most dangerous job on the team, said Lozier, was that of 'pitman', the unfortunate who had to be on the bottom end of the crosscut saw – under water. The redeeming feature was that, because of its hazardous nature, the pay rate was triple that of those working on the upper end of the saw. Lozier required several pitmen, but first insisted on strenuous tests being carried out on applicants. Each would-be pitman had to hold his breath and be timed. Those who managed to hold their breath the longest were taken on. It was reported that a number of men got in line more than once to see whether they could improve on their previous time.

Without modern-day communications, news of the preposterous plan did not reach other parts of New York so that no city officials were able to pour cold water on it. The workforce and the subcontractors kept the details to themselves for fear of missing out on what appeared to be a highly lucrative assignment. And none of them questioned how they were going to get paid – it was simply assumed that the Mayor would be footing the bill.

After several weeks of careful preparation, Lozier decided that he could stall no longer and announced a starting date. He told half of the 1,000 strong workforce to assemble at 6 a.m. at the junction of the Broadway and Bowery on the Battery end of the island, and the other half to meet at No. 1 Bowery, on the corner of Spring Street. From these locations, said Lozier, the men would march north, led by a fife and drum band, to the spot where Manhattan would be sawed off.

On the appointed morning the men turned up in their hundreds, backed by a cacophony of squealing pigs and clucking chickens. The only ones who weren't there were Lozier and DeVoe. With still no sign of the organizers, a delegation was dispatched to Center Market to find them. To their horror, the workers learned that the pair had fled the city the previous evening on account of their health. Gradually it dawned on those present that they had been tricked. There was no scheme to saw off Manhattan. The crowd slowly dispersed, some vowing to saw off Lozier and DeVoe if they ever caught up with them.

Having duped so many people, one might have expected Lozier and DeVoe to put as much distance as possible between themselves and Manhattan for the rest of their days yet after lying low in Brooklyn, they audaciously returned to Center Market several months later. This time it was different. Nobody hung on Lozier's every word: instead he was studiously ignored. The law may not have punished him for his hoax, but the manner in which he was ostracized by his fellow debaters proved equally painful.

Going For Gold

As city editor of the *Brooklyn Eagle* newspaper, 35-year-old Joseph Howard Jr had a sharp eye for finance. Always on the lookout for making a fast buck, he liked to dabble in stocks and shares and knew how volatile share prices could be, particularly in time of war. So in May 1864, with the Civil War still raging, Howard used his privileged position to plant a hoax story in two rival New York publications – an announcement that would enable him to make a swift killing on the gold market.

With the Union troops under General Grant advancing on Lee's

Confederate army near Richmond, Virginia, New Yorkers could finally see an end to the bitter, three-year-long war. For his part, Howard knew that any hint of a setback in the Union war effort would bring about an immediate rise in the price of gold. Therefore he decided to fake a proclamation from President Lincoln, ordering a day of fasting on 26 May plus the conscription of an additional 400,000 men into the Union army on account of 'the situation in Virginia, the disaster at Red River, the delay at Charleston, and the general state of the country.' Howard was certain that such calamitous tidings would send gold prices soaring, and on 17 May – the day before he intended the proclamation to appear in print – he invested heavily in gold.

His experience of newspapers meant that he knew precisely the best way to get a bogus story into print. The key was to deliver the information at the moment when the night foreman briefly assumed editorial control. Howard copied his false presidential proclamation onto forged Associated Press dispatches and, in the early hours of 18 May, with the help of *Brooklyn Eagle* reporter Francis A. Mallison, he arranged for them to be sent via couriers to the offices of various city papers. The messages were timed to arrive at 3.30am, shortly after the night editors and proofreaders had gone home, creating a situation whereby the night foreman was the sole person at each paper with responsibility for checking the dispatch and deciding whether or not to include it in the morning edition. As Howard knew only too well, the short period between the departure of the night staff and the arrival of the day shift was the one time during the entire 24 hours that a single person carried responsibility for reviewing any incoming news.

Howard had reckoned on the respective foremen not having the time or inclination to verify the story, but a number of city newspapers did decide to double-check it. They sent messengers to make sure that other publications had received the same story and their suspicions were aroused when it emerged that not every paper had. Consequently they decided against printing the proclamation until further checks could be made. However, the offices of the *New York World* and the *New York Journal of Commerce* were isolated geographically from the rest and were omitted from the messengers' check route. Thus when these two newspapers received the proclamation – and it was not uncommon to receive a telegram from Washington in the early hours – they saw no reason to suspect that it wasn't genuine.

That morning, readers of the *World* and the *Journal of Commerce* digested the ominous news that the war was likely to drag on for some time yet, placing a further strain on the nation's finances. At his home in Brooklyn, Howard waited in anticipation. Sure enough when the

New York Stock Exchange opened for business share prices plummeted in reaction to the news while gold, which was considered to be a safe investment, immediately rose in value.

After the initial shock had subsided, New York businessmen became puzzled as to why such an important proclamation had appeared in only two papers. By 11 a.m. a large crowd of merchants, beginning to suspect that there was no truth in the story, had gathered outside the offices of the *Journal of Commerce* on the corner of Wall and Water Streets to demand an explanation. The editors displayed the dispatch as proof that the story was genuine, but shortly afterwards the Associated Press issued a statement denying that it had sent any such dispatch. At 12.30 p.m. a telegram, signed by the Secretary of State, William H. Seward, was received from the State Department in Washington, declaring the proclamation to be 'an absolute forgery'. Word that the presidential proclamation was a callous hoax spread rapidly throughout the city but it was too late to prevent the damage to stock prices. And by then Howard had sold his gold and pocketed a handsome profit from his duplicity.

On hearing the news, President Lincoln angrily ordered that the *World* and the *Journal of Commerce* be closed down and their proprietors arrested. Acting on the President's orders, General Dix and a platoon of soldiers seized the offices of the two newspapers and suspended their publication for two days. Detectives investigating the hoax arrested Mallison on 21 May and he wasted little time in implicating Howard. Confronted with his partner's confession, Howard, too, admitted his guilt and served three months in jail before the President surprisingly ordered his release. This change of heart followed an appeal by Henry Ward Beecher, a friend of Howard's wealthy father, who pleaded that the young man was guilty only of 'the hope of making some money.' The President evidently sympathised with such pecuniary sentiments. He may also have been persuaded towards leniency by the fact that Howard's prophecy turned out to be alarmingly close to the mark. On 18 July – two months after the hoax – Lincoln did indeed issue a call for more men. The only difference was in the number. Howard had forecast 400,000; Lincoln demanded 500,000.

The Emulex Affair

A press release posted on the Internet on Friday 25 August 2000 briefly wiped a staggering $2.5 billion off the market value of Emulex, a California company which makes high-tech networking and fibre channel technology. The release indicated major problems within

Emulex, including the resignation of its chief executive and an official investigation into its accounting practices, but there wasn't a word of truth in it. As staff conducted a frantic damage limitation exercise, the story was revealed to be a financial hoax, devised by a 23-year-old student.

The first sign of trouble occurred at 9.30 a.m. Eastern Daily Time when a press release, purportedly from Emulex, appeared on Internet Wire, an Internet-based distributor of corporate news. According to the release, which contained formats similar to previous Emulex announcements and listed an actual investor relations executive as a contact, the company was restating its quarterly earnings from a profit to a loss, chief executive Paul Folino had quit, and the US Securities and Exchange Commission was launching an urgent investigation into the firm's accounting methods. Over the next hour the story was distributed to a number of bigger news services, notably Bloomberg and Dow Jones. The Emulex stock price plunged dramatically as the headlines did the rounds, sinking from a morning high of $113.06 to a low of $43 by 10.30 a.m. The stock of the company had actually dropped 62 per cent in just 16 minutes.

The three-hour time difference between the two coasts proved a major factor in assisting the spread of the hoax. Staffers on some of the wire services tried to verify the story with Emulex but were unable to contact anyone at the company's Costa Mesa base because it was barely breakfast time in California. This gave the bogus release over two hours to wreak havoc. When the truth was discovered, Emulex issued a press release rebutting the story at 12.45 p.m. EDT (9.45 a.m. California time), and officials with the Nasdaq Stock Market promptly halted trading in Emulex shares. An hour later Paul Folino repeated the denial on television, reassuring investors that the release was a hoax. 'This was a fictitious press release that was released this morning,' he said. 'We are not restating our fourth-quarter or annual earnings. Obviously I haven't resigned and am on the job.'

Emulex shares began to rise once more, closing at $105.75, down just $7.31. The nightmare scenario of corporate meltdown was over, but the market plunge had created panic in the minds of thousands of investors. Worst hit were shareholders who believed the release was genuine and sold as the price slumped, only to watch helplessly as the hoax was revealed and the shares recovered.

Internet Wire immediately proclaimed its innocence, maintaining that it had been tricked by a sophisticated group of con artists who, posing as a public relations firm representing Emulex, had sent the announcement to night staffers. They in turn had chosen to include the seemingly authentic press release among those for posting on the Internet in the morning. On learning of the hoax, Internet Wire pulled the fake release from its website and issued a press release of its own, explaining that it had been duped.

But far from being conceived by a group of sophisticated con artists, the Emulex hoax turned out to be the work of just one man – 23-year-old Mark Jakob, a student at El Camino Community College and a former employee of Internet Wire.

Jakob began trading stocks in the summer of 1998 with a $40,000 stake, some of which was borrowed. After enjoying a degree of success initially, he lost most of the money day-trading – a technique in which shares are bought and sold quickly, often in the same day. In April 1999 he started working at Internet Wire and had soon put aside sufficient money to commence trading again. Then in August 2000 he sold short 3,000 shares of Emulex. A short sale involves selling borrowed shares of a stock in the hope that the price will fall, enabling an investor to repay the loan at a lower price and pocket the difference. But instead of falling, shares of Emulex started to rise, leaving Jakob facing a potential loss of $97,000 together with a demand from an online brokerage that he deposit $20,000 in his account to cover anticipated losses. To cover his losses, Jakob decided to draft a fake Emulex press release, which he modelled on a genuine release that had caused shares of another company, Extended Systems, to drop sharply the previous month. Having left his job at Internet Wire on 18 August — a week before carrying out the hoax — Jakob was able to use his knowledge of the online service's system to get the release distributed. He sent the release at night via an e-mail from the library at El Camino Community College to Internet Wire. As the Emulex share price went into temporary freefall in the wake of Jakob's actions, he covered his short position by buying shares to replace those that he had borrowed at a lower price, making a profit of around $50,000. He then bought another 3,500 Emulex shares at $52, selling them three days later for a profit of $186,000.

Jakob had little time to enjoy his new-found wealth. He was arrested shortly afterwards and in December 2000 pleaded guilty to two counts of securities fraud and one of wire fraud. He was sentenced to 44 months in prison and ordered to repay all his profits from the hoax . . . plus interest.

Chapter 2

Literature

Faking Shakespeare

Shakespearean artefacts were big business in eighteenth-century England. Over a hundred years after his death, he was finally recognized as a true genius and the nation seemed gripped by Bard fever as the *literati* sought desperately to find out more about the man and his works. In view of the fact that much of his life remained shrouded in mystery at the time, there were numerous holes to fill in. Above all, so little existed that had been written in his own hand. This led the distinguished literary figure J.A. Boaden to speculate that someone had secretly collected the missing material and that one day 'a rich assemblage of Shakespeare papers would start forth from some ancient repository, to solve all our doubts and add to our reverence and our enjoyment.'

Another devoted student of Shakespeare was elderly antiquary, bookseller and artist Samuel Ireland. He had three children but Shakespeare was his real love. Particularly starved of affection was his son William Henry Ireland. Born in 1775, William proved a constant disappointment to his father who, not content with expressing the opinion that the boy would never amount to anything, even suggested that William was not really his son at all. Such statements did precious little for William's confidence and he appeared destined to live down to parental expectations by struggling at school before eventually being expelled for not attaining the required educational standards. He was then sent to school in France where, perhaps because he was removed from the disapproving gaze of his father, he performed considerably better. Inevitably Ireland Snr was still singularly unimpressed. Nevertheless in the summer of 1793, in a rare instance of bonding, Samuel Ireland took 17-year-old William on a pilgrimage to Stratford-upon-Avon. The old man was captivated by the place and bought a handful of Shakespearean relics, all of which were probably fakes. But there was no sign of the one thing he wanted above all else in life: Shakespeare's autograph.

Returning to London, Samuel Ireland furthered his obsession by penning a guidebook to Stratford. Meanwhile William was apprenticed to a lawyer, but found the job tedious in the extreme. His real ambition was to be a writer despite his father's typically blunt assertion that he had no talent. One day towards the end of 1794, between bouts of inactivity at the lawyer's office, William hit upon a way of pleasing his father. He found some old parchment gathering dust and a wax seal, and persuaded a local bookbinder to prepare a bottle of ink that would look suitably aged when quill was put to paper. Then, using an early seventeenth-century deed as his model, William painstakingly wrote out a title deed to a property in the Blackfriars district of London near the Globe Theatre, signing it in the names of Shakespeare and an actor by the name of John Heminge. He signed Heminge's name with his left hand and copied Shakespeare's signature from one of his father's books – a tome edited by literary critic Edmond Malone and which contained various facsimiles. He then presented the fake document to his father who was overjoyed when an expert declared it to be genuine. At last William was in his father's good books.

Naturally Samuel Ireland was curious to know how William had come by the document. William invented an elaborate story, saying that he had bumped into a wealthy country gentleman who, on hearing of his interest in antiquities, had invited him to his house in order to examine a chest full of old papers. The mystery man – named only as Mr H – invited William to take anything that caught his eye on condition that his identity and address remained secret. Listening to the tale, Samuel Ireland was scarcely able to believe his good fortune and begged his son to go back for more; William was only too happy to oblige.

Over the ensuing month young William produced a series of remarkable 'finds' – a letter from Shakespeare to the Earl of Southampton, thanking him for his patronage; a love poem to Anne Hathaway; and a letter of appreciation to Shakespeare from Queen Elizabeth I. These items were put on display in Samuel Ireland's shop off the Strand and drew visitors from far and wide, including the Prince of Wales, the poet laureate Henry Pye and noted biographer James Boswell. The last-named was so moved that he sank to his knees and kissed the artefacts in reverence, thanking God for having been allowed to live long enough to see 'the valuable relics of our bard'. Buoyed with enthusiasm, William then presented a 'Profession of Faith', supposedly written by Shakespeare in his dying days. Eminent scholar and clergyman Dr Samuel Parr was overcome with emotion at the quality of the prose, declaring: 'We have many very fine passages in our church service, and our litany abounds with beauties; but here is a man who has distanced us all!'

Not surprisingly, such lavish praise went to William Ireland's head. For a 17-year-old (especially one who had been told he had no future as a writer) to be compared, albeit unwittingly, to the greatest playwright in the history of English literature was bound to have a profound effect. He began to believe his own publicity, which left him, as he himself admitted later, 'fired with the idea of possessing genius to which I had never aspired.'

William grew bolder with each passing week. Next he announced that he had uncovered the original manuscripts of *Hamlet* and *King Lear*. Not satisfied with faithfully reproducing the plays in an imitation of Shakespeare's hand, Ireland displayed his newfound confidence by making what he considered to be his own improvements to the text. In doing so, however, he overstretched himself, strengthening the hands of those who were not taken in by the deception. For not every scholar was convinced of the authenticity of the documents. As speculation mounted about the identity – or indeed the very existence – of Mr H, William attempted to throw the hounds off the scent by enlisting the services of an aspiring actor, Robert Talbot, to claim that he had introduced young Ireland to the mystery man. William also composed a series of letters from the non-existent Mr H, among them one to Samuel Ireland extolling the literary virtues of his son. Clearly his father's approval remained of paramount importance.

Having seen his forged letters and poems widely accepted as the genuine article, it was a natural progression for William Ireland to embark on his most ambitious undertaking to date – a full-length Shakespearean work. He told his father that he had unearthed the manuscript of a previously undiscovered Shakespeare play – *Vortigern and Rowena*, loosely based on the life of an Anglo-Saxon king. The subject matter was inspired by a picture of Vortigern and Rowena that hung in his father's bookshop. William's play was set in five acts but he obviated the need for writing the whole thing out laboriously in Shakespeare's hand by claiming that Mr H would not allow him to remove the manuscript, only to copy it.

Ireland worked on his masterpiece throughout 1795 before offering it to playwright Richard Sheridan who owned the Drury Lane Theatre. Although Sheridan apparently had reservations about its authenticity, he agreed to stage the play in the belief that people would flock to see it, if only to decide for themselves whether or not it was genuine. The world premiere of *Vortigern and Rowena* was originally scheduled for the end of 1795 but was held over until the following spring. By then the sceptics were ranged in battle against the Irelands. A genuine signature from John Heminge had been discovered and bore little resemblance to William's forgery. Publications that had hitherto supported the finds now came out openly in opposition but, potentially most damning of all, Edmond Malone, an acknowledged expert on Shakespeare, was known to be preparing a detailed criticism of the documents entitled *Inquiry into the Validity of the Papers Attributed to Shakespeare*. Not only was Malone suspicious of Ireland's exaggerated Shakespearean spellings – 'ande' for 'and', 'forre' instead of 'for' – but also he was mystified by the supposed letter from Queen Elizabeth I to Shakespeare which referred to the anticipated presence of the Earl of Leicester at the Globe Theatre . . . the problem being that Leicester had died six years before the Globe opened.

Unfortunately for the Irelands, Sheridan had hired John Kemble to produce *Vortigern and Rowena*. Kemble was so convinced that the play was a fake that he wanted to open on 1 April but Sheridan, anxious not to pre-judge, insisted on 2 April instead. Edmond Malone's weighty criticism appeared just two days before opening night, but its 400 pages meant that the audience had little opportunity to digest the contents before taking their seats. As Samuel Ireland himself remarked: 'Let the public be judge.'

The 2,500 people crammed into Drury Lane Theatre that night were given more than a gentle nudge by Kemble, who seems to have done his utmost to sabotage the production. Kemble's most contentious piece of casting was to hand a role requiring immense *gravitas* to an actor with a distinctly high-pitched voice, as a result of which his every utterance provoked gales of laughter. Then in Act 4 the thespian playing one of the leaders of the Saxon army elected to die in the wrong spot and became painfully trapped under the drop-curtain as the scene ended. While the 'corpse' endeavoured to extricate himself from his ignominy, a drunk clambered on stage to lend a helping hand and was pelted with oranges. And in the final act where Vortigern contemplates death, Kemble, according to William Ireland's own account of proceedings, spoke the line 'And when this solemn mockery is ended' in a manner that suggested he was referring to the play itself. This, too, produced howls of derision from the audience, followed by a general free-for-all at the final curtain. There was no second night.

The farce of *Vortigern*, coupled with Malone's revelations, left few in doubt that the Shakespearean relics were forgeries. J.A. Boaden reluctantly joined the Malone camp. He wrote: 'In some instances credulity is no disgrace, strong enthusiasm is always eager to believe; I confess that, for some time after I had seen them, I continued to think they might be genuine; they bore the character of the poet's writing, the paper appeared of sufficient age, the water marks were earnestly displayed, and the matter diligently applauded; I remember that I beheld the papers with the tremor of utmost delight, touched the invaluable relics with reverential respect, and deemed even existence dearer as it gave me so refined a satisfaction.'

The one person who steadfastly refused to believe that the works were fakes was old Samuel Ireland. When the finger of suspicion was pointed at his son, for once he stoutly defended the boy, partly to protect his own reputation and partly because he insisted that William was not clever enough to have perpetrated such a complex fraud. This assertion hurt William, who had just completed a second Shakespeare play, *Henry II*, and had also started writing *William the Conqueror*. William Ireland felt obliged to admit to the hoax and when his father still refused to acknowledge it, William published a full confession in which he wrote: 'Had the play of *Vortigern* succeeded with the public, and the manuscripts been acknowledged as genuine, it was my intention to have completed a series of plays from the reign of William the Conqueror to that of Queen Elizabeth; that is to say, I should have planned a drama on every reign the subject of which had not been treated by Shakespeare.'

Samuel Ireland was appalled by the confession and never spoke to William again. Still unwilling to admit that the cherished finds were frauds or that someone whom he perceived as having no talent could have duped him, Samuel denounced Malone's claims and went ahead with the publication of *Vortigern* in 1799. He died four years later, insisting to the last that *Vortigern and Rowena* was a genuine Shakespeare play.

Meanwhile William married and went to live in France where he proceeded to write over a dozen novels and plays, thus underlining the fact that he did possess genuine literary ability. Sadly it was too late to impress his father.

Maria Monk's Awful Disclosures

Anti-Catholic sentiments were widespread in early nineteenth-century America. English colonists, in particular the puritans of New England, had brought with them a distinct hostility towards the Roman Church, as a result of which many of the colonies – and later states – had introduced measures discriminating against Catholics. There were laws to prevent Catholics holding office and against priests owning property, and special taxes were levied on Catholic servants. In this climate of mistrust, anti-Catholic literature flourished, books and pamphlets of that persuasion bearing such evocative titles as *Priestcraft Exposed, Forty Popish Frauds Detected and Disclosed*, and *The Female Jesuit, or a Spy in the Family*.

So when, in January 1836, a woman named Maria Monk published a book titled *Awful Disclosures*, in which she exposed a succession of scandalous events that, she claimed, had occurred at the Hotel Dieu convent in Montreal, the public lapped it up. Her shocking revelations about sexually rampant nuns and priests and allegations of mass infanticide were gleefully adopted by American Protestants who used them to denounce popery and all its attendant evils. They now thought they knew almost everything about Catholicism. What they didn't know was that Maria Monk was a complete fake.

Monk's story, as she told it in the book, was truly sad. Although raised a Protestant, young Maria apparently became interested in religious life after studying at convent school in Montreal. On completing her studies, she said she decided to become a nun and trained as a novice at the Hotel Dieu, which had the reputation of being one of the most respectable institutions in the whole of Canada. However, once admitted to the convent, Monk's illusions were quickly shattered by the Superior who told her bluntly that sex with priests was obligatory.

Monk described the scene thus: 'The Superior now informed me that having taken the black veil, it only remained that I should swear the three oaths customary on becoming a nun; and that some explanation would be necessary from her. I was now, she told me, to have access to every part of the edifice, even the cellar, where two of the sisters were imprisoned for causes that she did not mention. I must be informed that one of my great duties was to obey the priests in all things; and this I soon learned, to my utter astonishment and horror, was to live in the practice of criminal intercourse with them. I expressed some of the feelings which this announcement excited in me, which came upon me like a flash of lightning; but the only effect was to set her arguing with me, in favour of the crime, representing it as a virtue acceptable to God, and honourable to me.'

Monk went on to relate how the priests used the convent's network of underground passages to enter the building each night and have their wicked way with the nuns. Monk claimed that all babies born of these illicit liaisons were baptized before being killed and dumped in a lime pit in the cellar, a makeshift burial ground which was also littered with the bones of those nuns who had dared to resists the priests' amorous advances. Her stories of brutality included the account of a hapless nun who was tied to a mattress following some petty transgression:

'In an instant another bed was thrown upon her. One of the priests, named Bonin, sprang like a fury first upon it with all his force. He was speedily followed by the nuns until there were as many on the bed as could find room, and all did what they could do, not only to smother, but to bruise her. Some stood and jumped upon the poor girl with the feet: and others, in different ways, seemed to seek how they might beat the breath out of her body. After the lapse of fifteen or twenty minutes, Father Bonin and the nuns ceased to trample on her and stepped from the bed. They then began to laugh.'

Maria Monk said that after spending seven tortuous years in the convent ('speedy death', she wrote, 'can be no great calamity to those who lead the lives of nuns'), she, too, fell pregnant to a priest. Unable to contemplate the thought of her infant being killed and dumped in the basement, she escaped and made her way to New York where, after barely surviving the birth of her baby daughter in a charity hospital, she told her sorry tale to a sympathetic minister. The minister was apparently so moved by her story that he persuaded her that the world should know the truth about the horrors of convent life. The result was the *Awful Disclosures*.

This was Maria Monk's story as it was peddled to the American public. The truth was somewhat different, although equally miserable. She was born to a Protestant family in St Johns, Quebec, in 1817. Her mother later described her as un uncontrollable child, a trait she attributed to a brain injury suffered when a slate pencil was rammed into the young Maria's ear, penetrating her skull. From then on, said her mother, Maria was prone to wild fantasies. She had never been a novice or a nun and had never even been inside the Hotel Dieu convent. Her only known contact with a Catholic institution was as an inmate of the Magdalen Asylum for Wayward Girls in Montreal. When it was discovered that she had become pregnant while resident in the asylum, she was asked to leave. She drifted into prostitution and, at the age of 18, met Revd William K. Hoyt after soliciting him on the street. Hoyt was head of the Canadian Benevolent Society, an organisation that combined Protestant missionary work with vehement anti-Catholic activism. He took Monk as his mistress and together they travelled to New York with her baby in tow. The child that she claimed had been born out of having sex with a priest in the convent was actually fathered by a Montreal policeman.

In fact, although it was published in her name, Monk's contribution to the *Awful Disclosures* was minimal. She did little more than compose pen pictures of Montreal and of life at the Magdalen asylum. The driving force behind the book was the opportunistic Hoyt who recruited his fellow American Protestant extremists (or nativists), Revd John J. Slocum, Revd George Bourne and Theodore Dwight, to provide additional text. When the four men subsequently fell out over the profits, it emerged that Slocum had been the principal author. Hoyt and Bourne had also made sizeable contributions while Dwight, an accomplished linguist, had exaggerated Catholic 'crimes' by stealing ideas from Italian, French and German works on convents and torture. Monk was so impressed by Dwight's translations that she offered to elope with him, a gesture he apparently found able to refuse.

Instead she was taken under the wing of Revd W. C. Brownlee, author of a best-selling anti-Catholic work, *Popery*, and the New York-based editor of the *American Protestant Vindicator*. This newspaper had trailed *Awful Disclosures* for some months prior to publication, ensuring that sales were brisk. In the first six months alone, the book sold over 26,000 copies – a staggering figure for the time. Small wonder that Hoyt was angry at losing control of Monk whom he now labelled a 'damned jilting jade'. Monk's story proved so profitable that the editor of a rival nativist newspaper, Samuel B. Smith, tried to get in on the act by producing his own escaped nun from the Hotel Dieu and calling her Saint Francis Patrick. However, she was not such a born liar as Monk and doubts were soon expressed regarding the authenticity of her story. When the two bogus nuns took part in a carefully stage-managed tearful reunion, the association harmed Monk's own credibility.

Right from the outset, Monk's book caused a storm. Catholics denounced it as a tissue of lies, which prompted Monk to invite any doubters to visit the Hotel Dieu to compare the building with her description of it. This brazen bluff was obviously effective since there were no takers for the time being. Meanwhile Protestants demanded action against the convent, putting the Bishop of Montreal under such pressure that he eventually authorised an investigation into the workings of the Hotel Dieu. It failed to produce a shred of evidence to support Monk's account, but the nativists refused to accept the findings, claiming that the investigation had been carried out by Jesuits disguised as Protestants.

Impartial evidence remained at a premium until October 1836 when William Leete Stone, a Protestant moderate and editor of a New York newspaper, obtained permission from the Bishop of Montreal to explore the convent in search of the tunnels, prisons and mass graves, as described by Monk. Carrying Monk's book in his hand, he compared her description of the Hotel Dieu with the convent itself and found no evidence to suggest that Monk had ever been there. In Stone's eyes, Monk was a fraud, and when he published his views, support for her dwindled rapidly. Her cause was not aided by the revelations of her mother in Montreal who maintained that her daughter had never entered a nunnery. Even more damningly, she added that in 1835 Hoyt had offered her £500 to say that Maria had been at the Hotel Dieu.

Despite these setbacks, *Awful Disclosures* was reprinted at least six times through 1836. Monk saw little reward, however, as her share of the royalties had been appropriated by the Revd Brownlee's organization, the Society for the Diffusion of Christian Knowledge. Monk paid him back by running off with his young protégé, Slocum.

In August 1837 Monk turned up at the home of Philadelphia physician William Willcocks Sleigh, claiming that she had been abducted by a gang of lecherous priests. Her story had a familiar ring to it. At first Sleigh believed her but the more she talked, the more it became peppered with inconsistencies. He felt compelled to denounce her in the form of a pamphlet carrying the catchy title *An Exposure of Maria Monk's Pretended Abduction and Conveyance to the Catholic Asylum, Philadelphia, by Six Priests on the Night of 15 August, 1837: with Numerous Extraordinary Incidents During Her Residence of Six Days in This City*.

Incredibly Monk still had sufficient supporters and nerve to come up with a sequel to life at the Hotel Dieu. Lacking any new revelations, *Further Disclosures of Maria Monk* could not match the original and what money it did make was spirited away by Slocum. In 1838 Monk gave birth to a second illegitimate child, after which her life went downhill fast. Interest in her waned to the extent that she was reduced to making ends meet by picking pockets and returning to prostitution. In 1849 she was jailed for picking the pocket of a man who had paid her for sex, and later that year she died in prison on New York City's Welfare Island at the age of 32. But the legend of Maria Monk did not die with her. Even though her supposedly factual books were pure fiction, they remained in print for over a century, an edition of *Awful Disclosures* being published as recently as 1971. By then the title had sold in excess of 300,000 copies. Not bad for a hoax.

Ern Malley: An Australian Cultural Hero

One of the major outlets for avant-garde writers and artists in 1940s Australia was a magazine called *Angry Penguins*, published in Adelaide and edited by Max Harris, a literary visionary in his early twenties. It was dedicated to the spread of modernism in general but took a particular interest in furthering the cause of surreal poetry, Harris's pet project.

One day in 1944 the mail brought Harris a letter from a Sydney woman named Ethel Malley who said that her brother Ern had just died of a rare thyroid disease at the age of 25. She wrote at some length about her brother's short life. He had been born in England in 1918 before moving to Australia two years later following his father's death. Ern's mother had then died when he was 15, and the boy was left in Ethel's care. The Malleys, she said, were uneducated working-class folk. Having dropped out of school, Ern had worked as a garage mechanic in Sydney and subsequently as an insurance salesman and part-time watch repairman in Melbourne. He had barely managed to eke out a living and in 1943 had returned to Sydney. 'The weeks before he died were terrible,' she wrote. 'Sometimes he would be all right and he would talk to me. From things he said I gathered he had been fond of a girl in Melbourne, but had some sort of difference with her. I didn't want to ask him too much because he was nervy and irritable. The crisis came suddenly, and he passed away on Friday the 23rd of July. As he wished, he was cremated at Rookwood.' Ethel described Ern as a reclusive lad who rarely gave vent to his feelings and so it came as something of a surprise (particularly as he was known to have owned only one book – Thorstein Veblen's *Theory of the Leisure Class*) when she discovered among his possessions some poetry he had written. The ingenuous Ethel freely admitted to knowing nothing about poems, but wondered on the off chance whether they might be of any interest to Harris.

There were 16 short poems in total, among them *The Darkening Ecliptic*, *Sybilline*, *Colloquy with John Keats*, and his final work, *Petit Testament*. Harris was so impressed that he excitedly published them in the next issue of *Angry Penguins*, and had no hesitation in hailing Ern Malley as one of Australia's greatest writers. He was also one of Australia's greatest hoaxes.

Ernest Lalor Malley was not born in England in 1918 but on a quiet Saturday afternoon at the Victoria Barracks, Melbourne, land headquarters of the Australian army, in October 1943. Lieutenant James McAuley and Corporal Harold Stewart were two Sydney poets with a shared dislike for the type of surrealist work championed by *Angry Penguins*. They felt that some Australian intellectuals had become so infatuated with embracing new trends that they were in danger of no longer being able to differentiate between good and bad poetry. As McAuley and Stewart saw it, any over-written, pretentious twaddle was likely to be greeted as a masterpiece.

So they set about composing verse that would sound imposing but be utterly meaningless. As their inspiration, they consulted the books and documents on their desks, unashamedly lifting lines at random from Shakespeare, a dictionary of quotations and even an American report on the breeding grounds of mosquitoes. By mixing metaphors, using unnecessarily flowery language and incorporating 'confused and inconsistent hints at a meaning', they produced what they deemed to be bad poetry. One such passage ran:

> You have hawked in your throat and spat
> Outrage upon the velocipede of thriftless
> Mechanical men posting themselves that
> Built you a gibbet in the vile morass
> Which now you must dangle on, alas.

McAuley and Stewart named their creation Malley after the French word for bad ('*mal*') and called him Ernest because they were not. His complete works were written in that single afternoon.

It was not only the quality of Malley's verse and inventive vocabulary that thrilled Max Harris. One of the chief requirements for achieving cult status in any field has always been to die young, and Malley fell perfectly into that category, going to meet his maker at exactly the same age as Keats. He was thus accorded the status of tragic hero, underlined by the fact that a number of his poems appeared to contain premonitions of an early death.

Harris and his friends, including the painter Sidney Nolan, waxed lyrical about their new discovery, but their euphoria was cut short when, in June 1944, the press revealed the hoax. The events took a strange turn. The South Australian police pronounced some of the poems to be indecent and *Angry Penguins* ended up involved in an obscenity trial. One officer testified in court that, although no actual 'dirty' words were used, he was sure the poems contained sexual innuendo . . . even if only by virtue of their setting. Commenting on a poem about people in a park at night, he pronounced: 'I have found that people who go into parks at night go there for immoral purposes.' He did, however, go on to concede that 'my experience as a police officer might, under certain circumstances, tinge my appreciation of poetry.' The only surprise was that the officer himself was not also a hoax. When the farce was over, the judge fined Harris £5.

With Ern Malley's cover blown, one might have expected him to fade from the public eye. Not a bit of it. Harris and his associates stuck by their belief that Malley's poems had genuine literary merit. Despite the ridicule heaped upon them for being taken in by the hoax, they continued to promote Malley as a prime exponent of surrealism. To them, it was immaterial that the author did not exist. 'The myth,' Harris remarked, 'is sometimes greater than its creator.'

Others jumped on the Malley bandwagon and he has gone on to become as much a part of Australia's cultural heritage as that other literary giant, Sir Les Patterson. New editions of Malley's poems have been published on a regular basis, and the editors of the 1992 *Penguin Book of Modern Australian Poetry* saw fit to include all of Malley's verses in their anthology. And in 2000 the story of the hoax was turned into a musical called *Angry Penguins*. The legend of Ern Malley has mushroomed way beyond McAuley and Stewart's wildest expectations to a point where the original joke has frequently been overlooked. With Malley earning serious acclaim from respected academics, it has been suggested that the hoaxers have been hoisted on their own petard. Whatever the case, it has not been a bad return for an afternoon's mischief.

Lobsang Rampa and *The Third Eye*

Described as the autobiography of a Tibetan Lama, *The Third Eye* was one of the publishing sensations of 1956. It became an instant bestseller in a dozen different countries, shifting 300,000 copies within the first 18 months. Yet none of the book's captivated readers realized that the mystic Himalayan author who called himself Tuesday Lobsang Rampa was really Devon plumber's son Cyril Henry Hoskins, a man who could not speak a word of Tibetan and didn't even possess a passport.

Hoskins was born in Plympton in 1911 but left Devon in 1937 to work for a firm of surgical instrument makers. A few years later he moved to Thames Ditton, Surrey, and, after studying the occult in his spare time, completely reinvented himself. Shaving his head and growing a beard, he changed his name to Dr Kuan-Suo and told puzzled neighbours in the leafy suburb that he had been a flying instructor with the Chinese airforce and had suffered terribly while held captive in a Japanese prisoner-of-war camp. It was all a figment of his imagination.

Although Sir Edmund Hillary's conquest of Everest had awakened interest in the region, precious little was known about Tibet in the Western world of the 1950s. However, as horizons broadened following the slackening of post-war restrictions, people were eager to learn more about this land of mystery and spiritualism. Enter Tuesday Lobsang Rampa.

In his supposedly autobiographical tale, Rampa described how he had been born to a wealthy Tibetan family and, at the age of seven, had been sent to Chakpori Lamasery in Lhasa to study medicine and become a Lama. There he learned the mystic arts of astral projection, crystal gazing, aura deciphering and many more occult practices, all under the watchful eye of his guru, the Lama Mingyar Dondup. While at the monastery, Rampa, who acquired the 'Tuesday' prefix because, he said, each Lama bore the name of a day of the week, also learned about flying through the air, running at speeds exceeding 400 mph, and about past and future incarnations. But the key moment in his life was the operation on the middle of his forehead to open his third eye. According to Tibetan tradition the third eye is associated with the pineal gland (a tiny organ in the brain) and is said to be the centre of human psychic activity. Opening the third eye is believed to endow the subject with various mystic powers, including clairvoyance, and to enable him to discriminate between good and evil people via a study of their aura. In Rampa's case, the eye was opened by drilling a hole in his head, just above the bridge of his nose, and then inserting a specially treated sliver of wood.

He wrote of the operation: 'The instrument penetrated the bone. A very hard, very clean sliver of wood which had been treated by fire and herbs was slid down so that it just entered the hole in my head. I felt a stinging, tickling sensation apparently in the bridge of my nose. It subsided and I became aware of subtle scents which I could not identify. Suddenly there was a blinding flash. For a moment the pain was intense. It diminished, died, and was replaced by spirals of colour.' He then recounted how Lama Mingyar Dondup turned to him and said: 'You are now one of us, Lobsang.'

The book went on to relate how Rampa performed levitation, had an encounter with an Abominable Snowman and befriended the Dalai Lama, the spiritual head of Buddhist Tibet. Each page seemed to offer a new insight into the curious customs and religious practices of that far-flung land, containing a wealth of facts which really did appear to be stranger than fiction.

The Third Eye was rejected by three British publishers before being accepted by the respected house of Secker & Warburg. Experts in Tibetan culture were consulted as to whether the book should be classified as non-fiction or fiction, but their reaction was mixed. Some felt that the author had lifted his text from other accounts, and one academic went so far as to label the entire work a fraud. Nevertheless publication went ahead in the belief that the book was factual, and its success soon earned its author the princely sum of £20,000. In Germany alone it sold 100,000 copies.

However, a number of Tibetan scholars, including explorer Heinrich Harrer who had personally tutored the Dalai Lama, remained convinced that the book was pure fiction, containing, as it did, certain statements inconsistent with Buddhist beliefs. So they hired private detective Clifford Burgess to delve into the background of Tuesday Lobsang Rampa. What Burgess came up with was Cyril Hoskins, a man who had never been anywhere near Tibet, had no real knowledge of the country's language or indeed of Buddhism, and had certainly never had a hole drilled in his forehead. Any expertise had been gleaned from reading books in London libraries.

Confronted with the evidence in April 1958, Hoskins put on a brave show of defiance, concocting an explanation even more fanciful than any of his previous biographical 'facts'. Yes, he had been born Cyril Hoskins and he had lived at Thames Ditton, but since 1949 he had been bodily possessed by the Lama Lobsang Rampa. Hoskins said that the spiritual conversion took place after he had fallen from a tree while trying to photograph an owl. Lying concussed on the ground, he saw the figure of a Lama in saffron robes crossing his Thames Ditton lawn and entering his body. From that moment Cyril Hoskins became Lobsang Rampa.

Regardless of whether anybody actually swallowed his tale, Hoskins/Rampa went on to write over a dozen more books, among them *The Rampa Story*, in which he recounted how his body had first been taken over, and *Living With the Lama*, said to have been communicated to him telepathically through his cat Mrs Fifi Greywhiskers! Combining the occult, fantasy travel and astrology, these later works found a lucrative niche in the market, and it is estimated that Hoskins sold some four million books in total. He died in 1981 but, to this day, *The Third Eye* remains a classic of its kind. And many readers still believe every word.

Appleton's Dubious Dictionary

The six volumes of *Appleton's Cyclopedia of American Biography* make it potentially one of the most valuable reference works of its kind. Edited by James Grant Wilson and John Fiske and first published in New York between 1887 and 1889, it aimed to set the standard for competing biographical dictionaries, containing, as it does, hundreds of entries relating to native and adopted American citizens dating back to the earliest settlers. Many of the nation's leading academics sent in contributions that have shed new light upon colourful, long-forgotten lives. Unfortunately some unscrupulous scribes, taking advantage of the fact that contributors were paid by the word, invented fictitious persona in order to make more money. As a result it is estimated that as many as 200 of the biographical sketches in the encyclopedia concern people who never actually existed.

The hoax entries were not discovered until some 30 years after publication when eminent scientists and historians noticed alarming discrepancies. According to his entry, Miguel da Fonseca e Silva Herrera, a Brazilian historian, was presented with a gold medal by the historical institute of Rio de Janeiro in 1820. Yet that society was not founded until 1838. Nicholas Henrion, a French scientist, was said to have arrived in South America in 1783, just as an epidemic of Asiatic cholera broke out there. However, the first such epidemic did not occur until 1835. And the biography of Charles Henry Huon de Penanster, described as a French botanist, is almost identical to that of Nicolas Thiery de Menonville, who is also featured in the encyclopedia. The vast majority of the bogus entries relate to pre-nineteenth-century European scientists who journeyed to the New World to study the region's natural history.

A few of the false entries make extravagant claims, such as that for fifteenth-century Spanish geographer Vicente y Bennazar who allegedly published a map of the world clearly showing both North and South America 16 years before Columbus sailed across the Atlantic. His brief biography stated that he 'published at Antwerp in 1476 four charts, representing the four continents of the world. Unlike Columbus, he did not imagine America to be part of Asia, but represented it as a distinct continent and, what is more remarkable, as a continent divided into two parts by an isthmus. This publication, at so early a date, and before Columbus's discovery, has caused much discussion.'

It is still not known who was responsible for the tall tales in *Appleton's Cyclopedia*.

The Cruise of the *Kawa*

Following the hardships and restrictions of the Great War, the 1920s heralded a brave new age in fields such as fashion, music and travel. But while the names of Coco Chanel and George Gershwin have lived on, their reputations enhanced by the passing decades, that of intrepid explorer Walter E. Traprock has sadly fallen by the wayside. It is difficult to understand precisely why Traprock drifted into anonymity, although the fact that he did not actually exist may have had something to do with it.

Walter E. Traprock was the invention of writer George S. Chappell and publisher George Palmer Putnam who decided to send their hero on an imaginary expedition to the South Pacific and recount his exploits in a non-fiction book. Traprock, said to hail from Derby, Connecticut, and to have been the author of *Jumping Jean*, the book of a musical version of *Les Misérables*, set sail in the good ship *Kawa*, accompanied by Captain Ezra Triplett, scientist Mr Whinney, Bohemian artist Herman Swank, and First Mate William Henry Thomas.

Published in 1921, *The Cruise of the Kawa* was described by a straight-faced Putnam in the introduction as 'a supreme, superlative epic of the South Seas.' The book told how Traprock and his companions discovered the previously uncharted Filbert Isles, so named on account of their wealth of filbert nut trees. Readers were enthralled by stories of the natives' ability to remain underwater for hours and by encounters with such exotic natives as Zambao-Zambino whose name was apparently Filbertese for 'Young-Man-Proud-of-his-Waistline'. There was also an extensive course in the Filbertese language, featuring words like 'oo-pa' (a local vegetable delicacy) and 'hoopa' (a delicious milk, 27 per cent proof). Even more fascinating was the islands' wildlife, which included giant crabs capable of pulling boats, pearls the size of apples, the ooza snake (which lived on a diet of coconut milk), and the dew fish. When rising to the surface of the water at sunrise, this tiny creature was said to have turned 'the entire ocean to a pulsating mirror of silver'. But most remarkable of all was the expedition's discovery of the fatu-liva, a curious bird that laid square eggs! To support the find, the book contained a photograph purporting to be of the nest of the fatu-liva bird, showing its square, speckled eggs and a feather. The 'speckled eggs' were four dice . . .

The caption to the photograph read: 'This is without question the most extraordinary picture which has ever been taken of any natural history subject. It corroborates in most convincing manner the author's claim to the discovery of the wonderful fatu-liva bird with its unique gift of laying square eggs. Here we see the eggs themselves in all the beauty of their cubical form and quaint marking; here we see the nest itself, made of delicately woven haro and brought carefully from the tree's summit by its discoverer, Babai-Alova-Babai. An extremely interesting feature of the picture is the presence in the nest of lapa or signal-feather. By close observation, Mr Whinney, the scientist of the expedition, discovered that whenever the mother-bird left the nest in search of food she always decorated her home with one of her wing feathers which served as a signal to her mate that she would return shortly, which she invariably did. Sceptics have said that that it would be impossible to lay a square egg. To which the author is justly entitled to say: "The camera never lies".' A second photograph showed what was claimed to be the first-ever recording of a fatu-liva chick. The gawky fledgling looked uncannily like a baby parrot.

Amazingly, many readers swallowed the hoax and believed that Traprock and his colleagues had made a startling discovery. Traprock was even invited to a lecture by the *National Geographic* in Washington, DC. It is not known whether he accepted the invitation.

An Instance of Swift Retribution

The most popular form of literature in early eighteenth-century England was the almanac, a pamphlet that featured detailed astrological predictions for the forthcoming year. Anxious to discover what the future apparently held for them, people bought almanacs in their thousands. John Partridge was essentially a cobbler by trade but seeing the business possibilities in the burgeoning astrology business, he set himself up as a stargazer and started printing his own almanacs. His gimmick was to challenge his readers to try their hands at prophecy and see whether they could match his powers of prediction and it worked so well that Partridge's almanac soon became a bestseller. In more elevated literary circles, Partridge's scribblings were treated with the disdain they warranted until he made the mistake of over-reaching himself by attacking the Church of England. In doing so, he made a dangerous enemy in the shape of Irish satirist Jonathan Swift.

Ordained in the Church of England in 1694, Swift was later made a prebendary of St Patrick's, Dublin, the city where he established himself as a writer of note. Many of his works were penned under assumed names in a bid to protect himself from the type of libel cases that were being brought against his fellow satirists on a regular basis. Reading Partridge's attack on the Church, Swift decided to stand up for his employer and in February 1708 launched a counter-offensive. Partridge's recently published almanac had forecast that a fever epidemic would sweep through London in early April 1708. Using the name 'Isaac Bickerstaff', Swift published his own almanac titled *Predictions for the Year 1708*, and among its statements was the bold prophecy that Partridge 'will infallibly die upon the 29th of March next, about eleven at night, of a raging fever.'

An outraged Partridge was provoked into an immediate response, accusing Bickerstaff of being a fraud:

'His whole Design was nothing but Deceit
The end of March will plainly show the Cheat.'

On the night of 29 March, Swift, as Bickerstaff, printed a sombre, black-edged elegy announcing the death of John Partridge. It recounted how Bickerstaff had visited Partridge on his death-bed where the dying man had finally confessed to being a fraud and had admitted turning to astrology purely to earn sufficient money to support his wife. Although Swift's declaration of death was a hoax and Partridge was still very much alive, people believed what they read. When Partridge's maid heard the tolling of a bell and asked a passer-by who it was for, she was told: 'Dr Partridge, that famous almanac-maker, who died suddenly this evening.' Undertakers and embalmers turned up at the house, and Partridge heard that a joiner was fixing the screws to his coffin. Then Partridge was woken by the sexton who wished to know if there were any instructions relating to a funeral sermon. The self-styled astrologer scarcely slept a wink that night. His wife was understandably frantic.

The following day, using another alias, Swift circulated among Londoners a pamphlet titled *The Accomplishment of the First of Mr Bickerstaff's Predictions*. It claimed that Bickerstaff's foreboding had come true and that only its timing had been slightly awry, the unfortunate Partridge having died at 7.05 p.m. instead of 11 p.m. Swift even wrote a little epitaph for Partridge:

> Here Five Foot deep lyes on his back
> A Cobbler, Starmonger, and Quack.
> Who to the Stars in pure Good-will,
> Does to his best look upward still.

It was another three months before Partridge finally summoned the courage to venture out into the street and when he did so, acquaintances stared at him in disbelief. Some told him they thought he was dead; others said he looked exactly like someone they knew who had just died. Partridge was not amused.

He published a pamphlet of his own, in which he revealed that he was still alive and accused Bickerstaff of being a fraud. But nobody believed Partridge, principally because the Stationer's Register had already removed his name from their rolls, which meant that he was unable to vote or sue anyone for defamation. John Partridge was legally dead.

Swift's reply on Bickerstaff's behalf was savage and humiliating. He remarked that Partridge was obviously dead since no living person could have written the drivel that appeared in his last almanac and noted that even Partridge's own wife had admitted that her husband possessed 'neither life nor soul'.

The hoax had succeeded in discrediting Partridge to the extent that he was forced to give up astrology and cease publication of his almanac. By contrast Swift would go on to pen *Gulliver's Travels*.

George Du Pre: The Man Who Talked Too Much

Six years after the end of the Second World War, *Reader's Digest* magazine came to hear of an epic tale of heroism which clearly deserved a wider audience. It concerned a young Canadian, George Du Pre, who, recruited by British Intelligence, had apparently been trained for nine months to behave like 'the village half-wit' before parachuting into German-occupied Normandy. There, he had joined the Resistance and posed as a simple French garage mechanic to help smuggle allied airmen out of France. After saving countless lives by his selfless endeavour, he had finally been captured by the Gestapo. Tortured by the Germans, he was given an enema of sulphuric acid and had boiling water poured into his clamped-open mouth, but he had stubbornly refused to talk. And in one last dramatic act of bravery, he had somehow managed to escape back to his homeland where he was feted as a national hero.

Du Pre had recounted his war experiences to church and club meetings across Canada and when the story reached the ears of *Reader's Digest*, the magazine sent former war correspondent Quentin Reynolds to interview him and write an article. Reynolds was not a man to be taken in easily, but he was convinced that Du Pre was genuine. He body bore all the hallmarks of Nazi torture. He had a speech impediment, no teeth, a broken nose and hideous scars on his hands and throat, all of which, he claimed, were the legacy of his ill-treatment by the Germans. Reynolds duly wrote the piece for *Reader's Digest* but also believed that Du Pre's story had the makings of a compelling book, and so he approached Bennett Cerf, the head of publishers Random House. Cerf was suitably impressed, but prior to publication Reynolds submitted his manuscript to British Intelligence for verification. However, they refused to look at it because of their policy of never confirming or denying that any individual had been a member of the secret service. Nevertheless the book went on to become a 1953 best-seller under the title *The Man Who Wouldn't Talk*.

When Reynolds insisted on splitting the royalties from the book with Du Pre, the modest Canadian at first refused but then promised all income to the Boy Scouts of Canada. It seemed a truly magnanimous gesture, but one which was perhaps born more out of guilt than philanthropy.

For shortly after the book went on sale, a Royal Canadian Air Force officer walked into the offices of the *Calgary Herald* with a photograph of himself and Du Pre taken in Victoria, British Columbia, in 1942 – at a time when, according to his book, Du Pre was supposed to have been in France ruffling the Germans' feathers. Intrigued, the *Herald* dispatched reporter Douglas Collins, himself a former Intelligence operative, to talk to Du Pre. Initially Du Pre maintained the pretence but Collins soon tripped him up by getting him to say he knew Intelligence personnel and training camps that Collins had invented. Almost relieved that the truth was finally out, the 'man who wouldn't talk' did. He confessed to the *Herald* that the entire story was a hoax – that he had spent the whole war in Canada and England, and had never set foot in France. What had started out as the simple, fanciful exaggerations of a country boy had now grown dangerously out of hand. Du Pre himself admitted: 'The story eventually got bigger than I was.'

The editor of the *Herald* phoned Cerf who was dismayed to hear that Du Pre's scars were more likely to have been caused by farm machinery than the Gestapo. In turn Cerf rang DeWitt Wallace, the publisher of *Reader's Digest*, and suggested that the best way to deal with their blunder was to laugh it off. Sensing the business possibilities in a hoaxer's tale, Cerf urged the title of the book to be changed to *The Man Who Talked Too Much* and suggested that booksellers move it to the fiction section where it would be more at home. As for Reynolds, he was devastated at having been taken in. 'Trust George Du Pre?' he said. 'I'd have bet my life on that man!'

The Premature Demise of Gabriel Garcia Marquez

A poem seemingly signed by Colombian author Gabriel Garcia Marquez that entered literary circles in December 2000, and which appeared to predict his own imminent death, was subsequently exposed as a clever e-mail hoax.

Billed as a farewell, it lamented the impending demise of the renowned purveyor of magic realism whose novels included *Chronicle of a Death Foretold* and who was a close friend of both Bill Clinton and Fidel Castro. A brief note attached to the e-mail poem said the 72-year-old Nobel Prize winner had retired from public life as a result of worsening lymphatic cancer, and this was his goodbye.

Marquez had written his masterpiece, *One Hundred Years of Solitude*, after locking himself in isolation at home and smoking six packets of cigarettes a day, but in 1999 he was diagnosed with cancer. After that, he disappeared from public gaze.

Rich in imagery and written very much in Marquez's style, the fake poem fooled people all over the world. It began: 'If for a moment God were to forget that I am a rag doll and granted me a piece of life, I probably wouldn't say everything that I think; rather, I would think about everything I say . . . I would value things not for their worth but for what they mean. I would sleep less, dream more, understanding that for each minute we close our eyes, we lose 60 seconds of light.'

It also contained a number of South American references, so beloved by Marquez. One passage ran: 'My God, if I had a heart, I would write my hate on ice, and wait for the sun to show. Over the stars I would paint with a Van Gogh dream a Benedetti poem, and a Serrat song would be the serenade I'd offer to the moon.' Benedetti was a Uruguayan novelist and poet; Serrat a Catalan singer.

On learning of the hoax, Marquez, who was working on his memoirs and a book of short stories at the time, was furious that the fake poem had been sent to so many literary figures. Among those to receive it was novelist Susan Hill. 'Initially I thought it inspired,' she said. 'Halfway down I thought it began to be a bit sentimentally phrased. But I thought the first half was so true.' Another recipient was playwright Arnold Wesker. He, too, recognized weaknesses in the piece but decided: 'These are the thoughts of a dying man. Inevitably some will be sentimental, some wise and some unnecessarily humble.'

Meanwhile the true author of the e-mail poem was keeping a low profile.

Al Capone's Henchman

Hugo Baruch was an inveterate fantasist. In the early part of his life, his lies and deceptions repeatedly landed him in trouble with authority but then he hit upon the idea that would change – and make – his fortune. He reinvented himself as Jack Bilbo, one of Al Capone's most bloodthirsty henchmen, and set about writing a book recounting the murderous exploits of the Chicago mob. The resulting publication took the literary world by storm – even though scarcely a word of it was true.

Born in 1907 to a wealthy German father and an English mother, Baruch was raised partly in Holland where he proved such a rebellious child that he was dispatched to boarding school. Any hopes that the move might instil some discipline into young Baruch appeared decidedly optimistic, judging by his own account that he blackmailed the headmaster into promoting him each year by threatening that otherwise his father would take him out of school, thereby depriving the establishment of much-needed fees. In view of Baruch's subsequent career, it is difficult to determine how much of this tale is inventive bravado, but one thing is certain: he was not lacking in confidence.

On eventually leaving school, he travelled extensively in the United

States before returning to his native Germany to work for a film company. He proceeded to drift from job to job (journalist, theatre producer, artist) and from country to country, his wanderings curtailed only by a spell of three months in a German jail for fraud. By 1930 he was scraping a living as a Berlin taxi driver when he met Stephen Lorant, editor of the *Münchener Illustrierte Presse*. Seizing the opportunity to fulfil his dreams of becoming a writer, he passed himself off as one Jack Bilbo, supposedly a member of Al Capone's gang, and delighted Lorant with colourful tales of Chicago gangland. Lorant was sufficiently impressed to commission a book titled *Carrying a Gun for Al Capone* in which 'Bilbo' lifted the lid on life with the mob. In his 1948 autobiography, he revealed the irony of the situation. 'What I really wanted was to be a writer, but all my books, sent to publishers under pseudonyms, were returned. Now, with a juicy murder on every page, fifteen different publishers in fifteen different countries were rushing to get their filthy hands on it.'

Although he had never been to Chicago or carried a gun in his life, let alone been one of Capone's mob, 'Bilbo' played the part to the full, posing for publicity pictures in a trenchcoat and hat with the brim pulled down, and brandishing a pistol in his hand. The book described how 'Bilbo' started out working in an office for the gang before serving his apprenticeship as a gunman and finally graduating to cruising the streets of Chicago as one of Capone's personal bodyguards. To impressionable young men and women leading dull existences, the narrative was compelling, littered as it was with shoot-outs, punch-ups and even a gangland execution. It also offered a rare insight into the world of the gangster and his code of conduct, not to mention arguably the most in-depth portrait to date of Capone himself. The author wrote: 'Most of the pictures of Capone do not show him as he is. True, he did have a certain animal wildness in his face, but a wildness reminiscent of a wildcat rather than a gorilla.'

First printed in German, the book sold so well that it was translated into a number of other languages and published in many countries including the United States. It also attracted favourable reviews. The *Sunday Times* critic enthused: 'It contains dramatic glimpses into a sinister underworld, and . . . an excellent pen portrait of Al Capone.'

In 1934 – four years after publication – 'Bilbo' finally came clean and admitted the hoax: the contents of the book were a figment of his own imagination. It was a work of pure fiction. Curiously, his confession did nothing to harm sales and the book remained in print for years, becoming a worldwide bestseller and making its author a wealthy man. Nobody seemed to care – or remember — that he was a fake. When some of his paintings were displayed in London in 1939, *Time* magazine reported the event as an exhibition by a former Chicago gangster, while at least one newspaper stated as fact the erroneous claim that the artist had killed upwards of a dozen people.

Revelling in the full-time persona of Jack Bilbo and freed from any financial shackles, Baruch spent the rest of his life trying to live up to his reputation as a writer/adventurer. He worked as a journalist in Paris, became embroiled in political intrigue, wrote several more books as Bilbo, and opened a bar in Spain where he entertained the likes of actor Douglas Fairbanks and author G. K. Chesterton. In his autobiography Chesterton described mine host as an 'authentic American gangster who had actually written a book of confessions about his own organised robbery and racketeering.' Baruch was apparently happy to give the public what they wanted. After all, his was just too good a story to let the facts get in the way.

The Bard of Bristol

The tale of eighteenth-century poet Thomas Chatterton is a sad affair. Born of humble stock, he was a brilliant young author in his own right but chose instead to forge medieval verses and pass them off as the works of another. When he was finally exposed, London critics rejected him and rather than face starving to death, he chose to commit suicide by poisoning himself with arsenic at the tender age of 17.

Chatterton was born on 20 November 1752 into an impoverished Bristol family. His father, also named Thomas, was a choirmaster at the church of St Mary Redcliffe, but died three months before young Thomas was born. The boy's mother Sarah and older sister Mary were worried that Thomas was a slow learner and struggled to teach him the alphabet. Then suddenly, at the age of six, he picked up one of his father's old books – a fifteenth-century French songbook – and taught himself to read the ancient script, which was just as well since he was instructed in only the barest basics of reading and writing at the poor boys' school to which he was sent. Perusing through some more of his father's old documents, taken from the coffers of St Mary Redcliffe, he was inspired in 1764 to write a poem in medieval script titled *Elinoure and Juga*. The documents made mention of William Canynge, Lord Mayor of Bristol (who had died in 1474), and of his friend, a merchant named Thomas Rowley. Chatterton now decided to compose his medieval poem in Rowley's name and used obsolete spellings and words to make it appear genuine. As a finishing touch, he wrote it on a piece of parchment, which he rubbed first with yellow ochre and then on the dirty ground before crumpling it in his hand to give the manuscript that aged look.

Chatterton passed the poem on to Bristol antiquarian William Barrett who received it with such enthusiasm that Chatterton set to work forging further medieval poems in Rowley's name. In the course of these verses, 'Rowley' extolled the virtues of Bristol at the expense of 'cowarde Londonne', thereby winning local acclaim.

By now, Chatterton was serving an apprenticeship with a scrivener, Mr Lambert, but he still dreamed of seeing his poems reach a wider field. Above all, he craved acceptance from the London literary set and so, with the aid of Barrett, he wrote to Horace Walpole, the leading English writer of the time, for an assessment of 'Rowley's work, enclosing *A History of English Painters* and a selection of poems. Chatterton first wrote to Walpole on 25 March 1769: 'Sir, Being versed a little in antiquitys, I have met with several Curious Manuscripts among which the following may be of service to you, in any future edition of your truly entertaining *Anecdotes of Painting* – In correcting the mistakes (if any) in the Notes you will greatly oblige. Your most humble servant, Thomas Chatterton.' Chatterton took care not to give any indication as to his true social position.

Walpole was initially enthusiastic about the beautiful fifteenth-century poems and wrote back, offering to publish Rowley and asking Chatterton to send him more poems. Emboldened, Chatterton duly obliged, but this time mentioned his family's financial status and his own position as an apprentice. Walpole immediately became suspicious as to how a 16-year-old apprentice came to be in possession of one of the greatest literary discoveries of the century, and sought the opinion of a friend, the poet Thomas Gray. Sifting through the manuscripts, Gray detected some of his own style in Rowley and had no hesitation in declaring them to be fakes. Walpole wrote back to Chatterton, condemning the boy as a simple forger and strongly advising him against the continuation of the deception. Chatterton was deeply wounded and demanded the return of the manuscripts, insisting that they were genuine.

In May 1770 Chatterton extricated himself from his apprenticeship, borrowed whatever money he could from friends and family, and decided to try and make his fortune as a poet in London. He lived with an aunt, but barely eked out a living writing beneath himself for popular magazines. What little money he did earn was either dispatched to his poverty-stricken mother and sister back in Bristol or went towards fitting himself out in fine clothes so that he could mingle with the rich men of London, among whom he hoped to find a patron.

With no money left to spend on food, Chatterton's health and already fragile mental state began to suffer. The trickle of work dried up altogether. In desperation, he temporarily abandoned his literary ambitions and tried to obtain a post as a ship's surgeon with the East India Tea Company, but his old mentor William Barrett refused to provide a letter of recommendation on the grounds that Chatterton had no formal medical training. Chatterton felt rejection at every turn.

July saw Chatterton move to a tiny garret apartment in Gray's Inn. The room had inadequate ventilation for countering the oppressive heat of summer and by now its occupant survived on a loaf of bread a week, bought stale to save money. On 30 August he decided to end this miserable existence by committing suicide although his chosen method of arsenic poisoning was tortuously painful and slow. His body was found by his landlady Mrs Angell. Torn-up manuscripts were strewn across the floor – the final despairing act of a supremely gifted writer who saw himself as a failure.

Ironically Chatterton's greatest success was achieved posthumously. Although he didn't live to see an edition of his poems published, seven years after his death a collection of his Rowley poems appeared in print, with several more collections to follow. The same literary circles that had once shunned him now began to take an interest in Chatterton's life and work with the result that a number of biographies were written about the tragic young man. At the request of Chatterton's biographers, who donated a sum of money to the cause, the city of Bristol erected a monument in his name, situated outside the church of St Mary Redcliffe, his favourite haunt as a boy. It stood there for many years until renovations forced its removal and new church officials deemed it blasphemous to keep a monument to a suicide victim on holy ground. At last report, the monument was in storage and, alas, almost forgotten . . . rather like Thomas Chatterton himself.

The Hitler Diaries

That a small-time East German forger could hoodwink some of the world's leading historians, handwriting experts and students of Nazi memorabilia into believing that his home-made Hitler diaries were the genuine article remains one of the more endearing hoaxes of our times. It is difficult not to feel a degree of sympathy for the petty criminal who, operating from the back room of his shop in Stuttgart, composed the fake diaries to order and managed to milk around $4.8 million from the German magazine *Stern* simply because the experts were so desperate to believe that the volumes were genuine that they overlooked any number of glaring errors. What Konrad Kujau may have lacked in integrity, he made up for in sheer impudence.

Konrad Kujau ('Konni' to his friends) was born in Loebau, Saxony, on 27 June 1938. Raised in an orphanage, he perfected the art of forgery at an age when most youngsters are still mastering their 12 times table and was soon earning pocket money by selling fake autographs of East German politicians. He then studied art at Dresden but fled to West Germany in 1957 to evade arrest on minor charges of theft. Settling outside Stuttgart, he found legitimate work as a window-cleaner but quickly realized that such a menial job was hardly worthy of his talents and returned to a life of crime. He adopted a new identity – 'Peter Fischer' – under which name he was jailed twice, again for relatively minor offences. In 1962 he opened the Pelican Dance Bar in partnership with Edith Lieblang (a fellow refugee from the East) but the business flopped and Kujau ended up behind the wrong sort of bars, this time for forging luncheon vouchers. After that, he managed to stay on the right side of the law until the authorities discovered that Peter Fischer was really Konrad Kujau who was still wanted in East Germany. Another spell in prison beckoned.

Fortunately Edith was more reliable and had set up the profitable Lieblang Cleaning Company. Admiring her business acumen, Kujau decided to start collecting Nazi memorabilia for which there was a thriving market. He advertised in newspapers and by the end of the 1960s had amassed a sizeable collection of helmets, uniforms, medals and flags. He began to run out of space in his apartment and was forced to open a little shop in Stuttgart's Aspergstrasse. Business was brisk but, with his overheads also rising, he decided that a general price increase was necessary. To justify this, he started forging documents of authentication, including a note supposedly from Rudolf Hess declaring that a rusty, nondescript First World War helmet was the very one worn by Hitler himself in 1917. Unaware that the guarantees had actually been penned by Kujau and that they weren't worth the paper they were written on, collectors willingly paid extra for items carrying these assurances of authenticity. Seeing the potential for dramatically improving his profit margins, Kujau decided that what he couldn't acquire he would manufacture himself. To this end, he began to copy Hitler's handwriting and artistic style.

Among his regular customers was Fritz Stiefel, owner of a small engineering factory in the suburbs of Stuttgart. Having discovered Kujau's shop in 1975, Stiefel went on to spend more than 250,000 marks (approximately $110,000) there in the course of the next six years on 160 drawings and paintings plus poems, letters and speech notes, all supposedly in the hand of the Fuhrer. Stiefel's appetite was insatiable, encouraging Kujau to produce the ultimate Hitler collectable – his personal diary.

Taking the information from a 1935 Nazi Party yearbook, Kujau prepared a single volume titled Political and Private Notes. In a faithful copy of Hitler's handwriting, the tome covered the period from January to June 1935. It was decorated with a red wax seal, a black ribbon and the brass Gothic initials 'F H', Kujau having apparently mistaken the Gothic capital F for an A when he bought the type in Hong Kong! Stiefel could hardly contain his delight and wanted to know whether further volumes of Hitler's diaries were likely to become available. Kujau said he would see what he could do.

Stiefel's enthusiasm almost paled into apathy alongside Gerd Heidemann. A photo-journalist with *Stern* magazine since 1955, Heidemann's fascination with the Nazis bordered on obsession. Indeed his second wife had left him because she was tired of playing second fiddle to his collection of toy soldiers. In 1973 he achieved one of his great ambitions by buying and restoring Hermann Goering's former motor yacht, *Carin II*. In the course of the transaction, he met Goering's daughter, Edda, and embarked on a torrid affair with her, thereby, it has been suggested, fulfilling another lifelong dream. The affair eventually fizzled out and in 1979 Heidemann married Gina, a former airline stewardess. He promised her a honeymoon in South America. She visualized sun-drenched beaches. Instead he disappeared into the mountains to search for Nazi war criminals Martin and Bormann and Josef Mengele, Auschwitz's infamous 'Doctor of Death'. Bormann and Mengele remained typically elusive but Heidemann tracked down an acceptable substitute in the form of Klaus Barbie, the 'Butcher of Lyons'.

By 1979 Heidemann's career at *Stern* had reached something of a plateau. He was no longer the golden boy and needed a big story to re-establish his reputation. Meanwhile his new bride and his hobby were both proving expensive investments, the upkeep of the yacht alone eating up two-thirds of his salary. Desperate times called for desperate measures and he tried to sell his beloved yacht for 1.1 million marks, but found no takers. So he contemplated parting with some of his other Nazi memorabilia and was given the name of Fritz Stiefel as a possible buyer.

On meeting, the two men talked excitedly about their shared passion and when Stiefel revealed himself to be the proud owner of a genuine Hitler diary, Heidemann pleaded to be allowed to see it. On 6 January 1980 Stiefel showed the journalist the diary he had purchased in good faith from the man he knew as Peter Fischer. It was a slim, A4-sized book with over 100 lined pages, some half full, others blank. Some entries were written in pencil, others in ink. Many of the pages bore what appeared to be Hitler's signature. Heidemann was enthralled and wanted to know more. Stiefel was reluctant to give too much away, partly because he knew little about the source. All he could repeat was what Kujau had told him – namely that the source had influential relatives in East Germany and that it was rumoured that another 26 volumes might become available in due course. What they did not know was that this was dependent on how quickly Kujau could write them.

In Heidemann's mind every piece of the jigsaw began to fit into place. He knew from his studies of the period that one of the last flights to leave the besieged city of Berlin on 20 April 1945 had been carrying Hitler's personal papers to his Alpine retreat until it crashed near the village of Börnersdorf on the Czech border. Heidemann concluded that these personal papers must have contained Hitler's much-prized diaries, which had obviously been secreted in East Germany ever since the plane crash.

He informed *Stern* of his discovery, and at once his star began to rise. *Stern* shared Heidemann's interest in the Nazis purely because stories about the figures of the Third Reich were good for circulation, and gave the go-ahead for him to seek out the remaining diaries. An associate (a former junior member of the SS) told him he thought the first diary had come from a dealer called Fischer. Using the ex-SS man as an intermediary and with the cautious backing of *Stern*, Heidemann bid two million marks for the remaining diaries. In return he was given Fischer's telephone number and on 15 January 1981 Heidemann and Fischer (alias Kujau) made contact for the first time. It was an encounter that would change both their lives.

Kujau informed Heidemann that in addition to the diaries he also possessed a number of other Hitler manuscripts including a sequel to *Mein Kampf* and an opera that the Fuhrer had composed in his youth, *Wieland der Schmied* ('*Wieland the Blacksmith*'). Kujau also stressed the need for secrecy, claiming that most of the diaries were in the possession of a highly placed officer in the East German army and had to be smuggled into the West — often inside pianos — at considerable risk to all concerned. For Heidemann, it all added to the intrigue and, indeed, to the plausibility of Kujau's story.

Heidemann gleefully reported the news back to his superiors at *Stern*, pointing out that he could not name his source as secrecy was of paramount importance. Although there were some dissenters within the organization plus others who were kept totally in the dark, *Stern*'s publishers agreed to give Heidemann the funds to buy more diaries.

With a deposit of 200,000 marks and the gift of Goering's dress uniform (a present from Edda), Heidemann flew to Stuttgart to open negotiations with Kujau. At first Kujau expressed reluctance, claiming that someone in the United States had offered him $2 million for the diaries, but in the end Goering's uniform swung the day.

Over the next three weeks Kujau rattled off three diaries, writing what might pass as Hitler's daily thoughts in Gothic script into a black A4 notebook. To give the finished article an aged appearance, he would pour tea on to each page. He would then slap the pages together and batter them against the table to create the necessary impression of wear and tear. Finally he affixed two red wax seals in the form of a German eagle on the covers together with a forged note from Hess declaring the diaries to be the property of A. Hitler. The contents were taken from medical records, newspapers and a library of reference books, particularly the two-volume work *Hitler's Speeches and Proclamations*. Some of the entries were breathtakingly banal, scarcely worthy of such a forceful orator. One read: 'Meet all the leaders of the Storm Troopers in Bavaria, give them medals. They pledge lifelong loyalty to the Fuhrer, with tears in eyes. What a splendid body of men!' Another ran, 'Must not forget tickets for the Olympic Games for Eva'. On a bad news day the best Kujau could manage was 'On my feet all day long'. And there was the classic 'Because of the new pills I have violent flatulence, and – says Eva – bad breath.' *Stern* paid around $80 per word for this material.

Heidemann took the first consignment of diaries to *Stern* on 18 February 1981. Even though nobody present could read a word of the German script, all were convinced it was genuine and handled the diaries with extreme care and reverence. Due to the overriding need for secrecy, they decided against bringing in outside experts to examine the documents until a full set was in the company's possession. That day, without consulting a handwriting expert, a forensic scientist or a historian, *Stern* managing director Manfred Fischer committed the company to the purchase of 27 volumes of the Hitler diaries at 85,000 marks apiece plus another 200,000 marks for the third volume of *Mein Kampf* – a total outlay of around 2.5 million marks. It was not only Kujau who was to be handsomely rewarded for his efforts. Heidemann, too, would receive an advance of 300,000 marks when eight volumes of the diaries had been delivered.

Kujau slaved away on the diaries for the next three years. When the money started to roll in, Kujau's neighbours noticed a change in his behaviour. Whereas previously his girlfriend Edith had been forced to explain away the fact that he was spending so much time alone – he was working on a project for *Stern*, she said – now he made frequent, ostentatious visits to local nightclubs, often spending as much as $4,000 in the course of an evening. Sometimes he would arrive in uniform and insist on being addressed as 'General Kujau'.

Although he continued to preach the virtues of secrecy, Heidemann could not help boasting about his success and contacted an old SS friend, Wilhelm Mohnke, to read out a few extracts from the diaries. Mohnke immediately denounced them as fakes, but Heidemann remained unperturbed. Then Eberhard Jaeckel, Professor of History at the University of Stuttgart, announced that a collection of Hitler's poems, which he had obtained from Stiefel and Kujau, were forgeries. *Stern* worried in case the poems had come from the same source as the diaries and asked Heidemann to investigate. Instead of getting in touch with Jaeckel, he simply sent the poems to Kujau and asked him whether he had ever seen them before. Naturally Kujau said he hadn't. That was good enough for Heidemann.

In return for its colossal expenditure on the diaries, *Stern* was planning to sell extracts to magazines and newspapers right across the world. This required prior confirmation of authenticity. Three handwriting experts stated categorically that the writing in the diaries was Hitler's. They reached this conclusion by comparing it with other samples of Hitler's script – little knowing that the comparison samples had also been forged by Kujau. But when the West German Federal Police conducted a series of forensic tests on various items from the Hitler archive, their scientists found that six of the nine documents tested were fakes as they displayed traces of a paper whitener not in use until after the Second World War. A worried Heidemann rang Kujau who calmly shrugged aside his concerns. The documents must have become contaminated in the laboratories, he suggested. Heidemann was reassured.

In the meantime rights to the story behind the discovery of the Hitler diaries had been offered to Rupert Murdoch's Times Newspapers in London. The *Sunday Times* had been embarrassed 15 years earlier, in 1968, after spending £250,000 on the diaries of Mussolini, which turned out to be fakes, and was anxious to avoid a repeat performance. Accordingly the eminent historian Lord Dacre (Hugh Trevor-Roper, author of *The Last Days of Hitler*) was dispatched to Zurich to authenticate the diaries. Prophetically, the date was 1 April.

Trevor-Roper had grave reservations initially. He knew that Hitler hated writing and had virtually given up writing in his own hand after 1933. Moreover there had never been any historical evidence, either from German archives or from the accounts of colleagues, to indicate that Hitler kept a diary. On the journey to Zurich, Trevor-Roper was handed a 20-page document written by Heidemann, outlining the background to the discovery of the diaries (as he knew it) and containing several extracts. The most sensational suggested that Hitler had known of – and approved — Hess's abortive peace flight to Scotland in May 1941. This flew in the face of all known findings.

Trevor-Roper was taken to a Zurich bank where he was shown 58 volumes purporting to be Hitler's handiwork, along with a bound volume of the Fuhrer's original drawings and paintings and even the trusty First World War helmet. The historian was also invited to inspect the favourable reports from the three handwriting experts. In no time at all he was won over. He wrote in *The Times*: 'When I entered the back room in the Swiss bank and turned the pages of those volumes, my doubts gradually dissolved. I am now satisfied that the documents are authentic . . . Whereas signatures, single documents, or even groups of documents can be skilfully forged, a whole coherent archive covering 35 years is far less easily manufactured. Such a disproportionate and indeed extravagant effort offers too large and vulnerable a flank to the critics who will undoubtedly assail it . . . The archive, in fact, is not only a collection of documents which can be individually tested: it coheres as a whole and the diaries are an integral part of it. That is the internal evidence of authenticity.'

On 22 April 1983 *Stern* ran its exclusive story announcing to the world the discovery of the Hitler diaries, but no sooner had the publication hit the news-stands than *Stern* received the results of a second batch of forensic tests, which stated beyond doubt that much of the Hitler archive was a forgery. Trevor-Roper suddenly got cold feet but the *Sunday Times* went ahead and published anyway, to the delight of its rivals who denounced the diaries as a hoax. Heidemann was now under mounting pressure from *Stern* to divulge his sources. He began changing his story, further fuelling Trevor-Roper's doubts. *Stern* published its first instalment of the diaries on 25 April and attempted to defend them at a press conference in Hamburg. However, the occasion was hijacked by maverick English historian David Irving who pointed out a glaring inconsistency. In his diary, Hitler was supposed to have written about the July 1944 bomb plot, yet a promotional film made by *Stern* and screened at the press conference clearly showed him having to greet Mussolini a few hours after the explosion with his left hand. Yet his writing in the diary for that day was unimpaired. *Stern* executives shuffled awkwardly in their seats.

Somewhat belatedly the West German Federal Archives were asked to examine three of the diaries. The results of their forensic tests came through on 6 May and confirmed that the documents were forged. The chemical paper whitener present had not been used before 1955 while the labels stuck to the front of the books, supposedly signed by Martin Bormann and Rudolf Hess, had all been typed on the same typewriter! Tests on the ink proved that the Hess volume had been written in the last two years and that writing from a 1943 diary was less than a year old. The paper, the binding, the glue and the thread were all found to have been manufactured after the war. The archivists also discovered a number of factual errors within the diaries. A law passed on 19 January 1933 was entered in the diary under 19 January 1934 and other mistakes were copied from Kujau's main source, *Hitler's Speeches and Proclamations*. Hans Booms, director of the West German Federal Archives, declared the diaries to be 'grotesque and superficial forgeries'.

If Kujau was wounded by such damnation of his work, he did not waste much time brooding over it. Once the forgery was exposed and Heidemann was sacked by *Stern*, he knew that the trail would soon lead back to him. He went on the run but was apprehended by the West German police at the Austrian border on 14 May. By the end of the month he had confessed to producing the Hitler diaries and other fake documents purporting to be the work of the Fuhrer.

In 1985, at the end of an 11-month trial, Kujau was sentenced to four and a half years in prison for forgery. Heidemann, who protested that he had been duped by Kujau, was also implicated and sent to jail.

Kujau was released 18 months early when it was learned that he was suffering from cancer. Despite the fact that *Stern*'s money had never been recovered, he now told the world that he was in debt to the tune of some $250,000 – money he owed to lawyers and tax officials. He also insisted that he had told Heidemann all along that the diaries were fakes and that Heidemann had replied that he was merely passing them on to a former aide of Hitler's who was in hiding in South America. Kujau claimed to have been shocked when he saw his work in newspapers and magazines.

By now balding and portly, Kujau seemed to revel in the publicity he had received during the court case and decided to capitalize on his notoriety. He opened a gallery in Stuttgart where he sold 'genuine' forgeries of Hitler's paintings, and also turned his hand to producing Dalis, Monets, Rembrandts and Van Goghs, signing them with his own and the original artist's name. So successful were his efforts, which could fetch up to $70,000 each, that by the 1990s a counterfeit submarket had appeared in fakes of Kujau's fakes.

In 1994 Kujau stood unsuccessfully for mayor in his home town of Loebau. Two years later he ran for mayor of Stuttgart, securing 901 votes. He had always intended writing his memoirs but when a book appeared in his name entitled *The Originality of Forgery*, he denounced it as a fake. 'I did not write one line of this book,' he protested. It was just another bizarre twist in the life of Konrad Kujau.

Although he remained an essentially jocular figure, trouble seemed to follow him around after that. He was fined for keeping a number of forged driving licences in his apartment and for firing a semi-automatic weapon in a Stuttgart bar. The judge told him: 'You are very apparently a man who is attracted by that which is illegal.'

The cancer finally claimed him on 12 September 2000. On a wall in his home there used to hang a handwritten letter from Hitler. It was addressed to the young Kujau and gave him authority to 'compile' the Fuhrer's diary after his death, for posterity. The letter was, of course, a fake – Konrad Kujau's last laugh at the hoax that made his name.

Chapter 3

The Paranormal

Pictures from Mount Clemens

Dan and Grant Jaroslaw lived with their mother in a ramshackle house in Mount Clemens, Michigan. The building had been gutted by fire two years previously and Mrs Jaroslaw and the two boys lived in the basement, the remainder of the house being uninhabitable. The boys' father, divorced from their mother, lived a few miles away with his second family.

Grant, 15, was a high school freshman who had decided to skip school on the bitterly cold afternoon of 9 January 1967. Elder brother Dan, 17, had dropped out of high school and worked for a company making sails. He had always been fascinated by UFOs.

The Jaroslaw house was a mile from Selfridge Air Force Base and overlooked Lake St Clair where the local board of health had recently been carrying out pollution tests on the water. Yellow dye marker had been flushed into a septic tank. If sewage were polluting the lake, the yellow dye would then show on the surface ice. The brothers were eager to discover the results of the test and, armed with Grant's $20 Polaroid Swinger camera, stepped into their snow-covered yard at around 2.30 that afternoon to photograph the lake.

According to their account, Grant was holding the camera when Dan spotted a dark grey, saucer-shaped object suspended over the lake. 'It was hovering above the ice,' said Dan, 'but near open water, about a quarter mile from shore.' The boys estimated the object to be approximately the size of a helicopter, but were unable to detect any markings or windows. 'We've lived in Selfridge for 14 years and see a lot of planes,' added Dan, 'but never anything like this.'

The mystery object hovered motionless and in silence for about ten minutes. 'I was real scared it was going to land,' confessed Grant, 'but Dan told me to keep taking pictures and I did.' Then without warning, the object suddenly accelerated and sped off towards the south-east, leaving behind no vapour trail, no marks in the sky, just four photographs taken by Grant.

Five minutes later, a coastguard helicopter appeared over the lake and the boys photographed that too.

When the boys told their mother what they had seen, she contacted the *Detroit News* and supplied the paper with three of the photos, the fourth having apparently been lost somewhere in the house. The pictures were subsequently reproduced in a number of newspapers and magazines as proof of the existence of UFOs.

But cracks soon began to appear in the brothers' story. The frame numbers on the backs of the pictures indicated that the helicopter must have been over the lake during the time the boys photographed the object. The helicopter photo was number three in the series of five. The first two frames showed the object; the third was of the helicopter; the fourth was the one that mysteriously went missing, but which the boys said was of the mystery craft; and the fifth also showed the flying object. Yet the helicopter pilot saw nothing untoward. Similarly, the nearby Air Force base reported that no unidentified object had been picked up on the radar screens.

As speculation mounted as to the authenticity of the pictures and the story, the Jaroslaw family retreated into their shells. Despite pleas from Air Force and civilian investigators, they reclaimed the original prints and refused to allow detailed examination. They refused to be interviewed, twice changed their unlisted telephone number and posted large 'Keep Out' and 'Beware of the Dog' signs on their house to deter newshounds.

A variety of tests were conducted on copies of the original photos but these proved inconclusive. However, a more thorough investigation, led by Major Raymond Nyles of the US Air Force, found inconsistencies in the photographs, prompting UFO expert Dr J. Allen Hynek to suspect that they may have been faked. There was also the question of why the brothers would use a camera that took black and white pictures to photograph a yellow dye. The boys' father stood by their story and insisted that they submit to a polygraph test to prove whether or not they were telling the truth. They were extremely nervous when undergoing the test and the examiner felt unable to exonerate them.

The mystery lingered on for nine years. Some dismissed the Mount Clemens pictures as a hoax; others saw them as definite evidence of the existence of UFOs. Then in 1976, on behalf of his brother and himself, Grant Jaroslaw wrote to Dr Hynek, admitting that the whole story had been a fabrication.

'Dan suggested to make a model of a UFO,' wrote Grant, 'hang it up with a string, and if the photo turned out good, we could play a joke on our family and friends to see their reaction and then tell them the truth. Dan made a quick model. Then we wrapped plain white thread with paper tape around two poles several times, and then taped the model to the threads. I was reluctant to waste the film, because I thought the threads and tape would be visible on the photo. The weather conditions were just right, the photo came out so real-looking we took some more. At the same time we were taking the pictures, a helicopter flew over the area. Just for the heck of it, I photographed it, too. We showed our mother the photos and pretended they were real. But before we knew it, while we were in another room, she had called the newspaper.

'Dan and I for some reason decided to let the paper have a story. We made it up as the reporter asked his questions. We just didn't think the story would become as big as it did. We are sorry if we caused anyone any trouble over this.'

Fairies at the Bottom of the Garden

One Saturday afternoon in July 1917 at a house in the Cottingley area of Bradford, Yorkshire, 16-year-old Elsie Wright asked her father if she could borrow his camera in order to take a photograph of her young cousin, Frances Griffiths, down by the beck which ran along the bottom of the long garden. Arthur Wright was initially reluctant, partly because the camera was new and partly because Elsie had never taken a photo before, but eventually he relented and the two girls set off down the garden. The resultant photograph – which appeared to show five little spirits, with ballerinas' legs and dragonfly wings, dancing beneath Frances's face against the backdrop of a waterfall – would surely have been dismissed as a joke but for the intervention of no less an authority than Sir Arthur Conan Doyle. When the creator of Sherlock Holmes, possessor of the sharpest brain in literature and a man capable of solving the most intricate of mysteries, ruled that the picture was genuine, people sat up and took notice. And the riddle of the Cottingley Fairies rumbled on for another 70 years.

Frances Griffiths and her mother Anne had just arrived in England from South Africa and were staying with the Wright family that summer. Frances was an adventurous ten-year-old who enjoyed nothing more than playing with cousin Elsie, a former art student who had also worked as a photographer's assistant, in the small wooded creek behind Elsie's home. The secluded spot was a children's paradise, ideal for all manner of ingenious games. However, Frances's mother was not amused when her daughter repeatedly returned to the house with wet shoes and stockings after falling into the stream off the slippery stepping-stones. Eventually she told Frances to keep away from the water, but the girls disobeyed her and sneaked back to the beck whenever the opportunity arose. In exasperation, Anne Griffiths demanded to know why they spent so much time down there. What was so fascinating about Cottingley Beck? Frances told her they went there to see the fairies.

The statement was greeted with disbelief even though Elsie insisted that she, too, had seen fairies. Both mothers and Elsie's father attributed it to over-active imaginations. The Wrights had become used to Elsie's passion for fairies as she had regularly drawn or painted tiny elves and goblins since childhood. Now the girls decided to repay their parents for their scepticism by obtaining photographic proof of the existence of the fairies. Within half an hour of borrowing the camera, they were back in the house begging Arthur Wright to develop the plate. After tea, with an excited Elsie by his side, he set to work in his makeshift darkroom and produced the image of Frances with the dancing figures. He told his daughter sternly: 'You've been up to summat.'

Elsie's parents were astonished by the picture but her father, at least, remained unconvinced. He was certain that it was an elaborate joke, but the girls were equally adamant that the fairies were authentic. To support their case, two months later Frances borrowed the camera again and took a photograph of Elsie apparently playing with a gnome. However, Mr Wright still refused to believe the evidence that was seemingly before his eyes and, although the girls showed the two photos to friends, the story of the Cottingley Fairies looked likely to end there, not least because Elsie and Frances were denied permission to borrow the camera for a third time.

By 1919 the respective mothers – Polly Wright and Anne Griffiths – had begun to acquire an interest in the supernatural and they started attending meetings of the Theosophical Society in Bradford. One evening they took the two photographs along to a meeting of the society and asked the guest lecturer whether they could possibly be genuine. As a result, the pictures were brought to the attention of leading theosophist Edward L. Gardner, who wrote back to Polly Wright expressing the view that the photograph with the fairies was 'the best of its kind I should think anywhere'. Gardner obtained from the Wrights the original glass plates and sent them to photographic expert Harold Snelling, saying: 'What Snelling doesn't know about faked photography isn't worth knowing.'

For although photography was still in its infancy, certain practitioners had already perfected the art of what was known as 'spirit photography'. Using a simple double exposure, unscrupulous photographers were able to make sizeable sums of money by producing images of the sitter accompanied by the 'ghost' of a relative who had died in the Great War. Most people did not understand the mechanics of photography and were therefore incapable of detecting the ruse while spiritualists, in particular, were vulnerable, having been led to believe that the camera could see things that the human eye could not. Harold Snelling was on the lookout for any evidence of fake 'spirit photography' in the fairy pictures.

After careful examination, Snelling concluded that the first photo was a single exposure and that the dancing figures were not made of fabric or paper, nor were they painted on to a photographic background. Above all, he was firmly of the opinion that the little figures had actually moved during exposure. Taking everything into account, he had no hesitation in declaring both photographs to be genuine. Gardner also submitted the photos to Kodak who were markedly less impressed, refusing to award a certificate of authenticity on the grounds that 'they must have been faked somehow'. But Gardner was so desperate to prove that the negatives had not been tampered with that he ignored the possibility that the fairy figures themselves might be fakes.

Disregarding Kodak's opinion, Gardner contacted Sir Arthur Conan Doyle, an acknowledged authority on the supernatural and the spirit world, and a man all too eager to believe in the existence of fairies. 'Extraordinary and amazing as these photographs may appear,' wrote Gardner, 'I am quite convinced of their entire genuineness.'

Conan Doyle was wary at first. He got in touch with the girls' families but while he found their stories promising, he asked another photographic expert, Kenneth Styles, to take a look at the pictures. Styles was as sure of his diagnosis as Snelling had been – but in a negative way. 'One at least,' he told Conan Doyle, 'is a most patent fraud and I can almost tell you the studio it comes from.' Although Styles had jumped to the right conclusion, he was wrong about the photographs having been touched up in a studio.

Styles's unequivocal report left Conan Doyle a disappointed man. He so *wanted* to believe in the Cottingley Fairies. To sow further seeds of doubt in Conan Doyle's mind, the girls were not even willing to swear on the Bible that the photos were genuine. However, they were prepared to take more photographs. Conan Doyle gladly accepted their offer and so it was that in the summer of 1920, Gardner was dispatched to Cottingley where Elsie and Frances were once again given a camera and left on their own in the beck. The session produced three more photographs, all taken in the absence of any independent witnesses. Gardner saw nothing untoward in this, reasoning that the fairies were shy and would not appear in the presence of an adult male. One photograph showed Frances with a leaping fairy; another showed a fairy offering harebells to Elsie; and the last depicted fairies frolicking in the grass, bathed in sunlight. These new pictures clearly swayed Conan Doyle who duly wrote back to Gardner in enthusiastic terms. 'When our fairies are admitted,' he predicted, 'other psychic phenomena will find a more ready acceptance.'

Conan Doyle decided to go public and his opening article about the Cottingley Fairies appeared in the *Strand Magazine* in November 1920. The front cover proclaimed: 'AN EPOCH MAKING EVENT . . . DESCRIBED BY A. CONAN DOYLE'. Inside, his article was accompanied by the first two photographs. The story created such worldwide interest that Conan Doyle followed it up with a second piece in the March 1921 issue, this time featuring the last three fairy photos. Inevitably not everyone was as gullible as Gardner and Conan Doyle. The *Birmingham Post* wrote: 'On the evidence I have no hesitation in saying that these photographs could have been faked.' The critic of *John O'London's Weekly* simply remarked cynically: 'It is easier to believe in faked photographs than fairies.'

The Cottingley Fairies became the talk of spiritualists everywhere. Clairvoyant Geoffrey Hodson, a friend of Gardner's, visited Cottingley to see whether he could detect the spirits. The girls later admitted teasing the poor man by taking him on woodland walks and pointing out non-existent fairies. To their delight, Hodson claimed that he, too, could see the fairies. In Hodson's case, believing was seeing.

Conan Doyle and Gardner were both subjected to widespread ridicule for giving credence to the fairy story. Even Elsie Wright said later: 'My poor dad was very much disappointed in his favourite detective writer, Conan Doyle. I heard him say to my mother: "How could a brilliant man like him believe in such a thing?"' Apart from his undoubted desire to believe in the fairies, Conan Doyle did not think 'two children of the artisan class' capable of clever photographic tricks. In taking this lofty position, he overlooked the fact that Elsie, the prime mover in the hoax, was, at 16, no longer a child and also that she had once worked as a photographer's assistant.

Conan Doyle expanded his *Strand* articles into a 1922 book, *The Coming of the Fairies*, in which he wrote, with somewhat belated caution, that the contents 'represent either the most elaborate and ingenious hoax ever played upon the public or else they constitute an event in human history which may in the future appear to have been epoch-making in its character.' Perhaps because of the vociferous opposition to his support for the fairies, Conan Doyle seemed to be wavering a shade and wrote: 'If I am myself asked whether the case is to be absolutely and finally proved, I should answer that in order to remove the last faint shadow of doubt I should wish to see the result repeated before a disinterested witness.' His wish was never granted. The cousins drifted apart soon afterwards and no more fairy photographs were ever taken.

Gradually the Cottingley Fairies faded from the limelight, only to resurface in 1976 on the Yorkshire Television regional news programme *Calendar*, which reunited Elsie and Frances at the ages of 75 and 69. They were asked whether they had fabricated the photographs, but their answers were decidedly ambiguous. Frances challenged the interviewer: 'You tell us how she could do it . . . and then we'll tell you . . . Remember, she was 16, and I was ten.' Elsie added enigmatically: 'Let's say they are figments of our imagination, Frances's and mine, and leave it at that.'

Then in 1981 Frances finally confessed to author Joe Cooper, revealing that she and the artistic Elsie had traced and cut out the fairies from page 104 of a copy of *Princess Mary's Gift Book* and secured them to the earth with hatpins before taking the photograph. Talking about that famous first picture, Frances said: 'From where I was, I could see the hatpins holding up the figures. I've always marvelled that anybody ever took it seriously . . . I swore to Elsie I wouldn't tell anybody.'

The confessions were published in *The Times* in 1983. Elsie admitted that all five photographs had been faked; Frances said the first four were fakes but maintained that the fifth was genuine. The debate surrounding the fifth photograph arose from the fact that both women claimed to have taken it, but the mystery was solved when it transpired that it had been a simple case of double exposure. *The Times* article poured further scorn on Conan Doyle. 'Desperate for evidence of the paranormal, when he saw what was actually a hatpin holding down a cut-out illustration of a goblin, he described it as evidence of a fairy navel; proof, he told fellow researchers, that the creatures reproduced in the same manner as humans.'

A film of the Cottingley Fairies riddle was made in 1997 and, with both Elsie and Frances now dead, a collection of glass plates and negatives of the 'fairies' was sold at auction in March 2001 for £5,200. So the fairy story had a happy ending for someone.

The Strange Case of Hamilton's Heifer

In April 1897 a small Kansas newspaper, the *Yates Center's Farmer's Advocate*, ran a sensational story which subsequently made headlines in publications from New York to Berlin. It reported the terrifying experience of Le Roy cattle farmer and local civic dignitary, Alexander Hamilton, who claimed that he had witnessed one of his animals being kidnapped by a UFO.

Hamilton's narrative began: 'Last Monday night, about 10.30, we were awakened by a noise among the cattle. I arose, thinking that perhaps my bulldog was performing some of his pranks, but upon going to the door saw to my utter astonishment an airship slowly descending upon my cow lot, about forty rods from the house.

'Calling my tenant, Gid Heslip, and my son Wall, we seized some axes and ran to the corral. Meanwhile, the ship had been descending until it was not more than thirty feet above the ground, and we came within fifty yards of it.

'It consisted of a great cigar-shaped portion, possibly three hundred feet long, with a carriage underneath. The carriage was made of glass or some other transparent substance alternating with a narrow strip of some material. It was brilliantly lighted within and everything was plainly visible – it was occupied by six of the strangest beings I ever saw. They were jabbering together, but we could not understand a word they said.

'Every part of the vessel which was not transparent was of a dark reddish colour. We stood mute with wonder and fright, when some noise attracted their attention and they turned a light directly upon us. Immediately on catching sight of us they turned on some unknown power, and a great turbine wheel, about thirty feet in diameter, which was slowly revolving below the craft, began to buzz and the vessel rose lightly as a bird.

'When about three hundred feet above us it seemed to pause and hover directly over a two-year-old heifer, which was bawling and jumping, apparently fast in the fence. Going to her, we found a cable about a half inch in thickness made of some red material, fastened in a slip knot around her neck, one end passing up to the vessel, and the heifer tangled in the wire fence. We tried to get it off but could not, so we cut the wire loose and stood in amazement to see the ship, heifer and all, rise slowly, disappearing in the north-west.

'We went home but I was so frightened I could not sleep. Rising early Tuesday, I started out by horse, hoping to find some trace of my cow. This I failed to do, but coming back in the evening found that Link Thomas, about three or four miles west of Le Roy, had found the hide, legs and head in his field that day. He, thinking someone had butchered a stolen beast, had brought the hide to town for identification, but was greatly mystified in not being able to find any tracks in the soft ground.

'After identifying the hide by my brand, I went home but every time I would drop to sleep I would see the cursed thing with its big lights and hideous people. I don't know whether they are devils or angels, or what, but we all saw them, and my whole family saw the ship, and I don't want any more to do with them.'

Such was Hamilton's standing in the community – he was a member of the House of Representatives – that this bizarre tale of alien abduction was widely accepted. To dissuade any doubters, he had also gone to the trouble of asking ten of his most respectable friends to sign an affidavit supporting his story. With no shortage of credible witnesses, the Le Roy calf-napping joined the ever-growing list of close encounters with alien life forms across the USA. The truth was out there . . . but it would be another 80 years before it made itself heard.

Alexander Hamilton died in 1912. He did not exactly take his secret to the grave because, in May 1897, just a month after the alleged abduction, he had cheerfully confessed to the hoax in a Missouri newspaper, the *Atchison County Mail*. However, as is so often the case, the disclaimer did not receive the same degree of coverage as the original story with the result that many still believed that a calf really had been snatched by aliens in Kansas.

The legend lived on until 1976 when UFO historian Jerome Clark, conducting his own investigation into the incident, tracked down a woman whose mother had been at the Hamilton household in April 1897. A laughing Hamilton had been heard telling his wife: 'I fixed up quite a story and told the boys in town, and it will come out in the *Advocate* this weekend.' It emerged that Hamilton and his friends (the ones who had signed the affidavit) were members of a local liars' club who devoted their energies to making up tall stories. Among his fellow members was Ed Hudson, editor of the *Yates Center's Farmer's Advocate*. Reflecting on his career, Hudson had actually written an article about the hoax back in 1943, but this, too, had been largely overlooked.

Clark published his findings in the February 1977 issue of *Fate* magazine and the story was subsequently taken up by the *Fortean Times*, specialists in all things weird and wonderful. Hamilton's hoax had finally been exposed to the wide world. But it had been fun while it lasted.

A Ghost in the Forest

The hottest item on Thailand TV news programmes in late April and early May 2000 was the seemingly authentic footage of a ghostly séance that had occurred deep in the Kham Chanot forest, nearly 600 km from Bangkok. The video, which had been shot at night using an infra-red camera, showed a man dressed as a Buddhist monk making contact with various ghoulish figures. One spirit appeared as an impossibly tall and skinny man who wore no shirt and ran through the forest, howling, screaming, and waving his arms. The wobbly footage, featuring eerie sounds of the night-time forest, was shown repeatedly on news broadcasts, gripping a nation obsessed with the supernatural. After the release of the video, numerous people travelled to the area where it had been shot, in north-east Thailand's Udon Thai province, hoping to see the ghosts for themselves.

Police, however, harboured reservations about the authenticity of the footage, and suspected that it might be an April Fool's joke. They reported that two groups of people had been seen leaving the Kham Chanot forest on 1 April, the day the video was shot. One group questioned at around 3 a.m. told officers that they had come to make an offering to spirits in the forest. A search of their bags produced a video camera.

On 24 May a local cult leader, Kitti Papasarobol, was arrested and charged with creating the fake footage and with defrauding one of his female followers. It emerged that Papasarobol had told the woman he could contact ghosts and that, in return for 300,000 baht ($7,700), he would use his spiritual connections to improve her fortunes. After she handed over the money, he came up with the video as proof of his powers. On studying the video closely, the police identified Papasarobol as the 'Buddhist monk' and theorized that the lofty ghost was an acquaintance standing on a box.

Papasarobol vehemently denied the charges and insisted that he really could contact the spirit world. So the police gave him the opportunity to prove it by asking him to produce a Buddhist amulet from sand. When he failed the test, he was sent to jail.

The Queens of Rap

It is a sobering thought that the birth of the modern spiritualist movement can be traced back to two young American girls playing tricks with an apple and a piece of string.

Margaret and Katherine Fox lived with their elder sister Leah in Hydesville, a hamlet near Rochester, New York. The previous occupants of the farmhouse had reported hearing strange rapping noises in the night, and this seems to have been the inspiration for the antics of Margaret and Katherine.

Early in 1848, 13-year-old Margaret and 11-year-old Katherine began claiming that they could hear mysterious rapping noises on the walls of their bedroom. The sounds appeared to be emanating from another room. On the night of 31 March the noises reached such a crescendo that the family called in witnesses before fleeing the house. With no obvious explanation for the phenomenon, the house and the sisters became the focal point of local interest. The girls played to the gallery, reviving an old yarn about an itinerant peddler who was rumoured to have been murdered and then buried in the basement of the house five years earlier. By replying to the tapping with similar sounds, they managed to convince people that they were able to communicate with the deceased.

The sisters then gave a demonstration of their art at the Corinthian Hall in Rochester, drawing such an enthusiastic audience that the money-making possibilities were there for all to see. Under the shrewd management of Leah, they embarked on a profitable career as mediums, performing séances in private parlours throughout the United States. There was big money to be made from talking to the dead. Their fame spread abroad, and their act fooled even eminent scientists like Sir William Crookes who, after witnessing a séance in London in 1871, declared himself satisfied that the raps were 'true objective occurrences not produced by trickery or mechanical means.' Others – notably men of the cloth – were less charitable and denounced the sisters as frauds.

When Leah Fox ditched her husband, Fish, in favour of a wealthy New York banker, she decided that she no longer wished the burden of two younger sisters, and ceased to represent them. Left to their own devices, Margaret and Katherine appeared to lose heart until, in 1888, Margaret finally decided to admit that they were frauds. They produced their first rapping sounds, they confessed, by using an apple tied to a string. In the darkened rooms where these strange happenings always took place, nobody could see them tug the string and bounce the apple with a resounding thud against the wall. As their technique grew more sophisticated, they resorted to making the required noises by popping the joints of their big toes.

Margaret told the *New York World*: 'My sister Katie was the first one to discover that by swishing her fingers she could produce a certain noise with the knuckles and joints, and that the same effect could be made with the toes. Finding we could make raps with our feet – first with one foot and then with both – we practised until we could do this easily when the room was dark. No one suspected us of any trick because we were such young children . . . All the neighbours thought there was something, and they wanted to find out what it was. They were convinced someone had been murdered in the house. They asked us about it, and we would rap one for the spirit answer "yes", not three, as we did afterwards. The murder, they concluded, must have been committed in the house. They went over the whole surrounding country, trying to get the names of people who had formerly lived in the house. They found finally a man by the name of Bell, and they said that this poor innocent man had committed a murder in the house, and that these noises came from the spirit of the murdered person. Poor Bell was shunned and looked upon by the whole community as a murderer. As far as spirits were concerned, neither my sister nor I thought about it . . . I have seen so much miserable deception that I am willing to assist in any way and to positively state that spiritualism is a fraud of the worst description . . . I trust that this statement, coming solemnly from me, the first and most successful in this deception, will break the force of the rapid growth of spiritualism and prove that it is all a fraud, a hypocrisy and a delusion.'

Having made such a detailed confession, Margaret Fox soon recanted it and went back on the road with Kate, the pair's appeal apparently undiminished. But by now both were hopeless alcoholics, which rendered lecturing almost impossible, and Kate was arrested for drunkenness. The Fox sisters had genuinely made contact with spirits.

For the last few years of her life, Kate existed by begging, eventually dying in poverty in 1892. Margaret followed her into a pauper's grave a few months later. Given the circumstances surrounding their later lives, perhaps the only surprise is that spiritualism didn't die with them.

Abducted by Aliens in Swindon

Those who thought tales of alien abduction were confined to America were startled to read of a Londoner who had been paid £1 million ($1.6 million) in settlement by an insurance company after successfully proving that he had been kidnapped by aliens while on a trip to Swindon, Wiltshire. It was difficult to know which was the more surprising phenomenon – aliens lurking near Swindon or an insurance company prepared to pay up.

According to reports, Joseph Carpenter, a 23-year-old electrician and UFO enthusiast, had been visiting Swindon on 8 October 1996 with a UFO hunting group called 'Majestic Twelve'. Near RAF Lyneham he said he was suddenly struck by a strange beam of light and was confronted by a group of small beings with triangular heads and dolphin-like skin who communicated with him telepathically before he passed out. He was then 'beamed up' into the air – an act caught on video by his colleagues. When he awoke back on earth some 40 minutes later he thought he had dreamed the experience until he noticed inexplicable marks on his skin and an 'alien claw' stuck to his shirt sleeve.

By sheer good fortune Carpenter had recently taken out a £100 insurance policy with a firm called GRIP (Goodfellow Rebecca Ingrams Pearson Ltd) to protect him against being 'abducted, impregnated or eaten by aliens.' It looked like being a shrewd investment as insurance broker Simon Burgess, head of GRIP, announced that he was so impressed by the supporting evidence, which included the camcorder footage, testimony of witnesses and DNA samples taken from the claw, that he was willing to pay out in full. As an added bonus, he said that *X Files* star Gillian Anderson would be presenting the cheque to Mr Carpenter.

But sceptics smelled a rat. The story of an abducted ufologist seemed too good to be true. Then there was the name: Joseph Carpenter. Aside from the biblical connotations, it was the name used by the alien Klaatu when he came to earth in the 1951 science fiction movie *The Day The Earth Stood Still*. As for Burgess, he appeared remarkably eager to pay up and was already boasting that he had sold 1,100 policies against alien abduction and had received hundreds of enquiries a day since the Carpenter case.

After Gillian Anderson had failed to materialize, the *Sunday Times* exposed the scam. 'Joseph Carpenter' was really Joe Tagliarini, ex-courier and business partner of Burgess. They had cooked up the abduction story to publicize Burgess's extensive range of bizarre policies. In that respect, at least, the ruse had been successful. Burgess was no stranger to the unorthodox, having previously offered insurance against 'pregnancy by immaculate conception.' Naturally the British insurance industry, who regarded him as an 'unhelpful maverick', sought to distance itself from his activities.

Round and Round in Circles

On a glorious English summer's day in 1978, two middle-aged artists, Doug Bower and Dave Chorley, were enjoying their usual Friday drink at the rural Percy Hobbs pub near Winchester. They usually sat in a corner, quietly sipping their pints while showing each other their latest watercolour paintings, but on this occasion they were so taken by the beauty of the surrounding landscape that they ventured outside with their glasses and gazed admiringly at the fields of golden corn. As he looked out across the gently undulating Hampshire countryside, Bower was reminded of a story he had read when he and his wife Ilene had emigrated to Australia back in 1958. It concerned strange circles which had appeared in a cornfield in Queensland, prompting speculation that a UFO had landed in the dead of night and its occupants had left behind their own peculiar brand of alien graffiti. The practical joker in Bower began to wonder how such a phenomenon would be received in England.

'How would you like a bit of a laugh?' he asked his friend. Dave Chorley was game, and so they went to Bower's picture-framing shop in Southampton, collected the 5 ft-long iron bar which he used to secure the door to the premises, and returned to the cornfields that night. There, while Chorley stood firmly on one end of the heavy metal bar, Bower pulled it around in a circle, bending the corn carefully as he went. The result – a mysterious circle in the middle of a flat cornfield with no tracks nearby – looked impressively baffling from a distance. The great crop circle hoax was born.

Over the course of the next two years circles cropped up in cornfields across southern England. At first they attracted so little attention that Chorley was prepared to retire from the hoaxing business, but Bower persuaded him to keep going, convinced that one day their creations would be headline news. The breakthrough came when they made a circle at a well-known beauty spot – the Devil's Punchbowl. 'That was the turning point for us,' recalled Bower in a 1999 interview. 'I realized that for people to really take note of our circles we needed a site with a viewpoint, so people could sit having picnics and look down in wonder on our work. One day I was driving past the Devil's Punchbowl with Ilene and I noticed that corn was being planted there for the first time. Dave and I couldn't wait for the crop to grow. One summer night we went and made a crop circle. Twenty-four hours later it was on the television news.'

The deluge of publicity brought in a matching flood of so-called experts, each with his or her own view as to what may have caused the crop circles. Some stated categorically that the circles were evidence of spacecraft landings – that alien visitors had left their calling cards; others attributed the patterns to rutting hedgehogs frantically running around in circles. When an Oxford meteorologist suggested that downward-spiralling winds were creating a vortex that flattened crops with its circular movement, Bower and Chorley felt obliged to give credence to the theory by creating more elaborate, geometric designs. Bower would sketch the patterns in his studio workshop and then, armed with a plank and a rope, the pair would head off at night to a suitable cornfield where Bower proceeded to walk around with the rope in ever increasing circles before making a 'ladder' leading to another identical circle. To keep the lines accurate, Bower wore a baseball cap and peered through a 'sight' made from a loop of wire, which, when attached to the cap, hung over his left eye. Whereas copycat hoaxers used stilts to avoid leaving telltale tracks, Bower and Chorley insisted that they simply moved in a high-stepping, loping course that left no trace among the corn.

Bower recalled: 'It was just pure enjoyment on those beautiful summer nights for two artistic people under the stars amid all those cornfields. We were both nineteenth-century people really. We were in another world. Dave and I were a team in tune with nature.'

As the rash of crop circles spread, thousands of pilgrims turned up from all over the world to lie down in the circles and absorb the 'cosmic energy'. Enterprising farmers cashed in on the operation by charging admission fees to the sites. Bower, who often made nature recordings at night, helpfully told the experts that he would keep a lookout for any fresh circles. 'We'd make a circle at night,' he laughed, 'then I'd ring up the experts the next morning to say I'd spotted another one. We did about 200, mostly around Warminster in Wiltshire, because it is a well-known centre for UFO sightings.'

They even created a crop circle next to the home of Denis Healey, former Chancellor of the Exchequer, who promptly photographed it for posterity.

For seven years, the two pranksters kept their nocturnal activities a secret from their wives, but their cover was blown when Ilene Bower, who did her husband's bookkeeping, became puzzled by the increasing number of services their car needed. And when she realized that there was an extra 400 miles a week on the clock, she demanded an explanation. At first she was unimpressed by her husband's confession, so he presented her with a huge pile of press cuttings showing crop circle patterns, together with his original designs. When that, too, failed to convince her, he asked her to design a circle of her own and then to watch while he created it at night in a cornfield. It became their shared secret for another six years.

Then in September 1991 Doug Bower and Dave Chorley decided to tell all. *Today* newspaper ran a story headlined 'THE MEN WHO CONNED THE WORLD' in which the pair revealed how they used to infiltrate groups of scientists camped on hillsides waiting for circles to appear. When they heard the experts predicting bigger and more complex patterns, Bower and Chorley felt it their duty to oblige.

Chorley said at the time: 'They called us "superior intelligence". That was the biggest laugh of all. We weren't in it to make publicity – we just wanted to make fools of the experts who were springing up everywhere.'

However, those experts – most of whom had invested their reputations in the circles being the work of some unknown force – were not prepared to be humiliated. They immediately denounced the confession as a hoax in itself. When Bower and Chorley were invited to demonstrate their technique before the world's media, author Colin Andrews sniffed: 'Straight away we saw everything we would expect to see in a hoax. The plants were broken, it is extremely ragged and obviously a fake.' Yet when a newspaper later used the pair to create a secret crop circle, experts who were called in pronounced it to be genuine.

The row simmers to this day. Dave Chorley (who died of cancer in 1996) and Doug Bower were denounced as liars. Crop circle fanatics refused to believe that the cornfield patterns had been the work of two practical jokers, pointing to the fact that, despite the pair retiring in 1991, new crop circles have continued to appear every summer. So was the whole episode a double hoax? Doug Bower has a simple explanation: imitators.

He added: 'When I was a boy in Upham, ten miles from Southampton, there was a local man who'd go to the pub every night and on his way home he'd take off every garden gate and leave it further up the lane. He was a practical joker and it rubbed off on me. He was my hero, and the circles were my chance to emulate him. I don't consider being on a planet for over 70 years is much use if you don't leave your mark.'

Chapter 4

Medicine

The Miraculous Bullet

The American Civil War was a conflict rich in tall stories, but few reached loftier heights than the yarn spun by Dr LeGrand G. Capers who claimed that on a Mississippi battlefield he had witnessed the most bizarre instance of artificial insemination known to medical history.

Dr Capers stated that the event in question took place at around 3 p.m. on 12 May 1863 at the Battle of Raymond where Brigadier General John Gregg's Confederate forces encountered Unionist troops led by General John A. Logan. In his role as Confederate army doctor, Dr Capers was with his regiment at the peak of the fighting. Some 300 yards behind the Confederate lines stood a house, the occupants of which (a mother, her two daughters and their servants) were standing near the front door watching the battle and waiting to dash to the aid of any wounded Confederate soldiers. According to the medical man, he suddenly saw a soldier drop to the ground near him and at the same moment he heard a deafening scream from the house. Tending the stricken soldier, Dr Capers quickly ascertained that he had sustained a wound to the leg caused by a Minnie ball and that the bullet had 'ricocheted from these parts, and, in its onward flight, passed through the scrotum, carrying the left testicle.'

As he was dressing the soldier's wounds, the mother from the house ran up to him and begged him to come and take a look at her eldest daughter. Rushing to the house, Dr Capers observed that the daughter, too, had been hit by a Minnie ball and that the bullet had penetrated the left abdominal parietals, 'about midway between the umbilicus and anterior spinal process of the ilium, and was lost in the abdominal cavity, leaving a ragged wound behind.' With the battle raging fiercely, the doctor only had time to prescribe the girl an anodyne before he and his regiment were forced to retreat.

Over the next two months, Dr Capers was stationed with the wounded at the nearby village of Raymond, an arrangement which enabled him to monitor the girl's progress. She recovered fully but then, six months after her injury, when he visited her again, he was aware that her stomach had started to swell. Three months later she gave birth to an 8 lb son.

While the family were horrified that their unmarried daughter had given birth, the girl herself was mystified by the whole affair, and protested that she was still a virgin. Dr Capers examined her and found that her hymen was still intact.

Three weeks on, the baby's grandmother asked Dr Capers to examine the boy whose scrotum had now become swollen and sensitive. The doctor decided to operate and discovered to his amazement that a Minnie ball was lodged in the child's scrotum.

Dr Capers was truly baffled. At first he could think of no logical explanation as to how a bullet could have become embedded in the baby's scrotum until it dawned on him that it must have been the culmination of an unbelievable chain of events. Remembering the young soldier and the bullet which had passed through his left testicle, Dr Capers decided that the same bullet must have continued on its flight, transporting with it particles of semen, before coming to rest in the young woman's abdomen, impregnating her, and then working its way into the child's scrotum.

After the doctor had put forward his theory about the fluke pregnancy to the family, they asked to meet the soldier. Dr Capers said that the soldier and the young woman went on to be married and to produce two more children by more conventional means.

This then was Dr Capers's astonishing story as it appeared in a November 1874 edition of the *American Medical Weekly* under the heading 'Attention Gynaecologists! – Notes from the Diary of a Field and Hospital Surgeon'. The account was, however, a complete fabrication, the tale having apparently been concocted by Dr Capers as his way of exposing some of the ludicrous Civil War stories that were doing the rounds in the 1870s.

But the last laugh was on Capers. An eminent doctor in his own right, he had submitted the story anonymously to the journal, not wishing to damage his reputation by being associated with such a far-fetched article. Unfortunately, the editor of the *American Medical Weekly*, E. S. Gaillard, not only deduced at once that the piece was a hoax but also recognized the handwriting as that of Dr Capers. So he achieved a splendid revenge by printing the story in its entirety . . . and in the name of Dr Capers. Thus Capers was undone by being the only doctor whose handwriting could actually be read . . .

The Woman Who Gave Birth to Rabbits

In 1726 the wife of a lowly Surrey cloth-maker carried out a preposterous hoax which made her the talk of London society and also made fools of England's most eminent surgeons. Mary Toft claimed that she had given birth to as many as 20 rabbits – a story which, far from being dismissed as a tissue of lies, was embraced by the finest medical minds in the land, including the physicians who attended King George I.

Twenty-five-year-old Mary Toft lived in modest circumstances with husband Joshua and her three children at Godalming and was described as being of 'a healthy strong constitution, small size, fair complexion, a very stupid and sullen temper, and unable to read or write.' Nevertheless she proved smart enough to hoodwink her social and intellectual superiors over a considerable period of time.

Her tale began when she was weeding in a field one day and was startled by a rabbit suddenly jumping up beside her. She and a fellow worker chased the rabbit, but the animal escaped. According to her account, she was five weeks' pregnant at the time and the incident in the field started an inexplicable craving for rabbits. Shortly afterwards, another rabbit sprang up near the same spot. Again Toft tried to catch it, but once more the rabbit got away. That night she dreamed that she was in a field with two rabbits in her lap, only to wake from her slumbers in a terrible fit, which lasted until morning.

Over the next few months her yearning to eat rabbit meat grew stronger and stronger, but she possessed neither the skill nor the money to fulfil her craving.

Then on the night of 27 September she was taken seriously ill. Her doctor, John Howard, a respected man with more than 30 years' experience of delivering babies, was summoned to the house from nearby Guildford. Dr Howard examined the patient's abdomen and detected signs of life within. Soon afterwards, he helped her give birth . . . to a dead rabbit. If this came as something of a surprise to the good doctor, what followed was beyond belief. For over the next few days, he watched Mary Toft give birth to eight more dead rabbits. When a further seven rabbits were pulled out of the womb within the month, Howard was able to contain his excitement no longer and wrote to distinguished doctors and scientists, relaying full details of the miracle of Godalming.

News of these amazing births reached the ears of King George who was so intrigued that he dispatched his house surgeon, Dr Cyriacus Ahlers, to Godalming to investigate. Toft explained to him that she had recently miscarried, but that during the pregnancy she had begun to long for rabbit meat. She recounted her dream about the rabbits in her lap, and said that the next thing she knew, she was giving birth to rabbits. Ahlers had expected to be able to brand Mary Toft a fake but, after witnessing yet another bunny birth, he was forced to revise his opinion. He returned to London convinced that he had obtained tangible proof of the truth of Toft's story and furthermore he promised to try and secure a royal pension for this remarkable woman. This last development was music to Mary Toft's ears.

Hearing Dr Ahlers's recommendation, the King sought a second opinion and sent his anatomist, Nathaniel St Andre, a surgeon at Westminster Hospital, off to Godalming. Accompanied by Mr Molyneux, secretary to the Prince of Wales, St Andre arrived just in time to witness the birth of two more rabbits. St Andre decided to carry out some tests to confirm that the phenomenon was genuine. He placed a piece of the lung of one of the still-born rabbits in water and observed that it floated, indicating that the rabbit must have breathed air before its death, which could not have happened inside a womb. He also noted that no umbilical cords or placenta were produced at the birth. Despite uncovering this highly suspicious evidence, St Andre declared that the births were as they seemed. He even took some of the creatures back to court and dissected one before the King to show that it was a real rabbit. In December 1726, St Andre published his findings. They divided the medical profession, not to mention the royal court. For while King George agreed with his doctors that Mary Toft had indeed given birth to rabbits, Caroline, Princess of Wales, remained on the side of the sceptics and asked Sir Richard Manningham, Fellow of the Royal Society and of London's College of Physicians, to study the case personally. So that he could keep a closer watch on Toft, Manningham arranged for her to be brought to London, to a residence in Leicester Fields (the area now known as Leicester Square). Manningham sat with her throughout the first night and although he detected a leaping sensation in her belly, nothing untoward occurred. Thereafter he ordered that Toft be placed under constant surveillance by doctors and nurses in order to prevent the possibility of any rabbits being smuggled into her room. Just as miraculously as they had started, the rabbit births suddenly ceased.

By now, Manningham could smell a rat as opposed to a rabbit. A porter at the house, Thomas Howard, came forward to state that Toft had asked him to obtain a rabbit. Others admitted that they had earlier supplied rabbits to Toft's husband. Brazen to the last, Mary Toft tried to bluff her way through the furore despite warnings from a magistrate that she could be sent to prison if found guilty of deception. Initially there was a wave of sympathy from the general public, but then Manningham played his trump card, threatening to perform a dangerous operation on her uterus unless she confessed. Faced with possible death, Toft finally admitted the hoax. She said that the idea had been suggested by a woman friend as an ingenious method of earning money without having to work. In return for a cut of the royal pension, the woman had arranged for Toft to receive a regular supply of rabbits. Toft then secreted the rabbits in her bedding before inserting them into the appropriate orifice, when needed, to baffle, bemuse and bewilder England's finest physicians.

Instead of her royal pension, Mary Toft received a stay in prison for fraud, but she was eventually released without trial. The careers of Drs Howard, Ahlers and St Andre were wrecked, immortalized as they were in a satirical print by Hogarth titled 'The Wise Men of Godalming in Consultation'.

The Sad Demise of Ernest Flucterspiegel

In 1858 a San Francisco newspaper, the *Alta*, published a letter from a Dr Friedrich Lichtenberger, in which he recounted witnessing a death so shocking that he wished to alert the readership to the dangers.

The good doctor recalled how he and a Prussian gentleman by the name of Ernest Flucterspiegel were members of an expedition that, after setting off from San Francisco, had been forced to camp near a stream in order to take shelter from a storm. As it was still daylight when the storm subsided, some of the party began looking for gold. Unable to find any ore, they apparently amused themselves by breaking open geodes – described as rounded masses of quartz with hollow centres. Some of the geodes contained a transparent fluid, much to the delight of Herr Flucterspiegel who promptly drank half a pint of the liquid.

On his way back to camp, Flucterspiegel complained to the doctor of a pain in the epigastric and left hypochondriac regions, and was quickly rendered speechless. Dr Lichtenberger put him to bed, but the patient broke out in a cold sweat. His pulse was feeble; his heartbeat violent and irregular. Within 15 minutes of returning to camp, poor Flucterspiegel was dead. When informed that the deceased had swallowed the fluid in the geode, Lichtenberger concluded that he had died from some form of mineral poisoning, but could not conceive of any poison which acted so quickly nor caused such unusual symptoms.

The doctor then noticed a strange rigidity in Flucterspiegel's limbs that increased minute by minute 'until in the course of two-and-one-half hours the victim's entire body became stiff and inflexible as a board.'

Lichtenberger told how he decided to conduct a post-mortem examination. As he prepared to open up the dead man's stomach and intestines, his surgeon's knife made a grating noise and he noticed that Flucterspiegel's smaller blood vessels were solid and seemingly ossified. The doctor proceeded to remove the stomach of the deceased and on slitting it open, he found several lumps as hard as quartz. He said he also removed some muscle and lumps of undigested potato, all equally hard. The conclusion was inescapable: the contents of Flucterspiegel's stomach had turned to stone.

Next the doctor cut an opening in the victim's chest and discovered that his heart was a natural colour but rock hard. He went on: 'The larger blood vessels were all as rigid as pipe stems and in some cases the petrified blood could be cracked out from the veins.' Still mystified as to the precise cause of death, Lichtenberger later applied nitric, sulphuric and hydrochloric acids to the petrified blood, but none appeared to have any effect. In danger of exhausting every option, he then tried a small amount of fluorhydric acid and, to his great relief, this acted not only on the blood but also on the contents of Flucterspiegel's stomach. After conducting further tests, Dr Lichtenberger came to the conclusion that the liquid swallowed by Flucterspiegel must have contained a large quantity of silicic acid, which in turn had caused a petrification of certain substances within the body.

Although readers of the *Alta* were taken in by this tragic tale, the letter was, of course, a hoax, the perpetrator of which was never unmasked.

The Fictitious Fortescue

The reclusive J. Fortescue was renowned for being one of the leading medical scientists in 1930s San Diego. President of the International Board of Hygiene, he had earned widespread praise for his research into such diverse subjects as polio, the sexual habits of American males and beer. During Prohibition, he had apparently gone to the lengths of crossing the Mexican border to Tijuana in order to conduct detailed research into local beers – all in the name of science, naturally. And when Fortescue concluded that one of the beers was calorie-free, San Diego advertisers were so impressed by his findings that they subsequently advertised it as a slimming drink. Such was the influence of the man.

His reputation had also earned him an impressive entry in the 1936 edition of *Who's Who in San Diego* as well as a glowing write-up in the magazine of the San Diego Medical Society, penned by one of the few colleagues who professed to know him well, Clifford Graves, MD. However, for the rest of the Californian medical world, Fortescue remained a shy, reclusive figure, and so it came as no surprise when he politely declined an invitation to attend a banquet in his honour or to accept in person the $10,000 Fleischmann Prize for his copious research into yeast.

In truth, there was a very good reason why Fortescue shunned the limelight: neither he nor the International Board of Hygiene actually existed. For he was the invention of Rawson Pickard, a pathologist from La Jolla, California, and his drinking partners who included a certain Clifford Graves. They had created their imaginary scientist in a Tijuana bar, naming him after fifteenth-century British jurist Sir John Fortescue, the man who first put forward the notion that it was better that the guilty should escape than the innocent be punished.

The drinking friends managed to keep the Fortescue hoax going for almost 30 years until Pickard died in 1963.

A Most Uncommon Vice

William Osler was one of the leading Canadian doctors of his generation, a man who was Chair of Clinical Medicine at the University of Philadelphia before rising to the position of Professor of Medicine at Johns Hopkins University, Baltimore. Osler was also a renowned joker who coined the phrase: 'A physician who treats himself has a fool for a patient.' One of his favourite ploys was to console new female patients by telling them: 'You are in the most capable hands and don't worry, old Dr Kelly's senile tremor disappears as soon as it's time to operate.'

To satisfy his thirst for practical jokes, Osler invented an alter ego, Dr Egerton Yorrick Davis, described as a retired surgeon captain of the US army. In the guise of Dr Davis, Osler wrote numerous hoax letters to medical journals, outlining bizarre cases that he had supposedly treated. His most celebrated letter was to the *Medical News,* which printed it in its issue of 13 December 1884. Dr Davis recounted how he had been called out to attend 'an uncommon form of vaginismus' whereby a maid had experienced a violent vaginal spasm while in the act of sexual intercourse with her lover, the coachman. As a result of the spasm, the coachman had become locked inside her, and the doctor had been summoned to separate them – a feat he eventually achieved by relaxing the maid with chloroform.

The redoubtable Egerton Yorrick Davis penned many more letters on sexual matters, including a 1903 missive to the *Boston Medical and Surgical Journal* titled 'Peyronie's Disease – Strabisme Du Penis', which described 'an old codger' who experienced 'a most remarkable change in his yard'. As Osler discovered, there is never a shortage of new unsuspecting magazine and journal editors ready to be hoaxed.

Chapter 5

Sport

Rosie's Ruse

Susan Morrow had never previously paid much attention to the New York City Marathon. But in 1979 the freelance photographer and designer decided to go along as a spectator and lend moral support to a friend who was among the 8,000 entrants. Leaving her home in Greenwich Village, she caught a subway train at West 4th Street station and set off on the journey towards the race finish line at the Tavern on the Green in Central Park. Boarding the train, Morrow couldn't help but notice that one of the passengers was a woman in running clothes who was sitting with her head down and appeared to be upset. The adjacent seat was empty, so Morrow sat down next to her. After a while, the silence was broken by the athlete asking the time. When Morrow replied, the woman introduced herself: 'Hi, I'm Rosie Ruiz.'

The pair entered into conversation with Ruiz telling Morrow that she had injured her ankle at about the ten-mile mark. Both got off at Columbus Circle and made their way towards the finish line through a succession of barricades manned by police officers and volunteer race marshals. Morrow recalled later: 'Every time we got to a barricade, she (Ruiz) would put her arm on my shoulder, like she was leaning on me, and the police would let us through.' At one barricade the limping Ruiz stopped at a table, grabbed a can of juice, opened it and poured it over her head. 'I remember thinking it was a little weird,' said Morrow, 'but I figured that's what all runners do.' The final barricade was 50 feet from the finish line. As Ruiz reached it, she wailed: 'I'm an injured runner.' She was quickly surrounded by race officials who escorted her to the medical area right by the finish line. Rosie Ruiz was officially placed 11th in that year's New York City Marathon.

Six months later – on 21 April 1980 – Harvard students John Faulkner and Sola Mahoney were attending their first Boston Marathon. As it was an unseasonably warm day, they had chosen to jog over the Massachusetts Avenue Bridge and view the race from Commonwealth Avenue, little more than half a mile from the finish. The leaders in the men's race had just passed when Faulkner turned to see a woman in a yellow T-shirt 'sort of stumbling from the crowd onto the street. Her arms were flailing away, like she was swimming. She was very erratic. I told Sola, and we just stood there thinking, "The gall of that woman."' Shortly afterwards, Faulkner heard a loud roar from nearby Kenmore Square as Canadian runner Jacqueline Gareau came through. 'Those people thought that Gareau was the first woman,' recalled Faulkner years later. After the field had passed, Faulkner jogged back across the Charles River to his dorm, and forgot all about the mystery runner in the yellow T-shirt. He said: 'I figured that woman would just jump out before the end or somebody would stop her.'

Back at the finish the declared winner of the women's race was lapping up the adulation with scarcely a trace of sweat on her yellow T-shirt. The reason she hardly looked as if she had been in a race was because she hadn't. Her name was Rosie Ruiz.

Born in Cuba in 1953, Ruiz moved to Florida as a child. At the age of 20 she had a large tumour removed from her head and five years later surgeons inserted a plastic plate into her skull. Not long afterwards she moved to New York and filled out the application form to run in the 1979 New York Marathon. On the form she estimated her time of arrival at Central Park at 4 hr 10 min. Instead she crossed the finish line in 2 hr 56 min 29 sec – the 11th placed woman. The fact that Ruiz had chopped over an hour off her estimated time went largely unnoticed. She had simply run out of her skin . . . or out of the subway. Nobody thought to query her time, which was fast enough to qualify her for the Boston Marathon in the number W50 as the 50th-ranked woman runner. Her boss was so proud of her performance in the New York race that he paid for her to go to Boston that following April.

Her winning time in Boston of 2 hr 31 min 56 sec was the third-fastest marathon ever by a woman and a record for the race – an astonishing performance in such sultry conditions. Rosie Ruiz had seemingly come from nowhere. The men's winner, Bill Rodgers, was certainly puzzled. As the two stood side by side on the victory podium, Ruiz's head adorned by the winner's laurel wreath, he asked her simply: 'Who are you?'

Rodgers already had his suspicions. 'The second I saw her I was sceptical,' he said. 'I know a top runner when I see one. She didn't look tired. There were no sweat stains on the back or underarms of her yellow T-shirt. I remember thinking, "Oh no, somebody made a big mistake here."'

For someone who had apparently just run 26 miles at an incredible pace, culminating in a stunning sprint finish, Ruiz looked remarkably good. She wasn't even breathing heavily. And there was something about her legs – they were much softer than those of most champion athletes. Bill Rodgers's brother Charlie was convinced that something was amiss. 'I started to get sick in my stomach,' he recalled. 'Rosie looked like a housewife with two kids, not a world-class marathoner.'

While Charlie Rodgers searched out an official to whom he could voice his concerns, brother Bill sat at a table with Rosie Ruiz, awaiting the start of the post-race press conference. Bill Rodgers remembered: 'I asked her about her training and how many intervals she did. She didn't know what intervals were. You don't run 2:31 and not know about intervals.' If Rosie Ruiz thought her ordeal was over, she was wrong: it was just about to start.

Whatever her innermost feelings, outwardly Ruiz was savouring the moment, telling newsmen how surprised she was to have won. 'I thought I was one of a few women to cross the finish line,' she said, 'until someone pulled me over and put this wreath on my head. I expected to finish, but not to win. I don't know how to explain what I did – I just got up this morning with a lot of energy. This is all a dream.'

For the athlete declared runner-up – Canada's Jacqueline Gareau – it was more of a nightmare. Having fought her way to the front of the race, she had been cheered on by the crowd every yard of her journey, only to be told by a spectator on Commonwealth Avenue that she was actually in second place. Gareau thought the onlooker had got it wrong but noticed on the closing stretch that the cheers for her weren't as loud as they had been. She reached the finish two and a half minutes after Ruiz. 'I remember looking up to my right, at the winner's stand,' said Gareau 'and I saw Bill Rodgers and a woman wearing the wreath. It started to hit me. I didn't win.' Gareau quietly accepted her fate until, soon after the ceremony, she heard the first rumours that Rosie Ruiz might be a fake.

Suspicion mounted because no checkpoint officials or runners could remember seeing Ruiz on the course. Nevertheless she vehemently rejected the suggestion that she had cheated. 'I ran the race,' she sobbed, offering to submit to a lie-detector test. A few hours later race director Will Cloney met Ruiz at the city's Sheraton Hotel. She was accompanied by Stephen Marek, a small-time race promoter from New York, who had jogged the Boston Marathon that day in a Superman outfit and who insisted that he had seen Ruiz in the early stages of the race. Cloney told Ruiz that the race records failed to show her at any of the checkpoints, but she stuck to her guns, repeating mantra-like: 'I ran the race.'

That evening, John Faulkner was chatting to one of Harvard's leading women runners. She asked him whether he had heard about the furore surrounding the winner of the women's marathon. Faulkner's mind flashed back to the runner in the yellow T-shirt who had stumbled into the race through the crowd. He hoped the two incidents were unconnected, but when he picked up a newspaper the following morning his worst fears were confirmed. Faulkner contacted the media. The net was closing in on Rosie Ruiz.

Down in New York, Susan Morrow had been watching highlights of the Boston Marathon on TV. 'I saw this woman on the winner's stand with the wreath on her head,' said Morrow, 'and I almost fell out of my chair. That was the woman I sat with on the train. I remember starting to feel real nervous. I didn't know what to do.' When she heard that Ruiz's run in the New York Marathon was also under scrutiny, Morrow decided to get in touch with the *New York Times*.

While officials began studying over 10,000 photographs and reels and reels of videotape in an attempt to find any evidence that Ruiz had taken part in the race, she continued to protest her innocence in the face of increasingly hostile interrogation. Asked to describe any specific landmarks along the course, the best she could manage was 'beautiful countryside and lots of houses and churches'. As for any other questions – 'I ran the race.'

A few days later her only witness – Stephen Marek – withdrew his support, admitting: 'I'm not sure if she ran or not.' The marathon task of scanning every photo was concluded. There was still no sign of Ruiz in any picture. TV cameras showed no trace of her up until around half a mile from the finish, and not one runner (male or female) who finished shortly before or after Ruiz recalled seeing her at any point in the race. Furthermore many competitors stated that when they were running near Jacqueline Gareau, the crowd cheered her on as the first woman. These factors, taken with the testimonies of John Faulkner and Susan Morrow, made Ruiz's disqualification inevitable. Jacqueline Gareau was declared the new winner of the Boston Marathon.

Columnists had a field day with Rosie Ruiz. The jokes at her expense came thick and fast. David Kindred of the *Washington Post* asked: 'Did you hear about the Rosie Ruiz doll? Wind it up and it takes the subway.' The same writer added: 'Rosie Ruiz is taking this too seriously. Instead of crying on national TV, she could have written a book, *Shortcuts to Fame*. It would start on Chapter 20 . . . '

After the disgrace of Boston, Ruiz hit hard times. In 1982 she was placed on probation for stealing $60,000 from the Manhattan real estate company where she worked. She headed back to Florida and landed in more trouble with the law after allegedly selling cocaine with two other women to undercover agents at a Miami airport. She spent three weeks in jail before again being put on probation. Since then she has attempted to keep a low profile, never admitting her deception and steadfastly refusing to answer questions about the race. But her infamy has lived on to the extent that she has arguably become America's best-known marathon runner ever. Given her silence on the subject, nobody can be sure precisely what Rosie Ruiz did that day in Boston but, in view of her underground activities in New York, the popular theory is that she rode on the subway to within a mile or so of the finish and re-joined the race for the last 800 metres. There is even doubt that she intended to win in Boston. Had she merely been trying to impress her boss, only to mis-time the point at which she jumped in to the race?

In April 2000 – on the 20th anniversary of Rosie's ruse – an intrepid journalist tracked her down in West Palm Beach and tried to get her to tell her side of the story. All she would say was: 'I ran the race.'

The Swinging Postman

One golfer stood out from the rest of the would-be qualifiers for the 1965 British Open – Walter Danecki (US) whose two-round total of 221 left him a matter of 81 strokes over par. But behind a score which would shame even the humblest 'rabbit' lies a remarkable tale of a man who entered one of the world's majors under false pretences in the hope of realizing a dream.

Danecki was not even a professional golfer. He was a 43-year-old postman from Milwaukee. Nor had he ever been a member of any golf club or driving range, any proficiency at the game having been acquired from seven years of playing the municipal courses of Milwaukee at $1.50 a round. His handicap was never having had a golf lesson in his life. Nevertheless he was confident that he could hack it with the big boys and, desperate to play alongside the likes of Arnold Palmer and Jack Nicklaus, he attempted to join the US PGA tour, only to be told that he would first have to serve a five-year apprenticeship. That seemed to be the end of the dream until he somehow managed to get hold of an entry form for the British Open and when he reached the space where he had to indicate 'amateur' or 'professional', he lied through his teeth and wrote 'professional'. Then, taking part of his annual leave from the Post Office, he secretly travelled to Britain for the qualifying rounds. None of his workmates knew that he had left the country, let alone that he was competing in the Open.

Although Danecki had managed to fool the Royal and Ancient committee, who run the British Open, the fairytale ended the moment he picked up a golf club in anger. After posting a first-round 108 over the par-70 course at Hillside, Southport, he fared even worse the following day, recording an embarrassing 113 at Southport and Ainsdale. He missed the qualifying mark by no fewer than 70 strokes.

As it emerged that Danecki was a gatecrasher, he discussed his rounds in time-honoured tradition with puzzled reporters. Asked how he had enjoyed links golf, he replied straight-faced: 'Well, I guess your small British ball helped me some. If I'd had to play the big ball, I'd have been all over the place.' Danecki, who thought he might have fared better but for a sore right hand, was also asked why he had lied on the entry form. 'Because I wanted that crock of gold. My conscience made me write down "professional".' But, he was quick to add by way of explanation: 'I don't charge if I give a lesson . . .'

Defiant to the last, he reiterated his vow to join the PGA tour. 'What I'll do is win one of the big ones. Then they'll have to let me in.' Nearly forty years on, the golfing world is still waiting.

The exploits of Walter Danecki inspired other Sunday morning golfers to try their luck in the British Open. In 1976, it was the turn of Maurice Flitcroft, a 46-year-old crane driver from Barrow-in-Furness who had no handicap, was self-taught from an Al Geiberger instruction book, practised in a field near his home and, incredibly, had never played an 18-hole course when he stepped on to the tee at Formby in Lancashire for the first qualifying round of the Open. His subsequent score of 121 was the highest qualifying score in the 141-year history of the British Open. He went out in 61 and came back in 60, including a traumatic 11 at the tenth hole. In spite of his total, Flitcroft saw definite grounds for optimism. 'I've made a lot of progress in the last few months and I'm sorry I did not do better. I was trying too hard at the beginning but began to put things together at the end of the round.'

The Royal and Ancient were less impressed. They were so appalled that Flitcroft had been allowed to slip through the net that they refunded the £30 entry fees to the two unfortunates who had been drawn to play with him. And having entered as a professional, Flitcroft was effectively barred from future Opens for misrepresenting his playing status.

However, Flitcroft was nothing if not resourceful. In 1978 and 1981, in the guise of one Gene Pacecki, Flitcroft resurfaced at South Herts but on each occasion he was quickly rumbled by Royal and Ancient officials who promptly ordered him off the course. He tried again in 1983, this time masquerading as Swiss professional Gerald Hoppy. Playing in the qualifying round at Pleasington, Lancashire, he got as far as the ninth hole, by which time he had already taken 63 strokes. At that point, officialdom smelt a rat and politely suggested that Herr Hoppy might care to retire. Flitcroft lamented: 'Everything was going well and according to plan until I five-putted the second.'

Maurice Flitcroft's last reported appearance in an Open qualifying round was in 1990 when, as James Beau Jolly, he was removed from the third green at Ormskirk Golf Club. So it would seem that Flitcroft has finally decided to give up on his lofty golfing ambitions, but the Royal and Ancient remain ever-vigilant . . . just in case.

The Horse That Came Out of the Fog

On a foggy afternoon in January 1990 American jockey Sylvester Carmouche shocked punters at Louisiana's Delta Downs racetrack by romping home on 23–1 outsider Landing Officer. But there was more to Carmouche's victory than met the eye since he had used the prevailing weather conditions to perpetrate a gross deception, the severity of which resulted in him receiving a ten-year ban.

Shortly after the start of the one-mile race around the oval track, Carmouche pulled his horse up, hid in the thick fog that had enveloped the course, and waited. With even the most powerful binoculars unable to penetrate the gloom from the stands, he remained undetected until putting his master plan into action. As the field came round again, he waited until he could hear the approaching hooves and then set Landing Officer sprinting down the straight to the winning post. Unfortunately for Carmouche, the very fog that had inspired his action also proved to be his downfall. For he had seriously misjudged how far away the other horses were. He knew they were behind him, but had intended winning by no more than a few lengths. Instead Landing Officer crossed the wire 24 lengths clear of his rivals and in a time that was just 1.2 seconds outside the track record.

The margin of victory for such a moderate horse immediately aroused suspicion. The stewards held an inquiry. Two jockeys in the race insisted that no horse had passed them at any time, but Carmouche retorted: 'They never noticed me.' Track vet James Broussard examined the horse and observed that it wasn't breathing heavily after the race and that its leg wrappings were clean. He concluded: 'In my opinion, Landing Officer did not appear to have participated in a mile race.'

Carmouche and Landing Officer were disqualified even though the former continued to protest his innocence and the latter maintained a dignified silence. Carmouche finally confessed in 1993 but by then he had seen his jockey's licence suspended for ten years by the Louisiana State Racing Commission for 'failure to race the entire course'. The ban was lifted after he had served eight years of the sentence, and Sylvester Carmouche resumed his riding career, carrying with him the certainty that he would always be known as the 'fog jockey'.

Double Duplicity

First raced in 1921, the Comrades Marathon, run over 54 miles in KwaZulu Natal Province between Pietermaritzburg and Durban, is South Africa's most prestigious long-distance race, offering big cash prizes to the leading finishers, rising to $200,000 to the winner. As a result it was open to corruption and cheating, and in 1993 the seventh-placed runner was found to have covered only the last 18 miles on foot, having ridden the rest of the way in a taxi. Among the 13,000 entries for the 1999 event was 21-year-old Sergio Motsoeneng, a talented athlete who lived with his impoverished parents and ten brothers and sisters in a cramped two-bedroomed house in the former depressed black homeland of Qwa Qwa. Joining forces with his 19-year-old brother Fika – an almost identical lookalike – Sergio hatched a plan to get his hands on some sorely needed prize money. They would use their physical similarity to run the race in relays, passing themselves off as the same competitor.

So it was that on 16 June 1999 Sergio ran the first 45 minutes of the Comrades Marathon before nipping in to a mobile lavatory along the route and swapping kit and number with Fika who was waiting inside. They thought they had left nothing to chance, even remembering to exchange hats and the computer chip that was laced to each runner's shoe to capture the times and positions at various points on the course. While Sergio then went ahead in a car, Fika proceeded to pile on the pace for the next 18 miles until, around the halfway point, they met up once more in another mobile toilet where they exchanged equipment again before Sergio completed the race to the finish.

All seemed to be going according to plan when Sergio finished in ninth place in 5 hr 40 min 20 sec, enabling him to win a cash prize of $1,000. Sergio was preparing to hand the money to his father when things got even better. The second and sixth-placed finishers were both disqualified after returning positive dope tests, thereby promoting

Sergio to seventh and earning him a valuable gold medal as the champion novice.

However, dark mutterings were afoot, led by fellow competitor Nick Bester, a former Comrades champion who had been placed 15th. According to the electronic race records, Sergio had been behind him earlier but Bester claimed that he had counted everyone who had passed him in the second half of the race and that there was one athlete too many for Sergio to have been able to finish ninth. After studying the results of the computer timing system, the race referees could find nothing amiss and cleared Sergio of cheating. But the fuss would not die down. Bester's team-mate, Nic Schalkwyk, immediately appealed against the decision – a move which initiated the studying of photographs from the race. And therein lay the incriminating evidence. For although the brothers thought they had covered every eventuality when transferring clothes and chips, they had made a fatal blunder over their watches. Whereas Sergio wore his watch on his right wrist, Fika wore his on his left. When the Johannesburg daily newspaper *Beeld* showed the runner purporting to be Sergio Motsoeneng wearing two different watches at different stages of the race, the scam was exposed. Photographic evidence also revealed another discrepancy. Fika had a scar on his right shin, but Sergio had none. Thus the scar which Motsoeneng sported at the halfway point had mysteriously vanished by the finish!

Sergio desperately tried to bluff his way out of his predicament but, acting on the advice of his lawyer who warned him that the evidence was overwhelming, he duly confessed. He returned the medal and the prize money and was banned for six years.

The chairperson of the race's Jury of Appeal, Cheryll Winn, reflected: 'If it wasn't for the fact that he made a mistake with the watches, he probably would have got away with it. That's really scary.'

While the Motsoeneng brothers could be considered unlucky not to have tricked race officials after a well-rehearsed hoax, Algerian runner Abbes Tehami, who tried a similar ploy at the Brussels Marathon in September 1991, merits no such sympathy. In league with his coach Bensalem Hamiani, Tehami devised a cunning plan to claim the first prize of £4,500.

Wearing number 62, Hamiani ran the first seven and a half miles of the race before disappearing into dense woodland alongside the route. There, he met up with Tehami who had been hiding behind a tree. The two men swapped running vests and numbers before Tehami emerged from the forest and, with fresh legs, ran out the eventual winner. There were just two minor snags. Journalists and spectators could not help noticing that Tehami had grown considerably during the race and, perhaps more damning still, that although he had started the race with a moustache, he was clean-shaven by the finish. In all their meticulous preparations, it seems that the pair had overlooked this fact. As one race official remarked afterwards: 'They looked about the same . . . only one had a moustache.' Disqualification followed swiftly.

A Lesson From the Teachers

Wealthy New York stockbroker Morris Newburger (a partner in the firm of Newburger, Loeb and Company) was a huge fan of American football, but was annoyed by the fact that so much press coverage was given to small provincial teams. So in 1941 he decided to make his point by inventing a team, the Plainfield Teachers, and phoning a report of a non-existent game through to the offices of the *New York Herald Tribune*.

Newburger got such a kick from seeing the *Herald Tribune* report the Teachers' remarkable 20–0 victory over Beacon Institute that he began widening his field. He reckoned more people should hear about the Teachers' exploits and phoned further reports through to the *New York Times*, United Press and Associated Press. To make the hoax more plausible, Newburger also invented a fake sportswriter – Jerry Croyden – and every report he sent to the newspapers that season carried the by-line 'From the Desk of Jerry Croyden'.

The Teachers' coach was one Ralph 'Hurry Up' Hoblitzel (famed for his revolutionary W formation) while Newburger generously included himself in the team as tackle. But the undoubted star of the show was Johnny Chung ('The Celestial Comet'), a 212 lb Chinese American who, according to Croyden's colourful prose, ate bowls of rice between halves. Chung became a legend in his creator's imagination. Each week Jerry Croyden gave him such rave reviews that a genuine sportswriter, Herb Allen of the *New York Post*, felt compelled to write a feature about him . . . blissfully unaware that the subject of the article didn't exist.

By now, Newburger was enjoying himself immensely, his jape having proved more successful than he had dared to hope. But after the Teachers had run up a series of Chung-inspired triumphs, someone blew the whistle on Newburger to Caswell Adams of the *New York Herald Tribune*. Hot on the scent, Adams visited the real Plainfield, New Jersey, where he discovered that the townsfolk had never heard of the Teachers. Tracing Jerry Croyden's phone calls to the press, Adams followed a trail that led directly to Newburger's office.

Adams broke the story of the hoax in his newspaper on 14 November 1941. *Time* magazine were ready to print a follow-up and contacted Newburger prior to his exposure. He begged *Time* to enter into the spirit of the joke and wait until the end of the football season, but they refused. Thus the final report from the desk of Jerry Croyden stated that six of the Teachers, including the mighty Chung, had been declared ineligible for the team after failing their mid-term exams. Consequently the rest of the season's fixtures had been cancelled. The Plainfield Teachers were laid to rest.

The One That Nearly Got Away With It

When angler Jonathan Denny claimed he had caught a monster 52 lb 4 oz pike in 2001, it seemed that he had landed the British record for the fish. He posted a picture of himself proudly holding the giant on an Internet angling website, and said that he had caught it at the Llandegfedd Reservoir in Gwent, South Wales – the same location where the previous record holder had been hooked nine years earlier. But staff at the *Angling Times* reckoned there was something fishy about the photograph, and soon Denny, a 23-year-old telecommunications manager, was forced to admit that he had not caught Britain's 50 lb pike after all. The photograph was not quite what it appeared.

Instead the pike in the picture was actually a mere 22 pounder that he had caught in the River Kennet, not far from his home in Reading, Berkshire. But then his friend, Max Spenser-Morris, had tinkered with the image on a computer to make it look much bigger. 'Max made the image as a joke,' said an apologetic Denny afterwards, 'so I could see what it would look like to hold a real monster. For a laugh we posted it in the Trophy Room on the website to see if anyone would notice.'

The digitally enhanced pike certainly looked convincing, but the *Angling Times* remained sceptical, all the more so when they noticed that Denny said he had caught the fish at Llandegfedd on Sunday 7 January. For the reservoir is open to pike fishermen only on certain dates and that Sunday was not one of them. A series of probing e-mails left Denny wriggling on the hook, and finally he admitted the hoax.

Photographic experts subsequently spotted a tell-tale flaw in the doctoring of the picture – a tiny blue dot on the fish's head. The dot was actually part of Denny's blue sweater, but was transferred to the fish when the image was enlarged.

The British Record Fish Committee took a dim view of the deception. Secretary David Rowe said: 'We have no procedures in place at the moment that take into account the use of digital imagery, but we will be vigilant for any photos which could have been altered. If this type of hoax became commonplace, it could threaten the integrity of our record list.'

Nevertheless Max Spenser-Morris was proud of his work. 'If we hadn't owned up, no one would have been 100 per cent sure if it was real or not. It was so well done I believe the fish could have stood the test of time and become a legend.'

The Olympic Torch Hoax

Back in 1956 Australia was gripped by Olympic fever. That year the summer games were being held in Melbourne and the whole nation was high on anticipation. Well, most of the nation, because for a group of Sydney University students the elongated build-up to the Olympics was proving a monumental bore. What particularly irritated them was all the hype surrounding the traditional carrying of the Olympic torch – a journey that was to wend its way right down the east coast to Sydney before heading south-west towards Melbourne. So the student pranksters decided to register their protest by staging their very own torch ceremony at Sydney Town Hall with the help of a sawn-off broom handle, a used jam tin and a pair of old Y-fronts.

The fake Olympic torch was the brainchild of 20-year-old veterinary student Barry Larkin. Along with Peter Gralton and other colleagues from the university's St John's College, Larkin painted the broom handle and jam tin silver, stuffed some underpants soaked in kerosene into the tin and lit the hoax Olympic flame. With the real torch-bearer still some way behind, Larkin, Gralton and a third associate (all dressed in the official whites) made their way into the city's York Street en route for the Town Hall and an appointment with the Lord Mayor Pat Hills.

However, in York Street their bogus runner lost his nerve, dropped the flame and ran off. With their plan facing ruin, the co-conspirators quickly scooped up the torch and the burning Y-fronts and, against the backdrop of a cheering crowd, Larkin set off to fulfil a joke which he had intended watching safely from a distance. On and on he ran through the city streets, proudly carrying the torch aloft. All the while he was flanked by an escort of half a dozen police motorcycles since officials and spectators alike were convinced that he was the authentic Olympic torch-bearer. Finally reaching the Town Hall, he ran up the steps, handed the torch to the Lord Mayor who then embarked on his ceremonial speech.

Interviewed in September 2000, Larkin remembered: 'All I could think of at the time was, "Shit, what am I going to do now?" I thought if I play it cool, everything will be OK, so I just walked back down the steps and jumped on a tram back to the old Astoria coffee house in Newtown.'

The real torch turned up shortly afterwards, but by then most of the crowd had gone. All that remained were a few stragglers and a bewildered Lord Mayor.

The Loneliness of the Long-Distance Sailor

Donald Crowhurst was a complex man. Born in India in 1932, he was devoted to his mother who repaid that love by dressing him as a girl until he was eight years old. That Crowhurst should have been so close to his mother was hardly surprising in view of the fact that his father was a habitual drunkard who died when Donald was 16 – a year after the family had moved to England. Crowhurst joined the RAF before drifting through various jobs in the field of electronic engineering. He was something of an introvert at the best of times but after suffering a serious head injury in a car crash, he became prone to sudden mood swings and prolonged bouts of deep depression.

One pastime that always held his interest, however, was sailing. He kept a 20 ft sloop – *Pot of Gold* – moored near Bridgwater in Somerset and launched a company, Electron Utilization, to market his own invention – a sailing navigation device which he called the Navicator. He persuaded a Taunton businessman, Stanley Best, to help finance the venture but Best soon discovered to his cost that while Crowhurst's technical knowledge was excellent, his business brain was less well developed.

In May 1967, at the age of 65, Sir Francis Chichester returned to England and a hero's welcome at the end of his epic solo voyage around the world in his yacht *Gipsy Moth IV*. Chichester's achievement inspired the younger generation of sailors, including Donald Crowhurst, to contemplate similar feats. From the moment Chichester landed back at Plymouth, Crowhurst, too, became determined to circumnavigate the world single-handed. So when, in March 1968, the *Sunday Times* announced that it was sponsoring a non-stop, round-the-world solo yacht race with a prize of £5,000 for the fastest finisher and another prize – the Golden Globe — for the first boat home, Crowhurst wasted no time in entering. The question was: would his brittle temperament stand up to nine months alone at sea?

Crowhurst planned to race in a trimaran, but acquiring a suitable craft was easier said than done. Eventually he talked Best into financing the building of the boat on the understanding that victory would prove a veritable money-spinner for the company. Crowhurst also appointed a press agent, local journalist Rodney Hallworth, who suggested that Crowhurst should start from the South Devon port of Teignmouth. The BBC bought the TV and tape recording rights and supplied a camera and recorder for the trip. Crowhurst's voyage seemed sure to be headline news, and so it proved . . . but for all the wrong reasons.

The rules of the event stated that competitors could start from wherever they chose, provided their departure was before midnight on 31 October 1968. In the middle of that October, by which time most of the leading contenders had long since sailed, Crowhurst was still putting the finishing touches to his newly built 40 ft trimaran, christened *Teignmouth Electron*. The boat only arrived in Teignmouth 16 days before the race deadline, and its unsatisfactory trials showed that there was still much work to be done in order to rectify a number of serious faults. Also, an alarmingly high percentage of Crowhurst's electrical equipment remained in pieces. The situation did not bode well. It was a predicament which would have prompted the vast majority of sailors to withdraw, but Crowhurst had staked his reputation on taking part in the race. He could not afford to lose face.

Crowhurst and his yacht left Teignmouth Harbour on the morning of 31 October – a matter of hours before the deadline. In the first two weeks at sea he completed a mere 800 miles due to a combination of erratic steering equipment, faulty electrics and leaky hatches. Alone and miserable in his tiny cabin, he briefly considered docking at Madeira during the third week before hitting on an idea that he thought would solve his problems but which, as it turned out, merely served to guarantee his future notoriety. For it was there, with the vast, forbidding waters of the Atlantic stretching before him, that a desolate Donald Crowhurst made the decision to keep two logs of his voyage – one true and one false.

He began compiling his false log in the second week of December. Tape recording messages for the BBC, he pretended that everything was going smoothly and that on 10 December he had sailed 243 miles in one day – a record distance for a solo sailor. In truth, the greatest mileage he covered in any single day was 177. The fake record report earned Crowhurst widespread press coverage and was accepted by most seafaring experts as genuine although Sir Francis Chichester, for one, expressed grave doubts as to its veracity.

On 17 December Crowhurst deliberately transmitted another erroneous message: 'Through Doldrums Over Equator. Sailing Fast Again.' By Christmas he was claiming to be 550 miles ahead of his actual position, which was off the north-east coast of Brazil, and when he radio telephoned his wife on Christmas Eve, he refused to give his position. Fearing that continued radio contact would wreck his deception, Crowhurst began to imply that he was having trouble with the generator, as a result of which he was able to maintain radio silence for 11 weeks from 19 January without arousing too much suspicion. While the outside world assumed that he was speeding around Cape Horn and across the Pacific, he spent the whole of that period drifting aimlessly off Brazil, his boat in urgent need of repair. On 6 March he landed illicitly on the estuary of the Rio Salado near Buenos Aires where he finally managed to get the vessel repaired, and two days later he set sail again, heading south towards Cape Horn.

Crowhurst's two-month sojourn off the Brazilian coast had not been entirely wasted time. For all the while he had been listening in to radio messages from boats crossing the Pacific and Indian Oceans so that he would be able to enter plausible weather conditions in his false log. Now, having sailed almost as far south as the Falklands, he suddenly turned north again, and waited patiently until he felt it was safe to resume radio contact from the South Atlantic. As far as the race organizers were concerned, he was back in the Atlantic after rounding the Cape of Good Hope. They had no idea that he had never even left the Atlantic.

By now, many of the favourites for the race – including Chay Blyth and John Ridgeway – had dropped out, leaving just three competitors apart from Crowhurst still afloat. Robin Knox-Johnston in *Suhaili* was the favourite to win the Golden Globe for first boat home, but he was struggling so badly that the £5,000 prize for fastest voyage appeared to rest between Crowhurst and Nigel Tetley, also in a trimaran, *Victress*.

With everything seemingly going according to plan, it would appear that Crowhurst decided to let Tetley win, reasoning that nobody would bother to examine the log of the second boat home, thus allowing his chicanery to remain undetected. Then disaster. On 21 May, Tetley's boat sank off the Azores. The third man, Bernard Moitessier, also dropped out, leaving Crowhurst a certainty to collect the cash prize if he could just make it back to England. Press agent Rodney Hallworth excitedly prepared a hero's welcome for his client back in Teignmouth and cabled Crowhurst to inform him that over 100,000 people were waiting to greet him on his return. But far from giving Crowhurst extra strength over the final leg, the message had the opposite effect. He realized that as the winner his log books would be closely scrutinized and that he would inevitably be exposed as a cheat. He could not face the humiliation. Day by day, his mood darkened. His radio was now genuinely broken and, furthermore, he was short of food. With no assistance from its master, the *Teignmouth Electron* bobbed about on the ocean, still 1,800 miles from its destination.

Early on the morning of 10 July the Royal Mail packet ship *Picardy*, en route from London to the Caribbean, spotted the *Teignmouth Electron* drifting slowly. Sensing that something was amiss, the *Picardy*'s master, Captain Richard Box, altered course and tried to make contact with the vessel. The sound of a foghorn having elicited no response, a boat was lowered to investigate at close quarters. On board the trimaran, Captain Box found dirty dishes in the sink and radio receivers lying in pieces. The life raft was still in place, but there was no sign of either the chronometer or Crowhurst himself. The log books were stacked on the chart table. The last entry was 29 June.

From initial examination, the log books appeared to indicate a highly successful voyage, but then Captain Box discovered the second set – the true account of Crowhurst's positions. By then, Rodney Hallworth had already sold the log books to the *Sunday Times* for £4,000 and was flying out to collect them. On his arrival at the small Caribbean island of Cayman Brac, to where the *Teignmouth Electron* had been ferried, Hallworth was informed by Box that something was seriously wrong and that he should consider destroying the relevant documents in order to protect Crowhurst's family from the awful truth. However, Hallworth felt it his duty as a journalist to see that the truth was published, and so the story of Crowhurst's faked radio messages and positions became known.

Robin Knox-Johnston, who, as the only finisher, had collected the £5,000, graciously donated the prize money to the appeal fund for Crowhurst's family while Nigel Tetley, having virtually driven his boat to shipwreck in his struggle to stay ahead of Crowhurst, was awarded the sum of £1,000 as compensation.

It will never be known whether, in his disturbed state of mind, Donald Crowhurst jumped overboard or simply fell to his death. Whatever the truth, it was a tragic climax to an elaborate hoax and one which, but for the misfortunes that befell his rival competitors, might well have been carried off successfully.

Marathon Man

The marathon at the 1904 Olympic Games in St Louis was run over a hilly course in the middle of a scorching hot afternoon with the result that only 14 of the 32 starters made it to the finish. The patriotic spectators were hoping to acclaim an American winner and so they burst into spontaneous applause and cheering when the figure of Fred Lorz, a member of New York's Mohawk Athletic Club, bounded into view, apparently full of running. Lorz broke the tape in 3 hr 13 min and was immediately declared the winner. He was photographed with Alice Roosevelt, daughter of the President of the United States, and was about to be presented with the gold medal when word got out that he had travelled 11 miles of the race by car.

It was the weary, dishevelled state of the runner-up, English-born American Thomas Hicks, which first prompted Olympic officials to query Lorz's physical state. Like Rosie Ruiz 76 years later, Lorz simply looked too fresh to have run a marathon in such stifling heat. As the rumours spread and the cheers for Lorz turned to jeers, he owned up, insisting that the whole thing had been meant as a joke and that he would never have gone through with the medal ceremony. After suffering from cramp early in the race, he had dropped out at the nine-mile mark and accepted a lift in an official's car for the next 11 miles. When the car overheated and broke down, a rejuvenated Lorz had jumped out and run the remaining six miles, milking the applause all the way to the finish.

Hicks was duly awarded the gold medal while Lorz was banned for life for his joke that backfired. However, the ban was lifted the following year, allowing him to win the Boston Marathon.

Chapter 6

The Military

The Man Who Never Was

In the spring of 1943 the Allied forces carried out one of the most ingenious acts of military subterfuge since the Trojan horse. Implemented under the codename Operation Mincemeat, the deception involved the deliberate planting of fake documents on a dead body to relay false information to the Germans concerning the location of a forthcoming Mediterranean invasion. The anonymous corpse thus became an unlikely hero of the Second World War, and subsequently became known as The Man Who Never Was.

Having taken North Africa in 1942, the Allies' next move was to be an invasion of mainland Europe from the North African coast via a number of convenient island stepping-stones. There were three basic choices: Italy via Sicily, Greece via Crete, or Southern France via either Sardinia or Corsica. The opportunity of gaining a foothold in Italy was irresistible, encouraging Allied commanders to give the go-ahead for a mass invasion of Sicily. The Germans, who were anticipating an imminent strike, had also done their geography and had arrived at the same conclusion. Now it was up to the Allies to feed the Germans the tastiest of red herrings.

The importance of convincing the Germans that the invasion would not be taking place in Sicily cannot be over-estimated. For the might of the German army was sure to be waiting for the landing in the hills above the beaches, ready to pick off the Allied troops as they came ashore. The result would almost certainly be wholesale slaughter and the inevitable failure of the invasion. But if the Germans thought that the target was elsewhere in the Mediterranean, the chances were that the landing forces would encounter no more than token resistance.

The task of devising a suitable plan fell to British Intelligence who came up with the idea of producing a set of fake documents giving details of a different invasion site and allowing them to fall into enemy hands. The initial suggestion was for a British agent to be captured in possession of the papers, but this clearly posed too great a risk for the individual concerned, who would, in all probability, be subjected to torture and then death. Instead why not plant the documents on a corpse – one purporting to be that of a British Intelligence courier seemingly killed in a plane crash at sea? The body with its top-secret papers would then drift ashore to be found by eager German agents who would waste no time in informing Berlin of their spectacular discovery. The process of misinformation was under way.

In order to divert attention from Sicily, the first decision to be made was whether to set the body ashore in Spain or France. Neutral Spain was eventually selected in the belief that the Germans would have less opportunity to examine the body there than if it fell into their own hands, yet because of their intelligence network, they would still be able to obtain copies of the incriminating documents at the very least. Then the port of Huelva in southern Spain was pinpointed as the ideal place for the drop as it was known to house an active German agent who had established good contacts with Spanish officials.

The problem of finding a plausible corpse for Operation Mincemeat was addressed by Lieutenant-Commander Ewen Montagu of British Naval Intelligence. He approached noted pathologist Sir Bernard Spilsbury and outlined the requirements over a civil glass of sherry. To simulate someone who had supposedly died from exposure at sea, Sir Bernard proposed a pneumonia victim as possessing similar symptoms, the liquid in the lungs from pneumonia being consistent with a victim who had died while floating in choppy waters. At no stage did the pathologist ask precisely what the body was needed for. He knew that he probably would not have received an honest answer anyway.

A likely candidate was soon recruited – a man in his early thirties, of the right build for a serving naval officer, who had died from pneumonia followed by exposure. According to those involved in the operation, the deceased's family gave permission for his body to be used in the exercise on condition that his true identity remained a secret. Sir Bernard approved of the choice and offered reassuring news: 'You have nothing to fear from a Spanish post-mortem; to detect that this young man had not died after an aircraft had been lost at sea would need a pathologist of my experience – and there aren't any in Spain.'

The corpse was placed in cold storage until ready for use. Timing was all-important, and a check of the prevailing winds and tides around Huelva indicated that April was the perfect month for washing a body towards the shore. Operation Mincemeat was scheduled for the end of April 1943.

The unnamed body was given the ID of Major William Martin of the Royal Marines, Martin being a common surname among naval officers at that time. The story was to be that his plane had crashed at sea while he was carrying in a briefcase vital documents from the UK to Allied Forces HQ in North Africa. The papers related to the forthcoming Allied invasion of . . . Sardinia.

To back up the bogus invasion, two highly confidential letters were to be placed in the briefcase. One was from the Vice-Chief of the Imperial General Staff explaining to General Alexander in Tunisia why Sicily had been rejected as the landing location. It went on to state that an invasion via Crete and Greece would act as cover for the main operation, adding, by way of a double bluff: 'We stand a very good chance of making the Boche think we will go for Sicily.'

The second faked letter was from Lord Louis Mountbatten, Chief of Combined Operations, introducing 'Major Martin' to Admiral Sir Andrew Cunningham, Commander-in-Chief Mediterranean. It read: 'Dear Admiral of the Fleet, I promised VCIGS (Vice-Chief of the Imperial General Staff) that Major Martin would arrange with you for the onward transmission of a letter he has with him for General Alexander. It is very urgent and very "hot" and as there are some remarks in it that could not be seen by others in the War Office, it could not go by signal. I feel sure that you will see that it goes on safely and without delay.

'I think you will find Martin the man you want. He is quiet and shy at first, but he really knows his stuff. He was more accurate than some of us about the probable run of events at Dieppe and he has been well in on the experiments with the latest barges and equipment which took place up in Scotland. Let me have him back, please, as soon as the assault is over.'

As a mischievous last line above his signature, Mountbatten's letter concluded: 'He might bring some sardines with him – they are "on points" here!' The throwaway sardine joke carried a clear implication – Sardinia was to be the setting for the Allied invasion.

To establish Martin's identity and make him appear the genuine article, it was necessary to invent a background for him and to include about his person some relevant paraphernalia. It was decided that he should recently have become engaged to a girl named Pam, and so he carried a photograph of his beloved (in reality Jean Gerard Leigh who worked as a clerk in the War Office), together with a selection of love letters (composed by War Office secretaries) and an unpaid bill for the engagement ring. He also carried a letter from Lloyds Bank, dated 14 April 1943, demanding that he pay off an overdraft of £79 19s 2d, and one from his father in North Wales. Other belongings given to flesh out his character and render him all the more human included £8 in notes plus loose change, a book of stamps (minus two which had been used), a silver cross on a chain around his neck, two bus tickets, a box of matches, a packet of cigarettes, a bunch of keys, and two counterfoil stubs of tickets for London's Prince of Wales's Theatre, dated 22 April 1943.

The body of 'Major Martin' left Scotland on board the submarine *Seraph* on 19 April. To slow down the process of decomposition, it was kept in an air-tight container packed with dry ice. At 4.30 a.m. on 30 April, following a few words from the service for burial at sea, the body, now wearing the uniform of a major, Royal Marines, and a 'Mae West' life jacket, was deposited into the sea some 1,600 yards from the mouth of the Huelva river. A rubber dinghy was released separately nearby. To ensure that the briefcase containing the essential documents did not float away from the body, it had been chained to the dead man's wrist — a move that had the additional benefit of emphasizing the importance of its contents. The deed done, the *Seraph* slunk quietly away in the still of the night. Now it was simply a question of waiting and hoping.

Four long days passed before the British naval attaché in Madrid signalled to London that a fisherman had picked up the body of a British major on a beach near Huelva on 30 April. Knowing full well that these signals would be intercepted, it was essential for London to reply in a manner which indicated alarm. Accordingly, the attaché was urged to demand the return of 'Martin' and his documents as soon as possible, but while exercising discretion. The body was duly handed over to the British Vice-Consul and given a full military funeral. When the briefcase was returned to England, British Intelligence discovered that it had been very carefully opened, then resealed. Just as the Allies had hoped, the Germans had photographed every document on the body and in the briefcase before releasing them back to the Spanish authorities. Ewen Montagu was able to telegraph Winston Churchill with the message 'Mincemeat swallowed whole'.

The Germans translated the letters excitedly. Correspondence to Admiral Doenitz, the Commander-in-Chief of Naval Staff, began: 'The genuineness of the captured documents is above suspicion.' Doenitz saw Hitler about them on 14 May, convincing the Fuhrer that either Sardinia or Greece would be the principal Allied target. Hitler responding by issuing the order: 'Measures regarding Sardinia and the Peloponnese take precedence over everything else.' The German High Command quickly moved divisions of troops away from the south coast of Sicily and dispatched extra forces to Sardinia and Greece instead. Consequently when the Allies stormed ashore in Sicily on 10 July, they were met by just two German divisions. What was surely the most justifiable hoax in history had proved a resounding success.

The true identity of the Man Who Never Was remained a secret until 1996 when amateur historian Roger Morgan found the answer in the Public Record Office at Kew, West London. The body used in Operation Mincemeat was revealed as that of Glyndwr Michael, a 34-year-old down-and-out. Hitler had been fooled by a tramp.

Veterans of Future Wars

When an act of Congress advanced by ten years – from 1946 to 1936 – the date at which American veterans of the First World War would receive their controversial soldiers' bonuses, a group of students at Princeton University, New Jersey, saw the new legislation as ripe for satire. The act had been passed following intensive lobbying by the American Legion and the Veterans of Foreign Wars, but the Princetonians felt it to be an intolerable raid upon the United States Treasury for the benefit of an organized minority.

Led by Lewis Jefferson Gorin Jr, a politics major from Louisville, Kentucky, who was writing a senior thesis, appropriately enough, on Machiavelli, the students formed a joke organization called the Veterans of Future Wars, designed to poke fun at the bonus hunters. Its first manifesto, published in the *Princetonian* in the early summer of 1936, argued that sooner or later there would be another war and that therefore Congress should grant a cash bonus to all American men between the ages of 18 and 36. Legally the bonus would be payable in 1965, but since Congress seemed intent on paying bonuses before they were due, the Future Veterans suggested that the actual payment should be June 1936 with, of course, an additional 3 per cent annual interest compounded back from 1965 to 1936. In this way future veterans would receive their benefits while all were still alive to enjoy them. The organization adopted its own national salute, a modified version of the infamous Fascist greeting: an arm held straight out in the direction of Washington, the palm turned up receptively.

Newspapers all over the country picked up the campaign. Almost overnight, local chapters mushroomed on college campuses across America. By June 1936 there were over 500 chapters and a paid-up membership of more than 50,000 students. The manifesto reached the ears of Congress who, after much discussion, rejected the idea for advance payments. Nor did it find favour with the organized veterans' movement. The Commander of the Veterans of Foreign Wars, James Van Zandt, referred to the Future Veterans as 'insolent puppies', adding: 'They'll never be veterans of a future war for they are too yellow to go to war.' The Princetonians replied that since the Veterans of Future Wars was a wholly patriotic organization, Van Zandt was obviously a 'Red'.

The Future Veterans movement continued to attract media attention throughout the summer of 1936, appealing as it did to both conservatives and liberals. Conservatives enjoyed the joke on the basis that it lampooned government spending while liberals saw it as an opportunity to satirize war itself. But all jokes have their lifespan and Future Veteran activity had peaked by the close of the academic year. After the summer vacation the joke was stale and national attention turned instead to the forthcoming presidential elections. The Princetonians gamely issued a few proclamations and sent questionnaires to the presidential candidates about the bonus, but by April 1937 all operations were suspended. And with its campaign books showing an overall deficit of 44 cents, the Veterans of Future Wars quietly faded away.

The Flawed War Hero

Douglas R. Stringfellow's election to the US House of Representatives in 1952 was largely the result of a tub-thumping campaign in which he enthusiastically portrayed himself as a decorated all-American war hero. He talked up his military exploits at every opportunity to the extent that he became a national celebrity, appearing in countless magazines and receiving a Junior Chamber of Commerce award as one of America's ten outstanding young men of 1953. In January 1954 he was also given the accolade of featuring on television's *This Is Your Life*, following which President Eisenhower's press secretary James Hagerty sent Stringfellow a telegram: 'Congratulations on the wonderful presentation of your life and many outstanding accomplishments. The President has asked me to extend to you his very best wishes and congratulations.' Nine months later, when he ran for re-election, Stringfellow's story was exposed as a sham.

Born in 1922 in Draper, Utah, Stringfellow was crippled by a Second World War land mine after seeing just a few days' action in France. It was while recuperating in a Utah hospital that he met his future wife Shirley. On his discharge, he returned to the town of Ogden where he became a radio announcer. He then began touring Utah, preaching to Mormon Church groups and audiences of local dignitaries, regaling them all with extraordinary tales from his war service. His heroics grew all the more daring with each telling.

He claimed that he had been hand picked to serve as an agent with the OSS (Office of Strategic Services), the forerunner of the CIA, during which time he had undertaken numerous top-secret missions. His most perilous, he revealed, was a three-week cloak-and-dagger operation that saw a 30-strong OSS unit dropped behind German lines near Nuremberg to help the Allies in their assault on the Siegfried Line. Stringfellow said that his group held a key German communications centre for 11 hours, allowing them to misdirect German military operations. He also took the credit for capturing German atomic physicist Otto Hahn from behind enemy lines and taking him to England. The only survivor of that elite OSS team, Stringfellow said that he, too, had been captured by the Germans and held in the notorious Belsen prison camp where he had been brutally tortured. While stricken with terrible injuries, he had apparently experienced a profound religious vision and through his new-found faith, he had managed to escape from his incarceration. According to Stringfellow, he then made his way to France, only to fall foul of the land mine – wounds which left him a paraplegic. He said that he had been awarded the Silver Star for his gallantry, and all who listened to his moving story could not help but conclude that the honour was richly merited.

The image of the wounded war veteran discovering religion was an appealing one and Stringfellow's speeches soon brought him to the attention of the Republican Party. He served two years in Congress, in the course of which his star continued to rise. But there were some who thought his stories were just a little too good to be true.

Chief among the doubters was the *Army Times*, an unofficial military journal which, with Stringfellow standing for re-election, decided to seek confirmation of his service record from the US Defense Department. The latter's reluctance to provide corroborating evidence further stoked the publication's suspicions, as a result of which the *Army Times* conducted its own investigation and found so many holes in Stringfellow's story that the congressman was asked to come up with positive proof to support his claims. He was unable to do so, but maintained that the information necessary to substantiate his account was kept in secret files that only President Eisenhower could order to be unlocked. He then threatened a libel action against the *Army Times* whose senior editor, Harold Stagg, was warned by Stringfellow supporters that he would be accused of harbouring

Communist sympathies. Refusing to bow to threats and slurs, the journal went ahead with its exposé.

Douglas Stringfellow's glittering war record was revealed as pure fabrication. He had not worked for the OSS; he was a mere private in the Army Air Forces. His version of the seizure of Dr Hahn was ridiculed by a letter from the scientist himself and also by the genuine OSS officer to whom Hahn had surrendered months after Private Stringfellow had returned to the United States. Stringfellow had played no part in that, or any other, OSS operation. It almost goes without saying that he had never won the Silver Star. Nor was he even a true paraplegic. He had been seriously wounded by a land mine explosion in France, but it was during a routine mission, and he could walk with the aid of a cane. His academic qualifications were similarly discredited. He claimed to have attended Ohio State University and the University of Cincinnati, but neither institution had any record of his presence.

Stringfellow tried to bluff his way out of the situation at first, admitting that he might have used 'poetic licence' with regard to minor details, but insisting that his story in essence was authentic. 'The entire attack on me is politically inspired,' he ranted. But a mere two days later, after being quizzed by Utah's two Republican senators, Arthur Watkins and Wallace Bennett, and under mounting pressure from the Mormon Church, he decided to make a public confession, much to the delight of his Democratic opponents. In October 1954 – just 16 days before the new election – he appeared on television in Salt Lake City. Even that was unorthodox. The scheduled programme on KSL-TV was delayed and Stringfellow materialized on screen without any introduction. Joined by his wife, he gave a ten-minute broadcast in which he said that the exaggeration of his military record had arisen after he had been asked to give a series of talks to various groups following his release from hospital. 'Somewhere along the line, the thought came in during the introduction that Douglas Stringfellow was a war hero. As the stories grew, I did not correct these erroneous accounts, but rather thrived on the adulation and new-found popularity. Consciously or unconsciously I began to embellish the account and awoke to find that it had taken on an aspect that even I had never expected. I fell into a trap which was in part laid by my own glib tongue. I came here tonight to give you the facts. These here are the facts. I was never in the OSS. I was never on a behind-the-lines mission. I never captured Otto Hahn or any other German physicist. I come before this radio and television audience humble, contrite and a very repentant individual. I have made some grievous mistakes.' He apologized profusely to the people of Utah and, when it became clear that most of the electorate were not disposed towards forgiveness, announced his withdrawal from the campaign. Republican Party officials needed little persuasion to accept his resignation.

When the storm had subsided, Stringfellow attempted to capitalize on his infamy by embarking on a speaking tour, but nobody wanted to know. He returned to broadcasting, working at various radio stations in Utah, but always under a pseudonym. In 1966 at Long Beach, California, he reached the end of a short, turbulent life, but one that was not quite as colourful as he tried to paint it.

Chapter 7

Archaeology

A Giant Among Men

It has been called 'America's Greatest Hoax': the chance discovery on a farm in New York State of the fossil of a 10 ft 4½ in-tall man. Thousands flocked to see the bizarre specimen, apparently indifferent as to whether or not it was genuine, but, in doing so, ensuring that the Cardiff Giant achieved an unwavering popularity that has enabled it to remain part of American folklore for nigh on 150 years.

The Giant was born in the mind of George Hull, cigar-maker and atheist of Binghampton, New York. One day in 1866, while visiting his sister in Ackley, Iowa, Hull became involved in a heated debate with a fire and brimstone preacher by the name of Revd Turk who, quoting Genesis 6:4, declared: 'In those days and even later, there were giants on the earth who were descendants of human women and the heavenly beings. They were the great heroes and famous men of long ago.' Such beliefs were not shared by Hull who set about teaching a salutary lesson to Revd Turk and others of his ilk.

Hull bought an acre of land in Fort Dodge, Iowa, known as 'Gypsum Hollow', and began the quarrying of a five-ton block of blue-veined gypsum. The work attracted considerable attention from the local population, but Hull had prepared a ready-made answer to anyone who asked what he was doing: the stone, he said, was to be Iowa's gift towards a memorial to Abraham Lincoln in Washington, DC. The idea was to transport the stone block by rail to Chicago for sculpting, but its weight was such that the wagon carrying it to the railway station collapsed under the sheer weight. So Hull arranged instead for a smaller, 12 ft long section (weighing only one and a half tons) to be cut from the block and dispatched to Chicago. There, it came under the wing of marble cutters Edward Burghardt, Henry Salle and Fred Mohrmann, who began the laborious task of carving the solid block into a shape resembling a human.

Supervised by Hull – who himself modelled for the Giant's head – the trio made use of the natural dark streaks in the gypsum to create human veins and, with the help of a wooden mallet, they drove darning needles into the Giant's surface to simulate skin pores. The chosen pose suggested that the Giant had died in considerable pain, his right arm reaching across his abdomen and his legs contorted in discomfort. For the hoax to succeed, the figure had to appear of sufficient antiquity to be recognized as a fossil or an ancient statue, so the team of sculptors utilized sand, ink and sulphuric acid to render an ageing effect. When Hull was satisfied with his creation, he had it shipped by rail and sturdy wagon to the farm of his cousin and co-conspirator, William 'Stub' Newell, close to the village of Cardiff in upstate New York, the last leg of the journey by road taking a circuitous route through remote countryside to avoid detection. In November 1868 the Giant was secretly buried three feet deep near a tree behind Newell's barn. And there it would remain for the best part of a year.

On 16 October 1869, Newell hired two labourers, Gideon Emmons and Henry Nichols, to dig a well behind his barn. Although his farm already had a more than adequate water supply, he told the pair that he wanted a well that would be more conveniently located for his cattle. Hull was on hand to ensure that digging took place near the tree . . . and therefore directly above the burial site. It wasn't long before the workmen struck something solid. Thinking it to be an underground water line, they tried to dig around the object, only to find that it was a stone leg, at the end of which was a stone foot. Soon the entire stone effigy had been unearthed. News of the 'accidental' discovery spread like wildfire. By the afternoon a tent was in position over the Giant's grave, and visitors were being charged 25 cents admission to come and gawp at the 2,900 lb figure. Publicly, Newell expressed indifference at the find – even suggesting that the Giant be buried again – but when a neighbour offered the deed to his farm in return for sole possession of the Giant, Newell flatly refused to sell. Indeed his professed reluctance to cash in on his good fortune was somewhat at odds with his decision to raise the admission fee first to 50 cents and then to a dollar when wagonloads of scholars, geologists, clergymen, politicians and curious sightseers began arriving from the nearby towns of Syracuse and Albany and even as far afield as New York City.

Since the Cardiff area was once home to both Jesuit missionaries and Native American Indians, a historical find seemed entirely plausible. Theologians declared that the Giant was most likely a petrified man, but palaeontologists pointed out that the figure contained stone representations of soft-tissue matter that would not have left a fossil trace. Opinion was divided: some thought it was an ancient statue; others favoured a modern hoax. Meanwhile, with around 3,000 people a day arriving to pay homage to the Giant, farmer Newell continued to rake in the money, taking one-tenth as his cut and sending on the balance to Hull.

Having spent under $3,000 on the construction and transportation of his creation, Hull, too, was reaping the rewards. Retaining a quarter interest for himself, he sold shares in the Giant for $37,500 to a syndicate of three Syracuse businessmen led by banker David Hannum. The money-making potential of the venture came to the attention of legendary showman P. T. Barnum who offered Hull $60,000 to rent the Giant for three months and display it at his American Museum on Broadway in New York City. Hull rejected the deal and set about exhibiting the Giant himself, taking it to the Bastable Arcade in Syracuse where it drew large crowds in November 1869. By now, speculation as to the Giant's origins had become something of a national pastime. Noted sculptor Erastus Dow Palmer had no hesitation in declaring it a fake, a view shared by Andrew White, president of Cornell University, whose analysis of the 'body' revealed that it was made of gypsum but who, for the time being, decided against making his findings public. Arguments over authenticity did nothing to diminish the Giant's popularity and newspapers carried interviews with various people attesting to having seen the heavy cargo en route to Cardiff. Somewhere among this mountain of column inches, two Chicago sculptors told how they had carved the statue in 17 days but their story was deemed no more likely than any of the other far-fetched accounts.

Still seething about missing out on a share of the Giant industry, Barnum heard the hoax stories and, climbing on his moral high horse while keeping one hand on the financial reins, vowed to 'expose the swindle and punish the perpetrators.' He hired an artist to visit the Giant exhibition and to make a secret wax model of the star attraction before asking a friend from New York City, George Wood, to build a full-size plaster version of the model. Barnum shamelessly billed this hoax of a hoax as the 'genuine Cardiff Giant', maintaining that Hull's business syndicate had sold him the original while they exhibited a mere copy. By December 1869, the tour of the original Giant had reached New York City, only to discover Barnum's version on display at his Broadway museum and, more disturbingly, doing better business. As events became increasingly surreal, the syndicate sued

Barnum for calling their Giant a fake and applied for an interim injunction to stop the rival exhibition. The judge at the hearing said he would be happy to grant the injunction if their own giant would first appear before the court and swear to his 'genuineness'. When no such promise was forthcoming, the judge dismissed the motion and the competing Giants went on show just two blocks apart.

The public paid happily to see both, even after anatomist Dr Oliver Wendell Holmes had drilled a hole in the skull of the original and declared it to be almost certainly an ancient statue. He was by no means the only one to fly in the face of commonsense by proclaiming the Giant to be genuine. As late as 1872, Yale divinity student Alexander McWhorter persisted with his belief that the figure was a Phoenician god bearing clandestine inscriptions which only he was able to see. To compound his folly, the earnest McWhorter dedicated months to the translation of these inscriptions.

But by then the riddle of the Cardiff Giant had been solved. During the build-up to the court case, pro-Barnum journalists had retraced the journey of the figure to Cardiff and had also begun to delve into the backgrounds of George Hull and 'Stub' Newell. Large transfers of admission money from Newell's tent enterprise led directly to Hull, and people in upstate New York suddenly remembered Hull's journeys around the region in 1868 hauling a huge wooden crate. From there, the trail moved on to the Fort Dodge gypsum quarry and ultimately to the Chicago sculptors. Cornered by reporters, both Hull and Edward Burghardt cheerfully confessed, Hull stating that his intention all along had been to ridicule the clergy. On 2 February 1870, under oath in the Barnum lawsuit, Hull repeated his admission: the Cardiff Giant was a hoax. Naturally enough, the case against Barnum was dismissed.

It was estimated that Hull made as much as $100,000 from the hoax while, ironically, Barnum fared even better. Despite passing through the hands of several owners, the original Giant continued to be exhibited at State Fairs as recently as the 1940s. In 1947 it was acquired by the New York State Historical Association and put on display at the Farmer's Museum in Cooperstown. Over in Michigan, Barnum's copy can also be found in a museum – a legacy of the winter when America really did stage a battle of the Giants.

The Shaming of Shinichi

In Japanese archaeological circles Shinichi Fujimura was said to have 'God's hands' on account of his uncanny knack of unearthing priceless relics where others had failed. Some fellow experts privately considered his repeated good fortune to be highly suspicious but this was ascribed to jealousy on their part until, in November 2000, Fujimura was caught red-handed planting ancient artefacts at one of his digs. The fallout from the scandal not only threatened a region's tourism but also the very fabric of Japanese history.

Fujimura's career started out as a hobby. He was working at a manufacturing company in 1972 when he developed an interest in prehistoric Japan. Teaching himself archaeology, he devoted his time and energy to searching for age-old artefacts. He first made his name in 1981 with the discovery of stoneware dating back 40,000 years — the oldest stoneware ever to have been found in Japan. From there his reputation took off and over the next two decades he was involved in over 150 archaeological projects around Japan, including most of the country's Palaeolithic sites. Time and again he managed to uncover increasingly older artefacts that pushed back the limits of Japan's known prehistory.

Fujimura's remarkable talent for rewriting history boosted interest in archaeology in Japan to unprecedented levels. He achieved celebrity status. His work became front-page news, textbooks were continually revised to accommodate his latest discovery, and tourism flourished around areas where significant finds had taken place. Nowhere was this more apparent than in the town of Tsukidate in the Miyagi Prefecture, some 190 miles north-east of Tokyo. Ever since Fujimura had been instrumental in unearthing colourful Stone Age tools at nearby Kamitakamori in 1993, the 16,000 residents of Tsukidate found themselves at the heart of the Japanese archaeology boom. Overnight, primitive Japanese man had acquired a new identity – someone who was capable of using colours to differentiate among tools and to perform mathematical tasks. As the leader of the local board of education put it in an interview with the *New York Times*: 'Our idea of primitive man as someone who just wandered around eating rotten meat began to give way to another image. Suddenly we had a new picture, of someone with some intelligence.'

In the wake of Fujimura's discoveries, something akin to Stone Age fever gripped Tsukidate. Flintstone-like characters became the town's mascots; a special drink called 'Early Man' was sold to tourists; the Early Man Marathon became a popular event for athletes from all over Japan; and Tsukidate adopted an official slogan of 'The town with the same skies viewed by Early Man.' Tsukidate basked in its new-found fame and the wealth that came with it.

By the year 2000 Fujimura was 50 and had been appointed deputy director at the Tohoku Palaeolithic Cultural Research Institute. Once again he was back at Japan's oldest archaeological site, the Kamitakamori ruins. He had already announced a number of minor finds when, on 22 October, he came up with his most spectacular discovery to date – several postholes which, he hypothesized, had once held pillars supporting primitive dwellings. Along with a collection of eight stoneware pieces found simultaneously, these were believed to be over 600,000 years old, making them one of the oldest signs of human habitation anywhere in the world. Naturally the find made international headlines.

But then on 5 November it all turned sour. The daily *Mainichi Shimbun* newspaper published on its front page three photographs showing Fujimura digging holes at the site and burying the very same artefacts that he later dug up and announced as major finds. The paper had taken the pictures in secret and had not published them until confirming with Fujimura that he had buried the items himself.

Exposed as a fraud, Fujimura attended a press conference that same day where he admitted planting 61 of the 65 pieces excavated from the Kamitakamori site that year. He described how he had gone to the site shortly after 6 a.m. on 22 October when nobody else was around and dug holes in the ground into which he placed several stoneware pieces that he had brought from home, before covering the holes with soil. He insisted that the pieces in question had been unearthed previously in Miyagi Prefecture, and that he had kept them at home as part of his collection. He also confessed to having planted all 29 artefacts found earlier in the year at the Soshinfudozaka site in Shintotsugawa, North Japan.

His head bowed throughout the conference, Fujimura said: 'I was tempted by the Devil. I don't know how I can apologize for what I did. I wanted to be known as the person who excavated the oldest stoneware in Japan. I was impatient that the ruins have not produced as much in findings as the Ogasaka ruins in Saitama Prefecture.' The Ogasaka site features a layer of earth estimated at 500,000 years old.

In the light of the revelations, Fujimura's previous finds inevitably came under the spotlight. He protested that his work at other sites was genuine, but dark mutterings resurfaced about how Fujimura had repeatedly seemed able to unearth stoneware as soon as he arrived at a dig when such finds had eluded fellow archaeologists. Some researchers came forward to state that they had noticed that Fujimura's discoveries appeared inadequately stained for their ages, but said that they had been reluctant to challenge him on this point because of his glowing reputation. In a national newspaper one of the country's leading archaeologists, Toshiki Takeoka, poured scorn on the gullibility of scientists in accepting everything that Fujimura had laid before them. He added that he had written of his concerns earlier, but that academic journals had edited out his major reservations. Ken Amaksu, Chairman of the Japanese Archaeological Association, conceded that Japan's academic environment might have contributed towards creating a climate in which the hoax could prosper. 'We need to examine,' he said, 'whether enough information was disclosed and enough theories were exchanged among researchers with differing opinions concerning the new discoveries.'

While Fujimura was expelled from the Japanese Archaeological Association and his post at the Tohoku Palaeolithic Institute, publishers hastily tried to correct pictures of his artefacts that they had included in textbooks. More than twenty of his pieces which were exhibited at the Tokyo National Museum were swiftly removed from display. The credibility of Japanese archaeology lay in ruins.

The Beringer Stones

A Professor of Natural History at Würzburg University in the early eighteenth century, Dr Johannes Bartholomeus Adam Beringer had developed an intense fascination with fossils, or 'formed stones' as they were then known. Unfortunately he had also made enemies at the university and two of his foes decided to exploit his obsession by perpetrating a cruel hoax, calculated to destroy his reputation and make him an object of ridicule. They succeeded in making Beringer a laughing stock but, with a certain poetic justice, they did not exactly emerge unscathed from the affair either.

While acknowledged as a gifted scientist, Beringer was also perceived in some quarters as being arrogant, a trait which brought him into conflict with two of his colleagues in particular – J. Ignatz Roderick (Professor of Geography, Algebra and Analysis) and the Honourable Georg von Eckhart (Privy Councillor and university librarian). Eckhart was the finer scholar of the two, and was busy compiling a history of the Duchy of Würzburg; by contrast Roderick was described as a devious, somewhat unsavoury character. It is generally assumed, therefore, that Roderick was chiefly responsible for the plot to discredit Professor Beringer but it should be remembered that Eckhart was the one with the knowledge of prehistoric studies necessary to make the hoax appear credible, and was thus probably equally culpable. Both men knew that Beringer's Achilles heel was his collection of fossils and that he paid three local peasant youths — Christian Zaenger and brothers Niklaus and Valentin Hehn – to bring him any interesting stones they happened upon. Until the summer of 1725 the trio of searchers had failed to unearth anything out of the ordinary, but all that changed when Roderick and Eckhart infiltrated the gang and put 17-year-old Zaenger on their own payroll too.

Guided by Eckhart, Roderick set about hand-carving fake formed stones from a soft shell-limestone and either giving them to Zaenger to take directly to Beringer or planting them on the slopes of Mount Eivelstadt, a hill near Würzburg, which was Beringer's major fossil source and where the unsuspecting Hehn brothers would be sure to stumble across them. The first batch of three rogue stones sent Beringer into raptures. Two bore pictures of worms but, most exciting of all, the other featured a likeness of the sun and its rays. Convinced that the youths had uncovered a genuine set of remarkable fossils, Beringer hastily sent his search party back to Mount Eivelstadt. They returned with yet more stones – all between four and eight inches in diameter and bearing in bold relief images of animals, birds and plants.

Beringer's appetite for the stones was insatiable, forcing Roderick and Eckhart to come up with yet more intricate designs. One stone showed stars and comets while others bore Latin, Arabic and Hebrew characters. Beringer had the hieroglyphics translated by scholars and was ecstatic to learn that they spelt out the name of Jehovah. God had signed his own handiwork! Beringer enthused that the stones with Hebrew script were 'the work of benevolent nature, by which God demonstrates the wonder of his ways.'

Beringer himself joined in the excavations and had soon amassed a collection of around 200 stones, all depicting far clearer images than anything that had been discovered previously, not least because Zaenger had been busily polishing many before planting them. It appears that Eckhart felt that the joke was beginning to get out of hand and, gatecrashing one of Beringer's digs, he tried to denounce the stones as fakes. But Beringer was unmoved, even when Roderick demonstrated his technique of carving 'into some of the more impressionable stones Hebrew characters, the figures of a winged dragon, a mouse, a lion, a pomegranate, etc.' Far from harbouring doubt, Beringer simply saw this as a crude attempt to discredit him by planting a few fakes among his genuine finds and prepared instead to educate a wider audience. Never one to hide his light under a bushel, he decided that his discoveries were of such significance that they ought to be reproduced in a book, which, he thought, would guarantee that his name would go down in the history of geology. Indeed it did, but for all the wrong reasons.

The *Lithographiae Wirceburgensis* was published by Beringer at great personal expense in 1726 and featured elaborate plates of the stones. He could not be accused of underselling the contents, describing how he had discovered 'a hoard which like a cornucopia, holds everything formerly found only in the grottoes of other countries.' Addressing their importance to mankind, he added: 'God, the Founder of Nature, would fill our minds with his praises and perfections radiating from these wondrous effects, so that, when forgetful men grow silent, these mute stones might speak with the eloquence of their figures.'

He went on to outline his theory regarding the origins of the Würzburg iconoliths, as he referred to the stones. 'No intelligent person,' he wrote, 'could entertain the slightest suspicion that our iconoliths were petrified by the sea waters – whether in the general flood, or drawn from the ocean by some other channel.' He was contemptuously dismissive of his rivals' 'vicious raillery, their false rumours and gossip' despite the fact that, even prior to publication, scholars had pointed out that some of the stones showed evidence of a sculptor's chisel. Beringer acknowledged this and wrote that the figures were 'so exactly fitted to the dimensions of the stones, that one would swear that they are the work of a very meticulous sculptor . . . (and that they) seem to bear unmistakable indications of the sculptor's knife.' Beringer also observed that the upper surfaces of the stones were smooth (where they had been chiselled and polished) while the underneath areas were rough and unfinished, but this merely served to convince him all the more that the chisel was wielded by the hand of God while in the act of practising his skills as a sculptor. In view of the fact that many of the creatures which appeared on the stones were soft-bodied, it seems incredible that a professed expert such as Beringer could have believed that they were genuine fossils.

Eventually he saw the light and realized that he had been duped, apparently after finding a stone with his own name inscribed upon it. Having spent a vast sum of money on publishing his book, Beringer now desperately tried to salvage his reputation by spending another fortune on buying up every copy. Meanwhile young Zaenger was charged with falsifying, burying and selling the stones, to which he replied that Eckhart and Roderick had put him up to it. Legal proceedings were duly instigated against Eckhart and Roderick, both of whom made a full public confession, stating that they had sought to ridicule Beringer because 'he was so arrogant and despised us all.'

Eckhart was sacked immediately. Prevented from using the university library and its archives, he was unable to complete his historical research, which thus remained incomplete on his death just four years later. Roderick left Würzburg in disgrace to become a journalist, but his reputation was in tatters. Both hoaxers had paid a heavy price for their jolly jape.

Ironically Beringer lived for another 14 years – until 1740 – and wrote a further two books, both of which were well received. Even after the revelation, he remained adamant that most of the stones were authentic. He never did manage to recall every copy of his book, leaving just sufficient in circulation to ensure that they became collectors' items. Such was the public demand for reading this masterpiece of misguided faith that a publisher brought out a second edition some 25 years after Beringer's death. It outsold the first edition by several thousand copies – proof that the fallibility of man has universal appeal.

Two Petrified Men

When journalists in nineteenth-century America found themselves with time on their hands, they were apt to invent fake stories, many of which found their way into newspapers. Around 1860, there appeared a sudden rash of petrification stories, which came to the attention of a young reporter by the name of Samuel Clemens . . . or, as he later became known, Mark Twain. Throughout his career Twain was notorious for his hoaxes but the one that ridiculed the fad for petrified men had the distinction of being his very first.

Twain had moved to Nevada in 1861 but, after failing to find work as a miner, he submitted a number of articles to the *Territorial Enterprise* in Virginia City and was soon offered a job on its editorial staff. The paper's editor-in-chief, Joseph T. Goodman, had a reputation for encouraging his reporters to write interesting articles, regardless of whether or not they were actually true.

Relishing this journalistic licence, Twain set to work on his fake story about 'A Petrified Man'. As the author himself later explained: 'One could scarcely pick up a paper without finding in it one or two glorified discoveries of this kind. The mania was becoming a little ridiculous. I was a brand-new local editor in Virginia City, and I felt called upon to destroy this growing evil. So I chose to kill the petrification mania with a delicate, a very delicate satire.' Twain had also selected a second target for his piece – the region's new coroner and Justice of the Peace, a pompous individual named Sewall. Twain depicted him as a fool and deliberately misspelt his name in the article.

Twain's story appeared in the *Enterprise* in 1862, reporting that a petrified man had been found partially imbedded in rock in a desert cave south of Gravelly Ford. The deceased, who had been lying there for at least 100 years and maybe considerably longer, had turned entirely to stone. Even the man's left leg, which had been a wooden leg during his life, had turned to stone. Twain proceeded to describe how Justice 'Sewell' had travelled five days from Humboldt City, rushing to the scene to hold an inquest into the man's death (even though the victim had been dead for over a century and had turned to stone). The verdict was that the man had died from protracted exposure.

Having ascertained cause of death, 'Sewell' now presided over attempts to bury him, at which point it was discovered that the man of stone had become anchored to the rock. It seemed that water dripping down the man's back for so many years had deposited a limestone sediment which glued him immovably to the rock. Twain solemnly added that 'Sewell' had, 'with that delicacy so characteristic of him', forbidden miners from blasting the body from its position.

Twain had not expected anybody of sound mind to be taken in by his hoax. He had even described how the deceased's hands were arranged in an unusual position – with a thumb to the nose – to indicate that the whole thing was a joke. But such was the quality and depth of his prose that these minor details were overlooked and the story was accepted at face value, being reprinted as fact in a number of other newspapers. Twain decided to milk the situation by sending correspondence on the article to Justice Sewall and eminent scientists, some of who annoyed Sewall intensely by writing to him requesting further information on the case. Twain was clearly delighted to see Sewall suffer, as can be gauged from his subsequent comment about the petrified man hoax: 'I did it for spite, not for fun.'

The motive behind the petrified man hoax that adorned the front page of Wisconsin's *Rusk County Journal* of 21 January 1926 was far less sinister: journalist Manley Hinshaw simply had a space to fill.

The story began: 'Recently a firm in Chippewa Falls acquired a tract of land near here. Monday morning two employees of the firm, Art Charpin and Walter Latsch of Owen, set about clearing the land for their company.

'They noticed a large basswood, and felled it. Even though it had a large hole some 30 feet above the ground, it looked like good timber. Monday afternoon they struck their saws into the basswood at a point where they expected a cut would give them a 20-foot log and eliminate the portion affected by the large hole. All went well until about half way through the log, the saw stuck in a rock. Latsch and Charpin cursed because they knew their saw blade would be dulled.

'After some labour, the men turned the tree trunk over and began a cut on the other side. Before long the same difficulty was encountered, but by turning the trunk about, the cut was finally completed, and the log rolled away, revealing what threw the men into a bad fright.

'There, staring up at them, was the ashen face of a man. And there, encased in the living trunk of the tree, was the entire body of a man, fully clothed in a coarse homespun and buckskins, which fell away when touched, and the head had been covered with long hair which had been tucked up under a coonskin cap. With the mummified body in the hollow tree was an old muzzle-loading flintlock rifle and a muzzle-loading pistol of fanciful design.'

The story went on to reveal that the petrified man was identified as a French explorer, lost in 1663, and that the body was being sent to the State Historical Society in Madison.

Regular readers of Hinshaw's articles immediately spotted that it was a hoax, recalling perhaps the story he had once written about an inventor who extracted static electricity from the air, then used the electricity to run a large motor. However, less-knowing souls accepted the story in good faith and it was picked up by other local newspapers and a national news agency. Consequently people from all over the United States besieged the *Journal* with letters and telegrams demanding more information and photographs about the petrified man of Wisconsin. Visitors flocked to the State Historical Society's museum in Madison where the curator patiently announced that the mummified remains had not been brought to the museum, and probably never would be. He explained that for a body to be petrified, its decaying cells would have to be replaced by certain mineral matter – something that the sap of a basswood tree did not carry.

Although visitors to the museum turned away disappointed, Hinshaw's story was never widely exposed as a hoax. Indeed as recently as 1982 a book entitled *Wisconsin's Famous and Historic Trees* reprinted the article as if it were true.

The Schoolboy Saviour

Members of a society calling itself The Friends of Prehistory were made to eat humble pie at Hameln, Germany, in 1933 when the stone carvings that they had hailed as the oldest examples of Palaeolithic cave art in Northern Germany turned out to have been the work of a twentieth-century schoolboy.

The boy had been learning about Neanderthal man in history lessons at school and had also been studying a children's book titled *Cave Children In Our Land*. This inspired him to try his hand at the seemingly harmless pursuit of copying prehistoric art, so when he happened upon three flat limestone slabs he decided to make drawings of animals using a sharp stone. It took him just 15 minutes to produce three pieces of work.

One resembled a bear, another a wild horse, and the third a mammoth. Particularly dissatisfied with the mammoth, he tossed the slabs into a ditch but later reclaimed them and took them to school to see what his teacher's reaction would be. He admitted only that he had found the slabs and refrained from revealing that he had done the drawings.

The teacher was hugely excited by the finds and wasted no time in contacting the experts for their opinion. They were unanimous in their praise. Then the Friends of Prehistory became involved, declaring the boy to be the saviour of German heritage. His parents thought he ought to receive some recompense for his discovery and, operating under the age-old maxim of finder's keepers, arrived at a price of 20,000 reichsmarks for each slab. German art lovers, eager to prevent such national treasures being sold abroad, quickly raised sufficient funds to buy the drawings, only for the sale to be ruled illegal because their discovery had already been reported to the Landesmuseum of Lower Saxony.

There the three plaques were examined under a microscope. This revealed the presence of modern algae, which could not possibly have grown in the total darkness of the loess. Furthermore, when viewed under ultra-violet lamp, the incisions on the slabs were found to be recent. Even in the face of such damning evidence, the Friends of Prehistory defended the stones as genuine, but shortly afterwards the boy was arrested by police and made a full confession. He maintained that he had never meant any harm but that when the experts had told him how valuable the drawings were, he had been too embarrassed to tell the truth.

Dawson's Missing Link

For centuries anthropologists the world over had been looking for the so-called missing link, the key to the evolution of the human race. The second half of the nineteenth century was a particularly fertile period for significant finds, most notably the discovery near Dusseldorf in 1856 of the leg bone and skull of the creature that came to be known as Neanderthal Man. Smaller and stockier than present-day humans, with a strong jaw and prominent brow ridges on a sloping forehead, *Homo sapiens neanderthalensis* roamed the earth some 75,000 years ago. His excavation was a major breakthrough and, followed as it was by further important finds across Germany and France, it increased the pressure on British anthropologists to come up with a contribution of their own.

Hastings solicitor and amateur fossil hunter Charles Dawson had been scouring the Kentish Weald to good effect, unearthing a succession of fossil plants, fish and mammals. He had discovered three new species of iguanodon and the tracks of a megalosaurus, as a result of which he had been awarded fellowship of the London Geological Society at the relatively early age of 21. But, like everyone else in his field, what he really wanted to find was the missing link.

Among Dawson's closest associates was Arthur Smith Woodward, Keeper of Geology at the Natural History branch of the British Museum in South Kensington. In 1909 Dawson wrote to Woodward saying that he was 'waiting for the big discovery which never seems to come.'

In the hope of speeding up this 'big discovery', Dawson had put most of the quarrymen in Kent and Sussex on alert. If they should come across anything remotely unusual, they were to get in touch with him. In return, he would reward them handsomely.

One day towards the end of 1911 Dawson was strolling on Piltdown Common, near Uckfield in East Sussex, when a member of a gang digging gravel for road construction handed him a piece of skull bone which they had stumbled across. Dawson was fascinated by the find and intended to search for the remaining fragments of the skull, but was prevented from doing so by the winter rains which flooded the gravel bed. Nevertheless he was sufficiently optimistic to write to his friend Woodward on 14 February 1912: 'I have come across a very old Pleistocene bed overlooking the Hastings beds between Uckfield and Crowborough which I think is going to be interesting.' As the weather improved, Dawson returned to Piltdown and was able to write again to Woodward a few days later, claiming that he had found part of a skull which, in terms of significance, would rival the discovery of Heidelberg Man that had been unearthed in Germany five years previously. He invited Woodward to come to Piltdown.

In May 1912 Dawson and Woodward began a systematic search of the shallow gravel bed. On the very first day of excavation Dawson dug up part of a lower jaw, along with some fossilized animal bones and a selection of stone tools. Apparently Woodward did not think there was anything out of the ordinary in the fact that Dawson had conveniently come across the jaw straight away. Or maybe he was just too eager to believe.

There was more to come. In the autumn Dawson, accompanied by Pierre Teilhard de Chardin, a young Jesuit priest and amateur paleontologist, discovered the remainder of the skull bones and half of the lower jaw. Woodward had no doubt that the bones were human and he now had enough evidence to reconstruct the head, giving it an ape-like jaw and human braincase and large, pointed teeth. The resultant ape-man look fitted in perfectly with the commonly held theories of the time regarding human evolution.

The only note of discord came from Arthur Keith, conservator of the

Hunterian Museum of the Royal College of Surgeons, who argued that the teeth should be smaller and that Piltdown Man was of the earlier Pliocene, not the Pleistocene, period. This would put his time on earth between 5 million and 1.8 million, rather than 1.8 million and 10,000, years ago. Either way, his were the earliest remains in Europe.

On 18 December 1912 Woodward officially revealed Piltdown Man to a packed meeting of the London Geological Society. From the shape of the jaw, he felt able to announce with supreme confidence 'that the creature, when alive, had not the power of speech. Therefore, in the evolution of the human species, the brain came first, and speech was a growth of a later age.' This was clearly an enormous breakthrough, the most important archaeological discovery of all time — a member of a race from which both cave people and modern humans had developed. Possessing the noble brow of *Homo sapiens* combined with a primitive jaw, it was surely the missing link in Darwin's theory of evolution.

British palaeontologists certainly thought so, but their French and American counterparts were more sceptical, pointing out that the jawbone and the skull were clearly from two different animals and that their discovery together was simply coincidence. The British attributed these doubts to a nasty case of sour grapes.

Dawson was feted for his work, and Piltdown Man was named after him, *Eoanthropus dawsoni* – Dawson's man of the dawn. But a few other dissenting voices began to be heard, the most vociferous being bank clerk and amateur archaeologist Harry Morris who claimed he had been duped by Dawson. Morris said that Dawson had swapped Morris's genuine flints for counterfeit flints stained brown with permanganate of potash and now he challenged the Natural History Museum to test the Piltdown discoveries with hydrochloric acid. Morris was convinced that the brown stain of age present on Dawson's finds would be removed by the acid, thereby proving the fossils to be fakes. The accusations were swiftly swept under the carpet. Nobody in authority was willing to jeopardize the authenticity of Piltdown Man.

In 1913 de Chardin found a tooth at Piltdown which matched Woodward's model. That seemed to satisfy most of the sceptics, except for the Americans who continued to classify Piltdown Man as a mix of human and ape fossils. The British were quietly seething. After all, even Sir Arthur Conan Doyle, who had visited the site several times, had been impressed. If he was satisfied as to the validity of the finds, what right had the Americans to pooh-pooh them? But, as we have seen from the case of the Cottingley Fairies, Conan Doyle could be blinkered in certain areas and was therefore not always as sharp as his great literary creation.

Dawson died in 1916 and Woodward went on to make further discoveries at Piltdown which seemed to put an end to any speculation that Dawson might have planted the specimens. Woodward was knighted for his work in 1924, but two years later fresh doubts were cast about Piltdown Man when a comprehensive geological survey of the gravel at the site revealed that it was nowhere near as old as had been imagined. It certainly did not correspond to the supposed age of Dawson's relics. By way of further embarrassment, a number of other ancient human finds were made during the 1920s and 1930s – and Piltdown Man simply did not fit in with them. There seemed to be no rung for him on the evolutionary ladder.

Nevertheless the British maintained a stiff upper lip and stood by their Man. In 1931 Sir Arthur Keith wrote: 'It is possible that Piltdown Man does represent the early Pleistocene ancestor of the modern type of man. He may well be the ancestor we have been in search of during all these past years. I am therefore inclined to make the Piltdown type spring from the main ancestral stem of modern humanity.' Seven years later he unveiled a memorial to both Piltdown Man and Charles Dawson at the site. He told the gathering that Dawson had given them 'the entrance to a long past world of humanity such as had never been dreamed of, and assembled evidence which carried the history of Sussex back to a period to which geologists assigned a duration from half a million to a million years.'

Despite the British stance, the controversy would not go away and in 1949 fresh tests were carried out on the Piltdown remains, much more detailed than before. Four years later came the news that British anthropologists had been dreading – Piltdown Man was a fake. The results proved what American scientists had said all along – that the skull and jaw were incompatible. The skull was human all right, but only about 1,000 years old, while the jaw bone turned out to be that of an orang-utan, dating back some 500 years. De Chardin's solitary tooth came from a modern ape. None of these animal finds could possibly have been British in origin: they had evidently been planted there. Intensive examination of the teeth showed that they had been rubbed down artificially to make them look human.

There was more. The flint tools supposedly used by Piltdown Man showed traces of modern tool work – cuts which could only have been made by a metal blade. And the thorough chemical analysis carried out on the bones indicated that a solution containing iron had been used to stain them in order to give them an aged appearance. It was just as Harry Morris had said 40 years previously. Nobody listened then; they did now.

The leading lights of the British Museum had been the victims of an elaborate hoax – carried out by person or persons unknown – but the predicament in which they now found themselves was, in many respects, all of their own making. Right from the outset, they had been too eager to accept the finds as genuine, singularly failing to carry out sufficient detailed tests which would have exposed the hoax at once. An eminent dentist had long ago pointed out the incongruity between the heavy wear on the canine tooth found at Piltdown and its large pulp cavity, a sign of relative youth. But the dentist's suspicions were brushed aside. The teeth had never even been carefully examined under a microscope so that the erroneous wear pattern on the molars was not detected until 1953. Basically, the British Museum had always jealously guarded what it thought was its ground-breaking discovery and had refused to let experts handle the fossils. With a more open approach, the entire fiasco could have been avoided.

The finger of suspicion has since been pointed at a number of individuals, from Keith to Conan Doyle. But Dawson remains the most plausible perpetrator, particularly in the light of an article which appeared in the *Sussex Express* newspaper shortly after the hoax was exposed in 1953. The story read: 'Mrs Florence Padgham, now of Cross-in-Hand, remembers that in 1906, aged 13, when living at Victoria Cross, Nutley, her father gave Charles Dawson a skull, brown with age, no lower jaw bone . . . Dawson is supposed to have said: "You'll hear more about this, Mr Burley."'

Chapter 8

Television, Movie and Radio

Panic on the Streets of London

At the start of 1926 radio was in its infancy, the power of the medium still an unknown quantity. But a chilling warning as to its potential influence occurred on the evening of 16 January that year when a BBC broadcast inadvertently created scenes of panic in homes the length and breadth of Britain.

It all started innocently enough. The programme in question, *Broadcasting the Barricades*, was introduced as a 'burlesque' by Father Ronald Knox from the BBC's Edinburgh studio. Unfortunately the majority of listeners either missed – or failed to comprehend the significance of – the opening, and as a result thought that what they were hearing was real rather than an elaborate spoof. Thus a few minutes into Father Knox's sombre talk, they were horrified when the programme was suddenly interrupted by a report from London, stating that the capital was in the grip of a bloody revolution.

With unemployment and unrest rife (the General Strike was only a matter of months away), the BBC capitalized on the general unease in the nation by announcing, via news reports purporting to come from Trafalgar Square, that the unemployed had rioted and were laying waste to the city. Led by a Mr Popplebury – described as the Secretary of the National Movement for Abolishing Theatre Queues – the mob had apparently gathered in Trafalgar Square before sacking the National Gallery. From there the hordes were said to have surged down Whitehall, attacking government offices and destroying wildfowl in St James's Park with empty bottles. They then proceeded to blow up the Houses of Parliament using trench mortars. As Big Ben had crumbled to the ground in a heap of rubble, listeners were informed that in future BBC time signals would be sent out from Edinburgh.

As the news from London grew progressively more alarming, BBC announcers tried to calm the situation by announcing: 'We will now switch over to some light music.' Still it got worse. The Savoy Hotel was blown up and Mr Wutherspoon, the Minister of Transport, was reported as having been found hanging from a lamppost in Vauxhall after being seized by the mob. This was later corrected: he had in fact been found hanging from a tramway post. Anxious listeners rushed to telephones to contact relatives. Newspapers were besieged with enquiries, and callers rang the Admiralty demanding that the navy be sent up the Thames to quell the rioting. Even though Admiralty officials denied any knowledge of public disturbances, listeners refused to accept the assurances. The news must be true; they had heard it on the radio.

Father Knox's talk finished with the mob marching on the BBC's London headquarters. To an uninitiated audience, these news flashes must have sounded eerily realistic, backed as they were by sound effects of explosions and a baying mob. It was only when the programme was over that the BBC realized the monster it had created. To restore nationwide calm, it had to interrupt subsequent programmes with an official explanation of the broadcast and a repeat of the introduction that so many had misunderstood.

For the time being at least, the BBC learned its lesson and refrained from making any hoax broadcasts that were likely to induce mass hysteria. New Yorkers were not to be spared, however, and in 1938 CBS Radio unwittingly mirrored the events of a dozen years earlier with a dramatically updated version of H. G. Wells's *War of the Worlds*.

Devised and fronted by Orson Welles and his Mercury Theatre of the Air and scripted by Howard Koch, the CBS broadcast was, like its BBC predecessor, probably not really intended to fool anyone, but it was calculated to shock. At the outset – and on three separate occasions during the programme – listeners were told that they were tuning in to a play, but the overall effect was so realistic and, in the general context of the world at that time, so plausible, that the explanations went over many people's heads. In the autumn of 1938, with the world on the brink of war, it was nothing unusual for radio shows to be interrupted by grave news reports. So when, on the evening of 30 October, a live broadcast of the music of Ramon Raquello and his orchestra from the Meridian Room at New York City's Park Plaza was suddenly cut short for an urgent announcement, it was pretty much par for the course. Even the initial report – that astronomers had detected huge blue flames rising up from the surface of Mars – failed to create much interest, especially when the programme returned to the comforting music of Ramon Paquello.

A few minutes later there was a second news flash. A meteor had crashed to earth on a farm near Grovers Mill, New Jersey, forming a massive crater and causing untold damage. This was alarming enough, but what followed proved little short of terrifying to listening Americans. A reporter on the spot, 'Carl Phillips', revealed that it was not a meteor at all, but a spaceship, from which a sinister, tentacled creature, presumed to be a Martian, then emerged and began gunning down bystanders with a deadly heat-ray. Stumbling over his words and asking his panic-stricken interviewees (many of whom were played by actor Joseph Cotten) to speak louder into the microphone, 'Phillips' sounded frighteningly authentic, never more so than when he described how legions of Martians had exterminated 7,000 US soldiers who were ringing the crater and were now blasting people at will with their death-rays. At the same time the alien invaders were releasing a toxic black gas, which gas masks were proving powerless to combat. To the six million listeners at home, it must have seemed only a matter of time before the killer Martians seized the whole of New York.

Although further disclaimers were made on air, the most disturbing segment of the play had already been broadcast and it was too late to reverse the tide of panic for many. The special Halloween offering ended – again with echoes of the BBC production – in an announcer shouting hysterically from the top of the CBS building that Manhattan was being overrun. His commentary tailed off in a strangulated scream.

By then, carloads of residents were fleeing New Jersey and heading for the hills, many wearing wet towels on their heads in a desperate attempt to counteract the deadly gases. Others hid in cellars, praying that the gas would pass overhead. Restaurants emptied in New York, and in the Deep South women prayed on the streets. People rang newspapers and police stations, wanting to know the location of the nearest bomb shelter. A mother in New England reportedly packed her children and a stack of bread into her car, reasoning that 'if everything is burning, you can't eat money, but you can eat bread.' It was even claimed that marines were recalled to their ships in New York harbour, ready to defend the nation against the Martian invaders.

While newspapers probably exaggerated the sense of public panic (in an effort to discredit a radio industry which had quickly become a major competitor for advertising revenue), many did undoubtedly believe that the broadcast was genuine. When the hoax was revealed, they rationalized their fears by explaining that they had assumed the Martian invasion was really a cunningly disguised German attack. It was later revealed that most of those who panicked were middle-aged or older, as younger listeners recognized Orson Welles's voice as that of the hero in the popular radio series, *The Shadow*. In the aftermath of the broadcast, Welles and CBS were the butt of angry complaints and a number of lawsuits were filed against the company but all were subsequently withdrawn. Nevertheless new regulations were introduced to prevent US broadcasters practising a similar deception in future.

The episode certainly raised Orson Welles's profile and, as he himself would admit, presented him with the opportunity to become a major Hollywood player. And the other man who profited from the hoax was H.G. Wells. Although the day after the *War of the Worlds* broadcast, Wells labelled it 'a total unwarranted liberty', his attitude quickly mellowed, possibly because the publicity gave an enormous boost to the sales of his novel.

Daddy's Girl

A Channel 4 documentary that highlighted the 'unusually close' relationship between a father and daughter was pulled from transmission at the last minute when it was revealed that the couple at the heart of the programme were not related at all. Stuart Smith, 29, and his 19-year-old girlfriend Victoria Greetham had hoodwinked TV producers for over four months and their cover was only finally blown when Greetham's real father saw a trailer for the show and alerted Channel 4.

The 1998 production, titled *Daddy's Girl*, intended to focus on the relationships between three fathers and the daughters with whom they were living as single parents. Film-makers Blast! were using an agency to recruit suitable couples, but then a photographer suggested law student Victoria Greetham, who had previously done some modelling work for him. Greetham later insisted that her real father, Geoff, 52, had originally agreed to do the programme with her but when he dropped out, Smith, with whom she had been living for nine months, took his place.

Filming took place at the family home in Huddersfield, West Yorkshire (near where Smith worked in a pub) on two or three days a week over a period of some four months. Plumber's son Smith added ten years to his real age and created a new identity for Greetham's father, making him a racehorse trainer called Marcus. On camera, Marcus came across as intensely possessive towards his 'daughter', and there were even fights between him and Victoria's 'boyfriend' after a night out. Smith later revealed: 'I had to get my mate to play me when they wanted to meet Victoria's boyfriend. I pretended to hate him because he was only a plumber's son.' The undertone of the programme was that the father was incestuously obsessed with his daughter — a scenario that was manna from heaven to the film-makers, unaware that they were victims of a clever hoax.

Greetham's real father blew the whistle on the joke hours before the intended transmission. Smith admitted to having enjoyed the ruse: 'It felt good to be a middle-class racehorse trainer instead of a plumber's son. I swapped lives. But they could have blown my cover at any time. There is a book that lists all the trainers and they could easily have found out that I don't exist.'

Greetham added: 'We didn't think the programme would be that serious. It was all just a bit of harmless fun to us. When my dad pulled out, we thought that as Stuart is a bit older than me anyway, he could step in. My dad was fine about it – he thought it was hilarious. But we never meant it to go on this long.'

Film-maker Edmund Coulthard said he was 'shocked and betrayed' by the deception, while Peter Moore, who commissioned the film for Channel 4, felt angered and embarrassed by the hoax but conceded: 'Perhaps sometimes we believe the story presented to us because we so want it to be true.'

Greetham had one last trick up her sleeve. When a national newspaper reporter asked for her real father's phone number in order to obtain a comment, she supplied Smith's number instead. And he proceeded to supply a stream of outrageous quotes.

The Fake Film Critic

David Manning of *The Ridgefield Press* was one of Columbia Pictures' most cherished reviewers. The studio knew it could always rely on the small Connecticut weekly paper's film critic to put in a good word on new releases. In the first half of 2001 alone, Manning praised Heath Ledger of *A Knight's Tale* as 'this year's hottest new star!' and saluted *The Animal* as 'another winner!'. Small wonder that Columbia plastered Manning's rave reviews over four different movie advertisements at that time, including those for *Hollow Man* and *Vertical Limit*.

But a *Newsweek* investigation revealed that Manning's own life story should be called *Charade* because he doesn't actually exist. He was merely a product of the studio's advertising department.

The scandal came to light when *Newsweek* writer John Horn set out to write a story about the proliferation of junket ads – the blurbs from often-obscure critics that adorn movie advertising. Horn believed such ads were 'undermining the integrity and value of real critics.' As an example, he studied a newspaper ad for *The Animal* that ran in such papers as the *Los Angeles Times*. He noted that the ad contained a number of favourable quotes even though Columbia had not screened the Rob Schneider comedy for mainstream critics. Ringing round other studios to find out what he could about the obscure reviewers and their publications, Horn discovered that all checked out except David Manning. Two people at other studios said they had never heard of Manning and there was no trace of him on the Internet. As a last resort, Horn called the *Ridgefield Press* and was told that there was no David Manning working there.

When challenged by *Newsweek* about the reviewer's authenticity, Columbia's parent company, Sony Pictures Entertainment, was forced to concede that Manning was a fake. Sony expressed horror at the disclosure and vowed to take immediate action against those responsible for inventing David Manning whose name was thought to be that of a college friend of a Columbia advertising executive. Shortly afterwards two advertising executives were suspended for 30 days without pay and stricter checks were put in place to 'ensure the accuracy of quotes contained in future advertising campaigns.' Movie fans and bona fide critics were annoyed by the hoax, as was the unsuspecting *Ridgefield Press*, which received angry e-mails suggesting that it was somehow involved. The paper labelled the creation of the fictitious film critic 'unethical'.

But that was not the end of the story. In June 2001 two moviegoers – Omar Rezec of Los Angeles and Ann Belknap of Sierra Madre – sued Sony, claiming that they were duped into seeing *A Knight's Tale* by Manning's glowing appraisal of the film. They advocated that Sony should set up a $4.5 million fund to reimburse other movie fans who could promise under oath that they were misled into seeing any of the four films touted by the Manning blurbs. One of the plaintiff's attorneys remarked: 'We won't settle the case until the people who were deceived by the false advertising are paid. The bottom line is you can't cheat to compete.'

Peter Rainer, head of the National Film Critics Association, was not altogether surprised by the deception. 'It's been demonstrated in the past,' he told the *Los Angeles Times*, 'that studios will, in effect, create the kind of reviews they want by cultivating junketeers, who then provide quotes for the ads. Studios are in the business of getting good press now and if critics are perceived as not being part of "the team", they are marginalized. There are cadres of blurbmeisters who will do their bidding. This is the logical extension of that. They have taken out an added insurance policy by creating their own critic.'

Vague About Hague

By impersonating the then Conservative Party leader William Hague, radio disc jockey Steve Penk was able to penetrate the tight security around the Downing Street telephone switchboard and be put through to Prime Minister Tony Blair.

Penk made the call on a January 1998 edition of his morning show on London's Capital Radio. Blair's secretary was initially suspicious that the call was a hoax, but Penk's impression of Hague was so convincing that he was soon connected to the Prime Minister. However, Blair was not so easily fooled and rumbled the prank the moment Penk called him 'Tony'. As the Prime Minister's official spokesman later explained: 'William Hague never calls him "Tony".'

Nevertheless the pair chatted for a couple of minutes with the Prime Minister apparently enjoying the banter. 'I'm just trying to work out who it is,' he said at one point. 'You've done very well to get through the network – you must have taken them in very well on the switch-board.'

To which Penk (as Hague) continued: 'Well no, all it was is I was talking to John Prescott the other day and he said that you wanted that Cher exercise video . . . We went to the car boot sale, me and Ffion, and managed to find it and so perhaps I can let you have it in the Commons today.'

Blair replied: 'I think it would be very helpful, just hand it over at Prime Minister's Question Time. It will be a better exchange than usual!'

Blair later related the incident in the House of Commons during Prime Minister's Question Time, to the great amusement of MPs from all parties.

The Great Quiz Show Scandal

Of all the forms of television entertainment on offer to the American public in the 1950s, none grabbed the imagination more than the big money quiz shows. With producers cranking up the tension by the minute, these live shows put contestants through extremes of elation and frustration as the chance to win life-altering sums of cash was played out on a nightly basis in front of millions of captivated prime-time viewers.

Back in the 1940s the top prize money on a popular radio programme had been just $64, but the advent of television changed everything. When *The $64,000 Question* premiered on CBS in 1955, the stakes were raised a thousand fold. Sponsored by Revlon, the programme shot to the top of the ratings, watched by 85 per cent of the TV audience. Even the Las Vegas casinos were empty while it was on, and shops sold out of Revlon lipsticks. That show's instant success spawned a host of new quizzes – *Dotto, Tic Tac Dough,* and *Twenty-One* – and as ratings soared, so did the prize money. However, the opportunity to win a fortune led to greed, corruption and ultimately the scandal that threatened to destroy the US quiz show.

Most things in television are geared to ratings, and those quiz shows were no exception. All manner of gimmicks were introduced to heighten the drama. Contestants were placed in glass isolation booths with the air conditioning turned off to make them sweat while every grimace, every frown was captured by the cameras in tight close-ups that revealed studies in concentration. Meanwhile armed police guarded the supposedly secret envelopes containing the questions. The security was worthy of a courtroom . . . which, ironically, was where the quiz show would end up, on trial for duping the American people.

High on the list of requirements for top ratings was contestant appeal. Viewers who loved – or even hated – a particular contestant would most likely tune in next time to see that person win or lose. Indifference was a turn-off. With so much at stake, certain producers looked for ways of controlling the outcome, to ensure that the 'right contestant' won. And the way to do that was to flash the cash.

Herbert Stempel was a bespectacled, twentysomething graduate of the Bronx High School of Science with an IQ of 170. Fresh out of the army and attending City College of New York, he caught two episodes of *Twenty-One*, a complex NBC quiz show loosely based on the game of blackjack, in which two contestants competed against each other to answer general knowledge questions. Each question had a point value from one to 11 according to difficulty, the first to reach 21 points being declared the winner of that game. The winner received $500 for each point advantage over his or her opponent. Stempel thought he could do well on the show and immediately wrote to the production company in the hope of being selected as a contestant. A few days later he was invited to take part in the 3½-hour-long trial test. He passed with flying colours, answering 251 of the 363 questions correctly, and was awarded a placc on *Twenty-One*. In the meantime one of the show's producers, Dan Enright, visited Stempel at his home. 'Play ball with me, kid,' said Enright, 'and you'll win $24,000 just like that.' Stempel was hooked.

The plan was to feed Stempel the answers before the show, and over the next five weeks Enright sat down with him, going over the questions and answers and even scripting in deliberate mistakes so that the contestant would appear more natural. Stempel's on-screen movements and reactions were all carefully choreographed – when to pause, when to wipe his brow in order to achieve maximum impact. Stempel's role was the college nerd. As he himself recalled: 'The reason I had been asked to put on this old, ill-fitting suit and get this Marine-type haircut was to make me appear as what you would call today a nerd, a square.' Enright calculated that viewers would take one look at Stempel and be rooting for the other contestant to win. 'You want the viewer to react emotionally to a contestant,' explained Enright later. 'Whether he reacts favourably or negatively is really not that important. The important thing is that he react.'

Enright and Stempel enjoyed a good run for their money. Primed with the answers, Stempel had soon amassed the grand total of $50,000, but ominous clouds loomed on the horizon. People were no longer talking about him; the ratings were starting to slip. There was only one solution: Stempel must lose. Enright told him: 'We feel it is time for a change.'

The man chosen to unseat him was Charles Van Doren, a 30-year-old professor of English at Columbia University. Van Doren came from a family of high achievers. His father was the Pulitzer Prize winning poet Mark Van Doren; his mother, Dorothy Van Doren, was a novelist and writer; and his uncle, Carl Van Doren, was a respected historian whose works included a biography of Benjamin Franklin. Charles Van Doren himself was a serious and successful academic with a broad range of interests. He earned a BA at St John's College in Annapolis, Maryland, studying a 'great books' curriculum. He finished early, going on to study astrophysics at Columbia University's graduate school where he began turning his attentions to teaching and to study for an English PhD. After spending time travelling in Europe and studying at the Sorbonne, Van Doren returned to Columbia to join the faculty as a professor of English, on an annual salary of $4,400.

A friend of Van Doren's, who had appeared on *Tic Tac Dough*, told him of the vast amounts of money that could be won on quiz shows. Lucky contestants were walking off with as much as $200,000 — more than 40 years' salary for Van Doren. He knew he had the intellect to do well and so he applied to be a contestant on *Twenty-One*.

With Stempel's moon on the wane, the producers were looking for a handsome, intelligent, charismatic young man to replace him. Van Doren fitted the bill to perfection and as an added bonus he was single. Female viewers would love him; the ratings would soon be on the up.

But Van Doren would only be the answer to *Twenty-One*'s prayers if he were prepared, like Stempel, to play ball. According to Van Doren's subsequent testimony, another co-producer, Albert Freedman, persuaded him to take part in the deception by saying that quiz shows were entertainment and that fixing was a common practice. However, what really appeared to swing it was when the producers convinced him that the ruse would offer encouragement 'to the intellectual life, to teachers, and to education in general.' Thus Van Doren became reconciled to cheating by telling himself that he was performing a public service. Naturally the money played no part in his decision.

The producers had no desire to ditch Stempel overnight and, to build the tension to breaking point, arranged for three contests with Van Doren to end in ties before the clean-cut newcomer would eventually win the day.

Van Doren went into his first encounter with Stempel on 28 November 1956 and, carefully coached in his answers and mannerisms, came across as a TV natural. Viewers stared anxiously at the screen as, time and again, he appeared stumped by a question, only to come up with the correct answer when all seemed lost. It was edge of the seat television. Little did the studio audience or those watching at home suspect that he had been fed the answers in advance.

The intricate rules of *Twenty-One* stipulated that, in the event of a tie, the money wagered for points increased by $500. Therefore after the three pre-arranged ties, the pair were playing for $2,000 a point. On the evening of Wednesday 5 December an estimated 50 million Americans tuned in for what co-producer and host Jack Barry described as 'the biggest game ever played in the programme.' After a pair of matching blondes escorted the combatants to their isolation booths, the battle commenced. The first category was boxing, but Van Doren deliberately made a mess of it and soon trailed by 16 points to nil. At that juncture, Stempel was given the chance to stop the game. If he had done so, he would have automatically won, but he decided to stick to the script. The next category – movies – was more to Van Doren's liking. Stempel blundered badly over the 1955 Oscar Winner for Best Picture, answering *On the Waterfront* when he knew only too well that it was *Marty*, one of his favourite films. He later recalled that being forced to give the wrong answer to that question was the unkindest cut of all. Everything now rested on knowing the names and fates of the third, fourth and fifth wives of Henry VIII. By now, Van Doren had perfected the art of thinking aloud so that he took the audience with him every step of the way. The tension was tangible. Given the same question, Stempel answered the wives' names correctly but professed to having no idea about what happened to them. Barry pressed him for an answer. 'Well, they all died,' quipped Stempel to gales of laughter. Van Doren stopped the game and won the round. The king had been dethroned.

Stempel appeared gracious in defeat. 'This all came so suddenly,' he gushed. 'Thanks for your kindness and courtesy.' In reality, it was his finest acting performance to date. Inwardly he was seething at having been instructed to throw the game.

With Van Doren as champion, the ratings for *Twenty-One* started to rise again. Appearing to be knowledgeable about topics as diverse as George Washington and Broadway musicals, he quickly piled up the money, passing the $100,000 mark by outscoring a former college president, Edgar Cummings. Van Doren became the best-known quiz show contestant in America. He was pictured on the cover of *Time* magazine and received over 500 fan letters a week. So many people – journalists, Hollywood producers, single women – telephoned him that he was forced to get an unlisted number. It seemed that whole of America was in love with Charlie Van Doren.

Except Herb Stempel, that is. Just before his enforced exit he had been angry at overhearing two technicians saying they were glad the show was getting rid of the 'freak'. Now, seeing Van Doren on the cover of *Time* was too much for the embittered Stempel to take. It should have been him. So he decided to tell anyone who would listen that *Twenty-One* was faked. Nobody did listen.

Meanwhile Van Doren's spectacular run had come to an end, of his own volition. After amassing a cool $129,000 he bowed out in March 1957, beaten by lawyer Vivienne Nearing, whose husband Victor had lost to Van Doren the previous month. As with Stempel, there were three dramatic ties with Mrs Nearing before the champion was finally dethroned.

Although his reign had ended, Van Doren remained a much sought-after TV celebrity and in April of that year he signed a $150,000 three-year contract with NBC, which gave him a regular spot on the *Today* show where he discussed such topics as non-Euclidean geometry and recited seventeenth-century poetry. He had become the acceptable face of education.

Then in August 1958 the Great Quiz Show Scandal finally broke. The blue touch paper was lit by a standby contestant on *Dotto* who produced a page from a winner's crib sheet. Suddenly journalists started to listen to Herb Stempel's accusations. The whole thing went up after *Twenty-One* contestant James Snodgrass took the precaution of mailing registered letters to himself with the results of his appearances on the show predicted in advance. When these were made public, it became all too clear that the shows were rigged. Quiz show ratings plummeted, producers were fired, *Twenty-One* was dropped from the network schedule.

A New York grand jury convened by prosecutor Joseph Stone sat in October 1958 to investigate the allegations. There was actually nothing illegal about rigging a quiz show and so, rather than lose face professionally and personally, the majority of contestants called to testify behind closed doors decided to deny everything. Nearly a hundred committed perjury in preference to owning up that they had been party to cheating. At the forefront, inevitably, was Charles Van Doren. He steadfastly insisted that he was innocent, repeating the lie to his lawyer, the district attorney and finally the grand jury. 'It's silly and distressing,' he blustered, 'to think that people don't have more faith in quiz shows.' Prosecutor Stone lamented: 'Nothing in my experience prepared me for the mass perjury that took place on the part of scores of well-educated people who had no trouble understanding what was at stake.'

Although the judge presiding over the New York investigations ordered the grand jury's report to be sealed, Washington was not prepared to let the matter drop. From October 1959 the House Subcommittee on Legislative Oversight held its own hearings into the quiz show rumpus. Confronted by federal intervention and amidst rumours that the committee was probing communist links in the background of some witnesses, a number of network executives, producers and contestants alike suddenly felt the need to tell the truth. As many as 18 contestants, who had won anything up to $220,500 on assorted quiz shows, now pleaded guilty to perjury, and admitted that the shows were rigged.

However, the witness everyone wanted to hear from was Van Doren. He had been desperately trying to dodge a congressional subpoena by driving around the back roads of New England but finally he surfaced in November. Taking the stand in front of 500 spectators packed like sardines into the compact caucus room, he put on a performance that was every bit as riveting as any of his 14 appearances in the *Twenty-One* isolation booth. Opening his heart to his audience, he confessed: 'I was involved, deeply involved, in a deception.' He went on to testify how Albert Freedman had invited him to the producer's apartment before his first time on *Twenty-One* and told him that Herb Stempel was brilliant and unbeatable but also unpopular. He said Freedman asked him, as a favour, to agree to tie with Stempel in order to boost the show's entertainment value. Van Doren claimed that he asked to go on the programme honestly, without assistance, but was told that was impossible. He then related how Freedman had appealed to his intellectual instincts. 'I was almost able to convince myself,' said Van Doren, 'that it did not matter what I was doing because it was having such a good effect on the national attitude to teachers, education and the intellectual life.' He added that he had been 'living in dread for almost three years.'

As a result of the hearings, Congress made rigging a quiz show a federal crime. The consequences for the erstwhile golden boy of American television were equally dramatic. NBC immediately cancelled its contract with Van Doren, and his resignation was accepted by Columbia University. Such was his notoriety that he felt it necessary to pen books under a pseudonym for many years, not reverting to his real name until the mid-1980s. Just when it appeared that the whole sordid episode had finally been forgotten, along came Robert Redford's 1994 movie, bringing with it a new wave of negative publicity about those infamous quiz shows of the 1950s.

Ghostwatch

To mark Halloween night in 1992, the BBC aired a programme called *Ghostwatch*, which was promoted as a live investigation into reports of scary supernatural activity at a family's council house in the Northolt district of London. Over the next 90 minutes viewers looked on in horror as an apparition in a black dress glided across the screen, sinister scratches mysteriously appeared on a girl's body, and finally as presenter Michael Parkinson seemed to be possessed by demon spirits. Switchboards were jammed and those of a particularly nervous disposition hid behind the sofa . . . until it was revealed that the terrified family were all actors and that the entire programme had been a carefully scripted hoax recorded several weeks earlier in a studio.

Reasoning that a successful hoax needs a figure of authority at its heart, the BBC selected the experienced Parkinson as studio anchorman. He was joined there by Mike Smith while two other familiar presenters – Craig Charles and Smith's wife Sarah Greene – reported 'live' from the house. The aforementioned house was described as home to the Early family – single mother Pam and her two daughters, Suzanne and Kim. Viewers heard how the family had lived in fear for the previous ten months while witnessing increasingly disturbing phenomena. Furniture had moved of its own accord; apparitions had been seen floating through the air; the children had inexplicable cuts and lacerations on their bodies; and there were repeated sounds of something banging against a metallic surface. On account of these noises, the family had christened their malevolent spirit 'Pipes'.

Ghostwatch had placed cameras throughout the house, and parapsychologist Dr Lin Pascoe was on hand to comment on the happenings and to attempt to interpret them. No sooner had the programme started than things went bump in the night, but it turned out to be Craig Charles playing a joke on the crew. It was all a fiendish ploy to guarantee that subsequent incidents would be treated seriously. Then events appeared to take a more ominous turn. A lamp suddenly smashed into pieces. A wet patch appeared in the middle of the carpet. The howling of cats could be heard coming from the walls, and more scratches appeared all over the body of the older daughter Suzanne. Viewers called in on the special studio phone lines to report that they had seen a figure in a black dress lurking in many of the shots. A crew member noticed that his watch had suddenly stopped as he crossed the kitchen. It all seemed to be getting decidedly spooky.

Meanwhile a series of interviews with the neighbours uncovered some worrying facts about the history of the house. It emerged that a previous resident had hanged himself beneath the stairs after claiming that the spirit of a woman had possessed him. The man had owned a dozen cats, which had been locked inside the house without any food when he died. Consequently, they had tried to feed on his dead body.

Back in the house Suzanne went missing in the cellar. When her mother prepared to go in, the child was heard to scream, 'He's hurting me!' as a figure appeared briefly in the doorway. Sarah Greene was then shown searching for Suzanne while the sound of wailing cats echoed around her in the cellar. Outside, Dr Pascoe, in a state of high panic, explained that the spirit of 'Pipes' was now in the studio and the equipment. 'Jesus, Michael,' she yelled to Parkinson, 'we have created a séance, a massive séance!' It was explained that by having a live TV audience watching the investigation the four reporters had managed to channel tremendous psychic energies into the house, thereby multiplying the power of the spirit, which was now free to run rampant all over the country.

With Pam Early defying the crew's pleas by continuing to try and reach her daughter, held prisoner in the cellar, the pictures from the house suddenly went dead. The broadcast switched back to the television studio where the scene was similarly disquieting. A wind had whipped up inside the building and then all the lights went out. As Parkinson fumbled around in the gloom for a camera that was still working, the sound of howling cats was heard. The final, chilling image showed that Parkinson himself had become possessed by 'Pipes' and was spookily reciting nursery rhymes in the voice of the spirit.

Many viewers were convinced that they had just witnessed the forces of evil being unleashed upon the nation. Newspapers reported that several women were so scared by the programme that they went into labour, and that a teenager had committed suicide after watching it. When the hoax was revealed, the BBC came under heavy fire for irresponsible broadcasting.

Who Is Patrick Brannigan?

The world's movie stars descended on Canada on 7 September 2000 for the opening gala at the Toronto International Film Festival. Every few seconds a chauffeur-driven limousine would pull up, the doors would open and a famous name would parade along the red carpet to the accompaniment of camera flashes from the paparazzi and cheers and applause from the waiting fans.

One limousine pulled up and out stepped Patrick Brannigan. Fans immediately began calling out his name whereupon photographers asked him to turn and face them so that they could take his picture. Such was the clamour to get a piece of Patrick that the security crew had to push people back to allow him to walk into the festival hall. But then a strange thing happened. As Brannigan walked down the red carpet, he appeared to become confused and disoriented. Suddenly he started walking backwards before lurching into the crowd as if he was fainting.

It was then that the security staff realized that they had no idea who this man was. So they hauled him to his feet and shoved him back out on to the street.

It emerged that Brannigan's grand parade along the red capet was a publicity stunt carried out by a local web entertainment company, Trailervision.com. 'Patrick Brannigan' was not a real star at all – he was a little-known actor by the name of Ken Leonard whose claim to fame amounted to appearing in a handful of Trailversion's web movies. The fans and photographers who shouted out Brannigan's name were employees of the company.

Trailervision had actually perpetrated the same hoax the previous year when they smuggled people into the event simply by hiring fake paparazzi to scream out their names as they stepped out of limousines.

Albert Nerenberg, a director at Trailervision, defended the hoaxes. 'We think it's sad that so much of the intrigue and glamour of the festival comes from the fact that it's all about excluding people. To me that's fair comment for send up.'

Bowled Over By Hoax Caller

A Welsh caller pretending to be the new world indoor bowls champion fooled the BBC into putting him live on air and used the opportunity to make inflammatory anti-English comments. John Rabaiotti, 41, a trading standards officer from Swansea, phoned Nicky Campbell's Radio 5 Live show on 24 January 2000 after it had been announced that bowler Robert Weale, who had defeated fellow Welsh international John Price in the final of the world indoor singles the previous day, was going to be a guest on the programme.

Rabaiotti, who was introduced as a British world champion, told the radio audience: 'I won it for Wales. What you don't realize is that the English are the most hated race in the world.' He went on to boast about how brilliant a sportsman he was and to call for sexier groupies in bowls – traditionally an old people's game. Scotsman Campbell replied: 'How refreshing to have a competitor who is so hungry, aggressive and confident.'

The hoax was only rumbled when the genuine Robert Weale phoned in minutes later to conduct his interview with Campbell. At first the station told Weale that the interview had already taken place. Then the line went very quiet for a couple of minutes before a voice said: 'I think we've made a mistake.'

'I couldn't believe it,' said 36-year-old Weale afterwards. 'I was quite shocked at first and seriously worried that people might think that it was me and that those were my views. But I have begun to appreciate the funny side.'

Captain Janks: King of the Pranks

During a live report on ABC News after John F Kennedy Jr's plane plunged into the ocean off Martha's Vineyard, anchorman Peter Jennings took a call from someone claiming to be a coastguard representative. Jennings asked for the caller's location, and received the reply: 'Howard Stern thinks you're a ****.' Nonplussed, Jennings quickly dismissed the caller and explained that it was a fan of shock jock Stern's who has a tendency to interrupt crisis coverage on network and cable newscasts. Jennings was correct in his assessment. For the guy on the other end of the line was Captain Janks, a regular member of Stern's infamous Wack Pack, and the person responsible for successfully infiltrating reports about the Columbine High School shootings, the death of Princess Diana, and just about every emergency news report worthy of national coverage.

His real name is Tom Cipriano, a 34-year-old sometime gas station attendant from Philadelphia. He took the name of his alter ego from his old army captain, the butt of many a soldier's joke, and developed a taste for making crank phone calls from listening to comedy tapes from Jersey City's Tube Bar and *The Howard Stern Show*.

His first hoax call was to *Larry King Live* back in 1989, and he has since managed to get through to King on several occasions, unnerving and confusing guests like Dick Van Dyke, James Stewart and Donny Osmond.

'Larry King became my main target,' he said in a rare 1999 interview, 'along with other call-in shows such as Sonya Freedman on CNN and Phil Donahue. The calls to the news-gathering organizations didn't happen until 1992, when I called CNN as a witness after an earthquake in Southern California. I liked the challenge of getting on shows that did not take on-air calls. I remember getting through to the Jerry Lewis Labor Day telethon in 1991. In order to get on the telethon, I told the producers that I was representing Larry King and that he wanted to make an on-air pledge to Jerry. Then I put together several snippets of Larry King's voice to fool them into believing that he was actually on the phone. Once I got on the air I asked Jerry what he thought of Howard Stern. Jerry then called me a schmuck!'

With his catchphrase of 'How do you like them apples?' (based on an old saying of his mother's), the Captain has baffled and outraged America's most famous celebrities. Nobody is safe. Even rock group Crosby, Stills, Nash and Young were surprised to take a call on air asking whether Howard Stern had played guitar on a particular song. Not surprisingly, Janks has fallen foul of a number of people. Talk show host Rosie O'Donnell once bitterly criticized him on the *Charles Grodin Show*. 'In response, I got on her TV show disguised as the Mayor of Philadelphia. When I was put on the air with her, I called her a fat pig.'

He defends himself against accusations that many of his hoax calls are in dubious taste. 'I don't think JFK Jr's death is funny, nor do I think Princess Diana's death or natural disasters are funny. I pull my pranks on news-gathering organizations that are so gullible that, time and time again, they will put my calls through without checking the credibility of the call. They are so willing to get the scoop before anyone else that they can be very sloppy about getting the story on the air. At least I let the viewers in on the fact that it is a prank. I wonder how many times CNN has reported on breaking stories when they didn't have accurate facts. They never learn, and when they screw up and put a prank caller on the air, they cry "foul". My pranks are never about the story itself, just the organization that is covering the story.

'No one can trivialize a tragic event except maybe the news organization. As I recall, someone called in during the coverage of the Columbine school shootings claiming to be a trapped student on a cellular phone, which turned out to be a hoax. Even if that call had been authentic, why would a news station air it? That could only cause further problems, had the gunmen had a TV on in the school.

'Practical jokes are funny as long as no one gets hurt. Although my prank calls may evoke strong emotions, no one has ever gotten hurt. I don't do it to hurt people – I do it to make people laugh. Some people won't laugh, and I understand that. The majority will, though. Besides, for every one time I get through, there's ten times I don't.'

Alternative Three

As part of its ongoing series *Science Report*, Anglia Television screened a spoof 1977 documentary which claimed that the world's leading scientists were being kidnapped to work on Mars. Titled 'Alternative Three', it opened with the announcer revealing that the intention had been to produce a completely different programme but that a vast, global conspiracy had then been uncovered which forced a change of policy. Viewers were told that the original idea had been to focus on Britain's 'brain-drain', showing how British scientists were leaving the country to take better-paid jobs overseas, but in the course of their research, the programme-makers had found that these academics weren't just leaving Britain . . . they were leaving the planet.

Further investigation apparently led to a cover-up conducted by the uppermost levels of the American and Soviet governments. The story was that back in the 1950s environmental experts had concluded that, because of Man's folly, earth was heading inexorably for a catastrophe which would ultimately destroy humanity. In the face of this disastrous prognosis, world governments were left with just three options. Alternative One was to institute a programme to slash the Earth's human population. Alternative Two was to construct underground shelters to safeguard government officials until the crisis had eased. Alternative Three was to establish a colony of humanity's sharpest minds somewhere off the planet, ideally on Mars. It was no easy decision, but the stark reality of the situation had prompted high-level officials in American and Soviet governments to join forces and implement Alternative Three.

The Anglia documentary featured interviews with supposed scientists and astronauts who admitted that the collaboration between the Soviets and Americans had produced a landing on Mars as early as 1961. Furthermore the Apollo Space Programme was apparently nothing more than a publicity decoy to conceal the true reason for NASA's rocket launches, and, most alarmingly of all, it was disclosed that scientists were now being abducted to work on Mars.

The programme announcer was sufficiently earnest to persuade many viewers that the documentary was genuine and Anglia was inundated with calls to its Norwich studios. But the clues were there. For although the programme was transmitted on 20 June, the copyright date displayed on screen read 1 April.

Even after the show's producers confessed that the whole thing had been a joke, some people refused to believe the disclaimer. To this day, there are websites dedicated to the notion that Alternative Three is real and that the documentary was part of a sinister disinformation scheme perpetrated by world governments. These fanatics argue that, by making Alternative Three appear to be a harmless hoax, the world superpowers ensured that no one would ever suspect the terrifying truth.

Jerry Springer's Baby-Sitter Blues

At the forefront of the new wave of confrontational US talk show hosts was Jerry Springer. Tackling difficult, controversial subjects on a daily basis, his programme pulled no punches and exposed human frailties before a baying audience of millions. The more sensational the topic, the more the studio audience and the viewers at home loved it. No subject appeared too risky for Springer. However, when the call went out in December 1994 for guests who had slept with their kids' baby-sitters, Springer received a nasty surprise. The title of the show was 'Honey, Have I Got a Secret For You!', but the secret wasn't the one that Springer and his producers had been expecting.

For, unbeknown to everyone connected with the show, the cheating husband, his unsuspecting wife, the baby-sitter and her boyfriend who bared all emotionally before the prying cameras were not what they seemed. In reality they were members of a Toronto comic troupe called the Blockheads. And they had made a fool out of Jerry.

The hoax started out as an innocuous joke after one of the quartet – Ian Sirota – replied to Springer's on-air plea for men who had enjoyed sexual liaisons with their children's baby-sitter. Posing as his roommate Johnny Gardhouse (who would eventually play the philandering husband), Sirota phoned the show and was surprised when they fell for it hook, line and sinker. 'They never checked our references,' said 29-year-old Mini Holmes who would appear as the 18-year-old babysitter. 'It was just too easy. We kept thinking, "They're gonna catch on", but the next thing we knew we were at the airport, flying to Chicago.'

During phone dealings with Suzanne Muir, the fourth member of the group and the one who would play the wronged wife, the producers allegedly told her that the topic of the show would be how to restore the romance to her marriage. According to the comics, no mention was made of the shocking 'secret'. As the husband, Gardhouse said that he tried to back out a couple of times, telling the producers that the disclosure would devastate his wife. But, he claimed, they talked him out of it, telling him it would be safer if he revealed his affair to his wife on television because she might become violent if he told her in private.

The four – with Sirota playing the baby-sitter's boyfriend – arrived in Chicago for the 9 January taping of the show. Gardhouse and Muir went on first, and Gardhouse proceeded to reveal his 'secret' before a jeering studio audience, whereupon Muir burst into tears with total conviction. When Springer asked Gardhouse on air why he would choose to reveal 'something so intimate' on national television, Gardhouse replied that the show's producers had told him to. It was alleged that those remarks were edited out of the final tape. Meanwhile Holmes, posing as the baby-sitter tired of Gardhouse's amorous advances, was waiting off-stage. There, she claimed, a producer started inciting her like a trainer preparing a boxer for a big fight, urging: 'You're gonna let him have it, you're gonna let him have it.'

'It was a big joke to them,' said Holmes.

The hoax was exposed by a Toronto writer who saw the show when it aired on 7 February 1995 and immediately recognized the local comics. The comedians readily admitted the deception but added that what had started out as simply a joke had acquired a more profound significance as a result of their dealings with two of Springer's producers. 'We were doing this for a reason,' said Muir, 'which was to prove that these people are not honest in their dealings with the American public and on the level when they try to encourage them to come on.' Multimedia Entertainment Incorporated responded by threatening to sue the hoaxers for undermining the integrity of shows like Springer's. 'The truth is these people came on and lied to us about who they were,' said a Multimedia executive.

When the fuss had died down, the two Springer producers specifically named by the comics had both lost their jobs . . . although Multimedia stressed that their dismissal was not as a result of anything that had happened on the baby-sitter show.

Britain's own champion talk show hoaxer, Alex Smith, a 24-year-old unemployed man from Rochdale, was unmasked in April 2000 after appearing as no fewer than six different people on a variety of programmes since 1994. He made five appearances on the BBC daytime talk show *Kilroy*, hosted by former MP Robert Kilroy-Silk, of which four were as stage hypnotist Alex Leroy and the other as Alex Smith, a failed entertainer who had bounced back. On Channel 4's *The Big Breakfast* he was Dave Williams, a man with a talent for reading fortunes from belly buttons, and to Channel 5 viewers he was best known as Alex Alexander, a psychic who could read dogs' paws!

On an ITV daytime show in August 1997 Smith appeared as 'paper bag man', wearing a bag on his head in protest at the friendship of Diana, Princess of Wales, with Dodi Fayed. On a different ITV show he read fortunes from the movement of a garden hose. An edition of the BBC's *All Rise For Julian Clary* saw the versatile Smith posing as someone whose girlfriend had threatened to leave him unless he abandoned his collection of snails. Ironically, his real girlfriend did leave him after the appearance with camp comedian Clary because she felt so humiliated.

When he was eventually exposed as a multiple hoaxer, Smith was banned from any future editions of *Kilroy*. He remained unrepentant. 'Television wanted a performer and I was happy to play along,' he said. 'I never even had to disguise myself.'

The Bumper Spaghetti Harvest

Richard Dimbleby was the first giant of British television. Whether it was commentating on the coronation of Elizabeth II or fronting the BBC's flagship current affairs programme *Panorama*, his was always a calming, reassuring presence – someone upon whom viewers felt they could rely. An example of his unrivalled air of authority occurred at the height of the Cuban missile crisis in 1962 when a worried mother phoned the BBC to say: 'I won't send my children to school tomorrow unless Mr Dimbleby can promise me there will be no war. He himself lamented at the time: 'People think I'm a sort of national doctor who can cure all ills.'

So when in 1957 *Panorama* decided to present an April Fool's joke, who better to lend the necessary gravitas to the spoof item than Dimbleby? The last piece on that evening's programme featured Dimbleby reporting from the Italian-speaking Ticino area of southern Switzerland on that year's bumper spaghetti harvest. Dimbleby was seen walking between spaghetti-laden trees as farmworkers busily loaded the crop into baskets. His voiceover proclaimed earnestly: 'Spaghetti cultivation here in Switzerland is not of course carried out on anything like the scale of the Italian industry. Many of you, I'm sure, will have seen pictures of the vast spaghetti plantations in the Po Valley. For the Swiss, however, it tends to be a family affair. Another reason why this may be a bumper year lies in the virtual disappearance of the spaghetti weevil, the tiny creatures whose depredations have caused much concern in the past. After picking, the spaghetti is laid out to dry in the warm, Alpine sun. Many people are often puzzled by the fact that spaghetti is produced at such uniform lengths. But this is the result of many years of patient endeavour by plant breeders, who've succeeded in producing the perfect spaghetti.' As the item ended with a family sitting down to a meal, Dimbleby enthused: 'And it is, of course, spaghetti, picked earlier in the day, dried in the sun, and so brought from garden to table at the very peak of condition. For those who love this dish, there's nothing like real, home-grown spaghetti.' His sign-off line, 'And that is all from *Panorama* on this first day of April' was too subtle for those who had already been deceived.

Although it might seem inconceivable nowadays that anyone could be fooled by such a story, back in 1957 travelling abroad was the preserve of a tiny minority. Precious few viewers of *Panorama* had ever been to Italy or Switzerland and the majority knew relatively little about foreign food. Consequently hundreds of people rang the BBC, most wanting to know where they could obtain spaghetti plants. Producer Michael Peacock quietly informed them that many British enthusiasts achieved admirable results from planting a small tin of spaghetti in tomato sauce! Others wanted to know where they could see the spaghetti harvest when they went on holiday, but at least one viewer spotted that something was amiss. Spaghetti grew horizontally, he insisted, not vertically . . .

Brass Neck

Controversy has followed British satirist Chris Morris with the same certainty that night follows day and toothache follows a visit to the dentist.

The son of two respectable Cambridgeshire doctors, Morris studied zoology at Bristol University, starting his broadcasting career on BBC Radio Bristol in 1987. According to popular belief, he left his job abruptly after filling the news studio with helium so that a report of a serious motorway pile-up sounded as if it was being read by Mickey Mouse. He then moved to Greater London Radio where he edited the Queen's Christmas speech in such a way that made it sound as if she was swearing. His next brush with authority was on his Radio 1 show where he announced the fake death of disc jockey Sir Jimmy Savile, who was furious at the anguish caused by the hoax announcement. While interviewing Conservative MP Jerry Hayes, Morris broke off to say: 'And as soon as we have any news on the death of Michael Heseltine, we'll let you know.' Shocked by the news, Hayes delivered an impromptu tribute to his parliamentary colleague, only to discover that his death was no more genuine than Savile's.

But it was when Morris took his anarchic humour to television for the Channel 4 series *Brass Eye* that he really hit the headlines and upset middle England. In a succession of subversive hoaxes, he persuaded celebrities to appeal for help in rescuing an elephant that had its trunk stuck up its back passage, and to comment on plans for a non-existent musical about serial killer Peter Sutcliffe, better known as the Yorkshire Ripper. Morris's finest hour, however, was a disturbing (and entirely fictitious) report on the dangers posed to British youth by a new imported Czech drug called 'cake'. Among those tricked into denouncing the menace of 'cake' were Rolf Harris, comedian Bernard Manning, ex-footballer Jimmy Greaves, Margaret Thatcher's press secretary Bernard Ingham and DJ Noel Edmonds, himself a master of the practical joke. Each described horrendous accidents that had befallen youngsters who had taken 'cake', a drug said to play havoc with sense of time. Edmonds was seen sombrely describing a victim killed crossing the road . . . because he thought he had a month to do so. David Amess, Conservative MP for Basildon, was also fooled into taking part and was so perturbed about the threat of 'cake' that he promised to raise the question of the drug in Parliament. When told the programme was a spoof, Amess complained to Channel 4.

Morris was in hot water again in the summer of 2001 following a *Brass Eye Special* about paedophilia. The programme – a satire on the hysteria surrounding paedophiles in Britain the previous year – duped celebrities into endorsing two fabricated anti-paedophilia campaigns. Singer Phil Collins was furious after being filmed in a T-shirt bearing the words 'Nonce Sense' while dispensing advice to children. On discovering that he had been duped, he accused the programme of being in poor taste, adding: 'I did this in good faith for the public benefit. Unfortunately this will probably affect many celebrities' willingness to support public-spirited causes in the future, and it's not difficult to see why.' Among others to be taken in were comedian Richard Blackwood and disc jockey Dr Fox. The latter was seen to spout the following wisdom: 'Genetically paedophiles have more in common with crabs than you or me. There's no real evidence for it but it is scientific fact.' Afterwards Fox admitted ruefully: 'I have been had, and it was well done. He's a clever guy. It is just a shame it had to be about such a sick subject. But I did say those things and now I feel a right prat.'

While all hell broke loose with the usual suspects – the *Daily Mail* and Tory MPs – calling for Morris to be sent to the Tower, the man himself wisely opted to keep a low profile. The furore is unlikely to make him soften his approach given his general advice to viewers: 'If it's not for you, just don't bloody watch.'

Chapter 9

Religion

The Kinderhook Plates

In the first week of May 1843 the Mormon periodical *Times and Seasons* printed an article entitled 'Ancient Records' which reported the discovery of six age-old brass plates in an Indian mound near the town of Kinderhook, Illinois. A statement signed by W.P. Harris of Barry, Pike County, Illinois, told of the find:

'On the 16th of April last, a respectable merchant by the name of Robert Wiley commenced digging in a large mound near this place: he excavated to the depth of ten feet and came to rock. About that time the rain began to fall, and he abandoned the work. On the 23rd he and quite a number of the citizens with myself repaired to the mound, and after making ample opening, we found plenty of rock, the most of which appeared as though it had been strongly burned; and after removing full two feet of said rock, we found plenty of charcoal and ashes; also human bones that appeared as though they had been burned; and a bundle was found that consisted of six plates of brass, of a bell shape, each having a hole near the small end, and a ring through them all, and clasped with two clasps, the rings and clasps appeared to be of iron, very much oxidated. The plates appeared at first to be copper, and had the appearance of being covered with characters. It was agreed by the company that I should clean the plates: accordingly, I took them to my house, washed them with soap and water, and a woollen cloth; but finding them not yet cleansed I treated them with a dilute sulphuric acid which made them perfectly clean, on which it appeared that they were completely covered with hieroglyphics that none as yet have been able to read.'

The plates aroused enormous interest locally and a week later were taken to the town of Nauvoo, 55 miles north of Kinderhook, where they were shown to Mormon leader Joseph Smith. After claiming to have been granted divine revelation of the Book of Mormon, which was said to have been inscribed on gold plates and hidden a thousand years earlier in a hill near Palmyra in New York State, Smith founded the Church of Jesus Christ of Latter-Day Saints in 1830. Followers of the new sect were widely pilloried and the prophet Smith became an object of ridicule and hatred among zealots of other religions who saw him as a fraud. Consequently the Mormons were willing to embrace any new evidence which might support Smith's claims. An editorial in *Times and Seasons* underlined the potential significance of the Kinderhook Plates. It reported that Smith was now studying the brass plates, and stated excitedly that 'circumstances are daily transpiring which give additional testimony to the authenticity of the Book of Mormon.' According to a letter dated 2 May 1843 from a non-Mormon, Charlotte Haven, (who was visiting her sister in Nauvoo at the time), Smith 'said that the figures or writing on them was similar to that in which the Book of Mormon was written' and 'he thought that by the help of revelation he would be able to translate them.'

Smith arranged for the Mormon newspaper the *Nauvoo Neighbor* to promote his eagerly anticipated translation of the plates. On 24 June 1843 the *Neighbor* printed a facsimile of the plates, promising that 'the contents of the plates, together with a facsimile of the same, will be published in the *Times and Seasons* as soon as the translation is completed.'

Before Smith had the opportunity to go public with his findings, he was murdered in 1844, but his followers clung to the hope that he had managed to translate the plates before his untimely death. These prayers appeared to have been answered in 1856 when *The History of Joseph Smith* was serialized. It contained the following entry for 1 May 1843: 'I insert facsimiles of the six brass plates found near Kinderhook, in Pike County, Illinois, on April 23, by Mr Robert Wiley and others, while excavating a large mound. They found a skeleton about six feet from the surface of the earth, which must have stood nine feet high. The plates were found on the breast of the skeleton, and were covered on both sides with ancient characters. I have translated a portion of them, and find they contain the history of the person with whom they were found. He was a descendant of Ham, through the loins of Pharaoh, King of Egypt, and that he received his kingdom from the ruler of heaven and earth.'

But then in June 1879 Wilbur Fugate, who was among those present at the excavation of the Kinderhook Plates, gave a sworn affidavit that they were fakes. Under oath he swore that he, Robert Wiley and Kinderhook blacksmith Bridge Whitton had conspired to make the plates. Although the affidavit was 36 years after the fact, Fugate was able to describe in detail how the plates were made. 'We read the prophecy that "Truth is yet to spring out of the earth". We concluded to prove the prophecy by way of a joke. We soon made our plans and executed them. Bridge Whitton cut them out of some pieces of copper; Wiley and I made the hieroglyphics by making impressions on beeswax and filling them with acid and putting it on the plates. When they were finished, we put them together with rust made of nitric acid, old iron and lead, and bound them with a piece of hoop iron, covering them completely with the rust.'

A letter written in 1855, but which did not come to light until 1912, supported Fugate's story. Its author was W.P. Harris, the man who had penned the original *Times and Seasons* statement. In this letter he wrote that although he had initially accepted the plates as genuine, he had subsequently learned that they were fakes. 'Bridge Whitton said to me that he cut and prepared the plates and he and R. Wiley engraved them themselves, and that there was nitric acid put upon them the night before they were found to rust the iron ring and band. And that they were carried to the mound, rubbed in the dirt and carefully dropped into the pit where they were found.'

These confessions dealt the Mormons a bitter blow, all the more so because their leader had apparently, by means of divine revelation, translated the fake plates as genuine. Did this make him a false prophet? The object of the hoax had clearly been to embarrass Smith publicly and it had paid off beyond the plotters' wildest dreams. Some Mormons tried desperately to distance themselves from the plates by claiming that the incriminating *History of Joseph Smith* was not the work of Smith, but of his private secretary, William Clayton, and that Smith had not translated the plates at all. Others chose to adhere to the belief that the plates were genuine, but a series of microscopic tests conducted in 1980 proved conclusively that they were fakes. The tests showed that the plates were etched with acid, a practice not in keeping with the behaviour of the ancients. It was also found that they were made from a true brass alloy (copper and zinc). This was typical of the mid-nineteenth century whereas the 'brass' of ancient times was actually bronze, an alloy of copper and tin. Finally the tests revealed insufficient impurities for an alloy over 2,000 years old.

All things considered, the saga of the Kinderhook Plates is an episode in history that the Mormons would prefer to forget.

At the Church of Kurt Cobain

In a city that already boasted a Church of Elvis, a second rock-and-roll house of worship did not seem beyond belief. So when in 1996 it was announced that a new church in Portland, Oregon, was being devoted to the late Nirvana front man Kurt Cobain, the media turned out in force to hear the rallying cry of its leader and spokesman Revd Jim Dillon.

Indeed as many media representatives as potential followers flocked to the South Park Blocks on 28 May for the church's first public gathering. Only 12 disciples turned out to hear Dillon talk of a new religion in which sermons would draw on Nirvana lyrics. As an example he pinpointed the Nirvana track 'Rape Me', which, he claimed, was all about brotherly love. While Dillon spoke, members of his flock handed out information sheets and carried placards featuring Cobain's likeness and the words 'Peace, Love and Kurt'.

Wearing heavy framed glasses and a cap, Dillon went on to sermonize about Cobain's life and said that youngsters were in need of a new faith which spoke for their generation. He explained that the church's first goal was to win a $10,000 contest sponsored by a Portland radio station, and to donate the money to groups working to prevent drug abuse and suicide (Cobain, who was tormented by stardom and drug addiction, had committed suicide by shooting himself in April 1994). 'The church intends to create a positive effect from the loss of an artist who affected an entire generation,' said Dillon.

The media went away to file their stories, only to learn a week later that the Church of Kurt Cobain was a hoax and that Jim Dillon wasn't a reverend at all but a 34-year-old graphic artist by the name of Jerry Ketel. The whole charade had been designed to target the shallowness and insensitivity of the mass media, which, said Ketel, had both built Cobain up to idol status and contributed to his ultimate demise.

The Bride of Christ

When the daughter of an English farmer announced that she was the Bride of Christ and would eventually become the mother of the Second Messiah by virgin birth, believers fell at her feet in awe. She even specified the date on which the momentous birth would take place. But the day passed without incident. There was no birth; the woman wasn't even pregnant. Joanna Southcott was a fraud.

Southcott was born in April 1750 in the Devon parish of Ottery St Mary. Her early life was relatively uneventful, being split between domestic service and churchgoing until, in 1792, 'I was strangely visited, by day and by night, concerning what was coming upon the whole earth. I was then ordered to set it down in writing.' After claiming to hear voices speaking 'words so dreadful that they made me tremble', she began prophesying. At first nobody took her seriously but then she hit upon the idea of sealing her predictions and forbidding anyone to open them until after the event had happened. Among her predictions was that England would shortly be at war, that the country would be hit by a bad harvest, and that there would be a rebellion in Ireland. All three came true, but her detractors argued that in each case the omens were obvious to anyone with a degree of intelligence. The clergy were particularly hostile towards her so there must have been an unusual degree of satisfaction when, early in 1796, she correctly foretold that the Bishop of Exeter, who was in uncommonly good health at the time, would be dead by Christmas. Now even the doubters began to sit up and take notice of this strange woman. She pestered the clergy for official recognition of her divine powers and soon built up a following of over 100,000.

In 1802 she expanded her empire, decamping to London where, following further visions, she proclaimed herself to be 'the true and faithful Bride' of Christ who, by virgin birth, would one day bear a son, the Shiloh. Southcott said that the birth would lead to the Second Coming of Christ. She claimed to have been told that only 144,000 souls would be eligible for eternal salvation, but that those who contributed financially to her cause would receive in return a signed, sealed certificate protecting them as 'heirs of God and joint-heirs of Jesus Christ'. This proved a highly lucrative sideline. Her supporters maintained for years afterwards that the seals were not actually sold, but the distinction is so fine as to be practically invisible.

As time passed, her faithful followers started to grow impatient for the arrival of the new Messiah. Southcott finally quelled their fears by stating that the virgin birth would take place on 19 October 1814 – even though she herself would be 64 by then. From 11 October 1813 she cut herself off from society to prepare for the momentous event, apart from writing to every bishop, peer and Member of Parliament to advise them of the good news.

In the spring of 1814 Southcott began to feel unwell. Five months later – in early August – numerous doctors were summoned to check her health. Of 21 that studied her, 17 apparently diagnosed her as being pregnant even though she flatly refused to be examined internally. Of the four dissenters, one made his feelings known in the strongest possible terms by way of a letter to the *Morning Advertiser* on 26 August:

'Sir, It is stated in the *Morning Chronicle* of Saturday last, that two respectable Accoucheurs have given it as their opinion, that Joanna Southcott is with child, without their names or any reference.

'I consider that I should not be doing my duty to those poor deluded people who are in her belief and the public at large, were I not, after having had an opportunity of seeing her, to state the result of such a visit. I was informed, before I was introduced, that she was to express her own feelings, and I was to be allowed to judge accordingly; and I feel confident that no one will notice the mode of inquiry, but will see the imposition that was tried to be practised on me, or rather the trap in which I had like to have been caught. She desired that I would lose all idea of her being Joanna Southcott, and consider her a young woman about four or five and twenty years of age, and that she had been married about twelve months. She then described as her own feelings, the symptoms of pregnancy from first to last, and then again reminded me of the age she wished to be considered, and desired me to state what I should say of a person labouring under such symptoms. Had I answered the question in this shape, I certainly must have said such a person is pregnant; but the purport of my visit being to judge of her under all her circumstances, I told her she most decidedly was not in the situation she wished to impress upon the minds of those who follow her.'

The majority news that Southcott was pregnant prompted widespread rejoicing from her followers and as the date of the birth approached, crowds started to gather outside her house, three dying from exhaustion during the long vigil. Although she continued to insist that it would be a virgin birth, Southcott felt it necessary to acquire a husband and for this purpose chose John Smith, steward to the Earl of Darnley, whom she then married in a ceremony conducted in her bedroom.

The 19th came and went. With her followers becoming disillusioned, Southcott informed a doctor that she was going to die, and told him that she wanted an autopsy to be carried out four days after her death. She slipped into a coma and died on 27 December. The autopsy showed no sign of there ever having been a baby. Her appearance of pregnancy was now attributed instead to flatulence and 'extensive omental fat'. A medic in attendance, Dr Reece, put the enlarged breasts – one of the signs which had convinced so many doctors that she was pregnant – down to artificial stimulation and surmised that Southcott had planned to smuggle a baby into her room on the appropriate day, only to be somehow thwarted in her plan. Now utterly discredited, she was buried at night to avoid drawing crowds.

But that was not the last the world had heard of Joanna Southcott. She left behind a sealed box of prophecies which, if opened a century later in the presence of 24 bishops, would, she promised, cause 'crime, distress and banditry' to disappear. The First World War having just started in 1914, mankind was in dire need of an instant solution to all its problems but despite the pleas of the Southcottians (or the Panacea Society as they had become known), the Archbishop of Canterbury refused to open the box. Finally in 1927 the box was opened in the presence of only the Bishop of Grantham. Among the items contained within were a lady's nightcap, a horse pistol, a dice box, a handful of coins, a 1796 lottery ticket, a 1793 calendar of the French court, a puzzle, and a novel titled *The Surprises of Love*. The world continued much as before.

To this day, the few remaining members of the Panacea Society maintain that was the wrong box and that if the correct one is opened in the presence of the stipulated 24 bishops, all of the world's ills will be cured at a stroke.

Barney the Dinosaur: The Devil in Disguise

To millions of children, Barney the dinosaur is a harmless, lovable creature. But to Luscious M. Bromley and Jack Herman, fundamentalist Christian founders of a Florida-based group called Citizens Concerned About Barney, television's favourite dinosaur is conveying messages from Hell.

Bromley accused Barney of being 'the most powerful symbol of current evilness that is going to lead this country right down the tubes.' He added that Barney's message of 'Satanism, occultism and witchcraft' is leading the children of America by the hand inexorably towards the slippery slope of 'cocaine, gang violence, pornography, abortion, homosexuality, and maybe even marijuana.' Perhaps more dangerously, said Bromley, the mere inference that real dinosaurs existed millions of years ago threatens to undermine the Christian faith. 'If one truly believes in the Bible, the world is 6,000 years old, period! What we're seeing is the promotion of the evolution theory, and putting in the minds of children that the Bible is not necessary to explain the origin of man.'

The group's alarmist views were first reported by TV, radio and newspapers in the Tampa Bay region before being picked up nationally by CNN and Associated Press. But then someone saw through the cheap polyester suit that Bromley had bought from a charity shop especially for his press conference and recognized the two outraged individuals as John M. Bunch Jr and David J. Bennett – by day psychology students at the University of South Florida, and by night known collectively as Tampa Bay comedy team The Human Kennel.

Most of the journalists who had been hoodwinked took it in good part, but Thomas J. Billitteri, religious editor of the *St Petersburg Times*, was outraged, calling the hoaxers 'two puerile pinheads' and adding: 'What a sad commentary on our culture when religious bashing and thinly veiled hate can be viewed by two grown men as funny.'

'Bromley'/Bunch answered with an equally vitriolic letter to the newspaper's editor: 'Puerile? Sometimes. Pinheads? I doubt it. Religious bashing and thinly veiled hate? No way. Since Billitteri has found it necessary to stoop to name-calling, how's about I call him Mr Hyper-Inflated Pseudo-Intellectual Pumpkinhead?'

It was refreshing to see both parties behaving like Barney's target audience. But while the purple dinosaur may have many things to answer for, peddling the word of the Devil isn't one of them.

The Riddle of the Newark Holy Stones

In November 1860 amateur archaeologist David Wyrick made a startling discovery. In the course of excavations he uncovered a small rock bearing a figure of Moses, around which were carved what turned out to be a condensed version of the Ten Commandments, written in ancient Hebrew with a peculiar form of post-Exilic square lettering. The stone, which was to become known as the Decalogue, seemed to have been designed to fit into the hand, and experts concluded that it was probably used by its owner in daily prayers. They thought that it was a Jewish arm phylactery or tefilla of the Second Temple Period – dated at between 20BC and 70AD. Such a find would have aroused little more than passing interest if unearthed in the Middle East, but Wyrick had made the discovery near Newark, Ohio. So was this Hebrew artefact evidence that the 'Lost Tribes of Israel' had somehow ended up in North America, or was the whole thing just a hoax?

A number of basic spelling errors in the Hebrew text pointed to a definite hoax, and most scholars of the time suspected Wyrick of being the culprit. A few months before finding the Decalogue, he had also discovered another strange stone at a different site in Newark. The Keystone, as it became known, was shaped like a rounded arrowhead and it, too, was inscribed with Hebrew lettering. The fact that one person had managed to find two curious relics seemed more than just a coincidence and fuelled speculation that Wyrick was responsible for planting them in an attempt to prove a theory about the 'Lost Tribes of Israel'.

In 1861 Wyrick published his discoveries in a pamphlet, but the reproduction contained as many as 38 discrepancies in the lettering as well as mistakes in the figure of Moses. For example on the Decalogue stone Moses was wearing a turban; Wyrick drew him with a beret. Supporters of Wyrick insisted that he would not have made these errors had he been the hoaxer. Also, there was no indication in any of his work that he held a particular passion for solving the mystery of the 'Lost Tribes of Israel'.

The Newark Holy Stones proved to be Wyrick's ruination and in 1864 he committed suicide. He went to his death insisting that he was the victim – rather than the perpetrator – of a hoax. Found among his possessions was a Hebrew Bible, which led to renewed speculation that Wyrick had been guilty all along.

In the meantime other names had entered the frame. Principal among these was a local minister, Revd John W. McCarty, who was accused of planting the stones in a spot where Wyrick would almost certainly find them. The only piece of evidence against McCarty seems to be that he managed to translate the weird Hebrew script on the Decalogue in just two days after its discovery, suggesting that he must have had some prior knowledge of the contents.

However, one hoaxer was undoubtedly at work in Newark. In 1864 two more stones bearing Hebrew inscriptions were found during the excavation of a mound on a farm east of Newark. They were subsequently named the Inscribed Head and the Cooper Stone and caused considerable excitement until a local dentist, John H. Nicol, came forward to confess that he had carved and planted them to discredit Wyrick's earlier finds by demonstrating how easy it was to fake supposedly genuine Hebrew artefacts. The Inscribed Head reads in Hebrew letters as J-H-NCL. As short vowels are not represented by letters in Hebrew, that is precisely how one would write J-H-NiCoL. The Nicol hoax certainly achieved its aims in ridiculing Wyrick, and some began to suspect the demon dentist of being responsible for the Decalogue. Nicol never admitted as much, but he was standing worryingly close to Wyrick at the time of its discovery.

Although no one could be certain of the true identity of the hoaxer, most experts agreed that neither the Decalogue nor the Keystone were the genuine article. Then in 1998 fresh significance was attached to a stone bowl found with the Decalogue by one of Wyrick's companions when it emerged that such bowls were briefly made towards the end of the Second Temple period. The order that Jews should rinse their hands with pure water before eating had apparently created a short-lived Israeli Stone Age during which the manufacture of these bowls flourished since pure water could only come from a pure stone vessel. But after the destruction of the Second Temple in 70AD, the practice rapidly died out. Thus the stone bowl ties in chronologically with the Decalogue. And it must be doubtful whether Wyrick, McCarty, Nicol or indeed anyone else in 1860 Newark would have been aware of this little-known custom.

So could Wyrick's finds be genuine after all? The Newark Holy Stones: hoax or history? The debate goes on.

Mocking the Mormons

Mark Hofmann was brought up in a devout Mormon family. Although as a youngster he was never fully committed to the teachings of the faith, he entered the priesthood at 18 and served two years in England as a missionary. Returning to the United States, he enrolled at Utah State University with the intention of pursuing a career in medicine but dropped out to concentrate instead on his obsession for Mormon memorabilia.

Ever since the Mormon prophet Joseph Smith told how an angel led him to golden plates bearing the new message from which the Book of Mormons was translated, Mormons have been notoriously defensive about their history. Rumours abounded that while any documents supporting Smith's story would be trumpeted from the rooftops, anything that threatened to disprove it was quietly secreted away in locked church vaults. Hofmann saw the chance to cash in on Mormon paranoia, but what started out simply as a money-making hoax was to end in cold-blooded murder.

Although essentially a dealer in historical documents, Hofmann was also an expert forger. His first Mormon forgery was the Anthon Transcript that Joseph Smith claimed to have hand-copied from the golden plates. Clearly this was a key Mormon artefact and one which had never been located. So when Hofmann announced that he had discovered the original transcript, the Mormon Church of Latter-Day Saints excitedly secured ownership, totally unaware that Hofmann had written it himself. Realizing that he was on to a good thing, Hofmann then produced a letter from Smith's mother confirming precisely the prophet's account of the 1820 vision. The letter was exactly what the Mormon Church wanted to read. It, too, was a forgery.

Hofmann was also interested to see how the Mormons would react to bad news, and suspected that the Church hierarchy would pay even more for an item that cast aspersions on Smith's character. To this end, he offered a document which came to be known as the Salamander Letter. In the letter an associate of Smith's described how Smith had not been led to the plates by an angel, but by use of a seer stone – the same stone he had used to locate buried treasure on farmers' lands in his shady activities as a money-digger. Upon reaching the spot, Smith then found a magic white salamander in the box containing the golden plates. The implications were damning, raking up Smith's reputation as a money-digger, suggesting the use of folk magic (in which salamanders frequently featured), and calling Smith's own version of events into question. Hofmann also came up with a letter purporting to be from Smith to one Josiah Stowell in which Smith described some of the occult practices he used in pursuit of money-digging. Just as Hofmann thought, the Mormons were keen to buy the fake Salamander Letter in particular and paid $40,000 for it, the transaction being conducted through an intermediary, Salt Lake City collector and devout Mormon Steven Christensen. The letter to Stowell sold for $15,000. In total, Hofmann sold 48 documents to the Church of Latter-Day Saints, most directly but a few via local dealers such as Christensen.

However, dark clouds were looming on the horizon for Hofmann. Despite the steady flow of sales of his forgeries, his income was struggling to keep pace with an increasingly extravagant lifestyle. He needed a spectacular find and remembered the McLellin collection – an assortment of papers, letters and journals written by William E. McLellin, a former Apostle under Joseph Smith Jr, but who subsequently became disillusioned with the Mormon faith. Once again Hofmann calculated that the Mormons would pay good money to prevent the contents of the collection being made public. He was proved right when they handed him $185,000 to secure it. But Hofmann had been premature in announcing his find. He had yet to start work on the massive undertaking of forging the collection, and before long the Church was starting to demand a return on its investment.

Hofmann's answer was to forge an even more valuable document, the Freeman's Oath of 1639 – a groundbreaking statement about freedom of conscience and the first item to be printed on colonial America's first press. It was known to have existed in the form of a single leaf broadside, but had long since been presumed lost. In mid-March 1985 Hofmann visited a New York bookstore that, in addition to addition to rare prints, boasted bargain offers in a bin. In advance, Hofmann had prepared a worthless ballad sheet in olde worlde type, given it the heading 'The Oath of a Freeman', and planted it in the bargain bin. He then bought it, along with some other trivia, making sure that he obtained an itemized receipt bearing the shop's name. He now had proof of having purchased America's most valuable item of print at a New York store. He then set about simulating the early seventeenth-century document, taking great care that the print, ink and paper all appeared incontrovertibly authentic. The task took him barely two weeks and by April the newly discovered Freeman's Oath was being closely scrutinized by experts at the Library of Congress in Washington, and carrying a price tag of $1,500,000. The document passed the most stringent of tests; everyone was satisfied that it was genuine. Yet the Library declined to buy it.

The news came as a devastating blow to Hofmann who had been planning to use part of the money to repay his Church investors and claim that he had been unable to buy the McLellin collection after all. With the Church growing increasingly impatient, the net started to close in on Hofmann. He tried to buy more time by resorting to murder. On 15 October 1985 he planted a home-made bomb that killed Steven Christensen, his go-between to the Church on the McLellin deal. A second bomb, intended for one of Christensen's former business associates, accidentally killed the man's wife instead. The following day a third device – this time in a car – wounded Hofmann himself. The explosion had been intended to throw police off the scent but neither Hofmann's injuries nor the state of his car tallied with his story. Further investigations exposed Hofmann as a master forger.

Before his trial, Hofmann entered into a plea bargain, and in January 1987 received a life sentence for murder and fraud. The Church of Latter-Day Saints was left in the embarrassing position of having to explain how it had been duped by his forgeries. Worse still, the McLellin collection was reportedly found to be already in the Church archives, having been purchased back in 1908!

Alas, Poor Oric

In the increasingly wacky world of religious messiahs, Oric Bovar stands out as the one whose professed supernatural powers let him down with a resounding thud – ten storeys down, to be precise.

Born in 1917, Bovar first came to prominence as a showbusiness astrologer before branching out into religion. By the 1970s he had acquired a following of around 200 from New York to California, including celebrities such as Carol Burnett, Neil Simon and Bernadette Peters. He preached against the perils of tobacco, alcohol, drugs, and extra-marital sex yet despite this outwardly healthy approach to life, he deeply distrusted doctors and forbade them from entering his commune, as a result of which several of his flock gave birth without receiving proper medical attention. This did not overly concern Bovar as he had already hand-picked the mates for his devoted followers to marry.

On Christmas Eve 1975 Bovar told his followers to look up at the sky and they apparently saw him create a star. His behaviour now became even more eccentric as he convinced himself and his followers that he was Jesus and that as such he could last a year without going to the bathroom. Small wonder that his showbiz chums started to desert him. He then decreed that in future Christmas would be celebrated on his own birthday, 29 August. While his followers were put on strict diets and were forbidden from engaging in sex, Bovar watched endless showings of *The Exorcist* and began referring to himself as 'my son, Oric Bovar'.

His finest hour was yet to come. As Jesus, he believed he had the power to raise the dead so when a New York Bovarite, 29-year-old Stephanos Hatzitheordorou, died of cancer in the autumn of 1976, Bovar set about bringing him back to life. Accompanied by five of his fast diminishing flock, Bovar spent a two-month vigil over the corpse, chanting repetitively and ever more desperately: 'Rise, Stephan, rise.' They even paid the dead man's rent so that they would not be disturbed while trying to raise him. Eventually the police, acting on a telephone tip-off from ex-members of the cult, broke in to Hatzitheordorou's 79th Street apartment and charged Bovar and his followers with failing to report a death.

Disillusioned by their leader's abject failure to bring Stephan back from the dead, some of the flock began to question whether Bovar really did have divine powers. To allay their fears, he announced grandly that he would step out of the window of his apartment at 817 West End Avenue, 100th Street, flutter around outside for a few moments and then come back inside. Thus on 14 April 1977, Bovar stepped from the window of his 10th floor apartment . . . and dropped like a stone to his death.

Chapter 10

Exploration and Travel

The Visitor From Formosa

Few people in the London of 1704 had any knowledge whatsoever of Formosa, the present-day Taiwan. The vast majority would have been hard-pressed to pinpoint it to the nearest continent on a map, let alone relate anything about the country's natives and customs. To Londoners and indeed the rest of England, Formosa was simply some distant land.

Yet the English were eager to learn about new locations, this appetite manifesting itself in a popular wave of travel books. One in particular caused great excitement – a tome purportedly written by a native of Formosa who described in colourful detail the strange practices and rituals of that far-flung place. Unfortunately George Psalmanazar was not a native of Formosa, and had never even set foot there. His book, along with his entire persona, was a fraud.

What little is known of Psalmanazar's formative years comes courtesy his own memoirs that were published towards the end of his life. In view of his talent for deception and creative writing, these may not be wholly reliable. It seems that he was born in France but after a harsh Jesuit education, he headed north to Germany at the age of 16 in search of his father. On discovering that his father was as impoverished as his mother, George moved to Holland where he proclaimed himself to be Japanese!

Joining the Duke of Marlborough's forces, Psalmanazar came to the attention of Scottish army chaplain William Innes who quickly deduced that this curious young man was no more Japanese than he was. However, Innes saw definite potential in the situation and suggested that Psalmanazar change his nationality to Formosan and pretend that after escaping Jesuit persecution, he had been baptized a

Protestant by the good chaplain. Innes then took his protégé to England in the hope of impressing the Bishop of London, Henry Compton, with his story of how he had converted a heathen to Christianity. Anti-Catholic feeling was running high in England at that time, with the most fervent hatred reserved for Jesuits who were perceived as symbols of the Inquisition. So Innes reasoned that he could earn the Bishop's favour by claiming to have rescued this lost soul.

The fact that there was nothing Oriental about Psalmanazar's skin or hair turned out to be immaterial. Formosans, he said, bore much greater resemblance to Westerners than to Orientals. Conveniently, nobody was able to disprove this statement. Nor did the Formosan language become a barrier to his success. Although only around 20 in reality when he arrived in London (he added five years to his age to make his background appear more plausible), Psalmanazar was already fluent in six languages and was thus able to invent a Formosan tongue that appeared credible in both spoken and written form. He was also able to converse freely in Latin, which endeared him to the clergy. The Bishop of London was certainly impressed as was the Archbishop of Canterbury, and the former managed to obtain a sinecure for Psalmanazar at Christ Church, Oxford, where he translated the Church of England Catechism into his version of Formosan and trained missionaries. For it was the Bishop's dearest wish that Psalmanazar might spread Christianity on his return to his native country. The foreign visitor must have cut a bizarre figure at Oxford, often lecturing with a pet snake draped around his neck, which he said was the traditional Formosan way of staying cool.

While at Oxford, Psalmanazar also completed his majestic work, *A Historical and Geographical Description of Formosa*. It was seen at the time as the definitive book on that country, not least because competition was scarce. Published in 1704, written in Latin and dedicated to Bishop Compton, the book painted none too pretty a picture of life in Formosa, and, in doing so, pandered to the prevailing English mistrust of foreigners, especially Catholic foreigners.

Among the more lurid accounts was the annual slaughter on the island of 18,000 boys under the age of nine whose hearts were burned to satisfy the gods. The book also described how Jesuit plotters in nearby Japan had prevented the possibility of that country being converted to Christianity but, by way of a happy ending, Psalmanazar related that the Jesuits responsible were punished with a bloody death. He said that the Emperor of Japan had cunningly conquered Formosa under the pretext of offering religious sacrifices, legions of soldiers being disguised behind the heads of oxen and rams. When the beastly procession had gained the confidence of the natives, the soldiers suddenly leaped out and threatened the Formosans with death unless they surrendered. Thus the country was captured without bloodshed.

To reinforce the English view that Formosa – or anywhere east of Hamburg – was a land of savages, Psalmanazar detailed the deterrents for criminals on the island. Robbers and murderers were hanged head downwards and then shot dead with arrows, while the punishments for less serious offences included being buried alive, torn to pieces by wild dogs, having arms and legs hacked off, or having holes in the tongue bored with red-hot pokers. Psalmanazar also claimed that he had practised cannibalism in Formosa and that Formosan husbands were entitled to eat their adulterous wives. It was very much a man's world as, due to the shortage of males caused by the annual cull, polygamy was a popular concept. Here, however, Psalmanazar sounded a cautionary note: 'This kind of life is sweet and pleasant enough, as long as every one of them is of an agreeable humour; but if the Husband begins to love one Wife more than another, then arises Envy and Emulation.'

There were other plus points to living on Formosa. The natives had a life expectancy of around 100 – achieved apparently on a diet of raw meat and snake's blood – and there were several gold and silver mines on the island. Indeed, wrote Psalmanazar, 'their temples and houses were often covered with gold, both in cities and villages.' Such images of wealth and riches went down well with his readership.

No sooner was the book published than Father Fontenay, a Jesuit missionary on a visit to London, pointed out a number of basic errors, including the fact that Formosa was part of the Chinese, not the Japanese, empire. Fontenay noticed that sections of the narrative had been plagiarized from an account by George Candidius, a Dutch Jesuit missionary who was genuinely familiar with Formosa. Candidius in turn wrote Psalmanazar's book off as a work of pure fiction, maintaining that, far from being a harsh regime, the island's laws were practically non-existent. He also denied the existence of gold or silver mines in Formosa. But it was not lost on the English public that both Fontenay and Candidius were Jesuits. Why should their versions of events be trusted? Consequently the book sold so briskly that a second edition followed in 1705.

In the preface to the second edition Psalmanazar addressed 25 alleged factual errors that had been raised by various critics, but refused to yield on any point. He even argued that the discrepancies between his account and that of Candidius were proof that he

(Psalmanazar) was genuine, on the grounds that a hoaxer would have taken more care to adhere to the original. If nothing else, his nerve was breathtaking.

By 1707 Revd Innes had profited from his association with Psalmanazar by being appointed chaplain-general to the armed forces in Portugal. His departure left Psalmanazar without the necessary guidance and, with doubts as to his authenticity continuing unabated, the young man began to be taken less and less seriously. He drifted into obscurity, working as a humble clerk to an army regiment, but then in 1728 he fell seriously ill. Sensing the need for a deathbed confession, he finally admitted in a roundabout way that he had never been to Formosa and that he had invented his colourful background in order to lead a life of 'shameless idleness, vanity and extravagance'. Even when his fears of impending demise receded, he remained repentant and set about putting the record straight by writing his memoirs. He took his time over them and stipulated that they should be published posthumously. Therefore his full confession did not appear in print until 1764 – a year after his death.

In the meantime he contributed to a number of reference books, even having the effrontery to pen the chapters on China and Japan to Bowen's *Complete System of Geography*, borrowing heavily from the earlier writings of his old adversary George Candidius. The last few years of his life were spent shunning the limelight that he had once enjoyed so much. He wrote books without putting his name to them and decreed that, upon death, his body should be buried in an obscure corner of the common burial ground 'in a shell of the lowest value, without lid or other covering to hinder the natural earth from entirely surrounding it.' For all those who tried to unseat him in his youth but whose arguments were brushed aside contemptuously, it was indeed ironic that George Psalmanazar should end up his own worst critic.

Edgar Allan Poe's Balloon Hoax

The issue of the *New York Sun* on 13 April 1844 trumpeted a world exclusive – sensational news of the first-ever balloon crossing of the Atlantic. According to the full account that followed, based upon the diaries of two members of the eight-man crew, the balloon – the *Victoria* – had achieved the historic flight in just a little over three days. Even more remarkable was that it had apparently taken off from Wales bound for Paris, only to be accidentally carried across the Atlantic following damage to the propeller, and end up landing on Sullivan's Island, near Charleston, South Carolina. Such a sequence of events seemed almost beyond belief – and indeed it was. For there had been no balloon flight. Unbeknown to the *New York Sun*, its scoop was a lie from first word to last – an ingenious hoax dreamed up by Edgar Allan Poe.

In Poe's eyes, the key to a successful written hoax was to blind the readers with science. The more detail and minutiae he included, the more plausible the story became. He also took the precaution of making the pilot of his imaginary flight a real person – Monck Mason, who had travelled by balloon from Dover, England, to Weilburg, Germany, in 1836 and had described the journey in a book the following year. Mason's presence on the transatlantic trip immediately imbued it with the necessary air of credibility.

There were seven others on board for the journey that never was: Sir Everard Bringhurst; Mr Osborne, described as a nephew of Lord Bentinck; Robert Holland, a 'well-known aeronaut'; author Harrison Ainsworth; Mr Henson, 'the projector of the late unsuccessful flying machine'; and two seamen from Woolwich.

The first half of Poe's narrative was given to a lengthy description of the balloon itself, covering every aspect of the conveyance in fine detail and liberally dosing the account with his own interpretation of the laws of physics. He claimed that Mason had learned from the failings of Sir George Cayley and had 'conceived the idea of employing the principle of the Archimedean screw for the purpose of propulsion through the air.' He described the all-important screw as consisting of 'an axis of hollow brass tube, 18 inches in length, through which, upon a semi-spiral inclined at 15 degrees, pass a series of steel-wire radii, 2 feet long, and thus projecting a foot on either side. These radii are connected at the outer extremities by 2 bands of flattened wire; the whole in this manner forming the framework of the screw, which is completed by a covering of oiled silk cut into gores, and tightened so as to present a tolerably uniform surface. At each end of its axis this screw is supported by pillars of hollow brass tube descending from the hoop. In the lower ends of these tubes are holes in which the pivots of the axis revolve. From the end of the axis which is next to the car, proceeds a shaft of steel, connecting the screw with the pinion of a piece of spring machinery fixed in the car. By the operation of this spring, the screw is made to revolve with great rapidity, communicating a progressive motion to the whole.' And so on.

Apparently Mason was so delighted with his new developments that he decided to test the balloon on a flight across the English Channel, securing financial backing for the project from Sir Everard and Mr Osborne, 'two gentlemen well known for scientific acquirement, and especially for the interest they have exhibited in the progress of aerostation.' It was Mr Osborne's idea, continued the article, that the flight be kept top secret, which explained to Poe's audience why nothing had been heard about it in advance.

After early morning fog had been slow to clear, the *Victoria* took off at 11.07 a.m. on Saturday 6 April from the courtyard of Wheal-Vor House, Mr Osborne's seat, about a mile from Penstruthal, North Wales. In just ten minutes the balloon had reached an altitude of 15,000 feet and was heading south towards the Bristol Channel. High above the sea, the crew used the rudder to steer eastward in a line for the Paris destination and 'we set in motion the spring of the screw, and were rejoiced to find it propel us readily as desired. Upon this we gave nine hearty cheers, and dropped in the sea a bottle, inclosing a slip of parchment with a brief account of the principle of the invention. Hardly, however, had we done with our rejoicings, when an unforeseen accident occurred which discouraged us in no little degree. The steel rod connecting the spring with the propeller was suddenly jerked out of place, at the car end (by a swaying of the car through some movement of one of the two seamen we had taken up), and in an instant hung dangling out of reach, from the pivot of the axis of the screw. While we were endeavouring to regain it, our attention being completely absorbed, we became involved in a strong current of wind from the East, which bore us, with rapidly increasing force, toward the Atlantic.We soon found ourselves driving out to sea at the rate of not less, certainly, than 50 or 60 miles an hour, so that we came up with Cape Clear, at some 40 miles to our North, before we had secured the rod, and had time to think what we were about. It was now that Mr Ainsworth made an extraordinary but, to my fancy, a by no means unreasonable or chimerical proposition, in which he was instantly seconded by Mr Holland – viz.: that we should take advantage of the strong gale which bore us on, and in place of beating back to Paris, make an attempt to reach the coast of North America.'

After such high drama, the journals recorded that the remainder of the passage went smoothly, the Atlantic being crossed without difficulty and without any great apparent danger. The journey was even relatively comfortable, the ample space in the car enabling the crew to lie down at night under cloaks and blankets to keep out the cold, damp air. Mr Ainsworth's entry for 1 p.m. on Tuesday the 9th reported excitedly: 'We are in full view of the low coast of South Carolina. The great problem is accomplished. We have crossed the Atlantic – fairly and easily crossed it in a balloon! God be praised! Who shall say that anything is impossible hereafter?'

The *Sun*'s readers learned that the balloon came down near Fort

Moultrie, people rushing out of houses to welcome it to American soil. The 'journey' had taken just 75 hours. Not wishing to understate the significance of the achievement, Poe concluded: 'This is unquestionably the most stupendous, the most interesting, and the most important undertaking ever accomplished or even attempted by man. What magnificent events may ensue, it would be useless now to think of determining.'

Naturally the story, relayed to the *Sun* by Poe in the guise of a Charleston press agent, made banner headlines. Poe had carried it off beautifully, and the rush to buy a copy of the newspaper was unprecedented. The first anyone knew that the historic crossing had never actually taken place was when the post office at Charleston professed to having no knowledge of any balloon flight. Poe came clean, and on the day the article appeared in print, he stood on the steps of the *Sun*'s building in New York City and told onlookers that his story was a fake. He later summed up his attitude to hoaxing: 'A crow thieves; a fox cheats; a weasel outwits; a man diddles.'

Cook's Tour of Mount McKinley

The controversy over who was the first person to climb North America's highest peak, Mount McKinley, has raged for the best part of a century. Back in 1906 American explorer Frederick Cook claimed that he, together with Edward Barrill, had been the first to stand on the summit of the 20,320 ft-high mountain. To support their claim, they took a 'summit photo', a cropped version of which was published triumphantly by Cook in his book, *To the Top of the Continent*. However, rumours soon started to surface that they had not reached the summit at all. Cook's great rival, fellow American explorer Robert Peary, allegedly paid Barrill $1,500 for an affidavit stating that they had not climbed Mount McKinley and that the photograph was a hoax.

Both sides dug in to wage a bitter battle of words. Cook emerged the loser, and Hudson Stuck in 1913 is generally recognized to have been the first person to reach the summit. Cook's supporters maintained that their man had been wronged, cheated out of his just rewards, but then in 1998 author Robert Bryce produced fresh evidence which suggested that the so-called summit photo was indeed a fake and that Cook and Barrill probably didn't get any higher than 5,000 ft.

Frederick Cook was born in upstate New York in 1865. He was a determined, hard-working young man and, after going through medical school at New York University, he set up practice in Manhattan. He had already lost his father at the age of four, and now his new bride died giving birth to their only child. To compound

Cook's grief, the baby did not survive either. Seeking distraction from his grief, Cook began reading accounts of polar exploration, and in 1891 he spotted a paragraph in the *New York Telegram* announcing that a navy civil engineer by the name of Robert Peary was preparing an expedition to northern Greenland. Cook immediately wrote to Peary, offering his services as expedition surgeon – free of charge. Happy to keep costs to a minimum, Peary took him on. It was to mark the start of an intense rivalry between the two men.

At first they got on well enough but the relationship soured when Cook requested permission to publish an account of the expedition. Peary was not one for sharing the limelight and flatly refused, insisting: 'Not a word can be published by any member of any of my expeditions. Their work is my property for my use.' Put firmly in his place, Cook declined an invitation to join Peary on a second trip to Greenland, and could only suffer in silence as Peary became a national hero. For all his egotism and imperious behaviour, Peary had enormous energy and flair, which soon made him the darling of the National Geographic Society. Peary had charisma; Cook had a lisp.

The more success Peary achieved, the more resentful Cook became. While Peary appeared to have no difficulty in attracting sponsors, Cook struggled to raise money for his own Arctic jaunts and was forced to sign on with expeditions led by others.

At the end of the nineteenth century Alaska was still virtually unexplored. Then in 1902 Alfred H. Brooks, head of the US Geological Survey's Alaska branch, led an expedition to Mount McKinley, a peak whose very existence had only been discovered five years earlier. On his return, Brooks reported his findings, a copy of which Cook obtained and which spurred him to attempt to be the first to climb the summit – a feat that would surpass anything Peary had achieved to date. Encouraged by the moral and financial support of his second wife Marie, a wealthy doctor's widow whom he had married in June 1902, Cook set about organizing his own expedition to McKinley. It was still very much a low budget affair and, although Cook and his men completed the first circumnavigation of the base of the mountain, they failed to get anywhere near the summit.

Three years later he was approached by big game hunter Henry Disston who offered him $5,000 to organize a hunting expedition to the foothills of Mount McKinley. Cook took with him two members of the first expedition – photographer Walter Miller and guide Fred Printz – plus Arctic topographer R. W. Porter, cook S. P. Beecher, Columbia University physics professor Herschel C. Parker (who contributed $2,000 towards the costs), artist Belmore Browne, and

Edward Barrill, a tough but nearly illiterate hunting guide from Montana. Cook, Browne and Parker made up the first party to tackle the mountain. They tried to make headway from the south but the web of glaciers that protect the mountain from that direction proved impenetrable. So instead they had to settle for mapping new territories and surveying possible future routes. In fact the first successful climb from the south was not accomplished until 1954. Cook was not helped by the terrible weather conditions that summer. He later wrote: 'We had been over two months in the field, fording and swimming glacial streams daily; with an almost continuous cold rain pouring over us, with boots daily filled with water and our garments pasted to the skin, we were not in humour to prolong the torment.'

After two months of getting nowhere fast, Cook had concluded that the north-east ridge offered the only likely path to the summit. On 8 September, while the rest of the party carried out assorted tasks, Cook, Barrill and a prospector by the name of Dokkin suddenly headed up the Ruth Glacier. They travelled light, taking only enough supplies for about ten days, Cook having stated before departure that the object of the exercise was not to climb to the summit but to survey the north-east approach. His intention, he said, was to reach the top of the north-east ridge at around 12,000 ft. Nothing more.

Terrified by a succession of deep crevasses, Dokkin soon retreated, leaving Cook and Barrill to soldier on alone. Twelve days after setting off, the pair returned to base camp, and claimed that they had reached the summit of Mount McKinley. Cook said that the climb, interrupted only by a brief storm, had been 'ridiculously easy'. The rest of the party were almost lost for words. How could two men in their early forties have completed an 88-mile round-trip over such treacherous terrain in just 12 days? Browne was sure Cook was lying. He later wrote: 'I knew it in the same way that any New Yorker would know that no man could walk from the Brooklyn Bridge to Grant's Tomb (a distance of eight miles) in ten minutes.' Parker, who had left the expedition early in order to complete some outstanding college work, was equally emphatic in believing that Cook could not possibly have climbed Mount McKinley.

Cook opted to remain aloof from these petty squabbles, and went ahead with the publication of the 'summit photograph' in his book. On the basis of his McKinley claims, he received financial backing to conquer an even more significant landmark – the North Pole.

The race to the Pole was a straight fight between Cook and his arch enemy, Peary. Cook set off in 1907 and returned two years later to a hero's welcome from 100,000 New Yorkers after declaring that he had reached the Pole on 21 April 1908. He had recorded the moment in his diary: 'With a step, it was possible to go from one part of the globe to the opposite side . . . North, east, and west had vanished. It was south in every direction.' Peary eventually arrived at the Pole on 2 April 1909 – a full year after Cook claimed to have done so. Each man insisted that the prize was his.

As with those mysterious 12 days spent in the shadow of Mount McKinley, nobody seemed too sure of Cook's precise whereabouts between 1907 and 1908. His Inuit companions on the polar expedition later said that he never ventured out of sight of land. Others believe that he simply drifted aimlessly along the shores of Ellesmere and North Devon Islands. At first, however, Cook's account was accepted at the expense of Peary's but then the latter, backed by the influential National Geographic Society, set about discrediting Cook and, in the process, reviving the Mount McKinley controversy.

Two more members of the McKinley expedition, S. P. Beecher and Fred Printz, added their names to those who doubted that Cook had reached the summit. Printz told the *New York Sun* that Edward Barrill had confessed that Cook had offered him hush money. Printz added: 'I am just as sure as I'm living that Dr Cook never saw the North Pole. Any man who would make the representations he did as to his alleged ascent of Mount McKinley is capable of making the statements credited to him in the press about the North Pole.'

Then just as Cook was being presented with the key to New York City in honour of his achievement, Barrill came forward with a sworn affidavit (for which he was rumoured to have been paid by Peary). The affidavit, which appeared in the pro-Peary *New York Globe*, stated that he and Cook had never got near the top. Instead, said Barrill, they had climbed an 8,000 ft high peak nearly 20 miles away and it was there that Cook had faked the 'summit photo' of Barrill holding the American flag. Barrill also accused Cook of ordering him to fake diary entries which would support the successful ascent.

For the Cook camp, it just got worse. In 1910, Herschel Parker and Belmore Browne led a fresh expedition to climb Mount McKinley. They were unable to reach the top but Browne did discover what he maintained was proof that Cook's alleged photograph of McKinley's summit was taken on a hill on the southern side of the mountain, 20 miles away. The spot, known thereafter as Fake Peak, was almost identical to Cook's photo.

This revelation swung public opinion firmly against Cook. His claims to both Mount McKinley and the North Pole were largely dismissed as the words of a liar and in 1911 Congress officially acknowledged that Peary was the first person to reach the North Pole. Rather than fight his corner, Cook meekly backed down. His supporters were made of sterner stuff and pushed for their man to have a hearing before Congress, but just as it was about to materialize, Cook chose to disappear on a foreign expedition for the best part of a year. Peary's followers saw this as proof that Cook knew his story would not withstand the intense scrutiny of a congressional review.

Eventually turning his back on polar exploration, Cook formed his own oil company. In 1922 he created an oil-industry boom in Texas, selling stock in his new venture, the Petroleum Producers Association, based in Fort Worth. But even then he was dogged by controversy, and was arrested for mail fraud. He was convicted, fined $12,000 and sentenced to 14 years and nine months in prison. His loyal supporters blamed the Peary camp for the trial and complained that Cook's previous alleged misdemeanours had been used to blacken his character. A *New York Times* editorial, headlined 'A GREAT IMPOSTOR', showed just how far he had fallen from grace. 'Cook could go nowhere among men without being pointed out as the explorer who pretended that he had climbed Mount McKinley and beaten Admiral Peary to the North Pole, though the fact was that he had not got higher up on McKinley than a spur far from the summit.' Cook's appeal against the conviction failed and he was sent to Leavenworth Penitentiary on 6 April 1925 – perilously close to the 16th anniversary of Peary reaching the Pole.

Cook ended up serving five years behind bars. On his release, he lived a quiet existence, surfacing only occasionally to protest his innocence concerning the two exploration frauds. 'I reached the Pole, I climbed Mount McKinley,' he wrote. 'The controversy from my angle is at an end.'

Although Cook died in 1940, the arguments as to whether he was hoaxer or hero have shown no sign of diminishing. Any discussion on the subject inevitably involves Peary and there have been allegations that he, too, may have faked *his* polar expedition. The ongoing debate attracted the attention of countless authors, among them Robert Bryce who, in the course of researching a book about the epic rivalry between Cook and Peary, visited the archives at Ohio State University. There he came across a print of the infamous 'summit photo' of 1906, the image that has been described as 'the most controversial picture in the history of exploration.' But this was not the cropped version that had appeared in *Harper's Monthly* in 1907 and again the following year in Cook's own book: this was the original, unaltered print. According to Bryce, the broader vista showed geographical features which proved beyond doubt that Cook and Barrill were not standing on the summit of Mount McKinley but on Fake Peak. Bryce wrote: 'I don't think Cook ever had any intention of going to the summit. He apparently spotted this feature that he thought he could pass off as the summit and it was easy to stage the photograph because Barrill had to climb only a few hundred feet from the glacier floor.'

This therefore would appear to be the final chapter on that fateful 1906 expedition, yet somehow we all know that there is no more chance of the subject being laid to rest than of proving that Frederick Cook really did climb to the summit of Mount McKinley.

Murder on the Georgia Express

The edition of the London *Times* for 15 October 1856 carried a lengthy and disturbing account of one Englishman's highly eventful railroad journey in Georgia – a journey on which no fewer than six passengers, including a child, were apparently killed in a series of bloody duels.

The writer described how he boarded the train on 28 August in Macon, bound for Augusta. In the same carriage as him were about 25 people, including three women, one of whom was elderly and travelling alone. The other two were smartly dressed, one being around 20 years old, the other nearer 30. They boarded the train together, accompanied by a well-groomed man in his twenties. Soon a French barber entered and sat facing the two women and their companion, and almost immediately it became apparent that there was an uneasy atmosphere between the two men who were evidently rivals for the affection of the younger woman. As the row intensified, it was suggested that the situation be resolved by duelling with guns and the conversation became so animated that it was picked up by three or four different groups of passengers who began arguing furiously among themselves.

The writer continued: 'At length, attracted by the high tone of voice, I heard one of the disputants, a white-headed man past sixty at least, but hale-looking, accuse his opponent of ignorance of duelling and duels, and declare his belief that the other never saw a duel and would be afraid to face a man. Upon this the other, a respectable-looking man, of about forty-five, rose up and challenged the old man, telling his son, a fine little boy about six years old, to wait till he came back, followed the other into the smoking car, when, after arranging the preliminaries and making some written dispositions that occupied a quarter of an hour or so, the cars were stopped, and after they had descended with their witnesses, the cars moved on again leaving them behind. We learnt on the way – by telegraph – that the old man was killed.'

Following this diversion, the conversation reverted to the original challenge. A third male passenger – 'a hard-visaged man of about fifty' – had tried to intervene in the dispute between the barber and the ladies' companion, and ended up challenging the barber to a duel even though he had never met the two women before. Pistols were produced and passed among the passengers for examination. The train was stopped again and the conductor watched the duel, which resulted in the barber being killed. 'Whether the body was left behind or was put in the luggage car I do not know,' wrote the correspondent.

The victor then returned and proceeded to denounce the younger woman, saying 'that her conduct showed her to be no better than a common strumpet.' His hackles raised, he offered to fight anyone who would defend her character. The barber's father was willing to fight, but was turned down. However, shortly afterwards a young man stood up for the lady's honour and was led into the smoking car for a duel with pistols. The young man was killed, bringing the death toll to three.

The young man's son was so distraught by the news that he began to wail loudly, and was given to one of the women in the hope that he could be calmed. The crying irritated the father's killer who immediately threatened to kill the boy, too, if he didn't keep quiet. This merely served to upset the youngster further, prompting the killer's equally uncouth companion to take drastic action. The writer recounted how the man 'snatched the boy, carried him on to the platform, deliberately murdered him, and threw the body off from the car; the sudden silence of the child, the sound of his body falling down, had such effect upon me that, as soon as my mind could realize the murder as a fact, I became unconscious.'

He awoke to find yet another duel about to be fought. The conductor stopped the train and two more men were killed, further bloodshed only being spared by the fact that the child's murderer was left behind when the train moved off again and his associate was locked in a compartment of one of the carriages. The writer did not know what happened to the prisoner on reaching Augusta but since there was no account of the incident in the Georgia newspapers, he assumed that the killer had not been arrested. The piece concluded darkly: 'In Augusta I heard a person say that these were not uncommon incidents, and that scarcely a week passed without some fatal encounter on that road.'

The reason that the horrific railroad killings had not been reported in the American press was because they had never actually taken place. Americans protested about the story, and the president of the railroad wrote to *The Times* strongly denying that any such incidents had ever occurred. *The Times*, which had gleefully accepted the opportunity to ridicule Georgia, the South, and Americans in general, stood by the writer – named as John Arrowsmith of Liverpool – until a letter from the British consul in Georgia informed the newspaper that it had been comprehensively hoaxed.

The Last Tribes of Mindanao

Manuel Elizalde Jr was a wealthy, Harvard-educated Filipino, the playboy heir to an ancient island dynasty. In the eyes of Imelda Marcos, shoe-loving wife of Philippine president Ferdinand Marcos, 'Manda', as she called Elizalde, had class. So she persuaded her husband to appoint him Presidential Assistant for Tribal Minorities – a position which gave him enormous power and influence over the indigenous peoples. One day in 1971 Elizalde heard from a tribal frontiersman called Dafal about a primitive tribe of men, women and children living in the dense rain forest of Mindanao, a remote island some 600 miles south-east of the Philippine capital Manila. Dafal had apparently encountered them while on a hunting expedition with his father deep into the heart of the forest – an area usually avoided by tribes people who believed it to be the domain of evil spirits and savage beasts. Dafal eventually brought the tiny group of food-gathering natives pieces of metal and cloth in return for a choice forest vine and help in watching over his traps.

When the entrepreneurial Elizalde heard about the lost tribe, he immediately began to see dollar signs, the prospect of self-aggrandisement, and the chance to give a much-needed boost to tourism in the Philippines. He contacted *National Geographic* magazine in Washington with an offer of exclusive rights to the story about the last Stone Age tribe in the world. He said the tribe were called the Tasaday.

Elizalde volunteered to engineer the first-ever meeting between the Tasaday and the Western world. *National Geographic* snapped it up. The Tasaday were depicted as cave dwellers who used stone axes as tools and whose diet consisted primarily of yam-like roots, fruit, and nuts together with small fish, crabs and tadpoles from the forest streams. They knew nothing of agriculture, but had mastered a prehistoric device known as a fire drill. By whirling a wooden rod back and forth between the palms of the hand, a spark could be nursed into flame with the help of dried threads of vegetable fibre. Members of the 27-strong tribe (which included 14 children) wore no clothes except for a slim genital pouch for the men and a grass skirt for the women. Several adults tied their hair back with vines to make pony tails – hanging loose the hair was waist length. They were short in stature, the men being around five feet tall, the women slightly less. *National Geographic*'s cover story marvelled at the tribespeople 'huddled deep in the cave by fires where roots bake and leaf-wrapped tadpoles steam . . . leaf-skirted, bare-breasted, shapely young women knelt shyly beside us, smiling briefly in response to a light caress . . . a child clings to its mother, reflecting the affection that permeates all Tasaday life.' NBC paid Elizalde $50,000 for the exclusive television rights, its camera crew arriving in Elizalde's private helicopter and landing on a makeshift tree-top pad in the jungle. The resultant documentary, *Gentle Tasaday*, showed the tribes people to be 'wholly unaggressive, with no words for weapons, hostility, or war.' Speaking through interpreters who were able to translate the unique Tasaday tongue, they recalled a prophecy from their ancestors that told of an outsider who would come and love and protect them, and lead them out of the darkness. That saviour, they said, was 'Manda' Elizalde.

Accounts of the Tasaday lifestyle created a sensation in the Western world. Their discovery was hailed as one of the most significant anthropological events of the twentieth century, and experts concluded that the Tasaday had been isolated geographically and culturally for around 2,000 years. The media circus – supplemented by anthropologists – descended on the area en masse, ferried (at a price) by Elizalde's helicopter to the Mindanao rain forest. All visits were closely monitored, and in 1972 President Marcos declared some 19,000 hectares around the caves to be a Tasaday reservation. He said the measure was designed to safeguard the tribe but it also had the effect of sealing it off from prying eyes. Shortly afterwards Marcos also imposed martial law on the Philippines, thereby suppressing any locals who dared to question the authenticity of the Tasaday. Under such political restraints, the Tasaday story was carefully orchestrated and nobody was allowed the time to carry out a detailed scientific study of the tribe. The reservation was surrounded by soldiers from Elizalde's own private army. One anthropologist, who claimed he saw cooked rice being sneaked into the cave (thus casting doubts on the Tasaday's primitive existence), was swiftly ejected from the rain forest. Then in 1974 Elizalde put a halt to outside visits. The Tasaday vanished from the world's news pages as suddenly as they had arrived.

That was the last that was heard of the Tasaday until 1986. In February of that year the detested Marcos dictatorship finally crumbled, Corazin Aquino became president of the Philippines, and martial law was rescinded. Elizalde fled the country with $55 million. Without their 'saviour' to protect them, the Tasaday were once more open to visitors.

The first outsider to contact them was Swiss journalist Oswald Iten. He found a rather different story to that presented to the world 15 years earlier. The cave said to have been home to the Tasaday for thousands of years now lay deserted. Instead the tribespeople had blended into nearby villages where they no longer wore genital pouches and grass skirts but bedraggled T-shirts and jeans. Nor was there any sign of Stone Age tools. Men and women recognizable from the original media coverage were found living in everyday native huts, raising normal crops. Locals told Iten that the 'cave people' were just ordinary peasants who often came to market, fully clothed and smoking cigarettes. Furthermore they weren't even called the Tasaday. That was a name invented by Elizalde and the hunter Dafal.

Slowly but surely the scale of the deception became clear. Elizalde had bribed members of two tribes living on Mindanao – the Tboli and the Manobo – to pretend to be Stone Age people living in caves. They were actually farmers living in a village on the far side of the hill that housed the cave. At first the hoax had involved only two or three families who were persuaded to remove their clothes and act like Stone Age people for a couple of days for the benefit of American visitors. They had rehearsed beforehand with the stone axes and the fire drill, their Stone Age tools being nothing more than pebbles plucked from a nearby stream. Arriving by helicopter and touching down on a landing platform allowed any visitors to be taken to the cave without becoming aware of the pathways and village on the other side of the hill, thus creating the illusion of isolation from the outside world. Whenever Elizalde brought in visitors, the selected families left their huts, took off their clothes and played in the cave. As soon as the Westerners had departed, the villagers abandoned the cave and resumed their normal lives. Far from existing on forest produce, the 'Tasaday' had depended on rice handouts from Elizalde. That was the power he held over them.

'We didn't live in caves,' said one, 'only near them, until we met Elizalde. He forced us to live in the caves so that we'd be better cavemen. Before he came, we lived in huts on the other side of the mountain and we farmed. We took off our clothes because Elizalde told us to do so and promised if we looked poor that we could get assistance. He gave us money to pose as Tasaday and promised us security from counter-insurgency and tribal fighting.'

Another villager, who had featured as 'Lobo' on the cover of *National Geographic*, said bitterly: 'Elizalde promised us things so we changed our names and did whatever he wanted. He sent ahead messengers to tell us to take off our clothes and go to the caves. We did as we were told, but we got nothing.'

The emergence of the truth explained one thing that had puzzled many anthropologists – the absence of any 'midden' or trash layer, which decorates the floor of virtually every inhabited cave. As for the unique Tasaday language, it was simply a dialect of another local tongue. Iten's story appeared in the Swiss newspaper *Neue Zurcher Zeitung* under the banner headline '*Steinzeitschwindel*' or 'Stong Age Swindle', and was soon picked up by other publications and TV stations across the world. The myth of the Tasaday was well and truly debunked.

Elizalde ended up in Costa Rica, squandered all the money, became hooked on drugs and died destitute in May 1997. It could be argued that the simple tribespeople he so cynically exploited enjoyed infinitely more rewarding lives.

Chapter 11

Music

The Fake Philharmonic

Classical music fans living in Hong Kong were excited by the prospect of a series of concerts in the city by the world-renowned Moscow Philharmonic. The concerts, organized in association with the Hong Kong government, ran from 7–13 August 2000, and over 10,000 fans, each paying $30 for a seat, went to see the orchestra play. They were not disappointed. The performances won rave reviews, one paper enthusiastically praising the 'exciting accelerandos and heart-stopping rubatos'. The only problem was that whatever orchestra had performed to the citizens of Hong Kong, it was not the Moscow Philharmonic. It was a band of impostors.

When members of the real Moscow Philharmonic heard about the concerts in Hong Kong, they were somewhat puzzled. For, as its Russian agent, Yelena Tikhomirova, and principal guest conductor, Dmitri Yablonsky, pointed out, the celebrated orchestra was thousands of miles away on those dates, on a tour of France, Spain and Portugal. Ms Tikhomirova speculated that the rogue players were musicians from lesser Russian orchestras, playing without either her knowledge or the blessing of the real group.

The Hong Kong government angrily wrote to the agents who had organized the event, demanding clarification, but were unable to read the reply because it was in Russian. With some concert-goers asking for refunds even though they had thoroughly enjoyed the performances, Hong Kong's classical music buffs had to live with the embarrassment that they had failed to detect a bunch of second-rate musicians masquerading as one of the world's finest orchestras.

The Death of Paul McCartney

In October 1969 a rumour spread rapidly through the music world that Paul McCartney was dead . . . and had been for three years without any of his fans realizing it. The story went that he had been killed in a car crash towards the end of 1966 and that the surviving Beatles had recruited a lookalike replacement, William Campbell, whose face had been reconstructed through plastic surgery so as to render him indistinguishable from McCartney. Campbell in place, the group had apparently continued to play and record as the Beatles with no outsiders any the wiser.

Conspiracy theorists maintained that the car crash had been so serious that dental records were of no use in identifying the body. But there was proof, they insisted, and it lay within the group's lyrics and album covers. The following clues were cited as clear indications that McCartney was dead:

- The cover of *Abbey Road* was said to represent a funeral procession with John Lennon dressed as a minister, Ringo Starr as an undertaker, and George Harrison as a gravedigger.
- On the *Abbey Road* cover, McCartney is barefoot (another sign of death) and out of step with the others.
- The same album cover shows a Volkswagen parked nearby. It has the number plate 281F, which was taken to mean that if McCartney were alive, he would be 28.
- In 'Strawberry Fields Forever', Lennon supposedly mutters 'I buried Paul', although others claimed the words were 'cranberry sauce'.
- On the *Magical Mystery Tour* cover, three Beatles wear red carnations, but Paul wears a black one, indicating death.
- On the cover of *Sergeant Pepper's Lonely Hearts Club Band*, the band is standing on a grave.
- McCartney's uniform on the *Sergeant Pepper* cover has a badge on the sleeve saying 'OPD', interpreted by some to mean 'officially pronounced dead'.
- When the track 'Revolution 9' is played backwards, the fateful car crash can apparently be heard in its entirety.
- The cover of *Magical Mystery Tour* is supposed to reveal a London telephone number 231-7346 which, when dialled, allegedly answered: 'Paul McCartney is dead'.

Nobody was too sure precisely how the rumour had originated, but it seemed to have started in America's mid-west. It was ascribed variously to an Ohio University student, a story in a 1969 issue of the

University of Michigan magazine, and disc jockey Russell Gibb at WKNR, Detroit, who broadcast a special two-hour show on the death theory without a commercial break. When Roby Yonge, an all-night DJ on New York station WABC, also began discussing the rumours, the programme manager quickly took him off air.

By November 1969 mourners had started to gather outside McCartney's home. Newspapers and radio stations were besieged with calls from worried fans, and McCartney felt obliged to issue a statement. 'I am alive and well and concerned about the rumours of my death,' he said. 'But if I were dead, I would be the last to know.' However, the statement was released through the Beatles' Apple Organization: the absence of a personal appearance from McCartney merely added fuel to the speculation. Apple acknowledged the impossibility of the situation. 'Even if he appeared in public just to deny rumours it wouldn't do any good. If people want to believe he's dead, then they'll believe it – the truth is not at all persuasive.'

Meanwhile, at the request of a local disc jockey, Miami professor Dr Henry M. Truby put the McCartney riddle to a 'sound fingerprint' test. After subjecting dozens of Beatles records, pre- and post-1966, to 20 hours of testing on a sound spectograph machine, audio expert Dr Truby concluded that there was 'reasonable doubt' that three voices popularly attributed to McCartney were produced by the same set of vocal chords. 'I hear three different McCartneys,' added the professor, thereby guaranteeing that the death story would not fade away just yet. It even became the subject of a television courtroom special in which witnesses such as Peter Asher (brother of Paul's ex-girlfriend Jane Asher) and Beatles manager Allen Klein supplied testimony to famed trial lawyer F. Lee Bailey that McCartney was alive and well and living in Scotland.

In time most people came to accept that reports of McCartney's death had been greatly exaggerated. Those keen to perpetuate the mystery would not give up easily, however. Desperate to save face, they pointed to the overwhelming 'proof' and accused the Beatles of deliberately creating a hoax by planting misleading clues in their lyrics and album covers, either for sheer devilment or to boost record sales. Naturally the group ridiculed such allegations, and Ian McMillan, who photographed the *Abbey Road* cover, was at least able to defuse the claims relating to that album He recalled that the contentious Volkswagen 'just happened to be standing there. It had been left by someone on holiday – nobody with any connection with the Beatles – and a policeman tried to move it away for us, but he couldn't.' There was one other tiny problem. McCartney was born on 18 June 1942, which made him 27 – not 28 – in late 1969. As for McCartney's bare feet, 'It was a hot day,' said McMillan, 'and he just took his shoes off and left them on the pavement. It didn't seem symbolic to me.'

So the entire episode was either a prank or the result of someone's over-active imagination, perhaps from too much exposure to illicit substances. But just as there are people who firmly believe that Elvis is still alive and working in Burger King, there are those who contend that the real Paul McCartney died nearly 40 years ago and that his place ever since has been taken by an impostor.

The Fiddles of Fritz Kreisler

Austrian-born violinist Fritz Kreisler developed into one of the world's most accomplished instrumentalists. He performed many of his own compositions yet these received such lukewarm critical acclaim in his early years that he cleverly passed them off as the works of more famous composers so that his pieces could receive the recognition he thought they deserved. It was only some forty years later that he admitted to having fooled the critics.

A precocious and brilliant child, Kreisler first studied the violin at the age of four. He gave his first solo performance at nine and in 1887, by which time he was 12, he shared the Paris Conservatoire's top prize with four other students. His violin training was now complete, and he set about making his mark as a performer and composer.

He made his American debut in Boston in November 1888, followed by a nationwide tour with pianist Moriz Rosenthal. However, the critical response was not what Kreisler had hoped for; although his technique was admired, he was deemed immature in matters of interpretation. He became increasingly frustrated and briefly abandoned music in favour of medicine, only to realize that the violin was more rewarding than the stethoscope. Gradually he started to win over the critics, but remained angry that they would not accept a recital programme of his own compositions. He also felt there was a dearth of quality encore pieces in the established violin catalogue, and so began composing a number of 'salon' pieces, ascribing them to past masters such as Vivaldi, Pugnani and Couperin in order to avoid the contempt of the critics. Kreisler made no attempt to imitate the style of these composers – he merely borrowed their names. Speaking after his 1935 confession, he said of one of his Pugnani works: 'A child could have seen Pugnani never wrote it. There was a semi cadenza in the middle of it completely out of style with Pugnani's period.'

As Kreisler grew bolder and more inventive, he wrote *Posthumous Waltzes* by Joseph Lanner. Again, Kreisler kept his own involvement a secret, merely claiming to have discovered them. He unveiled them at a concert in Berlin. The following day a critic on the *Berliner Tageblatt*, a Dr Schmidt, drooled over the Lanner waltzes, saying they were 'worthy of Schubert', but attacked Kreisler for playing a piece of his own, *Caprice Viennois*, amid such gems. An indignant Kreisler wrote to Dr Schmidt, saying that 'if the Lanner pieces were "worthy of Schubert", then I was Schubert, because I had written them!'

Kreisler had made his point, but still nobody suspected him of having also written the Vivaldi, Pugnani and Couperin pieces.

His career as a violinist continued to go from strength to strength and his fake compositions went down well with audiences who appreciated his romantic flair and technical excellence, topped with a large helping of Viennese charm. Finally he decided to own up but in doing so, sparked a heated debate among sections of the music press as to his integrity.

Fritz Kreisler died in New York on 29 January 1962, having achieved widespread acclaim as a virtuoso violinist but, in terms of composition, more for his ability to fake the works of old masters than for anything written under his own name.

Milli Vanilli: Mime Artists

Dreadlocked duo Milli Vanilli thought they had conquered the pop world when they won a 1990 Grammy as Best New Artist for their hit single 'Girl You Know It's True'. Then a few weeks later their manager admitted that the pair – Rob Pilatus and Fabrice Morvan – hadn't sung a note on any of their songs. They were stripped of their Grammy and dropped by their record company. Milli Vanilli were left feeling silly.

The son of a German stripper and an American soldier, Rob Pilatus was born in Frankfurt in June 1965. At the age of four, he was adopted by a physician and his wife in Munich but ran away from home ten years later. He tried his luck at DJ-ing and modelling before realizing that his true talent lay in breakdancing. As a champion breakdancer, Pilatus took part in a 1986 competition in Los Angeles where he met up in a disco with Frenchman Fabrice Morvan who was attending a dance music conference. Morvan had been training to be a trampolinist until damaging his neck in a fall. Dancing, he decided, was less dangerous.

Back in Munich, Pilatus and Morvan teamed up and worked as dancers for various German groups. They also tried to find work as backing singers before electing to form their own act, taking the Milli Vanilli name from a New York club. Combining rap and soul, they came to the attention of German producer Frank Farian, the brains behind seventies disco sensations Boney M. Farian agreed to audition Milli Vanilli but didn't rate their vocals, so that although he duly signed them up, it was only as frontmen. There was no way Farian was actually going to allow them to sing.

The first Milli Vanilli album was recorded at a level of secrecy normally reserved for the KGB. Pilatus and Morvan were effectively locked out of the studio and the real singers (principally Johnny Davis and Brad Howell) were only allowed in and out under cover of darkness. Furthermore, Farian ensured that Davis and Howell each recorded separately, unaware of the other's role. Pilatus and Morvan didn't know their replacements from Adam. At the height of Milli Vanilli fever, Davis cheekily asked Pilatus for an autograph in the street. 'He had no idea who I was,' recalled Davis. 'It was quite funny.' Even Gina Mohammed, who sang Milli Vanilli backing vocals at weekend recording sessions, was unaware that Pilatus and Morvan were not the real group. She remembered being so thrilled for them when they stepped up to collect their Grammy Award . . .

But to the record-buying public, Pilatus and Morvan were Milli Vanilli. Between 1988 and 1989 they became international stars, tasting three US number ones thanks to a combination of their good looks, smooth moves and someone else's singing. Their breakthrough single, 'Girl You Know It's True', reached number two in the States and number three in the UK, and was followed by successive US chart-toppers – 'Baby Don't Forget My Number', 'Girl I'm Gonna Miss You' and 'Blame It On The Rain'. Lip-synching their way to success, the band sold 30 million singles and 14 million albums worldwide.

However, there is only one way to go from the top, and Pilatus and Morvan had made the mistake of not obeying the old adage about being nice to people on the way up. They had started to believe their own publicity, alienating press and fans alike by comparing themselves in interviews to Elvis and the Beatles. They were also perceived as being singularly ungracious at awards ceremonies, often declining to thank anyone for their elevated position on the pop ladder. Perhaps they felt that if they named names, their secret would be out.

The Grammy clearly went to their heads because shortly afterwards they began to think the unthinkable: they went to Farian and demanded to be allowed to sing on their next album, threatening to expose the scam if Farian refused. Fearing the contents of a forthcoming book on the band, Farian decided to get his retaliation in first and in November 1990 called a press conference at which he exposed the hoax himself.

'I'm relieved that the truth has come out,' he said. 'It was a crazy idea.' He added that the deception had failed because 'the success was too big. The situation became monstrous. Pilatus and Morvan wanted to sing on the second album. Their voices aren't that good. I couldn't fulfil that condition.'

Journalists attending the press conference were given video and audio tapes of Pilatus and Morvan singing so that they could compare the voices to the Milli Vanilli sound. A few sceptics in the audience goaded the duo into an impromptu 15-second version of 'Girl You Know It's True'. No further proof was required.

Pilatus bleated: 'We just hope our fans understand that we were young, that we just wanted to live life the American way.'

In the fallout, Arista Records cancelled Milli Vanilli's contract and the National Academy of Recording Arts and Sciences stripped them of their Grammy. Law suits were issued and eventually purchasers of 'Girl You Know It's True' were given the opportunity to ask for their money back.

In 1991 Farian launched the Real Milli Vanilli (using the studio session singers Brad Howell, Johnny Davis and Charles Shaw) while Pilatus and Morvan attempted to rebuild their careers as Rob and Fab. Both acts sank without trace.

Eventually Morvan went solo and Pilatus slipped into a downward spiral that included at least one suicide attempt and several arrests, mostly for drunkenness. Ironically on one occasion he was bailed out of jail by Frank Farian. In April 1998 Pilatus died of a drugs overdose in Frankfurt, Germany – a suitably sordid ending to the story of Milli Vanilli.

The Topless String Quartet

Musician and comedian Alan Abel has been one of America's most prolific pranksters over the past forty-odd years. He particularly relished the opportunity to put his own slant on topical stories, such as the time that he introduced his own candidate for the 1964 presidential election – Jewish housewife Yetta Bronstein, played by Abel's actress wife Jeanne. Under the campaign slogan 'Vote For Yetta and Watch Things Get Better', he earned plenty of media coverage from press releases outlining Yetta's policies, among which was a promise to put a picture of Jane Fonda in the nude on postage stamps 'to give a little pleasure for six cents to people who can't afford *Playboy*.' Then at the height of Watergate, when all the talk was about Bernstein and Woodward's mysterious 'Deep Throat', Abel decided it was time to introduce the informant to the world. So he hired a man to pose as

'Deep Throat' at a Washington news conference – an event which attracted over 100 reporters. One literary agent even turned up with a $10,000 advance cheque to buy the subject's life story, at which point 'Deep Throat' became embroiled in an unseemly argument with his wife who didn't want him to testify. After 'Deep Throat' had been whisked away in a limousine, the *Washington Post* ran a front-page story on the press conference. Abel recalled: 'When we exposed this a few days later, the *Post* didn't carry much of a story, but the rival *Washington News* ran a banner headline saying that the Post had been duped.'

In 1967 an Abel-scripted press release announced the arrival in the United States of a topless string quartet from France – 'France's first gift to America since the Statue of Liberty.' It explained that Madeleine Boucher, Michelle André, Maria Tonchet and Gretchen Gansebrust – a cellist and three violinists – played topless so as to produce pure and 'unhampered' tones. Abel hired four models for a photo session and sent the pictures to magazines and newspapers. The coverage surpassed Abel's most optimistic expectations with the *New York Post* running a story headlined 'BACH, BEETHOVEN, BRAHMS AND BOSOMS'. Hundreds of instant classical music fans requested autographed photos, agents queued up for the chance to promote concerts (purely on account of the group's musical merits, of course), and Frank Sinatra said that he wanted the quartet to record for his Reprise label! So frothy was the drool of anticipation that a lot of people never forgave Alan Abel when the hoax was revealed . . .

Piotr Zak at the BBC

Listeners to the BBC's classical music station, Radio 3, heard a highly esoteric piece being broadcast on 5 June 1993. It was introduced as the world premier of *Mobile for Tape and Percussion* by Piotr Zak, a 22-year-old Polish composer living in Germany and described as 'one of the youngest and most controversial figures in contemporary music.' The 12-minute track featured a mish-mash of cymbals, drums and xylophones, and drew scant praise from the music reviewers of national newspapers.

The Times critic wrote: 'It was certainly difficult to grasp more than the music's broad outlines, partly because of the high proportion of unpitched sounds and partly because of their extreme diversity.' The *Daily Telegraph* scribe was even less impressed, dismissing the performance as 'wholly unrewarding'. He added, with what would turn to be keen insight, that 'a succession of whistles, rattles and punctured sighs proclaimed, all too shamelessly, their non-musical origins.'

It was only later that the BBC admitted there was no such person as Piotr Zak and that the avant-garde piece was merely a random collection of sounds. 'It was an experiment,' said the BBC, 'to demonstrate that some contemporary compositions are so obscure as to be indistinguishable from tapes of percussion played at random.'

The hoax, conducted with official approval, was carried out by Susan Bradshaw and Hans Keller, two members of the BBC music division. 'We dragged together all the instruments we could find,' revealed Bradshaw, 'and went around the studio banging them. It was a serious hoax to set people thinking. That fake music can be indistinguishable from the genuine is a reflection on certain trends in present-day composition. We are sorry if we have embarrassed certain music critics.'

The BBC then announced its intention to run a discussion programme called *The Strange Case of Mr Piotr Zak*. The two hoodwinked critics were invited to participate.

The Britney Death Hoax

The pop music world was stunned by a story circulating on the Internet on 12 June 2001, which said that Britney Spears had been killed in a Los Angeles car crash and that her then boyfriend, Justin Timberlake of American boy band *NSync, was lying in a coma. The report, first broadcast by two DJs on the Dallas radio station KEGL-FM, gained added credence when a BBC Internet news page also carried the story, along with a picture of Britney's wrecked car.

Hospitals and fire stations in the Los Angeles area were bombarded with phone calls from concerned fans wanting to know whether or not the story was true and Britney's record company, Jive, fielded media calls from as far afield as Europe and Australia. However, nobody was more shocked by the news than Timberlake himself. On hearing it, the first thing he did was phone Britney because he thought 'maybe it got twisted, maybe something did happen to her.' He was hugely relieved to hear her voice on the other end of the line.

While Britney's spokesperson assured callers that the celebrity couple were in perfectly good health, the supposedly genuine BBC news page was revealed to be a mock-up, similar to a spoof MTV news page that had reported the fake death of rap star Eminem in 2000. In a sick twist, the Britney page contained a message of condolence from Eminem. The BBC pledged to track down whoever was responsible for copying its website.

The two Dallas DJs who started the rumour – Keith Kramer and Tony Longo – paid for their joke by losing their jobs. It was not the first time they had been in trouble, having previously been reprimanded for encouraging motorists to run over cyclists.

Chapter 12

Zoology

Nessie Exposed

Stories that a huge prehistoric creature was lurking somewhere in the depths of Scotland's Loch Ness have been circulating for centuries, but were mostly dismissed as fabrication or the result of one too many drams of whisky. Until 1933, that is. For that year began a run of reported sightings of weird beasties on and around the loch, culminating in the photograph that created the modern legend of the Loch Ness Monster. Yet the picture – the very backbone of the Scottish tourist industry – was exposed sixty years later as a hoax, dreamed up by an extrovert hunter probably in an act of revenge after finding himself on the receiving end of an earlier Loch Ness prank.

It was in 1933 that a new road was completed along the shore of the loch, offering the first clear views of the water from the northern side. One April afternoon a local couple were driving home when they spotted 'an enormous animal rolling and plunging on the surface.' Their account was published in the *Inverness Courier* where the word 'monster' was used to describe the vision before them. Then later that spring a couple called Spicer reported seeing one of the creatures lumbering across the shore road before disappearing into the water. The sightings sparked a flood of interest. Monster hunters descended on the loch from far and wide; small boys with fishing rods would row out on to the water in the hope of landing the catch of a lifetime; the narrow roads around the loch became jammed with tourists eager to snatch a glimpse of this beast from a bygone age; and a circus even offered a £20,000 reward for its capture.

London newspapers reacted by sending reporters north to cover the story. The *Daily Mail* went a step further and hired actor, film director and self-styled big game hunter Marmaduke Wetherell to try and bag the Loch Ness Monster.

A larger than life figure, Wetherell arrived at Loch Ness in December 1933, blessed with the unwavering conviction that he was the only man alive who could snare the monster. He had a photographer by his side to capture the moment for posterity. The locals treated Wetherell with thinly veiled contempt, not least because they were none too keen at the thought of an outsider claiming their prize.

A matter of days after embarking on his expedition, Wetherell reported finding huge footprints, just a few hours old, on the shore of the loch. Not given to false modesty, he boasted that his finely tuned hunting skills had led him to the precise spot. He estimated that the creature that had made the prints measured 20 feet in length. After making plaster casts of the footprints, he sent them off to the National History Museum in London shortly before Christmas. While the world waited patiently for the museum experts to return to work following their festive break, monster mania reached fever pitch. Inverness was floodlit for the occasion.

In January the experts delivered their verdict. The prints were those of a hippopotamus, but not just any hippopotamus – a stuffed hippopotamus. Suspicion fell upon a local resident with two mischievous sons who owned a Victorian umbrella stand in the shape of a hippo's foot.

Wetherell came in for some fearful stick from Fleet Street – the big game hunter unable to distinguish a dinosaur from an umbrella stand. The *Daily Mail* in particular was furious at having been made a laughing stock, and left Wetherell in no doubt as to its displeasure. Still smarting, the chastened 'Duke' told his son Ian: 'We'll give them their monster.'

Wetherell senior got in touch with his stepson, Christian Spurling, a skilled model-maker, and said: 'Christian, can you make me a monster?' Ian Wetherell bought the base, a tin toy submarine, for a few shillings from a shop in Richmond, Surrey, and Spurling constructed the monster, modelled on the idea of a sea serpent, in eight days. A head and long neck made of plastic wood was built over the conning tower of the toy submarine to create a creature that would baffle experts for over half a century. The end product was a foot high and about 18 inches long with a lead keel added to give it extra stability.

Armed with a camera, the Wetherells travelled up to Loch Ness and photographed their fake monster in a quiet bay before sinking the evidence. They then passed the undeveloped photographs on to a friend of a friend, respected Harley Street gynaecologist Colonel Robert Wilson who had the pictures developed and sold the best one to the *Daily Mail*. His story was that he had taken the photo on 19 April 1934 after he and London insurance broker Maurice Chambers had noticed 'something in the water' on Loch Ness.

The *Daily Mail*'s world exclusive created a sensation. The grainy black and white picture, which became known as the Surgeon's Photograph in honour of Wilson's occupation, showed a long neck rising from the depths and became *the* recurring image of the Loch Ness Monster. Experts speculated that it was a plesiosaur; sceptics suggested that it was an otter or a tree trunk. Nobody suspected for a moment that it was a toy submarine.

Those who saw the photo as proof of the monster's existence pointed to the telltale neck, which they estimated at over three feet long. In truth, it was just eight inches long.

If Wetherell had intended gloating to the *Daily Mail*, he was surely dissuaded by the amount of publicity his deception was attracting. Consequently the five conspirators decided it was wiser to keep their little secret among themselves. Wilson, the alleged photographer, gave only one interview, in 1956, and remained wary of saying that he believed the picture showed the monster. He had also been warned by the medical authorities that the publicity was bringing his profession into disrepute.

So it stayed until 1993 by which time all of the protagonists with the exception of Spurling were dead. Then two Loch Ness researchers, David Martin and Alastair Boyd, unearthed a press cutting from 1975 in which Ian Wetherell had said that the Surgeon's Photograph was a hoax perpetrated by his father. The claim was largely ignored at the time, but the two researchers were intrigued by certain aspects of the story, including the mention of Maurice Chambers. The man who had supposedly been present with Wilson at Loch Ness was now also revealed as a friend of Marmaduke Wetherell. Moreover Ian Wetherell stated that the photograph featured scenery of Loch Ness. The only picture that had ever appeared in the newspapers had been cropped to eliminate all background landmarks but Boyd himself had located the original uncropped version in the late 1980s and had seen the shoreline in the background. Boyd said of Ian Wetherell: 'Either he had a very long memory, or he took the picture.'

The pair managed to track down 90-year-old Christian Spurling who finally admitted that the famous photograph, which had sustained monster believers for so long, was nothing more than a hoax. Marmaduke Wetherell had enjoyed the last laugh on his detractors.

But, as the locals will tell you, just because one sighting of 'Nessie' has been proved to be a hoax, it doesn't mean that some of the others aren't genuine. After all, there are hotel rooms to be filled . . .

Mr Griffin's Mermaid

As a showman, Phineas Taylor Barnum was in a league of his own. He never allowed the truth to get in the way of a good story and possessed an instinctive feel for what would persuade the American public to part with their money. His speciality was the freak show. No freak was ever too freaky to appear in a Barnum line-up. Giants, dwarfs, bearded women, 161-year-old women; they were all integral parts of any Barnum spectacular. But arguably his most famous exhibit was the Fejee Mermaid – half monkey, half fish, and wholly profitable.

Mermaids had been exhibited in museums, taverns and fairs since the eighteenth century, and never failed to draw the crowds. In 1822 a Captain Eades of Boston, Massachusetts, brought one such creature – said to be part orang-utan and part salmon – to London and displayed it with some success in the West End. Eades had apparently acquired his mermaid in Calcutta, misappropriating $6,000 of his ship's money to purchase it in the belief that it would make him rich. However, after the initial surge of interest, he was obliged to go back to sea in order to pay off the money he had embezzled. Despite the misgivings of most zoologists, Eades never ceased to believe in the mermaid's authenticity. He valued it above everything else and when he died, it was said to be his sole possession. His son was less sentimental and sold it cheaply to a gentleman by the name of Moses Kimball who, in the summer of 1842, took it to New York to show Barnum. The mermaid was scarcely an object of beauty. Barnum noted: 'The animal was an ugly, dried-up, black-looking, and diminutive specimen, about three feet long. Its mouth was open, its tail turned over, and its arms thrown up, giving it the appearance of having died in great agony.'

Kimball was keen to share the profits with Barnum who, while intrigued by the possibilities the mermaid offered, decided to consult a naturalist before committing himself to any financial outlay. The naturalist replied, wrote Barnum, 'that he could not conceive how it was manufactured; for he never knew a monkey with such peculiar teeth, arms, hand, etc., nor had he knowledge of a fish with such peculiar fins.' So Barnum asked him why he thought it was manufactured. 'Because I don't believe in mermaids,' answered the naturalist. 'That is no reason at all,' said Barnum, 'and therefore I'll believe in the mermaid, and hire it.'

On 18 June 1842 Barnum and Kimball entered into partnership.

Barnum agreed to lease the mermaid for $12.50 a week (for a maximum period of 12 weeks) and to hire a manager for it (at no more than $8 a week, or a quarter of the net profits). At the end of this period Kimball was to have the opportunity of exhibiting it for up to 12 weeks in Boston and the nearby town of Lowell. Depending on how popular an attraction the mermaid proved, the respective managers would then share expenses and profits for up to two years while exhibiting it throughout the United States. Barnum promised to spare no expense in exhibiting it before the public and to 'take all proper and possible care of said curiosity and not allow it to be handled or in any manner injured or abused.' Barnum already had a manager in mind for his mermaid – an old accomplice called Levi Lyman who had helped promote one of Barnum's most profitable freaks, Joice Heth, 'the 161-year-old woman'.

With the agreement signed, the redoubtable Barnum publicity machine swung into action. His ingenuity in overdrive, he composed fake communications from correspondents in distant cities such as Montgomery, Alabama, and Charleston, South Carolina, and mailed them to various New York newspapers. To all intents and purposes these bulletins were genuine, containing as they did the type of stories one would expect to find in a local paper – crop updates, commercial news and political minutiae. But each letter also mentioned, almost casually, a certain Dr J. Griffin, British naturalist and agent for the Lyceum of Natural History in London. The paragraph reported that Dr Griffin, who was travelling through America on his way back to England, had with him 'a veritable mermaid', which he had just procured from the Fejee (Fiji) Islands.

As anticipated, the New York newspapers took the bait. Editors had no reason to doubt the authenticity of the letters since Barnum had gone to the trouble of asking friends in the relevant cities to post them, thereby ensuring that the postmarks were correct. Barnum later admitted: 'The corresponding postmarks did much to prevent suspicion of a hoax, and the New York editors thus unconsciously contributed to my arrangements for bringing the mermaid into public notice.'

With Dr Griffin continuing his journey up the east coast, a third letter was posted, from Washington, expressing the hope that editors might request a viewing of the curiosity before it returned to England. Their chance came when Griffin (alias Levi Lyman) arrived in Philadelphia and booked into a smart hotel. Before checking out, he invited the landlord to his room and showed him the mermaid. The landlord was so impressed with what he saw that he begged to be allowed to show it to his friends, among whom were several editors. Griffin had no intention of refusing the request.

By the time the doctor and his prized possession had reached New York, Barnum's craftily planned operation had aroused considerable interest in the mermaid. The supreme showman then put the next stage of his plan into operation, 'getting up woodcuts and transparencies, as well as a pamphlet, proving the authenticity of mermaids, all in speedy anticipation of Dr Griffin's specimen.' Barnum had at least four different woodcuts made of the mermaid, together with a written description, and took them round to the editors of the *New York Herald* and two Sunday papers. He explained sadly that he had commissioned the engravings with a view to using them in conjunction with an exhibition of the mermaid but had since been informed by Dr Griffin that the Lyceum of Natural History would not permit such an exhibition to take place in America. Barnum now said that, as a gesture of goodwill, he was allowing each editor to publish the engravings as an exclusive, free of charge, in next Sunday's paper. On Sunday 17 July 1842, each editor, convinced that he had an exclusive, printed the woodcut. Barnum wasted no time in capitalizing on his publicity coup and distributed 10,000 copies of the pamphlet throughout New York. With the populace clamouring for a glimpse of the oddity, Dr Griffin yielded to pressure and agreed to the mermaid and other curiosities being exhibited at Concert Hall on Broadway for one week only, commencing 8 August.

'THE MERMAID, AND OTHER WONDERFUL SPECIMENS OF THE ANIMAL CREATION' blared the newspaper notices, heralding an exhibition that also featured other apparent hybrids such as the duck-billed platypus and the flying fish. Vast crowds paid 25 cents a head to see the exhibits, encouraged, no doubt, by Barnum's inaccurate engravings of the mermaid, which depicted her as having the body of a beautiful, willowy woman. The truth, as the public soon found out, was that she looked more like a withered monkey. One critic went so far as to describe the mermaid as the 'incarnation of ugliness'.

Nevertheless most people were happy just to gawp at the creature and listen to Lyman's inventive lecture on the origins of such scientific oddities. The only hint of sacrilege occurred while Lyman was momentarily out of the room and a group of medical students lifted the glass bell protecting the mermaid and inserted a partially consumed cigar into its mouth. For once even Lyman was lost for words.

At the conclusion of the week-long engagement, the mermaid transferred to the American Museum, which had recently come under

Barnum's proprietorship, for another month. The museum's takings promptly rose three-fold as the crowds were lured inside by an enormous flag depicting an 18 ft mermaid. However, Lyman warned that the flag was taking exaggeration a little too far, and Barnum took down the flag after just a few days. In the face of an increasing number of sceptics, Barnum uncharacteristically began to tone down the advertising, proposing to Kimball that in future the mermaid should be presented as 'positively asserted by its owner to have been taken alive in the Fejee Islands, and implicitly believed by many scientific persons, while it is pronounced by other scientific persons to be an *artificial* production, and its natural existence claimed by them to be an utter impossibility. The manager can only say that it possesses as much *appearance of reality* as any fish lying on the stalls of our fish markets – but who is to decide when *doctors* disagree? At all events, whether this production is the work of *nature or art*, it is *decidedly* the most stupendous curiosity ever submitted to the public for inspection. If it is artificial, the senses of sight and touch are useless, for *art* has rendered them totally ineffectual. If it is natural, then all *concur* in declaring it THE GREATEST CURIOSITY IN THE WORLD.'

Barnum's new-found caution may have arisen from a stormy southern tour made by his uncle, Alanson Taylor, early in 1843. Taylor had replaced Lyman as the mermaid's exhibitor and had been doing excellent business until reaching Charleston. There he fell foul of a local naturalist and Lutheran minister, John Bachman, who wrote to the two principal local newspapers, the *Courier* and the *Mercury*, denouncing the mermaid as a fraud. Writing under the pseudonym 'No Humbug', Bachman further claimed that the whole scam was designed to extort money from a deceived public and enlisted the support of several distinguished Charleston scientists. Their opinion was that the mermaid was simply the body of a monkey clumsily sewn together to the tail of a fish. To illustrate their point, they observed that the creature possessed two chests and two abdomens.

With the help of Richard Yeadon, editor of the *Courier*, Taylor tried to fight back, but found that the odds against him were overwhelming. To prevent the mermaid being made into 'mince meat', it was secretly shipped back to New York. Barnum wrote solemnly to Kimball that 'the bubble has burst.' Barnum briefly entertained the idea of suing Bachman for libel and hiring Yeadon as an attorney, but the editor pointed out that he could only be confident of success if the mermaid was 'a genuine specimen.' So that was that.

The Fejee Mermaid was left to gather dust for the next couple of years until Kimball decided to resurrect both it and Dr Griffin. Lyman, who had been touring with a painting of *Christ and the Last Supper*, reprised his earlier role but the venture was short-lived. Barnum briefly lifted the mermaid out of mothballs to display it at his museum on April Fool's Day, 1855, and later took it to England to illustrate a series of lectures. It was treated there as an object of fun, and Barnum himself no longer made any attempt to pass it off as genuine. The English loved it, not least because it had fooled so many of their American cousins.

Alas, the original mermaid is thought to have been destroyed when Barnum's museum burned down in the 1860s. It was a sad day for the great impresario. Right to the end, the Fejee Mermaid occupied a place close to Barnum's heart – the space usually reserved for his wallet.

Cathouse For Dogs

'Cathouse for Dogs' began a 1976 advertisement in New York's *Village Voice* newspaper, 'featuring a savory selection of hot bitches . . . ' The ad invited any proud dog owner to reward his 'best friend' by getting him laid for just $50.

An accompanying press release sent to the media expanded upon the theme, suggesting that any owner whose dog had just graduated from obedience school, was having a birthday, or was just feeling horny, could enjoy sexual gratification with the female of his choice. This was not a breeding service, the release added, but one designed purely for canine sexual pleasure. However, unbeknown to the journalists and TV reporters, behind the crazy concept of New York's first brothel for dogs lay a face who would become all too familiar in years to come – arch prankster Joey Skaggs.

With Skaggs manning the contact number in the guise of doggie pimp, the phone rang non-stop. The advert not only attracted plenty of customers willing to pay $50 to please their pet, but also a fair proportion of weirdos who wanted to have sex with dogs or simply watch dogs having sex. Soon the newshounds got scent of the story whereupon Skaggs hired 25 actors and 15 dogs to create a bordello atmosphere in a Greenwich Village loft. Models posed with female dogs in look-alike outfits while the actors paraded with the male dogs waiting to view the bitches. A Skaggs associate, Tony Barsha, was on hand as a bogus veterinarian who told reporters that the female dogs were injected with a drug called Estro-dial, which would artificially induce a state of heat. He added that if a bitch were already naturally on heat, she would be given a contraceptive, Ovaban. Puppies were not the name of the game.

After listening to a lecture on the techniques of dog copulation, customers were asked to fill in a questionnaire about their male dog's age, medical history, and, most importantly, bitch preferences. A staff photographer was on hand to snap a memento of each passionate pooch's encounter, and a dog groomer stood by to brush the animals before and after sex. And all the while hostesses quietly served cocktails to the humans.

Among the media present at that inaugural event was a video crew from *Midnight Blue*, New York's first late night cable TV sex show. Hitherto believing they had shot every kind of sexual perversion known to man, the crew were blown away by the sight of female dogs being humped by male dogs for money. The cameramen even got down on all fours at one point to film the activity from the dogs' perspective.

The story received so much coverage that it alerted WABC TV who wanted to do a documentary on the Cathouse. Skaggs protested that harassment from the authorities had forced him to go underground, and he refused to take WABC to the facility. But he said he was willing to let the station have a copy of a video that had been shot at the Cathouse. Skaggs then got in touch with Alex Bennett, producer of *Midnight Blue*, let him in on the hoax and procured the tape for WABC.

The WABC programme portrayed proprietor Skaggs as a low-life exploiting innocent dogs for money. Even more organizations were now hot on Skaggs's tail, including the ASPCA, the Mayor's Office, the Bureau of Animal Affairs, and the NYPD vice squad. Eventually Skaggs was served with a subpoena by the Attorney General's office.

His response was to call a press conference at the Attorney General's office on, naturally enough, 1 April, when he confessed that the brothel for dogs had been a wind-up. It is said that WABC never retracted the story, partly because the producer of the documentary maintained that Skaggs had only said it was a hoax to avoid prosecution and partly because its hard-hitting exposé, having been nominated for a prestigious Emmy Award, had now been disqualified from entry.

A Tale of Two Serpents

New Yorkers fed on a steady diet of P.T. Barnum's imaginative curiosities had a new 'scientific sensation' to feast upon in 1845 when German archaeologist Albert Koch unveiled the 114 ft-long skeleton of what he claimed was an extinct marine reptile. Visitors to Broadway's Apollo Saloon were charged 25 cents each to view the monster, which Koch said he had dug up on an expedition to Alabama. With its slender body, undulating backbone, and head in a threateningly reared pose, it looked uncannily like the type of legendary sea serpent that had reportedly been seen in American waters for centuries. Koch gave it the Latin name *Hydrarchos sillimannii*, supposedly in honour of Professor Benjamin Silliman who had recognized the existence of sea serpents in 1827. But the suffix could just as easily have applied to anyone daft enough to have been taken in by Koch's creation.

From the outset it would appear that Koch set out to exploit the public's vague belief in the existence of sea serpents. For the exhibition he mounted the creature on stilts and deliberately arranged the head in that raised position so that it resembled the fabled images of menacing monsters of the deep. He claimed to have found all the bones in the ground together but his story was blown apart by anatomist Jeffries Wyman who, on visiting Koch's show, immediately denounced the exhibit as a fraud. Wyman pointed out that its teeth had the double roots characteristic of mammals but not of reptiles and proceeded to demonstrate that the skeleton, far from being a single creature, was actually a composite of several specimens of an extinct whale called the Basilosaurus or zeuglodon. A typical zeuglodon measured only 40 ft long; Koch had simply joined a few bits and pieces together.

When the truth emerged, Professor Silliman refused to have his name associated with such a blatant fake, but Koch was not about to give up without a fight and merely changed the beast's Latin name to *Hydrarchos harlani* after zoologist Dr Richard Harlan who had been involved in research on the zeuglodon.

In disgust at his treatment by American scientists, Koch packed his bags and took his serpent to Europe where he exhibited it with some success, particularly in his native country. In 1848, while it was still being exhibited to sizeable crowds, English palaeontologist Gideon Algernon Mantell wrote to the editor of the *Illustrated London News* to dismiss Koch's sea serpent as a hoax. Mantell revealed that it was not Koch's first attempt at a composite giant. 'Mr Koch,' he wrote, 'is the person who, a few years ago, had a fine collection of fossil bones of elephants and Mastodons, out of which he made up an enormous skeleton, and exhibited it in the Egyptian Hall, Piccadilly, under the name of *Missourium*. This collection was purchased by the trustees of the British Museum, and from it were selected the bones which now constitute the matchless skeleton of a Mastodon in our National Gallery of Organic Remains.

'Not content with the interest which the fossils which he collected in various parts of the United States really possess, Mr Koch, with the view of exciting the curiosity of the ignorant multitude, strung together all the vertebrae he could obtain of the *Basilosaurus*, and arranged them in a serpentine form; manufactured a skull and claws, and exhibited the monster as a fossil Sea-Serpent. But the trick was immediately exposed by the American naturalists, and the true nature of the fossil bones pointed out.'

There was no hiding place for Albert Koch; he had become a laughing stock on both sides of the Atlantic.

Despite Koch's exposure, American enthusiasm for sea serpents showed no sign of diminishing. Every state had to have one. Among the most enduring is the sea serpent of Silver Lake, which is honoured to this day by an annual Sea Serpent Festival in the nearby town of Perry.

Situated some 50 miles south of Buffalo in Wyoming County, New York, back in 1855 Perry was a sleepy town in desperate need of an image, something to put it on the map. Its prayers were answered on the night of 13 July that year when two boys and five men went out fishing from a boat on Silver Lake. After watching a floating log for several minutes, one of the party exclaimed in disbelief: 'Boys, that thing is moving!' According to the eyewitness reports published in the *Wyoming Times*, the shape disappeared beneath the surface for a while and then, all of a sudden, 'the serpent, for now there was no mistaking its character, darted from the water about four feet from the stern of the boat, close by the rudder-paddle, the head and forward part of the monster rising above the surface of the water . . . All in the boat had a fair view of the creature, and concur in representing it as a most horrid and repulsive-looking monster.'

The terrifying serpent appeared on a regular basis throughout the summer, manifesting itself to fishermen, residents and visitors alike. This prompted the *Wyoming Times* to conclude that 'the existence of the monster of the fish of serpent species in the quiet waters of Silver Lake was established beyond reasonable doubt.'

The arrival of the serpent provoked a mixed reaction. Locals were concerned for the safety of their families and a vigilance group armed with guns patrolled the shore of the lake. A tower was built at the north end to obtain a better vantage point for sighting the serpent. Serious attempts were made to trap or kill the beast, ranging from a solitary whale hunter with a harpoon to a company who put together the sum of $1,000 for the monster's capture. The Silver Lake Serpent had a price on its head. By contrast, the town's tradesmen had never had it so good. Hotels and restaurants were bursting at the seams as tourists flocked to the town by carriage, on horseback, or on foot, in the hope of catching a glimpse of the hideous green creature.

As monster mania swept through Perry, the descriptions of the beast grew ever more graphic, and newspapers carried fanciful stories about its capture. The *Chicago Times* reported that two visitors to the area had seen the serpent harpooned and towed to shore. The article added that at nightfall the creature had uprooted the tree to which it was tethered and returned to the lake. It was recaptured the following day, continued the *Times*, whereupon it 'awoke, threw its head 60 feet into the air; lurid eyes glared like balls of flame and its tongue, like flashes of forked lightning, 10–12 feet long, vibrated between its open jaws.'

By the end of the year the excitement had subsided. The tourists had gone and so, it appeared, had the serpent. Then in 1857 a fire broke out at the town's Walker Hotel. Firemen rushed to the scene to put out the blaze. They fought their way through the flames up into the attic where, to their astonishment, they discovered a great green serpent made of canvas and coiled wire.

The Walker in question was hotelier Artemus B. Walker who, together with a small group of local businessmen, came up with the idea of constructing a huge serpent in order to attract much-needed visitors to the town. Working chiefly at night so as to avoid detection, the conspirators built a 60 ft-long body, covered with a waterproof canvas and supported on the inside by coiled wire. It was to be operated from the shore by means of a large pair of bellows, connected to the serpent by a length of rubber hose. A 1915 account by local historian Frank D. Roberts revealed: 'The body was to be painted a deep green colour, with bright yellow spots added to give it a more hideous appearance. Eyes and mouth were to be coloured a bright red. The plan of manipulating the serpent was simple. It was to be taken out and sunk in the lake, and then when everything was ready, the bellows were to be operated and air forced into the serpent, which naturally would cause it to rise to the surface. Weights were to be attached to different portions of the body to insure its sinking as the air was allowed to escape.' Three ropes were attached to the forward section of the serpent's body, each rope connected to land in a different direction so that the monster could be moved around at will.

With construction complete, the mighty serpent was transported to the lake under cover of darkness and sunk to a depth of around 20 feet. When it was finally activated on Friday 13 July, it was undoubtedly bad luck for the fishing boat party who were given the fright of their lives. It seems that after the initial wave of tourists had been lured to the town, Walker and his associates decided to lie low for a while, partly through fear of discovery but also because they calculated that the sudden reappearance of the monster a few years later would spark even greater excitement and, with it, a new influx of visitors. However, the fire at his hotel scuppered his plans and forced him to take refuge in Canada until the heat was off.

Today everyone shares in the joke as the people of Perry parade all manner of inflated sea serpents through town. There are even hot-air balloons in the shape of creatures of the deep. And while there may not actually have been any sea serpents in Perry in 1855, hot air was one commodity that was definitely not in short supply.

The Rhinoceros of Lake Beebee

As an undergraduate at Cornell University, New York State, in the 1920s, Hugh Troy was a compulsive practical joker. One of his favourite jokes was played on a professor who frequently left his galoshes outside the classroom door during lectures. At an opportune moment Troy would sneak out and paint them to look like feet before covering them with soot to restore their black colour. When the professor walked in the rain, the soot would wash away so that it appeared as if he was walking barefoot.

The pleasure Troy derived from such a harmless prank led him to aspire to greater things, notably a hoax that was to become the talk of the campus. One winter he noticed that a friend owned a waste-paper basket shaped as the foot of a rhinoceros. Together with a classmate, Troy filled the basket with metal to give it weight and attached a clothes line to both sides. Then the pair stepped out into the Arctic night and, standing some 30 feet away on either side of the basket, gently raised and lowered the line so that animal tracks were left in the snow without any human ones. They continued this delicate manoeuvre down to the shores of Lake Beebee and out on to the thick ice where, about 50 feet from the edge, there was a huge hole in the ice. The rhinoceros footprints suggested that the animal had wandered down to the lake and out on to the ice before falling through it and drowning.

When the tracks were discovered the following morning, there was considerable concern. Lake Beebee was the source of Cornell's water supply and many students stopped drinking the water for fear that it would be contaminated by a dead rhino. Much to Troy's amusement, some learned scholars stated categorically that the water subsequently had a distinct taste of rhinoceros to it! Other sturdier souls waited impatiently for the ice to melt so that they could start dredging for the animal's body. The story even appeared in a local paper despite the fact that a check of all the zoos in the north-east of the United States had failed to reveal a missing rhino. With hysteria at a peak, Troy put everyone out of their misery by revealing anonymously in writing how the hoax had been carried out.

Troy, who had carried out his first hoax at the age of 14 when getting a fake poem published in the *New York Times*, went on to enjoy a fruitful career as an artist and illustrator. Wearing his artist's hat, he perpetrated an ingenious hoax while New York's Museum of Modern Art was staging an eagerly awaited Van Gogh exhibition. Unable to see the paintings because of the crowds, he went home and carved an ear out of a piece of dried beef. He mounted it in a velvet-lined box and typed out a note saying that this was the ear which Van Gogh had cut off. He then smuggled the ear and the note into the museum and hung it on a wall. As the sightseers immediately crowded around the new exhibit, Troy was left to enjoy the paintings in relative peace.

It took more than an international conflict to dent Troy's enthusiasm for pranks. During the Second World War he found his officer training hampered by the vast amount of paperwork involved. As a form of protest he invented a 'flypaper report' which he sent to the Pentagon on a daily basis to inform the authorities of the number of flies supposedly trapped on coded flypaper ribbons that were hanging in the mess hall. It did not take long for someone in Washington to question why other officers were not sending in their flypaper reports. Some of Troy's fellow officers began to conclude that they had been neglecting their duties, and one day two men from another unit confided to him that they were in trouble for not sending in their flypaper reports. They asked him if he knew what these curious reports were. 'Certainly,' he replied. 'I send mine in every day.' Hearing this, they protested that they had never been provided with the necessary forms whereupon Troy supplied them with the appropriate paperwork and they dutifully filled the forms in before sending them off to Washington. It is not known whether the Pentagon ever realized it was the victim of a hoax.

Waterton's Nondescript

Naturalist Charles Waterton is often portrayed as the archetypal English eccentric – a man who loved animals so much that he started imitating their behaviour. Guests arriving at his home, Walton Hall in West Yorkshire, would frequently find him lurking in the hallway on all fours. Then, as they hung up their cloaks, he would growl and nip them in the shin! However, even that must have been preferable to his behaviour at one dinner party where he rounded off the meal by dissecting a gorilla on the dining-room table.

Waterton was also an energetic traveller who undertook a series of expeditions to Guiana on which he observed the wonders of South

American wildlife. He was the first to record a detailed account of the slovenly lifestyle of sloths and to bring curare to Europe, having witnessed its medicinal use in the field. The book of his travels, *Wanderings in South America*, contained many examples of his typically unorthodox approach – how he rode a reluctant cayman (a South American crocodile) for several minutes and how he deliberately left a toe exposed from his hammock night after night in the hope of attracting vampire bats.

The Squire of Walton Hall, as he was known, was a keen exponent of the art of taxidermy and invariably returned from his journeys with hundreds of stuffed specimens. Such was the case when his boat docked at Liverpool in 1821 following one of his trips to Guiana, only on this occasion Waterton was in for a nasty surprise. Customs officials boarded the boat and informed him that new legislation, introduced that year, meant that he would have to pay a 20 per cent duty on all animals imported into Britain that were intended for his own or any other private collection. Waterton asked to see proof of their powers and was shown a letter signed by the Secretary to the Treasury. His name was J. R. Lushington.

There were few grey areas in Waterton's life; most things were firmly divided into loves or hates. Things that he detested included Protestants, Hanoverians, rats (the presence of which in England he blamed on Protestant Hanoverians), and, towards the end of his life, Charles Darwin. But for the moment J. R. Lushington was top of his list.

Waterton was particularly aggrieved by the high-handed tone of Lushington's letter, the perceived injustice compounded by the animal collection's prolonged detention at the Custom House while Waterton argued his case. This prevented Waterton from being able to further his study of taxidermy. The result was immense frustration and a desire for revenge.

Three years later Waterton set off on a fourth expedition to Guiana, this time returning with a fabulous specimen, which was unlike anything hitherto known to Man. Waterton labelled it the 'Nondescript' and loosely recounted its origins in *Wanderings in South America*. He wrote that, in the wilds of Guiana, he had procured an animal 'which has caused not a little speculation and astonishment. In my opinion, his thick coat of hair, and great length of tail, put his species out of all question; but then his face and head cause the inspector to pause for a moment, before he ventures to pronounce his opinion of the classification. He was a large animal, and as I was pressed for daylight, and moreover, felt no inclination to have the whole weight of his body upon my back, I contented myself with his head and shoulders, which I cut off; and have brought them with me to Europe . . . The features of the animal are quite of the Grecian cast; and he has a placidity of countenance which shows that things went well with him in life.' Waterton added that local tribes called the species the Itouli, pronounced 'I too lie'. The clues were there.

A drawing of the head and shoulders of the curiosity appeared on the frontispiece to the *Wanderings*. It seemed to have the body of an ape but the face of a human. Naturalists were suitably puzzled. Most concluded that it was human and Waterton was criticized for killing natives in order to demonstrate his skill in preserving their skins. When a letter was printed in the *Magazine of Natural History* calling into question Waterton's account of how he had come by the Nondescript, Waterton felt obliged to join the debate. His reply was deliberately vague. He said that he had intended to publish the details of his discoveries in the book but decided against it following the earlier impounding of his collection by customs officials. Instead he chose to illustrate the Nondescript on the frontispiece 'calculating that its appearance would give rise to much investigation by naturalists, especially by those who are connected with museums . . . My sole object has been to leave the thing in absolute doubt; and I have no wish whatever that it should pass for any other thing than that which the reader himself may wish it to pass for. Not considering myself anywise pledged to its identity, I leave it entirely to the reader's own penetration to say what it is or what it is not . . . I intentionally enveloped it in mystery on account of the illiberality of the British Treasury.'

The mystery lingered on for the remainder of Waterton's life. After Darwin had published *On the Origin of Species* in 1859, Waterton tried to claim that his Nondescript was the much talked about missing link in the evolution of Man from apes, but nobody took him seriously. It simply appeared to be an attempt to discredit Darwin, whom he held in high contempt. The remarkable Waterton died six years later (he had still been able to climb trees up to the age of 80) and, after his death, his friend and biographer, Revd J. G. Wood, threw some light on to the origins of the Nondescript. Revd Wood revealed that this 'wonderful specimen of Waterton's skill in taxidermy is formed from the head and shoulders of the Red Howler monkey. In manipulating it, Waterton has so modelled the skin that he has discharged from the face every vestige of the original features, and has substituted those of a man, grotesque enough, but still human. As bare skin becomes black when dry, the contrast of the black face with the fiery red hair has a very striking effect and adds to the resemblance.' Wood added that the difference in facial angles of a Red Howler monkey and that of a man made Waterton's task a most difficult one. He wrote that the preparation of the head would have been impossible 'if the skull, or any part of it, had been allowed to remain, and the really wonderful feat could only be performed by Waterton's system of removing the whole of the bones and having drawn all the bare skin until it was no thicker than ordinary writing paper.'

So the Nondescript was an elaborate joke, made in Britain rather than captured in Guiana. But what was the purpose behind its creation? It was not until the twentieth century that another Waterton biographer, Richard Aldington, was able to be more specific about the identity of the Nondescript. He stated categorically that the face was a caricature of Waterton's old adversary, J. R. Lushington, and cited as proof Waterton's sniping about Treasury illiberality. The suggestion that Lushington was the model for the Nondescript had been put to Waterton after the publication of the *Wanderings*. He had later denied it – in his usual enigmatic manner – but Aldington wrote: 'The way the denial is made in the 1837 edition of the *First Series of Essays* is such as to suggest the very thing the writer pretends to deny.'

It would appear, therefore, that Waterton had finally succeeded in making a monkey out of the man from the Treasury.

The Giant Penguin of Florida

Florida car dealer Tony Signorini and his pal Al Williams enjoyed nothing more than a good laugh. So when they saw a series of photographs of fossilized dinosaur tracks, they decided to try and baffle experts and local residents alike by creating their very own three-toed giant.

They began by getting a pair of heavy iron three-toed feet (each weighing around 30 lb) cast at a local foundry. In February 1948 the two pranksters, starting from a boat offshore near the town of Clearwater, West Florida, used their metal claws to make a trail of footprints that emerged from the sea, ran along the beach for two miles, and then disappeared back into the water. They removed any trace of their own presence by brushing away their footprints with a palm frond. The prints – 14 inches long and 11 inches wide – were found again on nearby beaches in March and April of that year. Then in October they moved their creation 40 miles up the Suwannee River to a point known as Suwannee Gables. This time operating from a car, they left tracks which suggested that the creature had swum inland from the coast.

Ivan T. Sanderson, an English zoologist and founder of the Society for the Investigation of the Unexplained, was asked to examine the Suwannee Gables tracks by New York radio station WNBC. Sanderson was excited by the find, noting that the tracks definitely indicated toe movement and therefore could not have been made by mechanical means. Flying overhead in a plane, Sanderson spotted 'an enormous dirty-yellow creature' on the surface of the Suwannee River. He estimated that the beast was 20 ft long and 8 ft wide, and came to the conclusion that it was a giant, three-toed penguin.

Certain he was on to something big, Sanderson set about tracking down other people who had seen the mystery creature. Two pilots came forward to say that they had seen a strange animal swimming in the sea off Hog Island on 25 July. They described it as being some 15 ft long with a 'very hairy body, a heavy blunt head and back legs like an alligator.' And the following month a Wisconsin couple reported that they had observed a neckless furry beast with a 'head like a rhinoceros', arms like flippers, and 'short, thick legs and huge feet' emerging from the bushes on an offshore island and waddling down to the sea.

The sightings, together with Sanderson's expert appraisal, made the locals wonder whether perhaps something strange was afoot in the vicinity and the giant penguin became part of Florida folklore. Then in June 1988 the *St Petersburg Times* solved the mystery of the tracks by printing Tony Signorini's full confession. He even produced the foot as cast iron evidence.

Yet the riddle of the various sightings remained. Did some oddity lurk off the coast of Florida back in 1948 or was it simply a case of over-active imaginations coming up with a creature to fit the tracks? Or were the witnesses hoaxers too? The truth is out there.

In Search of the Reetsa

Captains of industry are rarely associated with playing practical jokes but Brian G. Hughes was a notable exception. New York paper-box manufacturer and founder of the city's Dollar Savings Bank, the wealthy Hughes loved to spend his money on pranks calculated to deflate pomposity.

On one occasion he appeared before the Board of Aldermen to announce his desire to donate a plot of ground in Brooklyn as a public park. After accepting the generous offer and extending gracious thanks, the board appointed a committee to inspect its acquisition. On arriving at the location near Sixth Avenue and 63rd Street, the committee discovered that the proposed park was to be built on nothing more than an 8 ft by 2 ft concrete rectangle which Hughes had bought for just $35. In similar vein, he contacted a number of historical societies offering a mansion which Lafayette had supposedly occupied during the Revolutionary War. It turned out to be a derelict shack, inhabited by tramps, at 147th Street and Concord Avenue in the Bronx.

One of his favourite tricks was to leave expensive umbrellas unattended in public places. He then watched as thieves picked up the umbrellas and opened them, only to be showered with cards proclaiming 'This umbrella stolen from Brian G. Hughes'. He is credited with having been the first to drop a bag of imitation jewels outside Tiffany's and caused a huge security alert at the Metropolitan Museum of Art by deliberately leaving a set of burglar's tools and some empty picture frames on the doorstep.

Hughes also used to delight in buying alley cats or wagon horses, then cleaning them up and entering them in prestigious shows as pedigrees or thoroughbreds. He bought one alley cat for ten cents and made fools of some of the world's leading cat judges by entering it in a leading show as being of the famous Dublin Brindle breed named Nicodemus by Broomstick out of Dustpan by Sweeper. Amazingly, the carefully groomed feline won a first prize. He tried the same trick at a Madison Square Garden horse show. He'd bought a nag for $11.50 from the Metropolitan Street Railway Company, which was changing from horse to electric power. The animal could not be started until its rider, Miss Clara Hughes, jingled a little bell. He entered it as Orphan Puldeca ('Often Pulled a Car'), sire Metropolitan, dam Electricity, but confessed to the duplicity before the judges returned their official verdict. Whenever his mongrels won show awards, Hughes would produce bills of sale to prove their great value.

His longest-running hoax was one that kept naturalists and journalists on tenterhooks for over a year. He told the New York press that he was financing an expedition to South America to bring back the first reetsa to be viewed in the northern hemisphere. For the next 12 months he kept interest alive by leaking stories to the newspapers about his progress in tracking down the elusive reetsa. This little-known creature had previously managed to avoid capture by running backwards but finally the press reported excitedly that Hughes had succeeded in trapping one and was bringing it back by ship to New York. At the approach of the ship – hired by Hughes to pull into the docks for the occasion – thousands of onlookers lined the quayside in anticipation. The gangplank was put in position and Hughes tried to lead the animal down backwards, but it refused and had to be turned around. Necks were craned as the crowd tried to obtain the first glimpse of this curiosity. So imagine their disappointment when an ordinary steer was led down the gangplank. Hughes had conned them again, 'reetsa' being 'a steer' spelt backwards.

Brian G. Hughes died in 1924 at the age of 75. It was one thing he didn't fake.

The Jersey Devil

The myth of the ferocious, child-eating Jersey Devil dates back to around 1650. There are numerous legends relating to its origin, including one that suggests the Devil is the deformed son of a woman called Mother Leeds, but many of the so-called witnesses are agreed on a general description of the terrifying monster – that it is an animal hybrid with hooves, the bony structure of a horse's head, a body like a goat, claws, and bat-like wings which enable it to fly.

Like most Americans, Norman Jeffries, publicist for Philadelphia's Arch Street Museum and renowned hoaxer, was well aware of the stories about the Jersey Devil. So when the museum proprietor, T. F. Hopkins, admitted that it was in danger of closure unless Jeffries came up with something to boost attendances, the publicist decided that a captive Jersey Devil would be the ideal crowd-puller. In January 1906 he revitalized public interest in the legend by planting newspaper stories about fresh sightings of the Devil. Although frozen with fear, a New Jersey woman was apparently composed enough to describe 'the great wings, the frenzied countenances, half human and half animal, the long tail, the eleven feet, the deadly vapours which were exhaled in a mixture of fire and smoke.' That the same beast was reportedly seen in California on the same night might have aroused public suspicion had not aviation pioneer Samuel P. Longley helpfully asserted that the Devil's huge wings would permit it to fly from coast to coast in one night. As panic began to spread, Jeffries and his co-conspirator, the Arch Street Museum's animal trainer Jacob Hope, offered a $500 reward for the Devil's capture, claiming that it was a rare Australian vampire. Thus it was with some relief that readers learned that the Devil had finally been caught in Hunting Park, New Jersey, and chained to a tree. Jeffries proudly announced that he had arranged to have the creature exhibited at the Arch Street Museum.

The crowds flocked to the museum in such numbers that visitors were allowed only the briefest glimpse of the Devil. A curtain was opened, at which point the creature would lunge forward ferociously at the bars of its cage. Then the curtain was closed and a new audience brought in. That was all the paying customers saw, but it seemed enough to persuade them that they had just witnessed the legendary Jersey Devil. Apart from keeping the crowds on the move and therefore bringing in more revenue, there was, of course, an even more important reason for Jeffries not letting the public see the animal for longer than a few seconds. For his Jersey Devil was simply a kangaroo painted with green stripes, fitted with antlers, and with bronze wings attached to a harness made of rabbit skin. Its repeated attacks on spectators were the result of being prodded with a stick by a small boy hiding behind the cage.

Jeffries's publicity coup earned the museum a stay of execution, but he finally admitted the hoax to the *Philadelphia Record* in its issue of 8 December 1929.

The Society for Indecency to Naked Animals

While stuck in a traffic jam one day in 1958, American comedian Alan Abel watched two horses copulating in a nearby field. More to the point, he carefully studied the reactions of his fellow motorists who, no matter how hard they tried, found their gaze repeatedly drawn to the sex-crazed steeds. Many appeared downright embarrassed, judging the sight of animals mating in public to be an offence to morality. Abel quickly saw the comic potential in the situation and dreamed up an association dedicated to clothing all animals. He christened it the Society for Indecency to Naked Animals (SINA) and stated its goal as 'putting panties on pets, half-slips on cows, and Bermuda shorts on horses.' Under the presidency of one G. Clifford Prout Junior and with a slogan of 'Decency Today Means Morality Tomorrow', SINA began to wage war on naked animal flesh. It was to be a bigger cover-up than Watergate.

Abel originally saw SINA as the basis for a satirical short story but his submissions to several magazines were all rejected. Then while watching NBC's *Today* show in a Kansas hotel room and despairing over the quality of the guests, he came up with the idea of putting Prout on TV. In Prout's name he wrote to *Today* on hotel stationery, outlining the aims of SINA and revealing that he was fulfilling the desires of his late father, Clifford Prout Senior, whose dearest wish had been to see animals clothed. Meanwhile Abel had hired jobless actor Buck Henry to play Prout, and Henry made his debut as the moral guardian of beasts when Prout was duly invited to appear on *Today* in May 1959. Demanding that all animals over four inches high be clothed for the sake of decency, Prout begged his audience: 'Don't let your moral standards go lower and lower due to naked animals. It's a shocking situation, and I am spending every single minute of every day and every last dollar of my father's money to correct this evil.' He then asked rhetorically: 'Why do cows have their heads down in fields? Not because they're grazing, but because they're hanging their heads in shame.'

Prout's appearance really started the ball rolling and Abel furthered the cause by distributing thousands of SINA propaganda leaflets and hiring pickets to march back and forth outside the White House. He claimed that there were 55,000 SINA members. As enquiries flooded in, he set up a telephone answering service and rented a mail service with an address on New York's Fifth Avenue. Abel appointed himself SINA's vice-president (he was still relatively unknown as a comic and was thus able to pass undetected) and occasionally used a New York office to conduct interviews. When doing so, he decorated the walls with artwork done by a friend depicting farm animals and household pets with their sexual organs discreetly covered by clothing. For a photo session with *Life* magazine, Abel persuaded some more friends to bring along their dogs . . . suitably dressed, of course.

As SINA's profile increased so did its powers. The society managed to get a giant papier-mâché horse removed from the New York office of Northwest Orient Airlines when Prout complained that even a naked model horse was offensive. He received a fulsome apology from the company. His complaint about the HMV dog 'Nipper' was less successful, however. Abel drummed up more support via parades featuring the tone-deaf SINA Marching Band. 'It was horrible to hear and ridiculous to see,' admitted Abel, 'but because we were carrying the American flag and looking serious, everyone along the way applauded.'

Prout continued his work with missionary zeal, visiting parks and zoos and gaining ever more publicity. The *San Francisco Chronicle* ran a two-part feature on SINA including a photograph of Henry as Prout trying to put a pair of pants on a fawn at the city zoo. Newspaper editorials viewed SINA's prosperity as an indication that the United States was going crazy, but no matter how much they sniggered at the society's activities, they spectacularly failed to spot that the joke was really on them.

There were one or two close shaves. When Prout appeared on NBC Radio's *Dave Garroway Show* in June 1959, Garroway realized that it was a hoax but agreed to keep the secret. A Californian woman later offered SINA $40,000 and turned up at the office with her lawyer, ready to draw up the necessary paperwork. Abel knew that it would be fraudulent to accept such a donation and was also suspicious that it might have been a set-up, so he informed her that the society's rules forbade him to accept money from outsiders, and advised her to contribute to another charity instead. The woman stormed off, lawyer in tow. But the biggest threat to exposure was the Inland Revenue Service. Having read about the $400,000 that Proud said he had inherited from his father to set up SINA, the IRS wrote demanding back taxes on the inheritance money. Dissatisfied with the written replies, the IRS then decided to visit SINA's New York address and found it to be a broom cupboard. Realizing that the entire business was a harmless hoax, the IRS left Abel and Prout in peace.

The end finally came because Buck Henry's acting and writing career started to take off. He had just been hired as a writer on a CBS show when, as Prout, he was interviewed by Walter Cronkite on his CBS evening programme. Henry was recognized, and when he landed a part in a TV soap opera shortly afterwards, it was time for SINA's head to call a halt to television interviews. Abel and Henry had managed to keep up the pretence for three years, in the course of which some 40,000 letters had been delivered to their New York broom cupboard. Some correspondents called them cranks, but others were wholly supportive of the venture. Maybe it wasn't such a crazy idea after all.

Chapter 13

Art

The Real Eddie Burrup

Over recent decades the Australian arts world has seen a surge of interest in all things Aboriginal. Indigenous culture is currently very much in vogue with publishers and art gallery curators alike, but in 1997 two scandals broke which caused Australians to question whether or not these Aboriginal works are quite as genuine as they seem.

The previous year author Wanda Koolmatrie won the prestigious Dobbie Award for the best first book by a woman writer. The autobiographical *My Own Sweet Time* told how she had been kidnapped as a child in the South Australian outback and gave a revealing insight into Aboriginal hardships and the prejudices they encounter. The judges hailed Wanda as 'a distinctive voice in the growing genre of Aboriginal women's autobiography.' Wanda was an elusive figure. She did not collect her award – she was said to be overseas at the time – and was never available for interviews. Her publishers, Magabala Books, used to fend off the media by claiming that she was 'out in the bush, writing.' Not that they had ever met her either, but Bruce Sims, Magabala's publishing manager, was intent on meeting his star author before her second book hit the shelves. That was when, after two years of keeping up the pretence, the real Wanda Koolmatrie decided to come out of hiding. It came as quite a shock to those who had eulogized over her debut work to discover that not only was Wanda not an Aborigine, she wasn't even a woman. Instead 'she' was Leon Carmen, a 47-year-old white Sydney taxi driver who admitted that he didn't know any Aboriginal women. Carmen confessed all in a newspaper interview, saying that the hoax was designed to expose the prevailing atmosphere of political correctness in the Australian arts world. He complained: 'I can't get published, but Wanda can.'

The unmasking of Carmen created bitter recriminations, not least because it followed hot on the heels of the revelation that acclaimed Aboriginal artist Eddie Burrup was the alter ego of an 82-year-old white female painter, Elizabeth Durack.

Born to a wealthy family of Irish descent, Durack was raised in the far north of Western Australia where she immersed herself in the local Aboriginal culture. Settling in Perth, she blossomed as an artist and often illustrated books written by her sister, Dame Mary Durack. In the course of her career, Elizabeth Durack had 65 solo exhibitions, in Australia and overseas, and was one of the first white artists to adopt indigenous painting techniques. It was this fascination that led to the creation of Eddie Burrup.

Durack even invented a detailed biography of Burrup, which appeared on his own website. It said that he was born in 1915 at Yandeearra Station on the Yule River in the Pilbara region of Western Australia. From an early age he made drawings of native animals and station life and was encouraged in this field, first at convent school in Broome, and then while in jail in Fremantle. His intimate knowledge of the land led to him being invited to join a survey team mapping one of the new railway lines for the Pilbara iron ore development of the 1960s, but he then sustained serious injuries that left him with suspected brain damage. He eventually recovered and the compensation payment he received gave him greater independence and the desire to paint again.

Durack first painted as Burrup in 1994, signing his paintings in a childish scrawl and incorporating his trademark crab totem. Soon she was entering his works in Aboriginal art exhibitions. Burrup's first major showcase was in the 'Native Titled Now' exhibition at the Tandanya National Aboriginal Cultural Institute during the 1996 Adelaide Festival of Arts. After months negotiating with the Durack Gallery in Broome, Tandanya obtained three Burrup paintings to exhibit with the artist's notes alongside. It had been hoped that Burrup would put in an appearance at the exhibition, but he declined. Nor could the Durack Gallery provide a photograph because apparently Burrup was 'not comfortable' being photographed. Elizabeth Durack did attend the exhibition, however.

Burrup's paintings were part of an exhibition that critically explored indigenous influences and images in Australian visual art and were so well received that two of his paintings were selected for display at another Aboriginal exhibition, in Darwin, in October of that year.

With Burrup's fame spreading, Durack decided to 'out' herself in a March 1997 interview with *Art Monthly Australia*. She thought her intimate knowledge of Aboriginal people gave her the right to paint as one and felt that Eddie Burrup was building bridges between black and white. The Burrup persona, she said, had become important to her creative process and had freed her to paint as she wished. It had reached the point where she could not paint unless she was Eddie Burrup. 'Eddie is a real person,' she continued. 'Since working in direct unison with Eddie, I have experienced a feeling of tremendous happiness.'

Durack could scarcely have been prepared for the flak she was about to receive. She was accused of stealing indigenous culture and insulting Aboriginal people by her deception. Durack stood her ground, insisting that the spirit of Eddie Burrup had been channelled through her. 'Eddie Burrup is a compilation of several Aboriginal men,' she said, 'and I am astonished that it has hurt or offended anyone.'

Elizabeth Durack continued to paint as Eddie Burrup until two weeks before her death in May 2000 at the age of 84.

The Prisoner of Ibiza

For master art forger Elmyr de Hory it is the ultimate accolade. Over a quarter of a century after his death, his copies are in such demand that unscrupulous individuals have taken to painting fakes of his fakes. A genuine de Hory fake can fetch up to $25,000 so it is little wonder that an army of imitators are out in force.

Nobody knows exactly how many forgeries de Hory produced in his long career but the fact that he claimed to be able to paint a portrait in 45 minutes, draw a Modigliani in ten minutes and then immediately knock off a Matisse should give some idea as to the scale of his output. De Hory himself estimated the figure to be well in excess of 1,000.

Born in Hungary in 1911, de Hory grew up as part of a wealthy, cosmopolitan set for whom trips to Paris and Biarritz during 'the season' were very much the norm. He attended art school in Budapest, Munich and finally Paris, a city where, in the 1920s, the likes of Picasso, Matisse, Derain and Vlaminck were all part of café society. De Hory made a reasonable living selling his own paintings but at that stage money was of secondary importance to him since there was a plentiful supply from home. That all changed after the Second World War, however. Having survived a Nazi concentration camp by utilizing his talents as a portrait painter, he returned to Paris to find money in short supply. The seeds of his future success were sown in

1946 when a friend bought one of his drawings in the belief that it was a Picasso. It remains unclear whether the deception was intentional but the new horizons that were opened up were to change de Hory's life.

Although he would undoubtedly have preferred to pursue a legitimate career, the market for faking the masters proved more lucrative. He began by faking the styles of the Paris artists he had encountered in his youth. He maintained that he never actually copied other artists but produced work that they might have done. To de Hory it was of paramount importance that he was able to imitate an artist's technique down to the most delicate of nuances. For example, he observed that Matisse, while drawing, would often look up at the model, a habit which gave a slight hesitation to his line. So when doing a Matisse, de Hory always remembered to incorporate that tiny blip. De Hory later said that Picasso's early drawings were among the easiest to fake while the works of Cezanne, Braque and Monet were the most difficult.

De Hory spent most of the 1950s in the United States apart from a spell where he took refuge in Mexico to escape Federal charges. He sold his fakes to dealers in ten different US states, his success rate aided in no small part by his own demeanour. For his affluent upbringing gave him a definite air of plausibility and he was always able to drop a few names to smooth the transaction.

His most prolific – and profitable – period was yet to come, however. That began in the late fifties when he was spotted by Fernand Legros, an art middle-man. The pair went into partnership. De Hory, by then living on the island of Ibiza, was paid a salary to produce the work while Legros did all the selling. Between 1961 and 1967 they sold an estimated $60 million worth of oil paintings, watercolours and sketches. Their major customer was Texan oilman Algur H. Meadows who bought 32 works purportedly by such diverse artists as Dufy, Modigliani, Chagall, Gauguin and Degas. Meadows spent millions of dollars in adding these masterpieces to his collection . . . little knowing that de Hory painted each one.

Although de Hory was undeniably quick, the rapid turnaround eventually took its toll. He made the fatal mistake of hurrying the drying process on what was intended to be a 1906 Vlaminck with the result that the blue sky started to come away from the canvas shortly before the painting was due to be sold at auction in Paris. The French auctioneers could not help but be surprised that a supposedly 60-year-old painting was still wet.

The repeatedly duped Meadows had also finally become suspicious and by 1968 de Hory found himself languishing in Ibiza jail. The

Spanish authorities released him after two months but then expelled him from their country for one year on account of his being considered 'undesirable', due more to his reputation for being a flamboyant homosexual than a serial forger. In the meantime de Hory had sold his story to a fellow resident of Ibiza, a young American writer named Clifford Irving. Their collaboration, entitled *Fake!*, painted a colourful picture of de Hory's life, one during which, it is thought, he used as many as 100 pseudonyms. Yet it is difficult to distinguish truth from exaggeration in the text, particularly in view of the fact that a couple of years later Irving was responsible for one of the great literary hoaxes of the century when he received a $750,000 advance from New York publishers McGraw-Hill in return for the long-awaited authorized biography of Howard Hughes. Irving, who, like most of the Western world, had never met Hughes, gambled on the former Hollywood producer's obsession with anonymity. He said that Hughes had commissioned him to write an authorized biography but would not deal personally with the publishers. Hughes would only communicate with Irving. The plan might have succeeded had not Hughes, on learning about the forthcoming tome, broken the habit of a lifetime by going public to state that he had never met Clifford Irving. The bogus author was sentenced to 30 months in prison. The book was never published, but it is easy to see why Irving and de Hory were soul mates.

In the wake of his own exposure, de Hory lambasted art critics and experts who 'know more about fine words than fine art.' He went on: 'The dealers, the experts and the critics resent my talent because they don't want it shown how easily they can be fooled. I have tarnished the infallible image they rely upon for their fortunes.'

But strong words were not sufficient to keep the authorities at bay for much longer. Fernand Legros was extradited from Brazil to France in 1976 and duly sentenced to two years' imprisonment for swindling Algur Meadows. De Hory, too, was facing extradition to France and a lengthy term in prison. He had always vowed that he would rather kill himself than serve a jail sentence for his forgeries and in December 1976 he kept his promise by taking a fatal overdose of sleeping pills at his Ibiza home.

De Hory is now recognized as a genuine craftsman. His own creations were relatively moderate, but his forgeries were masterpieces. That is why visitors to art galleries will stand in front of a Modigliani fake and ask: 'Is that a real de Hory?' The old rogue would have been touched.

A Forgotten Artist

The several hundred artists, critics and dealers gathered at the Manhattan studio of pop artist Jeff Koons on 31 March 1998 represented the cream of the New York art world. They were attending a launch party for a new biography about the late Nat Tate who, most present agreed, was one of the most gifted yet sadly forgotten American artists of the twentieth century. A few days after they had exchanged memories of Tate and admired his all-too-brief contribution to American art, these same critics and dealers were horrified to learn that Nat Tate had never existed. Instead he was the creation of British novelist William Boyd, the fictitious artist's name being an amalgam of London's two leading galleries, the National and the Tate. Faces were as red as Van Gogh's *Field With Poppies*.

Tate first came to light in the April 1998 issue of the London-based magazine Modern Painters in which Boyd wrote an article promoting his forthcoming book, *Nat Tate: An American Artist, 1928–1960*. Boyd gave Tate, described as a second generation Abstract Expressionist, a tragic life in keeping with his perceived cult status. Born the illegitimate son of a housekeeper, Tate's obsession with a father who was thought to have drowned at sea fuelled the passion for bridges which would become so evident in the artist's most creative period. Indeed it was generally agreed (well, by Boyd anyway) that Tate's finest works were a series of drawings of bridges inspired by Hart Crane's famous poem 'The Bridge'. Boyd related how a meeting with Georges Braque in the autumn of 1959 seemed to drive Tate to despair, forcing him to question not only his value as an artist but also his very existence. He started to drink heavily and, a few months later, after destroying most of his work, he boarded the Staten Island ferry, removed his tweed coat, hat and scarf, and threw himself into the bay. His body was never found.

Anticipating queries about why nobody of any note seemed to own a Tate painting, Boyd wrote that Tate 'was one of those rare artists who did not need, and did not seek, the transformation of his painting into a valuable commodity to be bought and sold on the whim of a market and its marketers.' He made Tate a friend of Picasso and of museum founder Peggy Guggenheim with whom he enjoyed a torrid six-week virtual affair. Boyd's book quoted Guggenheim as saying that Tate was a great lover – 'almost in a class with Sam Beckett who had bad skin.'

For a short period Tate's drink-fuelled life and early death made him the toast of the New York art circle but he was soon forgotten. This was his rebirth.

Boyd made his creation all the more believable by inserting into the book cameo appearances by real art-world figures as well as a character from Boyd's other fiction. One passage ran: 'Gore Vidal met him (Tate) at this time and remembered him as an "essentially dignified drunk with nothing to say." Unlike most American painters, he was unverbal.' Vidal, who was in on the joke, contributed to the book's jacket, describing Tate mysteriously as 'an artist too well understood by his time.' The pictures in the book purportedly by Tate were actually drawn by Boyd while the photographs of the artist were of unknown subjects and had been collected over a period of years by Boyd from antique shops. The biography was published by a small Cambridge-based firm called 21 Publishing whose founders included David Bowie. The rock star was another contributor to the sleeve notes, observing in a deliberately pretentious manner that 'the great sadness of this quiet and moving monograph is that the artist's most profound dread – that God will make you an artist but only a mediocre artists – did not in retrospect apply to Nat Tate.' Fortunately none present at the launch were brave enough to ask Bowie what he meant.

Bowie's sombre reading of excerpts from the book was the highlight of the New York launch. The gathering at Jeff Koons's studio, which included artists such as Frank Stella and Julian Schnabel, listened intently as Bowie recounted details of Tate's sad life. Several pairs of eyes were seen misting over during the reading. Although Koons hosted the launch, he himself was not party to the secret. Most of the guests accepted Tate as genuine although they did concede that he was not particularly well known and did not have much of a reputation outside New York. However, several people at the party told Bernard Jacobsen, a London art dealer and another founder of 21 Publishing, that they had actually met Nat Tate. Karen Wright, the editor of *Modern Painters*, who was also fully aware of the hoax, said: 'We were very amused that people kept coming up to us and saying, "Yes, I've heard of him." There is a willingness not to appear foolish. No one wants to admit they've never heard of him – critics are too proud to admit that.'

The plan was for the truth to leak out slowly after the London launch on 8 April but smart detective work by the *Independent* newspaper's art editor David Lister exposed Tate as a fake. After hearing Boyd recall how he first saw a drawing by Tate at Alice Singer's 57th Street gallery, Lister decided to visit the gallery for a background piece. But there was no such gallery.

The New York art set were smarting at being made to look foolish although both author and publisher were quick to point out that was not their intention. Boyd explained: 'I wanted to see what illusions I could spin, what tricks I could turn. I wanted to play quite consciously with the ideas of reality and fiction in what amounted to almost a manipulation of our verification process. We decided to present it completely deadpan. We imagined there would be a slow burn of realization and a thrill at the peeling away of the layers, as the fictiveness slowly emerged.'

The denizens of the New York art world may have forgotten Nat Tate but they won't forget William Boyd in a hurry.

A Woman Scorned

When struggling art teacher John Myatt placed an advertisement in the satirical magazine *Private Eye* offering 'genuine fakes, nineteenth- and twentieth-century fakes from £150', he could have had no idea that he would end up as a key player in one of Britain's biggest-ever art frauds. In 1999 John Drewe, the man who masterminded the £1.8 million scam and who hired Myatt's cheap-rate services, was jailed for six years after being shopped to the police by the girlfriend he had recently walked out on. The art world listened in disbelief as the court case detailed the unlikely alliance between Drewe, suave conman and impostor, and the impoverished Myatt who fooled international art experts for nearly a decade by creating 'lost' works by modern masters using materials such as household emulsion paint, KY lubricating jelly and the contents of a vacuum cleaner bag.

While Myatt faked the paintings of the likes of Alberto Giacometti, Marc Chagall and Ben Nicholson – often for as little as £250 a time – Drewe infiltrated the archives of the Tate Gallery and the Victoria and Albert Museum to create bogus backgrounds for the works he had commissioned, thus making them much easier to sell.

The famous auction houses and plush art galleries to which these paintings were taken are a world away from Drewe's modest upbringing. He was born John Cockett in 1948, living in a farm cottage near the small Sussex town of Uckfield with his father Basil, a telephone engineer, and mother Kathleen. He left Haywards Heath Grammar School in 1964 with six O levels and went to work for the Atomic Energy Authority at Amersham, Buckinghamshire. His boss, Dr John Catch, found him clever but arrogant and disinclined to take advice. Dr Catch encouraged him to take A levels on day-release but he dropped out, complaining that the work was too easy, and eventually resigned from his job after two years. Dr Catch, whose name was later used by Drewe as the fake head of a modern art consortium, remembered: 'He was extremely clever and was able to talk about advanced physics very convincingly but did not understand the basics. He just memorized things from textbooks. He was unwilling to do A levels because he thought he knew it all already.'

By 1970 Cockett had changed his surname to Drewe, adding the letter 'e' to the second half of his mother's maiden name of Barrington-Drew. It was as Dr Drewe that he was appointed at the age of 22 to teach physics at Hazelwick School, Crawley, near his old Sussex stamping ground. He told staff that he had a PhD and was about to do research at Oxford but he was recognized by an old acquaintance and dismissed. He went on to teach at Pardes House, an orthodox Jewish school in North London, having falsely claimed to possess a degree from an American university. A former colleague recalled: 'He said he was a professor. Despite being an impostor, he was a good teacher but he tried to make a lot of himself, talking about spying and working for the government. He left suddenly under mysterious circumstances.'

Much of the remainder of Drewe's career is clouded in mystery. There is no official record of him holding a steady job or paying tax. He claimed to have been a highly paid nuclear physicist who also wrote papers on Western technology for the Soviet Union. A self-confessed communist, he spent time researching Nazi history and said he was employed by a South African secret agent to sell art to raise money for arms, but the international arms conspiracy was later dismissed in court. What is known is that in 1979 a mutual friend introduced him to an Israeli woman, Bathsheva Goudsmid. They moved in together in the North London Jewish community of Golders Green and had two children before the relationship ended acrimoniously in 1994. By the late eighties Drewe had all the trappings of wealth. He drove a string of expensive cars, dined in the most fashionable restaurants, and was a qualified helicopter pilot. Dozens of paintings, apparently by famous artists, passed through his home. He told Goudsmid that they belonged to John Catch, his old boss at the Atomic Energy Authority. He said that Catch had the title of Lord Chelmwood and was also a German baron. According to Drewe, Catch wanted to sell his collection of valuable paintings secretly and had asked Drewe to sell them on his behalf in return for a commission. Goudsmid later testified: 'I always believed the paintings were genuine. Over the years he said Mr Catch had supported him, helped him with his studies, given him money and was to leave him all his money. At one time I was told he would give him £2 million.'

The truth was somewhat different. In 1986 Drewe had answered Myatt's advertisement in *Private Eye*. A graduate of Gloucester Art

College and a former professional musician, Myatt was barely making ends meet as an art teacher in Staffordshire. To increase his sense of desperation, his marriage was on the rocks. So he didn't ask too many questions when Drewe told him that he was a research scientist, paid by the British government to inspect nuclear submarines. Myatt initially thought Drewe wanted the paintings for his home, but gradually realized that he was involved in fraud. He continued partly because Drewe frightened him (Myatt alleged that Drewe once threatened him with a gun), partly because it was a challenge to prove himself as an artist, and partly because the money was good. Although Drewe often paid him only £250 a time, Myatt was able to produce at least one painting every two months. As the fraud gathered momentum, he accepted Drewe's offer of a cut of the profits and had his own Swiss bank account in which to deposit the proceeds. Myatt's speed of delivery earned between £50,000 and £100,000 over the period of their illicit association. It once took him a mere five days to paint a fake Giacometti nude using household emulsion. The picture was then aged with dust tipped from a vacuum cleaner and the frame tacks were coated with salty water to give them a distressed look. Myatt used a mixture of emulsion and lubricating jelly to imitate the brushstrokes in oil paintings of Russian-French painter Nicholas de Stael and found that faking the works of French artist Roger Bissire became 'a kind of addiction.' He even took perverse pleasure in faking sketches by Le Corbusier, the French architect whose designs Myatt detested. Myatt also fakes signatures. After taking just two hours to complete a Nicholson, he forged the signature by copying it from a book about the artist.

Drewe had taken care to commission paintings by twentieth-century artists who were dead but he knew that any prospective buyer would want to inspect the picture's provenance – the record of its history. He realized that dealers, auctioneers and collectors would be less likely to question the authenticity of a fake painting if he created a provenance that was as bogus as the work of art itself. In order to do so, he needed to insert false information into the records of such establishments as the Tate Gallery and the Victoria and Albert Museum. With an IQ of 165 and a chameleon-like capacity to absorb other people's personalities, Drewe was able to appear wholly convincing in a variety of guises. And when in doubt he relied on the power of money. A £20,000 donation to the Tate led to officials trusting him as a serious researcher and gave him the required access to the gallery archives. He applied for a reader's ticket for the Victoria and Albert archives as Dr Drewe, the character reference (which described Drewe as an art historian of integrity) written by himself in the name of Dr Cockett, a throwback to his childhood. He also gained access to records at the Institute of Contemporary Art through the gift of two paintings that were probably fakes. The different archives contain records of thousands of paintings, including files from now defunct art galleries and dealers. Drewe tampered with this mine of information and inserted photographs of Myatt's paintings into the records, having produced the labels on an old typewriter. He even took the precaution of buying archive paper of the right age. After stealing a catalogue of an exhibition at London's defunct Hanover Gallery, Drewe replaced it with a bogus version that contained details of some of the fakes. Among the items he inserted was a forged receipt which showed that a Giacometti had been sold for £1,900 in 1958. The picture had been recently painted by Myatt. Drewe also wrote to the families of the artists concerned, tricking them into authenticating the forgeries, and, with threats of legal action, bullied a Roman Catholic religious order into providing fake histories.

When it came to selling Myatt's paintings, Drewe distanced himself from any dealings to reduce the chances of detection. Instead he used his considerable powers of persuasion and his unsurpassed capacity for lying to coerce assorted runners into doing his dirty work. One was told that the paintings were being disposed of by a man who wanted to keep the transaction hidden from his children; another swallowed Drewe's story that the paintings were being sold to buy archive material in Russia to prove that the Holocaust took place.

The pictures were sold to dealers in London and abroad for vast sums of money, as many as 15 passing through the world-famous auction houses of Sotheby's and Christie's. A fake Nicholson fetched $175,000 (£107,000) in the United States. An American gallery owner became worried about a Giacometti for which he had paid £105,000 and hired a specialist firm to verify it. Unfortunately the company he chose was run by Drewe who promptly charged the man £1,140 to authenticate a picture that he had arranged to be faked in the first place. On another occasion a London gallery owner complained after a de Stael turned out to be a fake, but was persuaded to accept four bogus Graham Sutherland sketches in exchange. Drewe's motives may have been highly questionable but his nerve was commendable.

Drewe's operation continued unhindered until 1995 when, in the wake of their bitter split, Miss Goudsmid went to the police and the Tate after discovering incriminating letters from Myatt to her former lover. She admitted to knowing nothing about art but said that when some canvases had arrived at the house without frames, she had seen

Drewe making frames in the garden from old bits of wood. She said he took photographs of the paintings and treated them in the garden. 'Once in the garden he put mud on a painting,' she recalled. 'He said it would make it look older because these paintings had been in a vault for many years and they looked new.' At about the same time two dealers also reported their suspicions to Scotland Yard over a Sutherland painting and some sketches by Jean Dubuffet. Drewe denied tampering with the records and claimed the fakes had been sold by arms dealers and countries desperate for hard currency. But Myatt confessed his part in the fraud and gave evidence against Drewe.

Determined to be the master of his own destiny, Drewe sacked his counsel on the second day of his five-month trial and thereafter conducted his own defence in a somewhat eccentric manner, punctuating his softly spoken charm with sudden roars and gestures. At one point a juror asked Drewe a question via a written note to the judge, then sent another note ten minutes into the defendant's rambling, incomprehensible reply, asking to withdraw the question! In February 1999, 50-year-old Drewe was found guilty of forgery, theft and conspiracy to defraud and was jailed for six years. Myatt received a prison sentence of one year. Even the prosecuting counsel said of Drewe: 'It was a waste of a clever, hugely retentive brain on a lifestyle which left a trail of victims in its wake.'

The police had recovered 60 of the forgeries but feared that as many as 140 were still in circulation. A detective warned: 'No doubt they are part of prized collections, able to command five- and six-figure sums on the market. The implications are horrendous.'

Chapter 14

Newspapers and Magazines

Batman on the Moon

In search of a publicity coup to make it the talk of the city in 1835, Benjamin Day's *New York Sun* came up with an outlandish tale of lunar discovery. On 25 August of that year the *Sun* reported excitedly: 'We have just learnt from an eminent publisher in this city that Sir John Herschel at the Cape of Good Hope has made some astronomical discoveries of the most wonderful description, by means of an immense telescope of an entirely new principle.' The story, credited to a supplement of the *Edinburgh Journal of Science* and eventually strung out over a period of four days, went on to state that noted British astronomer Sir John Herschel had been able to observe life on the moon in minute detail thanks to his invention of an ultra-powerful new telescope. But the report was a complete fabrication. There was no ground-breaking telescope, no startling discovery, and the *Edinburgh Journal of Science* had ceased publication some years previously. Indeed the only truth was that Sir John Herschel was in South Africa. And it was the very fact that he was conveniently out of the way in a distant land that enabled the *Sun* to carry off the circulation-building hoax so successfully.

The bogus account was written by Cambridge-educated *Sun* journalist Richard Adams Locke, who carefully built up the suspense each day, leaving readers in no doubt that there were more dramatic revelations to come. Locke filled his first article with technical jargon and complex diagrams, knowing full well that the paper's downmarket readership would not understand a word of it and would therefore assume that it was all true. He began by triumphantly listing a series of stunning astronomical breakthroughs that Herschel had apparently made 'by means of a telescope of vast dimensions and an entirely new principle.' Herschel, the article claimed, had established a 'new theory of cometary phenomena'; he had discovered planets in other solar systems; and he had 'solved or corrected nearly every leading problem of mathematical astronomy.'

Locke's second story reported that Herschel had discovered an inland sea on the surface of the moon, as well as white beaches, vast forests, deserts, and pyramids of amethysts. It sounded a truly wondrous place and *Sun* readers could hardly wait for the next instalment. They were not disappointed.

This time Locke revealed that Herschel had viewed animal life on the moon. Herds of bison had been seen wandering across the lunar plains while blue unicorns perched on hilltops and unidentified amphibious creatures inhabited the beaches. There were moose, reindeer, goats, cranes and pelicans, plus an advanced breed of beaver. Locke wrote of Herschel: 'Of animals, he classified nine species of mammalia . . . The last resembles the beaver of the earth in every other respect than in its destitution of a tail, and its invariable habit of walking upon only two feet. It carries its young in its arms like a human being, and moves with an easy gliding motion. Its huts are constructed better and higher than those of many tribes of human savages, and from the appearances of smoke in nearly all of them, there is no doubt of its being acquainted with the use of fire. Still its head and body differ only in the points stated from that of the beaver, and it was never seen except on the borders of lakes and rivers, in which it has been observed to immerse for a period of several seconds.' But as the lunar discoveries became the talk of New York, the best was yet to come.

For the fourth article announced a find of even greater significance – proof that there was indeed intelligent life on the moon. Herschel had spotted a race of furry, winged humans – creatures which he dubbed *Vespertilio homo* or 'man-bat'. He was quoted as saying: 'We counted three parties of these creatures, of twelve, nine and fifteen in each, walking erect towards a small wood . . . Certainly they were like human beings, for their wings had now disappeared and their attitude in walking was both erect and dignified . . . About half of the first party had passed beyond our canvas; but of all the others we had perfectly distinct and deliberate view. They averaged four feet in height, were covered, except on the face, with short and glossy copper-coloured hair, and had wings composed of a thin membrane, without hair, lying snugly upon their backs from the top of the shoulders to the calves of their legs. The face, which was of a yellowish colour, was an improvement upon that of the large orang-utan . . . so much so that but for their long wings they would look as well on a parade ground as some of the old cockney militia. The hair of the head was a darker colour than the rest of the body, closely curled but apparently not woolly, and arranged in two circles over the temples of the forehead. Their feet could only be seen as they were alternately lifted in walking; but from what we could see of them in so transient a view they appeared thin and very protuberant at the heel . . . We had no opportunity to see them actually at work. So far as we could judge, they spend their happy hours in collecting fruits in the woods, eating through the skies, bathing, and loitering about on the summits of precipices.'

Again Locke deliberately muddied the waters by repeating Herschel's detailed technical description of the creatures. 'We could perceive that their wings possessed great expansion and were similar in structure of those of the bat, being a semi-transparent membrane expanded in curvilinear divisions by means of straight radii, united at the back by dorsal integuments. But what astonished us most was the circumstance of this membrane being continued from the shoulders to the legs, united all the way down, though gradually decreasing in width. The wings seemed completely under the command of volition, for those of the creatures whom we saw bathing in the water spread them instantly to their full width, waved them as ducks do theirs to shake off the water, and then as instantly closed them again in a compact form.'

Subsequent reports told of the Temple of the Moon, constructed of sapphire and with its golden roof supported by pillars 70 feet high and six feet thick. Further man-bats were discovered but with *Sun* readers thirsting for more, they were informed that the all-powerful telescope had, alas, been left facing the east and that the sun's rays, concentrated through the lenses, had burned a hole 15 feet in circumference through the reflecting chamber, thus putting the observatory out of action.

The hoax had done its job. *Sun* circulation, which had reached 15,000 on the first day of the series, had soared to 19,360 with the announcement of bat-men on the moon, enabling proprietor, Benjamin Day, to declare that it now boasted the largest readership of any newspaper in the world. Rival New York editors were so impressed by the scoop that they shamelessly pirated stories for their own publications, claiming that they, too, had access to Herschel's data. Edgar Allan Poe decided to stop work on the second part of his own hoax story, *The Strange Adventures of Hans Phaal*, because he felt he had been outdone. It is estimated that 90 per cent of the *Sun*'s readership believed the story of Herschel's amazing finds. It was only later that the astronomer himself became aware that his name had been taken in vain.

Locke's downfall was in claiming that Herschel had compiled 40 pages of calculations based on his moon studies. When the New York Journal of Commerce asked to see these calculations, Locke was forced to admit authorship. Meanwhile the *Sun* came under fire from its competitors, angry and embarrassed that they had been duped. On 16 September 1835 the *Sun* wrote: 'Certain correspondents have been urging us to come out and confess the whole to be a hoax; but this we can by no means do, until we have the testimony of the English or Scotch papers to corroborate such a declaration.' This was the closest the *Sun* ever came to an admission of guilt.

The Great Moon Hoax, as it became known, established the *New York Sun* as a major force. It retained its increased circulation and went on to add many new readers by means of more conventional news stories.

The Abominable Showman

That the 1961 Broadway play *Subways Are For Sleeping* was not doing good business at the box office must have come as a surprise to readers of the *New York Herald-Tribune* who found an advertisement singing the production's praises in the most glowing terms. The names of no fewer than seven of the city's leading theatre critics appeared in the ad, alongside the rave reviews that each had given the play.

Howard Taubman declared that *Subways Are For Sleeping* was 'one of the few great musical comedies of the last thirty years, one of the best of our time. It lends lustre to this or any other Broadway season.' Walter Kerr enthused: 'What a show! What a hit! What a solid hit! If you want to be overjoyed, spend an evening with *Subways Are For Sleeping*. A triumph.' John Chapman was equally euphoric. 'No about it, *Subways Are For Sleeping* is the best musical of the century. Consider yourself lucky if you can buy a ticket for *Subways Are For Sleeping* over the next few years.' John McClain hailed it as 'A fabulous musical. I love it. Sooner or later every one will have to see *Subways Are For Sleeping*.' Richard Watts judged it to be 'A knockout, from start to finish. The musical you've been waiting for. It deserves to run for a decade.' Norman Nadel considered the play to be 'A whopping hit. Run, don't walk to the St James Theater. It's that rare class of great musicals. Quite simply, it has everything.' And Robert Coleman also waxed lyrical, describing it as 'A great musical. All the ingredients are there. As fine a piece of work as our stage can be asked to give us.'

But they were not just the sort of reviews a producer dreams of, they were actually the reviews a producer had dreamed up.

The advertisement was due to appear in all of the principal New York City papers but an editor at one publication spotted a curious anomaly in the tiny critics' photographs that accompanied their quotes. The picture of Richard Watts showed a black man, and the editor knew that Richard Watts the theatre critic was white. The editor warned the other papers that something was amiss with the ad and all pulled it except for the *Herald-Tribune*, which had already gone to press. Closer inspection revealed that Richard Watts was not the only irregularity. None of the seven pictures were those of the theatre critics of the same name. The photographs were of complete unknowns. What's more, none of the critics listed had said the quotes attributed to them.

The man behind the deliberately misleading ad was David Merrick, the producer of *Subways Are For Sleeping*. Since making his Broadway debut with the 1954 show *Fanny*, Merrick had acquired a reputation of being an astute impresario with a fearsome temper. This earned him the nickname of 'the abominable showman'. So when Merrick ordered his press agent, Harvey Sabinson, to track down seven people with the same names as the leading New York theatre critics, Sabinson did not need telling twice. He was instructed to take them to a preview of the play, wine and dine them in an expensive restaurant, and obtain written consent to quote them in an advertisement for the show. Sabinson then went through the archives of some of the biggest hits on Broadway and lifted quotes from old reviews, merely changing the title of the play. Everything was above board . . . just.

Merrick later admitted that he had wanted to pull that trick for many years but had been prevented from doing so because he had been unable to find anyone with the same name as Brooks Atkinson, renowned theatre critic of the *New York Times*. But when Atkinson retired in 1961, Merrick seized the opportunity to bring the play some much-needed publicity and to improve dramatically on the real reviews it had received.

Although the ad – headed '7 OUT OF 7 ARE ECSTATICALLY UNANIMOUS ABOUT SUBWAYS ARE FOR SLEEPING' – appeared in only one edition of one paper, it had the desired effect and *Subways Are For Sleeping* went on to run for 205 performances. Phyllis Newman won a Tony Award for her role in the musical. David Merrick never looked back either, going on to produce over 100 hit shows including *Oliver!*, *Hello, Dolly!* and *42nd Street*.

A Plague of Giant Grasshoppers

The front page of the *Tomah (Wisconsin) Monitor-Herald* for 9 September 1937 carried the headline: GIANT GRASSHOPPERS INVADE BUTTS ORCHARD EAST OF CITY. The story which followed related that a colony of grasshoppers had devoured some special plant food that local farmer A. L. Butts had scattered on his apple trees and, as a result, had ballooned to a length of around three feet. The monster mutants were so gross that their sheer weight snapped off the branches of trees as they hopped around the orchard.

The paper featured photographs of the huge insects being hunted by residents armed with shotguns and a picture of farmer Butts proudly displaying a dead specimen as a trophy. The story generated widespread panic, prompting homeowners to keep windows shut and to keep pets indoors lest their cats and dogs be attacked by malevolent grasshoppers. This was in spite of the fact that the paper printed a vague disclaimer on page four of that same issue: 'If there are those who doubt our story it will not be a new experience, inasmuch as most newspaper writers are thought to be the darndest liars in the world.'

Butts and the *Monitor-Herald* publisher, B. J. Fuller, subsequently confessed to concocting the hoax story.

Hollywood's Dream Girl

'If Allegra Coleman didn't exist, someone would have to invent her' ran the trail on the contributors' page of the November 1996 edition of the glossy men's magazine *Esquire*. What followed was a profile of a wannabe labelled 'Hollywood's It Girl', an actress described by the author of the article, *Washington Post* journalist Martha Sherrill, as 'the most compelling celebrity I've ever written about.' Ms Coleman was also the most fanciful celebrity ever written about. She didn't exist; Martha Sherrill and the staff of *Esquire* had invented her.

The piece was intended to be a parody of the type of gushing celebrity interviews so prevalent in magazines where the banal utterings of obscure actors are treated with the reverence once afforded to Einstein; where a favourite vegetable is elevated to the realms of rocket science. Sherrill chronicled the life of 'the Allegra Coleman nobody knows', from her minor role as a deaf swimmer in *Cliffhanger* to the scandalous nude photos of her with 'on-again, off-again boyfriend' David Schwimmer that appeared in the tabloid press a few months earlier.

Sherrill wrote that Coleman had a 'simple, irresistible vulgarity' that Gwyneth Paltrow could never match. She's 'one giant *kaboom* of a girl', added Sherrill, who also noted that the starlet was endowed with 'triumphant breasts'. She certainly appeared to have no shortage of admirers. Apart from Schwimmer, fans were said to include Woody Allen, Bernardo Bertolucci and new-age faith healer Deepak Chopra who was quoted as saying of Coleman: 'She is without blind vanities. Her nature is spongy and luminescent.'

Readers may have been puzzled as to why they had never heard of Allegra Coleman, but showbiz is such a transient field that careers can come and go in the time it takes to have a decent Hollywood lunch. Besides the girl on the cover, pictured beneath the headline 'Hollywood's Next Dream Girl', looked real enough.

Many were fooled by the spoof. After the piece appeared, *Esquire* fielded a series of 'increasingly frantic calls' from talent scouts at Twentieth Century Fox, desperate to get their hands on the budding starlet. Other journalists wanted to interview her. A gullible reporter at the *St Louis Post-Dispatch* angrily denounced *Esquire*'s apparent celebration of Coleman's brainless banality. And an irate friend of David Schwimmer called to protest about the magazine's invasion of privacy! They were finally put out of their misery when *Esquire* admitted that the profile was a hoax – 'a parody of the celebrity journalism that's run wild in the 90s.

The edition became *Esquire*'s biggest seller of the year. And there was a side effect which seemed to bear out the magazine's cynical view of celebrity. For Ali Larter, the unknown model who had posed as Coleman for the photo shoot, became famous overnight – a real-life starlet. As a result of the *Esquire* exposure, she has appeared in *Dawson's Creek* and in movies such as *Varsity Blues* and *House on Haunted Hill*. She also has a number of websites dedicated to her. Casting director John Papsidera, who cast Larter in *Flight 180*, said: 'There's a prime example of how hype discovered somebody. Ali's really talented but the hoax was certainly the initial reason I called and wanted an appointment with her.'

Allegra Coleman hasn't done too badly out of the deal either. She managed to work her way into the All-Time Glamour Girls Survey, an Internet poll rating '1,850 gorgeous women from all fields of entertainment.' Alphabetically, she nestled somewhere between Claudette Colbert and Joan Collins. Not bad for a virtual beginner.

The Winsted Liar

Not for nothing was Louis T. Stone, a reporter with Connecticut's *Evening Citizen* newspaper, known as the 'Winsted Liar'. For his journalistic career, which ran from 1895 to his death in 1933, was characterized by his innate ability to invent hoax stories centred on the

Connecticut town of Winsted. By selling his far-fetched tales to big city newspapers, he made Winsted so famous that visitors to the town were greeted with billboards that read: 'Winsted, Connecticut, founded in 1779, has been put on the map by the ingenious and queer stories that emanate from this town and which are printed all over the country, thanks to L. T. Stone.'

His first and best-known creation was the Wild Man of Connecticut – a naked, hairy man with an alarming tendency to jump out from behind trees and scare the living daylights out of people. Stone came up with the idea when he was a lowly paid young cub reporter in urgent need of making some quick money. He figured that the best way to raise ready cash was to sell a story to the New York papers and since there was nothing obvious that fitted the bill, he decided to invent one.

After the appearance of Stone's first story about the screaming Wild Man who roamed the forests, dozens of locals came forward to say that they, too, had witnessed this strange individual. Other newspapers picked up the story and visitors converged on Winsted to try and hunt him down. Eventually it was revealed that most of the sightings had been of a jackass belonging to a Mr Danehy.

The Wild Man may have faded from public view but the experience taught Stone that there was always a market for silly stories. Over the years he sold countless more tall tales. The majority of the editors who published them were all too aware that the reports were hoaxes, but the fact that their readers enjoyed them became the overriding factor. Thus readers in Los Angeles, New York and Washington were regaled with all manner of homely yarns from Winsted. These included:

- The farmer whose chicken laid a red, white and blue egg on 4 July
- The bald man who had so much trouble with flies buzzing around his head that he 'painted a spider up there and that sure did scare all them doggoned flies away.'
- The tree that grew baked apples.
- The cow that was so modest she would only allow women to milk her.
- The cat with a harelip that could whistle 'Yankee Doodle'.
- The chicken farmer who always plucked his chickens humanely – with a vacuum cleaner.
- The squirrel that brushed its owner's shoes with its tail.
- The cow that produced hot milk having grazed on a horseradish patch.
- And of course that old reliable, the talking dog.

So grateful were the Winsted townsfolk to Stone that they named a bridge in his honour. Appropriately it spans a stream known as Sucker Brook.

Mencken in Hot Water

In December 1917, with the world in the grip of war, American journalist H. L. Mencken decided to introduce a little light relief in the form of an article that appeared in New York's *Evening Mail* mourning the fact that nobody had thought to commemorate 'one of the most important profane anniversaries in American history, to wit, the seventy-fifth anniversary of the introduction of the bathtub into these states. Not a plumber fired a salute or hung out a flag. Not a governor proclaimed a day of prayer. Not a newspaper called attention to the day.'

Mencken's article appeared on 28 December and claimed that the historic anniversary should have been celebrated eight days earlier. He then went on to relate the history of the bathtub, describing how it had been introduced to England back in 1828 by Lord John Russell. Mencken wrote: 'The English bathtub, then as now, was a puny and inconvenient contrivance – little more, in fact, than a glorified dishpan – and filling and emptying it required the attendance of a servant. Taking a bath, indeed, was a rather heavy ceremony, and Lord John in 1835 was said to be the only man in England who had yet come to doing it every day.' According to Mencken, a visitor to England in the 1830s was Cincinnati cotton dealer Adam Thompson who immediately saw potential in the bathtub if only it could be enlarged to accommodate the entire body of an adult man. And in 1842, at his Cincinnati home, Thompson set about building the first modern bathroom, the water for his new bathtub being pumped from a well in the garden. The pump, wrote Mencken, was operated by six Negroes. The tub itself was some seven feet long and four feet wide and was built in Nicaragua mahogany by Cincinnati cabinetmaker James Cullness. To make it watertight, the interior was lined with sheet lead, soldered at the joints, but this had the effect of making the tub so heavy that the floor of the room had to be reinforced to support it.

Mencken said that it was in this tub, on 20 December 1842, that Thompson created his slice of American history. He apparently took two baths that day – a cold one at eight o'clock in the morning and a hot one (heated to a temperature of 105 degrees) in the afternoon. On Christmas Day he demonstrated the new contraption to dinner guests, one of who, a Frenchman, was brave enough to take the plunge. By the following day the whole of Cincinnati was talking about Thompson's bathtub. However, Mencken noted that the bathtub had a rough ride in its early years, being considered so unhealthy as to be banned in some cities. From 1845 Boston made bathing unlawful except upon medical advice. But the tide turned two years later with the invention of the zinc-lined bathtub, devised by Brooklyn plumber John F. Simpson. Medical opposition to bathing started to recede, even in Boston, and the bathtub gained the ultimate seal of approval when US President Millard Fillmore had one fitted in the White House in 1851. 'The example of the President,' continued Mencken, 'soon broke down all that remained of the old opposition, and by 1860, according to the newspaper advertisements of the time, every hotel in New York had a bathtub, and some had two and even three. In 1862 bathing was introduced into the Army by General McClellan, and in 1870 the first prison bathtub was set up at Moyamensing Prison, in Philadelphia.'

So there it was, a potted history of the bathtub. But not a word of it was true. Mencken had made it all up. 'This article,' he wrote when finally confessing to the hoax in 1926, 'was a tissue of somewhat heavy absurdities, all of them deliberate and most of them obvious. My motive was simply to have some harmless fun in war days. It never occurred to me that it would be taken seriously.'

But it was. Mencken's bogus history of the bathtub began to be reported as fact in countless publications, even working its way into medical literature and reference books. Mencken felt obliged to repeat his confession, but to no avail. He despaired: 'Soon I began to encounter my preposterous "facts" in the writings of other men . . . The chiropractors and other such quacks collared them for use as evidence of the stupidity of medical men. They were cited by medical men as proof of the progress of public hygiene. They got into learned journals and the transactions of learned societies. They were alluded to on the floor of Congress. The editorial writers of the land, borrowing them in toto and without mentioning my begetting of them, began to labour them in their dull, indignant way. They crossed the dreadful wastes of the North Atlantic, and were discussed horribly by English uplifters and German professors. Finally, they got into the standard works of reference, and began to be taught to the young.'

Having appeared as fact in countless magazines and newspapers, Mencken's hoax even infiltrated the White House and in 1952 President Truman used the bathtub story during a speech in Philadelphia. Trade manuals were no better informed. Writing about the history of plumbing in America, the July 1987 issue of *Plumbing and Mechanical Magazine* quoted the article as gospel, remarking that in 1845 'Boston forbade bathing except on medical advice.' And a trawl of the Internet reveals a number of sites which still maintain that Millard Fillmore had the first bathtub installed in the White House. Sometimes a hoax can be just too convincing.

Banana Spliffs

California hippies of the 1960s would smoke just about anything to get a high. As fast as the authorities clamped down on certain drugs, new ones would appear. It was a running battle between the men in suits and the men in beads. Then someone in the hippie camp came up with the idea of pretending that there was a new hallucinogenic drug called bananadine, extracted from bananas. As the story spread, the hippies watched in spaced-out amazement while the US government seriously considered whether it ought to make bananas illegal for the sake of America's youth.

The great banana hoax was instigated in March 1967 when a correspondent – believed to be Marvin Garson – wrote to a hippie paper in Berkeley, California, called the *Berkeley Barb*. The writer claimed that he had got high after smoking a dried banana peel, the sensation being similar to that derived from opium. The paper, delighted to have discovered a new psychedelic that was available to everyone, immediately printed the recipe. After peeling the banana, the user was advised to scrape off the white flesh, dry the peel out in an oven, roll the dried peel into a joint and smoke it.

The story was soon picked up by other hippie papers and then by national magazines such as *Time* and *Newsweek*. Hippies and students organised banana smoke-ins and grocery stores were inundated with scruffy hippies buying crates of bananas. The authorities were now in a state wondering how they were going to crack down on the banana trade. One Congressman jokingly proposed two new acts designed to counter the growing menace – the Banana Labelling Act of 1967 and the Banana and Other Odd Fruits Disclosure and Reporting Act of 1967. But not everyone saw the funny side. Some government departments took the threat seriously while banana importer United Fruit was so concerned about the adverse publicity that it, too, wanted scientific tests carried out to find out whether bananas really were hallucinogenic.

After an exhaustive examination, scientists concluded that while there are chemicals in banana peels that are distantly related to the likes of LSD, they are not present in sufficient quantities to get anyone high. The federal authorities also decided that the banana story was a hoax since the only mind-blowing experience people seemed to get from smoking banana peel was a severe headache.

Nevertheless the bananadine riddle has entered folklore. An extraction recipe has appeared in *The Anarchist's Cookbook* and the legend was allegedly the inspiration for Donovan's sixties hit 'Mellow Yellow'. But the truth is that the only trip you can take with a banana is when you slip on the peel.

Demolishing the Great Wall of China

One of the curiosities of history is that a seemingly harmless hoax story devised by four Denver journalists to appease their editors should culminate in thousands of people being slaughtered on the other side of the world. Yet the brutal Boxer Rebellion – among the most bloodthirsty episodes in Chinese history – was the tragic outcome to a fake Colorado report that the Great Wall of China was about to be demolished.

The unforeseen chain of events began when Jack Tournay, Al Stevens, John Lewis and Hal Wilshire – reporters on Denver's four papers, the *Times*, *Republican*, *Post*, and *Rocky Mountain News* – were dispatched to Denver's railroad station one Saturday evening in 1898 to cover the arrival of a visiting celebrity. When the celebrity failed to materialize, the hacks were left in desperate need of a story to keep their respective editors happy. Stevens suggested that since they couldn't find a suitable story, they should make one up, and so, in the time-honoured tradition of newspapermen, they adjourned to the Oxford hotel to lubricate their trains of thought. Their original intention was to come up with four phoney reports – one per paper – but as the beers flowed, they decided to concentrate their energies on one big story instead. Reasoning that a domestic tale would be too easy to check out, they started exploring foreign angles and eventually settled on China as being sufficiently distant and obscure.

It was Lewis who came up with the idea that they should announce exclusively that the Great Wall of China was soon to be pulled down. After all, it was one Chinese symbol that Americans were familiar with. But there needed to be a reason for the demolition. Over more beers they decided that the wall was being taken down as a gesture of goodwill by the Chinese government to welcome foreign trade, and that they had picked up this sensational story from four American engineers who had stopped off in Denver on their way to China. Wilshire harboured doubts but more beers overcame his reservations and by 11 p.m. all four had finalized their story. They then went to the Windsor Hotel and persuaded the night clerk to make out an overnight registration in four bogus names. He was told that, if asked, he should say the mystery guests had informed him they were engineers and that he recalled seeing them talking to reporters. Conveniently, the non-existent engineers had stayed only one night before departing for California early in the morning. This ensured that the story would be well nigh impossible to check out. The journalists had covered their tracks.

Unable to confirm or disprove the story, all four papers trusted their men and used it on the front page. The *Denver Times* trumpeted: GREAT CHINESE WALL DOOMED! PEKING SEEKS WORLD TRADE!

The story was so hot that it spread rapidly through the United States, overseas to Europe and eventually China. The timing was not good. There was mounting hostility towards foreigners within China, due to what was seen as the economic and political exploitation of the country by various Western powers and humiliating military defeats at the hands of Britain in two Opium Wars. A secret society of Chinese revolutionaries called the Righteous and Harmonious Fists, but known by Westerners as Boxers, had begun a campaign of terror against Christian missionaries in the north-eastern provinces. Although the Boxers were officially denounced, they were secretly supported by many members of the royal court, notably the dowager empress Tz'u Hsi. The Boxers' aim was to expel all foreigners from China. So when they read the story about the Great Wall with its supposed encouragement for foreign trade, they were incensed and stepped up the rebellion. European and US legations in the Chinese capital were besieged and thousands of Chinese Christian converts and missionaries were murdered throughout 1899. The following year a 12,000-strong force consisting of British, American, French, Japanese, German and Russian troops occupied the city to protect their own countrymen before a peace treaty was signed in September 1901. The Denver hoax had backfired dramatically.

As much for their own safety as to safeguard their jobs, the four instigators promised never to reveal the truth while any of the others were still alive. Consequently it was many years later that Wilshire, the last survivor, finally confessed to the hoax that had unwittingly destroyed thousands of lives.

Franklin's Witch Trial

Witches were everywhere in eighteenth-century America. Belief in the broomstick brigade had been heightened by the ludicrous trials at Salem, Massachusetts, in 1692 when 19 villagers and two dogs were executed on charges of witchcraft in a hysteria whipped up by the highly dubious evidence of two bored girls. Nearly 40 years on people continued to study their neighbours for telltale signs of sorcery – a situation which the more enlightened Benjamin Franklin chose to satirize in his role as owner and publisher of the *Pennsylvania Gazette*.

On 22 October 1730 the *Gazette* carried a report of a witch trial said to have taken place ten days earlier at Mount Holly, near Burlington, New Jersey. The account stated that almost 300 people had gathered to witness the trial of a man and a woman on charges of 'making their neighbours' sheep dance in an uncommon manner, and with causing hogs to speak, and sing psalms, etc., to the great terror and amazement of the King's good and peaceable subjects in this province.'

The accused were to be subjected to two tests. In the first instance each would be weighed in scales against a Bible. If the Bible was heavier, the accused was deemed guilty of being a witch. For the second test they would be bound and thrown into a millpond. If they floated, they were proved to be witches. If they drowned, they were innocent. Such was early justice.

Eager to prove their innocence, the two defendants volunteered to undergo the tests on condition that the most violent of their accusers – another man and woman – be tried with them. This was agreed and a time and a place set for the trial.

First up was the scales test. The biggest Bible that anyone could find was placed on the scales, 'which were fixed on a gallows erected for that purpose'. Against this charming backdrop all four took it in turns to be weighed after first being searched for any items of weight about their person, such as pins. Not altogether surprisingly, each individual proved considerably heavier than the holy book. Not satisfied with this, the mob demanded trial by water. All four were stripped (except for the women who were allowed to wear their shifts), bound hand and foot and thrown into the pond from a barge. One of the accusers, a particularly thin man, began to sink but the rest floated. The other accuser started to panic when she did not sink and asked to be ducked again. When once again she remained on the surface, she declared 'that she believed the accused had bewitched her to make her so light, and that she would be ducked again a hundred times, but she would duck the Devil out of her.' Meanwhile the accused man, 'being surprised at his own swimming, was not so confident of his innocence as before, but said, "If I am a witch, it is morc than I know."'

Sensing a stalemate, some of the more sensible spectators pointed out that anyone bound and placed in the water would swim till their breath was gone and their lungs filled with water, so the four were pulled from the pond. However, the general feeling was that the women's shifts and the garters with which they were bound had helped to keep them afloat. Consequently it was decided that they should be tried again, but this time naked, when the weather grew warmer.

While the account provided gripping reading for Philadelphians, it was pure fiction from Franklin's pen, but one that was nevertheless convincing enough to be reprinted in the British *Gentleman's Magazine* the following year.

The Ice Worm Cometh

Whereas the symbol of the Canadian town of Churchill is the polar bear and Pamplona in Spain is inextricably linked to bulls, the Alaskan port of Cordova is associated with a more humble creature altogether. For on the first weekend of February each year Cordova celebrates Ice Worm Day, beginning with a parade along Main Street led by a 100 ft-long 'worm'. The pageant, which sees the crowning of an ice worm king and queen, is a major tourist draw, pulling in visitors from miles around. And in the bars of Cordova those same tourists are served special ice worm cocktails, featuring strips of spaghetti frozen in ice cubes. Even more surprising is the fact that the popularity of the ice worm dates largely from a century-old story concocted on a slow news day by journalist Elmer J. White.

White's career began on the *Gainesville News* in Florida but by the time of the Klondike gold rush he and his family had moved north to Washington State. In the late 1890s he switched to Dawson City where, in addition to covering local news stories, he began a gossip column under the name of 'The Stroller'. He continued the column on becoming editor of the *Whitehorse Star*, and the greater freedom afforded by his elevated position gave him the licence to write whatever took his fancy – regardless of whether or not it happened to be true.

His most enduring piece of creative journalism was a far-fetched tale of giant ice worms and blue snows that were said to appear when the temperature dropped below minus 75 degrees Fahrenheit. White wrote up an interview he claimed had taken place with a native elder who was over 100 years old. The sage had described how, in times of extreme cold, the ice worm could swell to four feet in length with a head on either end of its slippery body. If the temperature remained between minus 70 and minus 80 Fahrenheit for a few weeks, the ice worms would start chirping lustily. Under those same conditions, wrote White, any snow that fell would be blue.

The story attracted the attention of the Smithsonian Institute, America's most prestigious scientific body, who wrote to the *Star*'s editor asking for more information about this fascinating discovery.

Learning of the Smithsonian's interest, newspapers in the southern states picked up the story. In January 1907 the *Philadelphia Ledger* carried a report from Yukon Crossing that the ice worms were in lusty voice because the temperature had dipped to minus 82 Fahrenheit. A week later, however, the paper informed its readers that the temperature had suddenly shot up to minus 45 Fahrenheit, causing the poor worms to suffer terribly in the stifling heat.

White may have been able to persuade his readers as to the veracity of the ice worm story, but he faced a tougher task over the blue snow. Nevertheless he gave it his best shot and when the snow remained resolutely white during a bitterly cold snap, he explained away the absence of blueness by claiming that the wind was in the wrong direction. For blue snow to occur, he wrote, the winter winds had to blow in from the coast. It is not known whether anyone was seriously convinced by White's excuse but one *Whitehorse* supplier did run an advertisement in the paper urging residents to buy warm clothes 'before the blue snow falls'.

White's journalistic inventions were immortalized in verse by the young poet, Robert W. Service, whom the editor of the *Whitehorse Star* encouraged in the early days of his career. In 1911 Service wrote a popular Canadian folksong 'When The Ice Worms Nest Again', the chorus of which contains the lines:

> In the land of the pale blue snow where it's ninety nine below
> And the polar bears are dancing o'er the plain.
> In the shadow of the pole, I'll clasp her to my soul
> To be married when the ice worms nest again.

Elmer White sold the *Whitehorse Star* in 1916 and moved to Douglas, Alaska, where he began publishing *Stroller's Weekly* and continued his practice of printing tall stories to amuse and bemuse his readers. As one who was often a stranger to the truth, it was perhaps fitting that he should eventually quit journalism to enter politics on being elected to the Alaska House of Representatives. He died in 1930 but his colourful legacy lives on in Cordova each February.

Chapter 15

Science and Technology

The Sokal Affair

In a May 1996 issue of the magazine *Lingua Franca*, Alan Sokal, professor of physics at New York University, explained the thinking behind a recent self-penned article. He wrote: 'To test the prevailing intellectual standards, I decided to try a modest (though admittedly uncontrolled) experiment. Would a leading North American journal of cultural studies – whose editorial collective includes such luminaries as Fredric Jameson and Andrew Ross – publish an article liberally salted with nonsense if (a) it sounded good and (b) it flattered the editors' ideological preconceptions? The answer, unfortunately, is yes.'

The explanatory piece made uncomfortable reading at the office of the trendy left-wing quarterly *Social Text*, which had just published Sokal's original article in its spring/summer issue and now realized that it had been the victim of an academic hoax. Ironically, *Social Text*, founded in 1979 and an organ that prided itself on its radical politics, was edited at Sokal's own university, New York.

Sokal's prank was part of an ongoing assault by 'old-fashioned' academics on the post-modern theorists of science studies who were viewed in some quarters as being all hot air and no substance. Cultural studies, it was argued, had precious little to do with real science or with anything else for that matter. It was just the latest fad of left-wing pseudo-intellectuals.

The first shots in the war were fired in 1994 by mathematician Norman Levitt and biologist Paul R. Gross in their book *Higher Superstition: The Academic Left and Its Quarrels With Science*. The authors savagely attacked the new breed for unacceptable ignorance about science, even accusing modernists of 'a widespread, powerful, corrosive hostility toward science.' Sokal shared these views even though he called himself a 'leftist and a feminist' and pointed out that he once taught mathematics in Nicaragua during the Sandinista regime. But he felt that cultural theorists such as Stanley Aronowitz, Marxist sociologist and co-founder of *Social Text*, had, along with the rest of the 'New Left', created 'a self-perpetuating academic sub-culture that typically ignores (or disdains) reasoned criticism from the outside.'

Sokal's hoax article was part of a *Social Text* collection dedicated to investigating what became known as the 'Science Wars', which pitted practising scientists against social theorists who studied sociology and the politics of science. He called his contribution 'Transgressing the Boundaries Towards a Transformative Hermeneutics of Quantum Gravity'. The airy title set the tone for the rest of the piece. Mimicking the verbal effluence of genuine articles in such journals, Sokal produced a jargon-laden work of academic gibberish in which he claimed a deep connection between quantum theory and radical politics. He repeatedly invoked philosophers, psychoanalysts and literary critics to back up his pronouncements about the most rarefied and speculative aspects of theoretical physics. Along the way, he called for a 'liberatory post-modern science'. Nobody asked him to explain what that meant.

The article was written in a deadly earnest style supplemented with hundreds of footnotes and dozens of references – at least ten times the number provided by other authors in the collection. *Social Text*'s hip co-editor Andrew Ross, who just happened to be chairman of the American Studies Department at Sokal's own campus, attributed the bewildering number of references to a novice's lack of confidence in new intellectual terrain. He did admit – at least once the hoax had been revealed – that Sokal's piece had seemed 'a little hokey' and 'outdated' but put this down to the young scientist's struggle to use the accepted modern terminology.

Sokal could not believe that the editors had failed to spot the hoax, claiming that any physicist would have 'laughed out loud' by the second paragraph, part of which read: 'It has thus become increasingly apparent that physical "reality", no less than social "reality", is at bottom a social and linguistic construct; that scientific "knowledge", far from being objective, reflects and encodes the dominant ideologies and power relations of the culture that produced it.' Sokal later said that anyone who believed this was welcome to jump out of his apartment window . . . which was on the 22nd floor.

However, he believed that part of the reason he managed to get the piece published was because it fitted in with *Social Text*'s agenda. Indeed he professed anger at 'how readily they accepted my implication that the search for truth in science must be subordinated to a political agenda.'

Sokal's confession made the front page of the *New York Times* on 18 May and was soon picked by up by publications in Britain, France, Italy and Scandinavia. Sokal was unremitting in his criticism of an academic world in which 'incomprehensibility becomes a virtue, allusions, metaphors and puns substitute for evidence and logic.' He said he was 'troubled by an apparent decline in the standards of intellectual rigour in certain precincts of the American academic humanities', and that the hoax was his way of calling attention to this decline. As he noted in *Lingua Franca*, 'The results of my little experiment demonstrate, at the very least, that some fashionable sectors of the American academic Left have been getting intellectually lazy. Throughout the (*Social Text*) article I employ scientific and mathematical concepts in ways that few scientists or mathematicians could possibly take seriously. For example, I suggest that the "morphogenetic field" – a bizarre New Age idea due to Rupert Sheldrake – constitutes a cutting-edge theory of quantum gravity. This connection is pure invention: even Sheldrake makes no such claim. I assert that Lacan's psychoanalytic speculations have been confirmed by recent work in quantum field theory. Even non-scientist readers might well wonder what in heavens' name quantum field theory has to do with psychoanalysis; certainly my article gives no reasoned argument to support such a link. In sum I intentionally wrote the article so that any competent physicist or mathematician (or undergraduate physics or maths major) would realize that it is a spoof. Evidently the editors of *Social Text* felt comfortable publishing an article on quantum physics without bothering to consult anyone knowledgeable on the subject.'

The leading players at *Social Text* were predictably indignant. While Andrew Ross attempted to claim the moral high ground, Stanley Aronowitz blustered that Sokal was 'ill-read and half-educated'. On the other hand, Norman Levitt thought Sokal's parody was 'a lot of fun and a source of a certain amount of personal satisfaction.' The debate raged on for months in various scholarly publications, via accusation and counter-accusation, briefcases at thirty paces. Whatever the merits of the respective camps, one thing is certain: few arguments provide as much entertainment as a falling-out among academics.

Redheffer's Perpetual Motion Machine

Back in 1812 there were not yet any physical laws to deny perpetual motion although common sense dictated that it was highly unlikely. Nevertheless city fathers clung to the slim hope that they might one day be able to drive their water pumps free of charge. So when Charles Redheffer arrived in Philadelphia in 1812 claiming that he had with him a perpetual motion machine that required no source of energy to run, local dignitaries sat up and took notice.

Backed by a publicity campaign in the *Philadelphia Gazette*, orchestrated by an accomplice, Redheffer set up a working model of his wonder machine on the outskirts of the city, close to the banks of the Schuylkill River. He lured the crowds by offering a sizeable bet that no one could debunk his contraption, covering himself by keeping spectators at a distance on the pretext that he was worried in case anybody damaged it. With no challenge forthcoming, he judged the time to be right to ask the state of Pennsylvania for money to develop his device. Before agreeing to provide the necessary funding, the state demanded an inspection of the machine at close quarters.

On 21 January 1813 eight state-appointed commissioners called on Redheffer. However, the building that housed the machine was locked and there was no sign of the key. Consequently the inspectors had to study the machine through a barred window. It was highly unsatisfactory but all part of Redheffer's plan to keep them at arm's length and prevent them seeing too much.

One commissioner, Nathan Sellers, took with him his young son, Coleman, who, unfortunately for Redheffer, was something of a mechanical genius. Redheffer had explained to the inspectors that his perpetual motion machine was providing the energy to power another, separate machine by means of a set of interlocking gears. But young Coleman noticed that the gear teeth were worn on the wrong side for that to be the case. Instead it was clear to the boy that power was being routed to the perpetual motion machine from the other machine. In other words, Redheffer was a fraud.

But instead of openly challenging Redheffer on the matter, Sellers Snr decided on a more subtle method of exposure. He instructed a local engineer, Isaiah Lukens, to build a machine that worked on the same principles as Redheffer's device, but whose power source was even more difficult to detect. Lukens's model was driven by hidden clockwork. It looked like Redheffer's machine, but anyone wishing to view it could walk right up to it. Next Sellers invited Redheffer to a showing.

Redheffer was alarmed at what he saw. Realizing that his duplicity had been uncovered and that this new machine was infinitely more convincing than his own, he tried to buy out Sellers, offering him a handsome share of the profits from the perpetual motion scam. When Sellers refused, Redheffer fled the city.

He turned up next in New York and once again put his machine on display. It attracted the attention of mechanical engineer Robert Fulton who could not help noticing that the machine wobbled from time to time and that its speed kept varying. Fulton deduced that the machine was being driven by a hidden hand-crank, and set out to uncover the operator. He offered Redheffer a challenge, claiming that he could expose the secret source of the machine's energy but adding that if he were unable to do so, he would pay for any damage that might have occurred. Redheffer confidently accepted, whereupon, encouraged by the crowd, Fulton knocked away the boards behind the table on which the machine stood to reveal a hidden belt made of catgut. Fulton followed the cord up a flight of stairs to where he found an old man sitting in a room, eating a crust of bread with one hand and turning a hand-crank with the other. Redheffer had been feeding the poor fellow nothing but bread and water while forcing him to turn the crank drive all day long.

When the onlookers became aware that they had been tricked, they turned violent and demolished the machine. Redheffer was forced to make another hasty exit, his speedy flight from New York being the nearest he ever actually came to achieving perpetual motion.

Von Kempelen and His Discovery

Inspired by the California gold rush of 1849, Edgar Allan Poe donned his hoaxer's hat to concoct a tale about an American scientist of German descent who had perfected a process for producing gold from lead.

Poe's article did not announce Von Kempelen's discovery as such; instead it operated on the premise that everyone knew about it already, referring to 'the very minute and elaborate paper by Arago', 'the summary in *Silliman's Journal*', and the 'detailed statement just published by Lieutenant Maury.' Of course Poe's readers knew nothing of these works, nor of the Mr Kissam of Brunswick, Maine, who, according to Poe, was telling the press that he had invented a similar process eight years earlier. In a classic case of double bluff, Poe went so far as to suggest that Kissam was a hoaxer.

Poe proceeded to blind his readers with science by asserting that Von Kempelen had based his discovery on crude experiments conducted by the noted British chemist Sir Humphrey Davy. The latter's invention of the miners' safety lamp had made him relatively famous and the inclusion of his name gave the article much-needed authenticity. He also had the advantage of being dead, thus rendering him unable to refute any of Poe's points. Poe suggested – and offered to prove it, if required – that Von Kempelen was set on the path to discovery by rough notes from Davy's diary, which should have been burned following his death but had somehow survived. For the uninitiated, Poe went on to describe Von Kempelen's background, saying that he was born in Utica, New York State, and was a distant relative of Maelzel Von Kempelen, inventor of the Automaton chess player. Poe recounted how he had met Von Kempelen the scientist some six years earlier while staying at Earl's Hotel in Providence, Rhode Island. From there, Von Kempelen had travelled to Bremen where, apparently, his discovery was first made public.

The disclosure itself was no ordinary affair. Poe told how, having been suspected of counterfeiting, Von Kempelen was traced by the Bremen police to a garret at the top of an old seven-storey house where they found him in the middle of a chemical experiment involving lead, a blazing furnace and some crucibles. Before being handcuffed, Von Kempelen threw the contents of the crucibles to the floor, but in another room the officers found a trunk, full of what seemed to be brass, 'all in small, smooth pieces, varying from the size of a pea to that of a dollar; but the pieces were irregular in shape, although more or less flat-looking, upon the whole, "very much as lead looks when thrown upon the ground in a molten state, and there suffered to grow cool."' Now, not one of these officers for a moment suspected this metal to be any thing but brass . . . And their astonishment may be well conceived, when the next day it became known, all over Bremen, that the "lot of brass" which they had carted so contemptuously to the police office, without putting themselves to the trouble of pocketing the smallest scrap, was not only gold – real gold – but gold far finer than any employed in coinage-gold, in fact, absolutely pure, virgin, without the slightest appreciable alloy.'

Poe glossed over Von Kempelen's so-called confession on the grounds that the details were well known to the public and, anyway, the scientist had yet to divulge the precise chemical formula for making gold from lead. But he did point out that, as a direct result of Von Kempelen's discovery, gold was now of no greater value than lead and of much less value than silver. Indeed he stated that in Europe lead prices had already risen 200 per cent.

Poe was able to carry off this – and other hoaxes – not only through his own imagination and skill with words but also because, in the days before 24-hour news, media communication was deathly slow. The information superhighway was still a bumpy old track.

The Von Kempelen yarn was published in the year of Poe's death, and it is generally believed that its motive was to prevent gold-diggers flocking to California. As Poe wrote when assessing the possible consequences of the discovery: 'If many were prevented from adventuring to California, by the mere apprehension that gold would so materially diminish in value, on account of its plentifulness in the mines there, as to render the speculation of going so far in search of it a doubtful one – what impression will be wrought now, upon the minds of those about to emigrate, and especially upon the minds of those actually in the mineral region, by the announcement of the astounding discovery of Von Kempelen?'

Chapter 16

Politics

The Queen Was Not Amused

Most DJ hoaxers are happy to settle for modest targets – gullible members of the public, bumptious civic dignitaries, perhaps even the occasional compliant celebrity. But Canadian comedian Pierre Brassard liked to aim higher. On his talk show with Montreal station CKOI-FM in April 1995 he phoned the Vatican and ended up chatting away to Pope John Paul II. His Holiness was particularly puzzled when Brassard asked him whether he would be prepared to attach a toy propeller to his hat, at which point the Pope laughed and said, 'God bless you and God bless Canada' before ringing off. The ease with which he had got through to the Pope encouraged 29-year-old Brassard, a member of a subversive comic troupe known as Les Bleues Poudres, to select another high-profile international target. So it was that on 26 October of that year Brassard enjoyed a 14-minute telephone conversation with the Queen.

It was a tense time for both the Queen and the Canadian government as on 30 October a referendum was to be held on whether French-speaking Quebec should become independent of the rest of Canada. The Queen was clearly worried in case the vote went in favour of separation and she had been in regular telephone contact with Canadian Prime Minister Jean Chrétien. In addition to possessing an iron nerve, Pierre Brassard was also an excellent mimic, one of his specialities being Prime Minister Chrétien's heavily accented English. Brassard knew that in the build-up to the referendum, Chrétien and his key staff would be out campaigning, making it the ideal opportunity to pose as the Prime Minister for a telephone tête-à-tête with the Queen.

Preparation for the escapade was thorough with Brassard employing a team of seven researchers to set up the hoax call. On Wednesday 25 October one of Brassard's researchers, claiming to be from Chrétien's office in Ottawa, called Buckingham Palace and said that the Prime Minister wished to talk to the Queen about affairs of state. A number was left for the Palace to call the following day. On the Thursday morning a senior member of the Queen's staff rang the number to arrange a time for the conversation. The aide was unconcerned that it was not the usual number, having been informed by the caller that the Prime Minister's staff were scattered around the country because of the impending referendum. Then the Queen's Private Secretary, Sir Robert Fellowes, called the Governor General's residence, at Rideau Hall in Ottawa, to discuss the proposed dialogue. By chance a senior member of Chrétien's staff was present at the time but expressed no surprise that the Prime Minister wanted to talk to the Queen.

Therefore at four o'clock that afternoon Pierre Brassard telephoned Buckingham Palace and was immediately put through to the Queen. The conversation began in French. Brassard (as Chrétien) warned Her Majesty: 'The Canadian political situation is very critical. Our latest polls are showing that the separatists are going to win the referendum.' The Queen replied: 'Well, it sounds as though the referendum may go the wrong way. If I can help in any way, I will be very happy to do so.' The bogus Prime Minister then suggested that the Queen could make a public intervention, in the form of a television broadcast, that would 'give back to the citizens of Quebec the pride of being members of a united country.' The Queen sounded receptive to the idea, remarking that 'in Canada I have tried to give the same message.' He added that her message would be broadcast on *Louvain à La Carte*, which, unbeknown to the Queen, was a Canadian chat show presented by a camp host. The Queen then switched to another line to consult her Private Secretary about a possible television speech before returning to 'Chrétien' and asking him to send her the proposed text.

From then on, the conversation degenerated into farce with Brassard suddenly switching into English. He told the Queen there could be a monetary crisis in Canada as a result of the referendum and debated whether it would be better to put her picture on a two-dollar bill or on a discount tyre store cash coupon. He also asked her whether she was wearing a costume for Halloween, to which she answered: 'No, no. It's for the children.' If the Queen suspected that this was a curious departure from the Prime Minister's usual line of conversation, she did not let it show although those who listened to the tape afterwards noticed a longer than normal pause by the Queen after the dialogue unexpectedly veered from French to English.

When the call was finished, Buckingham Palace officials contacted Chrétien's office at the regular number to arrange for the points for the proposed TV address to be faxed to the Queen. 'What points?' asked the Prime Minister's staff. That was when it dawned on everyone that the Queen had been fooled.

In the meantime Brassard broadcast the taped conversation on his radio show. He also sent a fax to Buckingham Palace, saying that it was an innocent joke and that no disrespect was intended. Buckingham Palace described the incident as 'irritating and regrettable' while the Queen herself was said to be 'philosophical' about the episode. Her main concern was that the revelation of her personal views might have adversely affected the outcome of the referendum. As it transpired, her fears were groundless. Not only did the people vote against separation but also the general consensus of opinion was that the fake interview showed her in a good light – well informed about Canadian events and deeply caring about the Commonwealth. And when the tape was broadcast, CKOI radio station was flooded with calls from people impressed by the Queen's fluent French. Pierre Brassard had unwittingly done her a favour.

The Rogue Republican

Of all the thousands of college pranks perpetrated down the years, only a handful are recounted to future generations as masterpieces of the genre. Principal among those to have acquired such immortality is a stunt pulled by the editors of Cornell University's student newspaper, *The Sun*, back in 1930. Their joke was to invent a statesman by the unlikely name of Hugo N. Frye who, they claimed, had been the founder of the Republican Party in New York State towards the end of the eighteenth century. And to celebrate what would have been Frye's 150th birthday, they were organising a banquet in his honour.

The editors sent out invitations to America's leading Republicans, reminding them, if they needed a memory jog, of Frye's historic campaigning slogans – 'Protection for our prosperity' and 'Freedom in the land of the free.' Vice-President Charles Curtis, Secretary of Labor James J. Davis and other members of President Hoover's Republican cabinet, plus senators, congressman, and New York State dignitaries all received invitations to the commemorative banquet. Most regretted that they would be unable to attend, but expressed their wholehearted support for the occasion. Secretary of Labor Davis went so far as to write: 'It is a pleasure to testify to the career of that sturdy patriot who first planted the ideals of our party in this region of the country. If he were living today, he would be the first to rejoice in evidence everywhere present that our government is still safe in the hands of the people.' He clearly held Frye in great esteem.

Then *The Sun* revealed the joke, asking readers to say out loud the name 'Hugo N. Frye'. The Democrats had a field day, Senator Pat Harrison of Mississippi gleefully reading out newspaper accounts of the hoax while Republican senators shuffled awkwardly in their seats, unable to conceal their embarrassment.

Report From Iron Mountain

Leonard Lewin's supposedly top-secret government document *Report From Iron Mountain* is a classic case of a hoax that was so convincing that, nearly forty years on, American right-wing militia groups still refuse to accept that it was a fake and see it as part of a vast political conspiracy. Published in book form, *Report From Iron Mountain* was promoted as a suppressed government report from the Kennedy administration, highly confidential but heroically revealed to the public by Lewin. Brilliantly mimicking government jargon and with footnotes that, apart from two, all referred to real publications, the book appeared utterly plausible. Its most astonishing claim was that the United States had become so dependent on military spending that it could not possibly reform to a peacetime economy should the Cold War end. The implication was clear: America had a hidden agenda regarding the Soviet Union, one designed to ensure the continuation of hostilities.

The spoof was conceived in 1966 by Victor Navasky, editor of the satirical political magazine *Monocle*, in reaction to a *New York Times* story which reported that the stock market had suddenly dipped following what was termed a 'peace scare'. Navasky and his cohorts, who included Lewin, then set about creating a sophisticated satire on the economic and social problems of peace, ostensibly authored by a panel of national security experts secretly convened by the government.

According to Lewin's book, these experts – 15 in total from diverse disciplines – had first been recruited by the US government in 1963 to examine 'the possibility and desirability of peace.' Known collectively as the Special Study Group, they usually met at a secret New York location ('an underground nuclear hideout for hundreds of large American corporations'), known as Iron Mountain. Lewin wrote in his introduction that he had been asked to disseminate the high-level report by an unnamed member of the Special Study Group.

Lewin claimed that the objectives of the SSG were to brainstorm on 'the nature of the problems that would confront the United States if and when a condition of "permanent peace" should arrive, and to draft a programme for dealing with this contingency.' These anonymous specialists appeared to favour a situation whereby the United States was on constant war footing, concluding that 'lasting peace, while not theoretically impossible, is probably unattainable; even if it could be achieved it would almost certainly not be in the best interest of stable society to achieve it.' Moreover the report grimly predicted a state of civil unrest without the nation-rallying opportunities provided by armed conflict. The American people, it argued, needed to be at war.

The alternative – peace – was too awful to contemplate, but, in the event of the worst-case scenario becoming reality, Lewin (as the SSG) suggested that 'alternate enemies' would have to be manufactured in order to preserve that siege mentality among Americans. The group advised that these enemies could perhaps take the form of 'an extra-terrestrial menace', 'massive global environmental pollution', or 'an omnipresent, virtually omnipotent international police force.' And if none of these measures were seen as sufficiently threatening to inflame the passions of the masses, the report advocated introducing 'a modern, sophisticated form of slavery', or maybe 'socially oriented blood games' recalling the halcyon days of witch trials or the Spanish Inquisition.

To facilitate the hoax, Dial Press, a division of Simon & Schuster, published *Report From Iron Mountain* as a non-fiction book. As soon as it appeared, it provoked widespread discussion in the media who were anxious to trace the book's unnamed writer and to verify its authenticity. However, by 1968, when anti-Vietnam protests were at their height, it almost became irrelevant whether or not the report was a fake. Its contents were seen as so pertinent to the changing face of America that it reached the *New York Times* bestseller list. *Esquire* magazine printed a 28,000-word extract, and dozens of other publications ran articles discussing the issues raised in the report. Even if it wasn't true, it could have been. Such were the fears about government manipulation.

In 1972 Lewin tried to put and end to the ongoing speculation about the authorship of *Report From Iron Mountain* by telling the *New York Times* that he wrote every word of it. But the very paranoia that the non-existent SSG had aimed to encourage ensured that right-wing groups disregarded Lewin's confession. Instead they view the attempts to persuade the American people that the report was a hoax as further proof that the government is trying to hoodwink the public. Its contents, they say, show that there is a conspiracy against citizens. It has also been used to back up allegations that a secret team of US military and intelligence officials were responsible for the assassination of President Kennedy.

When the book was updated in 1996, Victor Navasky looked back on its achievements. 'The report was a success,' he wrote, 'in that it achieved its mission, which in this case was to provoke thinking about the unthinkable – the conversion to a peacetime economy and the absurdity of the arms race. But it was a failure, given that even with the end of the Cold War we still have a Cold War economy.' Navasky also noted that, despite their best efforts, the Iron Mountain satirists have so far singularly failed to expose their own hoax to the satisfaction of all sections of the American public.

The Thatchergate Tapes

When members of the world's media received a tape of an apparent telephone conversation between President Reagan and Prime Minister Margaret Thatcher, they were united in dismissing it as a fake. The *Sunday Times* contended that the malicious content was clearly the work of the KGB while the US State Department agreed that the tape was evidence of 'an increasingly sophisticated Russian disinformation campaign.' Both parties received quite a shock therefore on learning that the tape did not originate from Moscow but from a north Essex farmhouse that served as the base for a little-known anarchist punk rock group called Crass.

Formed in 1977 at the height of the UK punk movement, Crass, whose lead singer, Steve Ignorant, was a less menacing version of the Sex Pistols' Johnny Rotten, were no strangers to hoaxes. They once duped a teenage magazine into offering a record called 'Our Wedding' by Joy de Vivre as part of a special bridal edition. The magazine promoted the disc as 'a must for the happy day', unaware that Joy de Vivre was a member of Crass and that the song, a track from the band's feminist album 'Penis Envy', was a 'sneering attack on love and marriage.'

In the summer of 1983, anxious to wreck Margaret Thatcher's prospects in the forthcoming General Election, Crass released anonymously to journalists what purported to be a tape recording of a discussion with President Reagan. A covering note claimed that the tape was a recording of a crossed line on which was heard part of the two leaders' telephone conversation. It added that the sender wished to remain anonymous for fear of retribution.

It was highly inflammatory stuff. Thatcher was heard virtually admitting that she had the Argentine warship *Belgrano* sunk during the previous year's Falklands War to end any chance of an agreement with Argentina.

'Why eliminate *Belgrano*?' Reagan was heard to ask. 'You directed this. The Argentinians were then going . . . Secretary Haig reached an agreement.'

Thatcher was heard to reply: 'Argentina was the invader! Force has been used. It's been used now, punishing them as quickly as possible.'

To which Reagan apparently exclaimed: 'Oh my God, it's not right!' He then went on to blame the Prime Minister for the loss of the British destroyer *Sheffield* in the Falklands conflict.

Reagan himself did not emerge unscathed. While talking about nuclear strategy, he seemed to say: 'In conflict, we will launch missiles on allies for effective limitation of the Soviet Union.'

'You mean over Germany?' asked Thatcher incredulously.

'Mrs Thatcher,' retorted Reagan, 'if any country of ours endangered the position, we might bomb the problem area, and correct the imbalance.'

The tape first surfaced in Holland, but failed to convince journalists there of its authenticity. Although the voices were definitely those of Reagan and Thatcher, they had obviously been spliced together and were not part of an actual conversation. Every word from Reagan was extracted from a lengthy November 1982 address on nuclear strategy. When, for instance, he seemed to blaspheme at Thatcher, he was in fact coming to the end of his speech and quoting a hymn, 'Oh God of love, O king of peace'.

The story came to the attention of the *San Francisco Chronicle* who contacted the US State Department for its reaction. Confirming that no such conversation had ever taken place between the President and the British Prime Minister, the State Department pointed an accusing finger at the Russians, saying: 'This type of activity fits the pattern of fabrications circulated by the Soviet KGB.'

Six months later, in January 1984, the *Sunday Times* ran the story under the headline: HOW THE KGB FOOLS THE WORLD'S PRESS. It quoted a State Department spokesman as saying that there was a pattern in the use of forgeries, which pointed unmistakably to the Russians.

Two weeks after the *Sunday Times* article, the *Observer* joyously revealed that its rival had been hoaxed. The tape was not the result of KGB propaganda, but of an Essex rock band. Crass reluctantly owned up and recounted how they had put the tape together over a period of two and a half months, using parts of TV and radio broadcasts made by the two leaders, then overdubbing with telephone noises. 'We wanted to precipitate a debate on the Falklands and nuclear weapons to damage Thatcher's position in the election,' said Crass. 'We believe that although the tape is a hoax what is said in it is in effect true. We were amused and amazed that the tape had been attributed to the KGB.'

The bogus tape had failed to undermine the Prime Minister's standing with the electorate but it did give Crass their 15 minutes of fame. 'The world's media pounced on the story,' said the eight-strong band, 'thrilled that "a bunch of punks" had made such idiots out of the State Department. Throughout the years as a band we had never attracted such attention, but all of a sudden we were media stars. We were interviewed by the Russian Press as American TV cameras recorded the event, we were live on American breakfast TV, we talked to radio stations from Essex to Tokyo, always giving the anarchist angle on every question.'

Chapter 17

April Fool's Day

FreeWheelz.com

It sounded like an offer that was too good to refuse: the opportunity to drive a free car in return for allowing it to be decorated with advertising. Readers of the April 2000 issue of *Esquire* magazine certainly thought so, even if it meant sitting behind the wheel of a pink Mini van painted as a huge billboard for tampons. But they should have studied the small print, which stated that the company in question, FreeWheelz.com, was being launched on the Internet on 1 April.

The *Esquire* article reported that the new Internet business was the brainchild of Skip Lehman, a graduate of Stanford University, California. Lehman said that his first Internet venture was I-Coli.com, a service that invited restaurants to post their health reviews and other ratings. He apparently sold the idea to Microsoft billionaire Paul Allen who put up the launch money and made I-Coli.com a local success. The idea for FreeWheelz came about while Lehman and some friends were discussing the various things that could be distributed free via the Internet – free computers, free music, free cigarettes, free booze, free dates. Then they thought: why not free cars?

Backed by an investment of $15 million, Lehman addressed a Chicago business conference in 1998 to look for advertisers. The article recalled how he entered the meeting 'in a rumpled white shirt, jeans, and a baseball cap with a hole for his ponytail. He clapped everyone to attention and said, "I'm told that in the new economy, if you don't have an idea, you should wear a suit. At least you look smart. Well, I don't have a good suit, but I've got a hell of an idea." Then he whipped off the baseball cap, to which his ponytail was sewn.

"Now that I've got your attention," he continued, "let me tell you how you can all get rich and possibly get a free car to boot."'

Lehman proceeded to explain how his company planned to provide drivers with free cars in exchange for the placement of large advertisements on the outside of the vehicle and the bombardment of non-stop commercials, specially tailored to the drivers' interests and needs, on the radio inside the car. To qualify for participation in the scheme, entrants had to guarantee that they would drive a minimum of 300 miles a week and complete a 600-question survey that enquired into such personal information as their sexual preferences, eating habits, political affiliations and whether they were concerned about hair loss. Finally they had to submit tax returns and a stool sample.

Despite the welter of red tape, Lehman told *Esquire* that the company had already tried out the idea successfully on a limited basis in Barrington du Lac, a smart suburb of Chicago, and that it had secured its first sponsor – StayFresh Tampons. He added that a fleet of Mini vans were already on the roads displaying the tampon advertisements. One of the first lucky recipients of a free StayFresh Mini van, PE teacher Jake Cameron, was quoted as saying: 'Getting the boys in the first time took some explaining. I tell the boys that a sanitary napkin isn't the best thing, but, hey, it's next to the best thing.' Other potential sponsors were said to include DearSkin.com, a company described as 'an eco-marketing venture that sells leather coats and gloves made exclusively from the hides of deer that have been humanely culled from suburban woods.' Lehman added that, in response to a request from Jimmy Carter, FreeWheelz had loaned the former President a 'Nuts for Peace' caravan sponsored by Planters.

The spoof article, written by Ted Fishman as a satire of the much-touted 'new economy' that had been created by the Internet, led to *Esquire*, who knew it was a hoax, being bombarded with phone calls from readers desperate to know how they could sign up to drive a StayFresh Mini van. It also sparked wholesale panic among chief executives of real Internet start-up firms with business plans similar to the fictitious FreeWheelz. *Esquire* revealed that David Guard, co-founder of Mobile Billboard Network, called an emergency meeting of his investors and thought it likely that he would have to come up with a new business idea. He rang the magazine in a serious panic, and was mightily relieved to be told that the article was a hoax. And Larry Butler, CEO of freecar.com, later told Fishman that he was so scared at the prospect of this new competition that he cried when he first read the article. Butler subsequently decided that the responses of readers who thought the parody was real actually validated his own business model. He ended up paying Fishman $25,000 for the rights to the FreeWheelz.com website. Fishman had originally paid just $75 to register the site.

Reflecting on his profitable prank, Fishman said that the concepts behind many Internet start-up companies were so ridiculous that he had wanted to invent 'something that seemed an incredibly grandiose idea and which people would find easy to dismiss. I was wrong.'

The Italian Gold Rush

Over 200 Italians rushed to the Roman hills and started digging frantically, hoping to find a £10 million pot of gold after being tricked by a classic April Fool.

On 1 April 2002 the Italian newspaper *La Provincia* printed details of a supposed excavation due to take place in the grounds of Montecassino, the monastery that had been a German stronghold in the Second World War until reduced to rubble by Allied bombers. It said Nazi soldiers had buried £10 million in gold bullion in a bunker at the site. For added authenticity, the paper quoted an SS soldier as saying he had been assigned to guard the gold bullion, which had been stolen from the King of Albania, and to ensure its safe burial before pulling out with the rest of the German troops.

Within hours of the paper going on sale, scores of people had read the story, grabbed shovels and rushed to the abbey 100 miles south of Rome. Police were called in to control the crowds heading for the site, and when told of the story, they contacted the editor who admitted that it was an April Fool. A police spokesman said: 'You can imagine the reaction of those that were in there when we told them they had wasted their Easter Monday looking for buried treasure which wasn't even there. I think the editor will be looking over his shoulder for a while.'

A Whopper From Burger King

On 1 April 1998 the Burger King Corporation published a full-page advertisement in *USA Today* announcing the introduction of a new item to its restaurant menus. The new line was a Left-Handed Whopper, specially designed to accommodate the 32 million Americans who are left-handed.

The advertisement said that the new Whopper was identical to the traditional version except that it had 'all condiments rotated 180 degrees, thereby redistributing the weight of the sandwich so that the bulk of the condiments will skew to the left, thereby reducing the amount of lettuce and other toppings from spilling out the right side of the burger.' Jim

Watkins, the senior vice-president for marketing at Burger King, was quoted as saying that the new product was the 'ultimate "have it your way" for our left-handed customers.' The advertisement added that the Left-Handed Whopper would initially only be available in the United States, but that the company was considering whether to market it in other countries with large left-handed populations.

The next day Burger King issued a follow-up release, revealing the Left-Handed Whopper to be an April Fool's Day joke. The company said that thousands of customers had been fooled by the bogus advertisement and had gone into branches of Burger King to ask for the new sandwich. And many more had specifically requested a right-handed version when placing their order.

Second Titanic Disaster

As an April Fool's Day joke destined to end in disaster, English local radio station Southern FM could not have chosen a better subject than the *Titanic*.

On the morning of 1 April 2001, presenters on the Brighton-based station excitedly announced that a full-size replica of the *Titanic* was sailing along the southern coast of England and would be visible from land. The best vantage point, they added, was from the top of the 400 ft-high cliffs of Beachy Head in East Sussex.

Taken in by the hoax, hundreds of sightseers rushed to Beachy Head, but the sheer weight of numbers caused a dangerous five-foot crack to appear in the cliff face and forced coastguards to evacuate the area. 'There was a real danger posed to the public because of a substantial crack,' said a coastguard spokesman. 'The cliffs at Beachy Head are notoriously dangerous at any time but they were also shrouded in fog. This has caused us a lot of problems.' To make matters worse, the crowd, in their eagerness to catch a view of the non-existent vessel, had also strayed on to parkland that had been closed to prevent the spread of foot-and-mouth disease.

One woman drove her two children more than 30 miles to see the ship. 'I felt such an idiot,' she said afterwards, 'but more than anything I was angry at the station for wasting my time. My kids were very upset.'

Southern FM was forced to apologize to its listeners, insisting, 'It was just a bit of fun.'

Redheads Beware

On April Fool's Day 1973, BBC radio broadcast a spoof interview with a geriatric academic who outlined the British government's policies in preventing the spread of Dutch Elm Disease, which was then ravaging much of the country's trees. He referred to the research of a Dr Emily Lang of the London School of Pathological and Environmental Medicine who had discovered that exposure to Dutch Elm Disease apparently immunized humans against the common cold. However, the expert warned that there was an unwelcome side effect to such exposure. Due to a similarity between the blood counts of redheads and the soil conditions in which affected trees grew, the disease was likely to make red hair turn yellow. So he strongly advised redheads to stay away from forests for the foreseeable future. The 'academic' was subsequently revealed to be legendary Goon Spike Milligan.

Canadian Minister's Shock Resignation

A joke Internet report that Canadian Finance Minister Paul Martin was quitting his job to breed Charolais cows and 'handsome fawn runner ducks' sent the Canadian dollar slipping to a one-month low against the US dollar on April Fool's Day 2002.

The author of the spoof report was Pierre Bourque who flagged it on his political gossip website, bourque.org. The article, which included links to sites with pictures of Charolais cows and large brown and white ducks, said that Martin was preparing to show his livestock at a country fair in Havelock, a small town near Quebec. It added that, in view of the shock news, the Bank of Canada was getting ready to intervene to defend the dollar.

As the Canadian dollar duly tumbled from C$1.5942 against the US dollar to C$1.6042, Bourque admitted to being baffled by the overreaction. 'It is 1 April, after all,' he told Reuters. 'The ducks were the telltale sign.'

The Canadian dollar recovered later in the day.

Stung Into Action

In 1949 Phil Shone, a disc jockey with New Zealand radio station 1ZB, warned listeners that a mile-wide wasp swarm was heading straight for the city of Auckland. He urged people to combat the threat by wearing socks over their trousers when leaving for work and by leaving honey-smeared traps outside the doors of their homes. Hundreds took his advice, resulting in some strange sights on the streets of Auckland that morning.

When Shone finally admitted that the deadly swarm was nothing more than an April Fool's joke, the New Zealand Broadcasting Service was so angry at what it saw as a betrayal of its good name that thereafter a memo was sent out each year before 1 April banning stations from broadcasting hoax stories.

A Guide to San Serriffe

An exciting new holiday destination presented itself to *Guardian* readers on 1 April 1977 – the Indian Ocean islands of San Serriffe, said to be celebrating ten years of independence from Portugal. To mark 'a period of economic expansion and social development probably unrivalled by any other new nation', the newspaper printed an entire supplement on the customs, history and economics of San Serriffe.

Guardian readers pride themselves on their knowledge of world affairs, so many must have been puzzled as to why they had never heard of San Serriffe. Yet there was something strangely familiar about the name . . . particularly to those who worked in the printing industry. For Sans Serif is a typeface, and virtually all the other locations featured on the map accompanying the article were printing terms. The two main islands of the archipelago were called Upper Caisse and Lower Caisse, principal towns were Bodoni and Cap Em, and there was a promontory on Lower Caisse known as Thirty Point. Furthermore, the indigenous natives went by the name of the Flongs. It goes without saying that there was no such place as San Serriffe.

Clues were littered throughout the article. The islands were described as being in the shape of a semicolon and their discovery in 1421 was said to be 'a punctuation mark in a long chapter of oceanic exploration.'

Readers were informed that San Serriffe was ceded to Portugal in 1815, but that a General Minion had seized power in 1969. The current President, M-J Pica, took control in 1971. The islands' wealth (its currency was the corona) had been established through phosphates, tourists and, latterly, oil, prompting the article to suggest that San Serriffe was an ideal spot for investment. 'In almost all the social and public services San Serriffe is much in advance of comparable countries, with three geriatric teaching hospitals and a pioneer pre-school psychiatric unit attached to the university at Perpetua.' An innovative education system allowed students to take subjects such as pearl-diving at A level.

The only warning note surrounded the geology of the area amid fears that constant erosion of the western coasts of San Serriffe would eventually bring the islands into collision with Sri Lanka.

The piece was accompanied by authentic advertisements. Texaco promoted a competition for which the first prize was a fortnight's holiday on San Serriffe's Cocobanana Beach. As a result the *Guardian*'s phones rang throughout the day with people wanting to know more about the islands. The spoof proved so successful that the

Guardian revived it in 1978, 1980 and 1999, each time changing the location of San Serriffe. It was last heard of somewhere in the North Atlantic.

Motorway Madness

On April Fool's Day 1991 *The Times* wrote that British government ministers were planning to introduce a unique one-way traffic scheme to ease congestion on the M25, the orbital motorway that encircles London. The Department of Transport was apparently planning to solve jams by making both carriageways one-way, with traffic travelling clockwise or anti-clockwise on alternate days of the week.

The scheme was said to have been inspired by similar projects on the continent where many cities apparently alleviated traffic congestion by allowing cars with odd and even number plates into busy areas only on certain days.

The plan for the M25 was to run traffic in a clockwise direction on Mondays, Wednesdays and Fridays, anti-clockwise on Tuesdays and Thursdays, and vice versa on alternate weeks. The scheme would not operate at weekends. The Road Haulage Association allegedly welcomed the measures. Said a fictitious spokesman: 'We have been advocating some such revolutionary solution for some time. Transport managers will be able to arrange clockwise deliveries on some days, and anti-clockwise on others. We will all know where we stand.'

However, residents of Swanley in Kent were said to be unhappy at the proposals. One resident was quoted as saying: 'Villagers use the motorway to make shopping trips to Orpington. On some days this will be a journey of two miles, and on others a journey of 117 miles.'

Taking a Liberty

When the *New York Times* ran a full-page ad on 1 April 1996 to announce that the fast food chain Taco Bell was purchasing the Liberty Bell, thousands of irate callers rang the National Historic Park in Philadelphia, where the bell is housed, to register their protest.

The offending advertisement said that 'in an effort to help the national debt, Taco Bell is pleased to announce that we have agreed to purchase the Liberty Bell, one of our country's most historic treasures. It will now be called the "Taco Liberty Bell" and will still be accessible to the American public for viewing. While some may find this controversial, we hope our move will prompt other corporations to take similar action to do their part to reduce the country's debt.'

An accompanying press release explained that people and corporations had been adopting highways for years. Taco Bell was simply taking it 'one step further'. Taco Bell finally revealed the hoax in a second press release at noon. Guardians of the nation's heritage breathed a collective sigh of relief.

The French Connection

The switchboard of BBC Radio Solent was flooded with callers taken in by a 1992 April Fool's broadcast which stated that the Isle of Wight was being claimed by France. The report said that the French were basing their claim on the basis of an ancient pipe that apparently linked the island to France. 'It would mean cheaper wine, better food, and topless women on the beach,' said the radio station. Most callers rang to say that they were in favour of their new nationality.

Every Pitcher Tells a Story

Baseball's best-kept secret was finally revealed in the edition of *Sports Illustrated* dated 1 April 1985. A feature by George Plimpton told how the New York Mets had discovered an eccentric rookie by the name of Sidd Finch who could pitch a baseball with deadly accuracy at an astonishing 168 mph – a speed 65 mph faster than the previous record.

Finch was apparently being kept under wraps at the Mets' training camp in St Petersburg, Florida, but the resourceful Plimpton managed to persuade a few people to talk about the game's most exciting prospect in decades. When he first came out to bat against Finch, John Christensen, a 24-year-old outfielder, was immediately struck by the fact that Finch wore a heavy hiking boot on his right foot. 'He had blue eyes,' Christensen remembered, 'and a pale, youthful face, with facial muscles that were motionless, like a mask.' He described Finch's peculiar pitching action as reminiscent of Goofy's pitching in a Disney film. 'I never dreamed a baseball could be thrown that fast,' said Christensen. 'The wrist must have a lot to do with it, and all that leverage. You can hardly see the blur as it goes by. As for hitting the thing, frankly, I just don't think it's humanly possible. You could send a blind man up there, and maybe he'd do better hitting at the sound of the thing.'

A catcher relayed his experience of playing ball with Finch. 'The first time I see him is inside the canvas coop, out there on the pitcher's mound, a thin kid getting ready to throw, and I'm thinking he'll want to toss a couple of warm-up pitches . . . Suddenly I see this wind-up like a pretzel going loony, and the next thing, I've been blown two or three feet back, and I'm sitting on the ground with the ball in my glove. My catching hand feels like it's been hit with a sledgehammer.'

Precious little was known about Finch's background, wrote Plimpton. He spent his early childhood in an English orphanage and was adopted by archaeologist Francis Whyte-Finch who was later killed in a plane crash while on an expedition in Nepal. At the time of the tragedy, the boy was in his last year at school in England. He entered Harvard in 1975, dropping the 'Whyte' from his name, but withdrew from college midway through the spring 1976 term. His roommate remembered Finch chiefly for his fondness for playing the French horn in the bath.

Finch left Harvard to study in Tibet and it was there in the mountains that he learned to pitch even though he had never played baseball before. Back in the US he introduced himself to the manager of the Mets' junior club and said that his name was Hayden Finch but he wanted to be called Sidd, which was short for 'Siddhartha', Tibetan for 'aim attained' or 'the perfect pitch'. Finch said that was what he had learned: how to throw the perfect pitch.

This young man of few words – the majority unintelligible to the Western ear – appeared remarkably ambivalent about baseball, often refusing to wear the proper uniform. In addition to his trademark hiking boot, he sometimes wore a tie over his jersey. In a bid to make Finch feel more at home, the Mets hired a specialist in Eastern religion who suspected that the strange ballplayer was an aspirant monk. They hoped to convince Finch that the two religions of Buddhism and baseball were compatible. But, the article concluded, he had yet to decide whether to pursue a career playing the French horn or baseball and had promised the Mets management an answer by 1 April.

The following week's *Sports Illustrated* told how Finch had decided against joining the Mets. Reading from a prepared statement at a press conference he had explained that the pinpoint accuracy required to harness his incredible fastball had suddenly deserted him. 'The perfect pitch,' said the mystic Met, 'once a thing of harmony, is now an instrument of chaos and cruelty.'

Sports Illustrated had received almost 2,000 letters in response to George Plimpton's original article, but on 15 April the magazine admitted that the story was a hoax. There had actually been a subtle clue in the sub-heading to the 1 April feature, which read: 'He's a pitcher, part yogi and part recluse. Impressively liberated from our opulent lifestyle, Sidd's deciding about yoga – and his future in baseball.' The first letter of each word, when spelt out, reads: 'Happy April Fool's Day'.

Slimline Tonic

A new line of socks designed to help people lose weight were unveiled in the *Daily Mail* on 1 April 2000. FatSox, as they were to be known, promised to 'banish fat for ever' by sucking the body fat out of a person's feet as they sweated.

The revolutionary socks incorporated a patented nylon polymer called FloraAstraTetrazine, invented by American professor Frank Ellis Elgood and previously only used in the nutrition industry. As a person's body heat rose and his or her blood vessels dilated, the socks, it was claimed, would draw any excess liquid from the body through the sweat. Having sweated out the fat, the wearer could simply remove the socks and wash them – and the fat – away.

Selling Off New York

Dozens of angry readers rang New York's City Hall to protest at a story that appeared in the East Side weekly paper *Our Town* and which stated that Gracie Mansion, the Mayor's official residence, was being sold to property developers.

The article said that the building 'will likely be sold to a developer who will tear down the landmark 1789 mansion and build luxury waterfront condos.' The newspaper claimed that the idea was 'part of Rudolph Guiliani's continuing programme of selling off city-owned properties in a last-ditch bid to close New York's billion-dollar budget gap.' It quoted Guiliani as saying: 'This is a wonderful opportunity for many New Yorkers – instead of just one family – to enjoy this particular piece of real estate.'

Donald Trump, named as the possible builder of a 50-storey tower on the site, was said to have described the project as 'the jewel in my crown.'

The article hinted that other landmarks – such as the Staten Island Ferry, Coney Island, and all the city libraries – would also be put up for sale. It added that city officials were considering invoking a law to seize churches and synagogues before selling them, too.

Such was the outcry that baffled officials at City Hall felt compelled to ring *Our Town* where publisher Tom Allon revealed that it was an April Fool's joke. Apart from the 1 April 1995 dateline to the story, there had been one other clue – the byline of Janet Cooke, the name of the *Washington Post* reporter who infamously won a Pulitzer Prize in 1981 for a report that was largely invented.

An Uplifting Hoax

On 1 April 1982 Britain's *Daily Mail* printed a story which claimed that there was a serious problem with 10,000 bras designed by a local manufacturer. It said that the support wire in the affected bras had been made out of specially treated copper, which had originally been intended for use in fire alarms, but which, when coming into contact with nylon and body heat, was producing static electricity. In turn, this static electricity was being emitted by thousands of unsuspecting women and causing widespread television interference.

Amazingly many readers swallowed the hoax report, including a chief engineer at British Telecom. After seeing the *Mail*, he allegedly demanded that all female laboratory employees disclose what type of bra they were wearing.

The Science of Chromo-Floristics

A 1996 article by Zola McMalcolm in the British journal *Everyday Practical Electronics* described how, in future, gardeners would be able to change the colours of certain plants by flooding them with light of particular wavelengths.

The two-page report said that horticulturists at a Kent laboratory had made the discovery accidentally, but that it had already stimulated interest from Jersey and Holland. The new phenomenon was called chromo-floristics. The article pointed out that plants' colours became brighter through the seasons – from winter snowdrops, to spring daffodils, to summer bedding – and explained that the 'changing light wavelength conditions' were responsible. Among the flowers said to be particularly responsive to light manipulation was *Primula Harlequina Apriliosii*, otherwise known as the April Harlequin.

Failing to spot the clear reference to April Fool, a *Times* reporter tried to follow up the scientific breakthrough by contacting first the laboratory and then Ms McMalcolm. Drawing a blank in both cases, she eventually got through to the editor of *Everyday Practical Electronics* and was put out of her misery. She was not alone in being fooled by the article, which was in reality penned by the magazine's technical editor John Becker. The long-running BBC TV science programme *Tomorrow's World* had also phoned in search of further information.

The Tasmanian Mock Walrus

The *Orlando Sentinel* of 1 April 1984 unveiled an exciting new form of pest control. It was called the Tasmanian mock walrus (or TMW for short), a tiny creature that had apparently been recently introduced to Florida from Australasia and which had a voracious appetite for cockroaches. The article claimed that one TMW could rid an entire house of cockroach infestation.

Described as a 'whiskered, four-inch long creature, which purrs like a cat and gets around efficiently on four tiny paws', the TMW was also blessed with the docile nature of a hamster and could be trained to use a litter tray. In fact, it was the ideal family pet.

Unfortunately the mock walrus was not welcomed by all. The report said that a Florida couple were hoping to breed the TMW in the USA but had fallen foul of the local pest-control industry, which saw the animal as a serious threat to its future prosperity and had pressured the Orlando city government to ban it. An accompanying photograph showed pro-TMW protesters picketing outside government offices brandishing placards reading 'FREEDOM TO BREED!' and 'SAVE THE TASMANIAN MOCK WALRUS'. Another picture showed the inoffensive little creature resting on the palm of a human hand.

It seems that many readers were touched by the plight of the TMW and dozens called the paper trying to find out where they could obtain one. That was when they learned that the Tasmanian mock walrus existed only in the imagination of the paper's editorial staff. The photo had been of a naked mole rat.

The Sound of Ancient Music

America's *Discover* magazine told how, in April 1997, a palaeontologist by the name of Oscar Todkopf had stumbled across some of the world's oldest musical instruments. The Hindenburg University scientist was said to have been hiking in Germany's Neander Valley when he tripped over what appeared to be a straightforward mastodon tusk. However, closer examination revealed the presence of 16 carefully aligned holes along the surface of the six-foot tusk, leading Todkopf to conclude that it was a Neanderthal tuba. He added that the number of holes suggested that Neanderthals used an octave scale.

The 50,000-year-old tuba was just one of Todkopf's reported musical finds. He also discovered a primitive bagpipe – possibly made from the bladder of a woolly rhinoceros – and a collection of bones of various lengths, which he called a xylobone. 'But,' said Todkopf, 'a colleague thinks Neanderthals hung the bones at cave entrances like big wind chimes. As for the bagpipes, well, it doesn't surprise me that we have Neanderthals to thank for them.' Todkopf believed that they played the bagpipes with their noses since wooden plugs attached to the instrument fitted perfectly into the sinus cavities of a Neanderthal skull found at the site. 'These fellows had nasal cavities as big as beer halls,' Todkopf remarked.

While excavating the instruments, Todkopf was said to have uncovered the first known example of a Neanderthal cave painting. It depicted musicians in groups of three, which he suspected was a form of musical notation – 'the origin of oompah-pah!' He believed that the Neanderthals' fondness for music may have led to their eventual extinction since the noise they made would have scared away all the game.

It came as little surprise to readers when the story of Oscar Todkopf was revealed to be an April Fool's Day hoax.

A Blast from the Past

The front page of the 1 April 1933 edition of the *Madison Capital-Times* contained a dramatic photograph that appeared to show the collapse of the dome of the Wisconsin State Capitol building. The accompanying story revealed that the 'beautiful $8 million capitol was in ruins today following a series of mysterious explosions which blasted the majestic dome from its base.' According to the report, the first explosion had occurred at 7.30 a.m., followed by a succession of lesser blasts that showered chips of granite on to the heads of pedestrians below.

Accident investigators believed that the first explosion had been caused by the ignition of large quantities of gas, generated through weeks of debate in the Senate and Assembly chambers. Hot air had then found its way into other rooms in the building, leading to the remaining blasts.

Although the story ended with the words 'April Fool', a number of readers expressed their view that the joke was in bad taste. One wrote to the editor describing it as 'a hideous jest'.

The Virgin Butterfly

A press release on the Virgin Atlantic Airways website for 1 April 2002 announced that the airline planned to begin advertising via butterflies, thereby becoming the first US advertiser to take advantage of research recently announced by the State University of New York at Buffalo.

It went on: 'According to a study published in *Trends in Ecology and Evolution*, Dr Antonia Monteiro at SUNY Buffalo is developing a genetic modification method that would allow companies to put markings such as logos on butterflies by scanning their wings with a laser beam. Virgin is confident that butterfly advertising will become a successful and popular new medium for airlines.'

John Riordan, vice-president of marketing, was quoted as saying: 'We think advertising via butterflies is a natural synergy for an airline, especially an innovative airline like Virgin Atlantic. We're always looking for new ways to promote our products and services, and what better way than via a constantly flying medium?'

Virgin said it hoped to be able to control the flight areas of the butterflies, keeping them within major park and recreational areas, and was intending to launch the project in the spring. This would allow time for final testing and lasering of the Virgin logo on the butterflies.

Before insect-lovers had a chance to complain, the release concluded with the words: 'Virgin Atlantic Airways wishes you a happy April Fool's.'

SECTION TWO

Con Artists

When Soapy Smith Cleaned Up The West

Jefferson Randolph Smith has been called the King of the Frontier Con Men. By means of the soap trick that earned him his nickname or the traditional shell game, Smith conned thousands of suckers out of their drinking money at a time when America's West was a place for guns and gambling, women and whisky. Smith, it seems, had a hankering for all four.

He was born in Noonan, Georgia, in 1860 to an aristocratic Southern family. His mother was sometimes known as the Pride of Virginia on account of her great beauty; by contrast, his lawyer father kept slaves and drank heavily. Jefferson was one of seven brothers. Three would go on to become doctors, two followed their father into law, and one opted for life as a farmer: all good, honest careers (apart from the lawyers, obviously). Jefferson, however, chose to take a different path in life.

His father faced financial ruin following the Civil War and the family moved to Temple, Texas, in the hope of building a new life. Money was still tight, but Jeff's mother prayed that the regular church-going to which he had been subjected since boyhood would stand her son in good stead. So it was with considerable disappointment that she saw him throw away his solid education to land a job as a cowboy.

Jeff joined his first cattle drive in 1876. After months on the trail, the drive ended up in Abelene, Texas, where, wandering the streets, he spotted a gambler who had set up a shell game. Three half walnut shells were laid out, one of which concealed a pea. After quick-fire manipulation, the challenger had to bet that he could nominate which shell the pea was under. Jeff tried it . . . and quickly lost his entire wages to the gambler. Although Jeff's pockets were now empty, his head was full of plans for the future. Life on the trail was too much like hard work when there was easy money to be made as a professional gambler. He reckoned he could make in minutes as a gambler what it would take him four months to rake in as a cowboy.

For the best part of ten years Smith roamed the frontier, operating gambling scams and furthering his ambition to become the best poker player in the West. In 1885 he turned up in Leadville, Colorado, and was immediately drawn to an old man surrounded by a crowd. The veteran in question was Old Man Taylor, whom Smith had heard of as a boy and who was known as 'King of the Shell Game'. Smith used his powers of eloquence to talk Taylor into a partnership and soon the pair had set up business on the corner of Harrison Street and Third Street, happily fleecing the locals of their money. The shell game proved highly profitable but they knew it had a limited life and so Smith, in particular, was always on the lookout for new cons. Then one day Taylor showed his young protégé the 'soap trick'. It was the scam that was to make his name.

Smith started his new enterprise by wrapping a $100 bill around a bar of soap, re-wrapping it with his own label, and putting it in a box with numerous other bars of soap, all bearing the name of his product, Sapolion. He then walked into one of the town's busiest saloons, offering the soap at $5 per bar. His silent partner 'bought' the loaded bar and, upon opening it in front of the other patrons, feigned surprise at finding a crisp $100 bill under the wrapping. A stampede followed as the rest of the drinkers all tried to cash in. Each was parted from five bucks for no reward. It was like taking candy from a baby.

Flushed with success, Smith moved to Denver where he unveiled an improved soap swindle. Setting up his little folding table on a street corner near the train station, he would entertain the crowds with songs and jokes before coming to his *pièce de resistance*. He loaded the bars with $10, $20, and even a few $100 bills, told the spectators to watch closely, and then gave them the chance to buy a bar of soap for $5. They all thought they were on to a winner but Smith had craftily swapped the bars, leaving only the corners showing. The only people to pick up the prizes were Smith's own accomplices. He took care to target visitors to the town rather than the locals in the belief that they were less likely to be around long enough to rumble him, but a complaint was eventually filed with the police. When booking him at the police station, the arresting officer couldn't remember Smith's first name but did recall that the swindle involved soap. The officer wrote 'Soapy' Smith on the log. The name stuck.

The scare encouraged Smith to veer towards pursuits that were marginally on the right side of the law and he opened the Tivoli Saloon and Gambling Hall. A sign above the door read '*Caveat Emptor*' (Latin for 'Let the buyer beware'). Luckily for Smith, nobody in Denver could read Latin.

The silver boom in Creede, Colorado, enticed Soapy to move his gambling operation there. He built his own gambling club and generally took over the running of the new town. He also met his future wife, saloon singer Anna Nielson, but it wasn't long before she tired of his increasingly heavy drinking and left him. Eventually he was kicked out of Creede whereupon he headed back to Denver and opened a railroad ticket office, advertising tickets to Chicago for $5. When customers arrived, they were told that the cheap tickets weren't sold every day, but they were shown instead to Soapy's gambling den in the back room. Smith and his cohorts were blamed for much of the lawlessness in Denver, a situation that brought them into conflict with Colorado governor Davis H. Waite. Determined to clean up the place, Waite mobilized the state militia. Smith raised his own army in opposition and became a colonel overnight. At one point he stood in the cupola of City Hall holding a stick of dynamite and dared the militia to open fire on him. Waite backed down and new city commissioners were appointed. Their first action was to run Soapy Smith out of town.

The Yukon Gold Rush of 1897 took Soapy to the port of Skagway, Alaska, where he soon opened a saloon/casino called Jeff's Place. Surrounded by his gang of helpers (whom he called his 'lambs'), Soapy ran such a tight casino that few gamblers made a profit. Those that did were likely to be relieved of their winnings by Soapy's 'lambs' in Skagway's back alleys. Smith ploughed part of the casino profits into building Skagway's first telegraph station, which opened less than a week after construction had begun. Business was brisk, the customers failing to realize that the telegraph wires extended only a few hundred feet into Skagway harbour. They did receive replies, however, most of which asked the men to 'send money' back home. Naturally the telegraph office was happy to assist.

When it dawned on the locals that they were being conned, they tried to run Soapy and his cronies out of town. Smith tried to cling to power but faced an armed uprising after swindling a miner out of $3,000 in gold. On 8 July 1898 Soapy Smith was shot dead during a gunfight. America's most slippery customer had been nailed down at last. He is buried in an unmarked grave in a Skagway cemetery.

Mary, Mary, Quite Contrary

Mary Bateman deceived her victims by professing to have supernatural powers. But in truth she was a heartless trickster who finished up on the gallows after one of her deceptions took a more sinister turn.

The woman who came to be known as the 'Yorkshire Witch' was born Mary Harker near the town of Thirsk in 1768. Her father was a farmer and both were parents were respected members of the rural community, but from an early age Mary showed a proclivity for theft. At the age of 13 she was sent to work as a domestic in Thirsk but was soon dismissed for petty pilfering. By the time she was 20 she had been sacked from so many posts that nobody in the immediate vicinity would employ her. So she tried her luck as a dressmaker in Leeds, supplementing her modest income by telling fortunes.

When Mary was 24 she married John Bateman, a wheelwright from Thirsk. He was one of many who had fallen under her spell but he quickly came to regret the union on learning of his wife's criminal tendencies. On one occasion she convinced him that his father was seriously ill. He hurried back to Thirsk and in his absence she sold his clothes and all their furniture to repay a victim who was threatening to contact the authorities.

Envious of the women for whom she made fine clothes, Mary tried to emulate their opulent lifestyle by resorting to theft and fraud on a grand scale. After a major fire in Leeds, she roamed the streets begging for money, sheets and blankets in support of the poor victims. Needless to say, all the proceeds ended up in her own home. As she began to lose interest in dressmaking, she concentrated increasingly on making a living from fortune telling and built up a reputation throughout Leeds as a warder-off of evil spirits and a miracle healer. Some were less charitable and viewed her as a witch.

To assist in her soothsaying activities, Mary invented a mythical character called 'Mrs Moore' who, as the seventh child of a seventh child, was supposed to be blessed with supernatural skills even greater than those of Mary herself. As Mary described her, Mrs Moore was the Wonder Woman of her day, capable of solving any crisis. An early victim was a Mrs Greenwood who was frightened into believing that her husband had been put in jail and that only Mrs Moore could secure his release. As requested, the gullible Mrs Greenwood handed over money to Mary and when her husband returned, she thought that it had been well spent. She was Mary's first satisfied customer . . . until she discovered that her husband had never been in jail at all.

Another victim, Mrs Stead, was tricked into believing that her soldier husband was considering an adulterous affair. Once again the non-existent Mrs Moore was wheeled out to save the day in return for a fat fee. The first instruction was for Mrs Stead to place pieces of coal outside her alleged love rival's front door and then set fire to them in order to consume her husband's illicit passion. If the gullible woman thought that was an end to the matter, she was gravely mistaken for Mary had all manner of hideous scenarios up her sleeve and foretold that Mrs Stead would be subjected to further dire happenings unless additional sums of money were paid to acquire the services of Mrs Moore. Eventually the hapless Mrs Stead handed everything she owned to Mary Bateman in the hope of averting these awful prophecies. Her life in ruins, she attempted suicide by drowning.

Mary remained untroubled by such trifles and by the autumn of 1806 she was trying out her latest scam in a Leeds tavern. Her hen had apparently started laying eggs inscribed with the words 'Christ Is Coming'. Believers took the divine inscription to herald the imminent approach of Armageddon, and prayer meetings were held throughout the town. Mary told the assembled throng that God had revealed to her that her hen would lay 14 similarly inscribed eggs and that the earth would then be consumed in flames. As she spoke, her hen laid another egg bearing the same portent of doom. Fortunately, said Mary, there was hope of salvation – but it could cost everyone present a penny to hear. Faced with almost certain extermination in a matter of days, a penny seemed a small price to pay, and everyone readily handed the money over to Mary.

Next she announced that God had decided that all those bearing a piece of distinct paper sealed with the inscription 'J. C.' would be allowed to enter heaven immediately after the 14th egg was laid. The price for this lucky ticket was a shilling. All who could afford it, paid up. With each additional egg that was laid, hundreds of desperate souls hurried to the tavern to purchase their single tickets to heaven. Mary's pockets were bulging.

Her luck ran out when news of the strange goings-on reached the ears of a local doctor. He decided to take a look for himself and, on close inspection, discovered that the wording on the eggs had been inscribed with corrosive ink. He notified the authorities who raided the tavern on the very day that the 14th egg was due to be laid. They apprehended Mary just as she was ramming an inscribed egg back into a distinctly apprehensive hen. Mary was arrested, but released shortly afterwards. Amazingly most of her victims were not worried about having been conned – they were simply relieved that Doomsday had been postponed.

The demise of the egg scam left Mary in need of a new avenue of revenue. She laid 'Mrs Moore' to rest and invented a new imaginary oracle, Mrs Blythe, who soon paid her way by persuading a family called Snowdon to give Mary a silver watch and 12 guineas in order to prevent their daughter from being drowned.

The couple that were eventually to prove her undoing were William and Rebecca Perigo of Bramley, near Leeds. When Mrs Perigo complained of chest pains, she was advised by the unseen Mrs Blythe to pursue various courses of action, all of which lined Mary's pockets and rendered the couple impoverished. At one point Mary visited the Perigos' home and told them that she would sew four money notes into their bed as a cure recommended by Mrs Blythe. In return they were instructed to give Mary four guineas with which she would recompense Mrs Blythe. The Perigos also received letters from Mrs Blythe, demanding cash and gifts so that Mrs Perigo could be restored to full health. Like so many before, they paid up without question. Yorkshire folk had clearly yet to acquire the reputation of being careful with their money.

To date the case had followed a familiar pattern, but now Mary realized that she had fleeced her victims of so much that the only way to preserve her own skin was to kill them off. Accordingly, the Perigos received another letter from Mrs Blythe ordering them to take half a pound of honey to Mary Bateman who would then put 'such stuff' into the honey as the helpful spirit advised. They then had to eat the 'pudding' mixture or face death from a terrible disease. Unbeknown to the Perigos the 'stuff' was mercuric chloride.

On 11 May 1808 the couple began eating the pudding and, when both fell violently sick, Mary kindly gave them an antidote. Unfortunately for the Perigos, the antidote was arsenic. Mr Perigo ate very little of the lethal cocktail or the antidote, but was nevertheless ill for days and his lips turned black. His wife forced herself to eat everything and died in agony on 24 May.

Gradually Mr Perigo recovered but was in no fit state to resist Mary Bateman who continued to weave her spells. Finally he decided to retrieve the money notes that had been sewn into the bed. Discovering them to be worthless pieces of paper, he realized he had been duped and arranged a meeting with Mary Bateman, at which she was arrested by two justice officers. A search of her house uncovered property belonging to the Perigos and a collection of poisons.

Her trial for murder took place at York in March 1809. She tried to lay the blame at the door of the fictitious Mrs Blythe but dozens of witnesses testified to her nefarious activities, which included fraud, extortion and performing abortions, and the jury quickly returned a verdict of guilty. As devious as ever she attempted to escape her inevitable fate by claiming that she was pregnant and that it was illegal for a pregnant woman to be hanged. A medical examination proved that she was lying again. Even while waiting for her appointment with the gallows she could not resist swindling her fellow prisoners out of money with promises of reprieves.

A huge crowd turned out for her execution at 5 a.m. on 20 March 1809. Those who believed she had supernatural powers were convinced that she would somehow cheat the hangman's noose, but for once none of her spells or imaginary friends could help her.

Afterwards her body was put on public display and thousands paid to view it, all proceeds going to charity. Later, strips of her skin were sold as charms to ward off evil. It was a scam of which Mary Bateman herself would surely have approved.

Frank Abagnale: Poacher Turned Gamekeeper

In a five-year spree of forgery, fraud and impersonation, Frank Abagnale earned himself a reputation as America's most notorious con man of the 1960s. Shamelessly using bogus diplomas and ID cards, Abagnale masqueraded as a paediatrician, a lawyer, a sociology professor and an airline pilot, in the course of which he was able to cash bad cheques to the value of $2.5 million. Perhaps the most remarkable aspect of Abagnale's career of imposture and deception is that it ended when he was just 21. In the world of the confidence trickster, he was a teenage prodigy.

The Frank Abagnale story begins in the affluent suburbs of New York City in April 1948. He was one of four children born to Frank and Paula Abagnale. His parents had met in a French village during the Second World War and Frank Snr owned a stationery store. Outwardly the marriage and the business were in good shape but soon there were clouds on both horizons. The family business ran into financial problems and, unable to secure a loan from the bank, Frank Snr had to move his brood downmarket.

Frank Jnr was a bright kid with an IQ of 136. He was, as he himself says, a 'very creative' child although he didn't always put his talents to the use that his teachers would have wished, on one occasion masquerading before class as a new French supply teacher. He would eventually drop out of high school in tenth grade.

The first person he swindled money out of was his father. 'When I first got my driver's licence, I asked my father if I could have a gas credit card to use and said that I would pay the gas bill. He and I having the same name, he gave me one of his cards for Mobil gas and said: "Go ahead and just use this, and then you be responsible for the bill." Several months later the Mobil people were calling my father because they wanted to know how he could possibly have a gas bill over $2,500! What I would do was go into a gas station and tell the attendant that I'd like to buy four brand-new tyres. He'd pull them down off the rack, I'd give him the credit card, he'd get an authorization and then he'd say: "OK, you want me to put them on?" I'd say: "No, but I'll sell them back to you for 50 per cent of what they're worth, and if you give me the money, that way you'll get the money from Mobil, plus you get to keep the tyres." They always said yes.'

Abagnale appeared to have few qualms about tricking his father and his disenchantment with his family was heightened when his parents obtained a divorce. It was a traumatic experience for the teenager. The judge asked him whether he would prefer to live with his mother or his father but it was a decision that young Abagnale was unwilling to make. Instead he walked out of the courtroom and basically ran away from home, ending up in New York City with no money and no job prospects.

'Nobody really wanted to hire a 16-year-old boy,' he says, 'but I was 6 ft tall, I had grey hair, and my friends always said I looked more like I was 26 years old.' So he changed the date of birth on his driver's licence, amending the '4' in 1948 to a '3', thus ageing himself by ten years. 'When I realized people accepted me for being 26, then I basically became that adult.'

One of the first things he did in New York was open a bank account. 'I was very much an opportunist. I didn't really sit there and premeditate these things. I didn't have a genius mind, but things would come to me. I went into a bank to open a cheque account with $100, which was all I had, with the intention that the bank would then print me cheques, and I had this phoney identification that I could go out and pass these cheques. So I walked in and opened the account. But when the New Accounts person came back, she said: "Here's your temporary cheques. We'll be mailing you your printed cheques in about ten days." Because I was young, I was inquisitive. I said, "What about deposit slips?' and she said, "No, they come from the cheque print, and they'll be with your cheque book. But in the meantime if you need to make a deposit, you can just go over to the table in the lobby of the bank, take a blank deposit slip, write your account number in, and just use that number until you get your printed ones."

'So I walked over and I took a big stack of them off the shelf. I went back to my hotel, but I couldn't sleep. I kept staring at them and thinking to myself, "I wonder." Then I bought some magnetic ink – the ink that banks use to encode numbers on account numbers and cheques – and I encoded my account number that the bank had assigned to me the day before. I then went back to the bank and put this stack onto the shelf . . . and everyone who came in put their cheque right in my bank account. I made about $40,000.'

Banks would prove a fruitful hunting ground for Abagnale. On another occasion he procured a security guard's uniform and positioned himself at the night deposit box of a bank's airport branch, having first written out a sign which read: 'NIGHT DEPOSIT VAULT OUT OF ORDER. PLEASE MAKE DEPOSITS WITH SECURITY GUARD.' By Abagnale's estimate, 35 unsuspecting souls dropped bags of cash into his container, and not one said anything more than 'Good evening' or 'Goodnight'. It was almost too easy.

By the end of 1964 Abagnale was living in Georgia and about to indulge his passion for impersonation. Using a forged medical school degree, he began posing as paediatrician Dr Frank Williams. It so happened that a neighbour was chief resident doctor at a nearby children's hospital and 'Dr Williams' was invited to look around. After reading every book he could find on children's diseases, he was appointed to the hospital staff, working his way up to the post of temporary resident supervisor. If he was ever puzzled by a particular term, he would hastily make an excuse to leave the room so that he could consult his pocket medical dictionary. He also read medical journals at length and, as a last resort, would bluff his way out of a tricky situation by spouting an appropriate line from *Dr Kildare*. For the most part he was only called upon to nod agreement with other doctors' diagnoses but he began to worry that his imposture was putting children's lives at risk and so, after remaining undetected for 11 months during which time he drew a sizeable salary, he shocked his colleagues by suddenly resigning.

Probably because he was forever searching for ways to bend it, Abagnale had always shown more than a passing interest in the law. Fabricating a Harvard law degree, but genuinely passing the Louisiana Bar exam, he practised law in Louisiana for nine months as Robert Conrad, conning his way into a position in the state attorney general's office. When in doubt, he once again resorted to a favourite TV character, this time repeating phrases he had heard on *Perry Mason*. He was finally unmasked when an authentic Harvard law graduate caught him out with regard to which professors he had studied under.

A new state meant a new career and a new identity. Wielding a bogus degree from Columbia University, he became sociology professor Frank Adams PhD at Brigham Young University, Utah. He taught there for three months without arousing the slightest suspicion. 'I just read a chapter ahead of the students and selected passages to emphasize.'

Abagnale's impostures to date had been rewarding enough financially but they had yet to bring him the glamour – and more especially the girls – that he craved. Having witnessed how stewardesses – and indeed pretty girls in general – went weak at the knees at the sight of a pilot, he decided on his most daring disguise yet: Pan Am pilot Captain Frank Williams.

Obtaining the uniform was a simple task for someone who, at 18, was already a seasoned con man. 'I called Pan American Airlines' corporate headquarters and asked to speak to somebody in purchasing. When they came on, I said I was a Pan Am pilot and that I'd flown into New York the night before and I'd sent my uniform out to be dry cleaned, but now the dry cleaners in the hotel say they can't find it. I said that I had a flight in a few hours and no uniform.

'The guy said, "What about a spare uniform?"

'I said, "Yes, back home where I'm based in San Francisco, but I'd never get it here for my flight."

'He said, "Well, you understand this would cost you, not the company, the price of a new uniform?"

'"Yes."

'He came back and said, "You need to go down to the Well Built Uniform Company on Fifth Avenue – that's our supplier – and they'll take care of you."

'I went down there and they fitted me out in the uniform, and when they were done they told me the uniform was $286.

'I said, "I'll write you a cheque."

'Of course the cheques were no good but he said, "No, we can't take cheques."

'So I said, "Oh well then, I'll just pay you cash."

'He said, "No, we can't accept cash. You have to fill out this computer card and in these boxes put your employee number, then we bill this back under uniform allowance and it comes out of your next Pan Am paycheque."

'I said, "That's even better. Go ahead and do that."'

Abagnale then set about obtaining a fake pass from 3M who manufactured Pan Am's identification cards. Posing as a purchasing officer for an expanding airline about to hire a number of new employees, he visited 3M on the pretext of putting a lot of business the company's way. After discussing quantity and price, he asked for a sample to take back to his bosses.

Abagnale remembers: 'At first he brought me out a coloured piece of paper with a picture of an ID card in the middle of it, kind of blown up with a name John Doe, and then someone else's picture and in bold red ink across the front: "This is a sample only."

'I said, "Don't you have the actual card?" before adding, "By the way, what's all this equipment on the floor?"

'He said, "We don't just sell this card, we sell the system, camera, laminator, the lot."

'"We'd have to buy all of this?"

'"Yes."

'"Well, I tell you what, since we have to buy it all, why don't you just demonstrate how it works, and use me?"

'So I sat down and he made up the card with my picture.'

But there remained one major snag. Although it had the correct colours, the card had no Pan Am logo or namc and because it was plastic, it was impossible to type or write anything on. Abagnale was feeling uncharacteristically despondent as he left the 3M building but on his way back to his hotel he passed a hobby shop. There he bought a model of a Pan Am cargo jet for about $2.40 and used the stickers of the Pan Am logo and name that were intended for the model's tail and fuselage to adorn his identity card.

As a bogus pilot, Abagnale spent the next two years 'deadheading' – the term for when a pilot who is not a member of the plane's crew gets a free ride to its destination. 'Basically I would board these planes and ride the jumpseat, deadheading from city to city, on different airlines. So I'd be a Pan Am pilot on a TWA flight. And when I got to a city I would be able to stay where the airline crew stayed. I didn't have to pay for the room – the room was billed to the airline.'

In this way, without ever taking control of a plane, Abagnale flew over two million miles for free. 'I partied in every capital in Europe and basked on all the world's most famous beaches.' His only scares came when fellow pilots occasionally caught him out over which carriers served which cities, but he always managed to talk his way out of any predicament.

He even acquired the pilot's standard accessory of a flight attendant girlfriend until he became so worried that she was getting serious about their rclationship that he decided to confess. He was not a 30-year-old pilot, he admitted, but an 18-year-old runaway wanted by the police. She burst into tears at the news and went back to her house. He gave her some thinking time and followed ten minutes later, fortunately by the back route as the front of the house was by now swarming with police cars.

At the time Abagnale felt bitter about the betrayal and saw it as a vindication of his determination to better himself by fair means or foul. 'If you're not a pilot,' he moaned, 'or if you're not parading as somebody, then people don't like you. And if you don't have a lot of money, then people don't care about you. The minute I told that girl the truth, she turned on me.' But with the wisdom born of maturity he later realized that she had probably acted with the best of intentions and had alerted the authorities to prevent him getting deeper into trouble.

Abagnale's travels on behalf of Pan Am enabled him to pass fraudulent cheques all over the world. The FBI calculated that he operated in every American state and in no fewer than 26 foreign countries. No sooner had he made money than he frittered it away, blowing the lot on women, clothes and food. The bogus pilot enjoyed living the high life and the massive ego boost it gave him. 'Modesty is not one of my virtues,' he admits. 'At the time, virtue was not one of my virtues. But money was just part of it. I had fun fooling people. It was exciting, and at times, glamorous. It was all just acting. I was always aware that if and when I were caught, I wasn't going to win any Oscars. I was going to prison.'

By 1969 the FBI and Interpol were closing in. Abagnale's face was on Wanted posters across the world. His luck ran out when an Air France stewardess recognized him from one of the posters and notified the authorities. Yet even when French airport officials accused him of being a fake, a number of his pilot colleagues steadfastly refused to believe it and loyally stood by him. The party was over, however. The man nicknamed 'The Skywayman' for his aerial exploits had come down to earth with a bump.

After serving time in French prisons, he was extradited to Sweden where he was convicted of forgery. He was then extradited back to the United States and sentenced to 12 years for forgery. He spent only five years in a Federal prison before being offered early release on the condition that he worked for the US government to help combat white-collar crime. Thus for over 25 years Frank Abagnale has been an adviser to the FBI – the ultimate poacher-turned-gamekeeper. As a secure document consultant to the FBI and thousands of worldwide corporations, he has established a new, legal reputation as one of the leading experts on document fraud. He heads his own risk management consulting firm in Washington, DC and the profits from his business have allowed him to repay the $2.5 million he stole in the 1960s. He was recently played by Leonardo Di Caprio in the Steven Spielberg-directed movie, *Catch Me If You Can*, based on Abagnale's best-selling autobiography that he wrote while he was in jail.

Looking back, Abagnale says: 'I don't think I was a real liar. I think I was just somebody who was always looking for the creative. I never felt I was a criminal. I was simply a poseur and swindler of astonishing ability.'

Drake's Progress

Oscar Merrill Hartzell was one of a rare breed – a victim of a scam who managed to turn it around and use it for his own ends. He was so successful that he defrauded over 70,000 people and pocketed some $2 million before justice finally caught up with him.

The person who unwittingly set Hartzell on the road to infamy and fortune was a con woman called Sudie B. Whiteaker. In 1919 she tricked an Iowa farming family out of several thousand dollars by means of a fraud involving supposed descendants of the sixteenth-century English seaman and explorer Sir Francis Drake. The family's name was Hartzell and one of the sons, Oscar, immediately saw the potential in the scheme. He tracked Whiteaker down in Des Moines, recouped his mother's lost money for himself and, with Whiteaker safely out of the way following her indictment, adopted her deception as his own. Hartzell claimed to have proof that Drake had had an illegitimate son who had been imprisoned to avoid scandal and had thereby been denied his rightful inheritance. The Drake estate, said Hartzell, was now worth $22 billion. With sums like that being tossed around, it was not difficult to gain people's attention.

Hartzell began by forming the Francis Drake Association and targeting America's mid-west where a number of the Elizabethan seafarer's distant relatives had settled in the eighteenth century. Passing himself off as a remote relative of Drake who had been appointed to conduct the legal formalities with a view to obtaining the family fortune, he told people that they could share in the estate if they were willing to pay him money up front to cover legal costs. When he held a public meeting in Quincy, Illinois, his 'spiel' was so convincing that virtually everyone present signed up. Originally he had named one Ernest Drake as the sole heir, but, ever on the lookout for ways of improving the fraud, he then declared Ernest to be a fake and insisted that the real heir to the Drake estate lived in England. Hartzell claimed that he had to go to London to exert pressure on the British government, which was desperately trying to hang on to the inheritance. He felt more comfortable operating from England – not least because it put considerable distance between himself and his victims. He made sure that all correspondence relating to the scheme was sent by American Express since it was a federal offence to use US mails for fraudulent purposes. He also selected his targets carefully. Whereas Whiteaker had swindled anyone who happened to cross her path, Hartzell deliberately aimed only for those who could be persuaded to believe that they might actually be descendants of Drake. Therefore he stipulated that only people with the surname Drake, or who were direct descendants of a Drake, could join his scheme.

Arriving in London in 1924, he sent a letter to a family he knew back in Iowa, the Shepherds, outlining the discovery of the estate and his urgent need for funds to fight the legal battle. He said he had traced the true heir who had given him authorization to sell shares in the estate. Once the claim had been settled in the English courts, wrote Hartzell, shareholders would be repaid at a rate of $500 for every dollar invested. Mrs Shepherd's maiden name being Drake, she was only too eager to become involved, and she and her husband mortgaged their home for $5,000. In return, Hartzell appointed them as his first agents. He spread his trusting agents across seven states of America, telling each that he needed $2,500 to be sent to London every week to cover his legal expenses. All agents and other financial contributors had to sign a pledge swearing secrecy, and were warned by Hartzell that violation of this pledge would automatically disqualify the guilty party from a share of the inheritance. The agents also had to swear to send money only by American Express.

The Drakes of Iowa alone raised over $170,000, encouraged all the while by Hartzell's assurances that settlement of the estate was imminent and that payday was therefore just around the corner. He stressed that negotiations with the British government were a delicate affair – particularly with the country in economic strife during the mid-1920s – but kept interest alive (and the money coming in) by announcing that the value of the Drake estate had risen to a colossal $400 billion. News of this exciting development further swelled Hartzell's coffers. Whenever he thought there was any danger of unrest among his investors, he strung them along by inventing a fresh story. At one stage he claimed that Queen Elizabeth I was the mother of Drake's illegitimate child and that, consequently, the British Royal Family were now involved. This sounded most impressive to those loyal fund-raisers in the mid-west who dutifully swallowed every lie.

Ironically it was an error by some of Hartzell's appointed agents that eventually led to the exposure of the scam. While they had apparently kept their promise of secrecy, several had slipped up regarding the method of posting money, and in 1932 were arrested on suspicion of using the US Mail in connection with a fraud. From London, Hartzell expressed outrage and urged those agents remaining at liberty to carry on the good work and to lobby their congressmen, even the White House, to see that justice was done.

In January 1933, it was – but not in the way that Hartzell had envisaged. For he was deported from Britain and arrested on arrival in New York. He was then handcuffed and transferred to Iowa where he was formally charged with fraud. Still he encouraged the faithful to send in the cash, claiming that his arrest was proof of the existence of the Drake inheritance and that the US government was in cahoots with its British counterpart. His appeal was so successful that he received another $130,000, sufficient to pay his bail bond and to tide him over until 1 July when he insisted that the estate would be settled at last.

Naturally there was no settlement, and for once Hartzell had run out of that most precious commodity – time. He was brought to trial accused of fraud on a grand scale. The majority of his agents and investors remained loyal to the last – unable or unwilling to believe that they had been duped all along – but sufficient numbers testified against him to guarantee a guilty verdict. In January 1935 Hartzell began a ten-year sentence, but remarkably the fraud continued. Word got out that British secret agents were planning to assassinate Hartzell to prevent him contesting the estate. The money began pouring in again – as much as $350,000 over the next 18 months.

But Hartzell was never able to enjoy these latest profits. Housed initially in the State penitentiary at Leavenworth, Kansas, he was then transferred to a prison hospital after being judged mentally incompetent. It was there that he died in 1943, never once having admitted that the Drake inheritance scheme was a scam.

The Lottery Liar

It all started with an £8 pair of shoes. Howard Walmsley, a sometime painter and decorator from Doncaster, South Yorkshire, was struggling to pay the bills. His marriage of five years was beginning to crack under the strain so when his wife Kathy fell in love with the shoes, which the couple couldn't afford, Howard decided to pretend that he had come in to some money. 'Get them,' he said. 'Get whatever you want. We've won the lottery!'

The trouble was, Howard Walmsley hadn't won a penny. But he couldn't bring himself to tell his wife the truth for fear that she would leave him. So over the coming months he kept up the fantasy that he had won a fortune on the National Lottery. 'One small thing led to a big lie,' he admitted afterwards. 'It just got out of control.'

Apart from keeping his wife happy and allowing him to buy time in their relationship, Walmsley also thought that if debt collectors and other creditors believed he had won the lottery, they would not keep pestering him for the money he owed them. They would just be patient, secure in the knowledge that they would soon be paid in full. At first he told Kathy to keep the news to herself but it soon spread to the rest of their family and neighbours on their crime-ridden council estate. What everyone wanted to know was how much Walmsley had won, but he refused to say. Suddenly everyone wanted to be his friend. He bought them drinks and meals. 'People paid more attention to me than if I hadn't won the lottery,' he said, almost sounding surprised. 'They seemed to want to be with me all the time.'

With borrowed money, Walmsley and his wife went on their first holiday abroad, to the Canaries. He warned her not to go on a spending spree out there, claiming that his winnings were in an offshore account and that, for the time being, they only had access to the interest. They made new friends on holiday and Kathy insisted that her husband would pay for the other couple's meals on account of his good fortune. It ended up being an expensive trip to the Canaries.

On their return Kathy was beginning to have doubts about the lottery win. Not only had she yet to see concrete evidence, but also bills and final demands were continuing to drop through their letterbox. She decided to telephone Camelot, who ran the lottery, and check for any large wins over the previous couple of months. The only date that tallied was 17 October 1998 when the amount won was £8,904,558. Armed with this information, she confronted Howard who coolly confirmed that just short of £9 million was indeed his winning sum.

Believing herself to be a millionaire, Kathy was delighted when Howard threw a celebratory party for family and friends. Howard's popularity was at an all-time high, having apparently promised the guests that each would receive a cheque at the party for a minimum of £50,000. Not surprisingly, the turnout was high. Sixty people left disappointed when the cheques failed to materialize.

By now, Howard Walmsley was leading such a fantasy life that he may even have convinced himself that he had won the lottery. Eager to keep up appearances, he set about acquiring the trappings befitting his new-found wealth. His first trip was to a Jaguar dealership in Doncaster where he agreed to spend £90,000 on cars for himself and his wife. Then he ordered a third Jaguar for another member of the family. The dealer was only too happy to let Walmsley borrow the car for a day. Walmsley later admitted: 'I put £50 in the tank. All I could think of was watching the petrol gauge go down and down.' The promised purchase of the cars finally convinced Kathy that the win was genuine. 'There were lots of times when I doubted that he'd won the lottery but buying the Jaguars, not just one but three, I kept thinking he wouldn't go this far telling porkies, but he did.' As a philanthropic gesture, Walmsley also announced that he was going to donate a tractor for the poor people of Africa.

The Jaguar's next outing was to the Derbyshire village of Marsh Lane where Kathy had spotted her dream home – a £285,000 farmhouse. It needed modernizing, but that was no problem to a couple with the Walmsleys' supposed funds. Howard commissioned an architect to draw up plans to add a courtyard, gymnasium, granny flat, snooker room, swimming pool and four garages. He told the swimming pool dealer that he wanted a pool cover he could dance on. Told that it would cost an extra £40,000, Walmsley replied: 'If it's what I want, I'll have it.' In all, he committed himself to £300,000 worth of alterations . . . even though he barely had £300 to his name. As a final fixture and fitting, he ordered Kathy a pedigree Labrador puppy.

All the while Walmsley was spending £60 a week on lottery tickets, hoping to pull out the win that would save his story from being a lie. One week, he thought he was in luck when his first four numbers came up. The last two didn't. A win of £70 was hardly the stuff of millionaires. As the hole into which he had dug himself became deeper and deeper, he became depressed and tried to drown his sorrows every night at his local club. Although he was broke, he found himself constantly having to buy drinks for everyone at the club just to maintain the pretence.

Yet the High Street banks were queuing up for Walmsley's imaginary money. They helped him open a dozen accounts. One bank said they would waive the £1,000 he owed them if he invested his fortune with them.

Kathy was becoming suspicious again and told Howard that he would have to prove that he had won the lottery because the bills were still coming in. So he wrote out a cheque for £8.9 million and paid it into one of his bank accounts, knowing full well that it would bounce, but not for several days. In the meantime he was able to print a cash machine statement that showed him with £8.9 million in his account. It was a trick he was to repeat over and over again, using an old cheque book to pay false cheques into his various accounts. Over a period of three months he bounced cheques on himself for millions of pounds. But his bank statements convinced businesses that he was a rich man and when the cheques bounced, he simply explained that he was having trouble getting the money transferred from his overseas accounts. The purchase of the snooker table for the Derbyshire farmhouse fell through when he failed to deliver the deposit. He was comfortable with promised money but the real thing was proving harder to come by.

The house purchase itself seemed to be going smoothly. The estate agent handling the transaction got in touch with Walmsley's bank and was assured that everything was in order. To speed up the sale, the vendors moved into a caravan. Then in April 1999, on the day of the proposed move, the police turned up at Walmsley's council house with a warrant for his arrest concerning a series of suspected frauds from a previous failed business. At first he told the police that there was no problem. He had won the lottery, he said; all his creditors would be paid back. But the hours in custody took their toll and eventually he broke down and admitted the truth for the first time in over six months. Telling the police he hadn't won the lottery was the easy part; telling his wife was much tougher. She threw him out, friends ostracized him.

As the police investigated the strange world of Howard Walmsley, they discovered that the holiday in the Canaries had been paid for by a loan which he had persuaded a former mistress to take out. Struggling to come to terms with the deception, his wife said: 'Howard was very good at it. He convinced professionals and the rest of his family. It got to the stage where I was doubting him on my own and people were telling me: "Why are you doubting him?" It was a nice dream while it lasted – and he did it all for me, because he loved me so much and didn't want to lose me.'

Howard Walmsley claimed that he never hurt anyone, but financially he did. His ex-girlfriend was duped out of £8,000 and the couple who were hoping to sell him the farmhouse lost around £30,000 on the aborted deal.

He stood trial in 2001 and admitted 12 offences of dishonesty, involving a total of at least £37,000. The court heard that he had three previous convictions for dishonesty and had served two prison terms. The prosecution said: 'He duped a number of people into giving him money or goods or kept them waiting for money owing to them with false promises and worthless cheques. He provided false documentation to give the impression that he was better off than he was. Defence counsel admitted that Walmsley had an 'impulsive, risk-taking personality.' Jailing Walmsley for three years, Judge Mrs Jane Shipley said: 'You conned your victims, but you will not con this court. I take the view that you lived in a fantasy world. You wanted to aspire to the high life, to appear successful, but you seem to lack what it takes to be a successful entrepreneur so you embarked on a scheme of lies and deceit.'

Wiping away tears outside Sheffield Crown Court, Mrs Walmsley declared that she would be standing by her husband. 'Howard did wrong,' she said. 'He knows and is very sorry. His motives, however, were not malicious. He did it to keep us together.'

Howard Walmsley's new prison nickname was 'Bonusball'.

'Doc' Brinkley: Kidding America

Of all the quacks in medical history, few have quacked louder and longer and ruffled more feathers than John Romulus Brinkley who promised thousands of American men that he could renew their sexual appetite by grafting on to them the glands or testicles of a goat. Over a 13-year period he performed more than 5,000 such operations which, at $750 a time, made him a very rich man indeed. But the transplants were worthless since the human body's immune system ensures that any animal tissue grafted on will quickly be rejected. Any benefit to the patient was therefore purely psychological. Brinkley was a fraud.

He wasn't even a proper doctor. Born in the remote mountain village of Beta, North Carolina, in 1885, Brinkley worked first as a telegraph operator for the Southern Railroad and then as a snake-oil salesman. But all the while he dreamed of becoming a doctor like his father and realized that ambition – after a fashion – by acting as assistant to a charlatan who handed out dubious cures for venereal infections. After divorcing his first wife, Brinkley headed for Greenville, South Carolina, where he teamed up with James Crawford, a man who would eventually be known more for his contribution to the field of armed robbery than medicine. Together they went into business as the grandly named Greenville Electro Medical Doctors and took out a series of newspaper ads which asked readers: 'Are You a Manly Man Full of Vigour?' Clearly few of the male population of Greenville fitted that description for they flocked to the two 'doctors' to have a rejuvenation jab at $25 a shot. The miracle liquid was nothing more than coloured water.

Skipping town, leaving behind a trail of unpaid bills, they alighted on Memphis where Brinkley married his second wife, Minnie Jones, the daughter of a genuine doctor. No sooner had he returned from his honeymoon than Brinkley was arrested for fraud, along with Crawford, by Greenville police. Fortunately Brinkley's new father-in-law exerted his influence and the charges were dropped. Brinkley was free to carry on masquerading as a medic.

In 1915 he acquired a medical degree, courtesy of the Eclectic Medical University of Kansas City, an infamous diploma mill which sold degrees to anyone with ready cash. This fake qualification –

purchased for $800 – allowed him to practice medicine in the state of Kansas, to where he and his wife soon moved. His first post was as medic at a slaughterhouse. What the job lacked in glamour, it made up for in opportunity for it was there that Brinkley watched the captive billy goats performing their mating rituals and started to wonder whether their rampant sexuality could not somehow be transplanted into humans.

A two-month stint in the US army – four weeks of which was spent under psychiatric observation – was followed in October 1917 by a move to the tiny Kansas hamlet of Milford (population 200) where he set up business as the local doctor. Outwardly respectable, the neat bespectacled Brinkley was every inch the rural, small-town doctor, trusted implicitly by his small dose of patients. Among them was an ageing farmer who, complaining that he had been impotent for 16 years, suggested that his sex drive might be restored if Dr Brinkley were to insert a couple of goat glands in him. Brinkley was initially sceptical but then read about the work of Dr Serge Voronoff who was implanting elderly Frenchmen with monkey glands to give them the sexual appetite of 20-year-olds. Remembering the animals at the slaughterhouse, Brinkley decided to use a young Toggenberg goat as the donor and implanted its glands in the farmer's testicles. Two weeks later, the farmer told Brinkley that he felt like a young man again and within a year he had fathered a son. Appropriately enough, he and his wife called the boy Billy.

Word spread like wildfire that Dr Brinkley was the man to revive a flagging libido and soon most of the old-timers in the area were begging for the operation. The goat symbolized sexual prowess to the average Kansan and now everybody wanted a piece of one. Luckily for Brinkley, goats' testicles were easy to obtain in the Midwest and as demand grew, the local slaughterhouses were filled to capacity with doomed goats. Business was so brisk that Brinkley was forced to move from his one-room office at the town drugstore to a larger building which became known as the Brinkley Gland Clinic. In return for $750 (cash up front) for a standard billy or $1,500 for a very young goat, Brinkley would carry out gland or testicle transplants. There were no apparent adverse side effects to the operation. The glands of the Toggenbergs were odourless which meant that the patients did not go around town smelling of essence of goat nor were they the recipients of unwelcome attention from other breeds. In his early days of experimentation, Brinkley did use Angora goats on two occasions but noted that his patients left the operating theatre smelling like a steamy barn on a hot summer's day. So he reverted to his trusted Toggenbergs. To ensure that they were getting an active goat for their money, patients were allowed to pick the billy of their choice from a herd of Toggenbergs kept in a backyard pen at the clinic. Brinkley was nothing if not fair.

As his fame spread, Brinkley became the subject of good-natured banter. A joke of the day went: 'What's the fastest thing on four legs? – A goat passing Dr Brinkley's hospital.' My, how everyone laughed . . . until they discovered they were being taken for a ride.

Although Brinkley knew that his work was highly unethical – he never once submitted a formal paper detailing the operation to a medical journal – he did actually believe in it, partly because he did not possess sufficient knowledge to realize that the operation could never live up to his claims. More to the point, the rich and famous started to believe in it too. Maharajah Thakou of Morvi travelled all the way from India for a transplant; *Los Angeles Times* newspaper magnate Harry Chandler was another grateful recipient and he sang Brinkley's praises to his friends in the blossoming movie industry; and E. Haldeman-Julius, publisher of the Little Blue Books, wrote numerous articles in support of Brinkley as well as allowing the 'doctor' years of free advertising because he believed so strongly in what he was doing. When Brinkley was eventually exposed as a fraud, Haldeman-Julius felt obliged to apologize profusely for his error of judgement. But in 1923 that was still a long way off.

That was the year when Brinkley, inspired by his friend Harry Chandler's purchase of Los Angeles' first radio station, KHJ, decided to start up a similar venture in Milford. And so KFKB ('Kansas First, Kansas Best') hit the airwaves with a signal so powerful that it could be heard all over America, its programming tailored to meet Brinkley's target audience – elderly men. At regular intervals the station churned out his advertising slogan: 'Let me get your goat and you'll be Mr Ram-What-Am with every lamb!' Subtle he wasn't.

Brinkley's saturation advertising worked a treat. In addition to promoting himself on radio, he enlisted the services of most of Milford's citizens to run his mail-order scheme. Up to 2,000 letters a day were sent out to prospective clients. He also planted friendly stories in newspapers and magazines, portraying himself as a God-fearing, devoted family man, medical pioneer and friend of the aged. These articles were invariably accompanied by photographs of Brinkley in a trim goatee beard, which not only gave him the air of a distinguished scientist but also reminded his readership of the very animal which, with his help, would restore their virility.

By 1927 'Goat Gland Brinkley', as he had become known, was

performing around 50 operations every month. Decrepit men converged on his Milford clinic from far and wide, all desperate to dip their toes in the fountain of youth. Everybody wanted a slice of the action . . . or at least a slice of the goat. Not satisfied with raking in nigh on $40,000 a month from the goat scam, the good doctor came up with a new radio show, *The Medical Question Box*, in which listeners wrote in about their ailments and he prescribed suitable treatments over the air. Needless to say, the medicines he recommended were always ones which he sold by mail order. He subsequently scrapped the mail order system and, in its place, enrolled hundreds of drugstore proprietors across the United States to sell his prescribed medicines at wildly inflated prices. The power of radio meant that some druggists participating in the Brinkley scheme took in $100 a day, and Brinkley himself creamed off $1 per prescription. He was a millionaire.

The devoted family man began to flaunt his wealth in the form of several houses, a private yacht, a fleet of cars and two private planes. He virtually owned Milford and acquired friends in high places. However, these did not include Dr Morris Fishbein, editor of the Journal of the American Medical Association, who accused Brinkley of 'blatant quackery'. Threatening to sue for libel, Brinkley launched a massive propaganda offensive against the AMA, but for once his empty bluster did not prevail. The *Kansas City Star* newspaper dealt him a further blow by running a damning exposé on the Milford clinic and its shady managing director, pouring scorn on his claims and qualifications. Brinkley was on the ropes, and in 1930 the Kansas Board of Medical Registration charged him with, among other things, gross immorality, malpractice and unprofessional conduct.

Brinkley defended himself vigorously, calling upon his many satisfied customers to testify on his behalf. But the Board were not to be hoodwinked, the judge summing up: 'The defendant has perfected and organized charlatanism until it is capable of preying on human weakness, ignorance and credulity to an extent quite beyond the invention of the humble mountebank.' Brinkley's licence was withdrawn.

In the same year the Federal Radio Commission took KFKB off the air after ruling that the station existed primarily to line Brinkley's pockets and that, in any case, his goat-gland operation was physiologically impossible and fraudulent.

Most people would have given up at this point, but Brinkley was determined not to go down without a fight and, reasoning that the surest way to regain his state-issued licence was if he controlled the state in person, he announced that he was running for Governor of Kansas. In both 1930 and 1932, he was only narrowly beaten but his third attempt, in 1934, resulted in a severe mauling. It was time for him to get out of Kansas.

The only states in which he was now licensed to practice his goat-gland sorcery were Arkansas and Texas, the citizens of which were subjected to new claims – that the transplant could return mental patients to sound mind. Since there was no shortage of mental instability in Arkansas or Texas, this proved another winner for Brinkley. So he moved his operation to Del Rio, Texas, and erected a huge radio transmitter across the border in Mexico for his new station, XER. The goats were finally dropped from his act, but he replaced them with a new rejuvenation technique, involving shots of Mercurochrome, which was equally worthless but even more profitable. He also marketed a cure-all composed of nothing more than blue dye and a splash of hydrochloric acid.

Just when everything seemed to be going well again, Brinkley fell foul of his old adversary, Dr Morris Fishbein, who, in a magazine article, labelled him 'the greatest charlatan in medical history.' Brinkley immediately sued Fishbein for $250,000. The case was heard in Del Rio, Texas, in 1939. Brinkley was confident of success and called the usual suspects to speak up for him, but the jurors were less impressed and found in favour of Fishbein. Brinkley was all but finished as a medical practitioner.

In a defiant last stand, he relocated to Little Rock, Arkansas, but was unable to prey on small-town ignorance in such a big city. The vultures were circling overhead. Former patients, realizing they had been conned, sued him for malpractice and he was forced to pay out huge sums in damages. At the same time, the US government billed him for over $200,000 in unpaid taxes. In January 1941 the millionaire quack declared himself bankrupt. Shortly afterwards he suffered a massive heart attack – possibly brought about by the fall of his empire – and the following year he died at the age of 56. America's goats could breathe easily again. The master of kidology was no more.

Gregor the First

When representatives of Venezuelan patriot Simón Bolívar arrived in London in 1811 to recruit officers for his Army of Liberation as part of the ongoing struggle to free Latin America from the Spanish Empire, one of those who joined up was a young Scottish soldier by the name of Gregor MacGregor. That same year MacGregor sailed for Caracas and proceeded to distinguish himself in battle with a series of notable victories, marked by his personal bravery and tactical genius. His successes did not go unrewarded and, after soaring through the ranks with indecent haste and being appointed to the noble Order of Liberators, he was granted the additional honour of marriage to Bolívar's niece, the beautiful Donna Josepha. Many men would have seen this as the ultimate accolade but MacGregor had developed a taste for wealth and fame. And now he wanted more of both.

In 1820, supported by an army of just 150 men in two small ships, MacGregor embarked on a number of raids on the Spanish forts that guarded the Isthmus of Panama. His mission complete, he then sailed up the east coast of modern-day Nicaragua, a land which had long since been abandoned by European settlers. With no Spaniards to fight, he landed on the Mosquito Coast and, offering nothing more than whisky and a few trinkets, persuaded the elderly chief of the Poyais Indians to grant him the rights to colonize a particularly inhospitable 70,000 square miles of coastland. Quite apart from the legions of insects that gave the area its popular name, the region was singularly uninviting – a mixture of arid hills and dense swamps. It was little wonder the Spaniards had given it a wide berth. But to the enterprising MacGregor it was the promised land.

Returning to Caracas, he collected his wife and set sail for London where he proudly introduced himself as His Serene Highness Gregor the First, Prince of Poyais. The average Londoner's knowledge of Central America was limited to say the least, and so nobody was suspicious as to why they had never previously heard of Poyais. Similarly there was no opposition to the new prince's glowing description of his country as being a land rich in gold and silver deposits, mahogany and cedar forests, and blessed with a fertile soil that was ideal for growing crops and fruit. As an added bonus, Poyais, he said, boasted a splendid capital city with a fine palace and opera house. Quite simply, he believed it to be the ideal area for overseas investment.

It was nothing new for the British upper classes to be endowed with more money than sense but on this occasion they surpassed themselves, welcoming the self-styled prince and princess into their elite circle and making them the toast of the capital. MacGregor knew that securing royal patronage was essential to the success of his scheme, and, to this end, he sent an associate, William Richardson, with letters to his 'brother sovereign', George IV. Richardson was duly received at court and official diplomatic recognition of Poyais achieved by means of that traditional method of oiling recalcitrant machinery – bribery. MacGregor was subsequently knighted for his services towards establishing Britain's relationship with the non-existent kingdom.

With interest in Poyais mounting by the day, MacGregor sought to cash in on the situation by distributing pamphlets extolling the virtues of the region to bankers and businessmen. Engravings of the capital of Poyais were sold on the streets of London and a handbook for prospective settlers was produced by another of MacGregor's cohorts, Thomas Strangeways. Lest there was anybody in London yet to hear of Poyais, MacGregor even hired musicians to sing its praises on street corners. The publicity campaign paid off in spectacular fashion. MacGregor persuaded the London banking firm of Sir John Perring and Co. to hand over a loan of £200,000 'for the purpose of consolidating the state of Poyais.' The share issue was fully subscribed, Perring being happy to accept the promised riches of the gold and silver mines of Poyais as security.

Having set up an immigration office in London selling Poyais land to potential colonists at four shillings an acre, MacGregor moved his operation to Edinburgh and worked the same trick. It proved so successful that in September 1822 over 200 would-be settlers sailed from Leith in two ships. Expecting to find a palatial city, they found dense jungle; instead of a land rich in gold, they found a land rich in mosquitoes. To make matters worse, a hurricane hit the region shortly after their arrival, destroying their ships and killing several of the sailors. Luckily for the survivors, help was at hand in the shape of a more reputable Scotsman, John Young, who acted as the Colonial Agent for British Honduras, located around 500 miles to the north. Young sent a full report back to Scotland, but 'Prince' Gregor dismissed it as a pack of lies composed by someone out to sabotage his enterprise and even threatened legal action against Young.

In the autumn of 1824 the swindled settlers returned to Scotland to hunt down MacGregor, but by then, realizing that he had been rumbled, he and his 'princess' had fled to France with the same scam. The French proved even more gullible and MacGregor was able to raise a further loan of £300,000, again using the fictitious gold mines as security. In 1825 the first French colonists sailed for Poyais from Le Havre, only to meet the same miserable fate as their Scottish counterparts.

When news of the ill-fated expedition reached Paris, creditors went looking for MacGregor, but once again managing to keep just ahead of the chasing pack, he escaped to London. However, there was nowhere else to hide and he was arrested and thrown into prison. Yet his charmed life continued by virtue of the fact that those pillars of society whom he had duped were so worried about the damage to their reputations that would result from the publicity of a trial that they dropped all charges.

He tried to revive the Poyais scam in 1836 but met with little response and shortly afterwards he and Donna Josepha returned to Venezuela where he was received as a hero for the part he had played in the quest for independence. The Venezuelan government was so grateful that it granted a generous stipend to support him. When he died in 1845, he was greatly mourned in his adopted country . . . if not in his native homeland.

Feathering Their Own Nests

A group of crooked British businessmen defrauded 3,000 investors out of almost £22 million in an 18-month period after persuading them that ostrich was the meat of the future.

The BSE scare that rocked Britain throughout the 1990s led to widespread fears regarding the safety of eating beef. The search began for alternative meats and in 1994 shop owner Brian Ketchell and second-hand car dealer Allan Walker launched the Ostrich Farming Corporation Ltd above a shop in New Ollerton, Nottinghamshire. A location further removed from the African plains was hard to imagine.

Their initial outlay was just £25,000, most of which was spent on advertising designed to persuade the public to see ostriches as an investment opportunity. The sales literature offered ostriches at prices ranging from £1,400 for a chick to £14,000 for a mature bird and promised high rates of return on breeding birds, suggesting a potential 270 per cent profit on an outlay of £10,000 in just five years. OFC's glossy brochures claimed that, because of BSE, there would soon be a huge demand for ostrich meat in Britain. Low in fat, cholesterol free and compared in taste to fillet beef, ostrich meat would, they said, become a safe and popular item on supermarket shelves and was quoted to sell at £20 per pound.

OFC projected that to replace 10 per cent of the domestic market for beef with ostrich meat, 1,000 breeding birds would be needed to produce the required number of offspring. Comparisons were made with the growth of the salmon farming industry, pointing out that salmon production had enjoyed a 7,500 per cent growth over a 13-year period. Virtually no part of the ostrich was left out of the sales pitch – hides for the leather industry, anti-static feathers as dusters for the electrical industry, oils for medical products, and even infertile eggs as ornaments.

To give the scheme a personal touch, investors were told that the birds would be microchipped with details of the owner. There would also be regular reports on each bird's progress and its progeny. The commercial breeding life of an ostrich was given as at least 25 years and buyers were promised a chick allocation that increased with the breeding maturity of the bird. OFC guaranteed to buy back all allocated chicks for £500 each at 12 months old. The corporation also guaranteed investors a minimum return on expenditure of 51.6 per cent per annum.

Sales representatives were hired to promote the cause and buyers, both individual and corporate, were invited to join the Ostrich Owners' Club. To emphasize the image of an expanding company, it boasted of having additional offices throughout much of Western Europe and the Middle East.

Within a mere 15 months OFC had attained a turnover of £21 million as investors queued to join up. Some clients were flown out to see their ostriches at the breeding farm near Ghent in Belgium where the birds were reared. It all appeared totally legitimate. Among those attracted by the scheme was former ITN newsreader Fiona Armstrong. After meeting Ketchell, she bought an ostrich for £12,500. It produced chicks which she sold back to the corporation for over £5,000. 'I thought it was an extremely good rate of return,' she said later, 'so I bought a second bird for £10,000. I thought the company was very professional. At the time the newspapers were full of this thing. It was very exciting.' Armstrong was so impressed that she appeared in a promotional video for OFC, hailing the ostrich-breeding business as 'the cash crop of the Nineties.' At the end of the video she said: 'Now that you know about it, what are you going to do? Put your head in the sand? The decision is yours.'

What Armstrong, her mother (who lost £10,000 on the venture) and the hundreds of other investors did not know was that their money was not being used to buy ostriches but to line the pockets of the OFC directors. At first OFC dealt directly with the legitimate breeding farm in Belgium but from July 1995 an offshore company called Wallstreet Corporation, based in Delaware, acted as an intermediary. Under the control of a third partner, Jack Bennett, Wallstreet opened bank accounts in the Isle of Man and the Cayman Islands to facilitate the laundering of money. While some birds were bought and raised on the Belgian farm, millions of pounds were being siphoned off. Instead of using the company's capital, based on the money received from customers, to purchase ostriches, the funds were being used by the directors to feather their own nests. Between them they received over £5.5 million via Wallstreet.

As the number of investors multiplied, OFC would have needed thousands of ostriches to fulfil the promises it had made. Instead just a fraction of the 'owned' birds could be found at the farm. The company continued to take orders from clients but they were investing in imaginary livestock. In many cases only the microchips were tangible. When the Serious Fraud Office began investigating OFC, it found that the ostriches were listed by serial number and status. The most common entry in the status column was 'dead'!

Of the 3,456 birds sold to customers or allocated under the guaranteed chick scheme, nearly 1,000 did not even exist.

OFC had been wound up by the Department of Trade and Industry early in 1996 after its activities had begun to arouse suspicion and, following a two-year investigation by the Serious Fraud Office, Ketchell, Walker and Bennett were charged with fraud. At their trial in 2000, the court heard how none of the trio had any experience of ostriches or farming, and none had purchased birds as a personal investment. Nevertheless they had made a fortune from duping clients. Bennett was jailed for four years, Ketchell for three and a half years, and Walker for two years ten months. All three were disqualified from acting as company directors for ten years.

And still nobody eats ostrich meat.

Queen of the Lonely Hearts

She looked and sounded like ideal wife material: pretty, young, and with a sizeable inheritance in the offing. No wonder she attracted a multitude of admirers when joining lonely hearts clubs. The catch was that the eligible miss searching for the perfect partner was really an elderly con woman who had ten children and weighed nearly 15 stone. There was no inheritance and the photographs she supplied were of the prettiest of her collection of daughters.

Susanna Mildred Hill was in her sixties when she began using a string of aliases to apply for membership to various lonely hearts clubs. Giving her age as anything between 18 and 23, she was not shy when it came to listing her virtues. But the real carrot was the money she said that she stood to inherit, and it was not long before replies to her advertisement began to fall through the letterbox of her home in Washington, DC. For obvious reasons, Mrs Hill went to great lengths to discourage callers to her home and made it a policy not to write back to any would-be suitor who lived within a 500-mile radius of Washington. Should any correspondent announce the intention of travelling to Washington, she tried to put him off by inventing a sudden family crisis. Nevertheless a handful slipped through the net and made their way to the Hill residence. On these occasions Mrs Hill cheerfully posed as the family housekeeper, and the callers left without ever meeting the beauty in the photographs.

The letters she sent purporting to be from a love-lorn young virgin were touching in the extreme. She would write that she was temporarily in financial difficulties because she had to look after her ailing mother and asked her suitor whether it would be possible for him to demonstrate his sincerity by making a small donation to such a worthy cause. She also casually mentioned a liking for jewellery. The recipients of her heart-rending epistles took the hint and sent money and jewellery in the hope of securing her hand in marriage. Little did they know that the person to whom they were writing was more likely to turn stomachs than heads.

She was able to string along most of her victims – and there were over 100 in total – without any problems, but occasionally a suitor would become impatient that, in spite of sending gifts, he had yet to meet the girl. In such instancces the redoubtable Mrs Hill would head off any potentially awkward encounters by writing back as the girl's mother to say that her daughter had run off with another man. If, however, Mrs Hill calculated that the suitor was a bottomless pit financially, she would visit him in the guise of the sick mother to make a personal plea for money to hasten her medical treatment so that her lovely daughter would at last be free to marry. Few men were able to resist the prospect of acquiring such a kind, considerate mother-in-law.

Mrs Hill was conducting one of these missions of mercy in 1945, visiting several likely husbands in the Chicago area, when she was arrested by US postal inspectors. Thousands of dollars in cheques and money orders were found in her possession, all from her hapless victims. At her trial the 'Queen of Lonely Hearts', as she was dubbed, persisted with the sick mother routine, pleading guilty from a stretcher, no doubt in the hope of receiving a lighter sentence. Sadly for her, the judge was hard-hearted and sentenced her to five years in prison.

No Stone Unturned

In the aftermath of the Civil War, rumours abounded that the American West was an area of enormous mineral wealth. Prospectors descended on the untamed territories in their droves, hoping to uncover precious stones. The vast majority returned home empty-handed, but Philip Arnold and John Slack were different, simply because they had decided not to rely on pure luck. They preferred to give Dame Fortune a little helping nudge in the right direction.

Arnold and Slack were veterans in their field, having caught the prospecting bug during the California Gold Rush of 1849. The summer of 1870 found them panning for gold in New Mexico. The quest was proving fruitless until they chanced upon a quantity of blood-red-coloured stones, which they thought were rubies. Excitedly they hurried back to San Francisco and took a sample of the stones to a jeweller for valuation, only to be told that they were worthless garnets. The jeweller sighed that what he really wanted to get his hands on were diamonds, similar to those that had recently been discovered in South Africa.

Momentarily disillusioned, Arnold and Slack retired to the nearest saloon where it needed only a drink or two to set them thinking about creating their own diamond field in Arizona. A friend who had once worked for a diamond drill manufacturing company agreed to obtain a few gems, following which Arnold and Slack visited a second jeweller and produced their newly acquired diamonds mixed in with the garnets. The jeweller was sufficiently impressed to award them a certificate of authenticity.

One day in 1872, Arnold and Slack ambled into the San Francisco branch of the Bank of California carrying a drawstring pouch which they handed to the teller, asking him to look after it while they went off to get drunk. As soon as they had left, the teller peeked inside the bag, expecting to find nothing more than a few pinches of gold dust. Seeing instead a collection of uncut diamonds, he rushed to tell his boss, banker William Ralston.

Fired with a desperate desire to track down the two wizened old prospectors as quickly as possible, Ralston trawled the city's bars for three days. When he eventually located them, they had clearly been celebrating excessively and were in a state of advanced incoherence. Patiently he waited for them to sober up before asking where they had discovered the diamonds. But they were giving nothing away, admitting only that they had found a diamond field 'bigger than Kimberley'.

Further convinced by the certificate of authenticity, Ralston was hooked. He continued to probe away at the pair as to the whereabouts of the field, but their lips remained tightly sealed. Even when he showed enthusiasm for investing in their discovery, they insisted that anyone who wanted to inspect the diamond field must make the journey blindfold. Ralston realized that he had little option for the time being but to comply with their conditions and arranged for his mining engineer, David Colston, to be taken to the secret site. Arnold and Slack postponed the visit for a couple of months, ostensibly to wait for better weather. In that intervening period, unbeknown to Ralston, they sailed to Europe and spent their life savings of $35,000 on buying diamonds from London and Amsterdam before depositing the gems on

Arizona soil. To cover their tracks, they left and entered the American continent via Halifax, Nova Scotia.

With the diamonds in place, engineer Colston was led blindfold to the site. He returned to San Francisco three weeks later, clutching a fistful of valuable diamonds for his master's inspection. Ralston now wasted no time in putting his money where his mouth was and securing his financial stake in the field. He paid Arnold and Slack $50,000 each upfront, set aside an additional $300,000 for them to develop the field, and promised an extra $350,000 once it started producing. He also proposed the formation of a syndicate with other wealthy San Francisco investors. These eminent financiers needed convincing too, so it was arranged for Charles Tiffany, America's leading jeweller, to examine the stones. Tiffany, whose expertise lay in silver as opposed to diamonds, immediately put a value of $150,000 on the gems. If Arnold was pleasantly surprised, he refrained from showing it.

In the hope of finding yet more backers, Ralston proposed sending another party to the field, led by Arnold and Slack. Prior to departure, the duplicitous duo decided to move their precious site to a more accessible spot, near the railroad in Wyoming. Carefully they sprinkled the rough stones across the ground, placing others in cracks and crevices. The diamonds were just waiting to be found.

The expedition set off in the late summer, travelling by Union Pacific to Rawlins Springs, Wyoming, where the two prospectors blindfolded mining engineer Henry Janin and the group of potential investors, and led them off into the hills. When the blindfolds were lifted several hours later, the visitors could scarcely believe their eyes. Diamonds were wedged in rock crevices, emeralds shone in tufts of grass, and tiny rubies twinkled in anthills. Some 600 diamonds were collected in the course of just two days. Reporting in the *Engineering and Mining Journal* of 3 September 1872, Janin wrote: 'I do not doubt that further prospecting will result in finding diamonds over a greater area than is as yet proved to be diamond bearing; and that I consider any investment at the rate of $4,000,000 for the whole property a safe and attractive one.' Like Tiffany, Janin was highly competent at evaluating gold and silver but struggled with diamonds.

With investors from New York joining the syndicate, a company – the San Francisco and New York Mining and Commercial Company – was formally created to mine the field. The first thing it did was buy out Arnold and Slack for a combined total of $700,000. They feigned reluctance but when Ralston threatened them with complex lawsuits which, he said, would leave them with nothing if they did not accept the offer, they decided to take the money . . . and skipped town without looking back.

Ralston and his associates thought they had managed to pull the wool over the two prospectors' eyes and land a hugely profitable deal into the bargain. Meanwhile Arnold and Slack were laughing all the way to the bank . . . but not Ralston's bank.

The first hint that anything was amiss came via a cable from London which revealed that a diamond merchant had a few months previously sold several lots of rough stones to two Americans. The purchasers were apparently unacquainted with precious stones and bought diamonds, rubies and emeralds without reference to size, weight or quality. The report was initially dismissed but the Wyoming find had aroused the suspicions of leading geologists Clarence King and E. W. Emmonds. Both men had earlier conducted detailed geological surveys in the region and had never detected the slightest sign of the existence of precious gems there. They could not believe they had missed such significant mineral deposits. And when descriptions of the site made King realize that the diamond field was located on the very spot where he himself had placed a survey marker, his worst fears were confirmed. He and Emmonds set off for Rawlins at once, arriving in early November. On finding the site, they were immediately concerned that it was only a few miles from the station at Rawlins yet the journey on foot had taken the party of potential investors several hours. The obvious conclusion was that Arnold and Slack had led them around in circles.

Arnold and Slack had undoubtedly heard of diamonds being found in termite mounds and anthills in Africa, but closer inspection of the Wyoming anthills showed them to be man-made. Furthermore, Emmonds noticed that certain diamonds bore the marks of a lapidary tool, the favourite instrument of a diamond-cutter. King went on to list ten separate reasons why diamonds could not occur naturally under the prevailing conditions before reporting back that the gems must have been planted there. On his return he sent a letter to the company directors in which he wrote: 'I have hastened to San Francisco to lay before you the startling fact that the new diamond fields upon which are based such large investment and such brilliant hope are utterly valueless, and yourselves and your engineer, Mr Henry Janin, the victims of an unparalleled fraud.' On 25 November 1872 the diamond company was dissolved. Ralston was a broken man.

Slack disappeared without trace but Arnold returned to his home town of Elizabethtown, Kentucky, where, ironically, he opened his own bank. Although an attempt was made to bring charges against him, the prosecution fizzled out because many of those prominent businessmen who had been conned were too embarrassed to pursue the matter. It was a familiar story: the con artist's safety net. Arnold never did mend his ways and paid for it a few years later when he was shot in the back by a business rival following another dodgy deal. Justice of a kind had finally caught up with him.

A Sick Pretence

Despite their misdeeds, some con artists elicit a degree of sympathy, even from their victims. Kristen Clougherty's fraud provoked nothing but disgust.

In the autumn of 1998, 23-year-old Clougherty from South Boston told her family and friends that she had been diagnosed with ovarian cancer, adding that because the treatment she required was not available in Massachusetts, she would have to travel to Connecticut. For a young woman in part-time employment and with student loans to repay, the financial burden would be unbearable.

Clougherty was part of a tight-knit Irish American community. Although she alleged that she had been brutally beaten by her stepfather since the age of four, she had over 200 cousins living in the area and hoped to count on their support in her hour of need. Friends, too, rallied round. Audrey McDonough, who was herself recovering from ovarian cancer, shaved Clougherty's head and obtained a wig for her in order to hide the effects of the chemotherapy that her friend would soon have to receive. In October 1998 Clougherty also persuaded her employer, Fidelity Investments, to promote her to a full-time position so that she could receive medical benefits.

Everyone was touched by her plight and in June 1999 supporters organized a fund-raising event at the Old Colony Yacht Club to help offset Clougherty's medical expenses. The function raised over $40,000, mostly in cash donations, which were duly presented to a grateful Clougherty.

In the course of the ensuing weeks the Clougherty bandwagon gathered pace and it was announced that the First Annual Kristen Clougherty Five-Kilometre Road Run would be staged to benefit the Ovarian Cancer Research Fund. Friends set up two Internet websites on her behalf and donations for the road race poured in, including a $250 contribution from the Boston Globe Foundation. The race was scheduled for October but two months before it was duc to take place, the Suffolk County District Attorney's office received an anonymous call claiming that Clougherty was not suffering from cancer at all.

The insinuation that Clougherty had faked having cancer purely in order to profit from charitable collections was so appalling that at first evcn detectives refused to believe it. However, as they probed deeper into the case, they discovered that Clougherty's story was nothing more than a scam. The tears, the pity, the shaved head were all part of a callous con.

In September 1999 the District Attorney's office took the unusual step of going public with its suspicions, warning people against making any further donations to the road race 'because of the very real and palpable expectations that the fraud will continue unless publicized.' The race was called off (a legitimate charity event took its place) and some $11,000 was seized from Clougherty's bank account, which was immediately frozen. Suffolk County DA Ralph Martin II went so far as to say of Clougherty: 'I'll eat my hat if she has ovarian cancer.'

Clougherty was charged with larceny. It emerged that the day after the Old Colony Yacht Club fund-raiser she had started transferring the money into her personal bank account. The cash that had been collected by well-wishers to cover her cancer treatment had indeed been used partly for medical expenses – it had paid for her liposuction and breast enlargement surgery. With the rest she had bought herself a new Nissan Altima, paid off her student loans, and treated herself to an expensive new wardrobe and a few weekends at a luxury hotel in Newport, Rhode Island.

As the scale of the deception became apparent, feelings ran high in South Boston. Clougherty became a social outcast. Family and friends refused to have anything further to do with her.

In October 2000 Clougherty pleaded guilty to larceny. Her defence attorney claimed that she had originally concocted the cancer story as emotional blackmail to prevent her boyfriend from dumping her, and that the lie had simply spiralled out of control. Clougherty was sentenced to two years' probation, ordered to do 300 hours of community service, and instructed to repay all the money she had been given – $43,411.13 – to the Ovarian Cancer Research Fund. Judge Carol Ball described Clougherty's act as 'breathtaking in its callousness' and stipulated that she wanted Clougherty's community service to be 'physical, menial labour like scrubbing graffiti as opposed to ladelling soup in a soup kitchen or handing out flowers to the sick.'

As South Boston turned its collective back on Kristen Clougherty, one former friend summed up the general view. 'It turns out she was infected with a disease even more deadly than cancer – the disease of greed.'

Beware of Persians Bearing Gifts

One morning in 1667 Louis XIV – the 'Sun King' – received word that His Most Serene Excellency, Riza Bey, and party had reached Marseilles. The envoy was said to have travelled via Constantinople to bestow upon the King of France sumptuous gifts from his own master, the Shah of Persia.

As the proud owner of 413 beds, Louis was quite keen on gifts, especially from someone as wealthy as the Shah. So although he had not been expecting the Persian delegation, he went to great lengths to accommodate them on their arrival in Paris, housing them in lavish apartments in the Tuileries Palace and laying on banquets for their delectation. Louis finally accorded them the great honour of receiving them in person on the third day, an occasion that was followed by a grand ball and supper. The envoy explained that the Shah's wondrous gifts had not yet arrived, but were expected any day. He told Louis that the Shah was keen to trade with France and made the monarch's mouth water by eulogizing about the fabulous riches of Persia. As a token of the king's appreciation, the envoy was presented with a portrait of Louis, set in diamonds, and other gifts worth millions of francs. In return, the envoy gave Louis several fragments of opal and turquoise, which, he claimed, had been found near the Caspian Sea. He promised that the region was littered with similar treasures and that the Shah intended to share them all with France when the alliance was finalized. Louis could barely contain his delight and watched entranced as the entourage left the court weighed down with gifts.

The following day there was still no sign of the Shah's presents, but one of the Persian party left Paris, ostensibly to go on an urgent mission abroad, taking with him his gifts from Louis. It was the same story over the next couple of days – nothing from the Shah, and more of the party heading off, clutching their gifts, on an urgent foreign mission. Meanwhile the envoy himself went on a shopping spree in Paris, returning with a quantity of expensive items. Louis insisted that payment be waived.

Soon only two members of the original entourage plus the envoy remained. The king was becoming impatient. Then at last Louis was informed by the envoy that the Shah's gifts had arrived and a date was arranged for their presentation at the royal palace of Versailles.

On the appointed day the king and the rest of the court waited and waited, but there was no sign of either the envoy or the promised gifts. Little did they know that at daybreak that morning three scruffily dressed men had sneaked out of the Tuileries with the last of their booty. The king's gifts had been smuggled out of Paris in stages. He had been well and truly conned. The Shah knew nothing of any visit or alliance, and the turquoises and opals turned out to be nothing more than coloured glass.

Although a nationwide search was launched for the men who had the effrontery to trick the king, they were never found. The prime suspect was a barber from Leghorn in Italy, who had once travelled in Persia, and had vanished from his home town at around the time of the deputation to Paris, but no charges were ever brought against him.

'The Darth Vader of Capitalism'

New Yorkers in the late 1970s and 1980s were bombarded on an hourly basis with radio and TV commercials for the Crazy Eddie chain of discount electronics stores. The ads were noisy and irritating, fronted by DJ Jerry Carroll as the manic, fast-talking salesman pitching Crazy Eddie's 'insaaaaane prices'. Some 2,500 different Crazy Eddie commercials aired in the New York area and a 1985 survey revealed that the Crazy Eddie character – personified by Carroll in grey turtleneck sweater and blue slacks – had greater face recognition than Mayor Edward Koch. The ads did wonders for the brand. Crazy Eddie was an advertising phenomenon.

Crazy Eddie was the brainchild of Eddie Antar, born in Brooklyn in 1947 to parents of Syrian-Jewish heritage. In the early sixties he dropped out of Abraham Lincoln High School and demonstrated his entrepreneurial ambitions by hustling televisions and radios in New York. He opened his first store, Sights and Sounds, on Brooklyn's Kings Highway, changing the name to Crazy Eddie at the start of the 1970s. Antar developed a reputation in the retail industry for saying anything to make a sale. He was brash, he was loud, the supreme salesman.

Boosted by the hugely successful advertising campaign, Crazy Eddie Inc. took off in a big way and over the next 15 years grew from that single family-owned store into one of the biggest retail electronics chains in New York with 43 stores and annual sales of $350 million. In 1984 the company went public. Apparently continuing to flourish, it became one of Wall Street's highest fliers until in 1987 Eddie Antar suddenly resigned as chief executive amid rumours that he was seriously ill. A group of company stockholders, headed by Houston businessman Elias Zinn, staged a takeover. To their horror, they found that the inventory was half what was listed on the books – a shortfall of $45 million.

The new owners tried to retrench but in 1989 the chain wound up in bankruptcy. Eddie Antar had already sold his shares, pocketing a cool $75 million, but other stockbrokers lost vast sums of money when the company went out of business. Not surprisingly, questions were asked. The Securities and Exchange Commission investigated the stock fraud and in February 1990 a US District Judge ordered

Antar to repatriate $52 million, which the SEC believed was obtained through insider trading and transferred to Israel. But Antar was nowhere to be found. He had gone on the run and was living off his ill-gotten gains.

As the SEC began delving further into Eddie Antar's affairs, they discovered that, far from being crazy he was very crafty. They were staggered by the depth of the fraud, prompting one official to remark: 'This may not be the biggest (financial statement) fraud of all time, but for outrageousness, it is going to be very hard to beat.'

The deception began after Crazy Eddie went public in 1984. The Antar family concocted a plan that not only skimmed cash from the company but also grossly inflated its value. By falsifying the books, they were able to convince financial analysts that the company was growing when in reality it was falling apart. Eddie flew to Israel with cash strapped to his body and deposited it in an Israeli bank. The money was then sent back through a dummy company in Panama to Crazy Eddie Inc. where it was used to persuade experts that the chain was growing. During this period the company's stock rose steadily, allowing Eddie to make $75 million over 38 months from selling shares even though he knew that the financial statements had been falsified.

Eddie's cousin, Sam Antar, who was the company's chief financial officer, later testified that one of the tricks used was to persuade an electronics buyer to write cheques totalling over $5 million, to reimburse him in various ways and then to count the money as new-store sales. Through these phoney invoices, business was seen to be booming.

Inventory numbers were also fabricated to suggest that the company's assets were much greater than they really were. Eddie and his associates would 'borrow' merchandise from friendly suppliers to boost the inventory account, ship stock from one store to another so that it could be double-counted, and, most audaciously of all, would unlock the auditors' desks and increase the inventory counts on the worksheets before photocopying the altered records. Sometimes it was even simpler. According to Sam Antar, the field auditors for Crazy Eddie's were young and inexperienced and, rather than climb over boxes in the warehouse, would ask company employees to assist them. Crooked employees volunteered and deliberately called out an inflated number. Repeated over and over again, this basic ruse helped to swell the inventory count enormously.

Eddie Antar also instructed his stores to hold the books open past the end of an accounting period so that sales revenues could be falsely inflated. Conversely, the liabilities for any given period were not usually recorded until the next one. Sam Antar regularly stashed unpaid bills in his desk, the liabilities either being entered after the end of the accounting year or held for long periods without being recorded. As a result neither the company nor the auditors ever really knew how much it owed.

And when the auditors were finally on the point of exposing the various frauds, company executives seized the falsified documents and threw them in the garbage.

In 1992 Sam Antar pleaded guilty to fraud and agreed to testify against cousin Eddie. But there was still no sign of Eddie. He had fled to Israel in 1990, calling himself first Alexander Stewart and then David Jacob Levi Cohen. He managed to stay one step ahead of his pursuers until making a fatal error in Switzerland. As Cohen, he went to the Swiss police and demanded help in gaining access to his $32 million bank account, telling them that the money in the account had been legally earned through the sale of gemstones to Alexander Stewart. The police were suspicious. The bank had already frozen the account at the request of US officials chasing Eddie and when police officers showed SEC officials the phoney Brazilian passport being used as Cohen's ID, investigators recognized their man. Eddie was picked up shortly afterwards near Tel Aviv, the end of his two and a half years on the run. In his room Israeli police found several passports, credit cards and $60,000 in several currencies. He was extradited to the United States in January 1993 to stand trial on 17 counts relating to the milking of Crazy Eddie shareholders of $75 million by inflating the value of their stock through a series of deceits. Two younger brothers, Mitchell and Allen, were also charged with various offences.

The trial lasted four weeks and featured Sam Antar's testimony. Asked why he had fled the country, Eddie claimed that he thought his ex-wife was trying to get more money from him following their acrimonious divorce (they had five children). The court heard how much of Eddie Antar's fraudulently obtained cash was placed in secret overseas bank accounts. Money was found in bank accounts in Israel, Canada, Luxembourg and Switzerland and in the names of a shell Liberian company and a foundation from Liechtenstein. Eddie also had dummy companies in Gibraltar and Panama. Via this intricate network, he was able to shuttle tens of millions of dollars around the world while on the run from the police. US attorney Michael Chertoff said that Eddie represented the 'epitome of the greed of the 1980s', adding that he had not been content simply to run his business but 'he had to steal and loot his firm of millions of dollars and defraud thousands of stockholders.' Antar was, he concluded, 'the Darth Vader of capitalism.'

Eddie was convicted on all counts and sentenced to 12½ years in prison. After also being ordered to repay $121 million to shareholders, he apologized for the 'pain and agony I caused my family.' Mitchell Antar was convicted on six of the eight charges, sentenced to four and a quarter years and ordered to pay $3 million in restitution, but Allen Antar was acquitted on all six counts.

Then in April 1995 a Federal appeals panel overturned the convictions of Eddie and Mitchell, ruling that the presiding judge had displayed prejudice against the men during sentencing. The following May, Eddie pleaded guilty to defrauding shareholders and, having been in custody since 1993, was sentenced to 42 months in prison.

The world had not heard the last of Crazy Eddie. Released from jail in March 1999, Antar and a nephew set up a new electronics store online, supported by a fresh batch of Jerry Carroll commercials. As Antar told the *New York Times*, 'Other companies are spending millions on brand awareness – we have instant name recognition. People keep asking, "Is this the real Crazy Eddie?"'

The Man Who Sold Titles

The son of a Hampshire clergyman, Arthur John Peter Michael Maundy Gregory was born into respectability. He exuded charm and intelligence and soon acquired friends in high places including government ministers and members of the Royal Family. But he used his connections to line his own pockets by perfecting the art of selling honours to those whose vanity was reflected in their bank balance – £10,000 for a knighthood, £35,000 for a baronetcy and £50,000 for a peerage. It was nice work if you could get it.

Maundy Gregory was born in Southampton on 1 July 1877. He went to Oxford University but left before obtaining a degree and drifted into teaching instead. Unfulfilled, he decided to become an actor but, after meeting with only moderate success, switched his attention to the business side of the profession. In 1907 he opened a theatrical agency on London's Charing Cross Road. It went bust two years later following the failure of a musical that he had backed but the venture had enabled him to establish some useful contacts.

In 1909 Gregory was recruited by the head of MI5 to compile dossiers on suspected foreign spies who were living in London. This undercover work provided him with inside information on some of Britain's leading politicians. Outwardly he began to mix in ever more exalted circles and could soon count among his friends the Duke of York (the future King George V) and David Lloyd George, the Chancellor of the Exchequer in the Liberal government that was formed after the 1908 general election. Gregory set up his own club, The Ambassador, in London's Conduit Street, bought a hotel in Dorking plus three other residences in the south of England, and acquired a splendid office at 10 Parliament Street, just around the corner from Downing Street. This enabled him to leave grandiose messages that he was 'over at Number 10'. He was clearly a man of influence although nobody knew exactly what his role was. He also launched a magazine, the *Whitehall Gazette and St James Review*, which was fiercely anti-Communist in content.

Lloyd George became Prime Minister in 1916. Ever since the House of Lords had rejected his 1909 budget, he had faced a constant battle with the peers and had been instrumental in pushing through an Act limiting their powers. Now he reckoned that the best way to ensure that he had plenty of supporters in the Lords was to fill it with his buddies. To achieve this, he turned to his friend Gregory who soon developed the selling of honours into a lucrative sideline.

Gregory's *modus operandi* was to discover, via his contacts, who was in line for an honour and whether the individual concerned wanted it enough to pay for it. The victim was then sent a letter proposing a confidential meeting to discuss a matter of considerable importance. Most paid up without realizing that they would have received the honour for free in due course. Alternatively Gregory would seek out a wealthy businessman who was said to be willing to pay for a title and use his government contacts to have the man's name added to a forthcoming Honours List. It was simple but effective.

Gregory's anti-Communist views had not gone unnoticed and in 1918 Special Branch asked him to investigate Victor Grayson, a former MP, who held left-wing views and was suspecting of working as an agent for the newly installed Communist government in Russia. Learning that Gregory was spying on him, Grayson retaliated with a little detective work of his own and ascertained that Lloyd George was using Gregory to sell political honours. Grayson denounced Lloyd George at a public meeting in Liverpool, declaring: 'This sale of honours is a national scandal. It can be traced right down to 10 Downing Street, and to a monocled dandy with offices in Whitehall. I know this man, and one day I will name him.' That 'monocled dandy' was Maundy Gregory.

Early in September 1920 Grayson was beaten up in the Strand – an incident that was probably an attempt by Gregory to silence him.

However, Grayson remained undaunted. He continued to make speeches attacking the selling of honours and threatening to expose the man behind the corruption. A few weeks later Grayson mysteriously disappeared off the face of the earth. No body was ever found.

Meanwhile Gregory carried on selling titles. But he was never far from controversy and in 1924 was linked to the fake Zinoviev letter that wrecked the chances of the Labour Party at that year's general election. MI5 had intercepted a letter supposedly written by Grigory Zinoviev, a prominent member of the Communist Party in Russia, which urged British Communists to promote revolution through acts of sedition. The letter was shown to Labour Prime Minister Ramsay MacDonald who was understandably concerned that any anti-red feeling might damage his party's chances at the forthcoming election. It was agreed that the letter should be kept secret but someone leaked its contents to pro-Conservative newspapers *The Times* and the *Daily Mail* just four days before voters went to the polls. Labour was duly trounced and afterwards it was claimed that Gregory had been involved in forging the letter and that Major Joseph Ball of MI5 had leaked it to the press. Ball later worked for Conservative Central Office where he pioneered the art of spin doctoring.

Ironically the installation of a Conservative government threatened Gregory's scam since new Prime Minister Stanley Baldwin confirmed his determination to stamp out the selling of political honours by introducing a 1925 Act of Parliament that made the practice illegal. Considering himself untouchable, Gregory went about business as usual, only to suffer a scare when someone to whom he had sold a baronetcy for £30,000 died before being able to collect it and the deceased's executors demanded the return of the money. Gregory managed to wriggle out of that predicament but in December 1932 he made the mistake that was to end his career. Over lunch, he offered a knighthood to Lieutenant Commander Edward Leake of the Royal Navy. Gregory confided that it cost money to open the right doors, but that £10,000 should do the job. He added that he had secured honours for money countless times in the past. Leake expressed sufficient interest to loosen Gregory's tongue but, instead of taking him up on the offer, went straight to Scotland Yard.

Gregory pleaded not guilty at first, to the horror of the many prominent figures who stood to lose everything should the defendant choose to name names in court. So he used his predicament to blackmail them in return for pleading guilty. They happily contributed to the Gregory coffers to ensure that no details of his criminal activities came out at the trial.

Gregory received two months' imprisonment and a £50 fine. On his release he became embroiled in yet another scandal, this time surrounding the death of Edith Rosse, with whom he had been living for a number of years. Once again Gregory emerged relatively unscathed but was persuaded by his influential friends to spend his remaining years in Paris. There he lived as Sir Arthur Gregory until his death on 28 September 1941.

The Shame in Spain

When big money first came into sport, corruption was only a short head behind. Canadian sprinter Ben Johnson had tarnished the name of the Olympics but it was hoped that at least the Paralympic Games – that platform for nobility and courage – might remain sacrosanct from accusations of cheating. Surely this more than any other sporting competition represented the original Olympic ideal that it was the taking part that mattered. Then along came the Spanish Paralympic basketball team.

In the wake of the hugely successful Sydney Olympics of 2000 – arguably the finest Olympics ever – the following month's Paralympic Games in the same city attracted greater media attention than usual. The surprise packages were Spain whose haul of 107 medals – 37 gold – put them third in the final medals table behind Australia and Great Britain. It was Spain's most successful Paralympics by some distance.

Among Spain's golds was an 87–63 victory over Russia in the final of the intellectual disability basketball tournament. But then it emerged that ten of the 12-strong Spanish squad had no disability whatsoever. The medals were handed back and a leading Spanish official was forced to resign.

The man who blew the whistle on the Spanish basketball team was one of its players, Carlos Ribagorda, who also worked as a journalist on the business magazine *Capital*. Despite having no mental handicap, Ribagorda had been playing for Spain's intellectually disabled national team for two years when Paralympic officials approached him about playing in Sydney. He decided to accept the offer with a view to exposing the scandal afterwards.

Ribagorda's story appeared in *Capital* a month after the Games. Under Paralympics rules, a player had to have an IQ of 70 or less to be eligible for intellectually disabled competition, but Ribagorda said that nobody ever tested him or asked him to provide any documentation to prove his disability. He claimed that at least 15 athletes with no incapacity at all, including ten basketball players, were signed up by the Spanish Federation for Mentally Handicapped Sports (FEDDI) and told to pretend they were handicapped. The goal, he said, was to win more medals so that the federation would qualify for additional funding. 'The FEDDI did not hesitate in signing up athletes without any type of handicap,' wrote Ribagorda. 'They just sent them an official letter. The aim of this policy was to win medals and gain more sponsorship. The FEDDI discovered that it could benefit from signing up athletes who had no physical or mental handicap. The only test they did was to make me do half a dozen sit-ups and take my blood pressure. We never had any medical or psychological tests.'

Apart from Ribagorda himself, the basketball squad also included a lawyer, an engineer and a number of students. Ribagorda claimed that members of the Spanish table tennis, track and field, and swimming teams at Sydney were not disabled intellectually or physically either.

In the ensuing hullabaloo an American Paralympic coach said that some nations allowed athletes who suffered only from dyslexia to play in basketball teams.

The Spanish Paralympic Committee reacted to the scandal by ordering the victorious basketball team to return their gold medals. Fernando Martin Vicente, president of FEDDI, was forced to resign 'for actions that were clearly contrary to the interests of the Spanish and international Paralympic movement.' And in January 2001 the International Paralympic Committee announced that it would no longer include athletes with intellectual or mental disabilities in its activities. A sporting outlet had been closed to many because of the actions of an unsporting few.

The Secret Lives of Philip Musica

Established for over a century, McKesson and Robbins Incorporated had risen to become the third largest pharmaceutical firm in the world. It had assets of $80 million, an annual turnover of double that figure and a highly respected president in the shape of financier Dr F. Donald Coster, a man described by his many business associates as being 'of good American stock.' So when Coster was sensationally arrested in December 1938 and trading in McKesson and Robbins stock suspended, the shock waves could be felt all along Wall Street.

Coster was arrested after corporation treasurer Julian S. Thompson discovered that some $20 million worth of drugs that were listed as the firm's assets were not only missing but also had quite probably never existed in the first place. The news came as a devastating blow to McKesson's 82 vice-presidents, especially as two of their number, deputy treasurer George Dietrich and trading agent George Vernard, were arrested along with Coster. Dietrich's seizure was of particular concern since he was a close friend and neighbour of Coster's in Fairfield, Connecticut. With Dietrich also under suspicion it made the New York commercial world wonder whether there really was some foundation to these unbelievable allegations against Coster.

On the face of it Dr Coster was a model businessman and pillar of the community. Born to American parents in Washington, DC, Frank Donald Coster was educated in Germany where he obtained a PhD from Heidelberg University. He later returned to his native country and practised for two years as a doctor in New York City. This background proved invaluable when, in 1926, he acquired McKesson and Robbins. In those 12 years at the helm he had overseen the firm's expansion into a world leader. Apart from the Fairfield mansion, which he shared with his loving wife Carol, and a 123 ft yacht, Coster was not one for flaunting his wealth. Nor was he a great socializer although he was a keen member of the New York Yacht Club. Instead he preferred to lead a quiet, family life and to put his money into worthy causes such as the heart clinic he had founded in Bridgeport, Connecticut. Coster himself had a heart condition. A director of three trusts and a member of the Bankers' Club, Coster was considered by his rival business magnates to be beyond reproach. If there was a criticism of him, it was that he was perhaps a little too conservative, too cautious and lacking in charisma for those changing times. But certainly nobody had reason to question his honesty.

If the news of Coster's arrest was greeted with incredulity, what followed was truly mind-blowing. On 14 December, the FBI routinely took his fingerprints . . . and found that they were a perfect match for a serial swindler who had not been heard of for nearly 20 years. Coster was really Italian-born Philip Musica who had served at least two jail sentences for fraud. He had no background in medicine and the degree certificate from Heidelberg University that was framed on his office wall was a fake. What's more, his two co-accused, George Dietrich and George Vernard, were found to be Musica's brothers, George and Arthur. It subsequently emerged that a fourth Musica brother, Robert, had been posing as Robert Dietrich, another senior executive with McKesson and Robbins.

The revelations were splashed over the front pages of the newspapers the following day. One assistant District Attorney who had prosecuted Musica earlier in his criminal career described him as 'the most diabolical, ingenious, sly man I ever came in contact with.' He added that outwardly Musica appeared a retiring type of individual 'and it only was when you looked into his eyes that you discovered a furtive look that aroused suspicion in you.'

No one was more surprised about the sensational disclosures than Carol Coster. The Costers had been married for 12 years – around the same time that he became head of McKesson and Robbins – and she knew nothing about her husband's former life or identity.

Bit by bit the true story of F. Donald Coster's background came to light. He was born Philip Musica in Naples in 1877 and the family moved to the US when he was six. His father Antonio was originally a barber by trade but in 1898 he set up a small business importing foodstuffs, notably cheeses, from his homeland to cater for New York's thriving 'Little Italy' community. Philip joined him in this venture and soon proved his worth by hatching a crooked scheme to avoid paying import tax. Customs inspectors were bribed to turn a blind eye, but after 11 prosperous years, the scam was uncovered and a number of customs weighers admitted to having accepted bribes from the Musicas. In court Philip protected his father and took full responsibility. He served five and a half months in prison before being pardoned by President Taft on the grounds that a dishonest customs officer had led him astray in the first place.

On his release, he embarked on a new enterprise with his father, setting up the grandiose United States Hair Company, manufacturing wigs from human hair specially imported from Italy. By forging invoices to create a stock that did not actually exist, Philip was able to borrow as much as $1 million from over 20 banks. The money was used partly to fund his increasingly extravagant lifestyle as he became a prominent figure in New York's Italian-American community, dining at the trendiest restaurants and making frequent excursions to the opera, invariably with a beautiful actress on his arm.

The hair scam was rumbled when Philip called at the offices of the Bank of the Manhattan Company in search of another loan. He said he had 216 cases of human hair, worth altogether around $370,000, and wanted a loan to cover the full value of the goods. As security on the loan he offered the bills of lading and the bills of exchange. By now the banks were anticipating repayment instead of further borrowing and stalled at $25,000. Musica accepted that sum as an advance and told the bank that the boxes of hair were stored on a pier in Brooklyn. Then a clerk, inspecting the bills of lading, noticed that the figures had been tampered with. He alerted his employers who sent investigators to the pier where they discovered that the boxes supposedly containing coveted strands of long hair actually housed tissue paper and clumps of almost worthless cropped hair. The shortfall was around $300,000. The Musica family made a run for it but were arrested in New Orleans on board a ship bound for Honduras. Philip was found to be carrying

$80,000 in cash and $250,000 in money certificates. One of his sisters had $18,000 secreted in a girdle, which she desperately tried to throw overboard as officers pounced. In custody old Antonio attempted suicide, prompting Philip to take all the blame once more.

Philip Musica was incarcerated in the Tombs Prison, New York, awaiting trial. There he ingratiated himself to the police by informing on other prisoners. In return, he was given a suspended sentence in 1918 for the wig fraud. Musica continued his role as police informer using the alias 'William Johnson'. In 1919 a Senate committee expressed its disquiet at the practice of using criminals in this way, but New York State's Deputy Attorney General, Alfred R. Becker, insisted that Musica was a reformed character and, indeed, had become a close personal friend. 'There is no person in the world I trust more than Philip Musica,' declared Becker in words that would come back to haunt him within just 12 months. For in 1920 William Johnson was charged with perjury after giving false evidence in a murder case. His days as an official informer were over. William Johnson promptly disappeared, as did the name of Philip Musica.

America was now in the grip of Prohibition, a law that inadvertently did more to encourage lawlessness than any other. With fraudsters on every corner, it was only natural that someone with Musica's track record would want a slice of the action. He resurfaced as Frank Costa, owner of the Adelphi Pharmaceutical Manufacturing Corporation, producers of hair tonics. His business enabled him to obtain a permit for 5,000 gallons of pure alcohol every month. Instead of going into hair tonics, the alcohol ended up being sold on as illicit booze. Adelphi was eventually raided, but Frank Costa evaded the long arm of the law.

It took more than a minor inconvenience to deter him from such a profitable scheme and in 1923 the Italian Catholic Frank Costa was transformed into American-born Methodist Dr F. Donald Coster, head of another firm of hair tonic manufacturers, Girard and Co. For his entry in *Who's Who in America*, Musica (as Coster) gave himself new parents, two college degrees and an impressive social backdrop.

With his real father dead, Philip was now head of the Musica family and appointed his three brothers to key positions in the company as the Dietrich siblings and George Vernard. Based in Alexandria, Virginia, Girard and Co. operated the same scam as its predecessor, Adelphi, but managed to avoid prosecution. The authorities had their suspicions but were unable to find 100 per cent proof.

The success of Girard and Co. gave Coster the taste for expansion. In 1926 he met his future nemesis, investment banker Julian S.

Thomson, with a view to securing a major loan. The carefully rigged books made Girard and Co. appear highly prosperous and thoroughly legal, as a result of which Thomson had no hesitation in offering his assistance. With Thomson's help, Coster obtained control of the long-standing firm of McKesson and Robbins and merged it with Girard and Co. Thomson was so impressed with Coster's business acumen and personal standing that he quit banking to join the new firm as a director and treasurer.

During Coster's reign everything at McKesson and Robbins looked rosy. Even the 1929 market crash, which wrecked so many apparently fireproof companies, failed to damage McKesson's profits. Soon it was marketing over 200 different pharmaceutical products and growing by the year. However, it was all an illusion. The firm survived and thrived on a diet of fictitious deals, forged invoices and imaginary assets, stored in non-existent warehouses. Like Girard and Co. before it, McKesson's crude drugs department was used to siphon off vast sums of money. Just as Girard and Co. had sold millions of dollars worth of bootlegged liquor through a company called W.W. Smith, so even greater sums of crude drugs were sold by McKesson through Smith's. But the drugs did not actually exist and W.W. Smith amounted to nothing grander than a solitary Brooklyn office staffed by George Vernard, alias Arthur Musica. Over the years some $3 million was paid in commission by McKesson to W.W. Smith.

In time Thomson became concerned about the listed assets of the crude drugs division. Coster and George Dietrich (alias George Musica) guarded that division fiercely from outside examination, further fuelling Thomson's suspicions. It took him eight months to accumulate sufficient evidence on Coster to demand a showdown.When he failed to receive satisfactory answers to his queries, he refused to sign the company's annual report unless he was permitted to inspect that division's assets in person. What he found – or rather, did not find – led to the arrest of the Musica brothers.

Having initially released Philip Musica on bail, the FBI called again at his mansion on 16 December to announce additional charges. By now, his past life was all over the papers. As two agents approached the house, Musica walked into the bathroom and shot himself through the head.

He left behind two letters – one to his wife, begging her forgiveness; the other, which ran to eight pages, trying to justify his own business actions and exonerate his brothers of any fraudulent dealing. For all his faults, he was loyal to his family to the last.

Carol struggled to come to terms with the death of her beloved husband and the sensations that surrounded it. In her eyes, he had just the one identity. And the name she put on his marble headstone was 'F. Donald Coster'.

Victor Lustig: King Con

With at least 24 known aliases, a fluency in five languages, and nearly 50 arrests in the United States alone, 'Count' Victor Lustig was truly a king among con men. He will forever be remembered for pulling what must surely rank among the most audacious stunts in history – selling the Eiffel Tower.

Despite the aristocratic title he later bestowed upon himself, Lustig was born to a conspicuously middle-class background at Hostoun, Czechoslovakia, near the German border, in 1890. At the age of 19 a fight over a woman left Lustig with a scar down the left side of his face. It may have added to his air of mystery but did not exactly enhance his prospects of anonymity – an essential weapon in the con man's armoury.

Lustig was an extremely capable student – in time he would be able to master Czech, German, English, French and Italian – but his real talent lay in the more recreational pastimes of billiards and poker. Seeing his future as a professional gambler, he took to boarding the transatlantic cruises where wealthy passengers offered easy prey for unscrupulous cardsharps. En route he learned the ropes from seasoned practitioners such as Nicky Arnstein. The First World War put a halt to the transatlantic trade and when peace was restored, Lustig decided to head for the United States on a more permanent basis. He was sure that he could make a living off his wits.

Calling himself 'Count' Victor Lustig, he entered negotiations in 1922 to buy a dilapidated Missouri farm that had been repossessed by the bank. He spun a sob story about how his noble existence in Austria had been destroyed by the war and how he had come to America in an attempt to rebuild his life with what remained of the family money. He said he had opted for a career in farming and offered the bankers $22,000 in bonds to purchase the farm. When the bank officials readily agreed to the deal, Lustig persuaded them to accept an additional $10,000 worth of bonds in exchange for cash so that he would have some operating capital until the farm was renovated and fully working. The bankers were so delighted at finally being able to sell the property that they failed to spot Lustig switch envelopes and make off with both the bonds and the cash. Lustig was subsequently trailed by the bank's private detective to New York but somehow managed to convince the moneymen that they would be better advised not prosecuting him on account of the bad publicity they would attract. Moreover, he persuaded them to hand over $1,000 for the inconvenience caused by his arrest. It was nothing less than a masterstroke.

Flushed with success, Lustig turned up in Montreal where he homed in on Vermont banker Linus Merton. The day after arranging for an accomplice to pick Merton's pocket, Lustig befriended the banker by returning his wallet with its contents intact. Having won Merton's trust, the Count regurgitated the family hardship yarn and told him about a sure-fire moneymaking scheme he was using to compensate for the losses he had endured during the war. He said that his cousin Emil worked at a bookie joint and was able to intercept the race wires. Consequently Emil could find out the winner of any horse race several minutes before the local betting windows were closed.

The banker was intrigued, particularly when he started winning. How was he to know the bookie joint was a fake? With Merton on a winning streak (albeit of relatively small amounts), Lustig went for the kill, informing him that Emil had to quit his job because his wife had suddenly been taken ill. Luckily there was just time for Merton to place one last bet. Since the system seemed foolproof, he made it a big one. This time he lost. Lustig took him for $30,000.

Lustig's most celebrated scam was hatched one afternoon in the spring of 1925. Leafing through the pages of a newspaper in a Paris café, he spotted a small article reporting that the Eiffel Tower was in such a state of disrepair that the government was exploring the possibility of having it demolished and rebuilt. Lustig immediately saw an opportunity to exploit this situation and decided to pass himself off as Deputy Director of the Ministre des Postes et des Télégraphes, the government department responsible for maintaining Paris's best-known landmark. Employing a counterfeiter to duplicate the ministry's headed notepaper, Lustig then wrote in deliberately vague terms to five scrap-metal dealers, inviting them to a clandestine meeting a week later at the city's Crillon Hotel.

On arrival the quintet were escorted into a suite by Lustig's 'private secretary', in reality a Canadian con artist by the name of 'Dapper' Dan Collins. Lustig proceeded to inform the gathering that the Eiffel Tower was in such a dangerous condition that repairs were needed as a matter of urgency. Howcver, he added, because the French government could not afford to carry out the necessary repairs, it had been decided, regretfully, that the tower would have to be pulled down and sold for scrap. He noted that the tower had been built back in 1889 and was never intended to be a permanent structure. As the dealers digested the news in stunned silence, Lustig stressed the need for secrecy since this highly controversial decision by the government would undoubtedly cause public outcry should word leak out. Pandering to their egos, he told the five that they had been chosen not only for their business expertise but also because they were renowned for their discretion.

Next Lustig took them to the tower in limousines and wined and dined them before inviting them to submit their sealed bids for the contract to demolish and dispose of the Eiffel Tower. As he pointed out, 7,000 tons of scrap metal had considerable value. The bids were to be sent to him at the Crillon Hotel within the next five days after which he would inform them of the government's decision.

By day four, all five had eagerly submitted tenders. But Lustig was not interested in who made the highest bid; he was only concerned with who was the best mark. That dubious honour, Lustig felt, should go to a provincial scrap metal merchant by the name of André Poisson whose evident hunger for social acceptance within the Paris business world seemed likely to override any commonsense. In short, M. Poisson was a fish out of water.

Five days after the meeting Lustig duly contacted Poisson to tell him that his bid had been successful. Poisson appeared surprised, almost hesitant, so Lustig quickly asked Collins to arrange a meeting with the 'Deputy Director' at the hotel on a matter so private that it could not possibly be discussed at the ministry. When Poisson arrived, he listened while Lustig bemoaned the fate of a public servant, saying how he was expected to entertain on a grand scale yet was paid a woefully inadequate salary. Poisson realized that Lustig was hinting at a bribe and with that all his doubts disappeared. If a French politician was asking for a bribe, he must be genuine! After handing Lustig a few large notes from his pocket, Poisson gave him a banker's draft for the contract. In return, he received a worthless bill of sale. With that, Lustig shook Poisson warmly by the hand, showed him out and headed straight for the nearest bank to cash the draft.

Within 24 hours Lustig and Collins were out of the country – in Austria. They made no attempt to lie low, instead enjoying the high life at the expense of the hapless Poisson. Each day, Lustig checked the newspapers for any story about the great rip-off but none appeared. He deduced that Poisson was simply too embarrassed to go to the police.

It has been suggested that Poisson's silence enabled Lustig to return to Paris shortly afterwards and pull the same stunt again, selling the Eiffel Tower to a second businessman. While nothing should ever be ruled out with regard to Victor Lustig, that particular story may well be apocryphal.

Having conquered Europe, Lustig fixed his attentions on the United States once again. Posing as a successful Broadway producer, he seduced a starlet called Estelle Sweeny whose CV amounted to runner-up in a Miss Illinois contest. He promised her a leading role in a musical and took her on the rounds of socialite parties where he would casually mention that he was looking for a financial backer for his next big production. Ronald Dredge, a New England businessman with a passion for the theatre and for seeing his name in lights, was immediately hooked and declared that he would be willing to provide the $70,000 that Lustig required. To have just taken Dredge's money would have been too easy. Lustig preferred a challenge and so, ever the gentleman, he insisted that he would not conclude the deal until he himself had raised at least 51 per cent of the capital. Impressed by Lustig's integrity, Dredge returned to his home in Providence, Rhode Island, and waited for the call.

Lustig deliberately let him stew for a few weeks before making contact. When he did, it was to announce that he had now raised the 51 per cent and was therefore happy to allow Dredge to invest his 49 per cent – a cool $34,000. Dropping Ms Sweeny for whom he had no further use, Lustig lured Dredge to a New York speakeasy. There, he accepted the businessman's $34,000 and exited the room for a moment, on the pretence of counting the money. Dredge was left with Lustig's case, which supposedly contained $36,000. When Lustig failed to reappear, Dredge became nervous and opened the case. He found a few dollar bills covering a wad of old newspaper. Despite pursuing him the length and breadth of the country, Dredge never saw Lustig or his $34,000 again. As for Estelle Sweeny, she ended up as a stripper at a seedy club in Havana.

By 1926 Lustig was in California, demonstrating a contraption known as the Rumanian Box, a fine mahogany piece which had been specially built for him by a New York City cabinetmaker. It was Lustig's money-making machine. In search of a sucker, he came across Herman Loller, a multi-millionaire who had earned his fortune manufacturing transmission flywheels for the automobile industry. But now his business was in trouble and he was looking for a get-rich-quick scheme so that he could continue living in the manner to which he had become accustomed. Lustig had the very thing. Spinning his familiar story about having been an Austrian count before falling on hard times, Lustig related how his fortunes had revived spectacularly thanks to a moneymaking device. Loller begged for a demonstration but Lustig feigned reluctance before eventually bowing to his request. In Lustig's hotel room he produced a box that had a narrow slot at either end. He twiddled a few knobs, adjusted a couple of dials and then into one slot fed a genuine $100 bill and into the other a blank piece of paper. He explained that the bill had to soak in the chemical bath for precisely six hours in order for all the images to transfer properly. He assured Loller that it was not a counterfeiting machine and that any bank would accept the finished article.

Exactly six hours later Lustig turned the knobs and the box spat out two identical bank notes. To prove its efficiency, Lustig persuaded Loller to take the two bills to a local bank. Both were confirmed as genuine, which of course they were. For Lustig had previously concealed a second bill in the box with the serial numbers altered so that they matched. Loller pleaded with Lustig to sell him the magic box and, after much persuasion, the 'Count' handed it over in return for $25,000. As Lustig made good his escape, Loller took the device back to his yacht and set about making money. Even when his first attempts failed to produce a bill, he persevered for days in the belief that he was somehow operating it wrongly. Finally losing patience, he opened the box and found to his horror that it was empty but for two rubber rollers and several sheets of blank paper.

Lustig's love of a challenge led him into dangerous territory when he contemplated swindling Public Enemy Number One, Al Capone. Invited into the mobster's inner sanctum, Lustig told Capone about a Wall Street scam he had planned that was guaranteed to double his money in sixty days. The minimum stake, he said, was $50,000. Capone counted out $50,000 and pressed a button on his desk. A wall panel slid open to reveal a hoodlum armed with a machine pistol. 'Sixty days,' muttered Capone. 'Understand?'

Lustig did not need the consequences of failure spelling out, but in truth he had no plan. He had simply been motivated by the thrill of taking money off Capone. However, now that he had $50,000 of Capone's cash he knew that he dared not spend it. Instead when the sixty days were up, he returned to Chicago and told Capone that, sadly, the scheme hadn't worked. A furious Capone was about to press the button when Lustig handed him the $50,000. Capone calmed down and listened as Lustig blurted out how embarrassed he was to have failed because, apart from anything else, he really needed the money. Honesty and Capone were not obvious bedfellows but he was moved by Lustig's apparent sincerity and handed over $5,000 to tide him on his way. Only Victor Lustig could have managed to squeeze money out of Al Capone.

In 1934 the United States was suddenly flooded with counterfeit bills. The chief suspect was a man named William Watts whose only known contact was Lustig. Secret Service agents arrested Lustig who had a key on him that opened a locker in Times Square, New York. Inside the locker they found a set of plates plus counterfeit money to the value of $51,000. Although Lustig pulled off a daring escape on the day before his trial, he was recaptured and sentenced to 20 years. On 9 March 1947 he contracted pneumonia and died 36 hours later. His death certificate gave his occupation as salesman.

Helpfully he left behind his 'Ten Commandments for Con Men'.

1. Be a patient listener (it is this, not fast talking, that gets a con man his coups).
2. Never look bored.
3. Wait for the other person to reveal any political opinions, then agree with them.
4. Let the other person reveal religious views, then have the same ones.
5. Hint at sex talk, but don't follow it up unless the other fellow shows a strong interest.
6. Never discuss illness, unless some special concern is shown.
7. Never pry into a person's personal circumstances (they'll tell you all eventually).
8. Never boast – just let your importance be quietly obvious.
9. Never be untidy.
10. Never get drunk.

A Teenage Tycoon

As the decade that taste forgot gave way to the materialistic 1980s, times were hard for young Barry Minkow. His father's real estate business had just gone bust with the result that money was in short supply around the family home in Reseda, just outside Los Angeles. When the gas company reacted to unpaid bills by disconnecting the heating, the family were often forced to take showers at neighbours' houses. It was scarcely the ideal environment for any teenager – especially for one with such low self-esteem as Minkow.

Short and skinny, Minkow epitomized the boy who got sand kicked in his face on the beach. He joined a gymnasium to try and improve his chances with girls but still feared that he didn't possess the college boy good looks to be taken seriously. The only thing he did appear to have in his favour was a sharp business brain. When he was a child, his mother used to save on the expense of hiring a babysitter by taking him into work with her. She worked for a small carpet-cleaning company and, even before he was a teenager, Minkow had proved himself adept at telephone sales. Customers appeared genuinely impressed by his boyish enthusiasm, allied to a shrewd grasp of the salesman's patter. He knew instinctively just how far to go in order to close a sale. The carpet cleaning business seemed to be in his blood and it came as no surprise when, in need of money, he landed a job after school cleaning carpets. Then one day in 1981 a friend from the gym lent Minkow $1,600 to set up his own business. Figuring that a 15-year-old entrepreneur might prove attractive to the opposite sex, Minkow accepted the generous offer and called his firm ZZZZ (pronounced zee) Best. The other kids thought he was mad, but to Minkow running a business was second nature. After all, he was Jewish.

Although his business was strictly a one-man operation at first (based in his father's garage, for which young Minkow paid rent), it made him feel good about himself. With all the family's financial worries, he saw himself as the knight on a white charger riding to the rescue . . . and putting one over on his father in the process. He knew that his market was a potential money-spinner but that there were any number of 'cowboy' operators. His task therefore was to establish a degree of public confidence in ZZZZ Best.

However, he felt unable to do that as a solo performer. It was important that he had a framework of subordinates, not only to convince the general public that he meant business but also to impress his schoolmates that he was the genuine article. So he hired his mother to work for him as a telephone sales rep, cold-calling people in the phone book to drum up custom. She did such a good job that Minkow had to expand. He outgrew the garage and leased space in a nearby warehouse. He acquired a truck – even though he himself wasn't old enough to have a driver's licence – and brought in more employees. Business was booming. But already there were worrying signs that Minkow's ego was in danger of spiralling out of control as he insisted that his mother call him 'Mr Minkow', particularly when his father was around.

From the outset Minkow had a flair for self-promotion. On one occasion he rang a local television news show in Los Angeles, posing as a satisfied ZZZZ Best customer, saying that the station ought to do a story about the 16-year-old who ran the carpet cleaning company. 'He's what's best about America,' said the caller. 'Here's his number.' Minkow then sat back and waited for his phone to ring. It took all of five minutes. From local TV he progressed to the *Oprah Winfrey Show* and the pages of *People* magazine, *USA Today* and *Newsweek*. He was a young man in a hurry – and that would eventually prove to be his downfall.

The growth rate of ZZZZ Best should have been enough to keep anyone satisfied but, although he was still at school, Minkow was becoming power crazy. In his desire to be the best, he worked unfeasibly long hours, driving himself into the ground. He addressed business schools and was hailed as a shining example to the youth of America. Yet ZZZZ Best's success was built on crooked foundations. Minkow had been submitting phoney financial statements to banks in order to secure loans and had also put through hundreds of thousands of dollars in fake credit card vouchers. On another occasion he made ends meet by staging a break-in at the company offices and filing an insurance claim. He took the call about the bogus burglary in class the next day. He believed that he could steal from the banks to build up a legitimate business empire, and for a while he got away with it. And if he were ever to get caught his attitude was that he was just a kid who was bound to make mistakes. He was fearless.

ZZZZ Best was doing well, but nowhere near as well as Minkow made out. By 1985, however, he was living in dreamland. He had left home for a smart, gated residence in the up-market suburb of Woodland Hills, the driveway of which was adorned by a Ferrari Testarossa. His neighbours included actress Heather Locklear. He needed to keep up appearances, and that meant further company expansion. So he announced that ZZZZ Best was branching out into the insurance restoration business, restoring buildings that had been damaged by fire, floods, and other disasters. According to Minkow, the company was undertaking several large insurance restoration projects that were expected to produce profits of up to 40 per cent and were collectively worth over $40 million. It was, said Minkow, a superb opportunity for an investor. All he needed was another $15 million to be able to take another giant chunk out of the lucrative restoration market.

By 1986 Minkow stated that 86 per cent of the company's business was now in the field of insurance restoration. The only problem was that none of it actually existed. True, there were thousands of pages of invoices, receipts, correspondence and payments, but they were all fakes, many copied on to false letterheads. There was not one genuine insurance contract. The entire restoration arm of ZZZZ Best was a scam to trick investors. But everybody fell for Minkow's smooth line in sales talk. Although his projected profit margins were clearly ludicrous (the standard profit on restoration jobs was nearer 7 per cent than 40), they were accepted because even hardened businessmen wanted to believe in the boy wonder. They never dreamed for a moment that they were being conned by a teenager.

When stock in ZZZZ Best was offered publicly in December 1986, some of Wall Street's leading companies clamoured for a piece of the action. At the age of 20 Minkow became the youngest chairman and CEO of a publicly traded company in the history of Wall Street.

Within a matter of months the share price had rocketed, based on stories about the company's high growth and reported income. In 1987, after only six years in business, ZZZZ Best had a market valuation of over $211 million, giving the genius at its helm a paper fortune of $109 million. *Business Week* quoted a member of a large brokerage house as saying that 'Barry Minkow is a great manager and ZZZZ Best is a great company.' The broker recommended his clients to buy ZZZZ Best stock. That same year, the Association of Collegiate Entrepreneurs and the Young Entrepreneurs' Organization placed Minkow on their list of the top 100 young entrepreneurs in America. And Tom Bradley, Mayor of Los Angeles, went as far as proposing a 'Barry Minkow Day', saying that Minkow had 'set a fine entrepreneurial example of obtaining the status of a millionaire at the age of 18.'

But the reality was that ZZZZ Best had never once made a legitimate profit. All of the documentation supporting these alleged profits was faked. Job folders bulged with contracts, cost accountings and receipts for raw materials, but they were all fictitious. A genuine firm specializing in start-up businesses had audited the company's early financial statements but it, too, had been duped by Minkow.

Part of the thinking behind the stock offering was that Minkow intended to use the money raised by it to repay most of his private investors and then create a legitimate carpet-cleaning enterprise. He believed that he would gradually be able to phase out the phoney restoration business and, indeed if the company stock performed well, he would have less need to invent jobs and contracts. It all looked good on paper – but then so did Minkow's fortune. Before he was able to put his plan into practice, he came under increasingly close scrutiny.

Taking on Wall Street had brought Minkow into contact with the highest investment bankers, lawyers and accountants in the land. When they demanded to see contracts, invoices and other paperwork relating to the insurance restoration revenues, he fobbed them off with more than 16,000 fabricated documents. Taking a keen interest in what was supposedly ZZZZ Best's largest restoration job, the accountants and lawyers asked for an inspection. This posed a problem for Minkow since neither the building nor the job existed. With help from his associates, he found a newly renovated tower block in Sacramento that matched the description. Fake blueprints and construction permits were created, and the professionals went away happy . . . for the time being.

Early in 1987 Minkow received another request from the company's external auditor, this time to see a building in San Diego that ZZZZ Best had apparently landed an $8.2 million contract to restore. Minkow had just a week to find and gain access to a multi-storey building in downtown San Diego that could support his story. He struck lucky. In the heart of the San Diego business district was the framework of a high-rise block that had been abandoned partway through construction because the developer had gone bankrupt. Minkow reckoned that, with a little dressing, it could pass muster as a building that had been gutted by fire on the upper floors. He gained access to the site by promising to buy the property, and then filled a nearby warehouse with hundreds of rolls of carpeting. On the day of the inspection, he arranged for a fleet of ZZZZ Best trucks to be positioned at the site, manned by workers wearing the company's T-shirts. The auditor and his colleagues were duly taken on a tour of the construction site and saw what appeared to be ZZZZ Best crews hard at work on another restoration job. Everything seemed to be in order.

Three months later the auditor asked to see the finished job. This spelt potential disaster. While Minkow had twice managed to find buildings that matched his description of projects in Sacramento and San Diego, this was an altogether tougher assignment, faced as he was with showing the inspectors an incomplete building to which he had no access. Since ZZZZ Best had, of course, pulled out of the deal to buy the property once the earlier visit had taken place, no work had been done on it in the meantime. Furthermore, the building's owners were furious with Minkow for reneging on their agreement. He knew he had to build bridges – not to mention eight-floor office blocks – fast.

Minkow flew overnight to Colorado to apologize profusely to the owners of the San Diego building for the earlier 'misunderstanding' and offered to pay $500,000 cash, in advance, for a six-month lease. The offer was accepted. A firm of architects was hired to draw up plans in double-quick time and as soon as the plans were approved, three construction crews began working round the clock. They finished six of the eight floors in just ten days. When the auditing team returned to the site less than three weeks after announcing their intention to do so, they found an authentic, newly renovated building which bore out Minkow's boast that ZZZZ Best could respond to a restoration emergency at lightning speed. However, not even they realized just how fast the work had been done. The auditor was suitably impressed and at the end of the tour, wrote a memo saying 'Job looks very good.' He was subsequently criticized for inspecting only what ZZZZ Best officials chose to show him, without making independent enquiries.

The elaborate lengths to which Minkow went to cover up his deception typified the story of ZZZZ Best. No expense was spared in creating an illusion. In one instance he decided that the ideal way to impress a bank's loan officers was to lure away a promising member of their junior staff and employ him in a legitimate area of ZZZZ Best at twice his original salary. As a result the bank saw ZZZZ Best as serious players.

By May 1987 Minkow was closing in on a $40 million deal to buy out KeyServe, the nation's largest retail carpet cleaning company, an acquisition that was being financed by the firm of Drexel Burnham Lambert. But two days before the deal was due to close, an old story returned to haunt Minkow. A reporter on the *Los Angeles Times* had learned that the police were investigating Minkow over suspected Mafia connections. Probing ZZZZ Best's finances, the journalist chanced upon the credit card scam and ran a story about credit card overcharges by a Minkow-owned flower shop. The incident in question had occurred two years previously and Minkow had attempted to deflect questions about it during the public stock offering by explaining it away as theft by some of his employees. To maintain his good name, he had immediately repaid the overcharged customers and sacked those responsible. But the *Times* story posed serious questions as to whether ZZZZ Best was entirely legitimate. The report sent the company's stock into freefall.

Minkow tried to bluff his way out of the mess but bankers, suppliers, investors and auditors now became concerned that an outwardly successful company reporting so much revenue and profit should have difficulty paying its bills. He spun a few more lies but the accountants were not taken in this time and resigned en masse. He responded by hiring a new firm of accountants who worked for over a month on ZZZZ Best's year-end audit without unearthing the fraud. He even convinced one of his board members to give him $1 million to invest in yet another fictitious restoration project. A few days later, convinced that the company he had built on a pack of lies was about to come tumbling down, Minkow resigned. ZZZZ Best collapsed instantly. The game was up.

Minkow was charged with 54 counts of fraud. He pleaded not guilty but on the final day of his four-month long-trial, faced with overwhelming evidence against him, he suddenly changed his plea to guilty. The judge was furious that Minkow had wasted so much of the court's time and threw the book at him, sentencing him to 25 years in prison. Ten of his ZZZZ Best colleagues were convicted of duping the auditors.

Minkow served most of his sentence at Englewood penitentiary, Colorado, where he converted to Christianity and earned a Masters degree in theology. He was released after seven and a half years whereupon he returned to his old stamping grounds of the *Oprah Winfrey Show* and *Donahue* to repent his sins and talk about his new way of life. He became head pastor of a church in San Diego, preaching against the evils of greed and corruption, and has served as chief consultant at the Fraud Discovery Institute, an online learning centre that teaches bankers how to spot fraud. Who says Americans don't do irony?

The Wandering Jew

Scottish social historian Thomas Carlyle called him the 'Prince of Quacks'. To others in eighteenth-century Europe he was known as the 'Wandering Jew' because he claimed to be over 3,000 years old, having successfully developed the elixir for everlasting life. He was, he told his followers, immortal. Yet when he died in 1795 Count Alessandro di Cagliostro, as he called himself, was a mere 52. His great age and medical prowess were as bogus as everything else in his life.

He joined the world not as a contemporary of Noah but in 1743 as Giuseppe Balsamo, son of a poor shopkeeper in Palermo, Sicily. When his father died, the boy was raised by an uncle and at the age of 13 entered a monastery where he learned a smattering of medicine. In Balsamo's hands, a little knowledge truly was a dangerous thing. With income at a premium, he made ends meet by forging theatre tickets and falsifying a will. Soon he was notorious throughout Sicily and, for his own safety, he decided it was wise to flee the island – a feat he accomplished by emptying a church collection box and robbing his uncle.

After roaming the Mediterranean, including a stint in Egypt, he settled in Rome where, in addition to continuing his trade of forging banknotes and wills, he developed several new lines of dishonesty. He claimed to be a clairvoyant, able to locate gold and buried treasure for paying clients. In return for a small fee, he would reveal to the gullible where he sensed riches and valuables were hidden. By the time these unfortunates came back empty-handed to complain, he had moved on. He also began peddling home-made creams and aphrodisiacs, but his biggest seller was yet to come.

Around 1768 he married a 14-year-old slum girl by the name of Lorenza Feliciani. He wanted to better himself and saw Lorenza's beauty as an ideal way of luring wealthy victims into his web of deceit. When Rome became too hot – due to victims seeking revenge rather than abnormally high temperatures – the husband and wife team moved on to Venice, Marseilles and London, arriving by the Thames in 1776 with £3,000 in ill-gotten gains. They used the money to transform themselves into Count Alessandro di Cagliostro and Countess Serafina. Servants were hired, coaches and fine clothes bought to enable them to enter high society in style.

Orders of Freemasonry were very much in vogue in Europe at the time and Cagliostro immediately realized the moneymaking potential of these lodges. With his new-found status, he joined a group of masons that met in London's Brewer Street. The lodge belonged to the Order of Strict Observance, which attracted some of the wealthiest merchants in the capital and had links with mainland Europe. Cagliostro was soon elected Grand Master and appointed to be the lodge's representative on the continent. He was thus able to travel around the cities of Europe as a seemingly respectable member of society, still promoting himself as a clairvoyant and faith healer. And he was being paid for doing it.

However, he preferred to be his own boss so he invented an Egyptian Rite order of Freemasonry in Paris and appointed himself as its head, or Grand Cophta. He also opened a lodge for women, run by Lorenza as the Queen of Sheba. The membership fees were exorbitant but that proved no bar to the Paris nobility, particularly when Cagliostro revealed that he had discovered the secret of longevity. He passed himself off as nearly 1,800 years old, claiming to have witnessed Christ's crucifixion and to have had regular conversations with angels. Moreover, he said that his wife, although she looked young, was really an old woman with a 50-year-old son. Since there was no denying that she did look young, men and women of all ages queued to buy his quack cures in the hope of achieving immortality. The pills he sold – beautifully wrapped in gold leaf – for whatever price he cared to name were merely cheap herbal remedies available from any apothecary.

Cagliostro's magical powers made him the talk of Europe. With his wife in tow, he journeyed from city to city, setting up a new Egyptian Rite lodge wherever he went. As soon as he was exposed as a fake in one place, he moved on. He practised as a doctor in St Petersburg but when Catherine the Great analysed his elixirs of eternal youth and found them to be worthless, she gave him 24 hours to leave. By contrast, the nobles of the independent Baltic state of Courland were so enchanted by his magic that they proposed making him king. Not wishing to restrict himself to one location when there was the whole of Europe to defraud, he declined the offer.

He was unmasked again in Warsaw but quickly moved on to Vienna, Frankfurt and, in 1780, Strasbourg. By now, he was claiming to be older than ever. He said that he had been born before the Flood, had studied under Socrates, and talked with Moses. He began dating his letters 550 BC. The elixirs did a roaring trade. Among those taken in by his quackery was Cardinal Prince Louis de Rohan who watched in amazement as his uncle appeared to be cured by Cagliostro of scarlet fever, thereby surpassing the efforts of Paris's finest physicians. From then on, de Rohan championed Cagliostro's cause and the charlatan's image began to appear on snuff boxes, medallions and shoe buckles. The sick and the needy begged to be treated by him, much to the annoyance of registered doctors who joined forces to make his stay in Strasbourg increasingly uncomfortable. When he was eventually forced out of the city, weeping crowds lined the streets and one woman cried out: 'The good Lord himself is abandoning us!'

Cagliostro retained de Rohan's patronage for five profitable years until both became embroiled in the Affair of the Diamond Necklace. Endeavouring to win back the favour of Marie Antoinette, de Rohan arranged for the purchase of a necklace that he believed the queen wanted. However, he neglected to pay the jeweller who, not unreasonably, complained long and loud. On investigating the sordid affair, Louis XVI discovered that de Rohan had been forging letters in the queen's name and had the archbishop and the Cagliostros arrested and thrown into the Bastille. For once, Cagliostro was innocent of any involvement and both he and his wife were subsequently cleared but under severe interrogation Lorenza had given away too many secrets, particularly with regard to the elixir for everlasting life. Realizing that Cagliostro was a fraud, Louis XVI kicked the couple out of France and warned them never to return.

Their star on the wane, they stayed in London for a while before the restless Lorenza persuaded him to head back to Rome. By now Freemasonry was considered heresy by the Catholic Church so when Cagliostro attempted to revive his finances by creating a new Egyptian Rite lodge in the eternal city, he was arrested by the papal police. Disenchanted by her rags-to-riches-to-rags story and with an innate feeling for self-preservation, Lorenza denounced her husband to the Holy Inquisition. His true identity was revealed and on 7 April 1791 he was found guilty of heresy and sentenced to death. For her part, Lorenza was ordered to be locked away in a convent for the remainder of her life.

In his wisdom the Pope decided to spare Cagliostro and had his sentence commuted to life imprisonment. For the next four years he languished in the dungeons of San Leo Castle at Urbino, a considerable comedown for a man who was once the toast of Europe. Then on 26 August 1795 the Sicilian swindler who turned himself into a count proved that he was not immortal after all.

Selling the Brooklyn Bridge

George C. Parker was a salesman supreme. The only trouble was, the things he sold weren't his to sell. In the course of his fraudulent career he struck deals to sell such monuments as the Statue of Liberty, Grant's Tomb and the Metropolitan Museum of Art. And he calculated that he sold New York's Brooklyn Bridge twice a week on average.

Parker began selling the bridge almost as soon as it had been completed in 1883. His method was breathtakingly simple. He would stroll over to a wealthy-looking sightseer, introduce himself as the bridge's owner and offer the victim a job manning a tollgate. He would then explain how he intended charging vehicles and pedestrians a few cents to cross the bridge. The dupe, who would invariably be a shrewd businessman, would inevitably express surprise at such a low fee and suggest that Parker could make considerably more money from his investment. At this, Parker would feign disinterest and doubt, making the businessman so frustrated at the lost opportunity that he would then offer to buy the bridge from Parker. Appearing initially reluctant to sell, Parker would eventually let the businessman twist his arm. Forged deeds and documents were always close to hand so that the transaction could be completed before the new buyer had a chance to change his mind or consider what a coincidence it was that he had happened to bump into the bridge's owner.

Before pouncing, Parker studied his potential victims carefully and ensured that the price he fixed on the bridge was within their reach. If he suggested a clearly unaffordable asking price, the victim would shy away and would almost certainly smell a rat if Parker lowered it dramatically. Resisting the temptation to go for a quick killing gave the scam a much longer life. Parker profited by viewing the big picture. In an instance where the buyer was unable to meet Parker's asking price but still wanted to go ahead with purchasing the bridge, Parker would graciously accept a deposit, followed by the balance in instalments.

No sooner had one sale of the Brooklyn Bridge been finalized than Parker sought out his next sucker. On several occasions his victims had to be forcibly removed from the bridge by the police when they tried to recoup their investment by erecting toll barriers.

Parker did not always escape unscathed and served four prison terms in total, the last from 1928. He died in Sing Sing nine years later at the age of 76, a con man to the last.

Although his output was unmatched, Parker was by no means the only person to sell the Brooklyn Bridge nor was he the only one to try and cash in on the Statue of Liberty. Arthur Furguson was a wily Scot who made his fortune in the 1920s by selling London landmarks to unsuspecting American tourists. In a scheme reminiscent of his contemporary Victor Lustig, he began by posing as the man from the ministry in charge of selling off Nelson's Column. Spotting a visitor from Iowa gazing intently at the column, Furguson lamented the fact that it was having to be sold in order to help repay Britain's huge war loan to the United States. After he had ascertained that the American was indeed interested in buying Nelson's Column, Furguson disappeared on the pretext of consulting his government superiors. He returned shortly afterwards to announce that, on behalf of Britain, he could accept a cheque for £6,000 on the spot. The buyer wrote out a cheque and Furguson gave him a receipt for the column plus the name and address of a firm that would dismantle it and ship it to the US. By the time the American had contacted the bemused demolition firm, Furguson had cashed the cheque and vanished.

Over the next few weeks Furguson repeated the trick, selling Buckingham Palace and Big Ben to American tourists for a £2,000 deposit and £1,000 respectively. He also succeeded in renting out the Palace of Westminster and the Tower of London for prices between £1,000 and £2,000.

His success with Americans persuaded him that the United States was the place to be and he soon managed to convince a wealthy Texan rancher that the President was having to lease the White House and move to smaller premises. The Texan was delighted at being able to lease the White House at the knockdown rent of $100,000 a year – the first year's rent payable in advance.

Although now wealthy beyond his dreams, Furguson could not resist another sting and found himself telling an Australian visitor to New York that the Statue of Liberty was due to be dismantled and sold as part of a plan to widen New York Harbor. The asking price, he said, was $100,000. Think how good it would look in Sydney Harbour . . .

Thc Australian took the bait, but his bankers were suspicious and advised him to notify the police. For once Furguson had slipped up, having allowed himself to be photographed with his potential victim in front of the Statue of Liberty. Furguson had a five-year jail sentence in which to reflect upon his error.

The Man Who Rewrote History

On being appointed to the prestigious post of librarian at the Paris Academy, scientist Michel Chasles immediately set about rebuilding the institute's collection of priceless historical manuscripts, his predecessor having removed a number of important items. It was such a mammoth undertaking that Chasles realized he could not hope to accomplish it alone and so he was delighted when a colleague wrote him a note suggesting the services of 'the industrious Lucas'.

'The industrious Lucas' was Denis Vrain-Lucas, a peasant's son from Châteaudun, some 25 miles to the south of Chartres. An ambitious young man, he abandoned rural France for Paris where he became a lawyer's clerk, but was denied further advancement by his lack of qualifications. He tried to get a job with a publisher, only to fail because he had no knowledge of Latin, and was similarly knocked back by the Royal Library who would not accept him without a university degree. Finally a dealer in rare manuscripts spotted Lucas's potential and, under his tuition, Lucas became an expert copyist. Such was his skill that two letters he faked as being from the sixteenth-century essayist Montaigne were instantly included in a scholarly edition by that writer. When the dealer died, Lucas inherited some valuable items and quickly discovered that he could sell copies of these old manuscripts as easily as the originals. The hopeful academic had metamorphosed into a forger and conman.

He teamed up with Chasles in 1861. Chasles was an inveterate patriot, eager to promote France as the centre of all things cultural, and as such was receptive to any document which might promote the French cause. This myopia made him an ideal fall guy for Lucas's forgeries.

Lucas selected his subjects almost by request. He would listen while Chasles waxed lyrical about a particular famous figure and then suggest that they consult the *Biographie Universelle* together so that he might be able to learn more about the individual concerned and share in the appreciation. Lo and behold, a few days later Lucas would suddenly produce a letter purporting to be from the very same person. Lucas had a ready-made story to support his miraculous 'finds'. An eighteenth-century French count had been shipwrecked while emigrating and the nobleman's elderly descendant was now obliged to sell off his splendid collection of ancient manuscripts. Chasles checked out the story and, as Lucas knew full well, there had indeed been such a count. So Chasles saw no reason to question Lucas's version of events, particularly as the letters he produced invariably painted the French in a glowing light. And in case Chasles wavered, Lucas invented a second descendant who was bitterly opposed to the sale of the letters and other documents. This unseen threat heightened Chasles's desire to buy for fear that the opportunity might suddenly be denied to him in the near future.

The first forged letter Lucas sold to Chasles was from the playwright Molière. Chasles paid 500 francs for it and then handed over 200 francs apiece for letters supposedly from Racine and Rabelais. When Chasles let slip that he was tracing the origins of the Paris Academy for a book on its history, Lucas took the hint and came up with correspondence between a seventeenth-century poet and Cardinal Richelieu that revealed the poet's involvement in founding the Academy. Chasles was understandably delighted. In his eyes, Lucas could do no wrong.

With such a willing market, Lucas began to take more liberties, delving further and further back into history. He unearthed a letter purporting to be from Lazarus to St Peter; one from Mary Magdalene to the King of the Burgundians that contained the line 'You will find the letter I spoke of to you which was sent me by Jesus Christ a few days before His passion'; one from Vercingetorix to Trojus Pompeius; a letter from Alexander the Great to Aristotle, giving him permission to visit Gaul in order to study the Druids; a letter from a French doctor to Jesus; and letters from Charlemagne and Shakespeare, the latter acknowledging how influenced he had been by French writers. Each missive was music to Chasles's ears. He bought the lot.

In 1867 Chasles confided that he was writing a book on Blaise Pascal's discovery of the scientific laws of attraction. Lucas responded by penning an exchange of letters between Pascal and Isaac Newton, which appeared to show that Pascal was the true originator of many of Newton's theories. Naturally this appealed enormously to Chasles's sense of patriotism. In July of that year Chasles read to the Academy two letters supposedly from Pascal to Robert Boyle in England, but doubts were raised as to their authenticity. Although Chasles refused to allow the signature on Pascal's letters to be verified, he did agree that copies of the letters to Newton should be examined by a British expert, Dr Grant of the Glasgow Observatory.

Grant found a number of discrepancies, not least the fact that at the time of the advanced scientific correspondence between the two men, Newton would have been just 11 years old. Also the data on which

Pascal based his alleged 1662 calculations had not been available until 1726. And another letter from Pascal contained a reference to coffee – a commodity that was not introduced to France until seven years after Pascal's death.

Meanwhile Italian experts were studying twenty letters said to be from Galileo. They dismissed the signatures as fakes and pointed out that a letter in which Galileo complained of eye strain was, according to the date, written three years after he went blind!

When Lucas's other compositions were investigated, it emerged that the letters allegedly dating from 350BC were written on paper, which did not become the chosen writing material of Europe until the fourteenth century. There was also the puzzle as to why the likes of Archimedes and Alexander the Great wrote in eighteenth-century French.

Although it seemed inconceivable that someone of Chasles's intellect would not have spotted such glaring errors, Lucas alone stood trial for deception. The court heard that he had faked no fewer than 27,320 items in a six-year period – which, if accurate, was a truly heroic output. He was sentenced to two years in prison. Chasles escaped with nothing more than a badly damaged reputation.

SECTION THREE

Impostors

Living the Dream

Ever since he tried to piece together an animal skeleton as a nine-year-old, Dennis Roark had set his heart on becoming a doctor. But rather than follow the conventional path through medical college, Roark decided to fake his qualifications. Over a seven-year period the bogus doctor used his phoney medical degree to land jobs at several American medical establishments, in the course of which he treated over 1,000 patients and assisted in, or was present at, such complex procedures as heart transplants, lung transplants, circumcisions, amputations, heart bypass operations, appendectomies and hysterectomies. It was only when a suspicious doctor in Lansing, Michigan, checked his application form for yet another medical post that Roark's reign of deception finally came to an end.

Roark's bizarre double life actually dates back over 20 years to his days at university. He was raised in Garden City, Michigan, where he was an average student and an apparently normal youngster, keen on football. Then on a family vacation he found a collection of animal bones and attempted to reassemble them. The task evidently captured his imagination because from then on he told anyone who enquired that his ambition was to become a doctor, preferably a surgeon.

On leaving high school he attended Wayne State University. He would later claim on job application forms that he graduated in 1981 with Bachelor of Science degrees in biology and chemistry 'with high honours'. However, while he did attend the university for a period, he did not obtain a degree there.

Nevertheless he told his parents that he was off next to study at Rush University Medical College, Chicago, paying his own way. For four years the Roarks dutifully drove their son to Detroit station and put him on the train for Chicago, meeting him when he said he was coming home on vacation. He would fill them in on all the campus gossip and chat about his roommate. Yet Dennis Roark never attended Rush.

His résumés went on to state that between 1986 and 1988, brandishing his diploma from Rush, he shone in postgraduate research and earned a doctorate at WSU-V.A. Medical Center, Detroit. He then said he was employed as a clinical assistant first at St Mary's Hospital, Livonia, and then at Northwest General Hospital in Detroit. All of these claims were false.

Precisely what Roark did during these years was shrouded in mystery. On his eventual arrest, he told police detectives that he had attended a medical school in the Dominican Republic, but this story, like so many of his claims, could not be verified. In view of the fact that he displayed sufficient medical knowledge to convince professionals that he really was a doctor, he must have acquired the information from somewhere, even if it was only from a library.

What is known is that in June 1990, armed with his fake qualifications, he was accepted as a first-year surgical resident by Western Reserve Health System in Youngstown, Ohio. Besides his Rush diploma, Roark presented a student transcript and a test score from the Federation of State Medical Boards. The transcript was real . . . but it belonged to another doctor who graduated in 1982 and not to Roark. Similarly the test scores were genuine . . . but were those of a graduate of the University of Damascus in Syria.

As a first-year student at Western, Roark spent much of his time observing, but he was present for 185 operations, and was the key junior surgeon at 28 of these including hernia repairs and leg amputations. However, he failed to meet the required standards and left a year later. From there, he became a surgical resident at St Joseph Mercy Hospital in Pontiac, Michigan, but once again he only lasted a year.

In July 1992 he joined the Medical College of Ohio Hospital in Toledo as a surgical resident. Hospital records showed that he participated in 75 operations during his two-year stay, including amputations, a heart bypass and biopsies. However, Dr David Allison, chairman of the hospital's residency programme, became worried by Roark's hesitancy in the operating room and during medical rounds. As a result Roark was allowed to leave in the summer of 1994. 'His résumé was terrific,' Allison told the *Detroit Free Press*, 'and patients apparently liked him because he was a very charming guy. But he was totally flat. I had no suspicion that he was a phoney but I just couldn't, in good conscience, see him as being a safe surgeon. He didn't have what it takes.'

Despite these setbacks, Roark continued to aim high and, with a view to becoming a thoracic surgeon (one who specializes in chest problems), he applied to join a programme at the University of Western Ontario in the Canadian town of London. In the meantime his talent for putting fake documents in official-looking envelopes earned a medical licence from the state of Michigan, which allowed him to prescribe drugs. He was subsequently accepted by the Canadian school, principally because of his letters of reference and seemingly impressive qualifications. But things quickly went wrong. 'It was immediately learned that his experience was invalid,' said Dr Neil McKenzie, director of Western Ontario's residency programme at the London Health Sciences Center. 'There were certainly discrepancies with his past experience and what he was comfortable doing. He couldn't be given responsibility.' After six months Roark departed by mutual consent. 'If he hadn't gone,' added McKenzie, 'we would have asked him to leave.'

Returning to Michigan, Roark was hired as a physician at Madison Heights Community Hospital and the Visiting Physicians Association of Southfield. At Madison Heights, Roark saw walk-in patients with minor complaints. One patient with a history of heart problems recalled: 'I had a bad cut in my thumb that wouldn't stop bleeding. He put a stitch in me without any Novocain. He was very good. He knew what antibiotics to give me that didn't conflict with my heart.' Roark was then employed for some six months by Visiting Physicians where he called on people who were homebound.

Towards the end of 1997 Roark, who by now was married with a young daughter, applied to the Ingham Regional Medical Center in Lansing for his dream position – that of thoracic surgeon. Unfortunately for Roark, Dr Linda Nash, a physician at Ingham, was not prepared to take his qualifications at face value. She set about rigorously checking each one and, in just three hours of telephone calls, managed to unravel Roark's years of carefully constructed deceit. Her very first call fuelled her suspicions: Roark was not on a computerized roster of medical school graduates. Thinking that there had perhaps been an oversight, she spoke to Rush Medical College registrar Joe Swihart who told her that no Dr Roark had graduated in 1986 or any other year. She then faxed Swihart a copy of Roark's diploma. The registrar rang back to say that it was a fake. With alarm bells now ringing loudly inside her head, Nash tried to contact Dr

McKenzie at Western Ontario on a number listed on Roark's application form. When she eventually got through to McKenzie via different means, he told her that he knew nothing of the number Roark had given. Nash decided that it was time to notify the Michigan Attorney General's office.

In May 1998, before his stunned wife, Roark was arrested at his home in Sterling Heights, Michigan, and charged with uttering and publishing false documents. Roark pleaded guilty. His attorney argued for a lenient sentence of between one and two years but the Attorney General's office pressed for a lengthy sentence, dismissing the claim that Roark really cared about his patients. If he had done, said Assistant Michigan Attorney General Amy Ronayne, he would have ceased practising medicine in 1991 when he was asked to leave Western Reserve Health System because his performance was inadequate. Ingham County Circuit Judge Peter Houk chose to impose a long prison term on the grounds that Roark's actions had shaken the credibility of the state's regulatory system and the medical profession, and had left several hospitals open to malpractice claims. 'Doctor' Roark was sentenced to between six and 14 years in jail. The dream was well and truly over.

The Abyssinian Delegation

With one spectacular hoax, Horace Cole and five friends (among them a young Virginia Woolf) achieved the not inconsiderable feat of embarrassing the British government and the Royal Navy by posing as the Emperor of Abyssinia and his entourage on a tour of a warship docked at Weymouth. Although the general public saw the funny side when details of the prank emerged, such were the potential implications of the *Dreadnought* hoax, as it became known, that questions were asked in Parliament. From then on, the name of William Horace de Vere Cole would be treated with deep suspicion in high places.

Educated at Eton, Cole served with the British Army in the Boer War and suffered wounds to the shoulder and lung. On his return from the war, he went to Cambridge University where he met Adrian Stephen, a fellow student with an equally anarchic sense of humour. Together they thought up a plan to poke fun at the establishment by impersonating foreign dignitaries on an official visit. At the time British imperialism was still a force to be reckoned with and all levels of government would bend over backwards to welcome official delegations from abroad in the belief that the visitors would return to their native land proud to be British.

The pair decided that the Sultan of Zanzibar would make an ideal subject but because the real Sultan was due to visit England, his photograph had already appeared in several newspapers, so they switched to the Sultan's uncle instead. In typical student fashion, they originally considered pulling the stunt on their own college, Trinity, but, fearing expulsion, concluded that the Mayor of Cambridge was a safer option. Joined by three friends, they hired costumes from a London theatrical outfitter and sent a telegram to the Mayor of Cambridge supposedly from a senior official at the Colonial Office. The telegram announced the impending arrival of the Sultan's uncle and his party and requested that they be given a conducted tour of the city's principal places of interest. After being wined and dined at the Guildhall, the bogus entourage were driven around the colleges of Cambridge in a hansom cab before being taken to a charity bazaar where Cole spent money in a manner befitting a member of a royal family. The party's credentials were never questioned and the occasion passed off without incident. Anxious to share the joke, Cole later sold his story to the *Daily Mail*.

The Zanzibar prank turned out to be a rehearsal for the celebrated *Dreadnought* hoax of 1910. The idea stemmed from a young naval officer friend of Cole's who wanted to play a joke on a fellow officer serving on HMS *Dreadnought*, the flagship of the Home Fleet. The proposed victim also happened to be a cousin of Adrian Stephen. In the early weeks of 1910 *Dreadnought* was at anchor in Weymouth Bay, Dorset, and Cole decided to time his official visit to coincide with the fourth anniversary of the ship's launch – 10 February. Once again he and his friends chose to impersonate representatives from an obscure African nation, this time masquerading as the Emperor of Abyssinia and his entourage. Cole and Adrian Stephen were the driving forces. Cole buried his thick mane of hair beneath a top hat to play Herbert Cholmondley of the Foreign Office, the party's official escort, and the 6 ft 5 in Stephen posed as the group's German interpreter. Anthony Buxton (who went on to become a noted author and naturalist) played the Emperor and Duncan Grant and Guy Ridley were recruited as princes. Suspecting that the group was a little short in numbers for an Emperor's retinue, they added Stephen's cousin Virginia (the future Virginia Woolf) at the last minute.

Appropriate costumes were obtained from the theatrical costumier's, Clarkson's. Early on the morning of the 10th, the four would-be Abyssinians blacked up their faces, donned false beards and colourful robes, and tucked their hair beneath turbans. Cole and Stephen were more sombrely attired, as one would expect of Europeans. They caught taxis to London's Paddington Station and boarded the 8.30 train to Weymouth. Meanwhile a confederate sent a telegram to Vice-Admiral Sir William May, Commander-in-Chief, Home Fleet, warning of an imminent visit by the Emperor of Abyssinia and his entourage, adding: 'Kindly make all arrangements to receive them.' It was signed 'Hardinge' to denote Sir Arthur Hardinge, permanent head of the Foreign Office. The telegram was deliberately sent at short notice so that nobody in authority at Weymouth would have time to check its authenticity.

That was pretty much the extent of the hoaxers' planning. Everything else was to be improvised as they went along. Over lunch on the journey down Cole did attempt to teach Stephen a few words of Swahili in the mistaken belief that it was the language spoken in Abyssinia, but the rest of the group remained in their compartment just in case eating ruined their make-up. As Weymouth drew nearer, all except Cole were filled with a sense of apprehension. Would they be arrested or, perhaps worse still, ignored?

They realized that their fears were groundless as soon as they stepped off the train. A naval officer in full ceremonial dress was waiting on the platform to greet them. A barrier had been erected to hold back onlookers and a red carpet laid out to lead the party to a fleet of taxis which would take the visiting dignitaries to the quayside. There they were met by a small launch that ferried them across the harbour to the warship HMS *Dreadnought*. As the launch pulled alongside, the ship's band played the national anthem of Zanzibar – the nearest thing it could find to Abyssinia.

Cole was the first to step aboard and be received by Sir William May whereupon he introduced the rest of the party to the Admiral. He momentarily threw Stephen by introducing him as 'Herr Kauffmann', the first time Stephen had heard that name. Stephen quickly found himself facing other potential traps. His cousin, who, along with the rest of the staff officers, was dressed in full uniform for the occasion, was standing worryingly near to him on deck. Luckily, although the lofty Stephen's only disguise was a moustache, the cousin was unable to see through it. Then Stephen realized to his horror that he knew the ship's captain through their shared love of country rambles. He had been aware that the man was a naval captain but did not know on which ship. Fortunately for the success of the hoax, the captain, too, failed to recognize Stephen as an impostor.

The party was then taken to inspect a guard of honour and, as Admiral May explained to 'Herr Kauffmann' why the marines wore two different uniforms, he suggested that the interpreter might care to relay this information to the Emperor. Put firmly on the spot, Stephen turned to Buxton and said: 'Entaqui, mahai, kustufani.' He had no idea whether or not they were words of genuine Swahili but figured that as long as he sounded authoritative he could probably get away undetected. However, he realized the need for extending his vocabulary and, drawing heavily on his classical education, came up with the idea of spouting lines from Virgil's *Aeneid*, deliberately mispronouncing the words so that they would not be recognizable as Latin. When he had exhausted his mental supply of Virgil, he turned to Homer, applying the same technique to Greek.

The 'princes' kept things simple. In her role of Prince Mendex, Virginia was worried lest her voice would betray her as a woman. So she pretended to have a cold and restricted herself to a gruff and utterly meaningless 'Chuck-a-choi, chuck-a-choi.' Her fellow royals invented a phrase to suit all occasions. Whenever they saw something that met with their approval (which was absolutely everything) they chorused 'Bunga-bunga!'. They were particularly excited at apparently seeing an electric light for the first time – a discovery which brought forth a wave of 'bunga-bungas'.

It was not all plain sailing. Grant's false moustache began to slip and when it started to rain, Cole hurriedly ushered the party below deck for fear that the Abyssinians' make-up would run. They also felt obliged to refuse an offer of lunch, being unsure what food their unknown religion permitted them to eat.

Before the party left the ship, Admiral May asked the Emperor, via his interpreter, what would be the correct number of guns to be fired as a salute. Stephen replied that no gun salute was necessary. He later wrote: 'The real fact was that I understood that firing salutes meant cleaning guns afterwards, and it seemed too much of a shame to cause such unnecessary trouble – besides, it was almost as grand to refuse a salute as to accept one.'

After spending just 40 minutes aboard the *Dreadnought*, the Emperor and his merry men returned to shore. They kept up the pretence on the train back to London, insisting that the waiters serving dinner wear white gloves, which necessitated a delay at Reading while an attendant went to buy some.

The adventure had been an unqualified success. Indeed their impersonations might well have remained uncovered had Cole not decided to boast about the pricking of naval pomposity to the newspapers. When the story broke, the British naval high command became the laughing stock of Europe. Poor Admiral May was reportedly chased through Weymouth by street urchins shouting 'Bunga-bunga!'. On a more serious note the *Daily Telegraph* sniffed that the hoaxers had committed a criminal offence by sending a telegram under a false name.

In the House of Commons Colonel Lockwood, Conservative MP for Epping, asked the First Lord of the Admiralty, Mr McKenna, whether the incident was true and, if so, what steps were being taken to prevent any repetition. McKenna replied: 'I understand that a number of persons have put themselves to considerable trouble and expense in pretending to be a party of Abyssinians, and in this disguise visited one of His Majesty's ships. The question is being considered whether any breach of the law has been committed which can be brought home to these offenders.'

Colonel Lockwood persisted: 'Does the Right Hon. Gentleman think with me that the joke was a direct insult to His Majesty's flag?'

McKenna answered: 'I hope that the Hon. and gallant gentleman will not ask me to go further into a matter which is obviously the work of foolish persons.'

The Irish Home Rule leader, William Redmond, eager for any opportunity to embarrass the British government, caused laughter by asking whether the impostors had in fact conferred the Royal Abyssinian Order on Admiral May, and whether the Admiral had written to the King asking for permission to wear it. McKenna said there was no truth in that particular rumour.

Some time later Adrian Stephen heard on the social grapevine that Admiral May was to be reprimanded officially over the affair. He did not want anyone to suffer because of the prank and, enlisting the aid of Duncan Grant (Cole was unwell), decided to apologize personally to the First Lord of the Admiralty in the hope of salvaging the Admiral's career. McKenna dismissed the apology out of hand, informing them that they had broken the law and were still liable to prosecution. He strongly advised them to lie low for a while. Stephen later wrote of his anger that McKenna should treat them so contemptuously 'even if he had rowed in the Cambridge boat before he was First Lord of the Admiralty.'

The Navy's hunger for revenge then took an unexpected twist. One day a group of officers turned up at Cole's house wielding canes, announcing that they intended to give him a sound thrashing to avenge the Navy's honour. Cole agreed on condition that he could return the punishment. Thus in a bizarre ceremony the parties concerned wandered round to a nearby mews where Cole submitted to six of the best over a dustbin before enjoying his turn with the cane at the expense of one of the officers. Afterwards both men shook hands.

A few days later another group of naval officers, also armed with canes, called at Duncan Grant's house. Bundling him into a taxi, they drove him to Hendon and administered a gentle caning.

By now the novelty of the *Dreadnought* hoax was beginning to wear thin on all of the conspirators except Cole. Adrian Stephen actually began to regret the prank. He wrote of the Navy: 'They treated us so delightfully while we were on board that I, for one, felt very uncomfortable at mocking, even in the friendliest spirit, such charming people.'

Although the Weymouth episode was undoubtedly Horace Cole's finest hour, it was by no means the end of his mischief. He could see the potential for mayhem in almost any situation. One day while walking in London he came across a gang of road repairers minus a foreman. In an act of spontaneity he filled that position and directed the men to Piccadilly Circus where he instructed them to excavate a huge trench in the middle of one of the city's busiest streets. A nearby policeman obligingly redirected the traffic all day, and it was several hours before officials realized that the chasm in their midst was wholly unauthorized.

Another stroll through London resulted in a humiliating experience for an old friend, Conservative MP Oliver Locker-Lampson. The pair were walking in the West End when Cole suddenly said: 'I'll race you to Bond Street.' Entering into the spirit, Locker-Lampson accepted the challenge but as they ran down Bury Street, Cole allowed his opponent to pull ahead, then shouted out: 'Stop thief! That man's stolen my watch!' Passers-by heard the commotion and gave chase, finally apprehending the puzzled MP. A policeman was summoned and when Cole's gold watch was found in Locker-Lampson's pocket, the latter was arrested. Cole felt the joke had gone far enough and explained that he had planted the watch in his friend's pocket. However, the police officer did not share Cole's amusement and promptly arrested him, too. The two men were charged with using insulting words and behaviour likely to cause a breach of the peace. Cole was detained in police cells overnight and the following day was fined £5 in court. The incident had put Locker-Lampson in an invidious position to the extent that a question was asked in Parliament with regard to his involvement in a felony. The then Home Secretary, Winston Churchill, stood up for his colleague, remarking acidly that Horace Cole was 'a dangerous man for his friends.'

When not hatching subversive plots, Cole wrote poetry, although more for pleasure than profit. He was married twice – on both occasions to much younger women – and later moved to France with his second wife. It was not a happy time for either of them. Most of his wealth had been invested in North American real estate but the Depression destroyed his prosperity and left him having to rely on handouts from his brother, a financier. His wife had an affair and Cole, by now partially deaf, refused to consider getting a proper job. He did at one stage contemplate writing his autobiography, but nothing came of it. In 1936 the 'prince of practical jokers', as he liked to be known, suffered a heart attack at Honfleur. But this time it was no joke. He was 53.

The Unknown Soldier

He has been Wayne Simms, Kenny Tyler, Thomas Michael Lamar, Brandon Lee Bailey, Eric Lee, Thomas McAfee, David Auni, Michael Simms, Robert Simms, Paul Robert Ritter and David Michael Pecard. And these are just the identities the authorities know about. Between stints as a bogus lawyer, emergency room technician at a hospital, and police officer, he joined the US Army on at least seven occasions, each time under a different name. He conducted federal investigations with the FBI, put criminals behind bars and married six women. So who is he? Will the real David Pecard stand up?

He started life as Wayne Hudson, born in 1956 on the south side of Chicago. He created his first false identity at the age of seven after being turned down for a paper round. He went back the following day to a different office, gave a different name and a different age, and was promptly given his own round. That episode taught the youngster that a little lie could open the right doors.

He claimed his childhood was an unhappy one, ruled over by a father who could become violent when drunk. At the age of 14 Wayne Hudson made a life-changing decision to get away from it all: he became 18-year-old Robert Simms and joined the Army. He was sent to Vietnam, but had no regrets. 'Even though I was going off to war, that didn't matter,' he told CBS's *48 Hours* in 2000, 'because I was someone. I was going to be like John Wayne.' But one night, while sitting around the fire relaxing with his Army buddies, he made the mistake of admitting that he was only 14. He was sent back to the United States.

Undeterred, he set about creating a new identity and within months he had tricked his way back into the Army. It was a ploy he would use over and over again. Ironically his military tasks included uncovering other people's fraud and deception. 'At one particular time I was responsible for the security of a tactical weapons site,' he said, 'which means verifying security clearances, verifying identifications.'

Whenever he felt in danger of being discovered, he moved on. 'When I reach a point where I can no longer safely be that person, I have one focus,' he said. 'I must survive and I must create a new person.'

Women seemed unable to resist this particular man in uniform. In 1974 during his first tour of Korea as 17-year-old Private Wayne Simms, he married Susan Kwon. He took her to America but disappeared when their second child was just six days old. Fifteen years and two wives later, this time going under the name of soldier Eric Lee, he met 19-year-old Angela Reed shortly after she had joined Army boot camp. They soon married and when he was sent to Korea, she dutifully followed. But before long she became suspicious and when she sneaked a look inside his briefcase, she discovered his guilty secret. She reported him to the authorities. He promised to mend his ways and, because she loved him, she agreed to stand by him. Forced to go on the run, they headed back to America and travelled from state to state. 'When he was changing his Social Security number,' she recalled, 'he would go to the office and claim that he never had one because he was out of the country all of his life as a missionary. And if the first person didn't believe him, he would keep going until somebody did. And they always did; somebody always believed him.' After two years of leading a nomadic existence, she finally decided to leave him.

Back in the summer of 1976 when he was between wives and stints in the Army, he moved to Houston, Texas, and worked for a private investigator. The experience instilled a yearning to branch out into other areas of imposture. He began studying medicine and law, picking up some qualifications and forging others, such as a degree from Columbia University. In 1984, posing as an Oregon lawyer, he managed to persuade a judge to grant the early release of a prisoner.

Over the next seven years the serial impostor journeyed through a number of foreign countries and 12 American states, finishing up in Phoenix, Arizona, where he adopted his most enduring identity, David Michael Pecard. As Pecard, he landed a job as an emergency room assistant at a Phoenix hospital. His supervisor remembered him as being good at his job.

In 1994 he joined the Army yet again, this time as a military policeman. Appropriately his speciality was tracking down con men. Two years later he was carrying out military inquiries in Phoenix when he met Maricopa County Sheriff Joe Arpaio who was so impressed with the man calling himself Pecard that he appointed him as his deputy. Left to his own devices, the new deputy put together a team of investigators, among them his neighbour, Joe Thomas.

Pecard continued his law enforcement work until November of that year when he was charged with sexually assaulting a female prisoner and improperly taking inmates out of the county jail. On arrest, he had been carrying a driving licence in the name of Thomas McAfee along with papers stating that he was an Army chaplain. A search of his house produced evidence of further identities.

As well as facing eight felony counts, including fraud, he had to appear before a court martial after the Army found that he had enlisted and deserted on at least seven occasions under seven different identities. This multiple identity crisis presented a problem for his lawyer who had to defend seven different people! Pecard pleaded guilty and was sentenced to six years in prison.

But there was a sting in the tail. Returned to Maricopa County Jail to await trial on the felony charges, he put his limited legal training to good use by claiming that the Sheriff's Department had violated his civil rights. Over a period of 11 months they had, he said, denied him meals, withheld medical attention, opened his legal mail, recorded phone calls to his attorney, and kept him in solitary confinement. Bravely taking on the system, he succeeded with a motion for the Arizona case to be dismissed and in July 1998 Maricopa County dropped all charges against him, including those of sexual assault. When the Army learned about this development, it reduced his military sentence to time served plus three months. Freed from prison, Pecard announced his intention to sue Joe Arpaio and the Maricopa County Sheriff's Department for $6 million.

The Royal Maid

At the age of 17 Sarah Wilson left her home in Staffordshire to seek employment in London. She was fortunate enough to be engaged as maid to Caroline Vernon, a lady-in-waiting to Queen Charlotte, the wife of George III. Sadly, no sooner had she been taken on than Wilson repaid this generosity by stealing from the Queen.

Finding herself alone in the Queen's closet, she began searching through the royal drawers and found a wealth of sparkling jewels. In the belief that some of the lesser items were not checked regularly and would therefore not be missed, she helped herself to a ring, some brooches and a miniature portrait of the Queen. She even took a dress. Scarcely able to believe how easy it was, Wilson planned to return a few nights later for further rich pickings. But unbeknown to her, a diligent German member of the Queen's staff, Frau von Schwellenberg, had discovered the original theft and fully expected the culprit to strike again. This particular lady-in-waiting was too smart for Wilson who was duly caught in the act.

At that time all theft of royal property automatically carried the death penalty but Miss Vernon pleaded with the Queen for clemency and the sentence was reduced to one of transportation. Thus in July 1771 young Sarah Wilson was taken by prison ship to Baltimore, Maryland.

Landing in America, she was put up for sale and was bought by William Devall of Bush Creek, Frederick County, Maryland. Having already mixed, albeit briefly, in high circles, she did not intend living a life of slavery and soon ran away. She still had some of the Queen's stolen possessions and used them to help pass herself off as Princess Susanna Caroline Matilda, sister of Queen Charlotte.

In her royal guise, Wilson journeyed south into Virginia and Carolina, to the delight of the locals who were thrilled to have a real princess in their midst. Spinning the line that Princess Susanna had been forced into exile after some unspecified quarrel with her family, Wilson travelled from one rich household to another and was received with warmth wherever she went. She relayed gossip that she had picked up from her time in the Queen's employ and regaled her audience with tales of English life. And if proof of her identity were needed, she was always able to produce the Queen's miniature in addition to linen that was embroidered with a crown and monogram. She even behaved with the decorum expected of a princess, again gleaned from her short period in royal service.

Naturally there was a financial motive for the impersonation. She informed her American hosts that she soon expected to be restored to favour at court and would then be able to use her considerable influence to land them prestigious positions. Their chances of such rewards would, she hinted, be improved enormously were they to cross her palm with silver. Most gave freely, believing that their generosity would be reciprocated in time. Incredibly these payments continued even after it emerged that the Queen's only sister was nearly 40 and a recluse.

Some were suspicious of Wilson. They wondered why they had never heard that the Queen had a younger sister and why, since she had apparently been born in Germany, did she refuse to speak German? They were also puzzled as to why her English was so good. Wilson countered the doubters by explaining that she had vowed never to utter a word of German until she was restored to favour at court as she blamed German-speaking enemies in London for her exclusion.

Princess Susanna's reign lasted for around 18 months. When Wilson's owner, Devall, heard that a girl answering her description was posing as a princess, he issued a circular to the effect that the person calling herself Princess Susanna was really his servant girl. He offered a reward for her return, and the wayward Wilson was eventually located on a plantation at Charlestown where she was in the act of regally allowing gentlemen to kiss her hand. Arrested at gunpoint, she was taken back to slavery at Bush Creek.

For the next two years Wilson obeyed her master's voice and knuckled down to work while forever on the lookout for an avenue of escape. The War of Independence brought just such an opportunity. With Devall away serving as a lieutenant in the Maryland Militia, a second slave girl by the name of Sarah Wilson happened to arrive in Maryland. Seizing on this remarkable coincidence, Wilson used her master's absence to substitute the new Sarah for herself. Running away again, she met and married a young English soldier called William Talbot.

When the war ended, Talbot realized a return to England was out of the question since his wife was liable to instant arrest. Instead she used the money that she had sensibly put aside from her royal career to fund her husband in a New York business venture. They settled in the Bowery district of the city and went on to have a large family, Sarah apparently making an excellent wife and mother. Against all the odds, a tale of greed and theft had a happy ending.

Billy Tipton: Songs For Swinging Lovers

Billy Tipton was one of America's most enduring jazz musicians. Part of the big-band scene of the 1930s and 1940s, then head of the popular Billy Tipton Trio in the 1950s, Tipton never quite made the major league but was nevertheless a highly regarded pianist and saxophonist. Off-stage Tipton was married five times, was stepfather to three sons and was an active Scoutmaster. So when Billy died in 1989 at the age of 74 it came as a shock to all who thought they knew him to discover that 'he' was a 'she'. The person they called 'Billy' or 'Dad' had actually been born Dorothy Lucille Tipton.

The last ten years of life had not been kind to Billy Tipton. Divorced from fifth wife, Kitty, in 1979 and, having long since stopped performing, Tipton barely eked out a living working in a musicians' booking agency. Home was a trailer park on the fringes of Spokane, Washington State, where his health began to deteriorate. He developed a bleeding ulcer but despite being too weak to get out of bed, always refused medical treatment. The reasons for this reluctance would soon become apparent.

His adopted teenage son William had been looking after him and had repeatedly begged his father to see a doctor. On the morning of 21 January 1989 Billy's condition seemed worse than ever and, after carrying him to the bathroom, William decided to call Kitty for advice.

She urged him to contact the emergency services. William made the call but before the paramedics could arrive, Billy collapsed unconscious. They showed up shortly afterwards and opened his pyjamas to feel for a heartbeat. At that point one of them turned to William and asked him whether his father had ever had a sex change.

Billy Tipton never regained consciousness and was pronounced dead later that day. The autopsy report stated that the body was female. A local newspaper was tipped off. Billy's secret was out.

No one was more stunned than his immediate family. Kitty Oakes, as she now was since remarrying, said that the reason she and Billy had never had sex during their 18 years together was because of her own poor health and emotional fragility. As far as she was concerned, they had been legally married and legally divorced. Trying to come to terms with the news that her husband was a woman, she sighed: 'No one knew.'

Gradually Billy's unusual habits started to make sense. It was reported that he had enjoyed a sexual relationship with some of his previous wives, but always with the aid of a prosthetic device since he claimed to have been left sterile and genitally disfigured as a result of a car accident. That same car smash was his excuse for wearing a jockstrap, and bandages around his chest at all times. His fractured ribs had never properly healed, he explained. His wives revealed that he was a very private person who always locked the bathroom door when washing or dressing. And in the bedroom he liked the lights off. Consequently they never saw him naked. Apparently only one of the five women who called themselves Mrs Tipton – the first – knew that Billy was female.

His other two adopted sons, John and Scott, found it hard to accept that Kitty had no knowledge of Billy's secret identity. A family feud erupted, illustrated by the fact that after Billy's cremation his ashes were divided into two boxes – one for John and Scott, the other for William. This bizarre situation led one journalist to remark: 'Even now, ironically, there are two Billy Tiptons.'

Dorothy Tipton was born in Oklahoma City on 29 December 1914. Her father was a machinist who, in addition to repairing and racing cars, was also a keen aviator; her mother was a housewife. It was a musical household with both parents playing the popular music of the time on the piano but when Dorothy was a child her parents divorced and she and her younger brother Bill were sent to live with an aunt in Kansas City. The aunt taught her niece piano and Dorothy continued her musical studies at Southwest High School where, rather than being called by her proper name, she preferred to be known as 'Tippy'. She was, it would appear, already having doubts about her female status. On finishing high school she made no attempt to ask for her graduation certificates, seen as proof that by then 'Dorothy Tipton' was an identity she was almost certainly planning to relinquish.

Kansas City had a flourishing jazz scene in the 1920s and by the time she was 16 Dorothy was heavily influenced by the new music, learning to play the saxophone as well as the piano. She began regularly attending jazz clubs and envisaged a career as a musician. At the age of 18 she auditioned for several jazz clubs in the region, only to be told by each owner that, while she was undoubtedly very talented, they would simply not consider hiring a woman. Disillusioned, she returned to Oklahoma City in the hope of finding work as a musician there but met with a similar response. Realizing that she would never be able to break into the male-dominated jazz world as a woman, she decided on drastic action. She taped her chest, cut her hair, and wore a suit to her next audition, taking her brother's name and calling herself Billy. As Billy Tipton, she immediately landed her first job. At 19, Dorothy Tipton was no more.

At first only close family knew the truth. Two female cousins assisted in the impersonation but Dorothy's father was so disgusted that he disowned her. Having taken the plunge, there was no going back, however, not while such discrimination existed in jazz circles. In order to play the jazz music she loved, Dorothy would have to continue living as a man.

Billy Tipton enjoyed some success musically and soon met up with Non Earl Harrell, who became known as the first Mrs Tipton. It seems that Harrell and some of the swing bands with whom Billy toured in the 1930s were privy to the secret. Whether Billy used his many romances as a cover or was really a lesbian remains open to speculation. His wives stressed that he was not overly fond of physical affection, but apparently they accepted that as part of the relationship. Around 1939 Billy moved to Joplin, Missouri, and fell in love with a vocalist named June. They, too, presented themselves as a married couple and spent a year playing at the Palmero Club in Corpus Christi, Texas, before returning to Joplin. By 1949 Billy had acquired a new wife, Betty Cox, and the pair moved to the Pacific Northwest in the company of clarinettist George Mayer. Happiness was short-lived, however, and in 1954 Billy met wife number four, Maryann, a former call girl.

After playing for a number of band leaders (including Jack Teagarden and Russ Carlyle), Billy felt sufficiently established to form his own group and in the early 1950s began touring with the Billy

Tipton Trio. They adopted Benny Goodman's 'Flying Home' as their theme tune – an appropriate choice as Billy had modelled his piano-playing style on that of Goodman's pianist Teddy Wilson. The Billy Tipton Trio recorded two albums. The cover for the second – 'Billy Tipton Plays HiFi on the Piano' – showed a woman in a low-cut dress perched on a piano, smiling flirtatiously at a grinning Billy. The trio became as popular for comic routines as for their music with Tipton dressing up as a woman in a bonnet for a rendition of an Ella Fitzgerald number. The irony was not lost thirty years later.

In 1958 the Billy Tipton Trio were offered their big break as house band in Reno, backing such famous artists as Liberace. But Billy, against the wishes of the other members, turned it down for fear that fame might lead to his secret being revealed.

Instead he settled in Spokane – one of his familiar hunting grounds while on tour – and the Billy Tipton Trio became the house band at a downtown nightclub. Billy supplemented his income by booking musicians with a local theatrical agency.

In 1962 Billy left Maryann and married ex-stripper Kitty Kelly. They began adopting a family – John (1963), Scott (1966) and William (1969) – and Billy became an active Scoutmaster and member of the PTA. He organized showbusiness charity events locally, having made the transition from jazz musician to all-round entertainer, albeit on a modest scale. He was quite a celebrity around Spokane. A lot of people knew Billy Tipton . . . or so they thought.

One of his adopted sons – John Clark – did not discover the truth until four days after Billy's death. A Spokane funeral director told him so that he wouldn't have to learn it from the death certificate. Clark said: 'He'll always be Dad, but I think that he should have left something behind for us, something that would have explained the truth.' Dick O'Neil, who played drums with the Billy Tipton Trio for a decade, recalled how Billy had sometimes been teased for having a baby-face and a high singing voice. But like so many others, O'Neil had never suspected a thing. Yet it emerged that the two female cousins to whom Billy had always been close had, over the last few years of his life, been writing to the person they still knew as Dorothy in an attempt to persuade Billy to join them in the Midwest and resume life as a woman. Even though he no longer had a jazz career and a marriage to Kitty, and his sons were grown up, Billy felt unable to come out of the closet and face the world.

In life, the name of Billy Tipton symbolized swing music; in death, it symbolized someone who took extraordinary steps to achieve her goal. A group of avant-garde female jazz musicians from Seattle acknowledged this by calling themselves the Billy Tipton Memorial Saxophone Quartet. One member said: 'Billy Tipton's story is a bittersweet one for us. On one side, here was this woman, Dorothy, who felt compelled to take her brother's name to pursue her passion for music. But on the other hand, here is someone who felt passionate enough about what she wanted to do whatever it took to get it and was courageous enough to live the life he (or she) wanted to live.'

The Tichborne Claimant

Lasting 291 days, the trial of the so-called Tichborne Claimant was the longest trial in British legal history. The Chief Justice's summing up alone took 20 days. The case divided the nation. For every man who supported the claimant, there was another who deemed him to be a brazen impostor. After over 500 witnesses had been called and £150,000 of public money spent (the equivalent of £2 million in today's terms), the second camp won the day and it was ruled that Arthur Orton, an overweight Australian cattle slaughterer from Wagga Wagga, was definitely not the wealthy English aristocrat, Sir Roger Tichborne.

Roger Charles Tichborne was born in 1829, the eldest son of Sir James Francis Doughty Tichborne, head of a leading Catholic family in Hampshire. Roger's illegitimate mother, Henriette, Lady Tichborne, was half French and kept the boy in Paris, seemingly against the wishes of his father. When Roger was 16, Sir James used the excuse of a family funeral to sneak him back into England and into the Catholic school of Stonyhurst. His mother was furious, all the more so when Roger joined the Army, securing a commission with the 6th Dragoon Guards.

At the age of 24, Roger fell in love with his cousin, Katherine Doughty, but, being Catholics, they were not permitted to wed. To help mend his broken heart, he resigned his commission and sailed for South America. In 1854, after enjoying a break in Chile and Argentina, he boarded a small ship, the *Bella*, in Rio de Janeiro for the journey home. The ship went down in a storm. Only her logbook and a few pieces of wreckage were ever found. All aboard were presumed to have perished.

However, Lady Tichborne refused to accept that her son was dead and over the next ten years or so placed advertisements in English and colonial newspapers around the world, appealing for information as to his whereabouts and offering a handsome reward. Her desire to locate her son intensified when her husband died not long after the shipwreck.

For years she heard nothing, but her optimism never wavered. Then in 1865 an Australian solicitor wrote to her to say that Roger Tichborne was living at Wagga Wagga under the name of Castro. Letters were exchanged but such was Lady Tichborne's will to believe in the correspondent being her son that she had made up her mind even before seeing a specimen of his handwriting or receiving one item of corroborative information. In her mind this Castro was her long-lost son.

From the subsequent trial it emerged that Castro's real name was not Tichborne but Arthur Orton. Born in 1834, the youngest of 12 children of a poverty-stricken butcher from Wapping in the East End of London, Orton became a merchant seaman, only to jump ship in South America. He returned briefly to England but in 1852 emigrated to Australia where he worked as a slaughterman, taking the surname 'Castro' from that of a Chilean family who had befriended him on his South American sojourn. He married an Irish girl but when she fell pregnant he found himself heavily in debt. It was then that he saw one of Lady Tichborne's advertisements and decided to pose as the heir to the family fortune. He contacted a solicitor, informing him that he had estates back in Britain and had once been shipwrecked. A pipe carved with the initials 'R.C.T.' was produced as supposedly conclusive proof.

Lady Tichborne begged him to come to Paris, where she was again living, and, on the strength of his anticipated inheritance, Orton managed to raise sufficient funds for the passage to France. Together with his wife and baby daughter, Orton arrived in Paris towards the end of 1866. In one of his letters he had written that he had 'grown very stout' – a wise precaution since Lady Tichborne was being asked to believe that the slim, sallow-faced young man who weighed barely ten stone when she last saw him 13 years previously had now ballooned into a ruddy-faced, 21-stone colossus. It was like replacing Stan Laurel with Oliver Hardy. In truth, Orton had always been fat. At 17 he had weighed 13½ stone and been known as 'Bullocky Orton'.

That first meeting between Lady Tichborne and Orton took place in a darkened room in Paris, Orton having insisted that the curtains were kept drawn. Even in the dimmest of lights she could hardly have failed to notice that he looked nothing like her son but her faith remained unwavering. This was in spite of the fact that Orton, while chatting about his supposed childhood, spoke of meeting a grandfather who had died before Roger had been born; that he now called her 'mamma' instead of 'mother'; that his handwriting had changed markedly; that he named his old school as Winchester instead of Stonyhurst; that the well-educated Roger now had difficulty with spelling even his own name (Orton spelt it 'Rodger'); that he got the names of the family estates wrong; that he referred to his early Army service in the ranks whereas Roger had been a commissioned officer; that he did not know where his own regiment had served; and that whereas Roger spoke fluent French, Orton could not understand a word when questioned by Tichborne's former language tutor. Orton did not recognize any members of Roger's family, nor they him. Most of Roger's friends looked at the impostor in disbelief. But a faithful old Negro servant named Bogle, the family solicitor, Mr Hopkins, and, most importantly, Lady Tichborne herself all maintained that the roly-poly figure before them was Roger Tichborne. As for the inconsistencies, she said that the poor thing was simply confused.

To prove her faith in his story, she invited him and his family to stay with her on the Tichborne estate in Hampshire and granted him an allowance of £1,000 per annum. Bogle was dispatched to accompany Orton back from Australia. Orton made good use of the journey, gleaning from the old retainer all manner of details about Roger and Tichborne family life in general. Orton was also assisted greatly by Lady Tichborne's generosity in allowing him access to all of Roger's diaries and letters. Once installed in Hampshire, Orton employed two former soldiers with Roger's regiment as servants so that he could pick their brains for anecdotes. Soon Orton knew his subject well – certainly better than Lady Tichborne knew the man who was pretending to be her son. Where once he had been vague and ignorant, suddenly he was able to recall trivial incidents from the past – sufficient to convince villagers living near the estate, local gentry and members of Roger's old regiment that he was the genuine article. However, the bulk of Roger's family remained visibly unmoved.

On Roger's death, his younger brother Alfred had inherited the family estates but he, too, had died young and the title of twelfth baronet had passed to his two-year-old nephew, Henry. Now Orton decided to take legal action to claim his inheritance from the child.

Then in 1868 his prospects were dealt a shattering blow. His champion, Lady Tichborne, died. Any thoughts he may have had of dropping the claim at that stage were overridden by the fact that he still owed a substantial sum of money to various creditors back in Australia.

Although the trustees of the estate bitterly opposed him, Orton pressed ahead with his claim. Another of his leading supporters, Hopkins the solicitor, died shortly before the trial but thirty of Roger's fellow Army officers signed an affidavit to the effect that Orton and their dead comrade were one and the same person.

The civil case began at Westminster before Lord Chief Justice Bovill on 11 May 1871. By then Orton weighed 24 stone and bore less resemblance to Sir Roger Tichborne than ever. The trial lasted 103 days, during which time Orton called over 100 witnesses to support his case. The Tichborne family could only find 17 to refute his claim, but their testimony proved the more telling. The jury heard how, when first arriving in Europe, the claimant could remember nothing of the first 16 years of his life and had no recollection of his hobbies, his family, or the names of the favourite Tichborne dogs. But what finally put an end to the charade was the revelation that Sir Roger had his initials tattooed on his left arm; Orton had none. At that point Orton's counsel gave up the fight. The foreman of the jury declared that there was a reasonable doubt that the claimant was Sir Roger Tichborne. Orton had lost.

Following the collapse of his case, Orton was immediately arrested and charged with perjury. A second hearing – this time a criminal trial – began just over two years later and lasted a further 188 days. Orton's cause was not assisted by his eccentric defence counsel, Dr Edward Vaughan Hyde Kenealy, who, between launching unfounded anti-Catholic tirades in court, repeatedly insulted the bench. On 1 March 1874 Orton was found guilty on all counts and sentenced to 14 years' imprisonment. On returning the verdict, the jury added a note of censure regarding Dr Kenealy's use of industrial language during the trial.

With his client languishing in Dartmoor Prison, Kenealy continued to fight Orton's corner. The doctor was given a loftier platform when elected MP for Stoke in 1875 and two months later put forward a motion in the House of Commons to refer Orton's conviction to a Royal Commission. The motion was defeated by 433 votes to one.

Orton was eventually released in 1884 and promptly began a fresh claim on the Tichborne estates. By now even the lower classes, who had staunchly supported Orton in the belief that his imprisonment had been a conspiracy by the rich against those who weren't terribly good at spelling, had lost interest in the campaign and it was doomed to failure. Disillusioned, Orton ended up doing the rounds of music halls as a novelty turn before dying in a seedy boarding house on April Fool's Day 1898.

Little Miss Nobody

When Rose Churchill stepped out into New York's high society, she was welcomed with open arms. Within days of her arrival in February 2001, the twenty-something London socialite was attracting a stack of media coverage. Wearing a winning smile and designer labels such as Gucci, Christian Dior and Vivienne Westwood, she was a photographer's dream. She quickly appeared on CNN and in the gossip columns of *Women's Wear Daily*. Her picture even made it into the *New York Times* – twice. She mingled freely at showbiz events with the likes of Julia Roberts and George Clooney, but just as soon as she had arrived on the scene, Rose Churchill vanished without trace.

Two months later the reason emerged for her whirlwind success and sudden disappearance. Rose Churchill was a fake. As revealed in the American edition of *Harper's Bazaar* magazine, she was the creation of 28-year-old English fashion journalist Jessica Brinton who had set out to discover how easy it was to live a lie in New York society.

'It's particularly easy if your clothes are a talking point,' she said after her exposure, 'because conversation at these cocktail parties is generally quite light. Clothes are a wonderful way of gaining access. Vivienne Westwood was good for that – I was just stared at.'

Miss Brinton, who shared a flat in Greenwich Village with two American girls, emphasized that confidence was all-important for carrying off the ruse. 'You have to be – or give the impression of being – enormously successful, either financially, professionally or socially. Combine all three and there are really no limits to what you can achieve. I just made it all up. I told people about my luxury apartment off Park Lane in London, and I really enjoyed telling people that I didn't do anything at all. I just told photographers I was a socialite. That seemed to be OK.'

Her finest moment was walking along the red carpet at an event staged in honour of Julia Roberts. 'Suddenly,' said Brinton, 'there was an avalanche of flashes. I was smiling for ages. What could be more satisfying for your vanity than a hundred cameras trained on you?'

Her brief period in the spotlight led to offers of modelling work and publishing jobs by New Yorkers who liked her style. She admitted that she could easily get used to being famous. 'It's really hard to resist. A couple more weeks of it and I'd have been taking it all very seriously.'

Michael Backman: Supreme Confidence

Like many young children, Michael Backman enjoyed pretending to be someone famous. He would tell his grade school teachers that he was Diana Ross's son and that he was simply living with a couple in Portland, Oregon, while the singer was on tour. The difference was that while most kids grew out of such fantasies, Backman continued to pass himself off as other people and was still claiming to be related to

Ross at the age of 31 . . . at the same time that he had also returned to his old high school to pose as a student.

That Backman should choose to go back to school at an advanced age is perhaps understandable in view of the fact that the happiest days of his troubled life were spent in the corridors of education. It was the equivalent of returning to the womb.

Adopted when he was 21 months old, Backman was a gifted child with a vivid imagination. His parents thought he had a talent for acting and enrolled him in children's theatre classes. His mother said: 'He wanted to be the star, right there and then, and begin acting, but he didn't want to learn to act.' Impatient for success, he lost interest after two sessions and stopped going to the classes. But he never stopped performing. By the age of 12 he would disguise his voice as that of a telephone operator and try to hook up with famous people.

After graduating from Grant High School, Portland, in 1986, his practical jokes soon developed a more sinister tone. He spent the next 12 years in and out of prison in Washington State, Oregon and California, convicted of passing bad cheques, opening false bank accounts under assumed names, and driving fast cars away from dealership lots before selling them across the border in Canada. In between his spells in prison, he tried looking for work but said that his criminal past always caught up with him. In the end he decided that the only way he was going to make anything of his life was to go to college.

So in January 1996, using fake transcripts and bogus recommendations from Beverly Hills High School and drawing on his childhood fantasy of being related to Diana Ross, he applied to Lewis & Clark College at Portland. Calling himself Adante Ross, he said he was the singer's nephew and, in a manner befitting his status, arrived on campus for his interview in a black limousine. At first glance, his academic qualifications appeared impressive, as was the claim that he had been a star member of the high school basketball team. But college officials became suspicious of the Beverly Hills material and of the fact that he was unable to submit a video to back up his basketball expertise.

Another small matter contributed to the cancellation of his college plans. In June 1996 he was convicted on six counts of theft for opening bogus accounts at several Portland banks. He served eight months in boot camp.

Backman later told the *Oregonian* that his boot camp experience had a profound effect on him. He recalled that members of his platoon were ordered to 'return to the base line' whenever they did anything wrong, meaning that they were directed to go back to the last thing they did right. 'In my mind,' said Backman in a 1999 interview, 'the last thing I think I did right was going to school. I thought, if I can go back and get the grades I should have the first time around, maybe I could get a (college) scholarship. If it meant doing high school all over again, I was going to do that.'

Therefore, after being released from another jail sentence, this time in California, Backman decided to redo his senior year at Grant High School. When on a visit to his old school he was told off by one of the teachers for loitering in the hallway, he realized that he might just be able to pull off the plan. With his boyish looks, slim build and short-cropped hair, he reckoned he could pass as a 17-year-old.

He sent off for a profile of Beverly Hills High School and used it to form the basis for a fake transcript, which showed that one Deandrea Deangelo finished his junior year at Beverly Hills ranked fifth in the class. He was also a star basketball player. The only clue, which went unnoticed, was the birthday of 1 April 1981 – April Fool's Day – that cut 14 years off Backman's age. The signatures and paperwork, which was embossed with the Beverly Hills logo, looked authentic with the result that in September 1998 – 12 years after he had left Grant High School – Michael Backman signed up again, as transfer student Deandrea Deangelo. Backman really was intending to concentrate on his studies this time and took a full schedule of courses including Government, Geometry, Global Studies and even Spanish, despite the fact that he could barely count to ten in that language.

Backman found his first week back at school distinctly unnerving. 'I was terrified that somebody was going to say, "Hey, don't I know you from somewhere?"' But they never did. In fact only two members of staff remained at Grant from Backman's first stint. One, vice-principal Joe Simpson, later reflected: 'When I saw him in the hallway, I looked at him and thought, "I know this guy." But I've been here so long that many names and faces are familiar.'

Backman's only real scare came when he looked out of the window in the middle of a lesson and saw a police car stop alongside his bright red Chevrolet Camaro that was parked in front of the school. He momentarily panicked and ran out of school to call a friend who was privy to the deception. It turned out that the car was parked in a ten-minute zone. Backman received nothing more than a ticket.

None of his classmates suspected that the newcomer was a fake even when he claimed once again to be Diana Ross's nephew. They just attributed it to wishful thinking. The girl whose locker was next to Backman's did notice that he had a bit of a bald patch, but thought nothing more of it. In every respect Backman/Deangelo was a model pupil, courteous in class and always one of the first to hand in his homework. He got straight A grades – apart from a B in Spanish – a feat that earned him a place on the school's list of honour students. He was also among several students who represented Grant at a Law Day symposium at Lewis & Clark College where students debated the proposed minimum mandatory sentencing guidelines for property crimes. Backman was a vocal opponent, maintaining that the proposals would unfairly punish African Americans and that extended sentences would not help towards rehabilitating offenders. Little did anyone present realize that he was talking from experience. His oratorical skills impressed John Bradley, first assistant to the Multnomah County District Attorney, and he invited Backman to visit his office. Backman declined the offer, fearing that at least two district attorneys might have recognized him, having prosecuted him in the past.

Backman stayed with friends in Portland, seeing his parents for the first time in years at Thanksgiving. He told them he was working for Nike, testing shoes.

Although Backman may not have been related to Diana Ross, he did have a decent singing voice and sang an a cappella solo at the school's 1998 Christmas production. A few days later, on 16 December, Portland police interrupted school choir practice and arrested Backman. They had received a tip-off. Sergeant Mike Hefley said: 'I thought it was strange, so I checked it out. I introduced myself and told him (Backman) I wanted some help in identifying someone. I opened up the 1986 high school yearbook and pointed to a picture of him. His reaction was one of shock. He knew and we knew.'

A search of his home revealed several false ID cards, a fake US Defence Department card, a laminator and a handful of other Grant High ID cards. Detectives began investigating how he had been able to afford a brand new car while living as a student. In May 2000 Backman was given 13 months in jail for falsifying school transcripts and forging cheques to support himself during the scam. Before beginning his sentence, he was allowed to finish his term at the college at which he had recently enrolled.

Reflecting on his second spell at Grant High School, Backman said: 'I never wanted to hurt anyone. The teachers and everyone there accepted me with wide-open arms. It felt good because I hadn't really experienced that. I did not repay them very well but the reality is that in that senior year I did that work. When it came down to it, I was in that class, and I was earning those grades. This was something I was doing legitimately.'

False Dmitry

Ivan the Terrible, Tsar of Russia, did everything in his considerable power to live up to his nickname. His excesses were the stuff of legends. One story attributed to him is that he was so pleased with the newly built Moscow church of St Basil that he blinded the two architects responsible so that they would never be able to come up with anything better. On another occasion, having fallen out with the Archbishop of Novgorod, Ivan apparently arranged for the cleric to be sewn into a bearskin and hunted down by a pack of bloodthirsty hounds. Ivan clearly felt that it was important to maintain standards and looked for a strong male heir to succeed him. To this end, he married a succession of wives – seven in total – but, after unfortunately killing his eldest son, Ivan, in a quarrel, was left with just two weak male offspring – Feodor and Dmitry.

Ivan died in 1584. For such a fierce warrior it must have been a shade disappointing to succumb while playing a game of chess. The childless Feodor succeeded him as Tsar with 16-month-old Dmitry waiting in the wings. As feared, Feodor was not up to the job. The country needed a strong ruler and one soon emerged in the shape of Feodor's brother-in-law, Boris Godunov, who took over as regent. One of his first acts was to banish Dmitry's mother from Moscow and send her to live in Uglich 80 miles away, claiming that she had been plotting for her infant son to become Tsar.

Dmitry was an epileptic. According to Godunov, when Dmitry was eight he had a fit while playing outdoors in Uglich and cut himself fatally on a knife. An official investigation was conducted into the tragedy, but it failed to throw much light on the mystery, partly because the boy's mother shut herself away. Rioting broke out in the town. Some blamed Dmitry's playmates for his death and one of the boys' fathers was lynched in an act of retribution. Others pointed the finger at Godunov, believing that he had arranged for Dmitry to be murdered in order to clear his own way to the throne. Then a fresh rumour began to circulate: that Dmitry was still alive.

Feodor died seven years later in 1598, enabling Godunov to seize power as Tsar of Russia. He was an unpopular ruler and acquired a number of enemies who were desperate to find a way of usurping his position. Such an opportunity presented itself when a Russian monk by the name of Yuri Otrefief, serving as valet to a Polish prince, declared himself to be Dmitry. He said that he had escaped the 1591 assassination attempt, engineered by the murderous Godunov, by substituting another youth in his place. Godunov's adversaries needed little persuading.

Otrefief certainly looked the part of a descendant of Ivan the Terrible, being broad-shouldered, well educated and an accomplished horseman. Many members of the Polish legislative assembly (or Diet) labelled him a fraud but Otrefief was not about to surrender without a struggle and embarked on a campaign to win over King Sigismund, a feat he achieved primarily by writing to the Pope and taking steps towards converting to Catholicism. If Sigismund, who had only recently signed a treaty with Godunov, still harboured any doubts as to the young man's authenticity, Godunov's headstrong deeds inadvertently removed them. For when Godunov dispatched two assassins to kill the pretender, they were intercepted and arrested. This, argued Otrefief, was surely proof of his identity. Godunov insisted that the man calling himself Dmitry was an escaped Kremlin monk and produced Otrefief's uncle and two fellow monks to back up the story. But by now the Tsar was so mistrusted that few believed a word he said, even when he was telling the truth.

Early in 1605 the bogus Dmitry led an army of some 2,500 Cossacks and Poles into Russia. They were greatly outnumbered by Godunov's troops but mass defections made the contest more equal. In despair at seeing his soldiers deserting him, Godunov took his own life in May and was succeeded as Tsar by his 16-year-old son Feodor II. However, the boyars – the Russian noblemen – switched their support to Dmitry and when the pretender's army reached the outskirts of Moscow, the boyars seized the city and had Feodor arrested. Feodor's reign lasted barely a month before he was butchered by a mob, almost certainly on the orders of the man posing as Dmitry. A few days later Otrefief entered the city in triumph and was crowned Tsar Dmitry.

Right from the outset, he made the mistake of alienating the Russian people by ignoring the country's customs and appearing to favour the Poles. As he rode up to the gates of the Kremlin he elected not to obey tradition and kiss an icon that was placed before him. Instead he entered the palace accompanied by two Jesuit priests and a Lutheran official – figures considered to be unclean by the Russians. Moreover he was clean-shaven – in public defiance of Orthodox teaching – did not drink alcohol and refused to take a bath even though one was prepared for him every morning. But it was the arrival of so many Poles in his wake and the presence of the Jesuits in his retinue that aroused most suspicion, convincing many Muscovites that their new Tsar was anti-Russian and a closet Catholic. This feeling was reinforced in May 1606 when he married landowner's daughter Marina Mniszech, a woman who, as a Polish Catholic, thus embodied the two great evils in one slender frame.

At this, the boyars turned against him and decided that he was an impostor after all. The real Dmitry, they said, had been murdered in 1591. Prince Vassily Shuisky, who had conducted the original inquiry into Dmitry's supposed death, declared that the pretender had only been put forward as genuine to rid the country of Godunov. Shortly after the royal wedding, Shuisky organized a counter-revolution. A mob surged into the palace, lynched the Tsar and left his body lying in a courtyard for three days before burning it. Popular legend has it that his ashes were then loaded into a cannon and fired off in the direction of Poland. Hundreds of his followers were also murdered.

Two years later there was a False Dmitry II who bore no resemblance to False Dmitry I but nevertheless secured the backing of both the mother of the real Dmitry and the wife of False Dmitry I. Marina took her support as far as living with him and providing him with a male heir. Alas, False Dmitry II suffered a similar fate to his predecessor and was murdered in 1610.

Hoaxing Hillary

Adelaide Abankwah's story was so pathetic that everyone who heard it was moved to tears. She told United States immigration officials that she faced genital mutilation if sent back to her native Ghana. Her plight touched the hearts of feminist campaigners including actress Vanessa Redgrave and First Lady Hillary Clinton. But they had been conned. For the woman at the centre of the case was an impostor – a former hotel worker called Regina Danson who concocted the story after being caught entering the US with forged documents.

It was in May 1997 that the name of Adelaide Abankwah first hit the headlines. A Ghanaian woman claiming to be her was arrested at New York's JFK International Airport in possession of false immigration papers. Her passport bore a number of suspicious alterations. She immediately demanded asylum to escape circumcision, which, she said, would be carried out on her body by the elders of her home village, Biriwa, if she were returned to Africa.

Later that year she testified before an immigration court in New York. She told how she was due to be elected 'queen mother' of her tribe following the death of her mother but was terrified that she would be rejected for the post because she was not a virgin. She said that the ceremony for the installation of the queen mother required that she pass a virginity test. The test apparently involved the queen mother designate being forced to cup her hands to hold water to the sound of beating drums. Should any of the requisites be violated, the water would spill. She was afraid the test would reveal that she was not a virgin and that the villagers would therefore impose upon her the mandatory punishments including the ritualistic killing of the boy with whom she'd had sexual relations and mutilation of her genitals. This would take the form of cutting her labia and clitoris. Even if by some miracle she passed – and she was sure she would not – she would still have to accept a husband appointed against her wishes and be required to participate in animal sacrifices and other blood rituals that ran contrary to her faith. She maintained that she could not simply hide away elsewhere in Ghana because she would undoubtedly be arrested and returned to her village. The only way out was to leave the country altogether, which was why she wanted to stay in the United States. Nor, she pleaded, could she return to Ghana and refuse to be queen mother. That, she claimed, would result in almost certain death.

To support her tale, she enlisted the help of a Pentecostal minister who testified that she, too, had seen ceremonies in Ghana where female genital mutilation was inflicted as a punishment for premarital sex.

However, Judge Donn Livingston ruled against Abankwah's claim, noting that Ghana had outlawed female circumcision in 1994 and that, in any case, it had apparently never been practised in the area around Biriwa. He also found that there was some doubt over her true identity. He ordered her to be deported. An appeal was launched but in July 1998 the Board of Immigration Appeals upheld the judge's ruling.

The case attracted extensive media coverage. How could a supposedly civilized nation such as the United States send this poor woman back to Africa to face mutilation and maybe even death? Politicians, celebrities and human rights activists took up the case and began lobbying the Immigration and Naturalization Service (INS) as well as the Clinton Administration. Gloria Steinem, Vanessa Redgrave and Julia Roberts all lent their support and a 'Free Adelaide' campaign argued that she should be released from detention and allowed to remain in the United States. But it was the women's rights group Equality Now who was able to play the trump card. It obtained the backing of Hillary Clinton who, according to the group's president Jessica Neuwirth, was 'very helpful in ensuring that the INS was aware of the case at the highest level.'

With the case now a liberal cause célèbre and pressure mounting by the day, in July 1999 a federal appeals court reversed the earlier decisions and awarded asylum to Adelaide Abankwah. The court found that the Board of Immigration Appeals had demanded too exacting a standard of evidence. It did not mention the concerns surrounding her identity. She was released from detention amid widespread rejoicing from feminists who hailed the decision as a victory in the fight against female circumcision. An official at the INS New York district office remarked caustically: ‘The White House wants you to release her, so they released her.’

The INS was far from happy at the outcome and began its own investigation of the woman calling herself Adelaide Abankwah. Agents in Ghana took statements from tribal leaders and local people and established that the celebrated asylum-seeker was really a former hotel worker, Regina Norman Danson, who had left Ghana simply because she had wanted to go to the United States. She did not have a drop of royal blood in her veins. Her mother was not even dead – she was working as a fish trader in Biriwa. And at no time had mutilation ever been practised in Biriwa. Danson had invented the entire story when caught trying to enter the United States on someone else’s passport.

The real Adelaide Abankwah was a former college student whose passport had been stolen in Accra in 1996. The daughter of a Ghanaian businessman, she was living in Germantown, Maryland, but had been afraid to come forward because she feared deportation from the United States due to immigration problems of her own. The passport Danson used to carry out her pretence had been sent for renewal by Abankwah to her father in Accra in 1996, but was then stolen from his car along with other documents. Although she managed to secure a new passport, she lost her student status in the process. In March 1998 she had received a letter from the INS ordering her to leave the US or face deportation. Not wanting to be found out, she went underground and watched Danson steal and misuse her name and identity.

In December 2000 the *Washington Post* blew Danson’s cover. The paper tracked her down to New York where she was selling cosmetics. She said she had started to use Adelaide Abankwah’s name when moving to Ghana in 1996 . . . at about the same time that Ms Abankwah’s passport was stolen.

The revelation came as no surprise to Emile Short, Ghana’s Commissioner of Human Rights and Administrative Justice, who said that the case should be a lesson to ‘gullible’ overseas authorities that tend to carry negative perceptions on the culture and traditional practices of African nations. ‘The commission is not surprised at the revelation that the allegations by the woman have proved to be false,’ he said. ‘We had our grave misgivings about these allegations when they were made and we were surprised at how the political authorities and women’s groups in the US rallied to her cause with such passion without conducting proper investigations in Ghana to verify the truth of the story. Danson had worked with the Biriwa Beach Resort for many years. If the proprietors of the resort had been contacted, they would have provided invaluable information, which would have debunked her claim. The authorities in the West should know by now that some Africans seeking greener pastures in their countries would put up some of the most outrageous and ingenious claims about conditions in Africa to support their unwarranted claim. By always putting us in a bad light, these Western authorities and groups quickly fall into traps set by self-seeking immigrants.'

INS investigators recommended that Danson be charged with fraud but the Justice Department was reportedly reluctant to prosecute for fear of embarrassing leading politicians who had supported her asylum bid so vociferously, not least Hillary Clinton.

The Reluctant Royal

Harry Domela came from a family of German settlers in Latvia. As such, he was regarded as something of an outsider and was frequently treated with mistrust and suspicion, particularly after Germany had invaded Latvia in 1915. In the course of the invasion Domela lost contact with his mother (his father had already died) and although the Germans withdrew from the region in 1918, Harry's future looked bleak.

The following year, at the age of 15, he joined the German Freikorps and was allowed to move to Germany. Being too young to join the regular Army, he took menial jobs, first as a gardener and then as servant to a baroness where he learned the high society manners that would play a major part in his life. Times were hard in the Germany of the Weimar Republic and soon the baroness was forced to lay off some members of staff, including young Harry. As a redundancy payment, he helped himself to a collection of her silver spoons but was arrested by the police. Charges were not pressed, however, and he succeeded in finding other short-lived jobs until the government passed a law that made it difficult for 'outsider Germans' such as Domela to find work.

Penniless, he began sleeping rough, drifting around northern Germany. The winter of 1922–3 found him on the streets of Berlin where he met up with a horoscope-seller calling himself Baron Otto von Luderitz. Like Domela, the baron had fallen on hard times. Taking one look at Domela's slim frame, blue eyes and pale complexion, the baron told him he resembled a nobleman. At the time the country was littered with former aristocrats, the Weimar Republic having abolished titles, and this situation prompted Domela to act on the compliment and pass himself off as a nobleman. He assumed the name of Count Pahlen, then Count von der Recke, but all he earned for his trouble were three separate prison sentences.

On his third release he headed south to Heidelberg where he had heard that, even in such troubled times, certain student clubs had maintained an air of aristocracy. He introduced himself as Prince Lieven of Latvia, but the students were convinced that the title was just a cover for someone of infinitely higher status. Before he knew it, Domela was admitting to being Prince Wilhelm von Hohenzollern, the Kaiser's grandson, and a future King of Germany in the event of the monarchy being restored. The students responded by treating him like royalty. It was a lifestyle to which the impoverished Harry Domela thought he could soon grow accustomed.

From Heidelberg he went north again, to Erfurt, where, in the guise of Baron von Korff, he booked into a plush hotel suite (complete with private bath). From the hotel he made a point of telephoning Prince Louis Ferdinand, one of the Kaiser's two sons, at the Cecilienhof Palace near Potsdam. Domela struck lucky on two counts. Not only was Louis Ferdinand out but also the hotel staff made a note of the call, leading the manager to conclude that 'Baron von Korff' was really Prince Wilhelm von Hohenzollern. The manager was so excited at this unexpected royal patronage that he refused to allow Domela to pay the bill. Harry was not going to argue.

Not wishing to outstay his welcome – or his good fortune – Domela set off for Berlin. Perhaps fearing another term in jail, he tried to play down the Kaiser association but his fame had spread and everyone insisted on calling him 'Your Highness'. So he decided not to try and fight it anymore. No matter what he said, people were convinced he was Prince Wilhelm. He travelled from town to town, being feted wherever he went. He stayed at no expense in castles and stately homes and attended operas in his honour. Returning to Erfurt, he signed the town's Golden Book as 'Wilhelm, Prince of Prussia'. Despite the fact that the real prince lived only 100 miles away, local politicians, bankers and industrialists insisted that Domela was genuine and paid all his bills.

Domela was now in too deep for his own good. One day he spotted a detective on the street; he was sure the authorities were on to him. So when he discovered that his hotel had a room booked for a Mr von Berg, which he knew to be the name of a senior member of the Prince's court, Domela panicked and fled. He decided to join the Foreign Legion, but was arrested on the border with France as he was about to board a train. It was only afterwards that he learned that the

Mr von Berg who had sparked his fateful flight was a banker from Frankfurt.

Domela was tried in the summer of 1927. His jail sentence of seven months was suspended and on 23 July he walked free. He later introduced himself to the real Hohenzollerns, who found him 'charming'. He went on to write his memoirs (which he had started while awaiting trial) and to be the subject of two plays. He starred in one of the plays himself and attempted to sue the actor who portrayed him in the second production. It was reassuring to know he retained some vestiges of grandness.

The Adventures of Louis de Rougemont

In August 1898 the English-based *Wide World* magazine published a captivating account of a modern day Robinson Crusoc who, following a dramatic shipwreck, spent 30 years living with the Aborigine tribes of Australia and mixing with cannibals. Modestly headlined, 'The most amazing story a man ever lived to tell', the narrative seemed to offer a fascinating insight into the Aborigine way of life.

The author, Louis de Rougemont, described how he had been on a pearling expedition to New Guinea when his boat, the *Veielland*, had gone down in a storm off the north Australian coast, between Melville Island and Bathurst Island. Apart from de Rougemont himself, the only other survivor was Bruno the dog who gallantly dragged his master through the rough waves to the safety of a tiny desert island, less than 100 yards long and ten yards wide.

For the next two and a half years man and dog lived a makeshift existence on that small strip of land. By his own account, de Rougemont was nothing if not resourceful. He had managed to salvage enough food from the shipwreck to survive and was able to supplement his diet by shooting sea birds with the help of a home-made bow and arrow. Raw meat was cooked on a fire he had created by striking a steel tomahawk against a stone one. He even managed to grow corn, having found a pile of seeds on the ship and planted them in compost made from a mixture of sand and turtle blood. The stalks were used to thatch the roof of the house that Louis built out of pearl shells. The house measured an impressive 10 ft long and 7 ft high, and he slept in a hammock made out of shark's hide. Another three months and he would probably have built a holiday complex . . .

One day the ever-alert Bruno spotted a boat off the island. Fending off sharks to reach the vessel, de Rougemont wrote how he found a family of Aborigines – a man, a woman, and two boys – perilously close to death. He managed to get them back to the island where he nursed them back to health and struck up a relationship with the woman, Yamba. De Rougemont had already begun building a new boat from the wreck of the *Veielland* and now, joined by the family, set sail for the Australian mainland, which he gathered was not that far away.

On landing he was invited to join an Aborigine tribe. With her husband's blessing, he took Yamba as his wife and wrote in glowing terms of her dedication. 'Ah! Noble and devoted creature! The bare mention of her name stirs every fibre of my being with love and wonder. Greater love than hers no creature ever knew, and not once but a thousand times did she save my wretched life at the risk of her own.' As the only white man for miles around, de Rougemont became something of a hero to the Aborigines. He killed huge alligators and whales, and lived on such delicacies as emu, snake, kangaroo and flying wombat. Other tribesfolk travelled great distances to marvel at the feats of the visitor who was duly made chief of his tribe. He reinforced his position as a great white warrior after defeating a neighbouring chief to win possession of two white girls – Blanche and Gladys Rogers, daughters of a sea captain, presumed dead. De Rougemont added the Rogers girls to his family but they tragically vanished one day when their canoe overturned during a fierce battle with a ship full of savages.

A high point for his readers back home in Britain was his reference to cannibalism and of seeing human bodies cooked in heated trenches, although he refrained from going into too much detail. He was more effusive when describing how a little chicanery saved the day after his position as tribal head came under threat from the medicine man. De Rougemont challenged the medicine man to a contest involving highly venomous snakes. As his adversary looked on alarmed, de Rougemont emerged unscathed after allowing the supposedly deadly snakes to bite his bare arm. What the medicine man did not know was that de Rougemont had taken the precaution of removing the snakes' poison fangs prior to the challenge. The medic lost his nerve and declined to take part, leaving de Rougemont still as top dog.

Eventually de Rougemont decided it was time to travel and he and Yamba set off across Australia, encountering various tribes along the way. At one point he was stricken with fever, and Yamba patiently supervised his recovery. The turning point in his condition came when he decided to try out an old native superstition, which claimed that a sufferer could be cured of fever by burying himself in the warm carcass of a freshly killed buffalo. Acting accordingly, de Rougemont somehow summoned the energy to kill a large buffalo, rip open its body and climb into the steaming intestines. With just his head protruding from the animal's chest, he stayed there overnight, only to discover the next morning that the carcass had become so cold and frigid that he had to be dug out. As he stepped out covered in congealed blood, his long hair matted, he was miraculously cured.

On regaining his strength, he noticed that his beloved Yamba was wearing a small packet round her neck. 'To my unspeakable horror,' he wrote, 'Yamba quietly told me that she had given birth to a child, which she had killed and eaten. It took me some time to realize a thing so ghastly and so horrible, and when I asked why she had done it, she pleaded: "I was afraid that you were going to die – going to leave me; and besides you know that I could not have nursed both you and the baby, so I did what I considered best.' The packet contained some of the baby's bones.

After some 30 years in Australia, de Rougemont returned to England . . . minus Yamba. There he sold his story to George Newnes, publisher of *Wide World*. The magazine's motto was 'Truth is stranger than fiction' and Newnes boasted: 'We have absolutely satisfied ourselves as to M. de Rougemont's accuracy in every minute particular.'

No sooner had the sensational article appeared in print than letters to newspapers queried its authenticity. Some of the tales were simply too preposterous to be true, wrote correspondents. Those which came in for particular ridicule were de Rougemont's claim to have ridden sea turtles (steering the creatures by poking them in the appropriate eye with his toe) and that a member of the original pearling expedition had been snatched from the boat by a giant octopus rising out of the water. Even more damaging was the scorn poured on de Rougemont's description of flying wombats since it was fairly well known that wombats could not fly. Publisher Newnes was momentarily ruffled before claiming that it was obviously a simple mistake – it should have read 'flying squirrels'.

De Rougemont was persuaded to appear before the Royal Geographical Society to answer the accusations. More wizened old man than mighty warrior, he certainly did not give the impression of someone who had slain buffalo or wrestled with alligators. The debate simmered for over a month until the *Daily Chronicle* printed a letter from a man claiming that the person calling himself de Rougemont had once passed himself off as a Mr Green. The *Chronicle* investigated further and discovered that de Rougemont's real name was Henri Louis Grin, son of a Swiss peasant. At the age of 16 he had run away from home with the ageing actress Fanny Kemble and had served as her footman, accompanying her on theatrical tours. After leaving Kemble in 1870, he had sailed to Australia and become butler to Sir William Cleaver Robinson, Governor of Western Australia. He then proceeded to drift through various jobs and although he did go on pearling expeditions and was once shipwrecked, the longest he was ever absent for was three years. One of these menial jobs was that of waiter in a Sydney restaurant. It was there that he borrowed and copied a diner's diaries to form the basis for the wholly fictitious adventures of Louis de Rougemont.

Grin was revealed to be a frustrated inventor, having perfected a potato-digger which didn't work and a diving suit that killed the man charged with testing it.

The *Chronicle* also tracked down Grin's mother in Switzerland and his wife who was living in poverty in Sydney with several children and claiming that Grin owed her a pound a week maintenance for some 20 years. The family rejected his story as pure fantasy. Having failed to trace the origins of the Rogers girls, the *Chronicle* found that two of Grin's own daughters were called Blanche and Gladys.

It transpired that the entire story had been thought up via the borrowed diaries and from information obtained in the Reading Museum of the British Library to which Grin was a frequent visitor.

Grin tasted his 15 minutes of fame, after which he became a musical hall turn, riding turtles in a vast tank on the stage of the London Hippodrome in 1906. The act went down quickly rather than well. During the First World War he briefly reappeared in the news as the inventor of a meat substitute but this met with little more success than his earlier efforts. He was last seen selling matches in London's Shaftesbury Avenue before dying penniless in 1920.

Mystery Boy

He was known as 'Mystery Boy' – a shadowy figure who would spring from nowhere to become an overnight sensation at American high school and university track meetings. In California he was a Swedish orphan raised on a Nevada farming commune; at Princeton he was a self-educated cowboy. In reality he was James Arthur Hogue, son of a Kansas City railroad worker.

Hogue was born on 22 October 1959 into a family of modest means. He attended Washington High School in Kansas City where he soon demonstrated an aptitude for distance running, competing for the school cross-country team and setting a national four-mile record. In 1977 he led the school team to its second successive league title and also won the Kansas City individual crown. This talent saw him recruited by the University of Wyoming in Laramie, which then boasted one of the finest collegiate running programmes in the United States. There he came up against world-class athletes from Kenya who had also been recruited to the team, but the competition was too hot for Hogue and he dropped out after two years.

The sense of failure never left him. Although he would soon be too old for college, his boyish looks enabled him to masquerade as a teenager even when hitting 30. In this way he set about recreating his dream of being a successful college athlete.

In the meantime Hogue returned to Kansas City. After a brief stint at a local community college, he left to study chemical engineering at the University of Texas at Austin but failed to graduate. In 1983 he had his first brush with the law, being placed on three years' probation for theft.

Two years later he enrolled for the senior class at Palo Alto High School, California. Hogue, 26 at the time, gave his name as Jay Mitchell Huntsman, a 16-year-old, San Diego-born, self-taught, Swedish orphan from a Nevada commune. He gave away little else about himself, other than revealing that his ultimate aim was to win a track scholarship to Stanford University, and came to be known around the campus as 'Mystery Boy'. When he created a major shock by winning the prestigious Stanford Invitational Cross Country Meet, even more questions were asked about his identity. A suspicious local reporter began digging and a police investigation revealed the teenage prodigy's true name. The real Jay Huntsman had died in infancy in 1969. Hogue had simply assumed the identity of someone born in the year that fitted his story. In the light of the revelation, Hogue agreed to withdraw from Palo Alto High just six weeks after enrolling.

After serving a 90-day jail sentence for forgery, Hogue began falsely claiming that he had a PhD in bioengineering from Stanford University. Unable to open any doors with his bogus qualifications, he landed a job working for custom bicycle frame builder Dave Tesch in San Marcos, Southern California. Within two months Hogue had stolen $20,000 worth of racing bike frames and tools from his employer.

In November 1987 the 28-year-old Hogue, now living in Utah, submitted an application to Princeton University in the name of Alexi Indris Santana. Once again Hogue invented a colourful background for himself. He claimed to be an 18-year-old ranch hand who had worked on the Western Plains with his horse Good Enough and had grown up in the Mojave Desert sleeping under the stars. He said he had educated himself by reading literary classics. The following March he went on a recruiting trip to Princeton and met with track coach Larry Ellis and admissions officers. Asked about his family, he said that his father had been killed in a car crash and that his mother was a sculptress living in Switzerland.

Unbeknown to Princeton, the police were on the trail of the applicant. Acting on a search warrant, they arrested him in St George, Utah, and charged him with being in possession of stolen bicycle frames. Detectives also discovered application forms to various Ivy League universities, all bearing the name of Alexi Indris Santana.

Hogue's double life was now becoming extremely complicated. No sooner had Alexi Santana's application to Princeton been accepted on the strength of his fake documents than James Hogue was being sentenced to a six-month sentence in the Utah State Prison for receiving stolen property. Having been granted a $15,000 scholarship to attend Princeton, Hogue was reluctant to let the opportunity slip by and so, as Santana, he wrote to Princeton requesting a one-year deferment because his mother was dying of leukaemia. Princeton agreed to the deferment, little realizing that the promising new student was really in jail.

In June 1989 he skipped parole in Utah and moved to Princeton, spending the summer working on a university grounds crew. Santana's fame had gone before him and the *Trenton Times* wrote an article about the incoming student headlined: 'A Different Path to Glory: Princeton's Self-Educated Santana Blazing a New Trail.' Less than two weeks later the state of Utah issued a fugitive warrant for the arrest of James Arthur Hogue.

That September, his imposture still undetected, he entered Princeton University as a member of the class of 1993. Over the next 17 months he proved a model student in both academic and sporting fields. While regularly obtaining A and B grades in such diverse subjects as Italian and Multivariable Calculus, he excelled for the university track team. He integrated sufficiently well to be admitted to the Ivy Club, Princeton's most select private eating club, although classmates recalled that he was a young man of few words who rarely looked people in the eye and often hid himself beneath a baseball cap. One track team-mate said that Hogue 'didn't want to create his own personality. He wanted you to create it for him.' His reticence was attributed to nothing more sinister than shyness.

Students and professors alike readily accepted him as a 21-year-old – even though he was over 30 – until his bogus world fell apart in February 1991. Competing at a Harvard-Yale-Princeton track meet in New Haven, Connecticut, Santana was spotted by a Yale senior who had once attended Palo Alto High School. Renee Pacheco immediately recognized Santana as the man who had masqueraded as a 16-year-old student in California and notified her coach. He in turn tipped off a journalist whose investigations revealed that Alexi Santana was really James Hogue, wanted in Utah for parole violations.

Hogue was arrested outside the geology laboratory at Princeton and charged with forgery, wrongful impersonation and falsifying records. In October 1992 he was sentenced to nine months' imprisonment and ordered to repay the $22,000 in financial aid that he had tricked from Princeton. The judge ordered the sentence to begin immediately but an appeal court agreed to let Hogue finish his semester at an extension programme in Massachusetts. While finishing his semester, Hogue saw an advertisement for a part-time cataloguer at the Harvard Mineralogical Museum and managed to con his way into a job there. He was only at Harvard for a few months but that was all the time he needed. The following year, shortly before Hogue's release from prison, Harvard curators discovered that over $50,000 worth of gems had gone missing from the museum. Sifting through the museum's employment records, the police searched Hogue's apartment at Sommerville, Massachusetts, where they discovered the missing gems, a stolen $10,000 microscope and other scientific equipment belonging to Harvard. The inevitable jail sentence followed, but in 1996 Hogue was up to his old tricks again, being arrested on the Princeton University campus and charged with trespassing after claiming to be a geology graduate student named Jim MacAuthor.

Not many impostors and petty criminals receive the accolade of being the subject of a film but in 2001 moviemaker Jesse Moss completed a documentary about Hogue's chameleon-like existence. Hogue, who had been working in construction at the time, agreed to co-operate with the film and on tape likened his impersonations to an addiction. 'If I were a drug addict or alcoholic there would have been millions of tedious AA meetings,' he said, 'but this is a different form of addiction not recognized as having a remedy.'

The only consolation for the authorities who have tracked Hogue for years is that, now in his early forties, he is surely too old to pass himself off as a teenage college athlete.

To most people he has encountered down the years 'Mystery Boy' remains just that. As one of his lawyers remarked: 'I understand what he did I didn't understand why he did it.'

Martin Guerre: A Family at War

In 1548 the village of Artigat in southern France was shaken by a major scandal when Martin Guerre, loving father and husband, disappeared without explanation. His family presumed that he was dead but then eight years later he turned up again just as suddenly. However, there was something not quite right about the new Martin.

Guerre and his wife Bertrande had been married for ten years when he vanished although both were still in their early twenties. She had been a bride at 13 and, with a dowry of a vineyard, was considered a good catch. His family were not without influence either and owned a tile factory in the village. They made a handsome couple – she was very beautiful, he was tall and agile – but, originating as he did from Basque country, he was sometimes treated as an outsider in the close-knit community of Artigat. Nevertheless the only thing that seemed to be missing from their marriage was a child and even this was rectified after eight barren years when a visit to the local 'wise woman' resulted in Bertrande giving birth to a son, Sanxi. Two years later Martin left amid rumours that he had argued with his father.

The grieving Bertrande was comforted by both families and when Martin's uncle Pierre married her widowed mother, Bertrande moved into their house with her young son. In Martin's absence, Pierre took over the running of the family business. Bertrande continued to pine for her missing spouse. As the years passed, she gave up all hope of him ever returning and came to the conclusion that he must be dead. Not for one moment, however, did she contemplate remarrying.

Then in 1556 her world was thrown into fresh turmoil when Martin's four sisters received word that he was back. Bertrande was taken to an inn some miles outside the village where Martin was said to be resting following his long journey. His sisters immediately embraced him as their Martin, but Bertrande was more cautious. Wasn't Martin taller and more athletic in build? And didn't he have warts, and a scar over one eye? But eight years was a long time to remember a face in the days before photography and when only the wealthy had portraits. Besides, if Martin's sisters were convinced that this man was genuine, who was Bertrande to argue? Any doubts dissolved when he asked about the long white stockings that she stored in a chest at home and which he liked her to wear. Such intimate knowledge of their married life finally persuaded Bertrande that the man was Martin Guerre.

They soon set up home together, reunited as husband and wife. If anything their life was even happier than before. Martin seemed more intelligent, less reserved than in his youth. They talked for hours, particularly about the old days, and she bore him two daughters, only one of which, Bernarde, survived. There were still a few whispers in the village – the local shoemaker noticed that Martin's feet had mysteriously shrunk – but Bertrande was so delighted to have her husband back that she disregarded any gossip about him being an impostor.

As he became more settled, Martin began to involve himself once more in the family business, which brought him into conflict with uncle Pierre. Whereas the old Martin had often appeared diffident, the new Martin had any number of bright ideas for building up the family wealth. He demanded to see the accounts that Pierre had been keeping since his brother's death, but the aged Pierre, resenting his interference, refused. Although local law was on Martin's side, Pierre stood firm and denounced him as an impostor. Soon the village was split down the middle.

Pierre started making secret enquiries and unearthed two men who could identify the newcomer as Arnault du Tilh, better known as 'Pancette'. Although Pancette and the real Martin had served as soldiers in Picardy, it is not certain whether they ever met but in 1553 – five years after Martin's disappearance – Pancette had been mistaken for him. It seems that this encouraged Pancette, who hailed from the north-west of the country, to head south and assume the identity of Martin Guerre.

Pancette was unwittingly assisted in his venture by the loyal Bertrande who obligingly filled in any gaps in his knowledge of Martin. Even after Pierre's accusation, she remained protective of the man she called her husband and together they went through times and places to make sure their stories tallied in the event of a court case. That scenario materialized in 1559 after Pancette was jailed on suspicion of arson. On release, he was seized by Pierre and his sons-in-law, who shared the old man's mistrust of the interloper, and imprisoned once again, allegedly on the orders of Bertrande. It seems highly unlikely that Bertrande was party to the incarceration. She simply buckled under family pressure.

In the region of 150 witnesses were called to testify in court at Rieux. Their opinion was divided but Bertrande refused to say under oath that the man before her was definitely not Martin Guerre. Despite her indecision, the defendant was found guilty. Although Pierre would happily have settled for an apology, the King's attorney asked for a sentence of death. Pancette immediately appealed to the Parliament of Toulouse where his case was heard in April 1560. Pancette acquitted himself admirably in court, appearing truthful in every respect, whereas Pierre had to be restrained for repeated outbursts. The judges were about to find in favour of Pancette when a one-legged stranger entered the courtroom. It was the real Martin Guerre, returned from the Flanders wars.

The support of the four sisters evaporated in a split second. They rushed to embrace their long-lost brother and realized that they had been wrong to put their faith in the impostor. Seeing this, Bertrande, too, turned on Pancette, claiming that he had tricked her. Pancette's time was up. While he went to the gallows, Bertrande and Martin were reconciled and produced another son.

The Bad Boy of Rap

Leicester-born rap artist Mark Morrison hit the big time in 1996 when his single 'Return of the Mack' reached number one in the UK and number three in the United States. But trouble followed him around. There was an incident with a stun gun – for which he was jailed for three months in 1997 – and various other allegations of bad behaviour. It seemed he was destined to spend more time in the slammer than in the charts.

The 25-year-old singer was then sentenced to 150 hours' community service by Leicester magistrates after being found guilty of affray. Morrison reckoned he was a star, and stars don't do community service. So he arranged for an impostor to take his place.

While Morrison spent part of the time sunning himself in Barbados and furthering his career, a stand-in, wearing a hat and dark glasses in order to avoid recognition, did the community service work at the Broadway Project Day Centre in London's Shepherd's Bush. Nobody at the centre knew precisely what Morrison looked like and so were unable to detect the impostor. In fact the substitute had a different build to Morrison and, unlike Morrison, had no scar on the right side of his face. The deception was eventually uncovered by *News of the World* journalist Mark Thomas following a tip-off. Thomas saw the impostor picked up in a chauffeur-driven Mercedes, which he tailed to Morrison's offices in Notting Hill. The impostor was dropped off, and then the Mercedes went to Morrison's home where the real singer got in. When a photographer asked the stand-in for an autograph, he refused in a desperate attempt to maintain the pretence, but exposure swiftly followed. The substitute had done 80 hours of someone else's sentence.

In 1998 Morrison was jailed for 12 months for sending an impostor to carry out his community service. Morrison said afterwards: 'The judge asked me whether I did my community service and I said "yes". I did 42 hours of it. I didn't do it all, but he didn't ask me that. I never lied – I just stretched the truth.'

The Nutty Professor

The son of a Philadelphia police officer, Marvin Hewitt, was something of a loner as a child. Whereas the other kids were into baseball and football, Marvin's consuming passion was advanced mathematics. He discovered the joys of algebra and logarithms at the age of ten and soon became so obsessed with his pet subject that neither family nor friends could converse with him. Unfortunately nothing else at school held any interest for him with the result that, instead of being able to continue his studies at university as he had hoped, he was forced to quit at 17 and take menial factory jobs. Anyway his family were too poor to pay for further education.

Over the next six years he drifted aimlessly through a succession of unrewarding posts – his talent looking certain to remain unfulfilled – until he spotted a newspaper advertisement for a senior preparatory school teacher at a military academy. Falsely claiming to be a graduate of Temple University, he applied and got the job. At last Hewitt was in an environment to which he could relate and quickly earned the respect of students and fellow teachers alike. He began to realize that with his natural aptitude for maths, allied to fake qualifications, he could achieve almost anything in the academic arena. So, borrowing a name and qualifications from a universities' *Who's Who*, he landed a post as an aerodynamicist at an aircraft factory. For Hewitt, the sky was the limit. Then his luck ran out. The name he had selected was too well known and he was forced to admit to the deception.

Hewitt was unfazed. Growing in confidence on almost a daily basis, he next took the name and qualifications of Julius Ashkin of Columbia University to apply for a job as physics teacher at Philadelphia College of Pharmacy and Science. With it came an annual salary of $1,750. His students did so well in their end-of-year exams that Hewitt felt he deserved better and circulated Ashkin's impressive credentials to other colleges, adding the Christie Engineering Company to his list of references. Ashkin's CV caught the attention of the Minnesota Bemidji State Teachers' College who duly wrote to Christie asking for a testimonial for Ashkin. The college received a glowing reply from Hewitt on fake headed notepaper. As Julius Ashkin, Hewitt got the job – this time on $4,000 a year. Things were looking up.

As fate would have it, the Bemidji president had been at Columbia University, like Ashkin, and wanted to talk about the old days. Hewitt felt increasingly uncomfortable under questioning. It was time to move on – to the physics department at St Louis University, on an annual salary of $4,500.

Life was good for Hewitt at St Louis. He felt he was finally achieving something, teaching graduate courses in nuclear physics and statistical mechanics. He certainly did not appear out of his depth although from time to time students would comment on what seemed to be glaring holes in his knowledge of basic physics. He had also got married to a woman who readily accepted his explanation for having two identities. He told her that because he had originally qualified under an assumed name, he had to continue using it. She was even willing to allow all mail addressed to 'Mrs Hewitt' to be delivered to a PO box.

There were a few nasty scares. A colleague at St Louis returned from a trip to Chicago to say that he had bumped into an old friend of Ashkin's, and then in the spring of 1948 an article appeared in the journal *Physical Review*, written by the real Julius Ashkin, now of Rochester University. Hewitt had to think on his feet. He went straight to see his superior and explained that he had signed the paper from Rochester University because that was where he had conducted the original research. His story was accepted but he knew that he was skating on thin ice and that it was best to move on again.

That same year he applied for a position as full professor at the University of Utah in Salt Lake City. The university received glowing references from St Louis and Columbia – unaware that they were for two different people – and nobody checked with Rochester. Hewitt's luck seemed in, especially when a dean at Columbia informed Utah that there had been two Ashkins on the university payroll. Hewitt's interview was successful. His new salary of $5,800 a year meant that, ironically, he had outstripped the man whose qualifications he had stolen. For the real Ashkin was still only an assistant professor.

Hewitt's elation lasted barely a month before he received a letter ominously addressed to 'Dr Julius Ashkin (?)'. It was from the real Ashkin who had finally discovered that an impostor was using his name. Ashkin's tone was surprisingly conciliatory. While ordering the deception to cease, he demonstrated sympathy for the usurper's plight and offered to help 'relieve yourself of what must have become an almost unbearable burden.' He promised not to inform the authorities immediately of the subterfuge. However, a colleague at Rochester showed no such compassion and tipped off Utah. Hauled before the Utah president, Hewitt confessed. The president, too, was reluctant to pillory Hewitt, who even in his short time there had shown himself to be a capable head of department, and offered him a job as research assistant so that he might be able to obtain the qualifications necessary to become a legitimate professor. Alternatively, the president offered to support Hewitt should he wish to qualify at another university. It was indeed a generous gesture but Hewitt felt so crushed by his exposure that he declined the offer and returned to Philadelphia a beaten man.

For the next 18 months Marvin Hewitt kept his head down but then reinvented himself as George Hewitt. Claiming to have been a research director with the RCA communications company, he applied for a job teaching electrical engineering at Arkansas University. He created a fictitious RCA vice-president with an address in Camden, New Jersey, to where any enquiries could be sent. Arkansas duly requested a reference . . . and received a laudatory testament, written by Hewitt. The old trick had worked again.

Then one day an RCA chief came to the university in search of engineering recruits and was told that his former research director was working there – George Hewitt. The RCA boss had never heard of him. Hewitt was off on his travels once more.

With twin baby sons to support as well as a wife, Hewitt could not afford to be out of gainful employment for long. So he bounced back as Clifford Berry, PhD, and secured a teaching post at New York State Maritime College. Then in 1953 he taught at the University of New Hampshire as Kenneth Yates, PhD. There he was undone by a particularly persistent student who, after growing suspicious of his tutor's frequent lapses in knowledge, thumbed through a copy of the *American Men of Science* catalogue and discovered that the real Kenneth Yates was working for an oil company near Chicago. Hewitt confessed and resigned, but this time the press picked up on the story and Hewitt's career as a bogus professor was at an end.

He was genuinely dismayed at not being able to teach any more and pointed out that he had never actually hurt anyone. 'If only they'd let me be a professor, I'd never want anything else or lie,' he said. 'I lied only to get those jobs. I was a good teacher.'

The Secret Life of Dr Barry

For 46 years Dr James Barry had served with distinction as a physician and surgeon in the British Army, rising from a lowly hospital assistant to Inspector General, a position that was second only in the Medical Department to Director General. Outspoken to the point of being downright cantankerous, Barry reluctantly retired in 1859 following a severe bout of influenza and bronchitis. Six years later, having settled in lodgings in the Marylebone district of London, Barry was stricken with diarrhoea. Despite a worsening condition, he refused to allow his valet to summon a doctor and quickly succumbed to the illness on 25 July 1865. The suddenness of his deterioration had caught the usually meticulous Barry unprepared. In previous instances where he had been seriously ill, he had issued strict instructions that he was to be buried untouched in the clothes he died in, his body sewn up in a sheet. This time there were no such orders. Dr James Barry's secret would be safe no longer.

Initially there was nothing untoward. The death certificate was signed by Staff Surgeon Major McKinnon, who had known Barry for some nine years, but a few days later McKinnon received a visit from Sophia Bishop, the Irish charlady who had laid out the body in readiness for burial but whose lack of education meant that she could only make her mark as a witness on the death certificate with an X. Bishop was aggrieved at having been denied access to the deceased's effects – a traditional perk of the job – but thought that she might be entitled to hush money on account of a discovery she had made while preparing the body. For although McKinnon had signed the sex as 'male' on the death certificate, Bishop said that the stretch marks on the body showed Dr Barry to have been female. Not only was James Barry a woman, added Bishop, but she had given birth to a child when very young. McKinnon asked her how she knew. 'I am a married woman,' replied Bishop curtly, 'and the mother of nine children and I ought to know.'

McKinnon wrote of the affair: 'I informed her (Bishop) that all Dr Barry's relatives were dead and it was no secret of mine, and that my own impression was that Dr Barry was a hermaphrodite.'

Rumours soon began to circulate. The Registrar General, George Graham, felt obliged to ask Dr McKinnon for Barry's true sex, purely for his own information. McKinnon explained that, having been 'intimately acquainted' with Dr Barry for so many years, it had never occurred to him to check the sex of the deceased when issuing the death certificate.

The story was suppressed for two weeks but on 14 August a Dublin newspaper broke the story of 'a female army combatant'. The *Medical Times* picked up the story, describing it as 'so extraordinary that were not its truth capable of being vouched for by the official authority, the narration would certainly be deemed absolutely incredible.' The article stated that Bishop 'was very positive indeed' about the fact that Dr Barry was a woman and added: 'Moreover she asserted, with equal assurance and decision, that there were undoubted signs of maternity. In these conclusions the woman was supported and corroborated by others.' The piece speculated that not everyone was surprised by the revelation. 'The deceased was very well known,' it continued, 'and many were the stories and surmises circulated during his (?) lifetime. The physique, the absence of hair, the voice, all pointed one way, and the petulance of temper, the unreasoning impulsiveness, the fondness for pets, were in the same direction.'

The Army desperately tried to hush up the affair and wheeled out Edward Bradford, Deputy Inspector General of Hospitals, to pour cold water on the allegations. While acknowledging Barry's 'singular appearance', Bradford insisted: 'He was quite destitute of all the characters of manhood . . . There can be no doubt among those who knew him that his real physical condition was that of a male.'

It was fighting talk, but to no avail. James Barry has gone down in the annals of history as a woman.

Throughout a distinguished career, Barry had always been vague about putting a date of birth in Army documents, instead referring to 'about 1799'. Barry's origins are obscure. Some believe she was the illegitimate daughter of a nobleman; others suggest she may have been the niece of artist James Barry. What is known is that by December 1809 she had signed the Matriculation Roll of Edinburgh University as a 'literary and medical student' in the name of James Barry – a 10-year-old girl dressed in boys' clothes. Fellow students remarked that young James became nervous when out walking in rough neighbourhoods and always walked with his elbows tucked in. One friend tried to teach him to box but noted that 'James Barry would never strike out but always kept his arms over his chest.'

At the age of 14 he joined the Army Medical Department at its Plymouth garrison and three years later was posted to Cape Town. In full dress uniform, his sword was almost bigger than he was. Barry's attributes soon led to him being appointed physician to the governor of Cape Town but as his fame spread so did gossip concerning his sexuality. Naval Captain William Henry Dillon, who had been treated by Barry, wrote some years later: 'This gentleman was in the Army and considered extremely clever. Many surmises were in circulation relating to him; from the awkwardness of his gait and the shape of his person it was the prevailing opinion that he was a female.' With his reddish hair, high cheekbones, long nose, short, slim build and dainty hands, Barry certainly made for a distinctive man, but it was the lack of a beard or any facial hair that aroused most suspicion.

However, there was no doubting his medical expertise and when the son of Napoleon Bonaparte's private secretary, the Count de las Casas, was taken ill, Dr Barry was recommended and duly dispatched to St Helena. On Barry's arrival in the company of a sea captain from the island, the count was immediately struck by the doctor's youthful appearance. He wrote: 'I mistook the Captain's medical friend for his son or nephew. The grave doctor who was presented to me was a boy of 18, with the form, the manners and the voice of a woman.' Nevertheless Barry's remedies proved successful. His star continued to rise.

Barry's attitude was not to everyone's taste. While plenty admired his gentlemanly behaviour that was entirely bereft of cursing or swearing, he did not always set out to endear himself to people, least of all his superiors. He could be vain, argumentative and impatient . . . except where ladies were concerned. For in order to continue the imposture, Barry went to great lengths to present the image of being a ladies' man, taking care to be seen with the prettiest girls at dances. One observer noted how Barry was a 'perfect dancer who won his way to many a heart with impeccable bedroom manners. In fact he was a flirt. He had a winning way with women . . . and his beautiful small white hands were the envy of many a lady.' He was also said to be fond of a racy story and a glass of wine.

Barry's humanitarian concern for the health of the poor black families of Cape Town inevitably made enemies of the influential whites who did not hesitate to report their dissatisfaction to the governor, Lord Charles Somerset. But Somerset soon had more pressing matters to deal with as rumours abounded that he and his personal physician were having an affair. Those who didn't suspect that Barry was a woman thought the relationship was homosexual. Either way the gossip did considerable damage to Barry's reputation and, under increasing pressure, Somerset abolished Barry's post and reduced him to the status of assistant staff surgeon.

Although highly indignant about his dismissal, Barry threw himself into his new challenge with customary conscientiousness. He made a name for himself for all the right reasons by performing an emergency Caesarean section on a pregnant woman. Barry had never witnessed a Caesarean and knew that in Britain no mother had yet survived such an operation. But thanks to Barry's care and commitment, mother and baby survived. He was quickly promoted to staff surgeon.

In 1831 Barry was posted to Jamaica where he served for four years before being transferred to St Helena to run the regimental hospital as the island's Principal Medical Officer. His duties there included responsibility for both the military and civilian wings and as usual it did not take him long to find fault with the existing set-up. He found the overcrowded, mixed-sex civilian wards 'confused and disgusting' and suggested converting an empty building next to the hospital into an area where men and women could be housed separately. Barry worked tirelessly to improve conditions but once again made enemies in high places after becoming frustrated with petty bureaucracy. When he went over the heads of the local commissariat and wrote directly to the Secretary of War, he faced a court martial for 'conduct unbecoming to an officer and a gentleman.' Barry was exonerated but the governor took the first opportunity that arose to send him home. Barry left the island in disgrace with his servant and dog.

Demoted back to staff surgeon, Barry was next dispatched to the Windward and Leeward Islands, a posting selected for its remoteness as it was thought he would find it difficult to embarrass authority from such a distance. In 1845 he contracted yellow fever and instructed the doctor treating him that, in the event of death, he should be buried in his night-shirt without an examination. Barry survived and was posted to Malta the following year and then in 1851, having been promoted to Deputy Inspector General, he was sent to Corfu. With the Crimean War raging, Barry advised bringing large numbers of the wounded to the Greek island. In this capacity, he met the crusading nurse Florence Nightingale, an equally forthright character. Nightingale later wrote that Barry had 'behaved like a brute' in her presence and considered him to be 'the most hardened creature I ever met throughout the army.' Not for one moment, it appears, did she suspect that Barry was also a woman.

Barry's last posting was to Canada where, in typical fashion, he spared no effort to improve conditions for the troops. It was there that the 60-year-old medic contracted the illness which brought about a premature and unwanted retirement from the British Army. His secret, however, was still safe . . . for another six years.

In the course of his career, James Barry ruffled more than a few feathers. Opinion was divided with regard to his personal attributes but, once he had overcome his distaste for the rougher parts of Edinburgh, all who encountered him were agreed about one thing – that he was utterly fearless. He fought a duel in South Africa, on another occasion engaged in a bare fist fight after being insulted, and suffered terrible physical pain when seriously wounded in the thigh. He battled authority and bureaucracy with commendable zeal. Yet even after being retired from the Army, Barry never had the courage to admit to being a woman.

A Sportsman For All Seasons

When Manchester United's soccer players lined up for the official team photo before their April 2001 European Champions' League match in Munich, they were surprised to see that they had acquired a 12th man – and one who, give or take a few pounds and inches, was the spitting image of their former French international striker Eric Cantona. However, this was no Gallic great, but a 33-year-old unemployed man from Droylsden, Manchester, who had carried out the challenge on behalf of a magazine.

According to family and friends, Carl Power – nicknamed 'Fat

Neck' – was something of a 'character'. One associate alleged that Power, a lifelong United fan, had once managed to get him into the directors' box at Old Trafford without a ticket. 'We went into the directors' box and drank about £40 worth of beer without having to pay. I don't know how he does it. He's a master joker. He's just so up front and cheeky it's unbelievable.'

After boasting of this and other hoaxes, Power was commissioned by the 'lads' magazine *Front* to infiltrate the United team photo in Munich as part of an investigation into how fans could travel the world watching their team for virtually nothing. The stunt took three weeks of planning. Power claimed afterwards that he had discovered from a club director which strip United would be wearing on the night. Dressed in their change kit of all white, he slipped past the gateman at Bayern Munich's stadium by pretending to be part of a television crew. Then spotting an entrance that was unattended by stewards, he made his dash to the side of the pitch and sat with a group of photographers. When the United team emerged from the players' entrance on to the pitch, Power tagged on behind. Although he made the fairly basic error of wearing a wristwatch, all of the United players were apparently too focused on the job ahead to spot the impostor in their ranks. Captain Roy Keane did throw an accusatory glare as Power lined up on the end of the row next to striker Andy Cole who even obligingly shuffled along to let the hoaxer into the picture. After the world's newspapers and TV stations had captured his moment of triumph, Power quietly rejoined the photographers.

Power later admitted that one of the United players, Gary Neville, had spotted the imposture at an early stage. 'As I ran on to the pitch,' said Power, 'Gary Neville tried to grass me up. He knew exactly what was going on and started waving his finger at me and telling me to get the hell out of it. But I just opened my mouth and yelled, "I'm doing this for Eric Cantona – now shut it!" I was as surprised as anyone when he did.'

Four months later Power struck again, this time posing as a member of the England cricket team during the Fourth Test with Australia at Headingley, Leeds. He hid in a toilet near the pitch for two hours waiting patiently for a wicket to fall. Finally he received the phone call from an accomplice to set off and he strode out on to the pitch in full batting gear, close behind England captain Nasser Hussain. It was only when Power removed his helmet and produced a mobile phone from the pocket of his trousers that the crowd realized it was a prank.

Power lamented: 'I was supposed to go all the way to the middle, where I was going to get a phone call from the people who helped me plan this. But I got a call before I got there and it was the wrong call. It was my mate. So I turned round and came back immediately.'

The Headingley hierarchy took a dim view of Power's antics and had him ejected from the ground. He probably considered it a small price to pay for another fleeting brush with fame.

The White House Impostor

For a lowly clerk, Stanley Weyman did rather well out of his career as an impostor. His various guises included the Romanian consul general, a US consul delegate to Morocco, a Serbian military attaché, and a Lieutenant Commander with the US Navy. He carried out this last-named deception with such flair and efficiency that he ended up being photographed on the lawn of the White House alongside President Harding. It was a remarkable triumph for the son of a poor immigrant family in Brooklyn,

He was born Stanley Weinburg in 1891 and although he subsequently chose to amend his name slightly to 'Weyman', that was as far as he went, even for the most elaborate impostures. He had no need for a string of aliases, preferring to keep his own name whether it be as Professor Weyman, Dr Weyman or Lieutenant Commander Weyman. A small man with big ambitions, Weyman relished the power invested from wearing a uniform. In his line of work, first appearances were everything.

His line of work was nothing special – at least not on the face of it. By day the 21-year-old worked as a lowly paid clerk in an unremarkable Brooklyn office, but at night he entered a totally different world. Pretending to be the US consul delegate to Morocco, he ran up hefty bills in the most fashionable Manhattan restaurants. While still in character, he made the mistake of stealing a camera and was sent to reform school. Released on parole, he impersonated a naval officer and was promptly returned to custody.

The naval masquerade was a dress rehearsal for his first major coup – a carbon copy of Horace Cole's famous *Dreadnought* hoax. In 1915 – five years after Cole had embarrassed the British Navy – Weyman telephoned the US Navy Department in New York, announcing himself as Stanley Weyman, the Romanian consul general. He said that the Queen of Romania had asked him to pay her respects to the US Navy, and a visit was quickly arranged to the battleship USS *Wyoming*, which was anchored in New York harbour. Looking very much the part in a light blue uniform with gold braid, Weyman was met at the quayside by a launch and escorted out to the *Wyoming* where the flag of Romania fluttered proudly alongside the Stars and

Stripes. After inspecting a guard of honour, during which he had the effrontery to pass a few mild criticisms, the official guest was wined and dined in the officers' wardroom. He told the officers that he was so impressed by the welcome that he wished to repay their hospitality by treating them to a lavish dinner at the Astor Hotel. To announce the occasion, the hotel issued an advanced press release, which happened to be seen by a New York detective. Recognizing the name of Stanley Weyman, he immediately smelled a rat and arranged for the Romanian consul general to be arrested at the dinner table. 'You could have waited until after dessert,' remarked Weyman.

Although the stunt earned him a short prison sentence, Weyman had little intention of mending his ways and he attempted to repeat the ruse in 1917, this time in the uniform of an Army Air Corps officer. However, he was arrested partway through inspecting a regimental armoury in Brooklyn. Hoaxes were all very well but they were not bringing in any money. It was time to put his talent for impersonation to better use and so, after posing as a hospital assistant, he quickly progressed to Dr Weyman. As a bogus doctor, he beat off other genuine applicants to land a lucrative post as medical officer to an oil exploration company. He was sent to Peru as a consultant on an engineering project and spent his time there living in a company villa and throwing extravagant parties.

But all good things come to an end and 1921 found Weyman back in the United States preparing his most audacious imposture yet. Princess Fatima of Afghanistan had just arrived in the States with her three sons on a private visit to New York. Although it was not a state visit, the appearance of this exotic Eastern princess in the Big Apple created quite a stir. Learning that there were no plans for Princess Fatima to be received at the White House, Weyman decided to arrange his own state visit. Posing as Lieutenant Commander Rodney Sterling Weyman, the State Department's Naval Liaison Officer (a post that Weyman created specially for the occasion), he called on the princess in her suite at the Waldorf Astoria and explained that he had been asked to arrange an official visit to Washington where President Harding was keen to receive her. Weyman then telephoned the State Department on behalf of Princess Fatima to reveal that she was keen to meet the President. The State Department told him to proceed with the necessary arrangements. With both parties agreed to the meeting, Weyman returned to the princess and mentioned that it was the American custom to give a cash present to the protocol officer involved in arranging such visits so that the money could then be shared out among various junior officials. Princess Fatima took the hint and handed Weyman $10,000.

Most impostors would have pocketed the $10,000 and fled but Weyman was not motivated solely by financial gain. He simply adored formal occasions and the chance to dress up. Accordingly the money was spent on hiring a private railway carriage to take the princess and her family to Washington.

The reception itself passed off without incident or without arousing a hint of suspicion. Weyman escorted the royal party into the Oval Office and introduced them personally to President Harding. The group – including Weyman – were then photographed on the White House lawn with the President, to whom the impostor chatted amiably for a few minutes. There was, however, a sting in the tail for the princess. As a parting shot, Weyman collected money from her supposedly to pay for her luxurious Washington hotel suite and to make payments to journalists, which he told her was another quaint American tradition. He promptly disappeared with a small profit from a great deal of hard work and organization.

Despite the non-payment of the hotel bill, the ruse was only discovered when a vigilant news editor recognized Weyman in the photo on the White House lawn. Weyman was eventually brought before the courts after being caught posing as a hospital official. The White House escapade was also taken into consideration, as a result of which he was given an additional two-year sentence for impersonating a naval officer.

When the dust had settled Weyman returned to medicine, notably at the funeral of Rudolf Valentino where he posed as the star's doctor. He then became Pola Negri's personal physician before turning his attention to the legal profession. Presumably his knowledge of the law left something to be desired because he was imprisoned twice for practising law without qualifications and eventually decided that a safer option was to lecture in both medicine and law on the university circuit. During the Second World War Weyman became a 'selective service consultant' whereby, in return for a small fee, he advised on the best way to dodge the draft. He and nine of his clients received prison sentences.

One of the few professions he had yet to tackle was journalism – a situation he remedied in 1948 when, using fake credentials, he became the United Nations correspondent for the Erwin News Service. In this capacity he made a number of useful contacts within the UN and was offered the job of press officer to the Thai delegation. However, he made the mistake of contacting the US State Department to ask whether accepting the post would affect his rights as an American citizen. The State Department discovered that it had a fat file on Stanley Weyman. End of job offer.

Weyman's policy had always been to maintain a high profile but now it seemed that he was just too well known in government circles to continue his career as an impostor. However, he remained alert to any job opportunity that required the wearing of a uniform and by 1960 was working as night manager at a motel in Yonkers, New York. One night there was an armed robbery at the motel. Weyman tried to intervene and was shot dead.

Lambert Simnel and Perkin Warbeck

The Wars of the Roses – the bitter conflict between the Houses of York and Lancaster – divided the English nation from 1455 to 1485. When Edward IV died in 1483, his 13-year-old son was crowned Edward V, only to be deposed within three months by his conspiratorial uncle, Richard of York, who claimed that the two sons of Edward IV were both illegitimate. On the orders of uncle Richard, young Edward and his brother Richard were imprisoned in the Tower of London where, according to popular belief, they were subsequently murdered. As Richard III, the new King's turbulent reign lasted just two years before he was defeated and killed by the Lancastrian Henry of Richmond at the Battle of Bosworth. Henry cemented an alliance between the two feuding houses by marrying Elizabeth of York and was recognized by Parliament as Henry VII, the first in the Tudor line of monarchs. Over the next decade hopes of a new era of peace and stability were repeatedly threatened, however, by the appearance of young pretenders to the throne, backed by power-hungry noblemen who sought to topple Henry and seize control for themselves.

Although the Houses of Lancaster and York had agreed a coalition pledging support to Henry VII, certain Yorkist factions were determined to reclaim the throne. In 1487, just two years after Henry's accession, they put forward a boy by the name of Lambert Simnel to impersonate Edward of Warwick, the 11-year-old son of Richard III's murdered brother the Duke of Clarence.

The son of an Oxford joiner, 10-year-old Simnel had fallen into the care of an Oxford priest, William Symonds, who, acting on rumours that the two princes in the Tower had not been murdered after all, plotted to pass Simnel off as one of them. Then he had a better idea and decided that Simnel should impersonate Edward of Warwick, who had also been detained in the Tower but was thought to have escaped.

Symonds took Simnel to Ireland where there was a strong Yorkist influence. The Earl of Kildare backed the claimant and he soon enlisted the support of other Irish lords and bishops. Two rebels from England – Lord Lovell (Richard III's great minister) and the Earl of Lincoln (whose mother was Richard III's elder sister) – joined the Simnel crusade. The Earl of Lincoln brought 2,000 German mercenaries with him to Ireland as an army to back the pretender in readiness for an invasion of England. Meanwhile Lambert Simnel was duly crowned in Dublin as Edward VI, a coinage was struck in his name and a parliament summoned to attend him.

Henry's response was simple: he brought the real Edward of Warwick from the Tower and paraded him through the streets of London. However, the rebels claimed that the boy in the Tower was the impostor and prepared to invade as planned. The German/Irish force landed in Lancashire in June 1487 and headed south-east towards London, hoping to pick up local support on the way. However, little was forthcoming and on 16 June the invading army was routed by Henry's troops at Stoke-on-Trent. The Earl of Lincoln was killed and Simnel and Symonds were captured. Both confessed. Symonds was imprisoned for life while Simnel – the boy who would be King – suffered the ignominy of being sent to work as a turnspit in the royal kitchens. Since he made no attempt to embarrass Henry further, he was treated well and eventually promoted to royal falconer.

If Henry had been able to crush the Lambert Simnel revolt with relative ease, the second pretender, Perkin Warbeck, proved a tougher nut to crack. The son of John Werbeque, controller of Tournai (now part of Belgium), he was favoured with good looks, an air of breeding and a flair for languages. He was already widely travelled when in October 1491, at the age of 17, he turned up in the Irish town of Cork where he was in the service of Sir Edward Brampton, a leading Yorkist, from whom he had learned a great deal about the court and family of Edward IV. When some of the townsmen saw young Warbeck dressed in his master's fine silk clothes, they immediately hailed him as the Earl of Warwick. But Warbeck swore on oath before the mayor of Cork that he was not Warwick, which was as well for the future of the imposture since it was unlikely that even the Irish would have swallowed another impersonation of the same prisoner so soon after the Simnel affair. Undeterred, the Irish proclaimed Warbeck to be the bastard son of Richard III and told him that he should not be scared of admitting it. Again Warbeck swore that he wasn't. So the conspirators said he must be Edward IV's younger son, Richard of York, one of the two princes in the Tower. This time Warbeck was not given the opportunity to disagree and thereafter was forced to dress and behave like a prince.

He was exhibited to the Earls of Kildare and Desmond in the hope of attracting wider support, but the reaction from the Irish nobles was generally lukewarm and was markedly less enthusiastic than that for Simnel four years earlier. The one thing in Warbeck's favour was that Henry could not easily prove that he was a fake since the real Richard of York was dead, smothered on the orders either of Richard III or Henry himself. So there was no chance of parading him through the streets of London.

Warbeck and his Yorkist supporters proceeded to do the rounds of foreign rulers. James IV of Scotland expressed interest, as initially did Charles VIII of France who received him as a prince. But his support ended with the Treaty of Étaples of November 1491, which included a clause stating that Charles would not help any of Henry's rebels. So Warbeck turned instead to Margaret of Burgundy, Richard of York's aunt and the exiled figurehead of the House of York.

Even though she had been out of England for 25 years – except for a short visit in 1480 when Richard was seven – Margaret immediately embraced Warbeck as her nephew, remarking that it was 'as though he had been raised from the dead.' She later wrote to Queen Isabella of Spain: 'I recognized him . . . not by one or two signs . . . but by so many particular signs that one man who has clues of this kind would scarcely be found among 10,000 individuals. Then I knew him from private conversations and acts which had taken place between him and me, and which assuredly no one else could guess at; finally I knew him from the question and conversation of others, to all of which re replies so correctly and expertly that it is clear and certain that this man is the one whom they once thought dead. I, in fact, when I considered that he is the sole survivor of our family through so many calamities and crises, was very much moved, and in that affection . . . embraced him as an only grandson or an only son.'

Warbeck was already a very convincing impostor, being able to recite the names of Edward IV's servants, and under Margaret's tutelage he became even more of an expert. Warbeck then invited the support of Isabella of Spain and in November 1493 was taken by Albert, Duke of Saxony, to Vienna to attend the funeral of Holy Roman Emperor Frederick III. There he was met by the Emperor elect, Maximilian, who received him as the rightful King of England.

Backed by Margaret and Maximilian, Warbeck landed at the Kentish port of Deal in 1495 with a small army of 1,500 men. The invasion was a disaster. It failed to muster any local support and Warbeck's men were quickly captured and executed. With a nose for self-preservation, Warbeck abandoned them and sailed for Ireland. Once again he made little headway there and moved on to Scotland where James IV befriended him. James may conceivably have believed in Warbeck at first but it is equally likely that he offered his support primarily to embarrass Henry. He even arranged for Warbeck to marry a relative – the daughter of the Earl of Huntly – in order to convince the Scottish nobles that the pretender was genuine. James's aid did not extend to supplying Warbeck with a viable army although Margaret of Burgundy did send a few more men to bolster the depleted force.

In September 1496 James and Warbeck invaded England from the north under the banner of Richard IV. Warbeck talked a good game and offered a reward of £1,000 for Henry's capture but he was not exactly warlike and professed shock at the devastation caused to the countryside by his brief incursion. Environmentally friendly he may have been, but it hardly made him an inspirational leader. His army took two days to progress just four miles into England but when James heard that an army of 4,000 Englishmen was approaching from Newcastle, it took the Scots a mere eight hours to retreat back across the border. It was a humiliating experience all round. James realized that Henry would not be easily shifted and became disillusioned with Warbeck. In 1497 Warbeck left Scotland and in the same year the Scots signed a truce with England. Becoming increasingly isolated, Warbeck was forced to try Ireland . . . again.

Out of luck in Ireland, Warbeck decided to take advantage of a Cornish uprising against taxation and sailed with 100 men to the west of England in two small ships. Stirring the rebels, he marched east and at Bodmin proclaimed himself Richard IV. He set off to take Exeter but in October 1497 his army was beaten back by the King's men. Warbeck was captured and made a full confession.

Henry spared him with a custodial sentence but unlike Lambert Simnel, Perkin Warbeck was not prepared to go quietly. He tried to escape and was thrown in the Tower for his trouble. A fellow prisoner there was Edward of Warwick, a persistent thorn in Henry's side, and now Henry hatched a plan to be rid of the pair of them. A letter allegedly written by Warbeck to Warwick outlining escape plans conveniently fell into the hands of the governor of the Tower who duly informed the King as to its contents. Both prisoners were tried for treason and executed in November 1499. Warwick went to the scaffold with dignity, but Warbeck pleaded that he was of royal descent. It seems that having been an impostor for eight years, he had come to believe that he really was Richard of York.

The Millionaire's Daughter

Whereas some impostors profess to nobler motivations, Cassie Chadwick was undoubtedly driven by sheer unadulterated greed. Indeed even before she turned her dubious talents to the art of impersonation, she had enjoyed a long and shameful career as a con woman.

She was born Elizabeth Bigley in 1857 on a farm in Eastwood, Ontario. Even as a child she was fiercely ambitious and in her teens printed up business cards that read: 'Miss Bigley – Heiress to $15,000'. The cards allowed her to run up large sums of credit with gullible storekeepers before staging a disappearing act. At the age of 22 she was arrested in Woodstock, Ontario, for forgery, only to escape conviction on the grounds of insanity. In 1882 she married Dr Wallace S. Springsteen of Cleveland, Ohio, but was thrown out 11 days later when her criminal background was revealed.

Although she then turned to fortune telling in San Francisco under the name of Madame Lydia DeVere, conning her victims by claiming to have healing powers, she failed to foresee that she would soon be the recipient of a ten-year sentence in the Ohio state penitentiary for forgery in Toledo. Her favourite scam – one that she would perfect in years to come – was to pose as a wealthy socialite so that banks and other financial institutions would fall over themselves to lend her money. She would breeze into a town, rent a mansion and throw lavish parties to convince everyone that she was a woman of wealth. She once bought on credit over two dozen grand pianos, which she then sold before swiftly moving on. She managed to stay one step ahead of the law for a while but eventually her luck ran out. Paroled after three years of her sentence on the orders of governor William McKinley, she returned to clairvoyance, this time combining it with blackmail for added rewards. She would hire a private detective to root out the darkest secrets of her clients who were then invited to pay her to forget what she had seen in her crystal ball. This proved a profitable number until one of her victims threatened to take her to court.

She fled back to Cleveland where she lived incognito as a 'Mrs Hoover' before moving into an up-market New York brothel. There she encountered Dr Leroy Chadwick, a member of one of Cleveland's most prominent families. She assured him that her role at the brothel was to help fallen women. He was completely taken in by her lies and, blissfully unaware of her chequered career, duly married her.

As Cassie Chadwick, she wanted for nothing financially but it was never enough. So in 1897 she came up with the scam that would mark her down as one of America's most infamous fraudsters. She arranged to bump into lawyer James Dillon, an acquaintance of her husband and a man with a liking for gossip, in the foyer of New York's Holland House Hotel. At that 'chance' meeting she invited Dillon to lunch with a group of her friends and afterwards asked him whether he would act as her escort on an errand. She requested to be taken to her father's house, which, to Dillon's amazement, turned out to be the address on Fifth Avenue of millionaire philanthropist Andrew Carnegie.

Clad in expensive furs, she strolled up to the front door, leaving Dillon waiting in his carriage. Earlier in the day she had called the house on the pretext that a domestic servant had applied to her about a job and had given the Carnegie residence as a reference. She now used this discussion as an excuse to be admitted into the house. Once inside, Chadwick invented a name for the non-existent employee. Naturally enough the housekeeper had never heard of her whereupon Chadwick feigned irritation and asked whether the woman in question might have been employed at another of Carnegie's several homes. The resultant search enabled her to spend almost half an hour inside Andrew Carnegie's house. When she finally emerged – with a friendly wave to the housekeeper who had come to the door to see her off – Dillon was left in no doubt that she was a frequent visitor to that illustrious address.

Back at the carriage while busily stuffing papers into an envelope, Chadwick deliberately let one fall to the floor. The lawyer helpfully retrieved it and with his trained eye spotted that it was a note signed by Andrew Carnegie permitting Chadwick to draw half a million dollars. Dillon could contain himself no longer. He simply had to ask Mrs Chadwick whether she was somehow related to Andrew Carnegie. Simulating reluctance initially, Chadwick was forced to admit that she was Carnegie's illegitimate daughter and that he had given her millions of dollars to assuage his feelings of guilt. Swearing the lawyer to secrecy, she said she stood to inherit $400 million. Even though Carnegie had the reputation of being a confirmed bachelor, Dillon swallowed the story and offered to help with her financial affairs.

As Chadwick had calculated, Dillon could not keep his discovery to himself for long. She knew her tissue of lies had spread throughout the business sector when she called in to a leading Cleveland bank and the president himself bent over backwards to be of assistance. Over the next seven years, posing as Carnegie's illegitimate daughter, she borrowed vast sums of money from Cleveland banks, using $5 million in certificates forged with Carnegie's name as security. It is estimated that she borrowed as much as $20 million in that period, expanding her activities across the United States and into Europe. And the banks were only too happy to lend it to her, no questions asked. The scheme appeared foolproof, not least because nobody dared to ask Andrew Carnegie for confirmation of Chadwick's identity.

Chadwick may not have had any problems taking money from banks but private individuals could prove more awkward, and it was one of these who eventually led to her downfall. She had borrowed a large sum of money from a Cleveland millionaire by the name of H. B. Newton who, in 1904, demanded the repayment of the interest which had accrued on the loan. Chadwick was indignity personified. How dare someone with over $10 million in the bank, as she claimed to have, be hounded like a commoner! Newton remained unfazed by her bluster and insisted on inspecting the promissory notes that were supposedly signed by Andrew Carnegie. They were found to be forgeries. Newton took her to court to recover the sum of $190,800. Meanwhile the *Cleveland Press* newspaper did some digging and discovered that Cassie Chadwick and convicted forger Elizabeth Bigley were one and the same person. When the news broke, Charles T. Beckwith, president of the Citizens National Bank of Oberlin (to whom Chadwick owed $1.25), is said to have fainted.

Chadwick fled to New York where she was arrested in the middle of another spending spree. She was wearing a money belt crammed with dollar bills; the rest she had already spent. Taken back to Cleveland to stand trial, she was convicted on seven counts of conspiracy, sentenced to ten years in jail and fined $70,000. She began her jail sentence in January 1906. A year later she died. By then Andrew Carnegie had broken his silence to declare that he was most definitely not the father of Cassie Chadwick, Elizabeth Bigley or even Lydia DeVere.

Old Before His Time

He called himself 'Brandon Lee', the same name as the late son of Kung Fu star Bruce Lee. And one of his referees was 'Marsha Hunt', which just happened to be the name of a singer who used to date Mick Jagger. He let slip that he clearly remembered the day Elvis died. Yet nobody guessed that Brian MacKinnon, posing as a 17-year-old student in 1993, was really a teenager in the seventies.

If ever there was a student imposture waiting to be exposed, it was that of Brian MacKinnon. He had even returned to his old school – Glasgow's Bearsden Academy – and been taught by some of the same teachers who had taken his classes 14 years earlier. Members of staff thought he looked too old but concluded that he was simply big for his age – 'a bit of an oddity.' Even his fellow students nicknamed him 'thirtysomething' because he appeared old before his time. As his form teacher commented when the imposture finally came to light: 'We were a right crowd of dopes. He stood out like a sore thumb.'

Bearsden Academy is one of Scotland's foremost state schools. MacKinnon first enrolled there in 1972 as an 11-year-old. He was an outstanding pupil and left in 1980, having gained four 'A's in his Highers. His dream was to become a doctor and his academic qualifications won him a place studying medicine at Glasgow University. Then things started to go wrong. He had health problems, failed his exams and dropped out in 1983. He tried to get back in, but the university refused his readmission. He was angry at being forced to abandon his dream. 'I felt devastated,' he said later. 'I felt as though I had been robbed and cheated out of my place at university.'

The resentment remained with him, but so did the burning ambition to become a doctor. Thus in the early 1990s he decided to reinvent himself, go back to Bearsden and resit his Highers in order to get into university by a route which ignored his previous academic record. In 1993 the 32-year-old Scot became 17-year-old Canadian Brandon Lee. Whereas MacKinnon's own parents had been a fireman and a nurse, Lee's were given as a professor of zoology and an opera singer. To facilitate the imposture, the deputy rector of Bearsden Academy was sent a fax from Lee's mother expressing her son's desire to attend the school, accompanied by a glowing report from 'Marsha Hunt', said to be Brandon Lee's former teacher in Canada. Another reference was supplied by a London professor of zoology, listed as a family friend. All of these documents had been written by MacKinnon. Fortunately for the health of MacKinnon's ruse, none of the referees were pursued by the school to corroborate his story. The deputy rector did interview 'Brandon Lee' and at the end of the meeting asked to see a birth certificate before fatally changing her mind and saying, 'No, I'll believe you.'

In a fake Canadian accent, 'Brandon Lee' told everyone that his father was dead and that he had been brought up by his mother with whom he had travelled extensively while she toured the world with various operatic companies. He added that she was currently on tour, and that he had come to Scotland to live with his grandmother. Bearsden headmaster Norman MacLeod said of his new pupil: 'He was very articulate and assured for a 17-year-old, quite polished really, which I put down to his cosmopolitan background.'

In truth MacKinnon lived on a Glasgow council estate with his mother. She thought he had gone back to school as an adult returnee – a fairly common practice in Scotland – and knew nothing of her son's double life until it was sensationally reported on the television news.

In the meantime he set about his studies with a vengeance. Even though a number of teachers remained from his previous time at the school, none recognized him. Although he didn't take people to his home, he was sociable and had many friends. Headmaster MacLeod described him as 'a well-spoken, polite, well-groomed, bright young man. He was a model pupil. He had lots of friends and was involved in all aspects of the school, including the school magazine.' Shortly after the start of term, MacLeod asked teachers to compile a report on the newcomer to make sure that he was settling in well. The teachers reiterated the statements of the bogus referees, saying he was making excellent progress in mathematics, biology, physics, chemistry and English. They added that he was a thoughtful and creative pupil.

Although MacKinnon was older than some of the teachers, his presence in class aroused few suspicions. He told one pupil who did question his age that he suffered from premature ageing. When he made the mistake of revealing that he could drive a car, he covered the slip by telling fellow pupils that 16 was the minimum driving age in Canada. Nobody at Bearsden knew otherwise. One fellow student recalled: 'He said he remembered when Elvis died and we wondered how that could be. We started thinking it was all a bit weird but we let it drop. It's amazing how he got away with it for so long.'

'The whole year went surprisingly smoothly,' admitted MacKinnon, 'and at times I was quite at ease. I was never comfortable with the role I was playing but I managed to put it to the back of my mind by concentrating on my work. I wanted to perform well but I had to keep my foot off the accelerator to a certain degree because I didn't want to end up in the newspaper for having won prizes or stood out from the others.' His one break with anonymity came as a surprisingly mature baritone when taking the lead in the school production of *South Pacific*.

'Brandon Lee' left Bearsden in May 1994 with five 'A' grades in his Highers and won a place on the first year of a medicine degree course at Dundee University. Everything, it seemed, was going according to plan until his very popularity proved his undoing. His wisdom beyond his years had impressed the girls at Bearsden and three of them joined him on holiday in Tenerife. While there, they caught a glimpse of his passport and realized that the lanky schoolboy they knew as Brandon was really 32 and called Brian. He admitted the ruse to them but when they came home an anonymous call was made to Mr MacLeod. The caller said, 'You had a pupil, Brandon Lee, who is Brian Lachlan MacKinnon,' before hanging up. The headmaster began checking through the school records and unearthed MacKinnon's first-year profile card from the 1970s, which had a photo of him aged 11. He could not help but notice the similarity to the student calling himself 'Brandon Lee'.

When initially confronted with the allegation, 'Brandon Lee' stuck to the pretence. MacLeod suggested he bring in his birth certificate or provide proof of his identity through his referees but he tried to stall for time, claiming that it was difficult to contact Marsha Hunt, his Canadian referee. This game of cat and mouse went on for a week until MacKinnon finally confessed. Amid the ensuing tabloid publicity, he lost his place at Dundee University.

MacKinnon was distraught. 'I'd go to Outer Mongolia if they spoke English and offered me the chance to practise medicine. I just want to help people.'

Headmaster MacLeod was philosophical about the affair. 'He produced references and we took them at face value and checked his address. Looking at his old profile card, there is a definite resemblance, but hindsight is a wonderful thing. We had no reason to doubt him at the time.'

The Captain of Köpenick

From its formation in 1618 Prussian power was built on its military strength. A Prussian soldier was a force to be reckoned with, even allowing for the occasional oddball like Field Marshal von Blücher who was haunted by the belief that he was pregnant with an elephant. For the most part the nation took great pride in its military and never was this truer than in the mid-nineteenth century when Denmark, Austria and France were defeated in three separate wars within the space of seven years. The seeds of future German military might had been sown.

Growing up in nineteenth-century Prussia, Wilhelm Voigt could only admire from afar the respect afforded to the nation's soldiers. On his good days, he was a humble cobbler; on his bad days, he languished in prison following another conviction for petty crime. He is thought to have spent almost half of the first 50 years of his life in jail.

In 1906, the 57-year-old Voigt had just been released from his latest spell of incarceration when he spotted a Prussian captain of the guards' uniform in the window of a second-hand shop in Potsdam, near Berlin. Voigt began to visualize himself wearing that formidable uniform, thinking how it would instantly transform him from one of society's misfits into a figure of power and officialdom. The price tag was as threatening as the uniform itself – equal to a whole week's wages as a cobbler – but he saw it as a potential investment. Posing as a captain in reserve, he tried the uniform on for size and bought it there and then.

The fact of the matter was that Voigt hated authority. He despised the arrogance of the Kaiser's government officials, particularly after they had refused to return his passport and identity card following his most recent term of imprisonment. He saw the acquisition of the uniform as not only a method of earning some long overdue respect but also as a means of pricking the pomposity of Prussian bureaucracy.

Before daring to wear the uniform in public, Voigt carefully studied soldiers around Berlin. He made mental notes of the way they marched, saluted, and issued commands, ready to imitate their every mannerism. The one thing he had neglected to study was the uniform itself. The first time he ventured out on to the streets he wore his cap badge upside down, but nobody noticed. Passers-by were too much in awe of the uniform to pay attention to detail. That first outing was to a brewers' exhibition in Berlin. As he strode into the crowded hall he was treated with the reverence associated with a Prussian captain. Complete strangers acknowledged his presence, ladies shot him admiring glances, but, most important of all in Voigt's book, junior soldiers jumped to attention and saluted stiffly whenever he passed. Voigt reasoned that if he could have this effect in Berlin, his power of authority in a small provincial town would be almost limitless.

On 16 October he polished his buttons, dusted down his uniform and set off once more on to the thoroughfares of Berlin. He headed towards a large barracks in the city and soon came across five grenadiers under the command of a corporal. Voigt demanded to know where the men were being taken.

'Back to the barracks, sir,' replied the corporal.

'Turn them round and follow me,' barked Voigt. 'I have an urgent mission for them on the direct orders of the Kaiser himself.'

Such an instruction was not to be argued with. So the six fell in behind the bogus captain and marched away from the barracks. A little further along the road he encountered four more soldiers whom he immediately assigned to his little platoon. Any initial apprehension that Voigt may have felt had long since disappeared. With each stride along the street he grew in confidence, knowing that the slightest hesitation would be interpreted as a sign of weakness or, worse still, imposture. By the time he reached a stationary bus, he was positively bursting with pride. Barely pausing for an explanation, he commandeered the bus in the name of the Kaiser, ushered his troops aboard, and ordered it to be driven to the outlying town of Köpenick.

Once in Köpenick, Voigt lined up his bewildered troops for an inspection before marching them off to the town hall. Placing guards on all entrances, he stormed into the office of the burgomaster, Dr Langerhans, and announced that he had orders to put him under arrest on suspicion of fraud. The burgomaster, himself a reserve officer, noticed that Voigt's cap badge was upside down but such was the captain's sense of authority that it seemed futile to argue. With the burgomaster under guard, Voigt marched down to the office of the Inspector of Police, berated him for dozing on duty, and then ordered him to deploy some officers in the town square to quell any possible unrest. The Inspector dutifully obeyed.

Voigt's next port of call was the town treasurer's office where, declaring that he had been sent to investigate the town's finances, he demanded not only the official accounts but also the entire cash treasury. Placed under arrest, the treasurer opened the safe and handed over its contents – 4,000 marks (approximately £650) – to Voigt who in return handed him a fake receipt in the name of 'Von Alesam, Captain, Guards Regiment'. While his men held the prisoners outside, Voigt, looking to repair the injustice he felt he had been done, ransacked the office in the hope of finding a passport and identity card, but the search proved fruitless.

Gathering himself together, Voigt ordered the Inspector of Police to commandeer two carriages from the wealthy citizens of Köpenick. The burgomaster was bundled into one and the treasurer into the other. When the burgomaster's wife became hysterical, the captain graciously allowed her to accompany her husband. Voigt then sent the carriages off under armed guard with instructions that the prisoners were to be taken to General Moltke at the Berlin military HQ for interrogation.

Arriving back in Berlin, the military escort took the town officials to General Moltke as ordered. Needless to say the general was completely baffled. He said that he knew nothing about any financial irregularities and had certainly not ordered their arrest. It dawned on the burgomaster and treasurer that they had been tricked by a clever impostor, one who had made off with the town funds. General Moltke immediately sent some of his men to Köpenick to arrest the bogus captain but it was too late. Voigt had changed into civilian clothes, which he had deposited earlier at the station's left luggage office, and caught the next train back to Berlin.

The exploits of the mystery man who had made fools out of the officials of Köpenick made front page news the following day. Even though a reward of 25,000 marks was offered for his capture, the bogus Prussian captain was perceived by many as a hero – the little man striking out against overbearing, self-important bureaucrats. The situation placed Voigt in something of a dilemma. On the one hand he had no wish to return to prison; but on the other hand he wanted everyone to know that he – Wilhelm Voigt, cobbler – was the brains behind the stunt that was the talk of the nation. As the days passed and with no arrest imminent, Voigt began to fear that he would never receive the acclaim to which he thought he was entitled. So he elected to offer the police a helping hand, planting a photograph that would lead them to his hiding place. Thus ten days after embarrassing both the government and the army, the captain of Köpenick was arrested.

Public sympathy was very much on Voigt's side – even the Kaiser is said to have referred to him as a 'lovable scoundrel' – but the authorities decided that he should be punished severely for his deception. He had, after all, escaped with 4,000 marks although the bulk of the money had been recovered. Consequently Voigt was sentenced to four years' imprisonment, as much for having the effrontery to ridicule the military as for any great crime he had committed. However, in view of his previous record, he could hardly complain.

In prison Voigt became even more of a hero to the masses, receiving over 100 marriage proposals. Public support never wavered, in the face of which the Kaiser pardoned him 20 months into his sentence after the Prussian Army had claimed that Voigt's continued imprisonment was giving it a bad name.

After his release Voigt capitalized on his fame by performing a vaudeville act in the United States . . . in full uniform. He later switched his stage career to German music halls until retiring to Luxembourg on a generous pension from a wealthy Berlin dowager who considered him to be a 'national treasure'. Indeed, unlike so many impostors, the years following his impersonation were the most profitable of Voigt's life and he lived in comfort right up to his death in 1922. Ten years later his famous escapade was celebrated in a motion picture, *Der Hauptmann von Köpenick*.

A Phoney Physician

When 63-year-old Gerald Barnes was sentenced to 12½ years in prison in 1996 for impersonating a doctor – his fourth such conviction – investigators hoped that it would be the last they heard of him. Partly because of his advanced age and mild manner, he was considered a low risk and was therefore sent to California's Taft Correctional Institute, a privately operated federal prison for minimum-security inmates.

Over the next four years, employing the same attributes with which he had convinced unsuspecting patients that he was a genuine doctor,

Barnes persuaded the Taft authorities that he was a model prisoner. So when he expressed interest in attending a rehabilitation programme in heating and air condition in Illinois, they deemed him to be a safe bet to travel unescorted to another minimum-security facility, at Marion, Illinois. They even gave him his bus fare. Unfortunately they failed to heed the words of the 1996 prosecuting counsel who had warned: 'He's been living a lie for 20 years. He's a serious danger to the community. He's a pathological liar. He's someone who can't stop himself.'

Barnes checked out of Taft on 29 August 2000. He was supposed to catch a bus from nearby Bakersfield to Illinois, arriving at Marion by noon on the 31st. When he failed to turn up, a warrant was issued for his arrest.

US marshals spent the next month hunting for the fugitive. They eventually tracked him down to a North Hollywood clinic where they found him with a stethoscope around his neck practising medicine yet again. It had taken him just a matter of days to talk his way into another medical job, still using the name of Gerald Barnes that he had borrowed from a North California physician two decades earlier.

Over that 20-year period 'Dr Barnes' had used his easy charm to secure posts at numerous medical establishments. He worked at community clinics treating the poor and flew volunteer medical missions to Mexico. He was appointed head doctor at a leading Los Angeles clinic where he performed company medicals on FBI agents, employees of the Federal Reserve Bank and other major corporations. Medicine, he thought, was in his blood. As soon he had served his sentence for one imposture, he was out looking for the next job. As one judge put it, he was incorrigible.

Yet his only legitimate connection with medicine dates back to 1958 when he graduated from the University of Illinois College of Pharmacy in Chicago. In those days he was known under his real name of Jerald Barnbaum and was an enthusiastic member of a local amateur dramatics group. He would put his talent for acting to good use in years to come.

He was working as a pharmacist in Illinois in 1976 but was then stripped of his licence by the state pharmacy board after being indicted on Medicaid fraud charges. However, a jury acquitted him.

Moving to California, he came across the name of Gerald Barnes, a respected Stockton orthopaedic surgeon, in a doctors' directory and legally changed his name to that. He had stationery printed in the name of Gerald Barnes and wrote to the Medical Board of California asking for a copy of Dr Barnes's medical licence. His excuse for requesting the licence was that his estranged wife had burned down the house and he needed the document to apply for a new job. Bizarre though the demand was, the board duly sent him a copy of the licence. Next the impostor contacted the University of Wisconsin, where the real Dr Barnes had graduated in 1965, to ask for a copy of his medical school diploma. Now in possession of the essential documents, the charlatan began working at clinics throughout Southern California, using the real Dr Barnes's medical credentials, Social Security number, and driver's licence.

But the bogus doctor's lack of training was soon to catch him out . . . with tragic results. In December 1979, while working at an Irvine clinic, he treated a patient who was complaining of a dry mouth, dizziness, sudden weight loss and an insatiable thirst – all symptoms of diabetes. After ordering a few tests, the impostor sent 29-year-old John McKenzie home and told him to avoid eating candy. The young man died two days later in a diabetic coma. The fake Dr Barnes had failed to detect that the patient had a serious diabetic condition. The misdiagnosis, coupled with the imposture, landed him on charges of involuntary manslaughter and unlawful practice of medicine. In 1981 he pleaded guilty to both charges and was given a three-year sentence.

The real Dr Barnes was mightily relieved. 'At first I joked that impersonation is the sincerest form of flattery,' he told the *San Francisco Chronicle* in 2001. 'At first it was just kind of annoying. I thought, well, they got the guy, he'll never do it again.'

The doctor's confidence was misplaced. Released after serving 18 months of his sentence, the impostor started up again in the same densely populated area of California, where he could easily be lost amid the hundreds of genuine medics, and using the same name. So confident was he of his ability to fool the authorities that he made no attempt to change his identity. 'Every time he's got out of prison, he has immediately taken on the identity of Dr Barnes,' said assistant US attorney Daniel Saunders. 'He's a charming man. He wants to be a doctor and he doesn't want to bother going to medical school. He believes that law enforcement is just interfering with his chosen profession.'

The bogus doctor resumed practising medicine at clinics in East Los Angeles and West Covina, earning $5,000 a month, but his cover was blown when a receptionist who had worked at the Irvine clinic recognized him and tipped off the authorities. In 1984 he pleaded guilty to grand theft and writing fraudulent prescriptions. He was sentenced to three years and four months but was again released early for good behaviour. In 1989 he was back in custody, this time for passing himself off as a doctor at a clinic in San Bernardino County.

By then, he had also begun fraudulently using the licence of a genuine San Francisco pharmacist, Donald Barnes. Pretending to be from the state pharmacy board, the impostor simply phoned Barnes and asked him to verify his Social Security number and licence number. The trusting pharmacist obliged. The deception was discovered when the bogus Barnes tried to land a post at a Los Angeles pharmacy using the San Francisco pharmacist's licence. The alert store was suspicious because of the San Francisco address and contacted Donald Barnes to ask whether he had applied for a new job.

Arrested again early in 1991 for parole violation and released in the October, the impostor spent the next four and a half years working in at least half a dozen different medical facilities in the Los Angeles district. During that period he earned over $400,000 while the facilities for which he worked billed insurance companies and individuals some $5 million for his services. All they got for their money was the expertise of a man with no proper medical qualifications.

One physician who hired him described him as charming, personable and seemingly knowledgeable, but another let him go because he had serious doubts about him. It was in June 1994 that 'Barnes' answered an advertisement placed by the Brandon Medical Group in Hollywood. The owner of the clinic, Scott Brandon, asked 'Barnes' to show him a copy of his medical licence. Handed the number, Brandon called the Medical Board of California to check that the licence number was valid. The Board said that it was, but, unbeknown to Brandon, the number belonged to the Stockton Dr Barnes. Brandon went ahead and hired the applicant but fired him two weeks later after he failed to produce proof of medical malpractice insurance, a Drug Enforcement Agency licence number for prescribing medicine, and his medical licence certificate. For once stringent checks had caught him out. But it was merely a blip.

Unchallenged despite his previous convictions, the phoney physician continued to live the life of a doctor to the full. When he met his future wife, Lisa, at choir practice, he described himself as a doctor and produced a business card to that effect. While he lived in a smart Brentwood apartment and drove a Cadillac, she was puzzled why such an apparently successful doctor had so little money. He claimed that he had spent all his savings caring for his terminally ill second wife. 'He could charm the socks off of any human being,' Lisa would reflect ruefully. The couple married in 1994. She thought she was his third wife; in reality she was his fourth. She remembered how they would watch *ER* together and her husband would delight in reaching the diagnosis before the screen doctors. 'People wonder why I didn't know he wasn't a doctor,' she said. 'How could I know? He worked as a doctor – he'd get up in the morning and go off to his clinic. He went to continuing medical education programmes. He did self-study courses at home. Sometimes he'd tell me a patient's name. I'd say, "Isn't that a breach of confidentiality?" He'd say. "Who's the doctor here? Have you been to medical school?"'

In 1995, still using the name and medical registration number of the Northern California Dr Barnes, he was hired by a health care organization as head doctor at its Los Angeles clinic. Among the group's major clients was the FBI. The impostor worked at the clinic for about nine months, during which time he carried out medicals on more than 70 FBI agents. He also wrote prescriptions and performed genital examinations on up to 25 patients a day. Acting on a tip-off, two Medical Board investigators went to the clinic in April 1996. One said: 'He showed me big drawers full of medical samples; it was like he was trying to convince me he really was a doctor. He said he had terminal prostate cancer and was going to take his own life. Then he grabbed his chest and said he thought he was having a heart attack. We got him a doctor but he was faking it.'

The false Dr Barnes pleaded guilty to charges including mail fraud, the unlawful dispensing of controlled substances and fraudulent use of a controlled substances registration. His lengthy sentence should have put him out of circulation until well into his seventies and guaranteed some well-deserved peace of mind for the real Dr Barnes who admitted that, because of the long-running imposture, he still had to fend off doubts regarding his own genuine credentials. 'Every time I go into the hospital here, the nurses or doctors say, "Are you sure you're the real Dr Barnes?" I've been putting up with that for umpteen years. I tell them, "Some days, I don't know."'

Princess Caraboo of Javasu

Late in the evening of 3 April 1817, a curious young woman called at a cottage in the village of Almondsbury, near Bristol, and asked for somewhere to sleep. Petite in stature, she was dressed from head to toe in black, wearing what appeared to be some form of turban wrapped around her head. Although she spoke no known language and thus had to communicate through a series of gestures, she generally exuded an air of Eastern origin. The cottage-owner sent her to the Overseer of the Poor for the parish of Almondsbury, and the Overseer in turn took her to Knole Park, home of Samuel Worrall, the Magistrate of the County.

On arrival at Knole Park the stranger took from her pocket a few coins – among them a bad sixpence – and implied that she had nothing else. The kindly Mrs Worrall took pity on the poor girl and allowed her to stay for the night. To add to the air of mystery surrounding her, she chose to sleep on the floor rather than in a bed. The magistrate's wife was enchanted by her and was eager to find out something about her background. This was an onerous task since the girl spoke only in a language unlike any other that the good folk of Almondsbury had ever encountered and did not respond to spoken words. However, she did react to pictures in travel books that Mr Worrall showed her and became particularly animated when the local vicar showed her some images of China. Not unreasonably, the Worralls deduced that she was probably from somewhere in the Far East although Mrs Worrall observed that her facial features were distinctly European, possibly Spanish or Greek. Another breakthrough occurred when the girl saw a picture of some bananas and repeated the word 'Caraboo' several times while pointing at herself. This, they decided, must be her name.

Mr Worrall made it clear that Caraboo's stay was purely short term but just a few days after their guest had been carted off to the Bristol poorhouse, Mrs Worrall persuaded him to relent and allow her to stay with them for a little longer. Visitors continued to try and unravel the riddle of the girl's language, but to no avail until a Portuguese sailor, calling himself Martin Eynesso, arrived in the area and claimed to be able to understand her. He managed to converse with her in her own tongue and, translating for the assembled throng, revealed that she was Princess Caraboo from the East Indies island of Javasu. Apparently she had been kidnapped from her home island by pirates and sold as a slave to the captain of a ship sailing to England via the Cape of Good Hope. As the ship neared Bristol, she had managed to escape by jumping overboard and swimming ashore. She was even able to draw a sketch map of her route to England.

As soon as Mr Worrall learned that he had royalty under his roof, he was more disposed towards allowing her to remain as a houseguest. Instead of worrying that the presence of a waif might jeopardize his standing in the community, he suddenly wanted everyone to know that a princess was residing at Knole Park. He informed the newspapers with the result that soon callers were coming from all over England to meet the glamorous Princess Caraboo. The centre of attention did not disappoint, displaying the eccentricities expected of an overseas visitor. To the bewilderment of the Worralls, she developed a habit of climbing on to the roof of Knole once a week and on one occasion made waves by swimming naked in the lake. She climbed trees, she fenced, and refused to drink out of any glass that she had not washed personally. She spent long periods praying to her god 'Alla Tallah', writing in a bizarre language with 36 letters, and practising a weird hopping dance on one leg.

She was in great demand. Lavish parties were held for her and she was showered with expensive clothes and jewels by tradesmen keen to secure her patronage. Artists drew her portrait. There was even talk of her being received in London by King George III with a view to encouraging trade between England and Javasu. Her life was a constant social whirl. One day she went to visit a society lady in Bath where she was observed by a Dr Wilkinson, proprietor of the Pump Room, who described her appearance and behaviour in a series of letters to the *Bath Chronicle*.

Dr Wilkinson wrote: 'Her head is small, her eyes and hair are black, her eye-brows finely arched, the forehead low and nose rather short. Her complexion is very trifling sallow, rather more corresponding to a brunette, with a pleasing colour on the cheeks. A sweet smile, her mouth rather large with beautifully white and regular teeth and lips a little prominent and full, the under lip rather projecting. Her chin is small and round. No ear-rings, but marks of having worn them, and hands unaccustomed to labour. In height five feet two inches. Her dress consisted of a black gown, with a muslin frill round the neck, a black cotton shawl on the head, and a red and black one around the shoulders, leather shoes and black worsted stockings. She appears to be about 25 years of age. Her manners are extremely graceful, her countenance of surprising fascination. Such is the general effect on all who behold her, that, if before she had been suspected as an impostor, the sight of her removes all doubt.'

Confident words indeed – but ones that would soon come back to haunt the doctor. For one of his letters in the *Chronicle* mentioned that Princess Caraboo had a distinctive scar on her back. This description – combined with other traits – was recognized by Mrs Neale, who ran a Bristol lodging house, as being reminiscent of a recent lodger – a woman who had a tendency to tell tall stories and to entertain children by speaking a nonsense language. Mrs Neale knew the woman not as Princess Caraboo of Javasu but as Mary Baker, a cobbler's daughter from Devon.

All of those who had invested so heavily in the story of Caraboo – emotionally if not necessarily financially – were aghast at the suggestion. The Worralls, in particular, faced the awful prospect of becoming a laughing stock for their gullibility. Equally, as an upholder of the law, Samuel Worrall appreciated the virtues of the truth and agreed that Mrs Neale should be allowed to meet the princess. Presented with Caraboo, Mrs Neale identified her at once whereupon Mary Baker broke down and confessed. The proposed visit to the King was hastily cancelled.

Her real life may have lacked the exotic locations of the princess's, but it had been equally traumatic. She had been born Mary Wilcox in Witheridge, Devon, in 1791. Her father was a strict disciplinarian and at the age of 15 she left home to work as a nanny to a local farmer's children before moving on to Exeter. Although she was uneducated, she had always dreamed of the finer things in life but her parents were convinced that the only way she had managed to afford the new clothes she wore was by selling her body. After yet another quarrel, she ran away from home for good and walked almost the entire distance from Devon to London. The walk was nearly the death of her and once in the capital she drifted into vagrancy but then found a job with an employer who taught her to read and write. She flitted from job to job until in 1813 she mistook a home for fallen women for a convent. Her somewhat confusing six-month stay at the Magdalen home on Blackfriars Road finally ended when she admitted that she had never been a prostitute. Shortly afterwards she married a man named Baker, who had travelled extensively in the Far East and regaled her with tales of the Orient. The information was stored away for later use.

These were deeply troubled times for Mary Baker. Her husband left when she became pregnant and then her baby died. In despair she returned to Devon for a short-lived reconciliation with her family. With everyone seemingly discussing the possibilities of starting an exciting new life in America, Mary became increasingly disillusioned with a rural existence. Learning that the fare to Philadelphia was £5, she resolved to raise the money by some means or another. She set off for Bristol but on the way fell in with a band of gypsies. Told that the ship sailed in 15 days, she needed to come up with a plan quickly. It was then that – with the help of her Portuguese sailor friend – she thought of passing herself off as Princess Caraboo of Javasu.

Given that she had tricked them so publicly, one would have expected the Worralls to have washed their hands of Mary Baker once the imposture was revealed. Yet Mrs Worrall, in particular, bore her no malice and not only forgave her for the deception but also gave her the £5 fare to Philadelphia.

Mary sailed in July. A few weeks later a story appeared in a British newspaper reporting that, en route to America, Princess Caraboo's ship had been blown off course and had drifted towards St Helena, where Napoleon was exiled. Apparently the princess had been so excited at the prospect of a rendezvous with Napoleon that she rowed out to the island in a small boat. After her knowledge of Chinese politics had convinced everyone that she was genuine, she was allowed to meet Napoleon who was said to have been fascinated by her story and instantly captivated by her charms. Overnight he was transformed from a sulky and difficult prisoner. The report stated that the former Emperor had begged Caraboo to marry him, but she refused. In fact the story was a work of pure fiction – a hoax of a hoax, designed to add another layer to the Caraboo myth.

The truth was that Mary Baker arrived safely in America without any detour near St Helena. Her fame preceded her and wherever she went she was gawped at by Americans curious for a sighting of the woman about whom they had heard such a great deal. After seven years the novelty of America had well and truly worn off and she returned to England where she occasionally tried to revive her flagging career by showing herself as 'the former Caraboo'. But there was little interest in the fallen star and she ended up making a living by selling leeches to a Bristol hospital. Some remarked that the leech trade was not unlike her previous activity. She died on 4 January 1865 and was buried in an anonymous grave in Bristol.

Son of Sidney Poitier

David Hampton was a bright kid – too bright, he thought, to spend the rest of his life in Buffalo. So in 1981, 17-year-old Hampton set off for the Big Apple to look for work as an actor. His method of preparing for his new career was highly unorthodox. Instead of the contrived setting of drama school, he preferred to act out role-plays on the streets, with real people in authentic locations. Ultimately it was his ability to slip effortlessly into a different character that would earn him fame, not as an actor but as the man who posed as the son of Sidney Poitier.

From his middle-class background in Buffalo (his father was a lawyer, his mother a nurse), Hampton had always idolized Sidney Poitier. Therefore playing his son was as much the fulfilment of a dream as the means to an end.

Hampton thought up his alter ego shortly after arriving in New York. Unemployed and unwilling to pound the pavements in search of an acting job, he decided that the best way to make valuable contacts was to mingle with celebrities. He and a friend tried to gain admission to Manhattan's prestigious Studio 54 club, but the doorman said the entry fee was $50 a head. Without access to that sort of money, they slunk away.

Hampton recalled in 1990: 'My friend said, "We have to get in there. There are celebrities in there we want to meet." And out of the clear blue sky, I said, "We'll lie. Think of who you can be. For me, it boiled down to a choice of being the son of three people: Sidney Poitier, Sammy Davis Jr or Harry Belafonte. I look like Belafonte the most but I had read in *People* magazine that he had a son, named David, who is a model. And I thought Sammy Davis Jr was too glitzy, too gaudy. Poitier has so much more class. He was the only one to have won an Oscar.'

So an hour and a half later, having rented a limousine (free of charge) from a hotel in the name of David Poitier, the pair returned to Studio 54 as the sons of Sidney Poitier and Gregory Peck. Not only did the Poitier name get them past the same doorman who had turned them away a few hours earlier, it earned them free drinks, too. 'We were swept into the centre doors like we owned the place,' said Hampton. 'It was a magical moment.'

Experiencing at first hand how a famous name could open all sorts of doors, Hampton realized he was on to a winner. After all, how many people knew that Sidney Poitier didn't really have a son – only four daughters?

Three days later a hungry Hampton called at a fashionable bistro on Columbus Avenue. He told the doorman that he wanted a table for two, that he had arranged to meet his father there, and that the last name was Poitier. At that, the staff jumped to attention. Hampton got the best table in the restaurant. Needless to say his 'father' didn't show up. Hampton was apologetic. Not to worry, the meal was on the house.

Hampton continued the imposture at Connecticut College, informing students that he was on campus to cast extras for the film version of *Dreamgirls* that his father, Sidney Poitier, was directing. He added that his father would be staying at the city's Pierre Hotel. People sat up and took notice. Three local news stations came to cover the casting. Hampton was finally receiving the attention he had always craved.

A few weeks later he 'borrowed' an address book belonging to wealthy student Robert Stammers. It was to prove his passport to success, containing as it did the telephone numbers and addresses of the rich and famous. Stammers reflected: 'I don't know why everybody fell for him. Maybe it was the strength of his persona. But when he identified himself as Sidney Poitier's son, no one suspected he could be anyone else.'

By making a few judicious phone calls and using the Poitier name as a guarantee, he managed to gain access to some of the wealthiest homes in Manhattan. He tricked fashion designer Calvin Klein and conductor/composer Leonard Bernstein and stayed at the apartment of actress Melanie Griffith while she was out of town. He turned up at Griffth's apartment at two o'clock one morning. Actor Gary Sinise was living there at the time. Hampton introduced himself as a friend of Griffith and her then husband Steven Bauer, and said that he had missed his flight to Los Angeles. He told Sinise: 'All my luggage and money is on the plane and I need a place to stay the night. My name is David Poitier and I've stayed here before.' He added that he had just come from a Diana Ross party.

Unable to contact Griffith, Sinise reluctantly allowed him to stay. They talked for a couple of hours. Sinise recalled: 'He told me he played a kid in the classroom in *To Sir With Love*, though it later occurred to me that Sidney Poitier was the only black in that classroom. He told me all about his background in Bel Air.' The following morning Sinise took him out to breakfast and gave him $10. When Sinise finally got in touch with Melanie Griffith she said that the guy in question had met Bauer in Florida while he was shooting *Scarface*. As a parting shot, she added that the guy was 'nuts'.

Each time Hampton targeted white middle-class liberals. He felt he had a point to prove and would later boast: 'The brilliance of what I did is that here you have a bunch of people that are snobby and insecure in their Park Avenue and Fifth Avenue homes, far removed from reality, and then you have this young black man and he can parlez-vous Français and walk around and comment on the art on their walls. It would have been easier if I had held a gun and tried to rob them. I never beat anyone over the head – I just asked and if I was given, fine. I sat at the table and was a gentleman and had perfect manners. I beat them at their own game: that is the thing that irks them the most, causes the most embarrassment.'

One who was not taken in by the Poitier persona was artist Andy Warhol. Three times Hampton tried to worm his way into Warhol's office or for dinner dates, but failed on each occasion. However, Warhol was very much the exception and over the next two years 'David Poitier' gained invites to all the right theatres, dinner parties, restaurants and clubs in New York.

One night in October 1983, Hampton phoned the East Side home of Osborn Elliott, dean of the Columbia University Graduate School of Journalism and former editor of *Newsweek* magazine. The Elliotts' daughter had attended college with Robert Stammers – their name was in the address book. Introducing himself as David Poitier, he said he was a friend of their daughter's. He explained that he had just been mugged and needed a place to stay until his father arrived in New York the next day. Elliott generously invited him to stay overnight and, feeling sympathy for his predicament, gave him $50 and some clothes to wear. To a man of Elliott's standing, the money was of no consequence and anyway he expected the young man to repay him as soon as his illustrious father reached New York. Hampton had asked Elliott's wife Inger to wake him early in the morning so that he could go jogging, but when she knocked on his door, she was alarmed to find him in bed with a scruffy young man. Hampton told her not to worry, that his companion was publisher Malcolm Forbes's nephew, who had got locked out of his place. She summoned her husband who promptly threw the pair of them out. As he left, Hampton asked to borrow some money so that he could send them flowers by way of an apology.

Concerned that the visitor might try his luck elsewhere, the Elliotts called their friends the Iselins, whose daughter Josie attended Harvard. John Jay Iselin was president of New York's public TV station WNET. The Iselins revealed that the same man had phoned them the previous night, claiming to be a friend of Josie's, and saying that he had been mugged on the way in from the airport. He had appeared particularly upset at losing his term paper to the muggers. His subject, he said, was the criminal justice system. Unable to contact their daughter because there was a phone strike in Boston and the lines were down, the Iselins had taken pity on him and had invited him to stay the night. They had lent him some money but had eventually become suspicious and asked him to leave.

Thrown out by the Elliotts, Hampton rang to apologize and proposed a meeting at a phone booth in Greenwich Village. The Elliotts notified the police who arrested him there. Sidney Poitier revealed that he had no son and Hampton was arraigned on charges of petty larceny, criminal impersonation and fraudulent accosting before eventually pleading guilty to the lesser charge of attempted burglary. Forgoing a trial, he was ordered to make financial restitution of $4,490 to his victims and was banned from setting foot in New York City. However, he failed to make the payments or to abide by the ban, checking into the Pierre Hotel and renting limousines, again in the name of David Poitier. In January 1985 Hampton was sentenced to 21 months in jail for the impersonation.

That was the last that was heard of David Hampton until 1990. Released from prison, he had worked as a waiter and bartender in Europe, returning to the United States in 1989 and settling in California where he delivered groceries and painted houses. Looking back on his ruse, he said: 'Once you're accomplished at what you do, you can get lazy, overconfident and sloppy. You forget what you've said. But you're having so much success that you think it can never end. That, along with greed, was my downfall. In a way I was happy that the game was over because it gets tiring after a while. You get paranoid.'

Moving back to New York, he heard that John Guare had written *Six Degrees of Separation*, a play based on Hampton's imposture. Hampton reacted by suing Guare for $60 million for the use of his life story. He protested to anyone who would listen: 'I'm not going to allow Guare to make millions of dollars off of me and not even send me a thank-you note. After all, I did create this character, David Poitier. And therefore it's no different from a painter painting or a writer writing a book.' Adding that he still wanted to carve out a career for himself in the arts, he insisted: 'I don't wish to become a victim of my notoriety.'

Hampton's case was thrown out and the play went on to become a big hit on Broadway. During one of the final previews, the cast were invited backstage to meet French film star Michel Piccoli. One of the actors, Evan Handler, was particularly excited at the prospect and told Piccoli: 'I met your son when I was in Paris.' Piccoli looked back blankly and replied: 'I have no son.'

The Pretender Princess

Stella Chiappini was a truly cosmopolitan pretender. Raised in Italy, she acquired through marriages estates in Wales and Estonia before trying to pass herself off as a member of the French royal family. It was an eventful journey but one which ultimately reaped little reward.

She was born in 1773 in the Tuscan village of Modigliana, one of seven children. Her father Lorenzo was the village policeman and when he earned promotion the family moved to Florence where Stella decided that her future lay on the stage. Before she could fully realize her musical ambitions, she caught the attention of Lord Newborough, an English widower who owned land in three Welsh counties. She was horrified by the courtship and protested that she would rather become a nun than marry him. Her disgust was understandable: he was 50, she was 13. Nevertheless the marriage went ahead, the none-too-happy couple remaining in Italy amid scenes of increasing acrimony. It was only when they finally escaped to Wales in 1792 that something approaching peace broke out in the relationship. Curiously the turning point was the death of Lord Newborough's only son by his first wife. Until then the marriage to Stella appeared destined to be barren but she then gave birth to two boys within the space of a year and they quickly became a source of great delight, not least to Stella's parents who were regular visitors from Italy.

Lord Newborough died in 1807 but Stella was not one to let the grass grow beneath her feet and she married the Russian Count Ungern-Sternberg, who owned estates in Estonia. Then in 1821 she received a letter from her sick father, in which he made a startling death-bed confession. He wrote: 'The day when you were born to a person I must not name and who has already passed away, a boy was born to me. I was asked to make an exchange, and in view of my financial circumstances at the time I fell in with the repeated requests, to some advantage. So it was that I adopted you as my daughter just as my son was adopted by the other party. I see that Heaven has made good my shortcomings by raining you to a better position than that of your real father, even though he was of almost similar rank. This affords me some peace of mind as I end my life.'

Stella was stunned and intrigued in equal parts. She set off at once for Modigliana in an attempt to unravel her father's bizarre admission. She doggedly tracked down anyone in the area who could remember her birth and learned that, back in April 1773, a French couple had arrived at the inn. They called themselves the Count and Countess de Joinville. The woman was heavily pregnant and gave birth to a girl on the same day that Signora Chiappini had a baby boy. Apparently the Count was bitterly disappointed at fathering a girl as he had wanted a male heir to secure the family estates and therefore suggested a swap with the Chiappinis in exchange for money. It was an offer which the impoverished Chaippinis could not refuse. The two babies were swapped, the Count's unwanted daughter thus becoming Stella Chiappini.

Stella continued her investigations and found further corroboration when it emerged that a Count de Joinville had been detained on Church orders near Modigliana in 1773. On the strength of this, she applied to the ecclesiastical court for her baptismal certificate to be amended. In 1824 a court at Faenza declared that the Count de Joinville had indeed exchanged his daughter for the son of Lorenzo Chiappini, and that the girl had been baptized as Maria Stella, 'with the false statement that she was the daughter of L. Chiappini and his wife.'

In the meantime Stella had traced the remnants of the Joinville family to a castle in Champagne where she discovered that they were linked to the ducal House of Orléans. Armed with confirmation of the exchange, she came to the conclusion that the boy for whom she had been swapped must have been Louis-Philippe of Orléans, heir to the French throne. Not only had Louis-Philippe been born in the correct year, 1773, but also his father, the Duke of Orléans, held the additional, but little used, title of Count de Joinville. To Stella, it was clear that the Duke and Duchess had been the couple travelling incognito in northern Italy, his desire for a son arising from the need to prevent his wealthy wife's inheritance reverting to her relations in the event of her death. If further proof were needed, said Stella, one had only to look at the portraits hanging in the Orléans palace. The similarity between herself and the Orléans princesses was, she maintained, so striking as to be beyond coincidence.

Stella certainly convinced herself that she had a good case. She began using the name of Marie Etoile d'Orléans (the 'Etoile' being a translation of 'Stella'), much to the dismay of her family who abandoned her and went home to Russia. In 1830 – the year of Louis-Philippe's accession – she published her proofs and her claim became a weapon for those who wished to discredit the 'bourgeois monarch' as the Elder Bourbon line disparagingly referred to him. For his part, the King treated the whole episode with amused contempt.

Stella persisted with her claim but her argument fell apart when it was revealed that Louis-Philippe had been born in October 1773, not April, and that his birth in Paris was witnessed by five people. A further three came into the room shortly afterwards and baptism was performed on the spot. The woman who craved a royal title was thus condemned to obscurity and was forced to live the rest of her life in Parisian poverty until her death in 1843.

One or two historians continued to champion her cause but in 1907 author Maurice Vitrac finally put an end to the speculation by gaining access to previously unpublished material in the French National Archives. Vitrac was able to prove that it was physically impossible for the Duke and Duchess of Orléans (or the Duke and a mistress) to have been in Modigliana in April 1773. According to the official *Gazette de France*, the Duke took part in the Maundy Thursday ceremonies at Versailles on 8 April, and from 7–14 April he constantly attended the Paris Freemasonry lodge of which he had recently been elected grand master. Moreover, it was impossible for the first prince of the blood royal to leave France without royal permission, and any absence would undoubtedly have been mentioned in the *Gazette*.

Vitrac went on to identify the real father of Maria Stella as Count Carlo Battaglini of Rimini, who died in 1796 without issue. The case, wrote Vitrac, was not one of substitution but of ordinary 'farming out' to avoid a scandal.

The Aristocratic Social Worker

To all intents and purposes Marc Philip Justin Onslow Berkeley St Leger, the 10th Viscount Doneraile and the Marquis St Leger, was an aristocrat whose family fortune allowed him to take a low-paid job as a social worker. He was privately educated, sported a silk cravat, had an entourage of loyal family retainers and boasted that he had met the Queen at Royal Ascot.

His connections enabled him to bank with Coutts (the Queen's bankers) and to join a committee of Irish peers. Then in March 2000 Bristol Crown Court heard that the marquis was a fake. His real name was Keith Andrews who, after attending a secondary modern school in Kent, lived with his elderly mother in a run-down house on an estate in Swindon, Wiltshire.

Andrews had lived a double life for over 20 years. The son of a labourer, he was born in Erith, on the barren eastern fringes of London, in February 1949. The family lived in a council house and after leaving school at 15 with no qualifications, Andrews took menial jobs in catering and with a firm of printers. He moved around between Oxford and London to no great purpose until, disillusioned by occasional spells of unemployment, he decided to better himself.

He created his noble alter ego after finding a book about the St Leger family, a clan with connections all over Kent and whose coat of arms was displayed in Canterbury Cathedral. The family dates back 1,000 years to before the Norman Conquest. In 1066 Sir Robert de St Leger left his lands near Dieppe in Normany to accompany William the Conqueror across the English Channel. According to family legend, it was Sir Robert who steadied William's arm as he stepped down into the cold English surf. Reading the history of the dynasty, Andrews discovered that the family was still locked in an inheritance dispute dating from 1785 when it had been alleged that John Gillis, the eldest son, was illegitimate. This meant that the title should have passed to his younger brother, James. However, John had kept the title and James had died childless. In 1975 Andrews invented a previously unrecorded marriage for James and set himself in direct descent through the new branch of the St Leger family. He claimed that his mother was Joy Chantal Helene de Burgoyne of Paris and Tours, and that he had been married to Marie-Louise, daughter of the Duc de Brissac of Paris. He called himself the Chevalier St Leger.

He supported his claim by creating headed notepaper, enhanced by photocopying the St Leger family crest from *Debrett's Peerage*. He then faked an appropriate birth certificate and typed up his own version of the family tree. Despite having no money, he used his title to open an account with Coutts.

By January 1980 he was ready to introduce himself to his intended relations. Journalist Moya St Leger received his first letter. Written in boldly sloping black ink, it began: 'I descend from William St Leger, son of John St Leger. I am just starting to write a family history.' Moya, who was herself planning a family history, was suspicious of his claim on the grounds that he sounded too forward. She answered, asking for details confirming his identity, and received an immediate reply. Over the next 15 years he proceeded to bombard her with requests, wanting to borrow microfilmed family records and other important documents. Whenever she suggested that they meet, he was unavailable.

In 1982, as a St Leger, he began a social work course at Mid-Kent College. He qualified in 1984 and, having illicitly obtained a second national insurance number in the name of St Leger and compiled a false CV, applied for a job with the Salvation Army in his new home town of Swindon. 'He was excellent,' recalled Captain Richard Cook. 'We found him a caring social worker. His work was impeccable.'

Even though he became a marquis after starting off as a chevalier, no one questioned his title. They did jokingly call him the 'marquee', but if they had seen his real house they would have known that a large tent would have represented a step up the property ladder. If anyone quizzed him about his humble choice of profession, he explained it by revealing that his wife and children had been killed in a car crash in Australia. He mentioned a period of depression and vaguely referred to having attended a drug clinic at some stage in his life. To his Salvation Army colleagues, he was simply trying to draw on his own sad experiences for the benefit of others. It seemed a noble gesture, and every 15 October, on the anniversary of the supposed car crash, he put a memorial notice to his wife and children in *The Times*. In truth, Andrews never married and had no children.

In 1990 he used his impeccable background to land a job as a social worker for Wiltshire County Council where he would work predominantly with deaf people. He wore cravats and corduroy trousers and always arrived for work in a Mini. He never socialized with colleagues and never gave the council a home address. Although he insisted on using his title, he gave away little about himself apart from airily mentioning weekends abroad and royal functions. His co-workers attributed such talk to aristocratic vanity but, in common with those at the Salvation Army, they were impressed by his desire to put something back into the community rather than be just another of the idle rich. They considered him at worst a harmless eccentric.

Remarkably he didn't see his boss in the six years that he worked for the council. Whenever a meeting was arranged, the marquis would be off sick or have an appointment elsewhere. His sick notes became collectors' items, written as they were on crested notepaper, penned by a fictitious private secretary, Colonel Villiers. Since his paperwork was always up to date, the council left him alone. All the time Andrews was claiming invalidity benefit under his real name.

In his noble guise Andrews talked of having a direct Windsor bloodline and even of having links with Bavarian royalty. He carried off the imposture in grand style. Given the confusion surrounding the St Leger family tree, his story sounded worryingly plausible and he succeeded in deceiving several members of the real St Leger family in both Britain and France. He was invited to stay in some of the finest stately homes in England . . . after which he would return unabashed to his mum and his housing association property in Swindon.

His aristocratic subterfuge remained unchallenged until Wiltshire County Council received an anonymous letter advising them to check the marquis's credentials. Challenged, he produced a long family pedigree plus a supporting letter from the redoubtable Colonel Villiers. While working at the council he wrote to his boss, as plain Keith Andrews, requesting a stair-lift for his elderly mother. As the correspondence dragged on, his letters became increasingly impatient, but when a meeting was suggested he said he worked too far away.

Andrews was now thoroughly immersed in his other world. In 1996 he took part in a BBC Radio 4 programme, helping to expose another fraudulent aristocrat even though the result was never broadcast. And when caught speeding, he wrote to complain, as Colonel Villiers, that the marquis had been undone by badly placed road signs.

After being satisfied with his work for so long, the council finally began to have second thoughts. His mileage expenses didn't tally and his reports seemed to be exaggerating his clients' ailments. In 1996 he was dismissed from his job and the council told the police about its suspicions. When he then tried to secure a huge mortgage against his imaginary French family-owned chateau, the makeshift marquis was arrested at his suburban home where he was not only at a loss to explain his suddenly reduced circumstances but also the display of birthday cards on the mantelpiece addressed to 'Uncle Keith'.

During the pre-trial hearings, Andrews adopted a number of ruses to delay the case, such as pretending to have been struck deaf and dumb.

This led the judge to declare: 'The inescapable conclusion is that he is playing silly devils with the court.'

Andrews, who cut a forlorn figure on crutches, was right to be concerned. When his case was finally heard he was found guilty of obtaining £19,500 by deception from benefit fraud and of obtaining pecuniary advantage by deception in his employment as a social worker. He was sentenced to 18 months' imprisonment.

He refused to give evidence, his sole public utterance coming after the trial when he insisted that he still wished to be known as Marc St Leger. Fearing that he would resume his imposture, genuine members of the St Leger family wrote to newspapers pointing out that Andrews was a fake and had no connections whatsoever with them.

Keith Andrews stands unique among impostors – the only con man to choose a lowly paid job.

Anastasia: The Final Solution?

In 1991 portions of nine skeletons were found in a shallow grave at Ekaterinburg in Russia. Two years later DNA testing identified the bodies as those of the last Tsar, Nicholas II, his wife Tsarina Alexandra, three of their five children, plus the imperial physician and three servants. However, no scientist could state positively whether one of the children found was the Grand Duchess Anastasia, whose fate had been the subject of the most heated debate surrounding any pretender of modern times.

Anna Anderson Manahan, the woman who had, since 1921, claimed to be Anastasia and whose authenticity or otherwise had divided historians throughout the world, had died of pneumonia in February 1984 at Charlottesville, Virginia. Although her body had been cremated, a portion of her preserved intestine had been discovered at the Martha Jefferson Hospital in Charlottesville. It was a pathology specimen from an operation she had undergone in 1979. This body tissue was subjected to DNA testing in 1994, which proved conclusively that she was not a daughter of Tsar Nicholas. Independent tests conducted on Anderson's hair reached the same conclusion.

There was, however, a match for her DNA, but not the one Anderson's supporters wanted to hear. For comparisons with DNA samples provided by Karl Maucher, great nephew of a Polish woman by the name of Franziska Schanzkowska, showed that, just as German newspaper reports of the 1920s had indicated, Anderson and Schanzkowska were almost certainly one and the same person.

Those who thought that scientific proof might put an end to the controversy had reckoned without the persistence of the Anderson camp. They insisted that the samples must have become contaminated, or that the tissue tested was not really Anderson's, or that the whole thing was a cover-up to discredit Anderson's rightful claim – anything but finally admit defeat. The Anna Anderson saga still has plenty of life left in it.

It is not difficult to understand why her followers have remained faithful for so long. Whereas some other pretenders lacked the expertise to prolong their claim beyond the initial wave of interest, her background knowledge of the Russian imperial family combined with an apparent recollection of the most trivial events meant that she was able to convince even hardened cynics. Whatever else anyone may say about her, she was very good.

When Nicholas II became Tsar of Russia in 1894, the country had been in turmoil for many years under the Romanov dynasty. As a 13-year-old boy hc had watched his grandfather, Alexander II, die in the Winter Palace after his carriage had been bombed by a terrorist group called People's Will. Whereas Alexander II was seen as a liberator, his son, Alexander III, took a much sterner stance, opposing reforms and persecuting minorities, especially Jews. Nicholas was 26 when he became Tsar – a role he was reluctant to assume and one for which he had received precious little training as it was assumed that his father would live for many more years. As a result he put great faith in his advisers who urged him to continue his father's hard-line policies, a stratagem that would eventually put him on collision course with militant groups of Socialist agitators.

Nicholas's wife, Alexandra, was born Alix, Princess of Hesse-Darmstadt, the daughter of Princess Alice of England and Grand Duke Louis of Hesse. A caring mother, she was nonetheless a cold, remote woman who would come to dominate her husband. The Tsar's family lived in the Alexander Palace at Tsarkoe Selo, one of eight imperial palaces that contributed to an overall wealth exceeding 20 billion dollars. Nicholas and Alexandra had four daughters – Olga, Tatiana, Maria and Anastasia – and a son and heir, Alexei. Born in 1801, Anastasia was the youngest, most intelligent and most mischievous of the daughters. She was an excellent mimic and enjoyed practical jokes, although she was not to everyone's taste. Her cousin, Princess Xenia, described her as 'frightfully temperamcntal, wild and rough.' Anastasia had light brown hair (sometimes described as reddish blonde) and bluc eyes, she inherited her mother's natural beauty although she showed an inclination to put on weight as a teenager. She shared a bedroom with Maria, whom she dominated, and was close to all of her sisters, as indicated by the fact that they sometimes signed themselves collectively by their initials, OTMA. She also looked after her sick brother, who suffered from haemophilia and was not expected to survive into adulthood.

Desperate to help Alexei, Alexandra turned to a controversial holy man, who had been nicknamed Rasputin – or 'dissolute' – on account of his drunken youth. After bringing Alexei back from the brink of death, Rasputin earned the imperial family's lasting trust and respect. When the First World War broke out and Nicholas personally took command of the Russian army, Alexandra ran the government in his absence with Rasputin – the mad monk – acting as her adviser. Rasputin quickly built up a number of powerful enemies and in 1916 he was assassinated. But the damage he had done to the imperial family was irreparable. Famine and unrest caused workers to riot in Petrograd and Moscow, mutiny spread throughout the military, and in March 1917 Tsar Nicholas was forced to abdicate.

The family were held prisoner at Tsarkoe Selo until August when they were moved to Siberia. The new Bolshevik government had no idea what to do with them but conditions in captivity steadily deteriorated. The guards were menacing. Anastasia and her sisters were not allowed to lock their bedroom door at night and were even followed into the bathroom. At the end of April 1918 the family were moved west to the town of Ekaterinburg where they stayed in a wealthy merchant's property known as the Ipatiev House. Eleven weeks later, on the night of 16 July, the family were rudely awakened and taken down to the cellar where, in the belief that they were going to be photographed, they lined up in two rows. Anastasia, carrying her pet dog, stood with her sisters, their doctor (Dr Eugene Botkin) and three servants. Suddenly armed soldiers burst into the room and began firing. Anastasia's parents and sister Olga died at once, as did Dr Botkin and two servants. But unbeknown to the assassins, Anastasia, Tatiana and Maria had sewn diamonds into their clothes so that they could smuggle them from place to place, and now the bullets bounced off the diamonds and began ricocheting around the cellar. The soldiers panicked but kept firing. Tsarevich Alexei lay groaning on the floor whereupon he was shot in the head. As the cellar filled with smoke, Anastasia was seen huddled against the wall, protecting her head with her arms. Soon Tatiana and Maria died; a maid who survived the gunshots was bayoneted to death. Some accounts state that Anastasia was also bayoneted, but her death remains shrouded in mystery and confusion. Indeed some people still refuse to believe that she died at all that night.

Intent on destroying all evidence of the massacre, the assassins hurled the bodies down a mine shaft and tossed in grenades. Later the corpses were removed from the mine shaft and some were burned while others were doused with acid. The remains were then thrown into a pit and buried. The circumstances surrounding the execution soon gave rise to all manner of rumours, notably that one or more of the children had survived. Several supposed Anastasias surfaced over the next few years. The most durable by far was the woman who called herself Anna Anderson.

Franziska Schanzkowska was born in Borowihlas in 1896, of Polish/German descent. Although her family were poor, young Franziska was intelligent and socially ambitious – friends remembered her as putting on airs and graces. Then at the age of 20 she sustained serious head injuries following a hand grenade explosion while working at a munitions factory, a blast that killed her supervisor. Thereafter she became increasingly unstable and spent two periods in mental hospitals. On her release she lived in a Berlin boarding house run by the Wingender family until early in 1920 she suddenly disappeared. On the night of 17 February of that year it is now believed that she tried to commit suicide by jumping off a bridge into the city's Landwehr Canal. What is known is that a woman was pulled from the canal that night and taken to a nearby hospital. She refused to give any clues to her identity and was committed to the Dalldorf Asylum where she maintained her vow of silence for nearly two years. During that period she read publications that contained photographs and articles on Russia's last imperial family, including a copy of a 1921 edition of *Berlin Illustrated* which detailed the executions and the belief that Anastasia had somehow escaped with her life. Her change of heart came after a fellow mental patient, Clara Peuthert, recognized her as the Grand Duchess Tatiana, presumed murdered three years earlier. She did not deny this immediately but, perhaps remembering that she herself was not the right build for Tatiana, stated enigmatically: 'I never said I was Tatiana.' She was then handed a list of the names of the Tsar's daughters and crossed out every one except Anastasia.

Learning of the claim, one of Alexandra's ladies-in-waiting visited her, but the patient hid furtively beneath a blanket. The lady-in-waiting called her an impostor and stormed off. However, there were plenty of others who were willing to believe, which meant that on her release from Dalldorf in 1922 she was able to live on the charity of various sympathizers. Most of these had their own agendas for wishing to promote this woman as Anastasia. Emigré nobles saw the restoration of the monarchy as a means of reclaiming their power in the land while others reasoned that association with the Grand Duchess would bring its own reward in the form of access to the imperial family fortune, particularly as it was rumoured that Tsar Nicholas had moved vast amounts of Russian gold out of the country during the 1917 revolution. But it was not only the ambitious and the greedy who latched on to her. Post-war Germany was an austere place and the rumoured presence of an imperial duchess brought some much-needed glamour and excitement to the ordinary people of Berlin.

Soon she revealed how she had managed to escape from the assassins. She said that although she had been bayoneted, she had survived because the soldiers' weapons were blunt. When the carnage was complete, one soldier (named Tschaikovsky) had apparently seen her moving and taken pity on her. Amidst the chaos of that fateful night, he somehow smuggled her out of the Ipatiev House and spirited her off to Romania. According to her story, they then married and, after her husband was killed during street fighting in Bucharest, she gave birth to his son, who was subsequently placed in an orphanage. The woman claimed that from Bucharest she walked to Berlin in search of her aunt, Princess Irene, although sceptics wondered why she had not instead sought out her parents' cousin, Queen Marie, while in Romania. She said that she eventually reached the palace where Princess Irene lived, but, seized with a sudden foreboding that nobody would recognize her, made no attempt to enter. Instead she opted to commit suicide by jumping off the bridge.

It was certainly an unlikely tale, but in some respects that was its strength, especially as the woman was deliberately vague about specifics. That was only to be expected following what must have been an unbelievably traumatic period in her life. Her supporters argued that it had to be true, if only because nobody in their right mind would invent such a preposterous story. The fact of the matter was that the woman was not always in her right mind and spent most of the 1920s in and out of hospitals, both general and mental.

At first she called herself Mrs Tschaikovsky but then wished to be known as Anna Anderson. She was quickly adopted by the Russian Refugee Office in Berlin, which was run by Serge Botkin, brother of the physician murdered at Ekaterinburg. The organization was essentially a monarchist support group and Anderson soon found herself surrounded by sycophants who encouraged her delusions and fed her nuggets of information about the Tsar's family.

But for every supporter there was a doubter. When Princess Irene did eventually get to meet Anderson, her first reaction was that she did not resemble Anastasia. Yet she later cried about the meeting and admitted: 'She is similar, she is similar.' Irene's son Prince Sigismund, a childhood friend of Anastasia, sent Anderson a list of questions and was so impressed by her answers that he became convinced that she was Anastasia. Another relative, Crown Princess Cecilie, was also a firm believer but Cecilie's son and daughter-in-law dismissed Anderson as a fraud. One of Anastasia's aunts, Grand Duchess Olga, visited Anderson on several occasions. She longed to accept her as genuine and frequently came close to doing so, but eventually declared, 'Not my niece.'

Anastasia's French tutor, Pierre Gilliard, had a Russian wife who wept for joy on first meeting Anderson and only changed her mind as a result of pressure from her husband. Gilliard himself wavered, too. Initially he conceded that Anderson might be Anastasia before disowning her completely and calling her 'a first-rate actress' and 'a cunning psychopath'. On the other hand, after spending two days with Anderson, Nicholas II's cousin, Grand Duke Alexander, exclaimed: 'I have seen Nicky's daughter!' And former ballerina Mathilde Kschessinka, who had been Nicholas's mistress before his marriage to Alexandra, was completely taken in by Anderson. She said Anderson had Nicholas's eyes and that she looked at her with 'the emperor's look'.

Anderson was extraordinarily well briefed. She was able to remember a private joke with an army captain, the colours of palace rooms and furnishings, secret passwords for family bank accounts (even though the real Anastasia would not have been privy to such information), and many other trivial details, all of which persuaded her followers that she was genuine. Yet she fell down on some of the basics. When quizzed by Romanov family representatives with regard to events from her youth, she would invariably change the subject or feign an emotional or physical breakdown to win sympathy and extricate herself from her predicament.

She did, however, reveal a family secret – namely that her German uncle, Grand Duke Ernst of Hesse, had visited Russia in 1916 while the two nations were at war. Ernst angrily denied making the visit (although the Kaiser's stepson testified in court in 1966 that he had been told that Ernst did secretly make the trip) and angrily set about proving that Anderson was an impostor. Rosa Wingender, daughter of the manager of the boarding house where Franziska Schanzkowska had stayed before her disappearance in 1920, revealed that Schanzkowska had returned equally suddenly two years later saying that she had been living in the interim with Russian monarchists who had mistaken her for someone else. Wingender identified Anderson's clothes as those worn by Schanzkowska and when a Berlin newspaper engineered a meeting between Wingender and Anderson, the former instantly recognized her as Schanzkowska. Anderson in turn recognized Wingender and hysterically ordered her from the room. It was time for another convenient breakdown. However, Anderson's supporters poured scorn on Wingender's account when she admitted that she had been paid for her testimony.

There is no doubt that Anderson and Anastasia were physically similar, prompting anthropologist Dr Otto Reche to testify in court in 1964 that they were either identical twins or the same person. Apart from the facial likeness, both had foot deformities and Anderson also bore scars that could have resulted from being shot and bayoneted. Her detractors maintained that the scars were the result of dropping the grenade when, as Franziska Schanzkowska, she worked in the munitions factory. But the point that arguably counted against her more than any other was her persistent refusal to speak Russian, Anastasia's native tongue. She claimed that it was simply a reaction to the murders and that she would never speak Russian again because it was the language spoken by those who had killed her family. This excuse was viewed by many as feeble, another way of hiding vast craters in her knowledge and thereby masking her true identity.

Anderson made a good living out of her imposture. Her faithful entourage solicited donations from affluent Russian expatriates and other prominent members of society in both Europe and America, all of whom gave generously to the cause. She toured extensively, staying at other people's expense in the finest hotels, attending fashion shows and socialite parties. Wherever she went she was feted as a celebrity, by press and public alike.

While she was on one of her publicity tours to the United States in 1928, a dozen of the Romanovs tried to call a halt to her imposture, issuing a formal document stating that her claim was false. This seemed to bring on another breakdown and she was committed to a mental hospital in the US after being certified 'dangerous to herself and others.' Further spells of incarceration would follow.

Fearful of missing out on the Tsar's fortune, her supporters retaliated vigorously but received a body blow in 1933 when German authorities, granting certificates of inheritance to the Tsar's surviving relatives, issued a statement on one certificate that Anastasia was dead. This ruling was challenged by Anderson who brought a case before a German court to prove her identity and her right to claim part of the inheritance. The case began in 1938 and, with a break for the war, dragged on for another 32 years. Handwriting experts and anthropologists queued up to give evidence but the court eventually ruled that Anderson had failed to prove that she was Anastasia. However, it did not go as far as to say that she definitely wasn't Anastasia. And there was no concrete proof that Anastasia was dead. Anderson's supporters still had hope.

For much of the case the moody, volatile Anderson lived in Germany, retreating in 1946 to a hideaway in the Black Forest. She rarely attended court in person, leaving her disciples to pursue her claim, but a steady stream of films, biographies and television documentaries ensured that her story remained in the limelight.

In 1968 she moved to America, settling at Charlottesville in a house with an overgrown garden and an assortment of dogs and cats. In December of that year she married John Manahan, a retired history professor and, between bouts of instability, finally achieved a degree of contentment as she began to lose interest in promoting herself as Anastasia. In 1979 she went so far as to describe her story as 'nonsense'.

Five years later she was dead. Her husband obeyed her wishes and arranged for her ashes to be scattered in the cemetery at Castle Seeon in Germany, which was owned by distant relatives of the Romanov family. The subsequent DNA tests indicated that she lived a lie for over 60 years. No one will ever know for certain whether Schanzkowska/Anderson was a calculating opportunist out to grab an inheritance or whether her mental state left her somehow convinced that she really was the Grand Duchess Anastasia.

The Heroine of Massachusetts

The name of Deborah Sampson may not appear in too many history books but her exploits have never been forgotten in her native America. In 1983, over 150 years after her death, Governor Michael Dukakis signed a proclamation declaring her to be the Official Heroine of the State of Massachusetts. Then two years later the United States Capitol Historical Society issued a commemorative medal in her honour. Sampson's right to recognition is indisputable as, disguised as a male soldier, she gallantly fought for her country in the Revolutionary War, treating her own battle wounds so that her secret would not be discovered.

Before experiencing the call to arms, Deborah Sampson's first vocation was schoolteacher. Yet from a very young age she was exposed to military tales that helped shape her destiny. She was born in Plympton, Massachusetts, on 17 December 1760 – the oldest of three daughters and three sons – her family being descended from the original *Mayflower* colonists. Her grandmother, Bathsheba Bradford, was a regular visitor to the Sampson home where she particularly indulged Deborah, favouring her on account of her lively mind and affectionate nature. The grandmother was French and used to regale little Deborah with stories about Joan of Arc, recounting how the Maid of Orléans led the French army to victory over the British.

There was also a history of cross-dressing in the Sampson family. Captain Simeon Sampson, a cousin of Deborah's father, had been taken hostage during the French and Indian Wars, eventually managing to escape by dressing as a woman. Deborah would later recall how, when she was four, she had asked Captain Simeon whether she could serve as his cabin boy, only for her offer to be rejected with laughter because she was a girl.

Deborah's childhood was far from idyllic, however. Her father Jonathan was considerably lacking in business acumen with the result that the family soon plunged into poverty. When Deborah was five, her father vanished. At the time it was thought that he had been lost at sea off the coast of England but in fact he had abandoned the family and gone to live in Maine. His fortunes fared no better there and he ended up being buried in a paupers' cemetery. With no husband to provide for her brood, Deborah's mother was unable to cope and was forced to send the children off to live with various relatives and neighbours. At the age of five Deborah went to live with her mother's cousin, Ruth Fuller, in Middleborough, Massachusetts. When Fuller died three years later, Deborah was taken in by the elderly widow of the Revd Peter Thatcher, minister of the First Congregational Church of Middleborough. She worked diligently and without complaint before becoming an indentured servant in the household of a local farmer, Deacon Jeremiah Thomas, the proud father of no fewer than ten sons but no daughters. Apart from Mrs Thomas, Deborah was the only female in a male domain.

As such, she was expected to muck in. Besides helping with the housework, she proved invaluable in the field where she turned out to be the equal of most men. She grew to a height of almost 5 ft 8 in – nearly a foot taller than the average woman of the day – and taller than the average man. The hours of strenuous farm work broadened her shoulders and toughened her muscles. While doing these chores she dressed in male clothing. She also learned how to handle a musket, often going on hunting expeditions with the Thomas boys and becoming as proficient at shooting as they were.

In common with most farm girls of that era, formal education was at a premium for Deborah. Only in winter, when there was less work to be done on the land, did she attend school, but she still managed to acquire an education by persuading the Thomas boys to discuss their studies with her each evening. The tactic obviously worked for, after spending ten years on the farm, 18-year-old Deborah was hired as a teacher at a Middleborough school.

She supplemented her income by spinning and weaving at various homes and at Sproats Tavern, a gathering place where men discussed the battles of the Revolutionary War, which, by 1779, had been going for four years. The conversation invariably revolved around the heroic exploits of local men, including Ebenezer Sproat, the 6 ft 6 in son of the tavern owner. Deborah listened intently, feeling ever more drawn to the conflict, until in the winter of 1780 she heard the news that would prompt her into taking drastic action. Deacon Thomas arrived at Sproat's Tavern to announce the death of two of his sons who had been fighting in Virginia, leaving Deborah grief-stricken for the boys she had to come to love as brothers.

Deborah was 19 at the time and living with Mr and Mrs Benjamin Leonard whose son Samuel was away fighting in the war. Aware that women were forbidden from serving in the military, she borrowed Samuel's clothes and decided to test her disguise by visiting a fortune teller at Sproat's Tavern. When the clairvoyant failed to recognize her, Deborah thought she could carry off the imposture and proceeded to enlist in the army under the fictitious name of 'Timothy Thayer of Carver'. However, as 'Thayer' signed the Articles of Enlistment, a Mrs Wood noticed that the new recruit, who was left-handed, was unable to bend the index finger of his left hand due to an old injury and remarked: 'Thayer holds the quill with his finger in that funny position, like Deborah Sampson.' Deborah's cover was blown. She was questioned about the incident by the deacons of the First Baptist Church, of which she was a member, but refused to admit to the deception.

While frustrated at being forced to return to civilian life, she never abandoned hope of joining the army. She decided to wait for the scandal over her previous attempt to subside and then to enlist elsewhere. In May 1782, 21-year-old Deborah donned male apparel and walked to Bellingham, Massachusetts, where her distant cousin, the Revd Noah Alden, who had served Deborah's congregation in Middleborough, now had a parish. His parsonage was just across the street from a tavern where recruits from the area were mustered in.

On 20 May, Muster Master Noah Taft of the Fourth Massachusetts Regiment looked up from his table into the cold blue eyes of a tall, rangy, fair-haired young man with a firm, jutting jaw and prominent nose. He gave his name as Robert Shurtleff (which Deborah took from her mother's first-born child, Robert Shurtleff Sampson, who had died at the age of eight). Taft paid the youth £60 bounty money, after first deducting his fee, and Shurtleff duly signed the Articles of Enlistment. The signature, bold and legible, still exists in Massachusetts records.

Three days later at Worcester, Captain Eliphalet Thorp mustered Shurtleff and 49 other recruits into Captain George Webb's company. The volunteers were marched to West Point, New York, where they were given uniforms and equipment. To maintain the subterfuge, Deborah bound her breasts tightly. The trick clearly worked because, apart from the fact that Shurtleff's fellow soldiers nicknamed him 'Molly' on account of his apparently being too young to shave, nobody suspected anything out of the ordinary. That was not the case back in Middleborough where Deborah was excommunicated from the First Baptist Church amid rumours that she had dressed in men's clothes and enlisted as a soldier in the army.

The clean-cut Shurtleff rapidly became a great favourite with the ladies, one of whom presented him with a watch, six shirts and a sum of money. Deborah broke off the relationship, signing the note 'your own sex'. Amazingly, the spurned woman chose to keep the secret.

The fear of exposure was constant. When Deborah's regiment was vaccinated against smallpox, she chose to risk her health by opting out rather than face the possibility of detection. Meanwhile she acquitted herself with commendable bravery in the line of fire, proving every bit as fearless as her male counterparts. Skirmishes were frequent and fierce and, after serving at West Point for 18 months, she was wounded twice in raids along the Hudson River. When her group were ambushed near Tarrytown, she suffered a forehead wound from a sabre slash and then at Eastchester she was felled by a musket ball in her left thigh. The Americans were rescued by the timely arrival of a regiment led by none other than Colonel Ebenezer Sproat who, in the heat of battle, understandably failed to recognize the heavily bleeding soldier as the prim schoolmarm who used to spin and weave in his father's tavern.

At a field hospital a French doctor treated the head wound, but was not advised of the thigh injury. Fearing detection – 'I considered this as a death-wound as it must, I thought, lead to discovery' – Deborah waited until the doctor was tending to another soldier and then limped out of the hospital. Later she displayed an iron nerve to remove the offending musket ball in her thigh with a knife. Although the wound never properly healed, she recovered sufficiently to be able to rejoin her regiment.

However, the reprieve was short-lived. A malignant fever set in and she lost consciousness. Robert Shurtleff was sent to a hospital in Philadelphia to be examined by Dr Barnabas Binney. Deborah later wrote: 'Thrusting his hand into my bosom to ascertain if there was motion at the heart, he was surprised to find an inner vest tightly compressing my breasts, the instant removal of which not only ascertained the fact of life, but disclosed the fact that I was a woman!'

She begged Dr Binney not to reveal her secret. He agreed to her request for the time being and took her to his own home so that she could recuperate. When her health was restored she returned to the army but Binney gave her a letter to take to General Paterson, which revealed details of the deception. In October 1783, Robert Shurtleff was honourably discharged from the army. It was all done very discreetly – perhaps to spare the army's blushes as much as Deborah's.

Although her army career was over, Deborah did not immediately abandon her male attire. This earned her short shrift when calling on her mother at Plympton and instead she went to stay with an aunt, Alice Waters. The aunt, not expecting a male visitor to the Waters farm, apparently jumped to the conclusion that the caller was Deborah's brother Ephraim.

For some reason Deborah continued to dress as Ephraim until meeting farmer Benjamin Gannett of Sharon, Massachusetts. In a manner befitting a fairytale, when she revealed herself as a woman, the two fell in love and were married on 7 April 1785. Money was tight but the union was blessed with three children – Earl, Mary and Patience. The family's financial plight came to the attention of Paul Revere, the famous night rider, who proposed that Deborah be awarded a pension for her sterling efforts in the war. Accordingly in 1792 the Massachusetts General Court voted to pay her a lump sum of $34 for past services in the US army where she 'did actually perform the duty of a soldier.' The all-male legislature added approvingly: 'The said Deborah exhibited an extraordinary instance of female heroism, by discharging the duties of a faithful, gallant soldier, and at the same time preserving the virtue and chastity of her sex unsuspected and unblemished, and was discharged from the service with a fair and honourable character.'

As well as teaching at a local school, from 1802 Deborah, although still troubled by her leg wound, travelled throughout New England and New York, delivering lectures on her military experiences. On these occasions she was billed as 'The American Heroine' and always made a point of wearing her full army uniform. The family income was further boosted when she was awarded a US pension of four dollars per annum, again thanks to the efforts of Paul Revere. She was also invited to meet President George Washington.

Deborah was thus able to live in relative financial – if not physical – comfort right up until her death in Sharon on 29 April 1827, aged 66. Her husband subsequently petitioned Congress for an increased pension on the grounds that he had 'burdensome medical bills as a result of her service-connected sickness.' In 1838, a year after Benjamin Gannett's death, Congress responded with an 'Act for the relief of the heirs of Deborah Gannett, a soldier of the Revolution', paying a total sum of $466.66 to her three children. Given their mother's unique contribution to the war effort, the family deserved nothing less.

The Monocled Mutineer

As a schoolboy, Percy Toplis was told in no uncertain terms by his headmaster that he would probably end his days on the gallows. As teachers' predictions go, that one proved uncannily accurate. The hangman would undoubtedly have had the pleasure of dispatching Toplis into the next world had not armed police officers beaten him to it.

It is not difficult to see why the head teacher arrived at such an ominous prognosis. Attending the village school at Shirland, near Alfreton, Derbyshire, Toplis was a quick-witted boy whose undoubted intelligence and interest in learning was undone by a wild, rebellious streak that resulted in him being a frequent visitor to the headmaster's study and an all-too-familiar face with the local constabulary. By the time he was 12, he had been birched for larceny, had run off after kicking a teacher who was about to cane him, had pulled off a number of money-making scams, and had entered school folklore one summer afternoon by passing a bottle of laudanum around during a history lesson. Overcome by the soporific drug, the entire class was soon fast asleep.

It was therefore a considerable relief to the school when, in 1910, Percy Toplis left the establishment at the age of 13. Sensing the need to instil some discipline into his life, an aunt got him a job as an apprentice blacksmith at nearby Blackwell colliery where her husband worked. Such an environment was grossly unsuited to Toplis whose talents lay in more artistic areas. An accomplished pianist and a promising actor – he starred in a production titled *Poor Little Johnny* at a local theatre – he clearly felt he was cut out for better things than the sweat and grime of a colliery. This frustration manifested itself in several more brushes with the law, albeit for minor misdemeanours, the last of which saw him incarcerated in Lincoln jail. On his release in 1915 he joined the Royal Army Medical Corps and set about taking advantage of the opportunities that wartime offered those with unprincipled ambitions.

A life in the lower ranks held no more appeal for Toplis than a career in the colliery. With his suave good looks, vivid blue eyes and smooth tongue, he visualized himself as officer material. Before returning to the UK on leave, he acquired a captain's uniform and a Distinguished Conduct Medal, put a bandage on his left knee in the belief that a wounded officer would not be challenged by the authorities and returned to Blackwell in the guise of an officer. Feted with champagne and beer, he regaled the locals with stories of his exploits at the front and told them how he had been shot in the knee. The limping hero was invited to review and drill the Local Defence Volunteers and had his photograph taken in his captain's uniform. That very photo would later feature on 'Wanted' posters distributed the length and breadth of the country.

Having successfully carried off his imposture in the provinces, Toplis decided to perform his act on a bigger stage – London. In the West End he masqueraded as an officer with a distinguished war record to great effect and no little arrogance. A friend later revealed: 'He would walk along the Strand with the air of a man with an important mission. I was with him one day when he stopped suddenly, turned round with a military air, and called out "Corporal". The non-com he addressed walked back. "Why didn't you salute me?" asked Toplis in an imperious manner. "I didn't see you, sir," replied the man, saluting. Toplis, with a wave of his stick, snapped out, "Then keep your eyes open in future, corporal," and passed on. I never saw anything done more properly. Not a shadow of doubt concerning the bona fides of the officer could have entered the non-com's mind. I certainly had none.'

Toplis never professed to be anyone in particular. That he could play the part of an officer was sufficient reward. Names were unimportant. In time of war, more than any other, the military were viewed as heroes and were warmly welcomed by a grateful public whenever home on leave. Pretty girls took it as an honour to be seen on the arm of an officer, particularly one as dashing as Toplis. He took to sporting a gold monocle (a trait which would eventually give him his nickname of 'The Monocled Mutineer') and to dining at the most expensive restaurants. He knew how to give a girl a good time. He also knew how to exploit the breakdown of the natural order of things that was an inevitable consequence of war. It was difficult to keep track of personnel; people would appear and disappear. Therefore, when he outstayed his welcome in one place, Toplis would simply move on. No questions asked.

Confidence is an essential commodity for any impostor and Toplis possessed it in abundance. He feared no one. This, allied to a natural cunning, made him a dangerous adversary. He was also a contradictory figure. Although he loved to dress as an officer and taste the opulent lifestyle of the upper ranks, he despised authority, just as he always had done at school. He was never one to abide by the rules.

As the First World War dragged on with no end in sight, morale in some sections of the British Army began to suffer. Hundreds of thousands of lives had been needlessly lost in the futile trench warfare conducted in Belgium and northern France. Every yard of land gained would be at the expense of casualties on a breathtakingly grim scale. Of course, the vast majority of soldiers accepted the orders from above without hesitation, no matter what their private thoughts may have been. They were doing their bit for King and country. Besides, invariably the punishment for disobeying orders was cold-blooded execution.

But not all soldiers were as compliant. Outside the British Army base at the French fishing village of Étaples a group of deserters and rebels had organized themselves into an underground network known as The Sanctuary. They lived in holes dug from the sand hills. Étaples itself was out of bounds to the men from the army camp and military police guarded the bridges into the village, but the common practice among soldiers was to sneak across the estuary at low tide away from prying eyes. One day in September 1917, a New Zealander, Gunner Healy, was cut off by the tide as he tried to return to the base and was left with no option but to cross one of the main bridges instead. There he was apprehended as a deserter and thrown into the guardhouse. The sense of injustice riled the rank and file who swarmed on to the bridge. Shots were fired in an attempt to quell the disturbance. The deserters in The Sanctuary saw the opportunity to make capital out of the situation. Among their number was Percy Toplis, nicknamed 'The General' by his fellow rebels, and it was he who used his intellect, supreme confidence and air of authority to dictate terms to Brigadier General Andrew Thomson and eventually reach a settlement that satisfied the men. The army later denied that Toplis was ever anywhere near that part of France during the war – probably for fear of promoting his status as a folk hero – but then again for the next 60 years (until 1978) it also insisted that there had never been a mutiny at Étaples. The whole episode was a massive army cover-up.

Toplis's role in the mutiny made him the army's most wanted man and British Secret Service agent Edwin Woodhall was brought in to track him down. Woodhall was a worthy foe for Toplis. Both men preferred to work alone, lived on their wits and were utterly ruthless. Each was also a master of disguise. Indeed the only real difference between them was that they operated on opposite sides of the law.

Knowing that he would be a marked man, Toplis did not hang around after Étaples. It was a shrewd move because Woodhall was swiftly into action, sticking up 'Wanted' posters wherever he went. The saturation publicity worked. In October 1917 Woodhall came face to face with his quarry in a French hotel. Toplis was arrested and thrown into jail pending trial. However, the agent's satisfaction was short-lived as Toplis managed to escape and flee to England. In an incredible act of bravado, Toplis went straight to the army recruiting centre in Nottingham and joined another regiment, the Royal Army Service Corps, under his real name even though he was the British Army's most wanted deserter.

The war was now over but Toplis seemed to want the army as much as it wanted him. Above all, he found it provided a cover for his various swindles. Having stolen the uniform of a captain in the RASC, along with a chequebook of the London County and Westminster Bank, he proceeded to write dud cheques to purchase whatever took his eye, always adding half a crown to the total as 'the mark of a gentleman.' It was a typically ostentatious touch, and one which convinced trades people that they were indeed dealing with an officer and a gentleman. When he was eventually arrested for passing dud cheques, the police failed to make sufficient inquiries into his background and he was sentenced to just six months' hard labour and given a dishonourable discharge from the army.

Released from jail in the summer of 1919, he once again presented himself at a recruiting office – this time in London – and re-enlisted in the Royal Army Service Corps as No. 54262 Toplis, Francis Percy. He was posted to Bristol, where he ran blackmarket deals in army petrol and food supplies, and then to Bulford Camp on Salisbury Plain. With the money he made from his illicit deals, he used to spend long weekends in London, dining at the Savoy Hotel and going racing at Ascot. He was rarely seen in the same uniform on two consecutive occasions. By now he had acquired a veritable collection of badges, from RAF to Army Remount. Sometimes he would appear as a private or a sergeant major, but more often as an officer wearing his trademark gold monocle. Occasionally he dressed in the uniform of a full colonel. Whatever the rank, he fulfilled it to the satisfaction of everyone he encountered.

Although he generally managed to stay one step ahead of the law, the nature of his activities ensured that he was walking a constant tightrope. He was arrested again, at Bristol, for stealing an army car but escaped after picking his guards' pockets while playing cards with them. The keys he plundered were then used to lock the hapless warders in his cell while he made his getaway.

Deciding that maybe it was time to take his leave of the army, Toplis joined the RAF in 1920, still using his real name. Three months later a Salisbury taxi driver was found murdered and Toplis was named as the prime suspect. His description was circulated throughout the country, stating him as being 'of smart appearance, affects a gold monocle. Sometimes has ginger moustache, cut à la Charlie Chaplin.'

Armed with a stolen revolver, Toplis went on the run for six weeks, first to Wales and then on to Scotland where the hunt intensified after he shot a policeman and a gamekeeper. It was hardly the behaviour associated with an officer and a gentleman but he was now a desperate fugitive, more dangerous gunman than working-class hero. Every British policeman – not to mention Edwin Woodhall – was on the lookout for Toplis.

Fleeing south from the Scottish Highlands, he found himself in Cumbria, on the road from Carlisle to Penrith, on the evening of Sunday 6 June 1920. Sitting down on the lawn of a Wesleyan chapel between the villages of Low and High Hesket, Toplis became so engrossed in a Sunday newspaper account of the Scottish shooting a few days earlier that the failed to notice the approach of PC Alfred Fulton, the village constable. PC Fulton eyed Toplis's army uniform suspiciously and asked to look in his kitbag. 'To my astonishment,' said Fulton in his subsequent account of the meeting, 'he threw it on the ground and stepped back a few paces. I then felt certain of my man, but knowing what a dangerous ruffian he was and as we were quite alone, I remarked jokingly, "You might be the likes of Toplis." He smiled grimly and replied: "I am not that fellow." The officer asked for his ID whereupon Toplis produced a driver's licence in the name of John Henry Thompson.

Although PC Fulton would later declare that he had already made up his mind that the man before him was Toplis, he decided to let him go on his way for the time being. Instead he rushed home and studied the 'wanted' descriptions over tea. His wife mentioned that she had seen a soldier pass by earlier in the day and thought that it could be Toplis. This seemed to convince Fulton and, after hurriedly mending a puncture on his bicycle, he set off in pursuit of the soldier. Pedalling furiously, he caught up with Toplis at St Mary's Church, High Hesket.

This time Toplis was ready for him. He pulled a gun on the policeman, levelled it at his head and announced, 'If it's Toplis you're after, I'm your man.'

Toplis spared the policeman's life and made his escape. After such a close encounter, PC Fulton decided that rather than risk becoming a dead hero, it was wiser to climb on his motorcycle and ride to Penrith for reinforcements. Over160 men were summoned from across the region, some issued with guns. Soon afterwards, Toplis was spotted, having changed clothes, near Plumpton, about four miles from Penrith. According to contemporary newspaper accounts, when the police caught up with him there, the cornered Toplis immediately drew his revolver and fired three shots at them. The police returned fire and Toplis fell to the ground, dead. Other sources state that Toplis did not open fire but was gunned down in cold blood by two plainclothes officers – Sergeant Robert Bertram and Inspector William Ritchie – who were under orders to silence him permanently as a legacy from Étaples. However, Ritchie protested that it had never been the intention to kill Toplis, merely to 'bring him down or disarm him.' What is certain is that few tears were shed over Toplis's demise.

Over the ensuing days lurid newspaper stories attempted to fill in the details of Toplis's life, disclosing how, posing as Captain Williams, he had apparently eloped with a pretty young motorist and had seduced at least six girls. Women never can resist a man in uniform. Neither could Percy Toplis, and that was primarily why his life ended in a violent shoot-out at the age of 24.

The Eternal Teenager

In the late summer of 1997 a fresh-faced girl with no education records sat in the principal's office at Evergreen High School in Vancouver, Washington State. She was a runaway who had been taken in by a local Christian family. She said that her name was Brianna Stewart and she was 16 years old.

The busy Evergreen administrators hesitated momentarily over a few gaps in her narrative but there was nothing to concern them unduly. She was clearly a lost soul who desperately needed some stability in her life and was duly admitted into Evergreen's sophomore class.

In fact, that autumn she was 28 years old. Her real name was Treva Throneberry and for the previous ten years she had drifted from state to state, assuming a variety of aliases, always claiming to be a teenager. However, it would be a further three years before the truth about Brianna Stewart finally emerged.

In the meantime she blended seamlessly into life among Evergreen's 2,000 students. She joined the tennis team, had a small part in the school production of *Man of La Mancha*, and became known as 'queen of the mall rats' for hanging out regularly after school and at weekends with friends at Vancouver Mall. She hid her full figure inside baggy clothes and if anyone looked too closely into her eyes, she would instinctively turn away. But nobody read anything sinister into her reactions: they all knew she had endured a tough life on the streets and was probably wary of letting anyone get too close.

The only aspect of Brianna's behaviour that aroused any negative comment was her habit of wearing her hair in pigtails every day. It was a fashion *faux pas* at Evergreen and one that seemed 'really weird' to her schoolfriends. Were the pigtails an attempt to make her look younger than she really was? For there was no doubting that, in other respects, she had a mature look about her. Classmate Joey Gambetta said: 'When I first saw her, I thought she was a teacher. Then she sat down at a desk like everyone else, and I put that aside.'

Teachers occasionally noticed a weariness in her demeanour but attributed it to the exhaustion of homelessness rather than adulthood. As the *New York Times* wrote: 'They were trained to look for kids who were stoned or violent, but they weren't trained to look for kids who weren't kids at all.'

Steve Nowacki, who taught Brianna psychology and sociology during her senior year, remembered: 'She looked older than the others, but street kids often have a lot of miles on them.'

The secret of maintaining a long-term imposture at any institution is to avoid standing out. Brianna came across academically as very much an average student except for an English essay that she wrote about her own street life, which, with its graphic tales of sleeping in doorways, sheltering from the rain under the awnings of shops and being rousted by the police at 3 a.m., so impressed her teacher that she was awarded an A grade. Otherwise she concentrated on drawing as little attention to herself as possible, just with being a member of the pack.

Acting as a typical teenager meant dating. One day she caught the eye of 15-year-old Ken Dunn when both were being treated at school for sports injuries. Ken had twisted his leg playing football; Brianna had gone down with a bad case of shin splints. Ken had never had a girlfriend before but found Brianna so easy to talk to. There was something different about her – she wasn't like other girls of her age. But at the time he didn't know why.

The friendship blossomed. She invited him to her local church, Glad Tidings, and soon they were a regular Sunday item. Finally he plucked up the courage to tell her he loved her, a declaration that brought a tender kiss. They dated for almost 18 months, holding hands in the hall at school and writing Valentines to each other. They would go to movies or sit and talk in coffee houses. Their topics of conversation were 'really intense', said Dunn. Often they talked about God, but on other occasions Brianna would recount her chequered past. She said her mother was dead, killed by her father. She talked freely about murder, rape and drugs. To a boy who still lived quietly at home with his parents, it was another world.

The peak of their romance was the Homecoming Dance, which they attended as a couple. Dunn remembered slow-dancing to a Shania Twain track and thought it was one of the best nights of his life. But the relationship was innocent. 'We never had sex – never,' said Dunn. 'I kept my hands to myself.'

If all was sweetness and light with Brianna's school life, it was a different story at home. It was in the spring of 1997 that she had first turned up at the 1,500-capacity Glad Tidings Church on the eastern side of Vancouver. There she proceeded to relate a torrid tale, which, with subtle variations en route, was one she had told many times before. She said she had been brought up outside Mobile, Alabama. Her mother had died when Brianna was seven, after which she had been raised by her stepfather, Alan Reeves, a Navajo Indian who worked for the sheriff's department. Reeves, she said, had a shady past. She claimed he had once worked for a gun-runner off the Ivory Coast and that he had subjected her to physical and sexual torture, making pornographic videos of her when money ran low. She said she had tried to turn her tormentor over to the authorities when she was 13, but when no action was taken against him, she ran away from home. She went on to reveal how, in desperation, she hitchhiked her way across the country in search of her real father – Michael Stewart of Vancouver. Her odyssey saw her beg for help from strangers, some of whom were kind enough to offer her a place to stay. She toiled away on farms to earn the bus fare to take her to the next dusty town on her journey. When she finally made it to Portland, Oregon, she said she tracked down a Michael Stewart in Aloha. Although he wasn't her father, he let her move in with him. It was the stuff of nightmares. He turned out to be a drug addict, she sobbed, who introduced her to crack cocaine and kept her prisoner in his apartment. She suffered this terrifying indignity for a couple of months before managing to escape. Taking to the streets, she met a youth pastor for Glad Tidings who encouraged her to attend services at the church.

Brianna's story touched the hearts of the congregation, and offers of help soon poured in. Church receptionist Debbie Fisher was so shocked by Brianna's tale of cruelty and hardship that she and her contractor husband Randy allowed the runaway into their home rather than see her end up back on the streets. Debbie Fisher immediately thought that Brianna seemed old for her age but whenever anyone remarked that she looked older than 16, the girl became 'very upset'.

At first, life at the Fishers appeared tolerable for all parties. Brianna successfully enrolled at Evergreen and began to make friends. However, as the months passed she became increasingly resentful of anything resembling parental authority and arguments erupted over household chores and bedtimes. Then there were the stories. She said her stepfather was involved in a satanic cult and that she was raised as a high priestess. Next she claimed that a senator from the Midwest had made her pregnant while she was working on his re-election campaign. While these accusations were far-fetched, they were relayed with such conviction, the Fishers didn't know what to believe.

These wild allegations also took their toll on her relationship with Ken Dunn. 'I would sit up and worry all night,' he admitted. 'She said people were following her, and I believed her.' In addition he was concerned about her apparent addiction to Ritalin, which had been prescribed for an attention-deficit disorder. Inevitably the friendship fizzled out.

By May 1998 the Fishers could take no more and after another row about vacuuming the living room, they gave her two weeks to move out. Using her student card as documentation, she persuaded caseworkers at the Washington State Department of Social and Health Services to put her in a foster home.

That autumn, however, her carefully planned imposture faced its first serious threat following a routine visit to the dentist. The dentist noticed that her wisdom teeth had been extracted and the scars fully healed. He considered this to be so unusual for a 17-year-old that he voiced his suspicions to Brianna's caseworker, Jan Shaffer. On 13 October Shaffer confronted Brianna, warning her that defrauding the foster-care system was a crime.

Far from being intimidated, Brianna decided that attack was the best form of defence and responded in characteristically belligerent fashion. She wrote a five-page, single-spaced letter in which she launched a blistering attack on her caseworker. 'I feel that remaining in foster care is not safe for my physical, mental and emotional well-being,' she wrote. 'I feel that I have been abused by the very system that I asked for help.' It was quite a letter for a 17-year-old. In the face of such a diatribe and perhaps fearful of adverse publicity, the

Department of Social and Health Services backed down. However, as far as Brianna was concerned, the rift was beyond repair. She had no intention of staying with anyone who questioned her integrity and instead took refuge with David and Theresa Gambetta, whose son attended Evergreen.

The Gambettas could not have done more to make Brianna feel at home. They cleared out the study so that she could have a room of her own and gave her a weekly allowance of $10 plus a stereo for Christmas. She repaid them five months later by calling 911 and accusing David Gambetta of spying on her. She said the light fittings in her room contained secret cameras and claimed that Gambetta had been making video recordings of her. She also said that he exposed himself to her and to his two young daughters. After thoroughly investigating the allegations, the police found them to be without any foundation whatsoever, but it had proved a traumatic episode for the Gambetta family.

The once popular classmate was gradually eroding her friendships as her behaviour became increasingly irrational. She started to feel alienated from her friends. She grew paranoid, falsely accusing a fellow student of spreading rumours about her and then reporting him to the principal. She felt that teachers were out to get her because they gave her Cs instead of As.

But there was always someone to pick up the pieces and in May 1999, a few weeks after leaving the Gambettas, she persuaded Portland police officer Richard Braskett to take her into his home. An officer for seven years, Braskett had numerous dealings with street kids, but something about Brianna touched him, not least the fact that she appeared to have good manners.

Over the coming months she went to enormous lengths to establish herself as Brianna Stewart. While Braskett delved into her version of her troubled background in an attempt to locate her real father, she wrote a six-page letter to Washington Governor, Gary Locke, asking for his support in obtaining a Social Security number. For she was due to graduate and knew that without a Social Security number she would not be able to work legally or to apply for financial aid for college. She allowed the *Mobile Register* to write an article about her and even contacted *The Montel Williams Show* about doing an on-screen session with a psychic. Every dramatic plea for information about her past life made her story seem all the more plausible.

Brianna Stewart graduated from Evergreen in June 2000. 'Evan, I DID IT!!!' she wrote to Evan Burton, an advocate at a Portland drop-in centre run by the Salvation Army. 'Thanks for all your help. I really appreciate all the great advice (+ verbal kicks in the arse when I needed it!!).' With her need for a Social Security number becoming ever more urgent, she contacted Portland lawyer Mark McDougal who specialized in helping the underdog. It was to prove a fatal miscalculation because, prior to petitioning for a Social Security number, McDougal covered himself by asking Brianna to submit her fingerprints to the FBI. When the results came back, her secret was out. For FBI records showed that the fingerprints belonged to Treva Throneberry, aged 31, who had been arrested in Altoona, Pennsylvania, in 1996 for making a false report to the police.

Brianna protested her innocence. 'I can't believe it. There must be some mistake,' she cried before storming out of McDougal's office and spinning a sob story to Burton. Listening to her story, Burton's mind flashed back to August 1997 (shortly before Brianna had enrolled at Evergreen) when she had been responsible for sending a man to jail. She had accused a 47-year-old security guard of raping her but instead he was convicted of statutory rape for having sex with Brianna in his car when she was – supposedly – only 16 years old. The guard, who admitted having sex with her, served 50 days in prison and lost his job as a result of the incident. Although he had always been supportive of Brianna, Burton had private misgivings about some of her more outlandish stories. Now as he scanned the FBI printout, he started to wonder whether the guard had been wrongly convicted for the bizarre reason that the girl with whom he had enjoyed sex had been 12 years older than she claimed.

The affair preyed on Burton's mind for a few days until, after a considerable degree of agonizing, he decided to inform the police. By then Brianna was taking a course at Clark College in Vancouver. Her misfortune was that the police investigation was handled by Vancouver Detective Scott Smith, the man who had arrested the security guard on suspicion of rape. She might have managed to fool him once, but lightning was not about to strike twice.

Over the next three months he sifted through police reports, child welfare records and an FBI dossier to build up the true story of the woman who had been calling herself Brianna Stewart.

She was born Treva Throneberry on 18 May 1969 in Wichita Falls, Texas, the youngest of five children of oilman Carl Throneberry and his wife Patsy, and grew up in the nearby town of Electra. Her sisters described the family environment as peaceful and loving, adding that, as befits the baby of the family, Treva was always 'Daddy's favourite girl'. The atmosphere changed dramatically in 1985 when Treva accused her father of putting a gun to her head and raping her. She pressed charges, which she subsequently withdrew.

As a result of the allegations, she was placed in foster care and in May 1986 was committed to a state mental hospital. She later moved to a girls' home in Fort Worth where she graduated from high school in 1987 – a feat she was to repeat 13 years later.

When she was 18 she left the home and rented an apartment in a suburb of Fort Worth, earning a living by working as a maid in local hotels. There were also spells of living on the streets. On a rare visit to one of her sisters, she told stories of ritual abuse – drinking blood and making sacrifices. Shortly afterwards she suddenly left town without a word to anyone. Treva Throneberry was consigned to the past.

Over the next decade she reinvented herself under a number of assumed names, always as a distraught runaway teenager peddling dark tales of abduction, satanic cults and sexual abuse. At each new town she would usually head straight for the nearest church where she would present herself as a sympathetic figure in need of shelter.

In 1992 she told police in Corvallis, Oregon, that she was 19-year-old Keili Smitt, and that her father had forced her into his car and raped her. The following year she claimed a Portland police officer was her father and accused him of sexually assaulting her. By 1994 she was calling herself Cara Leanne Davis and Cara Lewis in Coeur d'Alene, Idaho. She spent part of 1995 in a girls' home in Burlison, Texas, before turning up in Cleveland, Ohio, as Emily Kara Williams.

Then in August 1996 she hit Altoona, Pennyslvania. Wearing a short baby-doll-style dress and her hair in braids, she passed herself off as 16-year-old Stephanie Lewis, originally from Memphis, Tennessee. She told police that her stepfather molested her, shared her with his friends, pushed her into prostitution and forced her to take part in pornographic videos. Now, with the help of a religious underground movement, she said she was on the run from the satanic cult. But while 'Stephanie' was staying at a youth shelter in Altoona, a child welfare worker found out that she was really 27-year-old Treva Throneberry. She pleaded guilty to filing a false police report and spent nine days in jail. Less than a month after arriving in Altoona, she was on her way again – this time to the Pacific Northwest as Brianna Stewart.

In March 2001 Detective Smith arrested Throneberry at a YWCA shelter. Found among her belongings was a notebook with the words 'I AM 18!' written in big letters on the cover. Smith confronted her with overwhelming evidence in the form of fingerprints and dental records. Her parents identified her from photographs. Even then, she persisted with her story, saying there must have been a mix-up between her fingerprints and those of 'this Treva person'.

News of her arrest stunned those who thought they knew her. 'My reaction was one of shock and disbelief,' said Evergreen High School principal Jim Hudson. 'Most people are glad to get out of high school.' Richard Braskett, the duped Portland police officer, expressed anger, but surely it was nothing compared to the resentment that must have been felt by the security guard who had been jailed for having sex with a minor, only to find out now that the minor was really 28 at the time.

Throneberry remained defiant. 'I am Brianna,' she told police officers. 'I can remember being me since I was four years old.' She was assigned a public defender, whom she eventually fired, and she refused plea bargains because she did not want to appear guilty. After a psychiatrist ruled that she was mentally competent to stand trial, she chose to defend herself in court . . . as Brianna Stewart.

She was charged with defrauding the Washington State Department of Social and Health Services of $3,620 that was paid for her foster care and of defrauding Clark College in Vancouver out of $1,050 in tuition that was waived after she claimed to be a homeless teen. Her trial lasted three days, during which time Throneberry never wavered from her conviction that she was Brianna Stewart. 'There is nothing wrong with my mental capacity,' she insisted. 'I don't have any personality disorders that would cause distortion of reality.' However, the jury refused to accept that she was Brianna Stewart and, found guilty of defrauding the state, she was sentenced to three years in prison.

Throneberry was unlike other impostors who returned to high school: James Arthur Hogue, Michael Backman and Brian Mackinnon all wanted to seize an opportunity that, for one reason or another, had been denied to them previously. Throneberry's motives are less clear. It would seem that she had a terror of passing the age of 18 and therefore chose to become the eternal teenager.

Carl Throneberry recalled how, from time to time during her years of imposture, Treva would phone home but pretend to be someone else. 'I said, "I know you're Treva. I know your voice. You're my little girl." And she'd say, "I'm not . . . I wish I was."'

The Great Impostor

Surgeon-Lieutenant Joseph C. Cyr of the Royal Canadian Navy performed such heroic operations under heavy fire during the Korean War that his feats were reported in medical journals; prison officer Ben W. Jones of Huntsville, Texas, maximum-security prison was rated by the Director of the Texas Prison System as 'one of the best prospects ever to serve in the prison service'; and Maine language teacher Martin D. Godgart was considered to be the finest that the school had ever had.

All three men had one thing in common – they were alter egos of Ferdinand Waldo Demara, the man whose incredible life was immortalized in the 1960 Tony Curtis film *The Great Impostor*. Never was a title more richly deserved. Frank Abagnale Jr being a dishonourable exception, the majority of career impostors choose one specific field – perhaps medicine, education or the law – but Demara was able to turn his hand to just about anything. Quite apart from the aforementioned roles, he also masqueraded as a doctor of psychology, a biologist, a law student and a hotel auditor. His versatility knew no bounds.

Demara was born in Lawrencc, Massachusetts, in 1921 to a French-Canadian father and an Irish-American mother. It could be argued that being such a complex hybrid assisted his ability to adopt different guises. Known to his friends as 'Fred', his early ambition was to become a monk. Dropping out of high school, he joined a Trappist monastery in Valley Falls, Rhode Island, at the age of 14. He stayed for two years but was eventually rejected – a decision which left lasting emotional scars. For one who was supposed to be contemplating a life of abstemiousness and sobriety, he was already demonstrating an unhealthy interest in hoaxes. One of his favourite tricks was to borrow a dummy from a clothes shop, put a pair of boots on the feet, bury it head first in a snow drift by the side of the road and then watch from a safe vantage point as passing motorists screeched to a halt and rushed to the aid of the unfortunate victim.

In 1941 Demara joined the US Army but hated it with a vengeance and deserted by adopting the identity of a fellow soldier, Anthony Ingolia. Next he tried the US Navy with the hope of being accepted into hospital school, only to be turned down because he did not possess the necessary academic qualifications or have the right social background. To prove a point, he obtained an officer's commission and served on the destroyer USS *Ellis* on North Atlantic runs before deserting once again in spectacular fashion. Aware that Navy officials were closing in on his imposture, he faked his own death. When the heat had subsided and he thought that the coast was clear, he bought an honourable discharge and an officer's ID card for future use.

Meanwhile, with the assistance of a phoney PhD in psychology, he entered the Abbey of Our Lady of Gethsemane, a Trappist monastery in Kentucky made famous by Thomas Merton in his book, *The Seven*

Storey Mountain. Then, borrowing some headed stationery from Boston's Cardinal O'Connell, Demara proceeded to forge a letter of recommendation for his next creation, Dr Robert Linton French, ex-Navy officer (courtesy of the officer's ID card) and doctor of psychology. In this capacity he taught at Pennsylvania College and Gannon College, California. 'There's no mystery about psychiatry,' he said. 'Anybody with common sense could practise it.'

For the next few years Demara's impersonations followed thick and fast, his catalogue of aliases including Carl Shelby, R. C. Springarn, Arthur Moreland, Anthony Ingolia, Brother John Berchmans, Jefferson Baird Thorne, Dr Cecil Boyce Hamann and Brother Robert Copernicus. During this time he worked as director of publications at St Martin's School, Washington; a law student (Ingolia); a science teacher at a school in Arkansas; a doctor of zoology (Hamann); a Maine junior college instructor; a cancer researcher at the Cancer Institute in Seattle; a hotel auditor in Houston, Texas; an English teacher among Inuit at Point Barrow, Alaska; a deputy sheriff; an English teacher; and a Catholic brother at Trappist and other monasteries in ten different states. All of these posts were secured and held on the basis of forged or stolen qualifications.

He also found time to serve 18 months of a six-year prison sentence in California, imposed after military authorities finally caught up with him and charged him with desertion in time of war.

Early in 1951 Demara's crazy career took him to Canada where he resurfaced as Brother John, a physician turned theology student at a monastery in Grand Falls, New Brunswick. There he became friendly with a local doctor, Joseph C. Cyr, and proposed presenting Cyr's papers to the Maine Medical Board so that the 29-year-old doctor could practise in the United States. The trusting Cyr readily agreed, unaware that Demara intended using the credentials and medical certificate for his own benefit. In March of that year Demara went to the recruiting office in Saint John, New Brunswick, and, masquerading as Dr Cyr, offered his professional services to the Royal Canadian Navy. To gently twist the Navy's arm, he hinted that if they felt unable to use him, he was sure that the Army or Royal Canadian Air Force would gladly take him on board. At that stage of the Korean War and with Canada's new NATO commitments, qualified medical officers were desperately needed by all three services. Consequently no time was lost in recruiting him to the war effort. His credentials were accepted without verification and, three months after his visit to the recruitment centre, he was commissioned into the Navy as a Surgeon-

Lieutenant. The customary two-month enlistment process was completed in about a day.

Although his genuine medical experience was limited to a few weeks as an unskilled hospital orderly, Demara was assigned to the naval hospital at HMCS *Stadacona*. His quiet competence impressed colleagues and in June 1951 he was thrown into the front line, joining the crew of the destroyer HMCS *Cayuga*, which was shortly to leave for a second tour of duty in Korean waters. Demara found himself responsible for the welfare of 211 seamen and eight officers.

Easing himself into the post, he initially delegated many of the routine cases to his junior, Petty Officer Bob Hotchin, who was pleasantly surprised at being allowed to work with a minimum of direction and interference from his medical officer. Demara's gentle introduction to medical life at sea ended abruptly when he was informed that the ship's captain, James Plomer, was suffering from severe toothache. It had been a longstanding problem, one for which Captain Plomer had planned to obtain treatment back in Canada, but the rush to prepare the ship for her return to Korea had left him with no time to see a dentist. Now back at sea, the tooth was causing great pain. It was a job for the highly capable Surgeon-Lieutenant Cyr.

Usually a master of cool, for once in his life Demara was flustered. He might have been able to get away with a botched extraction on a lowly seaman but the mouth of the captain represented an altogether greater challenge. He spent all night reading textbooks and desperately trying to recall any dentistry he may have witnessed in the past. The following morning he gathered his equipment and headed for the captain's cabin. It was one of the few occasions when the dentist was more nervous than the patient.

After administering a liberal dose of local anaesthetic, Demara successfully removed the offending tooth and Captain Plomer promptly pronounced it to be as painless and professional as any dentistry he had ever experienced. What's more, he apparently had no further trouble with the problem area.

Mightily relieved, the bogus doctor now went about his chores with renewed confidence and happily performed the everyday tasks that he had earlier preferred to delegate. His newly acquired expertise was tested to the limit when the *Cayuga* reached the war zone. First he had to treat 19 badly wounded Korean civilians who had fought their way across the sea in a junk to plead for medical help from the Canadian vessel. 'I had to keep one basic principle in mind,' Demara recalled later. 'The less cutting you do, the less patching up you have to do afterwards.'

This episode proved just a foretaste of what was to come as the demands on his non-existent medical training became greater by the day. He removed an appendix in rough seas and when three seriously wounded South Korean guerrillas were brought aboard, he truly excelled himself. He successfully amputated one man's foot, operated on another whose chest had been smashed by a dum-dum bullet, and, under heavy enemy fire, removed a bullet from perilously close to the third soldier's heart. This emergency surgery was carried out on the spot, on the open deck and under the concerned gaze of a number of seamen. Those assisting him in the hazardous operation are said to have cheered wildly at its completion. It would have been a remarkable achievement by the most seasoned surgeon but for an impostor with no qualifications, no training and no previous experience, it almost defied belief.

Ironically Demara was to be a victim of his own success. News from Korea was in short supply at the time, so the Navy decided to publicize the heroic deeds of the surgeon-doctor. The story found its way into the Canadian papers . . . where it was spotted by the mother of the real Dr Joseph Cyr. Puzzled as to how her son had come to be performing emergency operations off the coast of Korea, she contacted him. He assured her that he was still in civilian practice in Grand Falls and, on seeing the accompanying photograph of the ship's surgeon, recognized him as the man who had called himself Brother John at the local Catholic monastery. Things began to fall into place for Dr Cyr – the missing medical credentials, the absence of which he had hitherto attributed to a recent move, and the fact that Brother John had disappeared at around the same time. Realizing that some form of skulduggery was afoot, Dr Cyr notified the Royal Canadian Mounted Police.

When the deception was first brought to the attention of the authorities, it was assumed that the surgeon had simply enlisted under a false name. Nobody doubted for a moment that the brilliant medic who had never lost a patient could be unqualified. But as the investigation intensified, it became all too apparent that the *Cayuga*'s popular doctor was a serial impostor. The shock news was relayed to Captain Plomer and arrangements were made for Demara to be returned to Canada with immediate effect. There he appeared briefly before a naval board of inquiry, at the end of which he was given an honourable release, several hundred dollars in back pay and orders to leave Canada.

In contrast to the glowing press release describing his feats at sea, the Royal Canadian Navy's communiqué on this occasion was markedly more succinct. It read: 'Ferdinand Waldo Demara, alias Cyr, will be discharged from the naval service at Esquimalt later today, November 21, 1951.'

However, his former shipmates did not forget the bogus surgeon and sent him a Christmas card.

Banned from Canada, Demara drifted south to Texas, where he became Mississippi-born prison officer Ben W. Jones at Huntsville maximum-security prison, which housed the state's death row. Although the bull-necked Jones looked eminently capable of dealing with any trouble, he also seemed able to relate to prisoners although nobody realized that it was because he himself had done time. He became a prison guidance counsellor but just when his senior officers were predicting a bright future in the service, Demara's past caught up with him. Hc spotted an inmate studying an article and photograph of him in *Life* magazine. It was time to move on.

In 1956 Demara turned up at North Haven High School in Maine as Latin teacher Martin D. Godgart but was sacked and charged with false pretence when it emerged that his qualifications were fraudulent. Although he served a short prison sentence, it was reported that his pupils' parents wanted him back, considering him to be the best teacher the school had ever had.

After inspiring *The Great Impostor*, Demara put his experience to good use when playing a doctor in the film *The Hypnotic Eye*. Yet his last role in life was as himself – a properly ordained chaplain at a 300-bed hospital in California. By a remarkable coincidence, the real Dr Joseph Cyr worked at the same hospital but chose to keep quiet about Demara's colourful past because he was 'doing a good job'.

Revd Ferdinand Waldo Demara died of heart failure in 1982. When asked why he had spent his life impersonating other people, the man who had finally fulfilled his ambitions of a church-related career replied simply: 'Every novice carries a bishop's mitre in his tunic.'

Uncle Steven

Although he was really a 25-year-old unknown from Iran, Anoushirvan Fakhran put on an Oscar-winning performance to pose as Steven Spielberg's 14-year-old nephew. For almost two years Fakhran fooled a prestigious Catholic high school in Virginia, claiming to be Jonathan Taylor Spielberg. Staff and students at the school were so honoured by the presence of the movie mogul's relative that, according to Fakhran, he was allowed to park his BMW in the principal's private space and to skip the occasional lesson if he felt tired.

After the deception was uncovered in 2000, Fakhran protested that there was nothing sinister behind the impersonation. He had merely craved celebrity and adoration. 'I always wanted to attend high school in America because I was abused and mistreated at school in Iran,' he said. 'But I thought if I go back to high school, I was going to be the most popular, trend-setting student. Being Steven Spielberg's nephew would give me the notoriety I wanted.'

Precious little is known about Fakhran's pre-Spielberg life. He was born into a wealthy Tehran family in 1973 and entered the United States via Hamburg on a student visa in 1992, accompanied by his mother Mehri. Mother and son headed for Fairfax City, Virginia, where a family of Iranian immigrants provided them with temporary accommodation. The boy was a quiet individual, usually spending the evenings after school watching TV or playing video games. Following a spell at the English Language Institute at George Mason University, he enrolled at Northern Virginia Community College. During this time, money wired by his father from Tehran enabled Fakhran and his mother to move into a smart two-bedroom apartment in Fairfax. Neighbours remembered them as being immaculately dressed and recalled Fakhran sometimes carrying out the garbage with a trash bag in one hand and a glass of wine in the other.

Following short-lived clerking jobs at two city stores, in August 1997 Fakhran legally changed his name to Spielberg, partly because it was his great-grandfather's name but also because it conveyed an instant image of Hollywood. With his new identity, he decided to acquire a new date of birth and to return to high school, this time at the exclusive Paul VI Catholic school.

In September 1998 the private school received a telephone call from someone pretending to be a representative of the Spielberg family. The caller (Fakhran) said that the famed producer's nephew would be in the Fairfax area filming a movie and wanted to attend a regular high school for background research on the film. School officials sent an application form, which was returned in the name of Jonathan Taylor Spielberg, listing his date of birth as 2 January 1984. Fakhran claimed that he then visited the school disguised as the family agent and met with the principal, Revd John Lyle.

The school welcomed its celebrity student with open arms. To help create the necessary image, he turned up on the first day flanked by hired bodyguards. The principal went to the trouble of escorting him around the cafeteria, introducing him to many of the school's 1,300 students, and then repeating the gesture in several classes. Needless to say, this was not a courtesy that was extended to other new students.

'They treated me like royalty,' said Fakhran. 'I was introduced to everyone as Spielberg's nephew. They gave me a free lunch. They asked for my autograph. It was heavenly.'

With his wealthy father unwittingly funding his fantasy from overseas, Fakhran quickly settled into his extravagant new lifestyle. He handed out $10 bills to his classmates and peppered his conversations with references to Hollywood and 'Uncle Steven'. He could have name-dropped for America, boasting of having friends like Jennifer Love Hewitt and Matt Damon and telling girls that Ben Affleck would be accompanying him to a school football game. He wore Armani, Gucci and Prada on non-school-uniform days and sported a diamond-encrusted Cartier watch.

Although he was supposed to be only 14, he drove a $24,000 leased blue BMW coupe to school, carrying the vanity licence plate 'SPLBERG'. When baffled students asked him how he had permission to drive, he told them he had a special Hollywood actors' licence. He even parked in the principal's parking space because, he said, the principal 'insisted'.

Fakhran said: 'It was such a hassle to park in the school parking lot so I complained. The principal offered me his space.'

Initially Revd Lyle allowed him to attend part-time (because of movie commitments) and waived tuition fees. Fakhran kept the principal sweet by hinting that his famous uncle might be donating money to the school in the future.

'To me, it was like the movie, *Never Been Kissed*,' admitted Fakhran in 2001. 'I was able to go back to high school and do it all over again. When I didn't feel like waking up for class, I was told I could skip first period so that I could rest. Sometimes I missed school for weeks at a time to "film" in New York, Australia and London. No one said a word. I had such a terrible time at high school in Iran but this time I was a somebody!'

Before taking on Fakhran as a full-time student, the principal requested high school transcripts. He was duly sent a transcript from the Beverly Hills Private School for Actors, listing excellent grades for Jonathan Spielberg. The school does not exist. Fakhran backed it up with a letter of recommendation that he printed on to notepaper bearing a fake logo of DreamWorks, Steven Spielberg's production company.

Impressed by the bogus documents, Paul VI accepted him as a full-time student in September 1999, following which the school started billing him. His appearances in class were as sporadic as before. Classmates estimated that he sometimes showed up as little as once every three weeks, but was still a frequent visitor to a nearby coffee shop where he could be seen leafing through fan magazines while holding court to those he sought to impress. Not all of the students believed his claims and some did remark that, even with his curious high-pitched voice, he seemed a lot older than 15.

Fakhran had no intention of wasting his father's money on school fees. As the school became increasingly anxious about the non-payment, he crafted another letter on DreamWorks notepaper. The letter, purportedly from Steven Spielberg's sister, stated that the family were already paying for a private tutor for Jonathan, which made it difficult for them to pay the school as well. However, she said that the family were trying to reach an agreement with the tutor and, with reference to Jonathan, added that 'making friends and being in public is very important to him.'

Fakhran was hoping to buy time. He was also hoping to launch a career as an actor or a model and, during his frequent vanishing acts from school, began taking his portfolio around various agencies, including William Morris.

But the school was beginning to lose patience. As its star student's absences mounted, a Paul VI official tried to contact the Spielberg family through the DreamWorks headquarters in Los Angeles. When word came back that Steven Spielberg didn't have a nephew named Jonathan, the police were called in. Fakhran was arrested in January 2000 and charged with forgery and submitting false documents to the high school. He pleaded guilty and in July of that year was given an 11-month suspended sentence and placed on two years' probation.

The impostor felt he had been harshly treated. 'They arrested me, they searched my house. I was devastated. I mean, I know it was wrong, but I didn't sleep with students, I didn't do drugs, I didn't stalk Steven Spielberg. What I did was really harmless. I didn't hurt anyone.'

Freed from the shackles of school at the age of 27, he was said to be concentrating on a career in Hollywood and had retained the services of a leading Beverly Hills lawyer to hawk his manuscript, *At Any Cost: From Fifteen Minutes of Notoriety to a Lifetime of Fame*. Nobody could accuse Anoushirvan Fakhran/Jonathan Taylor Spielberg of lacking ambition.

Bibliography

Abramson, Howard S. – *Hero in Disgrace* (Paragon House, 1991)
Allison, William and Fairley, John – *The Monocled Mutineer* (Quartet, 1979)
Arthurson, Ian – *The Perkin Warbeck Conspiracy* (Alan Sutton, 1994)
Blundell, Nigel – *The World's Greatest Crooks and Conmen* (Octopus, 1982)
Burton, Sarah – *Impostors* (Penguin, 2000)
Cheesman, Clive and Williams, Jonathan – *Rebels, Pretenders and Impostors* (British Museum Press, 2000)
Chrimes, S. B. – *Henry VII* (Eyre Methuen, 1972)
Cooper, Joe – *The Case of the Cottingley Fairies* (Robert Hale, 1990)
Dance, Peter – *Animal Fakes and Frauds* (Sampson Low, 1976)
Dukes, Paul – *A History of Russia* (Macmillan, 1974)
Gordon, Stuart – *The Book of Hoaxes* (Headline, 1995)
Harris, Neil – *Humbug: The Art of P. T. Barnum* (University of Chicago Press, 1973)
Kerr, Philip (ed.) – *The Penguin Book of Lies* (Viking, 1990)
Kohn, Alexander – *False Prophets* (Basil Blackwell, 1986)
Montagu, Ewen – *The Man Who Never Was* (Evans Brothers, 1953)
Moss, Norman – *The Pleasures of Deception* (Chatto & Windus, 1997)
Newnham, Richard – *The Guinness Book of Fakes, Frauds and Forgeries* (Guinness, 1991)
Raison, Jennifer and Goldie, Michael – *Caraboo* (Windrush Press, 1994)
Randi, James – *An Encyclopedia of Claims, Frauds and Hoaxes of the Occult and Supernatural* (St Martin's Griffin, 1995)

Rieth, Adolf – *Archaeological Fakes* (Barrie and Jenkins, 1970)
Rose, June – *The Perfect Gentleman* (Hutchinson, 1977)
Saxon, A.H. – *P. T. Barnum: The Legend and the Man* (Columbia University Press, 1989)
Sifakis, Carl – *Hoaxes and Scams* (Michael O'Mara, 1994)
Warnes, David – *Chronicle of the Russian Tsars* (Thames and Hudson, 1999)
Yapp, Nick – *Hoaxers and their Victims* (Robson Books, 1992)
The Museum of Hoaxes @ www.museumofhoaxes.com